Purloined Letters:

The Twelfth-Century Reception of the Anglo-Saxon Illustrated Hexateuch

(British Library, Cotton Claudius B. iv)

Medieval and Renaissance Texts and Studies

Volume 395

Purloined Letters:
The Twelfth-Century Reception of the Anglo-Saxon Illustrated Hexateuch
(British Library, Cotton Claudius B. iv)

By
A. N. Doane and
William P. Stoneman

ACMRS
(Arizona Center for Medieval and Renaissance Studies)
Tempe, Arizona
2011

Published by ACMRS (Arizona Center for Medieval and Renaissance Studies), Tempe, Arizona.

Library of Congress Cataloging-in-Publication Data

Doane, Alger Nicolaus, 1938-
Purloined letters : the twelfth-century reception of the Anglo-Saxon illustrated Hexateuch (British library, Cotton Claudius B. IV) / by A. N. Doane and William P. Stoneman.
p. cm. -- (Medieval and renaissance texts and studies ; v. 395)
Includes bibliographical references and index.
ISBN 978-0-86698-443-0 (acid-free paper)
1. Bible. O.T. Hexateuch--Manuscripts. 2. British Library. Manuscript. Cotton Claudius B. IV. 3. Bible. O.T. Hexateuch--Criticism, interpretation, etc.
I. Stoneman, William P. II. Title.
BS132.D63 2011
222'.10529--dc23

2011026486

∞
This book is made to last. It is set in Adobe Caslon Pro, smyth-sewn and printed on acid-free paper to library specifications.
Printed in the United States of America

Table of Contents

Preface *vii*

I. Introduction 1

II. The Textual Evidence 13

III. English in the Annotations 185

IV. Scripts and Codicology 213

V. *Historia Scholastica* and the Annotations 255

VI. "Jerome" and the Annotations 297

VII. Normannus at St. Augustine's and those Purloined Letters 339

Appendix I: Analysis of English Language in the Notations 361

Appendix II: Glossarial Index of English 371

Works Cited 383

Index 391

Preface

This book is the first full account of the cycle of Latin and English annotations added in the late twelfth century to the mid-eleventh-century illustrated manuscript of the Anglo-Saxon Heptateuch (Cotton Claudius B. iv) in the British Library. These notes have multiple tales to tell. Hidden in plain sight for eight hundred years in a famous and otherwise well-studied manuscript, acknowledged to exist but otherwise virtually ignored by scholars since the seventeenth century, these are true "Purloined Letters" that yield up much unexpected fruit to careful study. They represent a rare laboratory for examining the patterns and methods of Old Testament scholarship of typically learned, diligent, interested, and *au courant* twelfth-century English Benedictine monks of no extraordinary talent in themselves. What will be of most interest, perhaps, to students of English language and literature, the notes are a rare serious, detailed, and sustained—indeed, the most massive—instance of interactive medieval reception of Old English texts in an age—post-1180—when English was virtually out of use as a written language. And when the full story is spun out, and questions of "why" and "how" are addressed, this cycle of annotations reveals a fascinating saga of monastic political maneuvering and textual deception. It is also, not incidentally, a powerful illustration of the perils of modern medieval scholarship whenever it becomes balkanized according to conventional disciplinary, period, and linguistic divisions that cause "mixed" phenomena to be conveniently overlooked, however obvious: in this case Anglo-Saxon vs. Norman, the vernacular vs. Latin, the textuality of editions vs. manuscript margins, the canonical vs. the undocumented.

But what first and last caught *our* attention and astonishes us still, these annotations are the medium of "the last Old English"—English texts composed sometime after 1180 to a late-West-Saxon standard but informed by the "new" literal biblical exposition of the Victorine school as transmitted by Peter Comestor. This aspect will be fully discussed in the following pages: here is the place to say a few words about how this book came to be. About twenty-five years ago, one of us, William P. Stoneman, noticed that a few of the Latin and English notes corresponded exactly to extracts from the *Historia Scholastica* and he announced these results in a session on the Sources of Anglo-Saxon Culture at the 19th International Congress on Medieval Studies at Western Michigan University in Kalamazoo. An abstract of that paper was published in the *Old English*

Newsletter 17.2 (1984), A-37. Meanwhile, about twelve years ago, unaware of Stoneman's discoveries, A. N. Doane, in the course of preparing the description of Cotton Claudius B. iv for *Anglo-Saxon Manuscripts in Microfiche Facsimile* (the description appeared in Vol. 7, published in 2002), was mildly surprised to find that dozens of the Latin annotations were verbatim extracts from the *Historia* and astounded that many of the English notes also matched this source.

At any rate, by spring 2001, Doane had undertaken to identify the sources of all the notes, Latin and Old English, and to make an edition of them. This work proceeded through mid-2003, when Tim Graham, knowing about Stoneman's work and having found out that Doane was working on essentially the same problem, brought the authors together, and as a result they have been collaborating on this book since. Chapters One, Two, and Three, on the English notes, and the final arrangement of the seven chapters, are the result of full collaboration of both authors. Chapters Four through Seven were written by Doane prior to and since joining up with Stoneman, with his consultation.

We owe a special debt to Benjamin Withers, who has graciously shared with us selected images from his photos of Claudius B. iv and allowed them to serve as photographic stock this book. These photos are available on-line at www.bl.uk/manuscripts/.

In the course of the long preparation of this study we have received much other help and incurred many debts: first, our thanks to Tim Graham, for making us aware of the opportunity and need for collaboration; then to the staff of the British Library Manuscript Department who were always ready to give friendly and expert advice over several long periods of study there, especially Michael Boggen, Michelle Brown, David French, and Andrew Prescott; to Dr. Christopher de Hamel and Ms. Jill Cannell of the Parker Library, Corpus Christi College, Cambridge, for making their many copies of the *Historia* available; to Dr. David McKitterick of Trinity College Library, Cambridge, for help and hospitality on various occasions. Many friends and colleagues have shown interest, offered advice, and encouraged the work, especially Michael Gullick, Sandra Hindman, Maryanne Kowaleski, Yuri Kleiner, Franz van Liere, Roy Liuzza, Tim Machan, Richard Marsden, John D. Niles, Andy Orchard, Kathryn Salzer, Elaine Treharne, Jonathan Wilcox, and Kirsten Wolf. We had much appreciated help at different stages with the Latin translations from Carole Newlands, Martin Pickens, Sherry L. Reames, and Justin Stover. The authors take responsibility for all the remaining errors.

We are deeply grateful to Mr. David Way, the British Library Publications Director, for granting permission to use images of the manuscripts of Claudius B. iv and Cotton Nero A. viii in the book; to Dr. John R. Pollard, Fellow Librarian of Trinity Hall, Cambridge, and to the Masters and Fellows of Trinity Hall, Cambridge for granting permission to reproduce images of Trinity Hall MS. 1, and to Dominique Ruhlmann, Director of Library Services, for her help in making the digital images available; and to the Masters and Fellows of Trinity

College, Cambridge, for granting permission to use images of Trinity College MSS. B. 2. 34 and O. 4. 7.

Finally, we wish to thank Prof. Robert Bjork, Director of the Arizona Center for Medieval and Renaissance Studies, and the other marvellous members of its staff, Roy Rukkila, Managing Editor, Todd Halvorsen, Director of Design and Production, and Leslie S. B. MacCoull, copy editor and *Latinitatis magistra eximia*, for making the publication of this book not only possible, but a pleasant and rewarding experience.

Nick Doane thanks his wife Marty Blalock for her never-failing love, help, and encouragement over the many years of our life together and dedicates his share of this work to her. Bill Stoneman thanks his partner David Shapero who may not have been around for all of the twenty-five years this work has been in gestation, but realizes it may certainly seem so.

I. Introduction

> Aurisia est quando homines habent apertos oculos et non uident. . . . Fiat etiam aliquando quod homines rem habent aliquam in manu et non uident et hoc est etiam aurisia.[1]

One of the British Library's most famous treasures—often on public display and frequently studied—is Cotton Claudius B iv, known as the Old English illustrated Hexateuch, from its contents of the first six books of the Bible, Genesis to Joshua, in Anglo-Saxon. It has been well known since the seventeenth century by scholars of Old English for its text, an adaptation and translation, in part by Ælfric and in part by several anonymous authors, of the first six books of the Bible; its opening leaves contained Ælfric's preface to Genesis addressed to Æðelweard.[2] Its spectacular cycle of 418 colored illustrations, one of the largest

---

[1] "'Aurisia' is when men have open eyes and do not see. . . . It may also happen sometimes that people have something in their hand and they don't see it and this is also 'aurisia'": Cotton Claudius B. iv, f. 30r (no. 122).

[2] S. J. Crawford, ed., *The Old English Version of the Heptateuch, Ælfric's Treatise on the Old and New Testament, and his Preface to Genesis*, EETS, o. s. 160, repr. rev. N. R. Ker (London, 1922, rev. ed. 1969); see now Richard Marsden, ed., *The* Old English Heptateuch *and Ælfric's* Libellus de Veteri Testamento et Novo, Vol. 1, EETS 330 (Oxford, 2008): as Marsden's base text is Bodleian Library Laud Misc. 509, it does not supersede, for our purposes, Crawford's edition, which is based on Cotton Claudius B. iv. The "Preface to Genesis" was first printed, with a translation, from Oxford, Bodleian Laud Misc. 509, by William L'Isle, *A Saxon Treatise concerning the Old and New Testament* (London, 1623); the text of the Old Testament books was first printed from Laud by Edward Thwaites, *Heptateuchus, Liber Job, et Euangelium Nicodemi; Anglo-Saxonice. Historiae Judith Fragmentum; Dano-Saxonice* (Oxford, 1698). The first leaf of Claudius, containing the beginning of the "Preface to Genesis," was already missing when the manuscript came into the possession of Sir Robert Cotton. For the early history of Claudius B. iv and Laud 509, see A. N. Doane, "Anglo-Saxon Bibles and 'The Book of Cerne'," *Anglo-Saxon Manuscripts in Microfiche Facsimile* 7, MRTS 187 (Tempe, AZ, 2002), 72–73. The view that there are three hands besides Ælfric involved in the translation of the Hexateuch has been advanced by Richard Marsden, "Translation by Committee? The 'Anonymous' Text of the Old English Hexateuch," in *The Old English Hexateuch: Aspects and Approaches*, ed. Rebecca Barnhouse and Benjamin C. Withers (Kalamazoo, 2000), 41–89.

assemblages of pictures of any medieval manuscript, famous among Anglo-Saxonists, has become a staple to art historians because many of the pictures were left in various stages of incompletion, allowing insights into the stages of the artistic processes of early medieval book-art.[3] Finally, this important manuscript has been studied by codicologists concerned with the integration of text and image, most recently by Benjamin Withers, who deals with the codicology and art historical aspects in great detail.[4]

Not least, the manuscript is widely familiar because as one of the most photogenic and visually "legible" of Anglo-Saxon manuscripts, having a vast repertory of subjects, its illustrated pages are often reproduced, either in books on Anglo-Saxon art and antiquities in general or as exiguous cover decorations or illustrations of editions of literary texts; perhaps the most familiar to a generation of students is the colored reproduction of the Sacrifice of Isaac (f. 38r) as the frontispiece of most editions of the Cassidy-Ringler edition of Bright's *Old English Reader*.[5] It would seem, then, that this manuscript and all its components—text, art, and codicology—have been at least adequately addressed.

But this is manifestly not true: on that same page presenting the sacrifice of Isaac, we see, if we wish to see, not only a strikingly complex zigzag three-register colored illustration of Abraham's entourage ascending the mountain towards the sacrifice, and, above the picture, the handsome bold square insular writing of the main text itself, but also in the upper margin two passages of alien-looking Latin writing, three lines in the top margin and, conspicuously in the picture space, six short lines playfully interacting with Abraham's hovering sword and Isaac's threatened head. The style of script belongs to the late twelfth century; it, or variations of it, appear on almost every page of the book on a massive scale—the approximately 360 discrete annotations amounting to nearly half the bulk of the

[3] The text, paleography, illustrations, and their interrelations have been conveniently available for study for many years thanks to the excellent black-and-white facsimile of C. R. Dodwell and Peter Clemoes, *The Old English Illustrated Hexateuch: British Museum Cotton Claudius B. iv*, Early English Manuscripts in Facsimile 18 (Copenhagen, 1974). Very recently, an excellent CD-ROM facsimile has become available, accompanying Bejamin Wither's 2007 book (see the next note). The following study is heavily dependent on the Dodwell and Clemoes facsimile, the CD-ROM, as well as on Doane's first-hand examinations of the manuscript itself in 1996 and 2002.

[4] Benjamin Withers, *The Illustrated Old English Hexateuch, Cotton Claudius B. IV: The Frontiers of Seeing and Reading in Anglo-Saxon England* (London and Toronto, 2007), hereafter *Frontiers*; several perspectives on the art and layout of the manuscript are included in Barnhouse and Withers, *The Old English Illustrated Hexateuch*.

[5] F. J. Cassidy and Richard Ringler, eds., *Bright's Old English Grammar and Reader, Third Edition* (New York, 1971); cf. the rear dust jacket of Jonathan Alexander's 1983 Lyell lectures published as *Medieval Illuminators and Their Methods of Work* (New Haven, 1992).

main Old English text itself.[6] Yet, while the existence of these inscriptions has always been acknowledged, this writing, these "annotations," have been almost completely ignored. One supposes this is because they are regarded, at best, as irrelevant to the concerns of Anglo-Saxonists and students of the manuscript and, at worst, as acts of monastic vandalism, mere graffiti.[7] These neglected annotations are the subject of the present book: their study reveals that they represent the most massive and interesting evidence of reception of Anglo-Saxon language and culture during the Middle Ages and, moreover, contain the "last Old English," hitherto unrecognized as such. In spite of the fame and availability of this manuscript, it is nevertheless still not really known for what it is (or has become), because such a large part of its writing has been written off regardless of the fact that this writing is manifestly relevant to the main text and illustrations.

To study these annotations means crossing academic and conceptual borders, borders between "Anglo-Saxon" and "Norman," between Old English and Latin, between insular minuscule script and proto-gothic, between patristic biblical exegesis and twelfth-century historicism; and it means entering the no-man's-land between Old English and Middle English. The present study, then, is partly against the "aurisia" of modern scholarship, which is sometimes blinded by seeing only what it is primed to see within disciplinary boundaries. It is also about the fascinating story of late twelfth-century Benedictine monastic biblical scholarship that this manuscript documents, scholarship itself on the borderland between ancient monastic learning stemming from patristic exegesis and the hot new biblical scholarship that was beginning to come from the Paris schools that was about to put Benedictine preeminence into permanent eclipse. We shall attempt to show how for reasons of institutional pride and rivalry a venerable book of St. Augustine's Abbey was "enhanced" after about 1180 with diverse material old and new purloined from a few direct and identifiable sources and refashioned into a usable icon of antiquity meant to reflect distinction on St. Augustine's and its contemporary community of monk-scholars. This was done, we shall argue, for reasons of institutional pride connected with its nearby rival, Christ Church. This appropriation and reformulation of an old book to new uses has been hidden in plain sight for more than eight hundred years, while the "Saxon" book has continued to increase in fame.

---

[6] Crawford's edition of the two manuscripts, plus Vulgate parallel text, occupies just over 400 pages; the twelfth-century annotations, with translations and information about the manuscript layout, etc., occupy 174 pages in the present book.

[7] The status of these annotations is neatly symbolized on the cover art of a recent anthology of Old English literature that features a detail of Cotton Claudius B. iv, f. 15v, showing most of the page with the Old English text—but the Latin/Old English annotation along the bottom (no. 61) has been cropped (*The Cambridge Old English Reader*, ed. Richard Marsden [Cambridge, 2004]).

Humfrey Wanley placed Cotton Claudius B. iv just before the Norman Conquest, Ker (on the basis of the script) to the first half of the eleventh century, Francis Wormald (on the basis of the art) to the second quarter of the same century, and Withers, on the basis of comparative codicology, to 1020 × 1040.[8] The manuscript was in the possession of St. Augustine's Canterbury by 1491–1497, the inclusive dates of its first catalogue. This positive identification is confirmed by the agreement of the second folio incipit given in the catalogue.[9] Dodwell and Clemoes conclude that "Unless contrary evidence is discovered we may reasonably suppose that our manuscript was made at St. Augustine's, Canterbury, in the second quarter of the eleventh century and remained there throughout the Middle Ages."[10] Yet, until now, there has been no positive evidence that the book was in St. Augustine's before the fifteenth century. It found its way into Sir Robert Cotton's library some time before 1621; it was annotated by Robert Talbot (d. 1558) and William L'Isle (d. 1637). The present study will present positive paleographical and codicological evidence that the book was at St. Augustine's at the time the annotations were entered, which can be dated on various grounds between 1180–1200, and in the light of this evidence it is all the more likely that the book was always at St. Augustine's and was produced there, as Dodwell and Clemoes surmised. The underlying premise of this book is that it is a St. Augustine's product.

Before proceeding with the detailed evidence and arguments, the annotations need to be characterized in general. The extensive web of twelfth-century notes appears on almost every page of Genesis and Exodus and on many pages thereafter. These annotations are not inconspicuous but they are somewhat confusing to the modern eye, particularly to the eye of the Anglo-Saxonist trained in the relatively clear and unambiguous writing of late insular square minuscule. Their bold ductus of thick vertical strokes and black ink, contrast with the more willowy ductus and slightly browner ink of the Old English and make them leap

[8] Humfrey Wanley, *Antiquae literaturae septentrionalis liber alter*, in George Hickes, *Linguarum veterum septentrionalium thesaurus* (Oxford, 1705), 2:253–54; N. R. Ker, *A Catalogue of Manuscripts Containing Anglo-Saxon* (Oxford, 1957; rev. ed. 1990), no. 142; Francis Wormald, *English Drawings of the Tenth and Eleventh Centuries* (London, 1952), 26–29; Withers, *Frontiers*, 53–85.

[9] M. R. James, *The Ancient Libraries of Canterbury and Dover* (Cambridge, 1903), lxxxiv, 201; the St. Augustine's catalogue has been re-edited by B. C. Barker-Benfield, St. Augustine's Abbey, Canterbury, 3 vols., Corpus of British Medieval Library Catalogues 13 (London, 2008), Claudius B. iv. being no. 95, 1:405-06. As Barker-Benfield's edition became available after this book was already in proof, only minimal reference could be given to it, and James' edition remains the primary resource.

[10] Dodwell and Clemoes, *Illustrated Hexateuch*, 15–16. A brief and accurate summing up of our external knowledge of the manuscript heretofore is given by Mary C. Olson, *Fair and Varied Forms: Visual Textuality in Medieval Illuminated Manuscripts*, (New York and London, 2003), 100–1.

out at anyone using the manuscript. The proto-gothic script of the annotations is intrinsically somewhat more difficult to decipher, partly because the letter forms are more compressed and potentially ambiguous, partly because of the frequent abbreviations, partly because of the somewhat individualistic or idiosyncratic styles of these particular scripts, partly because the inscriptions are sometimes squeezed into small or irregular spaces; they are sometimes continued from one leaf to another and sometimes hop around the page, often making it very hard to see where individual notes stop or start without recourse to the their sources — and few attempts have been made to ascertain what those might be. On the other hand, their placement in the illustration spaces, along the tops and bottoms of picture frames, using the double lines as rules or "ledgers," and in margins; the obvious attempt to size the ductus of the annotations to that of the Old English and often to place them as run-ons or continuations of the Old English text at the end of blocks of writing so that they may become part of the text; not to mention three added leaves full of annotations in the same style, show that they are intended as enhancements and tributes to the original production. Study shows that the annotations have been entered with care, both so that they in most cases relate immediately to the Old English text and/or pictures on the same or facing pages, and so that they enhance, or at least do not spoil, the appearance of the page. Just as the original artist and scribes designed the book so that placement of texts and pictures would comment on one another and openings would present coherent overall patterns, so the annotations respect this quality of the book: when annotations are in picture spaces, they occupy only blanks and never interfere with the drawn figures; added text blocks within picture spaces carefully respect the shapes of the pre-existing figures (note the way the annotations avoid and often interact with them in meaningful ways);[11] comments that run on to the next page almost always go from the bottom margin of the verso to either the top of the facing recto or directly across to the facing bottom margin, very seldom do they run from recto to verso; an elaborate system of *signes-de-renvoi* and continuation marks and letters steer the reader during protracted or complexly displayed comments; the double outline frames are often utilized as ledgers to guide the annotations; and there is a general protocol that notes from older materials go in the margins and notes from "modern" sources go near or in the picture spaces. When large spaces are available for one reason or another, the annotations are carefully planned as to both content and appearance; the most

[11] For example, notice how on f. 70v the added script avoids the heads of the figures and follows the "steps" of the frame in the lower picture, or how on f. 25v in the upper frame it avoids the feet coming into the frame and in the lower frame responds to the play of the spear points coming into the top of the frame. A good general impression of the *mise-en-page* of the notes may be gained from the frontispiece to Dodwell and Clemoes' facsimile edition, showing f. 14r. See Withers' excellent discussion of the original design and construction of the book, *Frontiers*, 17–52.

spectacular instance of this being on the page with Noe's rainbow (f. 16v), where a medley of comments fills up the inner space of the arc with thirteen lines of writing. So this is neither occasional nor random annotation, though the project may have been carried out in stages over a relatively long time: we are witnessing a sustained and thoughtful reaction to the text and to its accompanying images, with comments chosen and placed so that they might illuminate (by the lights of mid- to late twelfth-century scholarship) the biblical text (as translated) with additional literal information, give etymological explanation of names, fill up gaps in the Old English translation, or provide continuities between one biblical event and another. The annotations show an extensive, we might say specialized, interest in chronology. Moreover, as we shall attempt to show in greater detail, the annotations are not merely *ad hoc* or incidental, but are part of a larger plan to remodel the Old English partial Old Testament that was found into a more complete representation of the entire Old Testament from Creation to Incarnation on a plan incorporating the Ages of the World and chronology according to the system Anno Mundi.

Among these twelfth-century annotations are more than three dozen notes in English. These were edited by Crawford, who took them as mid- to late-century copies of earlier Old English notes; Ker dated them "s. xii med."[12] No doubt, therefore, what will be most interesting to Anglo-Saxonists is the surprising discovery that these annotations, clearly in a late form of West Saxon / Kentish Old English, are in large part exact word-for-word translations of the famous biblical compendium, the *Historia Scholastica* of Peter Comestor, written no earlier than 1169; in fact the exact form of the text's exemplar is that of the revised recension issued by disciples of the Comestor about 1180.[13] This indisputable *terminus a quo* means that these notes, whatever else, are the last—unexpectedly late—example of extensive *original composition* (including translations) in language recognizable as Old English; they are the attempt—achieved with difficulty and ultimately with scant success—to put the new wine of twelfth-century literal commentary into the old bottle of "regular" or literary English, undertaken in an age and place where the preservation and copying of Old English documents was still a serious or at least possible enterprise.[14]

[12] Crawford edits them in his edition of the *Heptateuch*, EETS o.s. 160 and in "The Old English Notes in B. M. Cotton Claudius B. iv," *Anglia* n.s. 35 (1923): 124–35, with more extensive comments on their language; on p. 418 of *Hept.* Crawford says "we may date the notes about the second half of the twelfth century," a very general formulation; Ker's dating implies a margin of years either side of 1150, cf. Ker, *Catalogue of Manuscripts containing Anglo-Saxon*, 178.

[13] See ch. 5, 255–62.

[14] Of course there exist a number of manuscripts written in the last quarter of the twelfth century and the first years of the thirteenth that contain more-or-less linguistically intact *copies* of Old English works written at much earlier periods. See the essays

Few attempts, and those quite misleading, have been made to identify the nature or sources of the notes. Thomas Smith, the late seventeenth-century keeper of the Cotton library, says:

> . . . brevibus scholiis et annotationibus, partim Latinis, partim Saxonicis ex Beda aliisque.[15]

Humfrey Wanley is more circumstantial:

> Quod Cod. hunc attinet videtur scriptus paulo ante Conquisitionem Angliæ, per totum illustratur Iconibus Historicis, rudiori tamen manu delineatis, quam plurimis in locis, manu recentiori, insignitur Adnotationi[b]us Historicis Latinis, nonnullisque Saxonicis ex *Josepho, Methodio,* etc.[16]

Though Smith was somewhat closer to the truth (Joseph Planta, in *A Catalogue of the Manuscripts in the Cottonian Library deposited in the British Museum* [1802], simply repeats Smith), Humfrey Wanley's authority and specificity carried the day, leading S. J. Crawford, the only editor of the Old English notes, to forego any further chase: "these notes are derived mainly from the writings of Josephus, Pseudo-Methodius, and an authority who is called Normannus." M. R. James, ever the questing beast, in a private communication to Crawford added genuine though minor information, correctly attributing at least a few of the entries to the "History of Assenath, enough to show that he [the annotator] was using the larger Latin text and not the abridgment" (Crawford's words).[17] It is odd to think that the enormously learned James overlooked the much more obvious sources of the bulk of the notes: perhaps he recognized them but did not think it worth mentioning. Ker's *Catalogue* makes no identification of the notes at all. It is true that Josephus, Methodius, Normannus appear as prominent proper names in *English* notes, but what is oddly overlooked are the vast numbers of references to "Jerome"—but these are in the Latin notes.[18] The fact is that there are about 180 distinct Latin extracts from the *Historia Scholastica*, and "Jerome" and "Josephus"

---

in *Rewriting Old English in the Twelfth Century*, ed. Mary Swan and Elaine M. Treharne (Cambridge, 2000).

[15] From his catalogue of the Cottonian manuscripts, cited from Dodwell and Clemoes, eds., *The Old English Illustrated Hexateuch*, 14; repr. as Thomas Smith, *Catalogue of the Manuscripts in the Cottonian Library, 1696*, ed. C. G. C. Tite (Woodbridge, 1984) where the quotation is presented in English only, on p. 50.

[16] *Antiquae literaturae septentrionalis liber alter* (Oxford, 1705), 253–54.

[17] Crawford, ed., *Heptateuch*, 418. Dodwell and Clemoes (*Illustrated Hexateuch*, 14) are satisfied to simply quote Wanley and rest with Crawford (15); see also Marsden, ed., *The* OE Heptateuch, xlix.

[18] There is one mention of "Jerome" in the English notes (no. 46) but this appears to have been overlooked.

were the Comestor's most frequent sources and so naturally he often mentions their names. There are about twenty-four English notes translated directly from the *Historia Scholastica* and over a dozen more translated from other sources. The remaining Latin notes, upwards of 250, are citations from ancient works of biblical commentaries in the literal mode, providing information geographical, chronological, and cultural, citations overwhelmingly in the Hieronymian tradition, whether the works are by Jerome himself, thought to be by Jerome in the Middle Ages, or by Bede, following in Jerome's foot-tracks.

The works that have been correctly adduced up to now need a little further discussion. The "History of Aseneth" noticed by M. R. James is a quasi-mystical romance elaborating the details of Joseph's marriage to Aseneth (mentioned at Genesis 41:45 as a daughter of Putiphar), who is converted to purity by an angel. The longer Latin version was translated from Greek in the mid-twelfth century and a shorter version (the "abridgement") is found in Vincent of Beauvais' *Speculum Historiale.*[19] In fact, only two of the more than 360 notes are from this source.[20] James' contribution furthered the impression that the sources of the notes are diverse and fragmented, though in fact the full Latin history of Aseneth, being a twelfth-century confection that enjoyed some contemporary popularity, points towards the truth, that the sources, despite their various ancient pedigrees, are of recent origin.

Wanley's "Josephus" and "Methodius" are names indeed frequently mentioned in the notes, both Latin and English. The Latin Josephus was made originally at the instigation of Cassiodorus but came into high popularity in the Middle Ages, particularly in the Anglo-Norman area during the twelfth century,

[19] The longer Latin version is edited by P. Batiffol, *Le Livre de la Prière d'Aseneth*, Studia Patristica 1–2 (Paris, 1889–1890), 1–115. On the manuscripts, see Marc Philonenko, ed., *Joseph et Aséneth: Introduction, texte critique, traduction, et notes*, Studia Post-Biblica 13 (Leiden: Brill, 1968), 14–15. Two copies appear in Prior Eastry's Christ Church list (s. xiii/xiv), among the books of W. de Bocwelle and Iohannes de Crundale (James, *Ancient Libraries*, nos. 521, 1375 [62, 117]). James was in a position to recognize this source at once, since one of his earliest scholarly projects was an edition of the Greek and Latin versions of the History of Aseneth, stimulated by his finding complete versions in Corpus Christi College Cambridge MSS. 288 (13th century) and 424 (12th century) and Bodleian MS. Barocc. 148 (other English manuscripts listed by Christoph Burchard, *Untersuchungen zu Joseph und Aseneth: Überlieferung—Ortsbestimmung*, Wissenschaftliche Untersuchungen zum Neuen Testament 8 [Tübingen, 1965], 13–14). In 1888, James turned over his transcripts of those manuscripts to Batiffol when he learned that the latter was already well advanced with his edition (see Richard William Pfaff, *Montague Rhodes James* [London, 1980], 72–73). On James' view of the work, see idem, "Asenath," in *A Dictionary of the Bible*, ed. J. Hastings (New York, 1898), 1:162.

[20] See nos. 212 and 228.

which produced its own recension.[21] However, despite the many citations of "Josephus" in the Claudius notes, in fact only four of them can possibly be drawn directly from Josephus (though there probably are unknown intermediate sources even for these).[22] The rest are cited directly from the *Historia.* "Methodius" is a short apocalyptic work of the seventh century or earlier, translated into Lain in the eighth, which attracted to itself the name of the bishop of Patara in Lydia martyred about 311; the Latin version exists in many manuscripts, and was especially popular from the twelfth to the fifteenth centuries.[23] "Normannus," a name mentioned more than a dozen times in the notes, requires a chapter of its own. However mysterious, this name denotes a real presence behind the signed notes and probably many others. Thomas James correctly noticed the many attributions to "Bede," who is indeed an independent source of many notes. "Rabanus" is mentioned once or twice, but as drawn from the *Historia.* As already noted, most often mentioned by the annotator, but overlooked by scholars, are the dozens of attributions to "Jerome."

These various attributions mask the primary fact that the sources are modern and for the most part drawn from only two distinct books that would have been easily available to anyone with access to the St. Augustine's library: one was a single-volume collection of works attributed to Jerome, a type of collection that came into being only in the later eleventh century; and the other was the very recently written compendium of literal biblical commentary arranged in the order of the narrative known as the *Historia Scholastica.* This last is the unified

---

[21] The Latin *Antiquitates Iudaicae*, first translated in the sixth century and reaching the crest of its popularity in northern Europe, especially England, Burgundy, and France, in the twelfth and thirteenth centuries, and represented by over 200 extant medieval manuscripts. See Franz Blatt, ed., *The Latin Josephus, I: Introduction and Text, The Antiquities: Books I-V,* Aarsskrift for Aarhus Universitet 30.1, Humanistisk Serie 44 (Copenhagen, 1958), 14–15, 87–94.

[22] See notes 9e, 139, 268, 269a.

[23] Edited by Ernst Sackur, *Sibyllinische Texte und Forschungen; Pseudo-Methodius, Adso und die Tiburtinische Sibylle* (Halle a. S., 1898). Details are conveniently given by Marbury B. Ogle, "Petrus Comestor, Methodius, and the Saracens," *Speculum* 21 (1946): 318–24, at 318–19. A copy of "Methodius" was included in a volume among the books of the Christ Church canon N. de Sandwicus, jr, according to Prior Eastry's list (s. xiii/xiv) (James, *Ancient Libraries*, no. 536 [64]). Recently Katherine Scarfe Beckett (*Anglo-Saxon Perceptions of the Islamic World*, CSAE 33 [Cambridge, 2003], 158–64) saw the "Methodius" notes in Claudius as deriving directly from the medieval "pseudo-Methodius" tradition (perhaps, she says, written from an earlier examplar by a scribe who understood English imperfectly), and this is repeated by Michael W. Twomey, "The Revelations of Pseudo-Methodius and Scriptural Study at Salisbury in the Eleventh Century," in Source of Wisdom, ed. Charles W. Wright, Frederick M. Biggs, and Thomas N. Hall (Toronto, 2007), 370-86, at 378-79; Twomey's article is nevertheless a fount of useful information about the medieval Methodius-tradition.

source of nearly half the annotations but it is never mentioned by name. Rather the annotator carries over into his notes the many attributions of the Comestor to "Josephus," "Methodius," and others. Besides these, only two other books, or maybe even one, need be supposed: one is a copy of Bede's *Nomina regionum atque locorum de Actibus Apostolorum*; the other a source for the Anno Mundi dates from Bede's "World Chronicle," Chapter 66 of *De temporum ratione.*[24] The citations from Aseneth, the Josephus citations independent of the *Historia Scholastica*, and a few dozen isolated mixed citations could have come from the margins of the copy or copies of the *Historia* being consulted.

The chapters which follow form a single long argument. Those primarily interested in the English notes may turn first to chapter 3; those eager for general conclusions may turn directly to the end of chapter 6, "Planning" and all of chapter 7. Many may wish to pass over the long chapter 2 (essentially a diplomatic edition of the annotations) and refer to it as needed. However, this work is not aiming to be primarily an edition of the annotations, but a study of them and of the intellectual endeavor they document, so, as structured, the book lays out the annotations as the problematic evidence in what seems its logical place (in chapter 2), before the argumentation from the evidence commences, and thereafter we follow the trail as it leads, with discussions, discoveries, and speculations arising from this already presented material. We consider the Claudius annotations to be clearly the most remarkable recorded instance of reception of any Old English document during the English Middle Ages. We see the annotator, in our view probably only one person, though an argument must be made for this, meticulously working his way through the already ancient book and harmonizing it with his late twelfth-century ways of reading and writing, drawing from a couple of up-to-date books at hand to provide the comments he deemed relevant and worth entering. The result seems to be a negotiation between the book's older tradition of learning and textuality and newer ideas of what these ancient traditions ideally might have been, in the process transmuting the Old English Hexateuch into a different kind of biblical document from what it originally had been. The Hexateuch ceased to be an innocent mediator of the Latin text and became the problem, one calling for supplements, clarification, and explicit alignment with the modern literal methods of exposition. While its obscurities and lacks prompted commentary, its irreduceably vernacular status precluded it from carrying the traditional signals for spiritual commentary of the Latin Bible, but made it serve all the better as an indexical framework consisting of text and pictures around which the annotations could be placed for convenient reference and retrieval. Moreover, its venerable status as an ancient possession of the house, testifying to biblical activity there going back for unknown generations in the eye of the annotator, made it both a guarantor of the truth of the comments

[24] The latter might be taken from the margins of a copy of the *Historia*, or a chart. The two Bede works in question do not normally occur in the same volume.

being added and required that it be adorned with jewels of learning, like the relic that it was.

The chapters that follow are arranged thus:

Chapter 2 presents the primary evidence of the notes themselves in the form of a diplomatic edition. They are presented with minimal interference as they appear on the page so far as regular typography allows, along with translations, identification of the source of each item, and such commentary as seems needed to explain the physical relation to the original Old English text and illustrations; a bare minimum of necessary interpretive information is included to make this section of the book reasonably self-contained and comprehensible. The reader may want to become acquainted with this section first or or may prefer to use it as a reference when reading the chapters that follow it.

Chapter 3 discusses the English notes, showing the indubitable source of about two dozen of them in the *Historia Scholastica*, and therefore the late date of all of them; it goes on to show by a linguistic analysis that the language, though tending in some features towards Middle English with Kentish colorings, is the product of an effort on the part of the writer to conform to a standard West-Saxon graphoelect of a kind still being read, though not commonly written, in a few monasteries. The chapter then discusses in some detail the typical techniques of translation and writing used by the annotator and some of the practical difficulties he faced in producing these notes; they were probably conceived as a more grandiose project of English translation before being abandoned as too difficult a task.

Chapter 4 discusses the scripts. Although the handwriting gives a first impression of being by several hands—Ker attributes the Latin writing to one hand and the English to another, and the "Jerome" notes differ in character from the "Historia Scholastica" ones—a detailed analysis leads to the conclusion that all the late annotations, Latin and English, are by the same hand, a hand systematically altering the appearance and ductus in a regulated way to make a certain impression. This chapter also adds to the evidence for the book being a St. Augustine's production, since it shows that it was certainly there and being physically altered at the time the annotations were being added.

Chapter 5 discusses the use of the *Historia Scholastica* in the Claudius annotations. These notes must be among the earliest copyings of the *Historia* extant in England—if not the very earliest, and it is shown how the monastic annotator freely selected and rearranged the *Historia*—ransacking its earlier parts without ever acknowledging its use—to transform it from a new type of continuous literal commentary based for its structure on narrative to an older-style monastic commentary based on biblical "places" and their categories. We aim to show how, at their best, the annotations are in lively interplay with the Old English text, the pictures, and the commentary being drawn from the *Historia*. It is argued that the English notes are fully integrated into this scheme of reconceptualizing the source work.

Chapter 6 is on the use of the ancient literal tradition of commentary deriving from Jerome, including the use of genuine works and spuria commonly attributed to Jerome during the twelfth century. The source for these, it is shown, was a single "modern" one-volume edition of the literal expositions of Jerome, a now-lost but reconstructable book that can be identified as among those in the library of St. Augustine's in the twelfth century, plus a single additional work by Bede. These comments are used more mechanically for the most part than the *Historia* is, to gloss the meanings of place names, geographical relations of places, and a few other categories, but they have also been carefully selected and arranged so as to give the annotations—and the ancient book, regarded as incomplete by the annotator since it ends with Joshua—an overall programmatic shape.

Chapter 7 concludes the book by attempting to recover the "actuating" moment for this sustained program of annotation of an old and, one would think, already long-obsolete book. The search focusses on the mysterious "Normannus," a name mentioned about a dozen times in the notes. We identify him with a documented monk of St. Augustine's who lived there ca. 1176–1200. It is argued that the occasion was not antiquarian in the usual sense of curiosity about old things, nor merely practical glossing (though both of these play a part, no doubt), but a self-conscious act of cultural appropriation of an old book juxtaposed with new learning in order to validate the scholarship of St. Augustine's and to reassert the antiquity and priority of this house, a desire powered by the anxieties and possibilities of a shifting cultural moment in the life of the house in the late twelfth century.

Benjamin Withers opens his recent study[25] by reminding us that to understand this impressive book properly we must consider all its components, texts, pictures, and structure and seek to imagine the "horizon of expectations" of its early users. And by the same token we should extend this "horizon" to take in its twelfth-century additions, accepting them as an artifact of a larger ongoing dynamic situation, the life of a book with its texts, pictures, structure, and annotations, as they formed part of the horizon of expectations of generations of St. Augustine's monks who venerated and preserved it from the twelfth to the sixteenth centuries. They elevated it to the first place of their library, with the Genesis volumes, on the first shelf of the first bookcase,[26] and we get closer to what it must have meant to them and how they thought of it when we put the annotations into our line of vision.

[25] Withers, *Frontiers*, 9–13.

[26] James, *Ancient Libraries*, 201; it should be kept in mind that this was its place at the end of the fifteenth century, the date of the catalogue in which it was mentioned, and also that James makes a notation indicating that this item was added to the catalogue later than when it was first compiled; see now also Barker-Benfield, *St. Augustine's Abbey*, 1: 405–6.

II. The Textual Evidence

When one focuses on the twelfth-century additions to Cotton Claudius B. iv, one sees a rich, pervasive pattern of interventions that were no doubt intended as enhancements of the book. They form textual, intellectual, and visual patterns in complicated interplay with the preexisting Old English texts and with the original illustrations. The placement of the notes is usually in rational relation to the Old English text and pictures. Sometimes the interrelation of the note as comment to the text is complex or obscure. Very often relationships are explicitly marked with *signes de renvoi*. The best way to study this, is of course, by following the texts given here as they actually appear on the page, as can be seen in the generally available complete printed facsimile and by the recently published CD-ROM facsimile.[1] The following semi-diplomatic edition of the Claudius annotations is based on two collations of the manuscript, a collation of the CD-ROM, and constant reference to the printed facsimile.

The reader may want to scan the annotations quickly and proceed to Chapter 3, referring back to this chapter as discussions warrant. The annotations constitute an interesting body of texts in their own right, most of them translated into English for the first time here. The presentation of the notes is meant, however, to form the basis of the present study. Necessary biblical references are supplied. The twelfth-century English and Latin notes are keyed to the Vulgate as in Crawford's textual edition[2] of the earlier Old English text; citations of the original Old English text of the Hexateuch are printed in **bold**; when placement on the page is significant or a note is especially difficult to locate, its location is specified. Exact punctuation is retained and manuscript lineation is indicated. Manuscript lines indicated by (|), run-ons by (/). Years Anno Mundi as they appear in the text, taken from Bede's *De temporum ratione*, are given in bold and, as far as possible, with the note they stand nearest to, though they are never strictly part of the note.[3] The resolution of abbreviations, which are generally standard for the late twelfth century in the Latin and are few in the English, are

[1] Dodwell and Clemoes, *Illustrated Hexateuch*; the CD-ROM facsimile accompanies Withers, *Frontiers*, also now available online at the British Library website.

[2] Crawford, ed., *The Old English Version of the Heptateuch*, hereafter "Crawford".

[3] But in most cases this is not possible and they are merely keyed to their place on the page. For a discussion of the Anno Mundi dates, see ch. 6, 330–33.

indicated by italicized letters. In English notes, accents are retained when they are "flagged," but hairline strokes are not noted; in Latin notes, hairline strokes usually function as the dot of an "i" and normally are not specially noted; such marks over other vowels are shown when the mark seems to be that of the writing hand; seemingly accidental and vagrant hairline strokes and strokes not over vowels are normally not noted. The Claudius text is presented as it is, with minimum necessary corrections indicated in brackets after *recte*; only such mistakes as might cause doubt or confusion are marked *sic*. The edited text of the HS cited in the notes is that of Patrologia Latina, volume 198 (by column), unless Sylwan's edition is expressly indicated.[4] Translations of biblical quotations generally follow the wording of the Douay-Rheims version. Substantial differences and significant textual issues that arise from consultation of Sylwan's edition are mentioned in the footnotes, using Sylwan's sigla.[5] When an excerpt from the received text is substantially rearranged, or the excerpt is a combination of two disparate passages, the breaks are indicated by a back slash in the translation (\), or in the original text, if untranslated. The translations tacitly correct errors in the Latin *ad libitum* and add biblical citations. Omissions of words or phrases from the source text are indicated by ellipses in the translations at the analogous point.[6] Brief notes on the contents of illustrations are given; all labels of pictures

---

4 Agnete Sylwan, ed., *Petri Comestoris Scolastica historia: Liber Genesis*, CCCM 191 (Turnhout, 2005).

5 Sigla, following Sylwan (see discussion, ch. 5, 255n1, 263–68), are:

X hypothetical ancestor of Peter Comestor's original version, ca. 1170
- **P** Paris, BN Lat. 16943 (dated 1183, Corbie) best extant representative of X

Y hypothetical ancestor of the revised version of ca. 1179, represented by
- **S** Porto, Bibl. Pub. Mun., Santa Cruz 42 (s. xii^{ex}, Sens or Troyes), elements of the revised text inserted into the **X** text

β integral revised text **Y**, represented by
- **Tr** Troyes, Bibl. Mun. 290 (1184–1200, Troyes)
- **W** Wien, Österreichische Nationalbib. 363 (1180–83, Mondsee)

γ is **Y** text with post-1179 revisions, represented by
- **Pa** Paris BN 14368 (s. xii^{ex}, St. Victor, Paris)
- **To** Tours, Bibl. Mun. 42 (s. xii^{ex}, Paris)

δ is mixed text containing elents of **X**, **Y**, and γ, represented by
- **L** Lyon, Bibl. Mun. 187 (s. xii^{ex}, Paris)
- **T** Troyes, Bibl. Mun. 451 (s. xii^{ex}, Paris)
- **Cl** London, BL Cotton Claudius B. iv (s. xi^{med}, notes s. xii^{ex}, St. Augustine's Canterbury)

6 Commonly used abbreviations are:

B-T: J. Bosworth and T. N. Toller, *An Anglo-Saxon Dictionary and Supplement* (Oxford, 1898, 1921)

CCCM: Corpus Christianorum, Continuatio Mediaevalis

CCSL: Corpus Christianorum, Series Latina

mentioned below have been added in late twelfth-century script unless otherwise noted. Annotations are sequentially numbered for reference; Old English notes are placed in their sequence among the Latin ones, and are flagged by boldface item numbers.

F. 1v OE 39 lines = Preface + Genesis 1:1–5

1. § Fiat lux. et facta e*st* lux. i*d est* u*er*bum genuit: i*n* quo erat: ut fieret lux. i*d est* tam facile: ut | quis u*er*bo. Et appellauit luce[m] die*m*: á dian: q*uo*d e*st* claritas. sic*ut* lux d*icitu*r. q*uia* luit. i*d est* purgat tenebras. (HS 1057B/C)

"Let there be light and light was made." That is, he brought forth the Word in which he existed in order that light could come into being, that is, as easily as anyone (might indicate) by a word. . . . "And he called the light day," from (Greek) 'dia', that is 'clearness,' just as light is so called because it expiates, that is, it clears away the darkness. (Gen. 1:3, 5)

F. 2r Full-page picture of Fall of Angels

CD:	Ps.-Jerome, *Commentarius in canticum Debborae*, PL 23
CPL:	E. Dekkers, ed. *Clavis patrum latinorum*, 3rd ed. (Steenbrugis, 1995)
CSEL:	Corpus Scriptorum Ecclesiasticorum Latinorum
DTR:	Bede, *De temporum ratione*, PL 86
HS:	Petrus Comestor, *Historia Scholastica*, PL 198, cited by column
HQG:	Jerome, *Hebraicae quaestiones in libro Geneseos*, PL 23
Laistner:	*see* NLA
LJ:	*The Latin Josephus*, ed. Franz Blatt, *The Latin Josephus, I: Introduction and Text, The Antiquities: Books I-V* (Aarhus, 1958)
NLA:	Bede, *Nomina regionum atque locorum de Actibus Apostolorum*, ed. M.L.W. Laistner, *Bedae Venerabilis Expositio Actuum Apostolorum et Retractio* (Cambridge, MA, 1939; rpr. New York, 1970), also ed. Laistner, CCSL 121; pr. in PL 23 and PL 92, cited from PL 92 by col. and CCSL 121 by page and line
QH1P:	Ps.-Jerome, *Quaestiones Hebraicae in I-II Paralipomenon*, PL 23
PL:	Patrologia Latina
Sackur:	E. Sackur, ed., *Sibyllinische Texte und Forschungen: Pseudomethodius Adso und Die tiburtinische Sibylle* (Halle a.S., 1898)
SNLH:	Jerome/Eusebius, *De situ et nominibus locorum Hebraicorum*, PL 23, also P. de Lagarde, ed. Onomastica sacra (Göttingen, 1887)
Sylwan:	A. Sylwan, ed., *Petri Comestoris Scolastica historia: Liber Genesis*, CCCM 191 (Turnhout, 2005), cited by page and line
VSC:	Video Spectral Comparitor (at British Library)

F. 2v *Illustration:* Second day, God creating and dividing the Firmament **OE** = Genesis 1:6–13

F. 3r *Illustrations:* Upper panel: Third day, God creating plants; lower panel: Fourth day: God creating sun and moon **OE** = Genesis 1:14–19
2. Et d*icitu*r sol:· q*uia* solus lucet. i*d est* nullu*m* cu*m* eo:· luna:· luminu*m* una. i*d est* p*r*ima ut una dierum. *ue*l una | sabb*at*oru*m* d*icitu*r. Sol 7 luna d*icuntur* magna luminaria:· in duobus. 7 ex duob*us*:· i*d est non* solu*m* pro | qu*a*ntitate luminis:· s*ed* 7 corp*o*ris. 7 n*on* t*antu*m co*mparati*one stellarum s*ed* 7 sec*und*um se. q*uia* sol d*icitu*r | octies maior t*er*ra. et luna etiam maior d*icitu*r terra:- (HS 1060A)

And the sun is called 'sol' because it shines alone, there is nothing with it. The moon is one of the luminaries, that is first, as day one, it is called first day of the Sabbath. The sun and the moon are called "great lights" (Gen. 1:16) in respect to those two and from the two, that is, it is not only because of the quantity of the light but also because of their size and not just in comparison to the stars but in themselves, because the sun is said to be eight times the size of the earth and the moon is said to be bigger than the earth.

F. 3v *Illustration:* Fifth day: God creating fish and birds **OE** = Genesis 1:20–27

3.[7] S*ed* dum. Methodi*us* e*ss*et in cárcere martyre.[8] reuelatu*m* est ei a sp*irit*u de p*r*incipio. 7 fine mundi:· q*uod* et oraue|rat. et scriptum licet simpliciter reliquit. dicens q*uod* uirgines egressi súnt[9] de paradiso: (HS 1076B)

But when Methodius the martyr was in prison what he had prayed for about the beginning and ending of the world was revealed to him by the Spirit, and he left a writing, though in a simple style, saying that they (sc. Adam and Eve) went from Paradise as virgins.[10]

4.[11] § Cete. neutri:· i*n*declinabile e*st*. declinatur t*ame*n hic cet*us*. ceti. 7 omne*m* anima*m* uiue*n*tem atq*ue* mo|tabile*m* qu*a*m p*r*oduxerunt aque. Motabiles au*tem* d*icuntur* a*nim*e pisciu*m*. 7 auiu*m*:· respectu anime homi|nu*m*. Ille. *enim* mouent*ur* de e*ss*e ad n*on* e*ss*e. Illa:· n*on* q*uia* p*er*petua e*st*. Vel q*uia* forsan animas non h*abe*nt:· | Ip*su*m animal anima*m* uocauit:· i*d est* uiuens- (HS 1061D/1062A)[12]

---

[7] This note uses insular *r* and *g*.

[8] So CD-ROM; Sylwan 26/5: "Sed Methodius martyr orauit dum esset in carcere, et reuelatum. . . ."

[9] "sunt" is correct; the scribe appears to have written "fínit."

[10] Cf. Sackur, 60: "Sciendum namque est, quomodo exeuntes Adam quidem et Eua de paradiso uirgines fuisse."

[11] In margin there is an insertion mark and the letter 'b' referring to the picture of the whale above, marked with a similar insertion mark and 'a'.

[12] *Sylwan* neutri generis] generis *om. Cl S γ* ‖ *Sylwan* est indeclinabile est] i. e. *Cl Pa* ‖ *Sylwan* declinatur] tamen *add. Cl S β γ δ* ‖ *Sylwan* huius ceti] huius *om. Cl S* ‖ *Syl-*

'Cete' whale, when neuter . . . is indeclinable; it is also declined masculine 'cetus,' . . . 'ceti'. "And every moving and living creature which the waters brought forth" (Gen. 1:21): 'Moving' is to say the life force of fish and birds, (as well as) in respect to the life of men. For those are moving from being to nonbeing, but this (the soul) is not because it is perpetual or perhaps because those (animals) do not have souls. . . . An animal is so called from its 'anima', that is, it lives.

F. 4r *Illustration:* Sixth day: God creating Adam amidst animals **OE** = Genesis 1:27–31

5. Faciam*us* homine*m* 7 loq*uitur* p*ate*r ad filiu*m*. 7 sp*iritu*m s*anctu*m. Vel e*st* qu*as*i uóx c*ommunis* triu*m* p*er*sonaru*m*∵ faciamus. 7 n*ost*ram∵ (HS 1063C)

"Let us make man" (Gen. 1:26) . . . and the Father says this to the Son and Holy Spirit; or rather it is like a shared voice of the three persons: 'Let us make' and 'our'.

6a. .Methodi*us* cw̄æð. adam wǽs gescéopa mán on wlíte óf ðritig wíntra. 7 naþeles on áne dǽge. 7 géara | 7 æfter ðam `án 7-´ twa wintra. 7 þri wíntra. 7 alla ða oðron.[13]

Methodius said Adam was created a man in appearance of thirty years and yet in one day and a year and after that (one and) two years and three years and all the others.

6b.[14] P*r*ima e*st* e*r*go hui*us* mu*n*di etas ab ada*m* usq*ue* / ad Noe—id *est* a[d] diluuio | **annos. ī.dc.lvi.**[15] (Bede, DTR, PL 90.520D)

Therefore the first age of this world is from Adam to Noe, that is to the flood; 1656 years.

---

wan produxerant] -unt *Cl γ* ‖ *Sylwan* respectu hominis] anime *add. Cl S β γ δ* ‖ *Sylwan* ista non] illa n. *Cl Pa T* ‖ *Sylwan* sed ipsum] sed *om. Cl S Tr γ δ* ‖ *Sylwan* uocauerit] -uit *Cl S Pa γ*

[13] OE = HS 1076B: "Et si enim factus est Adam quasi in ætate triginta annorum, tamen fuit unius diei, et anni; et post, duorum annorum, et trium, et sic de cæteris." That is, though appearing to be 30, 31, 32, 33 years old, he is actually only 1 day and then 1, 2, 3 years old, etc.

[14] This continues unbroken from the previous note on the same line, the ink and nib apparently the same, beginning blackest with 'Methodius' and gradually becoming browner at 'wæs gesceopa', etc. with the tendency of the ink to occasionally become darker even within single letters; for example 'óf' is dark and in 'dǽge' the lower part of 'ǽ' and 'g' apparently have been retouched with blacker ink. The added superscript 'an 7-'is in a darker ink. The color alternates as if getting lighter as the ink runs out of the pen and this situation continues through 6b.

[15] Anno Mundi date; see headnote to this chapter and ch. 6, 330–33.

F. 4v *Illustration:* God in mandorla blessing creation **OE** = Genesis 2:1–7

7. (around top of frame, 3 lines) Joseph*us* (. .) cw̄æð. þ*æt* wǽs in syrie on áne felde abute damasco. of rædra yrþe. þ*æt* is mæden yrðe. | þ*æt* ís úniwemð yrðe. lánd huniréped- | þat is cláne land[16]

Josephus said that was in Syria in a field near Damascus, of red earth, that is virgin earth, that is uncorrupted earth, land untouched, that is pure land.

8.[17] § Tria. *enim* op*er*a fecerat. *cre*auit. disposuit. ornauit:- Quartu*m* opu*s* *pro*pagationis non desinit op*er*ari:' | Et benedixit diei septimo:' (HS 1065B)

For he did three works: he created, he ordered and adorned. A fourth work of propagation he did not fail to accomplish. . . . "And he blessed the seventh day" (Gen. 2:3).

F. 5r *Illustrations:* Upper: God, between two trees, planting the garden; lower: River Phison, represented by a green band of color. **OE** = Genesis 2:8–12; the notes 9a-f are a more-or-less continuous series in six spaces of ff. 5r-v.

9a. Et fluuiu*s* uel fons egredieba|tur ad irrigandu*m* paradisum. | i*d est* ligna paradisi. fons p*otes*t intelli|gi uel abissus. i*d est* matrix om*n*ium | aquaru*m*:' uel p*ro* fontes. p*er* sil*l*epsim | .Irrigare au*tem* positu*m* e*st* *pro* | ministrare[18] hu-|more*m* (HS 1068B)[19]

"And a river" or fountain "went out to water paradise" (Gen. 2:10), that is the trees of paradise; 'fountain' can be understood either as the 'abyss', that is the source of all waters or for 'fountains', by syllepsis [the singular for plural] . . . . 'To water, irrigate' is put for 'to supply moisture'.

9b. fison. qui et. á gangaro rege indie:' ganges. ⁊ int*er*pretat*ur* phison. s*ecundum* ysidoru*m*:' cate|rua. q*uia*. x flumina recipit. Vel mutatio oris. q*uia* mutat*ur* a facie

[16] There is a hairstroke through the *d* of 'land', not like the usual "flagged" stroke through *ð*; the passage is derived from HS 1071A/B: "Similiter sicut hoc nomen Adam fuit proprium illi homini, nunc vero est commune, et Adam sonat *rubreus*, vel *rubra terra*, quia, secundum Josephum, de rubea terra conspersa factus est. Talis est enim virgo tellus, et vera, vel rubea . . . (Additio 1) Terra proprie adhuc virgo erat, quia nondum corrupta hominum opere, nec sanguine infecta" (this Additio is in recensions *S β Pa γ*); cf. no. 15 which partly reflects the wording of this HS passage.

[17] Bottom two lines, with *signe de renvoi* 'hwǽr' referring this comment to the main OE text at line 17, 'hǽr'; the small 'b' in the margin opposite note 7 may be to indicate that it should be read after note 8.

[18] 'hu' cancelled after 'ministrare', and 'humore*m*' written on next line.

[19] *Sylwan* fons uel fluuius] fl. u. f. *Cl γ* ‖ *Sylwan* pro] *add. Cl S Tr γ δ* ‖ *Sylwan* silensum] sylempsin *Tr*, sillepsim *Cl*, *q.l. Sylwan*

qu*a*m h*abe*t i*n* paradiso- | hic circuiuit [*sic*] t*er*ram euilath. i*d est* indiam. 7 trahit aureas arenas: (HS 1068B/C)[20]

Phison, which is also . . . from Gangarus, King of India, (called) Ganges. And according to Isidore, Phison is interpreted 'crowd' because it receives ten rivers, or as 'change of face' because it changes its appearance from what it had in Paradise. . . . This "goes around the land of Evilath" (Gen. 2:11), that is, India and it carries down golden sand.[21]

F. 5v *Illustrations:* Top: River Geon, represented as four men; middle: River Tigris, represented by stylized waves and four men on the right gazing to the left; bottom: River Euphrates, represented by a green band with an outlined wave on the left. OE = Gen. 2:13–14

9c. Géon. q*ui* et nilu*s*. et sonat hya|tus t*er*re. Vel t*er*reus. q*uia* turbidus est. hic circuit ethiopiam: et irrigabat | t*er*ram egipti \`ut´ ubi uenit locusta-[22] (HS 1068C / 1066A)

Gehon . . . which is also Nile and called 'opening of the earth' or 'made of earth' because it is turbid. This "flows around Ethiopia" (Gen. 2:13) . . . and waters the land of Egypt . . . (as) where the locust comes (cf. Ex. 10:4).

9d. Dic*it* ioseph*us* q*uod* tygris d*icitu*r diglat. q*uod* sonat acutu*m* uel an|gustum. tygris animal e*st* uolocissimu*m*. [*sic*] 7 i*de*o fluuius ille. a sui uelocitate tygridi[23] eq*ui*uocatu*s* | est. Hic uenit[24] contra assyrios. (HS 1068C)

Josephus says that the Tigris is called 'Diglat' which means 'pointed' or 'narrow'. The tiger is a very swift animal and this river because of its swift current is likened to a tiger. It comes "along by the Assyrians" (Gen. 2:14).

9e. (insular *f*, *g* and *r*) § eufrates. 7 tygris. in mare. rubru*m* ferunt*ur*. (LJ 128. 21–22)

The Euphrates . . . and Tigris are carried into the Red Sea.

---

20 *Sylwan* qui a] et *add. Cl γ T* ‖ *Sylwan* indie dictus est ganges] d. e. *om. Cl Pa* ‖ *Sylwan* physon] phison *Cl S* ‖ circuit *Sylwan & mss*] circumit PL

21 Is the top illustration on f. 5v an out-of-place illustration of the River Ganges, the four figures representing a "crowd" ('caterua') or by a linguistic/visual pun men engaging in "an exchange of speech" ('oris mutatio')?

22 *Sylwan:* "irrigabat terram ut Nilus Egyptum" (26/21) . . . "ut ibi: Venit locusta" (26/27); the latter phrase is from an Additio lacking in *β γ δ*.

23 The scribe wrote the 'g' of 'tygridi' in insular form and altered it to proto-gothic script.

24 *Sylwan:* "uadit."

9f. **Seo feorðe ea is gehaten eufrates.**[25] frugifer vel fructuosu*s* | de quo p*er* quas t*r*ansiret regiones. d*icitu*r. *enim* ganges na`s´ci in locis cau`cau´casi[26] montis. Nilus; | non p*ro*cul ab athlante: Tygris et eufrates: ex armenia:- hec. iiii^{or}. flumina ut | diximus ab eode*m* fonte emanant.[27] et sep*ara*nt*ur*. (HS 1068C/D)

The fourth river is called Euphrates, 'fertile' or 'fruitful', concerning which regions it passes through [Moses is silent] . . . It is said that the Ganges arises in places in the Caucasian mountains. Nile is not far from the Atlas mountains. The Tigris and Euphrates are out of Armenia. . . . These four rivers as we said arise from the same source and become separated.

10. (f. 5v, bottom 4 lines)[28] Me red on bóc. be paradisu*m* in eden þ*æt* is neorxna. wanga. eden þ*æt* is inne estnysse. ⁊ inne blisse. eden is at anhǽfede[29] | angynne on hésdele þysre wórlde. se stéde is swyþe on suóte breðe. ⁊ swyðe suóte sḿelle. ⁊ wénsæm wúnyunge. | ⁊ láng hidráan an héstdele. anlǽnges ðare sǽ, bútan úre wuniaghe. ut usq*ue*. ad lunarem globum attíngit. þ*æt* ís | tó þas mónas træenle hí táeh`e´. ⁊ ðaer þa wæteræ dilúuii ne ne cóme. ðat is Nóes floð.[30]

It is read in a book about paradise in Eden, that is "Neorxnawang," Eden that is in pleasure and in bliss. Eden is at the (furrow) end, the beginning in the east parts of this world. The place is very much into [*sic*] sweet breath and very sweet smell and a pleasant dwelling-place and extended far into the east parts alongside the sea outside of our country *so that it reaches up to the globe of the moon*, that is to the moon's orbit it draws and there the waters *of the flood* do not come. That is Noe's flood.

---

[25] The Latin note is written as if continuing or completing the main OE text and continues three lines into the lower picture frame.

[26] Second 'cau' cancelled then added above.

[27] *Sylwan* manant] emanant *Cl γ δ*

[28] The accents represented in this transcription are the large bold hooked ones of the scribe and occur on Latin words as well as Old English ones; other hairline strokes typical of the regular *i*-dot strokes have been added, some over *i*'s but also over some vowels, and are not represented here.

[29] The MS spacing is 'atan hǽfede'. Crawford incorrectly reads "atanha ðam." Apparently it is for *andheafdu*: the place where the plow is turned at the end of the furrow, marking the boundary of a field, a late (s. xii) charter term. See *Dictionary of Old English*, s.v. and ch. 3, 202.

[30] Cf. HS 1067A/B ". . . vel a principio, id est a prima orbis parte. Unde alia translatio habet, paradisum in Eden ad orientem. . . . Ergo idem est paradisum voluptatis quod paradisum in Eden, id est in deliciis. Sed a principio, idem quod ad orientem. Est autem locus amœnissimus longo terræ, et maris tractu a nostra habitabili zona secretus, adeo elevatus ut usque ad lunarem globum attingat. Unde, et aquæ diluvii illuc non pervenerunt." PL's "terræ et maris tractu" is reading of *S δ*; Sylwan reads "maris et terre tractu" which better matches the English.

F. 6r *Illustration:* God instructing Adam in Paradise and presenting the animals. 13 lines above large picture space, God placing Adam in Paradise = **OE** Genesis 2:15–20; an apparently early (s. xi) gloss on line 1, **on `eden´ neorxnawange.**

F. 6v *Illustration:* Double picture in frame: God creating Eve, God uniting Adam and Eve.[31] **OE** = Genesis 2:21–25

11. (insular *g* and *r*) Vnde. ⁊ euigilans: p*ro*phetauit de *con*iu[n]cictione [*sic*] chr*ist*i. ⁊ ecclesie. etiam de diluuio futuro. ⁊ iudicio | futuro p*er* ignem. ibidem cognouit. ⁊ liberis suis indicauit. (HS 1070B)[32]

Whence, waking up, he both prophesied of the joining of Christ and the Church and also learned of the future flood and future . . . judgment through fire and (afterwards) revealed (it) . . . to his offspring.

12. § Diabolu*s* elegit Quodda*m* serpentis gen*us*. ut ait beda. ui*r*gineu*m* habens uultu*m*. q*u*ia similia similib*us* | ,ap[p]laudunt. ⁊ mouit lingu*a*m ei*us* ad loque*n*du*m*: t*am*en nescientes [*recte* -tis] sicut ⁊ p*er* phanaticos. ⁊ inerguminos l*o*q*u*itur. | Nestie*n*tes [*recte* -tis]. ⁊ ait. Cur p*re*cepit uobis d*eus* ut n*on* comede*r*`e´tis de omni ligno paradisi:· i*d est* ut co*m*mede*r*etis. de ligno. s*ed* | n*on* de omni:· (HS 1072B)[33]

The devil chose a certain kind of serpent, as Bede said, having the face of a virgin because like approves like, and he moved its tongue in order to make it speak, although it did not know how, the way he also speaks through the mad and the possessed, ignorant as they are, and says: "Why has God commanded you that you should not eat of every tree of Paradise?" (Gen. 3:1) that is, that you may eat of some tree but not of all.

F. 7r *Illustration:* Eve accepting the fruit from the serpent, turning to Adam, who eats. 26 lines below picture frame **OE** = Genesis 3:7–19

13a. § Hic q*u*ida*m* dicunt ficum | fuisse arborem p*ro*hibita*m* | ⁊ audier*unt* uoce*m* d*om*ini- (HS 1073C)

Here some say that the fig-tree was the forbidden tree, and they heard "the voice of the Lord" (cf. Gen. 3:8).

---

[31] The two faces of Eve appear to have been retouched by a later hand.

[32] *Sylwan* 31/21, et] etiam *Cl To T* ‖ *Sylwan* de iudicio] de *om. Cl γ* ‖ *Sylwan* suis postea] postea *om. Cl Tr γ δ*

[33] *Sylwan* genus serpentis] g. s. *Cl β γ* ‖ *Sylwan* uultum habens] h. u. *Cl β γ* ‖ *Sylwan* ad loquendum linguam eius] l. e. ad lo. *Cl Tr* ‖ *Sylwan* sicut et] et *add. Cl W*

13b.[34] hic sup*er*ba. 7 stulta r[es]|ponsio quasi displice|ret nudu*s*. qui | tal*is* fuerat factu[s] (HS 1073C)

Here is a proud and stupid response, as he was displeased being naked, who was created that way.

13c. § et sic*ut* naturale e*st* odiu*m*[35] i*n*ter equos. 7 gryfes∵ lupos 7 cánes∵ sic int*er* homine*m* et serpentem. | sic*ut*. *enim* uenenu*m* serpentis homine*m*∵ sic sputu*m* ho*min*is ieiuni p*er*imit. serpente*m*∵ et q*ui*a nudi erant | adhuc∵ serpens m*od*o nud*us* [*recte*-um] homine*m* timet. 7 fugit 7 [in] uestitu*m*∵ insilit. (HS 1074A)

And just as there is natural enmity between the horse and the griffin and between the wolf and the dog, so there is between man and the serpent. Just as the serpent's poison destroys a man, so the spittle of a man who is fasting destroys a serpent. And because up to then they were naked, inasmuch as a serpent fears and flees a naked man and . . . leaps (on) one who is clothed.

F. 7v *Illustration:* Upper: God to left of tree confronts Adam and Eve, who attempt to hide; lower, two panels: left, God expels Adam (partially clothed) and Eve (fully clothed) from Paradise; right, Adam and Eve, now fully clothed, do labor, an angel to the right.[36] **OE** = Genesis 3:19–24

14. Me cwæð. þ*æt* | hi wære inne | neorxna wange | vii. tide[37]

It is said that they were in paradise seven hours.

15.[38] In syrie. abute damasco. | ón áne felde. | þanon hé | com | þær cayn abel | ofsloh. 7 beside | þan wǽs adam. 7 | eue. bebyríg|de. on þan týw|féalde scrǽfe-[39]

---

[34] In right margin, 4 lines, trimmed, insular *h* and *r*; underlined in main text is **Adam hwær eart ðu?**

[35] *Sylwan* (43/34): Et ita, sicut naturale odium est inter] nat. e. o. *Cl W γ* ‖*Sylwan* in uestitum] in *om. Cl*; there are other casual word-order changes not attested in Sylwan or PL.

[36] Adam is digging with a spade; Eve is holding what appears to be a pick but must represent a distaff. On the facing fol. 8r, lower right panel, Cain's spade mirrors Adam's and Adam's pick mirrors Eve's.

[37] HS 1075D: "Quidam tradunt eos fuisse in paradiso septem horas" (an Additio in *S β γ δ*, Sylwan 45/11, note).

[38] In the right panel of the lower picture the English is in three irregular short lines and six regular short lines; a *signe de renvoi* 'hær' with a slanting line and two dots is matched by 'hwær' with the same code on f. 8r, lower frame left panel, top 4 lines, referring to the Latin text (no. 19), which is the one the English is translating here.

[39] HS 1075B ". . . in agrum scilicet Damascenum, de quo sumptus fuerat, in quo Cain Abel suum fratrem interfecit, juxta quem Adam et Eva sepulti sunt in spelunca duplici" (= no. 19). The verb 'wæs' is perhaps the result of the scribe misreading the 'sūt' in no. 19 on the opposite page as "fuit." See also no. 7.

In Syria near Damascus in a field from where he came, there Cain slew Abel and beside it Adam and Eve were [was] buried in a double cave.

16. (ink is light brown) Met`h´odi*us* cw̄æð. adam slép be ís wífe. 7 hi gestrínde sunes. | 7 dohtra.[40]

Methodius said (that) Adam slept with his wife and begot sons and daughters.

17.[41]§ Si q*u*erit*ur* q*u*id co*n*sumebat ignis ille. potest dici q*uo*d q*ue*da*m* spe*ci*es ignis e*st*. sic*ut* (. . . . .)[42] legit*ur*. cui si | manu*m* adhibes ardore*m* sentis. s*ed* non pat*er*is adustione*m*. n*e*c eget mat*er*ria [*sic*] qu*a*m co*n*sumat. 7 talis urit | sp*iritu*m. Si q*u*erit*ur* qu*a*re d*eu*s p*er*miserit[43] temptari. cu*m* sciret homine*m*[44] lapsuru*m*. 7 de multis in hu*n*c ‖ modu*m*[45] dicim*us*. qu*a*ntu*m* ad p*re*sens op*us* actinet [*sic*] q*uia* sic uoluit. Si q*u*erat*ur* cur uoluit; insipi`d´a est / questio. (HS 1075C/D)

If it is asked what this fire consumed, one can say that it is a certain kind of fire, as is read (in the life of St. Nicholas): if you hold out your hand to it, you feel the heat but do not suffer burning; nor does it lack material to consume; and such (a fire) burns the spirit. . . . If it is asked why God would have permitted man to be tempted, when he knew he would fall, and concerning many questions of this sort, we say, as far as it pertains to the present work, because he willed it so. If it is asked why he willed it, that is a foolish question.

F. 8r *Illustrations:* Upper, two panels: left, two cherubim, one with sword; right, gate of Paradise and two trees; lower: left, Adam to left and Abel tending his sheep to right; right, Cain digging, with Adam to right. **OE** = Genesis 3:24–4:2

18. Eftter [*sic*] fyftene wintra. 7 is súster[46] chalmana.[47]

After fifteen winters, and his sister Chalmana.

[40] HS 1076A "Adam cognovit uxorem suam . . . et plures subticet Adæ filios et filias." The ascription in the English to Methodius is extrapolated from the fact that two sentences in this chapter of the *Historia* ("De generationibus Ade," ch. 25) are ascribed to Methodius; the next sentence in the *Historia* is a Methodius comment, already copied on f. 3v in Latin, concerning the virginity of Adam and Eve in Paradise (no. 3).

[41] F. 7v, bottom margin, 3 lines, carrying over to f. 8r top, 1 line; *signe de renvoi* 'hwær' with cross which is referenced to main OE text about fiery sword at top of f. 8r.

[42] In erasure: 'i⟨n⟩ uita beati nicolai' (VSC).

[43] *Sylwan*: "permisit Deus hominem temptare."

[44] hominem] *add. Cl Tr To.*

[45] Imperfectly altered from 'modis'.

[46] Or 'sueter'; cf. the gloss immediately above the lower frame where the same hand writes '7 suester'.

[47] This item is not noted by Crawford. It is along the bottom of the left panel in the upper picture frame. The Latin sources are lower on the page, in the right panel, see no.

19.[48] Emisit eu*m* d*eu*s de paradiso uol*uptatis*. ut op*eraretur* t*erram* de qua | su*m*p-t*us* e*st*. i*n* agrum i*d est* damescenu*m*. un*de* su*m*pt*us* fuerat. | in quo caym abel occidit. iuxta quem ada*m* et | eua sepulti su*n*t. in spelunca duplici. (HS 1075C)[49]

"And God sent him out from the paradise of pleasure to till the earth from which he was taken" (Gen. 3:23) to the field, that is, of Damascus, whence he was taken in which Cain . . . killed Abel, near which Adam and Eve are buried in a double cave.

20.[50] Abel fuit pastor. et cayn agricola. post multos | dies obt`u´lerunt[51] d*omi*no munera. Caym de frugib*us*:. | Abel:· lac 7 p*r*imogenita agnorum. Credit*ur* ada*m*[52] in | sp*irit*u docuisse filios. ut d*e*o offerre*n*t decimas.[53] et res|pexit d*omi*n*u*s ad[54] abel. ad cayn u*er*o n*on* respexit. Irat*us* | est cayn. Increpans *ergo* d*omi*n*u*s cayn:· ait. Q*uare* irat*us* es:· | n*on*ne[55] si bene egeris:· recipies p*remiu*m. s*cilicet* a me. (HS 1076D-1077A/B)

"Abel was a shepherd and Cain a farmer; . . . after many days they brought the Lord gifts," Cain of his produce, Abel . . . of milk and the firstlings of his lambs. . . . It is believed that Adam taught his sons by the Spirit that they offer tithes to God . . . "and the Lord had respect to Abel . . . to Cain truly . . . he had not respect. . . . Cain was angry." Speaking loudly, the Lord thus said to Cain: "Why are you angry? If you do well will you not receive" the reward, namely from me? (Gen. 4:2, 3–7)

21.[56] Et anno uite Ade q*u*into decimo nat*us* e*st* ei caim. | et soror ei*us* Calmana. 7 potuit an*te* cain m*u*ltos | genuisse q*u*i tacent*ur* hic. 7 p*ost* alios. xv. annos | nat*us* e*st* ei abel. 7 soror ei*us* delbora. Anno uite | ada*m*. c°.xxx. chaim occidit abel. 7 luxeru*n*t- | eu*m*. ada*m* 7 eua .c. annis. (HS 1076B)

---

21. Related to this item, in the main text, are added late 12c glosses: **Eft** `ofer oðra xv.´ **he ge|strynde abel** `7 suester delbora´.

[48] In the lower frame, left panel, 4 top lines; the English note, no. 15, on the facing verso, lower right panel, translates this passage; the *signe de renvoi* refers to this English note.

[49] Sylwan (47/33): dominus] deus *Cl Tr γ* ‖ *Sylwan* assumptus] sumptus *Cl Tr γ T* ‖ *Sylwan* de quo] unde *Cl β γ* ‖ *Sylwan* suum fratrem interfecit] occidit *Cl*

[50] In the lower frame, left panel, 7 lower lines.

[51] Scribe wrote 'obtilerunt' and corrected.

[52] Looks like 'aða' but the flagged stroke is probably a reflex for the abbreviation stroke.

[53] Sylwan (49/1) Deo] domino *Cl S Tr δ* ‖ *Sylwan* (49/5) offerrent decimas Deo] deo o. dec. *Cl W γ To*.

[54] Corrected from 'ab'.

[55] Looks like 'ūne'.

[56] In the lower frame, right panel, upper 6 lines.

And in the fifteenth year of Adam's lifc Cain was born to him and his sister Chalmana.[57] . . . And before Cain he could have begotten many who are not mentioned here. And after another fifteen years Abel was born to him and his sister Delbora. In the one hundred and thirtieth year of Adam's life Cain killed Abel and Adam and Eve mourned him for a hundred years.

22.[58] Methodi*us*. 7 Joseph*us* | .cc. 7 xxx. annor*um* cu*m* [*recte* eum] fuisse sc*r*ibunt; cu*m* | gen*uit* seth. forte moyses. c annos luct*us* ade | p*r*et*er*misit. q*u*ia ut dixim*us*. ab adam i*n*cipit[59]| p*r*ima*m* etate*m*. alii a[60] Noe. Noe. x*imus* ab ada*m* i*n* q*uo* | p*r*imo [*sic*] etas terminata e*st*. (HS 1080C, 1081A)

. . . Methodius and Josephus write that [Adam] was 230 years old when he begot Seth. By chance Moses neglected to mention a period of 100 years of mourning by Adam because, as we said, from Adam he begins the first age of others up to Noe. Noe is the tenth from Adam, in whom the first age is terminated.[61]

23.[62] Supputa p*er* si*n*gulas | etates annor*um* numeru*m*. et inuenies ab ada*m* | usq*ue* ad natiuitate*m*. Noe annos. mille. | l. vi.[63]

Count up through the individual lifetimes the number of years and you will find from Adam to the birth of Noe is 1056 years.

24. Ab[64] ortu. Noe usq*ue* ad diluuiu*m*. annos sexsentos. a diluuio usq*ue* ad generatione*m* habraha*m*. annos | ducentos nonaginta duos. iuxta hebreos. et generatione`s´ vndecim. viuebat *er*go Noe. et | ad huc. xxx viii annis. sup*er*uixit.

57 See no. 18 (English).

58 Next 5 lines in the lower frame, right panel.

59 Over erasure, of 'incipiunt', *Sylwan* (57/2–3) incipiunt ab A.] ab a. incipiunt *β γ*.

60 'se' [seth] cancelled, text jumps from 1080C to 1081A, *Sylwan* 58/11–58/9–57/4-59/33.

61 The text is corrupt. See the English note on f. 10r (no. 38), which seems to be trying to translate the phrase from 1080C "Unde quidam incipiunt ab Adam primam ætatem; alii a Seth" ("whence some begin the first age from Adam, others from Seth"). Here the annotator is attempting to remodel this statement into the more familiar formula, "Adam begins the first age, Noe the second."

62 In the lower frame, right panel, final 4 lines.

63 This is apparently an original note. The information is from Bede, DTR, A.M. 1056, but the wording imitates Jerome, Ep. 73, "Ad Euangelum Presbyterum de Melchisedech" (ed. Hilberg, CSEL 55, 19.10): "Supputa per singulas aetates annorum numerum et inuenies ab ortu Sem usque ad generationem Abram trecentos nonagenta annos."

64 'Ab' altered from the "de" ligature.

ab `ortu´ abraha*m*. usq*ue* ad Iosue `i*d est* ad mortem. m.´ annos. ccccc qua[d]-raginta.[65]

From the birth of Noe up to the flood was 600 years, from the flood up to the generation of Abraham was 292 years according to the Hebrews and Noe therefore lived to the eleventh generation and up to this he lived 37 years after the birth of Abraham; up to Joshua (that is, to his death one thousand) 540 years.

F. 8v *Illustration:* divided into two panels: left, God enthroned, flanked by Cain and Abel in attitudes of worship; right, Cain killing Abel. **OE** = Genesis 4:3–15

25a.[66] Methodi*us* cw̄eð. | þa adam wæs ah`u´nd wíntra. 7 xxx. cayn ofsloh abel. þa wǽs | abel c. | wíntra | æfter þán. adam. 7 | eue. híne bewyppe. húnð | wín-tra.[67]

Methodius said when Adam was 130 years old Cain slew Abel when Abel was 100 years old: after that Adam and Eve wept for him for 100 years.

25b.[68] Se steðe ís ycwæðen. si dénæ of tǽran. besyde hebron þe adam. 7 eue. wypen.[69]

The place is called 'the vale of tears' beside Hebron where Adam and Eve wept.

F. 9r *Illustrations:* upper frame: God addresses Cain while turning his back on him; middle: Cain builds a city, his son Enoch and wife; lower, three panels: Line of Cain, left, Enoch with Mauiahel,[70] middle Mauiahel with Mathusala, right Mathusala with Lamech.[71] **OE** = Genesis 4:16–18

---

[65] After 'qua[d]raginta' is a mark '. ᴗ .' that might be interpreted as roman numeral '.v.'; but it is unlike any numeral or conclusion mark in the annotations. Source of the passage is unidentified. The addition above the line, including part of the numeral, shows that this is being copied from an exemplar, not improvised on the page.

[66] Irregularly runs from the left to the right panel, 1 short line on left, 3 on right; labeled 'a' under the last word.

[67] HS 1076B: "Anno vitæ Adam centesimo tricesimo Cain occidit Abel, et luxerunt eum Adam et Eva centum annis" (cf. no. 21). Pseudo-Methodius has (Sackur, 61): "Anno autem triginsimo et centisimo vitae Adae occidit Cain fratrem suum Abel et fecerunt planctum super eum Adam quoque et Eva annis C^{a}."

[68] One line, in lower ledger of picture frame, labeled 'b'.

[69] HS 1076 D (Add. 1): "Locus in quo luxerunt dicitur vallis lacrymarum juxta Hebrom" (cf. no. 21).

[70] Following the OE text, which omits "Irad"; cf. Dodwell and Clemoes, *Illustrated Hexateuch*, 19.

[71] Dodwell and Clemoes, *Illustrated Hexateuch*, 19, suggest that the child reaches for a double branch to signify his future bigamy, the topic of the comment written immediately beneath (no. 30).

26. Joseph*us* cwæð. fæle cenne lándes | ywilcon caym. 7 calmana is wyf. | forð hi cómen to hæra stede | þe me cw*æðe* naida.[72]

Josephus said, many kinds of land Cain overwalked,[73] and Calmana his wife. They came forth to the place which is called 'Naid'.

27.[74] § Naid t*er*ra in q*u*a habi|tauit cain. Vertit*ur* au*tem* in salum id e*st* motu*m* siue | fluctuatione*m*. (SNLH 23.912D; Lagarde 141.24)

Naid is the land in which Cain lived. Then it was changed into the sea, that is, motion or fluctuation.

28. (insular *r* and *g*) jerony*mus* dicit `non e*st* t*er*ra naida´ s*ed* habitauit in t*er*rra [*sic*] nod. i*d est* instabilis. 7 (. . . . . .) uágis quod sonat nod. 7 dicitur cayn nod. (HS 1078B)

It is not the land of Naida, says . . . Jerome, . . . but he lived in the land of Nod, that is, 'unstable' and 'wandering', which Nod means, and Cain is called Nod.

29a.[75] agǽn þ*æt* lǽnd óf | hestnysse. þ*æt* ís | eden neorxna|wange[76]

Towards the land of pleasure, that is Eden in paradise.

29b. (words added to OE text) **Soðlice enoch gestrynde** `irad. q*ui*´ **máui`a´hel. 7 maui`a´el gestrynde | mathsael**[77]

30.[78] **7 mathúsael gestrynde lámech** q*ui* septim*us* ab adam. et pes|simus: | § Quia prim*us* bigamia*m* introduxit. 7 sic adult*er*rum [*sic*] fecit co*n*tra lege*m* nat*ur*e. et d*ei* decretu*m*. In prima e*ni*m crea|tione unica unico f*ac*ta est mulier. 7 de*us* p*er* os ade decreuerat.[79] (HS 1078D–1079A; cf. no. 45)

Mathusael begot Lamech who was the seventh from Adam and the worst. For he was the first to introduce bigamy and so committed adultery against the

---

[72] 'cwæð(e)' is written 'cw̄ð', 'cw̄e'. HS 1078B, as given by Sylwan (52/42): "Iosephus ait: Et multam peragrans terram cum uxore sua Caym collocatus est in loco qui Nayda nuncupatur." The *Historia* literally cites LJ (I. 60, Blatt, 131); the addition of Cain's wife's name is a feature of the *β* recension.

[73] Taking 'ywilcon' as for *gewēolcon*, pret. of *gewealcan* strong 7, for "peragrans."

[74] These three irregular lines of Latin follow directly on the English in a darker ink.

[75] In margin, four short lines, with bracket enclosing three lines of main text. This note is written in the same brown ink as the added words 'non est terra naida' in no. 28.

[76] Cf. item 10.

[77] The inserted words are in Norman script.

[78] Beginning above the lower frame, as if completing the OE sentence, and then at § continuing below the frame.

[79] Scribe wrote 'decreauerat', cancelling the first 'a'.

law of nature and the decree of God. For at the first creation one woman was made for one man and God through the mouth of Adam so decreed it.

F. 9v *Illustrations:* Upper frame: Lamech with his two wives, Ada and Sella, with son Iabaal to right (in margin is added in large Norman script 'Iabaal'); lower frame: a son of Lamech (Jubal or Jabaal), with sons of Jabal, above left, "who have cattle" and above right, "who dwell in tents" and a son of Jubal, below left, "who plays the lyre," on right an unidentified man and woman look to center. **OE** = Genesis 4:19–21

31. Que inuenit arte*m* uarie texture. (HS 1079C)

[The sister of Tubalcain, Noema] who invented the art of multicolored weaving.

32. ⁊ Mulieres sue sepe male tractabant eum:· | Vn*de* ip*s*e irat*us* dicebat eis. Cur me uultis int*er*ficere:· Grauius puniet*ur* q*ui* me i*nter*ficiet q*u*am q*ui* / cayn: (HS 1079D-1080A)

And his wives often treated him badly, whence he [Lamech], angry, said to them. . . . Why do you want to kill me? He who kills me will be more heavily punished than he who kills Cain (cf. Gen. 4:24).

33.[80] **He gestrynde íaba`a´l.** ⁊ iubal [*recte* iabal] . | q*ui* adi*n*uenit portatilia pastor*um* tentoria ad mu`t´anda pascua. ⁊ greges ordina|uit et caract*er*ibus distinxit. sep*ara*vitq*ue* *secundum* gen*er*a greges ouium a gregibus / hedorum:· (HS 1079A)

He begot Jabaal and J[a]bal, who devised portable tents of shepherds for changing pasturelands, and regulated flocks, and distinguished markings and separated flocks of sheep according to their kinds from flocks of goats.

33a. (in left margin, below picture frame and alongside the OE text that has been altered by a late hand to 'iu**bal**') *ue*l. iubal

34.[81] lamech. ⁊ hís sunes hífúnde[82] fæle `cenne´ cræftæs: éac he wés | gód scétte. ⁊ mid his scéte ofsloh caym. ⁊ mid is (. . .) bóhe is `agene´ mán. of|sloh. hím to mycele sorhe. for þa*m* caynes sénne bið acorede seófonfealð | wyte. ís bið acorðe septuagies septies. wyten. þ*æt* byð syxti. ⁊ seofontene. | saulen. (. . . . . . .) of lámech; forfe[r]den in diluuio;[83]

[80] An indexical 'Iabaal' written in large letters in the margin and the first two words of the passage written above, as if continuing the OE. HS begins "Genuitque Ada Iabal. . . ."

[81] Five lines 2/3 across picture space; attributed to 'joseph*us*' in the left margin, as it is in HS, but this story is not in LJ.

[82] I.e., "gefunde."

[83] Epitomizes HS 1079C/D, *Sylwan* (55/40): "Lamech autem secundum Iosephum res diuinas sapienter sciens. . . . Lamech uero sagittarius uir diu uiuendo caliginem

Lamech and his sons invented many kinds of skills; and he was a good archer and with his shooting he slew Cain and with his bow his own man he slew to his great sorrow. Therefore Cain's sin is reckoned for sevenfold punishment. His (Lamech's) is reckoned for *seventy-seven* punishments, that is, sixty plus seventeen souls from Lamech perished *in the flood.*

35a. § Que sint septuaginta. septem uindicte q*u*e in lamech exsoluende sint: | Aiunt ab ada*m*. usq*ue* ad chr*istu*m generationes septuaginta septe*m*. Relege luca*m* euang*e*lista*m*. et i*n*uenies ita | esse ut dicim*us*. (Jerome, Ep. 36 to Damasus, PL 22.455)

What could be the seventy-seven punishments which may be unloosed on Lamech? They say from Adam up to Christ are seventy-seven generations. Review the Gospel of Luke and you will find it is as we say.

35b. (bottom line) IN̄S[84] ut putabat*ur* fili*us* Joseph: q*u*i fuit heli. q*u*i fuit Melchi: 7 *cetera:* (Luke 3:23–37)[85]

Jesus that is reckoned the son of Joseph who was (of) Heli . . . who was (of) Malchi, etc.

F. 10r *Illustrations:* Three frames, upper frame: Lamech and his two wives and his son Tubalcain at a forge; middle frame: presumably Adam, enthroned, with Eve and Seth; lower frame: Seth with his wife and his son Enos, the hand of God reaching towards him. OE = Genesis 4:22–26

36a. Methodi*us* cwæð of abele næs nan báren. 7 al caynnes | ofspringe furwurðen in diluuio.

Methodius said none was born from Abel and all of Cain's offspring perished *in the flood.*[86]

36b.[87] Adam se fór|me mán. seth se oder.[88]

---

oculorum incurrit, et habens adolescentem ducem . . . casu interfecit Caym . . . estimans feram. Quem quia ad indicium iuuenis dirigens sagittam interfecit, iratus illi cum arcu ad mortem uerberauit eum. . . . Et ideo cum peccatum Caym punitum esset septuplum, ut diximus, suum punitum est septuagies septies, id est septuaginta anime et septem egresse de Lamech in diluuio perierunt" (cf. Gen. 4:23–24 and Andrew of St. Victor, *Hept. (In Gen.)*, 1307–22, ed. Lohr and Berndt, CCSL 53.1, 43–44).

[84] So it is written (not IH̄S "Iesus"), for "Iesus Noster Salvator."

[85] The citation of Luke is not in Jerome, but supplied by the Claudius annotator.

[86] HS 1080C: ". . . quibus assentit Methodius, et ideo hoc dicit, quia de Abel nullus natus est, et generatio Cain tota periit in diluvio."

[87] As if continuing the previous note, in a different script and browner ink.

[88] Cf. no. 22, which may contain a garbled version of the source for this, HS 1080C: "Unde quidam incipiunt ab Adam primam ætatem; alii a Seth" (in 22, "incipiunt"

Adam the first man, Seth the second.

37. (insular *r*) Forte moyses .c. ánnos. luetus [*recte* luctus] ade pretérmisit q*uia* ut dixim*us* (HS 1080C)[89] **cxxx.**

Perhaps Moses neglected to mention the 100 years of mourning by Adam because as we said . . . [A.M. 130]

38. (continuing the previous note, in English) þa hundseófentig wenðeres. ⁊ methodi*us*. ⁊ Joseph*us*. gewríten. þ*æt* adam wæs twa | hund wintra. ⁊ xxx. þa he gestrínde seth.[90]

. . . the seventy translators and Methodius and Josephus wrote that Adam was 230 years old when he begot Seth.

39a.[91] (insular *r*) cilias. ḿ . annoru*m* e*st*. | i*n* p*r*imo millena|rio. scilias. sciliadis. | Mille interpretatu*r* / `xxx.´ anno p*r*ime cili/adis[92]

A chiliad is 1000 years in the first millennium; chilias, chiliadis is interpreted 1000; in the [one hundred and] thirtieth year of the first chiliad.

39b. (isolated in bottom left of middle picture frame) cv° annor*um*[93] (in right margin) **.cc.xxx.v.** [A.M. 235]

40. § q*uo*d sonat homo. u*e*l uir qu*as*i r*ati*onal*is* et fortis. qui cepit i*n*uocare | nomen d*omi*ni. forte: in|uenit u*er*ba depreca|toria ad inuoca*n*du*m* | d*eu*m- (HS 1080B)

[Enos,] that means 'man', or 'male person' as being rational and strong, who . . . "began to call on the name of the Lord" (Gen. 4:26). Perhaps he discovered the intercessory words for invoking God.

F. 10v *Illustrations:* Upper, divided into two: left, Adam and Eve with Seth, right, corpse of Adam held by two of his sons (labeled 'adam obiit'); middle frame,

---

changed to 'incipit').

89 Same as in no. 22, f. 8r, right lower panel, lines 8–9; see preceding note. The MS note is followed by '⁊c̄' in different ink but the same script; this properly belongs with no. 39a.

90 HS 1080C: "Septuaginta et Methodius, et Josephus ducentum triginta annorum eum fuisse scribunt, cum genuit Seth." The Latin has already been copied in no. 22, on f. 8r. right lower panel, lines 6–8.

91 In the margin, 4 lines, with last line running back inside the picture frame.

92 Source unidentified. The second sentence will correctly refer to the age of Adam at the birth of Seth in Bede's calculation ("130") if the isolated '⁊c̄' is brought down from the end of no. 37; '-adis' is in darker ink.

93 A fragment of a sentence from Bede, DTR, 90.522C: "Seth, annorum cv, genuit Enos."

right, Seth flanked by two daughters and two sons, left, corpse of Seth held by two of his sons (labeled 'seth obiit'); bottom frame, left, Enos flanked by four daughters and three sons, right, corpse of Enos flanked by grieving woman on left and man on right (labeled 'enos obiit'). **OE** = Genesis 5:5–11. In the outer margin, against the middle picture, is **.cccc.xxv.** [A.M. 325].

41. Me reð on bóce. þ*æt* adam hæfede .xxx. súnes- | 7 swa fela dohtra. bútan cayn. 7 abel.[94]

It is read in a book that Adam had thirty sons and as many daughters, not counting Cain and Abel.

42a. (as if continuing preceding, in darker ink and larger script) Et sepult*us*que e*st* | in cariatharbe. que distat ab | ier*usa*lem .xxii. milib*us* | ad australe*m* plagam.[95]

And [Adam] was buried in Cariath Arbe, which is twenty-two miles south of Jerusalem.

42b. (inserted in third line of OE in erased(?) space) **Seth wǽs** hund wíntre. 7 v. **ða he gestrynde enos** (Genesis 5:6)

F. 11r *Illustrations:* Upper frame, two panels: left, Cainan flanked by seven daughters and two sons; right, corpse of Cainan flanked by a daughter and two sons (labeled 'caynan obiit'); lower frame, two panels: left, Malalhel flanked by two daughters and a son; right, corpse of Malalhel held by two sons (labeled 'malaléél obiit'). **OE** = Genesis 5:12–20. At top of page **.ccc.xcv.** [A.M. 395]; against upper frame, in margin, **.cccc.lx.** [A. M. 460]; in margin, against lower frame, **.dc. xxii.** [A. M. 622]

42c. (inserted in OE, third line up, in erased(?) space) **Iáred gestrynde enoch ða hé wæs** húnd wíntre∴ twa and syxtig. (Genesis 5:18)

43.[96](insular *h* and *r*, brownish ink) Enoch quasda*m* literas i*n*uenit. quosda*m* lib*r*os sc*r*ipsit: sub q*uo* adam credis[97] mortu*us*∵ (HS 1081B, Add. 1, Sylwan 58/14)

---

[94] HS 1080B (Add. 1): "Legitur Adam triginta habuisse filios, et totidem filias præter Cain et Abel."

[95] An epitome of Isidore, *De ortu et obitu patrum*, PL 83.131B: "Sepultus est autem in loco Arbee, qui locus nomen a numero sumpsit, hoc est quatuor [i.e., cariatharbe] nam tres patriarchae ibidem sunt sepulti, et hic quartus Adam. Distat autem locus iste non procul ab Hebron . . . . Est autem civitas sortis Judae in sacerdotibus separata distans ad australem plagam millibus xxii ab Hierusalem." Similar information, but not the phrasing, occurs at HS 1093C. The information does not seem to be from Jerome.

[96] Bottom margin, fifth line up,

[97] So, apparently the MS, over an erasure (CD-ROM); the reading "creditur" (so *β γ*) is probably what the exemplar had; *Sylwan,* PL: intelligitur.

Enoch discovered some kind of letters . . . (and) wrote certain books, in whose lifetime Adam is believed [*or* you believe] to have died.

44. (continuing in the same ink and script) Sethes súnes. yhérden adames wytegunge be twám dómon. 7 þa yfu[n]donne créftes. ne forwurþon. | wríten hí on twám colúmban. þ*æt* bið twéan pilíres. ín hæder ǽl.[98] in þan lánde óf syria. Joseph*us* | cw̄æð. áne of márbra. oðra of ysódene tíhele. þa áne se flód[99] ne mihte forwæhshe. | þa ódra féer ne formélta.[100]

Seth's sons heard Adam's prophecies about two judgments, and, lest the invented arts be lost, wrote them on two columns, that is two pillars, everything on both, in the land of Syria. Josephus said one of them was of marble, the other of fired[101] tile. The one the flood could not dissolve, the other fire could not destroy.

F. 11v *Illustrations:* two frames: upper, divided into two panels, on left Jared with four daughters and a son, right, corpse of Jared with two grieving daughters and two sons (labeled 'Jared'); lower frame, divided into two panels, on left Enoch with three daughters and a son; right, Enoch ascending into heaven on a ladder, above, God with cross nimbus and book, takes him by the hand (labeled 'Enoch'). **OE** = Genesis 5:21–27. In left margin against upper frame, **dc.lxxx. vii** [A.M. 687]; in left margin against lower frame (trimmed), **[d]ccc lxx `ii´ii** [A. M. 874].

45. (in left margin, 'Lamech') Eal swa of caymes ofsprínge se seófonde wǽs þúr|utlige hunwarst,. swa wǽs of sethes ofsprínge. | se seófende. þurutlyge swyþe gód enoch.[102]

Just as of Cain's offspring the seventh was absolutely corrupt, so of Seth's offspring the seventh, Enoch, was absolutely very good.

98 i.e., hwæðer eall.

99 Written 'f́lod'.

100 HS 1079A/B: "Et quia audierat Adam prophetasse de duobus judiciis, ne periret ars inventa, scripsit eam in duabus columnis, in qualibet totam, ut dicit Josephus [*sic* PL, *marg.?*], una marmorea, altera latericia, quarum altera non diluetur diluvio, altera non solveretur incendio. Marmoream dicit Josephus adhuc esset in terra Syrica [*add. Tr*]." This summarizes LJ I.70–71, Blatt, 132, whose edited text reads "in terra Syrida."

101 Cf. B-T "séoþan II metaph. (1) with the idea of purification, to subject to a fiery ordeal, to try as with fire . . .". The sense in Claudius of "baked in fire" (rather than "boiled") seems unique, but implied by its transferred use as documented in B-T.

102 HS 1080C/D: "Sicut ergo in generatione Cain, septimus, scilicet Lamech [lamech *add. β γ δ*], fuit pessimus, ita in generatione Seth, septimus, scilicet Henoch [enoch *add. Tr L*], fuit optimus." Cf. no. 30.

46. fæle cynne wenughe me telleð be matusalemes geáren. þa lxx. `hundseofentig wríter´[103] cw*æ*ð þ*æt* he lefede `xiiii. wíntre´ hefter þan | flode. hác me ne reð þ*æt* he wéra[104] in þara árcæ. ne hé ne ferde míd gode. swá enóch deða. súme | cw̄æð þ*æt* he forþférde .vi. wíntre hǽr þan flode. Jer*onymus* cw̄æð[105] þán ylcan geáre þe se floð wæs.[106]

There are many sorts of opinions about the age of Mathusala. The Septuagint (70 writers) said that he lived (fourteen years) after the flood. But it is not read that he was in the ark, nor did he walk with God as Enoch did. Some say that he died six years before the flood. Jerome said that (he died) in the same year in which the flood occurred.

47–48. (ff. 11v-12r; same ink and script as preceding; in left margin 'Norman cwæð') Matusale*m* gestride. lamech da he was .c.l.xxx.v.ii. wintre. lamech. nóe þa he wǽs .c.l.xxx.ii. / wíntre. ‖ Forþan Mat`h´usalem wæs (. . . . .[107]) ðri hund wíntre. 7 l.x.ix. þa nóe wǽs ybore. Æfter ðam he | léfede. sixhund wíntre. nóe wǽs sixhund wíntre ær ðan flode. nemeð þa .c.c.c. hund wíntre | 7 .l.x.ix. dot hy to dan. six `hun´ wíntre. þ*æt* bið nygon hun wintre. (.) 7 l.x.ix. swa fele léuede matusale*m* hær / ðan flode.[108]

---

103 The descender of the *r* is curtailed, but definitely not intended as *n*.

104 i.e., wære.

105 MS: cw̄e.

106 HS 1080D-1081A: "De annis Mathusalem diversae sunt opiniones. Secundum computationem LXX, vixit annos quatuordecim post diluvium, sed non legitur fuisse in arca, nec translatus ut Henoch. Quidam dicunt quod mortuus fuerit ante diluvium sex annis. Hieronymus asserit, quod eodem anno, in quo fuit diluvium mortuus est." The last phrase in PL is added in the *W* recension. The English accords exactly with Sylwan's text.

107 Erasure, of about five letters with three dots inserted.

108 It is not certain whether this is two notes or one and whether only the material on f. 11v is attributed to "Norman." The material on f. 12r is to be traced to Jerome, HQG 5.27–28, 23.947B/C, CCSL 72.8–9: "Siquidem et in hebraeis et Samaritanorum libris ita scriptum repperi *et uixit Mathusala CLXXXVII annis et genuit Lamech. Et uixit Mathusala, postquam genuit Lamech DCCLXXXII annos. Et genuit filios et filias. Et fuerunt omnes dies Mathusalae anni DCCCCLXVIIII, et mortuus est. Et uixit Lamech CLXXXII annos et genuit Noe.* A die ergo natiuitatis Mathusalae usque ad diem natiuitatis Noe sunt anni CCCLXIX: his adde DC annos Noe, quia in sexcentesimo uitae eius anno diluuium factum est: atque ita fit, ut DCCCCLXIX anno uitae suae Mathusala mortuus sit, eo anno quo coepit esse diluuium."

(Indeed, in the Hebrew and Samaritan books it is to be found written "and Mathusala lived 187 years and begot Lamech. And Mathusala lived after he begot Lamech 782 years. And he begot sons and daughters. And all the days of Mathusala were 969 years and he died. And Lamech lived 182 years and begot Noe." Now from the day of the birth of Mathusala to the day of the birth of Noe are 369 years. Add these 600 years of

(Norman said) Mathusalem begot Lamech when he was 187 years old. Lamech (begot) Noe when he was 182 years old (Genesis 5:25, 28). Therefore Mathusala was 369 years old when Noe was born. After that he lived 600 years. Noe was 600 years (just) before the flood. Take then 369 years, add it to that 600 years so that it is 969 years, so many (years) Mathusala lived before the flood.

F. 12r *Illustrations*: Three frames: upper, divided into two panels, left, Mathusala flanked by four daughters and a son; left, the corpse of Mathusala held by a grieving daughter and a son (labeled 'matusalem'); middle frame: Lamech flanked by a daughter and a son sits on a plowed field, from the toil of which he will be released by a son (Gen. 5:29); lower frame: Lamech flanked by three daughters and two sons; left, corpse of Lamech with two daughters and a son (labeled 'ob*iit* lamech'). **OE** = Genesis 5:28–31. In right margin, against upper frame, **ī.lvi** [A. M. 1056].

49. Anno nongentesimo sexagesimo nono uite ei*us* | quo cepit diluuiu*m*. obiit Mathusa/lem.[109]

In the 960th year of his life, when the flood began, Mathusala died.

50. (bottom, four lines) § æfter adames forðsiðe. seth ytwǽmde his ofspríng. frám caynes ofsprínge. þ*æt* hí ywende to hære | ybora lánda. ⁊ seth wúneda on ána munte beside paradise. Cayn in ðon felde þe he ís broþer ofsloh, | ǽlswa adam hít hét hær is forðsyðe. þar hí ne scolde hí ymegg`h´e. Jose[phus] cwað. sethes súnes[110] belyfen góde. | to ðan seofende ofsprige. hác seþe hi gewéndon to mycelon heuele. Enoch se seofende. `man fram adame.´ Noe se tynde.[111]

Noe because in the six-hundredth year of his life the flood occurred: and so it was that in the 969th year of his life Mathusala died, at which year the flood began.)

The point of this question is that when the years given in the Septuagint version are calculated, Mathusala lives fourteen years beyond the flood. The Hebrew and Samaritan versions keep his years within the acceptable range; the calculation is simpler in "Norman"'s version than Jerome's but comes out the same and seems based on Jerome, whose words are frequently repeated. Given that a copy of HQG was at hand and frequently used in Claudius, this work is doubtless the immediate as well as ultimate source.

[109] Cf. Jerome, HQG 23.947C; CCSL 72, 9.17.

[110] Appears to be 'sńnes'.

[111] HS 1081C/D, 1081B: "Mortuo Adam, Seth separavit cognationem suam a cognatione Cain, quæ [qui *Sylwan*] redierat ad natale solum. Nam et pater vivens prohibuerat ne commiscerentur, et habitavit Seth in quodam monte proximo paradiso. Cain habitavit in campo, ubi fratrem occiderat. \ Josephus autem dicit quod usque ad septimam generationem boni permanserunt filii Seth, post ad mala progressi sunt" (cf. Isidore, *De ortu et obitu patrum*, PL 83.131).

After Adam's death, Seth separated his offspring from Cain's offspring so they went to their native lands and Seth dwelt on a mountain beside paradise, Cain in the field where he slew his brother, just as Adam commanded before his death that they should not mix there. Josephus said Seth's sons remained good to the seventh generation, but afterwards they turned to great evil. Enoch was the seventh man from Adam, Noe the tenth.

F. 12v *Illustration:* frame in two panels: left, Noe with wife and three sons, hand of God reaches from top of frame; right, Noe with wife in center, flanked by sons and their wives.[112] OE = Genesis 5:32–6:10. At top of text space, large initial 'N' marks major division of text.

51a. **ī.d.lvi** [A.M. 1056[113]] § Porro noe fu`i´t .x^{mus}. ab ada*m* i*n* quo p*r*ima etas t*er*minata e*st* itaq*ue* 7 ip*s*e in ea fuit. hui*us* etatis | annos: lxx. ponunt: duo milia. ducentos .xl.iiii^{or}. Ier*onymus* non plene duo milia. Methodi*us* | duo milia. Ip*s*e t*am*en p*er* ciliades s*ecu*la disponit. Nec apponit annos si s*up*ersint. 7 i*de*o nichil c*er*tu*m* de nu*mer*o / annorum tradidit- (HS 1081A, cf. no. 22, f. 8r)

Furthermore, Noe was the tenth from Adam in whom the First Age ended and so he was within it. The length of this Age the Septuagint gives as 2244 years, Jerome not quite 2000 years, Methodius 2000. The latter in any case arranges the ages into 'chiliads' [1000-year periods], but does not reckon years if they go over the chiliad and therefore he transmitted nothing certain down from the number of years.[114]

51b. (exdented) § .septingesimo anno[115] filii seth. co*n*cupier*un*t filias c`h´aym. et orti s*un*t gigantes. Potuit:[116]| Et in[117] t*er*cia ciliade i*n*undauit diluuium. Sic ordinauit Methodi*us*. (HS 1081D)

In the seven-hundreth year (of the second chiliad . . .) the sons of Seth lusted after the daughters of Cain and . . . the giants were born. And in . . . the third thousand-year period the flood inundated. That is the way Methodius arranged it.

---

[112] There are five heads of "sons" showing in this picture.

[113] A mistake for the date correctly appearing on f. 14r.

[114] Pseudo-Methodius (ed. Sackur, 63): "In explicionem secundi miliarii factum est diluuio."

[115] secunde ciliadis] *om. Cl β γ* || cupierunt] concup- *Cl β γ δ*

[116] 'Potuit' with a cross-shaped *signe de renvoi* refers to the comment beginning at the bottom of the page (no. 51f) with the same mark, and seems meant to refer it up to this place, where there is no more space to write it; it is all from PL 1081D. It also appears to refer, via the *signe* 'ȁ' to a place in the main OE text, line 7 up ('7 | **cwæð ȁ ic adylgie ðone mán ðe ic gesceow fram ðære eorðan**').

[117] PL, Sylwan have "incoepta," which provides the correct sense, that this took place at the beginning of the third chiliad, the sense of Methodius.

51c. (left margin) N *þæt* is Sethes | súnes gewemðe | hí. wyð cáines | dohtra. of hám | cóman þa | mycele mén.[118]

N[orman]: that is, Seth's sons polluted themselves with the daughters of Cain; from them came the giant men.

51d. (margin) Qui solent in | solempnitatibus[119]| op*r*imere mulie|res.[120]

Who (sc. incubi and demons) are accustomed to take possession of women in their rituals.

51e.[121] Tempus q*uando* hoc factum fuerit. utr*um* sub noe. *u*el. an*te*. *ue*l mu`l´tum uel parum an*te*. non det*er*minat:˙ (HS 1081B)[122]

The time . . . when this happened, whether under Noe, or before or much before or not much, is not determined.

F. 13r *Illustration:* In one large frame, four "giants". **OE** = Genesis 6:11–17

51f.[123](ff. 12v-13r) § Potuit *etiam*[124] e*ss*e u*ero* [ut] incubi demones genuer*un*t gigantes. a magnitudine corp*orum* sic dictos denominatos[125]| a geos q*uo*d e*st* ter*r*a *. . . .*[126] *sed* etia*m* i*n*manitate [*recte* -tati] corp*orum* respo*n*debat inmanitas a*n*i-mor*um*. Post diluuiu*m* *tame*n nati sunt:˙ ‖ alii gigantes in ebron. ⁊ post fuer*unt* in thani ciuitate. egypti. a qu*a* tytanes dicti s*un*t de | quor*um* stirpe fuit enachi*m*. cui*us* filii habitauer*unt* in[127] ebron. de q*u*ibus ort*us* e*st* golias:˙ ⁊ q*u*ida*m* alii. | § Irat*us* (. . .) d*eus* peccatis hominu*m* dixit. (HS 1081D/1082A)

---

118 HS 1081D, as in no. 51b.

119 PL: "in nocte."

120 HS 1081D; this is presented in PL in the passage here excerpted as no. 51f at the place marked *. . .*. This sentence does not appear in Sylwan's text or apparatus, though it obviously made its way into some early text, perhaps from a margin, and perhaps still was a loose note at the time the annotations were assembled.

121 In lower margin, with *signe de renvoi* 'hwær', apparently referring to OE main text below the picture, lines 1–4 ': **Entas wǽron eac swilce ófer eorðan on ðam dágum | æfter ðan ðe godes bearn tymdon. wið manna dohtra | ⁊ hí cendon ða synd mihtige fram wórulde . ⁊ hlisfulle | wéras.** 'hær'

122 *Sylwan* quidem quando] quidem *om. Cl* ‖ *Sylwan* hoc factum fuerit] h. fa. fu. *Cl β*

123 In the lower margin, last two lines and running over to 13r, 3 lines; keyed to the main OE on f. 12v text by a *signe de renvoi* (å) here and in OE at line 7 up; see nos. 51b and 51d.

124 Abbreviated '⁊'. The first word of the excerpt, "potuit," is preserved in the middle of note 51b, q.v.

125 *Sylwan* denom. sic d.] sic d. denom. *Cl β γ* ‖ etiam *add. Cl β γ*

126 See no. 51d.

127 in *add. Cl γ*

It is possible however (that) incubi (or) demons begot the giants, so called (and) named from the great size of their bodies from (Greek) 'geos', that is, 'earth'. . . . but the monstrousness of their bodies corresponded to the monstrousness of their souls. But after the flood other giants were born in Hebron and they were later in the Egyptian city of Than, from which . . . they are called 'Titans'. From their race were the Enachim whose sons lived in Hebron from whom was born Goliath and certain others. God said he was angry at the sins of men.

F. 13v *Illustration:* One frame, left, God speaks with Noe, right, Noe works on ark ('noe' twice). **OE** = Genesis 6:17–7:7, no annotations.

F. 14r *Illustrations:* Upper frame: God speaks with Noe (labeled 'noe'); lower frame: The completed three-story ark, with animals and Noe and family at top (labeled 'noe'). **OE** = Genesis 7:7–8

52. (top, as if a gloss to OE) **ðry súna. ⁊ hís wíf. ⁊ his súnu wif** `phiarphara. semes wíf parsia. ⁊ cahmmes wíf cataphua. iaphetþes wíf fúra.´[128]

53.[129] Moyses dic*it* | Cubit*us* aute*m* dicit*ur* sex palmi a pollice usq*ue* | in extremum digiti:´ (Ps.-Bede, *In Pentateuchum Commentarii*, PL 91.225B)[130]

Moses says a cubit is said to be six hands from the thumb to the end of the finger.

54. (insular *g* and *h*) Dicit Raban*us* cubitos arche geometricos. alioquin tanta ca*pere* non ualeret:´ | Continet. *enim* cubitus geometricus sex[131] n*ost*ros. *ue*l noue*m*. P*ro*prie. *enim* cubitu*s* pedem et dimidium h*abe*t:´ (HS 1083B)

Hrabanus says the cubits of the ark (were) geometrical cubits; otherwise it would not have been capable of containing such large things; a geometrical cubit contains six or nine of our modern cubits. Strictly, a cubit comprises a foot and a half.

55a. (insular *g* and *h*) Sescentesimo uite sue anno ingressus est noe. in archam cum omnib*us*:´ que dixerat ei d*omin*us. (HS 1084B)

---

[128] HS 1084C, Add. 1: "Uxor Noe Phuaphara, uxor Sem Pharsia, uxor Cham Cathaflua, uxor japeth Fliva"; this is in the *β γ δ* recensions, Sylwan (64/3, note) giving the names as "purphara," "parfia," "cathafluia," "fluia," citing as source Smaragdus, *Collect. in epist. et euang.* PL 102.265A.

[129] Three short lines to right of central figure in the upper picture space, with a word erased before this; in the next line 'pedes' is written to the left of the central figure.

[130] See *Clavis Patristica Pseudepigraphorum Medii Aevii* (hereafter CPPM), ed. Iohannes Machielsen, vol. 2A (Turnhout, 1994), no. 2026. At HS 1185D, Add. 2, is a definition of a "palm" not a cubit.

[131] PL "septem" as *P To.*

In the six-hundreth year of his life Noe went into the ark with everything the Lord had told him.

55b. die septima | decima mensis s*ecun*di. | .(.)ī.**dc.lvi**[132] (cf. Bede, DTR, CCSL 123B. 467)

The seventeenth day of the second month, (A.M.) 1656.

56. § dicit iosep*hus*. q*uo*d ab adam. usq*ue* ad hoc tempu*s* fuerunt anni .ii°. milia .d.c. lxvi: q*uo*d in sacris literis con|scriptu*m*. integritate signatu*m* est: (HS 1084B)

Josephus says that from Adam up to this time were 2666 [PL "2656"] years; which, being written in sacred scripture, its truth is guaranteed.

57. Norman*us* dicit. mille. sexcentos. l (.) vi- iuxta heb*r*`e´os-[133] (cf. Bede, DTR, CCSL 123B. 467, A.M. 1656)

Normanus says 1656 [A.M.] according to the Hebrew.

F. 14v *Illustration:* One large frame: the ark is closed. **OE** = Genesis 7:10–23

58. (underlined letters in contrasting brown ink) Se*cun*da se*cu*li etas á diluuio usq*ue* ad Natiuitate*m* abre p*ro*tendit*ur*. Quasi pueritia fuit generis | populi d*e*i. 7 ideo i*n* li`n´gua inuenta e*st*(. . . .)id e*st* hebrea. a puericia eni*m* incipit homo nosse | loqui. post infantia*m*. q*ue* hinc appellata e*st*. q*uo*d fari n*on* potest.[134] Et annos ducentos Nonaginta | duos.(. .)iuxta hebreos. duaru*m* au*tem* simul etatu*m* ab ada*m*. ad abram. mille. nongentos. 7 | q*ua*draginta octo.[135] Q*u*i septuaginta q*u*inq*ue* erat annor*um* q*ua*n*do* p*ro*missione*m* d*e*i accepit. | p*ro*missionis anni qu*a*dringenti triginta. ducat*us* moysi[136] anni qu*a*draginta. q*ui* f*ui*t o*mn*es duo | millia q*u*adringentes Nonaginta `trium´ annor*um*.[137] Normano testante. iuxta hebraicha*m* ue*ritate*m.

The second age of the world is extended from the flood to the birth of Abram. . . . It was as it were the childhood of the people of God and for that reason it is found in a language, namely Hebrew, because from childhood a man begins to learn how to speak,[138] following infancy which is so called because (an infant) is not able to speak. And [the second age is] 292 years according to

---

[132] Altered from '.īī.dc.lvi' to the correct date, A.M. 1656.

[133] See no. 55b; 'iuxta heb*re*os' is written in a different, reddish ink but the same script.

[134] Bede, DTR, 90.521A.

[135] Cf. Bede, DTR 90.526C.

[136] The 'y' is altered from *f* or *s*.

[137] Cf. Bede, DTR 90.528A.

[138] "fari," pres. part. "fans, fantis," etc.

the Hebrews, also the two ages from Adam to Abram [comprised] 1948 (years). Abram was seventy-five when he received the covenant of God, a covenant of forty-three years. Moses led for forty years which makes in all 2493 years. Testified by Normanus according to the Hebrew truth.

F. 15r *Illustration*: One large frame, the closed ark, a raven pecks at a human head fixed on the stem-post. **OE** = Genesis 7:24–8:9

59. (lines 3–2 up) § Ergo[139] sescentesimo p*r*imo anno. p*r*imo mense. p*r*ima die mensis. ap*er*uit noe tectu*m* arche: ⁊ uidit(.)q*uo*d | exsiccata e*ss*et sup*er*ficies t*er*re: s*ed* egrediendi expectabat domini preceptum. (HS 1085C)

Therefore "in the 601st year (of the life of Noe), . . . in the first month, on the first day of the month, Noe opened the roof of the ark and saw that the face of the earth was dried," (Gen. 8:13) but emerging he looked for the teaching of the Lord.

60. P*r*ima ei*us* die q*ui* e*st* uice|simus septim*us* mensis s*ecun*di id e*st*. Maii. silicet [*sic*] .iiii°. Kł. Junii feria p*r*ima egressu*s* e*st* Noe de archa-[140]

On his first day, which is the twenty-seventh of the second month, that is May, to wit four before the kalends of June, the first day of the week, Noe came out of the ark.

15v. *Illustration:* One large frame, the ark is opened, at top dove returns with green branch and Noe addresses God, who stands on the deck, while below left, the family of Noe (three males, four females) leaves the ark, birds fly away to left and right, and animals parade on lower right. **OE** = Genesis 8:10–18

61. Manasses damascenus de eisde*m* sic aít. Est sup*er* numadam[141] excelsus móns ín | armenia: qui baris appellatur. ubi requieuit archa. ⁊ Noe. ⁊ his hiwscípe eode of ðán múnte / heriænðe gódes[142] náme.[143]

Manasses of Damascus[144] about these matters says: "There is upon Numada a high mountain in Armenia, which is called Baris," where the ark rested. And Noe and his family went from the mountain praising God's name.

F. 16r OE = Genesis 8:20–9:17; no illustration or annotations.

139 *Sylwan* igitur] ergo *Cl Tr*

140 Cf. Genesis 8:4, 8:14; the exact source is unidentified.

141 PL "Numidiam," with no evident support of MSS.

142 The 'o' of 'godes' is written with a little 'c'-shaped stroke above it; a twelfth-century hand has added this mark above **god** throughout the eleventh-century text.

143 The Latin corresponds to HS 1085B; English roughly = HS 1085C as in no. 59.

144 Probably the mid-twelfth-century Byzantine author of a poem on the Holy Land, *Hodoiporikon*.

F. 16v *Illustration:* Very large frame covers most of page: the rainbow arc with Noe (labeled 'Noe') bowing to God (labeled 'd*ominus*'), to left Noe's family (three male and three female figures). **OE** = Genesis 9:17–19

62. (first line in rainbow frame, brown ink) Næs nán wúna hér ða flode. flæsches to notiéna. aéc her fyrst.[145]

There was no custom before the flood to eat flesh, but now was the first time.

63. (lines 2–5 within rainbow frame) § Joseph*us* refert: Posuit arcu*m* suu*m* i*n* nubib*us*. 7 e*st* signu*m*[146] duor*um*. iudicii p*er* aqu*a*m p*re*t*er*iti: | ne time`a´*tur*. 7 futuri p*er* igne*m*: ut expectet*ur*. In*de* e*st* q*uod* duos habet colores. ceruleu*m*: q*u*i | aqueus e*st*. 7 e*st* exterior. q*uia* preter*it*: 7 rubeu*m*: q*u*i e*st* igneu*us* [*sic*] q*u*i e*st* i*n*terior. q*u*ia fut*urus* e*st* | ignis. et t*ra*dunt s*anct*i q*uod* xl annis. ante iudiciu*m* n*on* uideb[i]t*ur* arcus: (HS 1086D)[147]

Josephus reports . . . (God) placed his arc (rainbow) in the clouds and it is a sign of two (judgements), . . . of judgement by water already past, that need not be feared, and of future (judgement) by fire so it might be awaited. Therefore it is that it has two colors: blue, which is watery and exterior because past; and red, which is fiery and interior because the fire is still to come; and the saints laid down that for forty years before the Judgement the arc (rainbow) will not be seen.

64. (lines 5–11 within rainbow frame) Repugnare uid*etu*r | huic q*uo*d sup*ra* dictu*m* e*st*: *quingentesimo*[148] anno Noe. Natu*m* sem. 7 sesce*n*tesimo i*n*undasse diluuiu*m*. *ergo* po*st* | diluuiu*m* ce*n*tenariu*s* erat sem. 7 biennio po*st*: c. 7 duor*um*. annor*um*. s*ed* mos e*st* scripture se|pe limites num*erorum* ponere. paucis annis si sup*er*fuerint. tacitis: potest *ergo* dici q*uo*d | sem erat. ć. annor*um* 7 duor*um* s*ed* duos tacuit scriptura. Vel Noe cu*m* gen*uit* eu*m*: *quingentorum*[149] 7 duor*um* annor*um*. | Vel duo anni deerant ad sesce*n*tos: cu*m* i*n*undauit diluuiu*m*. Uel ita legat*ur* litera. Sem: | .c. annor*um* erat po*st* diluuiu*m*. 7 erat biennio po*st* diluuiu*m*: q*uando* gen*uit* arf*axat*. (HS 1090C/D)[150]

---

145 HS 1086D, Add. 1: "Esus carnium ante diluvium non erat, set post statim concessus est"; only in *β T*. The version given by Sylwan (71/46, note) better accords with the English: "esus carnium ante diluuium non erat. hic post statum est et hic primo concessum."

146 *Sylwan* in signum] in *om. Cl S β γ T*

147 The end of the excerpt is marked by an 'X' placed above 'arcus'.

148 Expressed 'd*simo*'.

149 Expressed 'ð'.

150 *Cl* differs from Sylwan in word order and several omissions and in this regard is close to the PL text; particularly note: natum esse sem] esse *om. Cl S β γ* PL ‖ mos est sacre scripture] sacre *om. Cl* ‖ centum annorum erat] e. c. a. *Cl β* ‖ et duorum annorum erat] erat *om. Cl*, an. erat *om.* PL

[Sem was 100 years old when he begot Arfaxad. (Genesis 11:10)] Disagreeing with this is what is said above, that Sem (was) born in the 500th year of Noe and when he was 600 the flood covered the world. Therefore after the flood Sem was 100 years old, and two years later he would be 102. But it is the frequent custom of . . . scripture tacitly to round off a few years. Therefore it can be said that Sem was 100 plus two years old but Scripture does not mention the two, or, alternately, Noe, when he had him, was 502 or he was two years short of 600 when the flood covered the world; or so it literally reads. Sem was 100 years old after the flood and it was two years after the flood when he begot Arfaxad.

65. (last two lines within rainbow) Si quis *er*go huic expositioni n*ost*re co*ntrarius* e*st* q*u*erat alia*m* solutione*m*. & tunc ea que | recte a nobis dicta sunt imp*ro*babit (Ps.-Bede, *Quaest. super Gen.*, PL 93.302B = Wigbod, CPL IIA [1994], no. 2049)

Anyone who disagrees with our explanation, let him seek another solution and only then will he properly reject those which are pronounced by us.

66.[151] Sem filiu*s* Noe cu*m* centu*m* (.) annor*um* i*n* diluuio esset. biennio po*st* diluuiu*m*. gen*uit* arfaxat [*insert from above:* po*st* uixit annos q*u*ingentos. Noe[152] e*st* simul sescentos.] Arfaxat ig*itur* | iuxta euangelista*m* luca*m* annor*um* centu*m* t*r*iginta q*u*inq*ue* gen*uit* cainan. S*ecun*d*u*m hebreos au*tem* arfaxat annor*um* t*r*igin|ta q*u*inq*ue* gen*ui*t sale. Cainan `non e*st* in numero.´ luca teste annor*um* centu*m* t*r*iginta gen*uit* sale. sale annor*um* t*r*iginta gen*uit*. heber. | heber t*r*iginta `quatuor´ annor*um* gen*uit* phaleg. Phaleg annor*um* t*r*iginta gen*uit* Reu: Rev annor*um* t*r*iginta duor*um* | [*in left margin:* gen*uit*] seruch. Seruch annor*um* t*r*iginta gen*uit* Nachor. Nachor annor*um* xx^ti^. et ix^uem^ gen*uit* thare. || Thare annor*um* septuaginta genuit abRAM.[153] 7 nachor 7 aram. Supputa annor*um* num*er*u*m* et i*n*uenies | ab ortu sém usq*ue* Ad natiuitate*m* abram t*r*ecentos. et nonaginta duos.[154] Mortu*us* e*st* au*tem* abram. c. et lxxv^to^ etas sue \ anno.[155] Sem sup*er*|uixisse abrahe | annos t*r*iginta v. | iacob. et esau | ginta.[156]

[151] Bottom margin, 5 lines, with line above (beginning 'post vixit . . .') meant to be inserted with *signes de renvoi* in first line after first 'arfaxat', and continuing on to the top of f. 17r for two lines and then in the margin.

[152] Written 'hoe'.

[153] The smaller duct begins at this point.

[154] Written 'du,os'.

[155] Text goes into right margin and the larger duct resumes after 'anno'.

[156] The place for numeral is left blank at end of line above 'ginta'. The passage is loosely based on Jerome, Ep. 73, PL 22.679–680, with reference to the Gospels and perhaps other sources; cf. Genesis 11:11–26 and Luke 3:35–38; note also HS 1091C, Add. 1 (not in Sylwan): "Qui invenitur in glossa super Lucam. In quadam enumeratione generationis Christi de Cainam reperies, per quam Magister locum istum correxit"; the material is not taken from HS 1089C–1090D, for which, see no. 70f below.

Sem, the son of Noe, was 100 years old when he was in the flood. Two years after the flood he begot Arfaxad and afterwards lived 500 years. Noe at the same time is 600. Arfaxad therefore according to the Gospel of Luke was 135 when he begot Cainan. According to the Hebrew however Arfaxad was 135 years when he begot Sale. Cainan (he is not counted [in Genesis]) according to Luke was 130 when he begot Sale. Sale was thirty when he begot Heber. Heber was thirty (-four) years old when he begot Phaleg. Phaleg was thirty when he begot Reu. Reu was thirty-two when he (begot) Seruch. Seruch was thirty when he begot Nachor. Nachor was twenty-nine when he begot Thare. Thare at the age of seventy begot Abram and Nachor and Aram. Count up the number of years and you will find from the birth of Sem to the nativity of Abram is 392 years. Abram was dead in the 175th year of his life. Sem outlived Abram by thirty-five years, and Jacob and Esau by [-ty] years.

F. 17r *Illustrations:* Upper: Noe with spade tending a vine on a trellis (labeled 'Noe'); lower frame, a large winepress, on left a woman on ground, and two men on press (labeled 'sem', 'noe') tend a vine, on right a man on ground and a woman and man on press (labeled 'cham', 'phiarphara') do the same.[157] **OE** = Genesis 9:20–22

67.[158] hær ða flode nás ná wíngeard[159]

Before the flood there was no vineyard.

68.[160]§ Centesimo ann`o'(. .)*ter*tie ciliadis. nat*us* est noe. fili*us*. 7 dixit eu*m* Jonithu*m*. Trecentesimo(. . . .)anno dedit⁖ | noe. donationes filio suo Jonitho. 7 dimisit eu*m*. i*n* t*er*ra etha*m*. 7 i*n*trauit ea*m* Jonith*us*. usq*ue* ad ‖ mare. q*uod* d*icitu*r helioschora. i*d est* sol*is* regio. hic accepit a d*omin*o donu*m* sapi*enti*e. 7 i*n*uenit astronomia*m* ad que*m* | uenie*n*s n`e´mroth[161] gigas⁖ x cubitor*um* erudit*us* e*st* ab eo. 7 accepit ab eo co*n*siliu*m* in q*ui*b*us* ge*n*tib*us*. regnare | cepisset. Jonit*us* iste fut*ur*os q*uo*sda*m* reru*m* eu`e´nt*us* p*re*uidit. 7 maxime de ortu. iiii. regnor*um* 7 occasu / eo*rum* p*er* successiones;- (HS 1088B/C)[162]

---

157 The winepress is shaped like a boat, with the "mast," which effectively divides the picture into two panels, representing the long screw of the press. The label 'phiarphara' is in a Norman script using insular *r*.

158 In lower frame; in upper ledger is a blotted and smudged inscription.

159 Cf. *Adrian and Ritheus*, ed. Cross and Hill, 37: "Saga me hwa sette ærest wineardas of þe hwa dranc ærest win."

160 Two lines at bottom and to top of 17v, 4 lines.

161 Corrects 'nomroth'.

162 *Sylwan* terram] terra *Cl α β To T* ‖ *Sylwan* Eliochora] helioschora *Cl S* ‖ *Sylwan* gigas erudita] x cubitorum *add. Cl β γ* ‖ *Sylwan* ab illo] ab eo *Cl α Tr* ‖ *Sylwan* euentus] rerum euentus *Cl Tr* ‖ *Sylwan* successionem] -nes *Cl TR Pa*

In his hundreth year, in the third chiliad, a son was born to Noe and he called him Jonithus. In the three-hundredth year Noe gave gifts to his son Jonithus and sent him into the land of Etham and Jonithus entered into it up to the sea . . . which is called Helioschora, that is, the country of the sun. Here he received from the Lord the gift of wisdom and invented astronomy. Coming to him, Nemrod the giant, ten cubits tall, was instructed by him and received from him counsel with which he began to govern among nations. Jonithus foresaw certain outcomes of things to be and especially the rise and fall of those four kingdoms by their successions.

F. 17v *Illustrations:* Upper frame has a smaller frame defining a space on lower left and this frame forms a sort of stage for the figures in the upper left and a room for the figures entering into the larger scene: upper left, Noe, enthroned, with a wine jar, flanked by his wife and a son; lower left and entire right, Noe sleeping within a tent, Cham peeping through a wall or doorway, and, left, going back to tell his brothers of Noe's "nakedness"; lower frame: backing into a tent, Sem and Iaphet cover the nakedness of their father, while Cham, half in and half out, looks on, label written in roof of tent 'Noe. sem. cham. 7 Japhet'. **OE** = Genesis 9:23

69. (bottom) § Cham fili*us* Noe gen*uit* chuh [*sic*]. et mesraim. 7 phut. et cahnaan [*sic*]. filii chus saba 7 euila et sabatha 7 sabathecha. | et regma. filii Regma saba et dadan \`*ue*l iudam´. Porro chus: gen*uit* ne*m*rod. de quo belus descendit. Ipse cepit pote*ns* | e*sse* i*n* te*r*ra. et erat robust*us* uenator cora*m* d*omi*no. Fuit au*tem* p*r*incipiu*m* regnu*m* ei*us* babilon. et arach. 7 archad. [*sic*] et calanné. | Chanaan \`fili*us* cham´ aute*m* gen*uit* sidone*m*. p*r*imogenitu*m* suu*m*. 7 etheu*m*. 7 gebuseu*m*. 7 amorreu*m* . 7 gergeseu*m*. 7 eueu*m*. 7 aracheu*m* . et | sineu*m*. 7 aradiu*m*. 7 samarithen.[163] 7 amatheu*m*. 7 p[ost] \`h´os disseminati s*un*t p*op*u*l*i chananeor*um*. hos p*op*u*l*os expulit isr*ahe*l.[164] (= Genesis 10:6–19)

"Cham the son of Noe begot Chus and Mesraim and Phuth and Chanaan. The sons of Chus: Saba and Hevila and Sabatha and Sabatacha and Regma. The sons of Regma: Saba and Dadan (or Judan). Then Chus begot Nemrod from whom Belus descended. He began to be powerful on the earth and he was a stout hunter before the Lord. The beginning of his kingdom was Babylon and Arach and Achad and Chalanne. Chanaan (the son of Cham) begot Sidon his firstborn and the Hethite and the Jebusite and the Amorrhite and the Gergesite and the Hevite and the Aracite and the Sinite and the Aradian and the Samarite and the Hamathite and after these, the peoples of the Chanaanites were dispersed." These peoples Israel drove out.

[163] Final *n* shaped like an insular *r*.

[164] Ascenders of several cut-off letters visible at lower edge.

F. 18r *Illustrations:* Upper frame: Within tent, Noe awakens, blesses Sem and Iaphet, who stand by and curses Cham, who flees on left (labeled 'cham'); lower frame: corpse of Noe, flanked on left by five male figures, on right by seven figures, probably two female and five male (labeled 'Noe obiit') **OE** = Genesis 9:24–10:2

70a.[165] Texuntur a*utem* ex eis. lxx. ii^e^ g*ene*rationes. xv; de iaphet: xxx. de cam .xxvii:' de sem:' | § hii tres disseminati sunt[166] in trib*us* partib*us* orbis s*ecun*d*um* alquinum. Sem:' asiam:' cham. africam:' | Japhet. europam:' sortitus est:' (HS 1087D)

However, seventy-two generations are composed of these: fifteen from Japhet, thirty from Cham, twenty-seven from Sem. The three of these were disseminated through the three parts of the world according to Alcuin: Sem was allotted Asia, Cham Africa, Japhet Europe.

70b.[167] Narrat a*utem* philo in libro q*uesti*onum sup*er* genesim. q*uo*d ex trib*us* filiis | noe adhuc ip*s*o uiuente nati su`n´t .xx iiii^or^. milia[168] uiror*um* ⁊ .c. extra mulieres et paruulos. habe*n*tes ‖ sup*er* se tres duces. quos prediximus. (HS 1088D)

Also Philo recounts . . . in his book of Questions on Genesis that from the three sons of Noe, while he was still living, were born 124,000 men besides women and children, having over them three leaders whom we have mentioned above.

F. 18v *Illustrations:* Two frames: upper, a symmetrical group of 14 seated figures (4 female) apparently representing the descendants of Noe's sons (Gen. 10); lower frame, men making bricks in a fire (cf. Gen. 11:3). **OE** = Genesis 10:2–11:9

70c. (top, lines 1–2) Post obitu*m* uero noe. mouentes pedes suos ab oriente:' conuenerunt | duces in unum campu*m* sennaar. ⁊ timentes diluuiu*m* consilio nemroth. uole*n*tis regnare:' cep*er*unt. ⁊ *cetera.* (HS 1089A)

After the death of Noe, moving their feet from the east the leaders came together in a certain plain of Sennaar and, fearing the flood, by Nemrod's counsel, who desired to hold sway, they began (to build a tower, etc).

[165] Bottom, lines 4–2 up; insular *g* and *h*; the group of comments 70a-f + 72 are from related passages in HS and in the same script, with insular *g* and *h*, extending to f. 19r and mixed at top of f. 18v with notes in different script.

[166] sunt *add. Cl S β γ*

[167] Bottom two lines continuing to 18v.

[168] *Sylwan* quatuordecim milia] xxiiii *Cl β Pa T*^p.c.^

70d.[169] q*uo*d p*r*imi regnarent de cham:· | [p]ost de sem:· medi. ⁊ p*er*se. ⁊ greci. post. de japhet:· romani: (HS 1088C)

Because the first [rulers] reigned from Cham, . . . afterwards from Sem (came) the Medes and Persians and Greeks, afterwards from Japhet the Romans.

71.[170] He itaq*ue* vii. gentes qu*as* de japhet. stiripe [*sic*] uenire m`e´moraui. | . ad aquilonis partem habitant:· (Jerome, HQG 23.951A; CCSL 72, 11.23)

And so these seven peoples, whom I mentioned as coming from the line of Japheth, occupied the regions to the north.

70e.[171] chus dicitur filius cha*m*. ⁊ filius chus ne*m*rod:· `de quo belu*s* descendit´[172] qui cepit p*r*im*us* potens e*ss*e in t*er*ra. ⁊ robustus uenator ho*m*inu*m* \ .⁊ coram deo[173] | i*d est* extinctor ⁊ oppressor amore d*om*anandi [*recte* dominandi] . ⁊ cogebat homines \ ignem adorare:· (HS 1088A/B)

The son of Cham is called Chus and the son of Chus Nemrod (from whom Belus descended) who first "began to be powerful on the earth and was a powerful hunter of men (and in the sight of God)" (Gen. 10:9), that is, a destroyer and oppressor for the love of dominating, and he forced men to worship fire.

70f.[174] Sem; c. annor*um*. erat. q*uando* genuit arfaxat. biennio post diluuiu*m*. po`te´st ergo dici q*uo*d sem erat. c. | annoru*m*.[175] ⁊ duoru*m*. post diluuiu*m*. q*uan*-*do* genuit arf*axat*. arf*axat* `q*u*i i*n* luca uocat*ur* cainan. q*u*i condidit salem:´ genuit sale. qui:· heber a quo hebrei dicti sunt. s*ecundum* iosephu*m*:- | heber genuit phalec. ⁊ iectan: phalec hebraice: diuisio. eo q*uo*d in dieb*us* ei*us* p*ro* diuisione linguaru*m* diuise sunt- ‖ gentes. ⁊ diuisio terraru*m* facta:· Phalec genuit reu. u*el* rogau. qui saruch. qui nachor qui:(. .)thare:· (HS 1090C/D,-1089A)[176]

Sem was 100 years old when he begot Arfaxad two years after the flood; . . . it can be said that Sem was 102 years old . . . after the flood when he begot Arfaxad. Arfaxad . . . who is called Cainan in Luke and founded Salem . . . begot Sale . . . who (begot) Heber from whom the Hebrews are named according to Josephus. . . . Heber begot Phaleg and Jectan. In Hebrew Phaleg means 'division'

[169] Short line, shifted to right, between lines 1 and 2 + line 3, shifted to left; this entry is in brown ink.

[170] Follows no. 70d immediately on line 3, in black ink and the larger script, no insular letters.

[171] In lower border of upper frame and continuing in upper border of lower frame.

[172] Inserted from HS 1088D.

[173] *Sylwan* domino] deo *Cl W*

[174] Bottom of f. 18v, 3 lines, over to bottom of f. 19r, 1 line. The left halves of the bottom two lines on f. 18v are faded.

[175] *Sylwan* centum annorum erat] erat. c. a. *Cl β*; this passage is considerably rearranged in *Cl*.

[176] Cf. no. 66 above, which has similar material, but not from HS.

because in his days the peoples were divided for the sake of the division of languages and the division of the world was made. . . . Phaleg begot Reu or Rogau who (begot) Saruch, who (begot) Nachor who (begot) Thare.

F. 19r Full-page illustration of the building of the Tower of Babel, no OE

72.[177] Propterea babilonia*m* contigit uocari: ciuitate*m*. babel *enim* hebrei confusione*m* uocari de campo u*er*o sennaar in regione | babilonis meminint sib[y]lla[178] dice*ns*: (HS 1089B/C)

Therefore it happened that the city is called Babylon. For 'Babel' in Hebrew means 'confusion'. . . . Of the plain of Sennaar in the region of Babylon . . . (the Sibyl) makes mention, saying: . . .

73–74.[179] Turris au*tem* altituto [*sic*] cui*us* causa diuise s*un*t lingue. duo[180] milia ce*n*tum septuaginta. | .iiii^{or}. tenere dicit*ur* passuu*m*: paulati*m* altiu*s* angustior coartata erat ut pond*us* immine*ns* facili*us* suste*n*taret. | Hanc turre*m*. nembroth gigas construxit. Qui po*st* confusione*m* li`n´gua|ru*m* migrauit i*n*de ad p*er*sas. eosq*ue* igne*m* colere docuit. (Ps.-Isidore, *Chronica* (A.M. 2643), 22, ed. Mommsen, MGH, AA.9, pp. 429–30)[181]

The height of the tower, which is the cause of the division of language, is said to be 2174 feet high. As it gradually rose higher it became crowded into narrower space the more easily to support its enormous weight. Nemrod the giant constructed this tower, who after the confusion of tongues migrated thence to the Persians and taught them to worship fire.

75.[182] Moyses dic*it* | regma filliu*m* cuhus [*sic*] duos h*ab*uisse fillios. saba. 7 dadan. Joseph*us* u*er*o dic*it* saba 7 iuda*m*. quor*um* iudas egiptiaca*m* gentem | hesp*er*ior*um* i*n*habitans. inde [*sic, edd.* iudeis] cognome*n* suu*m* reliquit. q*uo*d au*tem* subd*icitu*r de t*er*ra sennaar. egressus e*st* assur. intelligendu*m* || est q*uia* nenroth expulit eu*m* ui a t*er*ra sua et turre. que erat ei iure hereditario- Vel non e*st* i*n*telligendu*m* / de

[177] At top of f. 19r, using the script of nos. 70 a-f, with insular *g* and *h*.

[178] The scribe's eye has skipped up from "meminit Esitius" (Sylwan 76/19) to "meminit sibila" (76/16).

[179] Top, lines 2–3 and in upper picture space, between sky and tower, 2 lines, in black ink.

[180] Received text is "v̄ milia," but variant "īī milia" occurs.

[181] Cf. also Hrabanus, *De Univ.*, PL 111.336D.

[182] Bottom, line 3 up, last two words on right, continuing over to f. 19v top. This item is in the same ink and script as no. 73–74. Immediately preceding it on the line is the end of no. 70f, in different script and lighter ink.

assur filio sem q*ui* i*n*uenit purpura 7 unguenta. | (*left margin*) a q*uo* caldea. 7 assyria | est dicta. (HS 1089C)[183]

Moses says that Regma the son of Chus had two sons, Saba and Dadan. Josephus however says that they are Saba and Juda, (from whence) Juda, living among the Egyptian people of the west, left his cognomen (of Jew). When it is also mentioned that Assur went out of the land of Sennaar it is understood that Nemrod forcibly expelled him from that land and tower which was his by hereditary right; or, alternatively, it is to be understood not of Assur son of Sem who invented purple cloth and ointment . . . from whom Chaldea and Assyria are named. . . .[184]

F. 19v *Illustrations:* Three frames: top, Thare at table with his wife and three sons, "Abram, Nachor, and Aran"; middle frame, in front of a mound of drapery, Aran with his wife and his son Loth; lower frame, corpse of Aran (labeled 'aran obiit'), held by four male figures, presumably Abram, Nachor, Thare, and Loth.[185] **OE** = Genesis 11:27–28

76.[186] Thare cum e*ss*et. lxx. annoru*m*: \ **Þare gestrynde abram.** | **7 nachor. 7 aran** 7 est ordo preposterus. aran. *enim* primogenit*us* 7 abram. | ultimus fuit (HS 1091A)

Thare was 70 years old when **Þare begot Abram, Nachor, and Aran** and the order is backwards, because Aran was the first born and Abram the last.

77. Witodlice áran gestrynde lóth. 7 lasca þé is sarai. | 7 melcha.[187]

Truly Aran begot Loth and Lasca [Iescham] who is Sarai, and Melcha.

78.[188] .bede. Chaldeoru*m* regio int*er* babiloniam*.* 7 arabia*m*. tigrin et eufraten. (NLA PL92.1036C; CCSL121.170.88)

[183] *Sylwan* iosephus dicit] uero *add. Cl β γ* ‖ *Sylwan* est quod] quia *Cl α* ‖ *Sylwan* eius erat iure] erat ei i. *Cl γ* ‖ *Sylwan* intellegendum non est] n. e. i. *Cl β γ*

[184] HS goes on: "sed Assur, id est regnum Assyriorum, inde egressum est, quod tempore Sarug, proavi Abrahæ, factum est."

[185] On this page and f. 20r, facing, are added designs resembling basket-work.

[186] Top, line 2, skipping a line and jogging down to end of first main OE passage, insular *g* and *h;* the note skips "genuit Abram, Nachor, et Aran," letting the intervening OE text stand for it. The note is in brown ink.

[187] *Sylwan*: "Porro Aram genuit Loth et Iescam et Melcham, et mortuus est . . . ." After "Iescam" is added the gloss (from the Vulg.) "que est sarai" in *S β γ T.* The letters of the added English text are unusually large, an apparent attempt to match them to the size of the main OE text.

[188] Bottom of middle frame, 1 line; '.bede.' exdented; further into the left margin 'bel' is written twice in faint reddish brown ink.

Bede: The region of the Chaldeans is between Babylonia and Arabia and the Tigris and Euphrates.

79.[189] (insular *g* and *h*) Et est nomen civitatis. ur. se*cund*um ioseph*um*. hebrei:· ur ignem dicunt:· p*ro*iecerunt abram:· 7 | aran. qui [*recte* quia] nolebant ignem adorare `et aran ibi expirante´ abram d*e*i auxilio liberatum:· | Thare *ergo* h*abe*ns odio terram *propter* luctum aran:· statuit p*er*egrinari. et dedit na`c´hcor uxorem. | melcha*m*. abre u*er*o sarai. (HS 1091B)[190]

And the name of the city is Ur according to Josephus; . . . in Hebrew 'Ur' means 'fire'. . . . They expelled Abram and Aran, who (because they) did not want to worship fire (and, Aran dying there,) Abram was liberated with the help of God. . . . Thare therefore, holding the land in contempt, and because of his grief for Aran . . . decided to wander in foreign parts and gave Nachor Melcha as a wife, and Sarai to Abram.

80a.[191] Jer*onymus* dic*it*. Aran a q*uo* syri: q*uo*ru*m* metropolis e*st* damascus. filii aran. hus. 7 vl. 7 gether. | 7 Mesli. hus. t*ra*conitidis et dama`s´ci co*n*ditor. i*nter* palestina*m* & celen syria. tenuit p*r*incipatu*m*. a q*uo* .lxx[ta]. in|terp*re*tes.(. .) in libro iob. ubi i*n* hebreo sc*r*ibit*ur*. te*r*ra hus regione*m* ausitide*m* qu*a*si usitide*m*. t*r*anstulerunt:· ‖ vl a q*uo* armenii. Gether a q*uo* acarnani. seu etharii.[192] Porro mesli p*ro* q*uo* . lxx. int*er*p*re*tes mosoch dixerunt:· | nunc meones uocant*ur*:· (Jerome, HQG 23.955A/B, CCSL 72, 18.8)

Jerome says, Aran from whom the Syrians (descend), whose chief city is Damascus. The sons of Aran: Hus and Ul and Gether and Mesli (Mes). Hus is the founder of Trachonitis and Damascus, he held power between Palestine and Coele-Syria, on whose account the Septuagint in the Book of Job translates 'Husitidis' where in the Hebrew it is written 'terra Hus', a region of Ausitides. Ul, from whom the Armenians, Gether, from whom the Acarnanians or Carians. Then Mes, for whom the Septuagint says 'Mosoch' . . . which now is called 'Maeones'.

F. 20r *Illustrations:* Two frames: upper, Abraham and Nachor with their wives; lower, four male figures with walking sticks, representing separately Thare leading Loth and Thare leading Abram to Haran, Thare being the figures first and third from right. **OE** = Genesis 11:29–31

[189] Written in the upper and lower ledgers of the lower frame. The first insert is in a blacker ink than the rest.

[190] *Sylwan* hur] ur *Cl y* ‖ *Sylwan* odio habens] h. o. *Cl y*

[191] Bottom, 3 lines and to top of f. 20r. Hairline accents have been supplied for a few vowels (besides 'i') and "flagged" OE-type accents for a few others.

[192] *edd.* Carii.

80b. Necdum quippe i*nter* patruos. et fr*atru*m filias. nuptie fu*er*ant lege p*ro*hibite. q*ue* in p*ri*mis hominib*us*. | etia*m* int*er* fr*atre*s. et sorores inite[193] sunt. (Jerome, HQG 23.956C, CCSL 72, 19.19)

In those days the law did not prohibit marriage between paternal uncles and the daughters of brothers, which among the first men was begun even between brothers and sisters.

81. Egressis e*st* e*r*go thare cu*m* illis ut iret in t*er*ram canaan.[194] uener*unt*q*ue* raab[195] aram mesopotamie ciuitatem. (HS 1091C)

Thare therefore left with them so "he went into the land of Canaan and they came to [Raab] Haran," a city of Mesopotamia. (Genesis 11:32)

82a. (in right margin '.bede.') Carra ciuitas Mesopotamie ap*ud* romanos crassi clade: ap*ud* nos au*tem* hospitio abraha*m* pat*r*ia[r]che. | et parentis ei*us* morte nobilis. (NLA, PL92.1036B; CCSL121.170.85; cf. no. 84)

Bede: Carra, a city of Mesopotamia, among the Romans known from the defeat of Crassus, among us because of its harboring the patriarch Abraham and by the death of his noble parent.

82b. Ier*onymus* dic*it*. Mesopotamia. regio int*er* fluminia tigri*n*. 7 eufraten. | que 7 ip*s*o uocabulo. g*r*ece i*n* medio fluminu*m* e*ss*e. posita monstrat*ur*. huic ad meridie*m* succedit | babilonia. deinde chaldea. uel cedar. nouissima arabia eudemon. (NLA PL92.1038C; CCSL121.173.194)[196]

"Jerome" says Mesopotamia is a region between the rivers Tigris and Euphrates which by that Greek word is shown "to be placed between rivers." To the south of this come first Babylonia and then Chaldea (or Cedar), and finally Arabia Felix.

83. (underlined words in contrasting brown ink) **.ii.xx.iii** [A.M. 2023] | Tertia etas ab abraha*m* usq*ue* ad dauid. annos. dcccc.xl duos; co*m*plectens. | § Ab abraham usq*ue* ad dauid. generationes q*u*atuordeci*m*. a dauid usq*ue* tra*n*smig*r*at`i´one babilonis `annos cccc.l.xx.iii.´ generationes | qu*ar*tuordeci*m* et a t*r*ansmig*ra*tione

[193] Written 'nute'.

[194] A *signe de renvoi* over 'canaan' is repeated in the right margin and refers to second line, middle passage of main OE, **to úr chaldea**.

[195] *Sylwan* irent] iret *Cl W* ‖ *Sylwan* uenerunt usque] ueneruntque usque *β γ T*; *Cl* shares this dittographic reading. 'raab' is to be deleted; it comes from a following sentence in HS, an explanation of aspiration: HS 1091D "Unde et filium Noe Habam dixerunt Cham. Inde est quod varie legitur Oreb, vel Choreb, Raab, vel Rachab."

[196] The previous note, 82a, is correctly ascribed to Bede, and this, an immediately following passage from the same work, is ascribed to Jerome, which it sometimes was; this suggests that at this point the Bede comments were taken not from a manuscript of NLA but from marginalia.

babilonis usq*ue* ad chr*istu*m `annos dl.xxx.ix.´ generationes qu*at*uordeci*m*. Id est simul generationes | Qua`d´raginta due:· quas tam*en* euangelista matheu*us* certi mysterii gra*tia* ponit:·[197]

The third age is from Abraham to David, comprising 942 years. From Abraham to David was fourteen generations, from David to the Babylonian exile (473 years), fourteen generations and from the Babylonian exile to Christ (589 years), fourteen generations. That is all together 42 generations, which Matthew the Evangelist established according to a certain mystery.

F. 20v *Illustrations:* Two large frames: upper, Thare (on right) and Abram; lower, corpse of Thare held by Abram and Loth (labeled 'thare obiit').[198] **OE** = Genesis 11:31–32

84. (upper frame, 2 lines) § Charan ciuitas Mesopotamie t*r*ans edessa*m* que usq*ue* hodie carra d*icitu*r. V*b*i roman*us* cessus [*recte* cesus] e*st* | exercit*us*. & crassus dux capt*us*. (Jerome, SNLH 23.888B, Lagarde 112.1)

Haran is a city of Mesopotamia beyond Edessa which up to the present day is called Carra, where the Roman army was abandoned (destroyed) and General Crassus captured.

85a. Et septuaginta anno*rum* genuit [Thare] abra*m*. ⁊ pos*t*ea uixit | centu*m* t*r*iginta q*ui*nq*ue* annis. (Sylwan 81/6bis) Si *ergo* p*ost* morte*m* p*at*ris abra*m* erat annor*um* .lxxv. patet q*uo*d dixim*us* | q*uo*d thare plusq*uam* .lxx annos. Habebat cu*m* genuit abra*m* (82/6) agusti[n]*us* dic*it*. (82/15) Abra*m* eg`r´essus est de | aram relinque*ns* ibi p*at*rem ⁊ fr*at*rem. (82/8) Si *enim* i*n* illa etate genuit abra*m*:· tunc po*st* morte*m* patris | erat abra*m* cxx`x´ xv. annoru*m*. (82/13) Adhuc *enim* uiuente patre eum e*ss*et. cxlv. | anno*rum*:· et abra*m* lxxv. egr`e´ssus est de haram:·[199] (HS 1091A, 1092B, rearranged)

And (Thare) was 70 years old (when) he begot Abram and afterwards he lived for 135 years.[200] If therefore after the death of his father Abram was 75 years old it shows what we said, that Thare was more than 70 years old when he begot Abram. Augustine . . . says . . . Abram went out of Haran leaving his father

[197] Based on Matthew 1:17, elaborated from mixed sources, resembling Jerome, Bede, DTR, Hrabanus, *De Universo*, PL111.307B, etc. The material was frequently repeated.

[198] Norman script, insular *r*.

[199] *Sylwan* Aran] haram *Cl* aram *S Tr γ*

[200] This is not in HS and contradicts PL Add. 1 (not in Sylwan), though the same total of years is reached: "Thare ergo erat centum triginta annorum cum genuit Abram, Abram septuaginta quinque cum pater obiit" ("Thare therefore was 130 years old when Abram was born, Abram 75 when his father died"). This corresponds to the details in Sylwan 82/9–10 (not in *Cl S β γ*): "qui erat [Thare] ducentorum quinque annorum quando mortuus est."

and brother. Therefore if at that age he begot Abram, then after the death of his father Abram was 135 years old. . . . For his father was still living when he was 145 years and Abram was 75 when he went out of Haran.

85b. (lighter ink) Septuaginta. v. anno*rum* erat abram cum egredetur de haram.[201]

Abram was 75 years old when he went out of Haran.

86. § N(. . . . .)[202] dic*it.* et cum | diuina*m* scriptura*m* diligenter euolueris. a Natiuitate abre. usq*ue* ad totiu*s* orbis diluuiu*m* inuenies | retrorsu*m* annos [dcccxlii] (Jerome's version of Eusebius, *Chron.*, PL 27.57A; Helm, *Eusebius Werke*, 15)

N[ormanus] said: and when you diligently consider divine scripture, from the nativity of Abr[ah]am back to the deluge of the whole world you will find [942] years.

F. 21r *Illustrations:* Two frames: upper, God, with cross nimbus and cross-marked book, telling Abram to leave Haran for Canaan, with city on right; lower, Abram, with ass, and Loth, their wives to left, complying. **OE** = Genesis 11:32–12:6

87. (inserted as a gloss in OE in third line between frames) **hí cómon to þam lánde chanaan** ˋ7 uenit ad syche*m*. q*ue* corrupte sychar[203] sepe legit*ur*ˊ 7 **abram sceáwode ðæt | lánd.** (HS 1092C)

They came to the land Chanaan (and [he] came to Sichem which is often read corruptly as Sychar) **and Abraham surveyed that land.**

88. § Berosus dicens. po*st* diluuium decima *gener*atione fuit ap*u*d caldeos uir in celestibus rebus exp*er*tus:ˊ (HS 1092D)

. . . Berossus saying ten generations after the flood there was among the Chaldeans a man learned in celestial matters.

89.[204] damasc*us* nobilis urbs fenicis. q*ue* 7 q*u*onda*m* i*n* omni Syria tenuit p*r*incipatu*m*. N*un*c sarraceno*rum* metropolis | e*ss*e perhibet*ur*. (NLA, PL92.1036D; CCSL 121.171.114)

Damascus, a noble city of the Phoenicians, which once was the capital of all of Syria. Now it is considered to be the chief city of the Saracens.

---

201 Unsourced.

202 Erased letters 'N..man*us*' (VSC).

203 *Sylwan* sichem, sichar] sychem, sychar *Cl Tr*

204 Bottom 2 lines, 'damas' was written at the end of line 3 up, smudged out, and rewritten on the next line.

90. (bottom line) Messe. Regio indie: in q*u*a habitauerunt filii iecthan.[205] filii heber: (Jerome, SNLH 23.908B; Lagarde 136.26)

Messe, a region of India in which lived the sons of Iectan, the sons of Heber.

F. 21v *Illustrations:* Upper, left, God with cross on head (no nimbus) and book gives land to Abram, who is bowing to God at an altar; right, Abram worships at altar, a tent pitched (between Bethel and Hai); lower, Abram and Sarai, shown on both left and right, and Egypt (city in center). **OE** = Genesis 12:7–12

91a. Vr chaldeor*um*. Vbi mortuus e*st* ara*n*. f*rate*r abrahe. Cui*us* hodieq*ue* sic*ut* joseph*us* refert. tumulus ostendit*ur*. Et sup*er* hoc | quid nob*is* uideat*ur* i*n* lib*r*is hebraicaru*m* questionu*m* diximus: (Jerome, SNLH 23.926B; Lagarde 158.17)

Ur of the Chaldees, where Aran the brother of Abraham died, whose burial mound is still shown, as Josephus mentions. And I have already given my views about this in the books of "Hebrew Questions."

91b. Vlammaus: p*ro* qua i*n* heb*r*eo sc*r*iptu*m* habet*ur* luza. Eade*m* e*st* au*tem* que & bethel sic*ut* sup*ra* dixi: (*ibid.*; Lagarde 158.22, cf. 100.8)

Ulammaus for which in Hebrew is written Luz. But it is the same name which is also Bethel, as I said above.

92. Habitauit. a*utem* in damasco. Vn*de* et nomen ei*us* usq*ue* nunc: . . . et uicus[206] ostend*itu*r qui ab eo dicitur habit*ati*o abraam:[207]| Vn*de* nicholau*s* dama`s´cenus. Abraam rignauit [*recte* regnauit] in damasco: ueniens aduena cum exercitu de terra que sup*er* babi|lonem dicitur caldeorum.[208] (HS 1093A)

Abram lived in Damascus, therefore his name is up to now [held in glory in the city of Damascus] and the place is shown which is called from him the 'Dwelling of Abram'. Therefore Nicholaus of Damascus[209] (said), "Abram reigned in Damascus, coming as an alien with his retinue from the land which once was called Babylon of the Chaldeans."

93. Facta est autem fames in terra. et descendit in egyptum: (cf. HS 1093A, but almost exact wording of Genesis 12:10)

There was a famine . . . in the land . . . and he went into Egypt.

---

205 Written 'iecthān'.

206 *Sylwan* uicus ibi] ibi *om. Cl S W γ*

207 'abraam' 2x in this passage (also *To*) is found only here for "Abram" in *Cl*; it occurs in 120, 127a, 153b incorrectly for "Abraham."

208 so *Sylwan Cl*] hur chaldeorum *Tr PL*

209 Nicholaus of Damascus was a first-century B.C. Jewish historian consulted by Josephus.

94. § farfar fluuius damasci:· (Jerome, SNLH 23.898B; Lagarde 124.7)
Pharphar, the river of Damascus.

F. 22r *Illustrations:* Two frames: upper, Abram and Sarai before Egypt; lower, two soldiers bring Sarai before Pharaoh, who is flanked by two others, while on left Abram is given coins in payment.[210]

F. 22v *Illustrations:* Two frames: upper, Abram with his wealth in "sheep, [oxen,] he-asses, menservants, maidservants, she-asses, and camels"; lower, Pharaoh, with gesture of distress, returns Sarai to Abram, two figures of authority seated on right; **OE** = Genesis 12:12–13:4. No annotations on ff. 22rv.

F. 23r *Illustrations:* upper, on left Abram returns from Egypt with Sarai and Loth,[211] on right Abram and Loth worship; lower, Abram and Loth with their tents. **OE** = Genesis 13:4–10

95. (bottom) Nageb. auster ap*u*d hebreos nageb d*icitu*r q*uo*d symmach*us* int*er*p*re*tat*ur* [*recte* -tat] Meridie*m*. Scie*n*du*m* au*tem* q*uo*d | eadem plaga ap*u*d hebreos t*r*ibus uocabulis appellat*ur* nageb.(. .) theman. darom. q*uo*d nos | possim*us* austru*m*. africu*m* & meridie*m*. siue euru*m* int*er*pretari. (Jerome, SNLH 23.913A/B; Lagarde 142.7)
Nagab, 'south', it is called among the Hebrews 'Nageb', which Symmachus interprets as 'south'. Moreover it is to be known that this same area by the Hebrews is named with three words, (to wit) 'nageb', 'theman', 'darom', which we are able to interpret as 'south', 'southwest', or 'southeast'.

F. 23v *Illustration*: Three frames: upper, Loth with his tents and herds (labeled 'loth'); middle, Abram with his tents and herds (labeled 'habra*m*'); lower, Loth (labeled 'loth') seated in a city (Sodom), to right six men (of Sodom) encircled by a scroll held by a devil, the scroll labeled 'diabolus'.[212] **OE** = Genesis 13:11–13

96. § ANteq*u*am sodoma*m*. p*er*uenirent. qu*a*tuor reges p*ro*fecti de babilone. int*er*fecerunt. gygantes.:· (Jerome, HQG 23.959; CCSL 72, 22.18)
Before they came to Sodom, the four kings set out from Babylon and killed giants.

---

[210] Dodwell and Clemoes, *Illustrated Hexateuch*, 22, point out that this accords with the Old English text (⁊ **abra*m* | underfeng féla scéatta for hyre**) rather than the Vulgate.

[211] Perhaps the third male figure represents "all that he had" (Gen. 13:1).

[212] The script on the scroll is in an 11c hand not that of the main scribe.

97a.[213] Jer*onymus* dic*it* (up in margin, in brown ink) | § Factu*m* est au*tem* i*n* illo te*m*pore. ut amraphel rex sennaar. i*d est* babilonis. ⁊ c*etera*. Ia*m* p*r*ocesserat t*antum*[214] libido dominandi. q*uo*d [queque][215] ciuitas | regulu*m* habebat. quor*um* pl*ur*imi alicui regi maiori seruiebant. tan`d´em[216] om*nes* subditi erant monarcho assiryorum | Sane. v. ciuitates sodomor*um*. sodoma. gomorra. adama. (.) sebonis.[217] bala. que et segor:· v. reges habebant. ‖ has subiungau*er*at s*ib*i codorlahomor rex elamitaru*m*. ⁊ t*r*ibutarias sibi fecerat. ⁊ xii. annis seruierant | ei i*n* t*r*ibuto:· xiii°. anno.[218] noluer*unt* s*ib*i dare. P*r*oinde. xiiii° anno:· codorlahomor a`s´sumens secu*m* tres reges | babilonis. ⁊ ponti. ⁊ ge*n*tiu*m* collecto exercitu conuener*unt* i*n* uall*em* siluestrem. i*n* qua erant putei- | que p*er* ira[m] dei po*st* uersa est in mare mortuu*m*. ⁊ ci*r*cumiacentia loca depopulati sunt- (HS 1094A/B)

Jerome says: "And it came to pass in that time that Amraphel, king of Sennaar" (Gen. 14:1), that is of Babylon, etc. Now the desire for domination had gone so far that [every] city had a ruler to whom many others bowed down as their great kings; in the end all were subdued by the monarch of the Assyrians. Indeed, five cities of the Sodomites, Sodom, Gomorra, Adama, Sebonis, Bala, which is also Segor, had five kings. These Chodorlahomor, king of the Elamites, had subjected to himself and made tributaries to himself, and for twelve years they served him with tribute. In the thirteenth year they did not want to contribute to him. Therefore in the fourteenth year, Chodorlahomor taking with himself three kings, of Babylon, and of Pontus, and of nations, they came together with an army in the Vale of Woods in which there are wells (of bitumin), . . which through the wrath of God afterwards was turned into the Dead Sea, and they plundered the surrounding areas.

F. 24r *Illustrations:* Two frames: upper, God, cross on head, no nimbus, blessing Abram in front of his tents (labeled 'd*omin*us', 'abram'); lower, Abram, with a boy moving his tents to Hebron, and worshipping before an altar (labeled 'abraham-'), hand of God descending. **OE** = Genesis 13:14–14:10

98.[219] Jer*onymus* dic*it*. ARbe q*u*atuor. eo q*uo*d ibi q*ua*tuor pat*ri*arche sepulti sunt. (Jerome, SNLH 23.862A; Lagarde 84.10)

---

213 Bottom, three lines, continuing (with marks) to bottom of f. 24r, three lines; on f. 23v *signe de renvoi* 'hwær' refers to 'hær' just above the lower section of OE main text on f. 24r, rendering Gen 14:1.

214 MS tm̄; *Sylwan* "iam tunc processerat," which emends MSS: tamen *P*, tantum *S β T*.

215 *Cl* incorrectly reads 'qn̄'; 'queque' is the correct reading.

216 Corrected from 'tamem'.

217 *Sylwan* sebois] seboys *S Tr Pa T*

218 Corrected from 'annis'; anno *add. Cl Tr*

219 Above lower picture frame, 1 line.

Jerome says Arbe means 'four' because four patriarchs . . . are buried there.

99. Ebron ciuitas est. que et cariatarbe d*icitu*r i*d est* ciuitas .iiii^{or}. Arbe *enim* q*ua*tuor: cariath: ciuitas. Ibi *enim* situs est adam | maxim*us*. 7[220] abram. ysaac. et ialcob. [*sic*] cum uxoribus suis. Josephu*s* dicens. habitabat. a*bram* ci*r*ca ilicem que uocatur agigi: (HS 1093C/D)

Hebron is a city which is also named Cariatharbe, that is 'city-four'; for 'arbe' is 'four' and 'cariath' is 'city'. Adam the greatest (of prophets) is located (buried) there and Abraham, Isaac, and Jacob with their wives, . . . Josephus . . . saying that Abram lived near that holm-oak which is called Ogygi.

97b. (on lower ledger of bottom frame, phrases to be inserted into main OE text) **Hyt gelamp ða on þære tíde þ*æt* ða** et egressi sunt .v. reges . ut pugnarent. adu*er*sus .iiii. **cyningas wúnnon hi*m* be twynan. iiii.**[221] (OE = Gen. 14:1–2; the wording of the insertion is from HS 1094B; cf. Gen. 14:9)

It happened then at that time that those also the five kings went out . . . so that they might fight against four **kings fought amongst themselves four** (kings against five).

F. 24v *Illustration:* One large frame divided into two scenes without register lines: above, battle and defeat of kings of Sodom, below Loth bound as a prisoner in a city (labeled 'loth'),[222] to right the escapee with walking stick observes this from behind a curtain-like landscape. **OE** = Genesis 14:11–13

100. § Et reu*er*tentes uenerunt. ad fontes [*recte* -em] iudicii. Hec e*st* cades. p*er* anticipatione*m* d*icitu*r. q*uo*d p*os*tea sic uocatu*m* est. | Significat au*tem* locu*m* apud pet*ra*m. Qui fons iudicii nominat*ur*. quia de*us* ibi populu*m* judicauit: (Jerome, HQG 23.960A; CCSL 72, 23.4)

And returning they came to the Fountain of Judgement; this is Cades. It is said by way of prolepsis because only later it came to be so named. It signifies the place near a rock which was named the Fountain of Judgement because there God judged the people.

---

220 *Sylwan* sepultus] situs *Cl γ* ‖ *Sylwan* prophetarum maximus] proph. *om. Cl S β γ T*; et *add. Cl T γ*. See no. 292d 'adam magnus' in same context, *ex* Hrabanus from earlier sources.

221 At this point L'Isle has entered "cyningas´ wið V.' from the Laud manuscript. It appears that the twelfth-century annotator is trying to make up this same omission.

222 Loth, handcuffed, is arrested by *two* kings; Dodwell and Clemoes, *Illustrated Hexateuch*, 22–23, point out that because of a textual omission in the OE (in no. 97b, f. 23r, line 4 up), the illustration shows only four kings in the battle, two beheaded.

101. § Damasc*us*. Nobilis urbs fenicis [*recte* -es]. Eode*m* au*tem* uocabulo & masech ancille abraha*m* fili*us* a`p´pellat*ur* e*st*. | Porro masech q*u*id sibi uelit i*n* libris( . . )heb*ra*icaru*m* questionu*m* pleni*us* disputauit [*recte* -aui]:· Hic tantu*m* | in-te*r*p*re*tis sum funct*us*. o`f ´ficio:·[223] n*on* q*u*o ancilla*m* abrahe masech nuncupata*m* p*ro*bemus:· (Jerome, SNLH 23.890B; Lagarde 114.21; cf. no. 89)

Damascus, the noble city of Phoenicia. The son of Abraham by the slave woman Masec is called by the same name. Some time ago in the "Hebrew Questions"[224] I discussed more fully what 'Masec' means. Here I am only carrying out the duty of an interpreter; we are not demonstrating how the slavewoman of Abraham Masec got her name.

F. 25r *Illustration:* Three frames: upper, Abram receives the messenger; middle, in two registers ("he divided his forces"), Abram's expedition; lower, Abram's forces attack kings' attendants. **OE** = Genesis 14:14–15

102a. pugnare non ualentes effugerunt. et p*er*secutus est eos usq*ue* hoba. que est ad leuam / damasci. 7 reduxit loth:· (HS 1094C)

. . . not being able to fight, they fled "and he pursued them to Hoba . . . which is on the left hand of Damascus and brought back Loth." (Gen. 14:15)

102b.[225] et tres[226] p*re*dictos f*ra*tres. Manbre. 7 anel.[227] 7 escol. 7 p*er*secut*us* e*st* eos usq*ue* dan `fenicis oppidum´:·[228] q*u*i e*st* fons unu*s* de fontib*us* | iordanis. 7 ab eo opidu*m* dan dictu*m* est. q*uo*d n[u]nc paneos dicit*ur*. Alt*er* *enim* ior dicit*ur*. q*u*ib*us* in unu*m* fed*er*atis:· / Jordanis dicitur.; (HS 1094C)

. . . and "three" already-mentioned brothers, "Mambre, Aner, and Eschol, and pursued them to Dan" (a town of the Phoenicians), which is one of the springs of Jordan and from it that town was named 'Dan', which is now called 'Paneos'. The other is called 'Jor', which when they are joined into one is called 'Jordan'. (Gen. 14:13, 15).

103.[229] ior:· q*uo*d int*er*pretat*ur* piopon. [po *cancelled*][230] id e*st* riu*um* siue fluuiu*m* heb*re*i uocat*um*; (Jerome SNLH 23.890C; Lagarde 114.28)

---

[223] The added 'f' is insular.

[224] HQG, CCSL 72.1.1 25.1.

[225] Bottom, 3 lines, *signes de renvoi* 'hwær / hær' keyed to OE text between top and middle frames.

[226] The first words 'et tres' and (above) 'hwær' are spaced so as to avoid the foot and leg of the figure.

[227] *Sylwan* aner] anel *Cl W y T*; cf. no. 106.

[228] Phrase unsourced.

[229] Bottom line, left; it has a mark indicating it is to be read with the words of the previous note: 'Alter enim ior dicitur'.

[230] i.e., ῥεῖθρον.

'Jor' which is interpreted in Hebrew as 'hreithron', that is, stream or river.

F. 25v *Illustration:* Two frames: upper, Abram's forces defeat kings, Abram victorious, exits towards right; lower, Abram, helmeted and blessed by hand of God, and his army (with women, as booty?) returns victorious to king of Sodom. **OE** = Genesis 14:16–20

104. § Dan. uic*us* in q*u*arto a paneade miliario euntib*us* tyru*m*. q*u*i usq*ue* hodie sic uocat*ur*: T*e*rmin*us* iudee p*ro*uin|cie c*on*tra septent*r*ione*m*: de q*u*o & iordanis flum*en* eru*m*pens: a loco sortit*us* e*st* nom*en*: (Jerome, SNLH 23.890B; Lagarde 114.26)

Dan, a place four miles from Paneadis in the direction of Tyre, which is still so named up to the present day. It is the northern boundary of the province of Judea from which the River Jordan rises and this place gets its name. (cf. no. 102b)

105.[231] Ceteru*m* bersabee | ut sup*ra* dixim*us* ad austrum uergens. uic*us* e*st*. maxim*us* .xx^{mo}. á chebron miliario: (Ps.-Eucherius, *De situ Hierusolimae*, ed. Fraipont, CCSL 175, sec. 14 [239])

But Bersabee, as we mentioned above, is a place towards the south, at most twenty miles from Hebron.

106. Mambre u*ero*: et anel:[232] et escol: fr*at*res fuerunt. et confederati sunt abre: (HS 1093C)

Mambre indeed and Aner and Eschol were brothers and allied with Abram.

107. abana fluuius damasci (Jerome, SNLH 23.876A; Lagarde 97.26)

Abana, a river of Damascus.

108. Ob hoc a*utem* institutus est quinquagesimus: quia tunc erat loth ut dicunt quidam .l. annor*um*: *u*el t*unc* | erat q*u*inqu*a*gesim*us* ann*us* ex q*u*o d*omin*us locut*us* est abre in uia. *u*el ex[233] q*u*o eg*r*essus est de charam: (HS 1095A/B)[234]

From this was instituted "quinquagesimus" (Jubilee) because then Lot was fifty, so some say, or because then it was the fiftieth year since the Lord spoke to Abram on the way, or from when he went out of Haran.

---

231 End of second line, continuing through bottom of upper frame; marks at upper right and lower left corners of frame show where the text continues.

232 *Sylwan* aner] et anel *Cl β Pa*

233 MS: 'ex ex'.

234 *Sylwan* locutus erat dominus] d. l. erat *W γ* (Sylwan also reports *Tr*, perhaps in error) ‖ *Sylwan* erat de aran] erat de charam uel *Tr*

109. Jer*onymus* dic*it*. (up in margin) Sich*em*. 7 sal*em* que latine 7 gr*e*ce. sic(. .) ima uocata e*st* ciuitas iacob. in t*r*ibu manesse. loc*us* in suburbanis | neapoleos iuxta sepulchru*m* joseph: fu`i´t au*tem* 7 alt*er*a sich*em* i*n* monte ephrai*m* ciuitas fugitiuor*um*: (Jerome, SNLH 23.918B/C; Lagarde 148.20)

Jerome says: Sichem and Salem, which in Latin and Greek is called Sicima, is the city of Jacob . . . in the tribe of Manasses, . . . a place in the suburbs of Neapolis by the tomb of Joseph; . . . there was also another Sichem on Mount Ephraim, a city of refuge.

F. 26r *Illustrations:* Two frames: upper, Abram and Melchisedech (with bread), an altar between them; lower, God blesses Abram (labeled 'habram', 'd*omin*us'. **OE** = Genesis 14:26–15:8

110. Et tunc p*r*imu*m* decime legunt*ur* date: Primicie uero: ab abel. (HS 1094D)

And for the first time it is read of tithes being given, but in truth the first was from Abel (Gen. 4:20).[235]

111a. Josephus refert que sal*em*. sub rege melchisedech. fuit (.) au*tem* in t*r*ibu beniamin (Jerome, SNLH 23.904C; Lagarde 132.13)

Josephus tells . . . that Salem under King Melchisedech was nevertheless in the tribe of Benjamin.

111b. § Jebus. Ipsa e*st*. que et ier*usa*lem. (*ibid.*)

Jebus is also the same as Jerusalem.

112.[236] Et Nota. q*u*ia ier*usal*em usq*ue* ad melchisedech. dicebat*ur* jebus. a q*uo* dicta e*st* sal*em*. Postea a dauid. dicta e*st* | Jebusal*em*. S*ed* postea mutata b. i*n* R. dixit ier*usa*lem q*u*asi munita*m* sal*em*. Jero enim(.)hebrice: muni|tio e*st*. Tradit Iosephu*s*. q*uo*d hanc littere mu*tat*ione*m* ab hom*er*o facta*m* q*u*ida*m* putant Postea dicta e*st* a salomone ‖ jerosolimia. et tande*m* p*er* sincopam: ierosolima- (HS 1329B)

And note that whereas Jerusalem was called 'Jebus' up to (the time of) Melchisedech, by whom it was called 'Salem', after David it was called 'Jebusalem'. But after the 'b' was changed to 'r' it was called 'Jerusalem', the fortress of Salem. 'Jero' in Hebrew is 'fortress'. Josephus reports that this change of letter was thought by some to be made by Homer. Later it was called by Solomon 'Jerosolimia' and finally, by syncope, 'Jerosolima'.

---

235 The comment applies to the word **teoðunga** in the top line of the OE immediately above this text.

236 Bottom, 3 lines continuing to top of f. 26v.

F. 26v *Illustrations:* Two frames: upper, God, cross-nimbed, shows Abram the stars of heaven (labeled 'habram', 'd*omin*u*s*'); lower, Abram drives the birds of prey away from the altar-offerings with a sling. **OE** = Genesis 15:8–11

113.[237] Et ab anno natiuitatis. ysaac usq*ue* ad annu*m* eg*re*ssionis ab egipto nu*mer*at. cccc.v. annos. S*ed* scrip|tura subticet q*u*inq*ue*. 7 legit litt*eram* sic⁚ seme*n* tuu*m* p*er*egrinu*m* erit. cccc annis .siue *enim* i*n* t*er*ra canaan. siue i*n* egipto. | p*er*egrinu*m* fuit. donec h*ab*uit hereditate*m* ex p*ro*missione dei. q*u*od(. .)au*tem* dictu*m* e*st*. ˋin quarta generatione eos redituros⁚ˊ[238] s*ecun*d*um* t*r*ibu*m* sacerdotale*m* i*n*telligendu*m* | e*st*. leui *enim* gen*uit* cahat.[239] q*u*i gen*uit* a*m*ram. q*u*i gen*uit* ááron. q*u*i gen*uit* eliazar. q*u*i cu*m* aaron egressu*s* est. Ne dicas .iiii^or^. genera|tiones p*er*sonas. s*ed* successiones. ut tot sint generationes. q*u*otiens ibi leligit*ur* [*sic, recte* legitur] genuit. Q*u*od alia lit*te*ra h*abe*t. q*u*inta⁚ s*ecun*d*u*m ‖ regia*m* tribum est. Judas. *enim* genuit phares. Q*u*i gen*uit* efron. [*recte* esron] | Q*u*i gen*uit* aram. q*u*i. gen*uit*[240] aminadab. Q*u*i gen*uit* naason⁚ Q*u*i cu*m* p*at*re egressus est. Et factu*m* [*recte* facta] e*st* caligo⁚ (HS 1096A/B)

And from the year of the birth of Isaac to the year of departure from Egypt numbers 405 years. But scripture does not mention 'five' and reads thus according to the letter: "your seed will be wandering for 400 years, both in the land of Canaan and in Egypt your wandering has been, until it has its heritage according to the promise of God" (cf. Gen. 15:13). That also is said (in four generations they will return); this is understood as applying to their priestly tribe: Levi begot Chaat, who begot Amram, who begot Aaron, who begot Eliazar, who went out with Aaron. You should not say four generations of persons but successions of entire generations as many times as the word 'genuit' occurs, but other literal passages have five generations depending on who is the head of the tribe. Judah begot Phares, who begot Efron, who begot Aram, who begot Aminadab, who begot Naason, who with his father went out. "And there arose a mist" (Gen. 15:17).

F. 27r *Illustrations:* Two frames: upper, the great darkness, the hand of God descends as a vision of the fiery oven appears over Abram asleep by an altar; lower, God with cross nimbus and book, making the covenant with Abram, beside the altar (labeled 'habra*m*', 'd*omin*u*s*'). **OE** = Genesis 15:12–21

---

[237] Bottom 5 lines, plus 2 lines above upper picture on f. 27r; *signes de renvoi* '+hwær /+hær' key the annotation to the OE version of Genesis 15:17, f. 27r/10 **mycel mist**; and a continuation mark takes the note from bottom of f. 26v to middle of f. 27r.

[238] The insertion seems to be in the same script, but written with a finer nib.

[239] *Sylwan* chaat] cahat *Cl To*

[240] *Sylwan* genuit *add. Cl δ*

114. (f. 27r, gloss to line 3 up of OE) **fra*m* þære egyptiscan ea** / i*d est* riuo corula Flumine egipti[241] (HS 1096B)

. . . **from the Egyptian river**, that is from the Corula Stream, From the river of Egypt.

F. 27v *Illustrations:* Three frames: upper, interior setting, Sarai, kneeling and pointing, presents Hagar to enthroned Abram; middle, right, Abram in bed with Hagar, Sarai, on left in another room, lies alone; lower, interior of a house, on left Sarai admonishes Abram about Hagar, on right, Hagar in listening posture in another room. **OE** = Genesis 16:1–6. No annotations.

F. 28r *Illustrations:* Two frames: upper, divided into two panels, on left under archway, Sarai, seated on left, deals with Hagar, who makes a gesture of grief, on right Hagar in wilderness is greeted by angel with (empty) scroll; lower, divided into two panels, left, postpartum Hagar, Ismael being washed by two female attendants, right, Abram and Sarai seated or enthroned together under a gable. **OE** = Genesis 16:6–16. Within the upper picture space, **īi.xxxiiii.** [A.M. 2033].

115.[242] § Uolens redire in pat*r*iam. q*uia* egiptia erat: iuxta putæu*m* q*ui* e*st* i*n* uia in / deserto sur. (HS 1096C/D)

(Hagar) wanting to return into her own country because she was an Egyptian woman; . . . next to the well which is on the road in the desert of Sur.

116.[243] Q*uo*d t*ame*n non de ip*s*o legitur: sed de filio ei*us* cedar. T*ame*n de genere ipsius hoc p*re*dictum est: Methodi*us* dic*it*.[244] q*uando* | .iiii^{or}. p*r*incipes de g*ene*r*e* hismael: q*u*os etia*m* filios uinee uocat: forte p*ro* uesania tanqu*a*m ebrios: oreb. s*cilicet* et[245].zeb. | et zebee. et salmana- egressi s*un*t de solitudine cont*r*a filios isr*ahe*l. q*u*i uicti p*er* gedeon: retrusi s*un*t in solitudinem | de qua prodierant; |

---

[241] *Sylwan* rinocorula] riuo corula *Cl α W T*; 'Flumine egipti' appears to be written in a separate stint. (A misunderstanding of the place-name Rhinocorula.)

[242] Two lines in top margin; an erasure of several words below the first two words of this passage.

[243] The passage is broken into several parts: top of upper frame, four lines, one line along bottom of that frame, two lines at very bottom (after no. 117), but the latter belongs with the text up under the arch, and is so marked. The *signe de renvoi*, a smallish 'hær' in margin, corresponds to 'þær' at line 12 of the OE text so that the comment on Hagar and Ismael should be read at the word '**gebroðra**': **and hé gewíslice arǽrd æfre hys getéld onnemn hys gebroðra: Agar þá clypode godes náman.** The other details of textual arrangement are given in the following notes.

[244] HS: "erat secundum Methodium, quando . . ."

[245] *Sylwan* hismael *om. Cl S Tr Pa T* ‖ *Sylwan* scilicet et *add. Cl β γ δ*

Hic[246] erit ferus homo: heb`re´us h*abe*t: phara. q*uod* sonat onager. p*rop*ter hoc ut dic*it* M*ethodius* dictu*m* e*st*: Onager | et capréé á deserto omne*m* bestiaru*m* sup*er*g*re*dient*ur* rabiem. et mansuetor*um* n*umer*us co*n*teret*ur* ab eis; | :Uocauit[247] d*omin*us `hismael´ onagru*m*. In sac*r*is locis int*er*ficient sacerdotes . Ibidem.[248] | cu*m* mulierib*us* dormie*n*t. ad sepulcra s*anct*or*um* religabunt iume*n*ta. Et hoc: p*ro* neq*u*icia chr*ist*ianor*um* q*u*i tunc erunt; (HS 1096D-1097A/B)

. . . which is read not about him but about his son Cedar. But this was mentioned above concerning his lineage. . . . Methodius says when "four princes of the family of Ismael," he calls these "sons of the vine," perhaps because of their madness, as if drunk, namely Horeb, Zeb, and Zebee and Salmana came out of the desert against the sons of Israel, who were conquered by Gideon, they were thrust back into the desert from which they were bred. . . . "He will be a wild man" (Gen. 16:12), the Hebrew has 'phara' which means 'wild ass'. Accordingly, as Methodius says, it is said, "the wild ass and the roe will surpass all the madness of wild beasts from the desert, and the portion of the tame will be destroyed by them." . . . The Lord called (Ismael) a wild ass. In hallowed places they will kill priests. At the same time when they are sleeping with women they will tie up their beasts at the tomb of the saints and this stands for the wickedness of Christians who are to come.

117.[249] Hic erit rusticus homo manu*s* ei*us* s*upe*r om*ne*s. p*ro* Rustico in hebreo sc*r*iptu*m* e*st* faran. | q*uo*d in[ter]p*retatu*r onager. (Jerome, HQG 23.963A; CCSL 72, 20–21)

"Here will be the wild man, his hand against all" (Genesis 16:12) . . . for 'wild' in Hebrew is written 'faran' which is interpreted 'wild ass'.

F. 28v OE 38 lines, no pictures = Genesis 17:1–22

118. (left margin) Quo cultello fieret | non est preceptu*m*. | Q*uare* aute*m* fiat lapi|deo:[250] post dicemus. (HS 1098A)

With which knife [circumcision] would have been done is not prescribed; of how it would be done with a stone (knife) we will speak later.

[246] This segment is in the bottom margin, two lines, with a mark indicating that it should be read after 'prodierant' just under the large colored arch in the upper picture, which is its place in the order of the text of HS.

[247] This segment follows immediately after 'prodierant', fourth line of annotation above the upper picture.

[248] After 'Ibidem' is an indexical letter 'a' in right margin, and the text skips to 'b' at 'cu*m* mulieribus' etc. in lower ledger of same frame.

[249] Top of bottom frame, two lines.

[250] *Sylwan* fiebat lapideo cultro] cultro *om.* *S β γ T*

F. 29r *Illustration:* Full-page picture of renewal of covenant, God, cross behind head and holding book, descending from heaven on ladder, eleven angels surrounding him, some flying, some holding the ladder; God, standing, blesses and renames Abraham, who is prostrate with Ismael praying behind him, no OE.[251]

119. (below picture frame) legit*ur* (. . . . .)[252] q*uo*d habraha*m* aliu*m* ha*buit* filiu*m*. de agar. [qui][253] dict*us* est Heliosdros a quo p*er*se duxerunt / originem. (HS 1097, Add. 1; Sylwan 94/45, note)[254]

It is read [in the Life of Clement] that Abraham had another son by Hagar, who was called Heliesdros, from whom the Persians descend.

F. 29v *Illustrations:* Two frames: upper, Abraham emerges from his tent, and then falls prostrate before three men, the first crowned with cross and holding out book, the second with book; lower, Abraham and his servant slaughtering and boiling an animal for the meal. **OE** = Genesis 17:23–18:7

120. (above upper frame) Abraam tunc erat nonaginta. ix. annorum. 7 hismael.[255] x.iii- (HS 1098C)

Abra(h)am was then ninety-nine and Ismael thirteen (when they were circumcised). (cf. no. 129)

F. 30r *Illustration*: One frame, a tent on right, Abraham sets out the meal before three figures.[256] **OE** = Genesis 18:8–22

121.[257] (in margin, as a gloss to **ic cúme éft tó ðe ón þísne tíman**) *id est* eode*m* die. reuolu|to anno. (HS 1085D)

That is, **I will come back to you at this time** on the same day a year later.

122. Aurisia e*st* qu*a*ndo homines habent aptos [*recte* apertos] oc*u*los et n*on* uide*n*t. q*uo*d magi faciunt incantationib*us*. Fiat | etia*m* aliqu*a*ndo q*uo*d homines rem habe*n*t aliqu*a*m i*n* manu et n*on* uident. et hoc e*st* etia*m* aurisia: (HS 1100D (cf. 1100C), Add. 1)[258]

---

[251] Inscribed on lowest angel's scroll in eleventh-century hand (not main hand): 'EGO su*m* d*o*m*inus* deus tuus'. Other angels hold (empty) scrolls.

[252] In erasure is 'in vita clementis', VSC.

[253] The word is smudged out.

[254] *S β γ δ*; eliesdros] heliesdros *Cl β*

[255] *Sylwan* ysmael] hysmael *Tr Pa T*, hismaehel *To*

[256] None are nimbed or carry books; the first and second men hold up hands in blessing.

[257] In the main OE text, line 3, '7' rewritten above as 'and'.

[258] This Additio appears in PL, but not in Sylwan text or apparatus; her text has "aorisia" (99/41), "acrisia" *β T.* Closer versions to *Cl* appear in BL, Royal 4.D.vii, f. 21r,

Aurisia is when men have capable [open] eyes and do not see, which sorcerers bring about with spells. Sometimes, too, it may happen that people have something in their hand and they do not see it, and this is also 'aurisia'.[259]

F. 30v *Illustration:* One frame, Abraham, gesturing towards the city, pleads for Sodom before the three men, now with divine attributes. **OE** = Genesis 18:23–32. No annotations.

F. 31r *Illustrations:* Two frames, above, the three divine figures enter Sodom, while Abraham departs to left; below, on right, Loth sitting at the door of his house, left, Loth prostrating himself before two hovering angels holding a blank scroll. **OE** = Genesis 18:33–19:1–4. No annotations.

F. 31v *Illustrations:* Two frames showing interiors, above, Loth entertaining two angels at a feast, on right, a servant (?), below, Loth vainly attempting to warn his sons-in-law elect. **OE** = Genesis 19:4–5, 12–14. No annotations.

F. 32r *Illustrations*: Two frames: upper, the two angels lead Loth, his wife, and two daughters out of Sodom; lower, Loth and his family, blessed by hand of God, approach the city (labeled 'segor'). **OE** = Genesis 19:15–22

123. (bottom, 3 lines) Tradunt hebrei hanc urbe*m* primo dicta*m* bala*m*. ⁊ post salisa*m*. ⁊ i*n* ysaia: uitula*m* cont*er*nante*m*.[260] q*u*ia t*er*cio t*er*remotu ab|sorpta sit: post subu*er*sione*m* aliaru*m* .iiii^or^. ciuitatu*m*. Qua*m*diu *er*go loth fuit i*n* ea: pep*er*cit ei d*omin*us. Ier*onymus* \`dic*it* ´ timens. loth | consuetu*m* ei*us* t*er*remotu*m*: egressus mansit in monte. ⁊ suspicate s*un*t tale aliq*u*id factu*m*: quale in dieb*us* noe: (HS 1101A, 1101D)

The Hebrews hold that this city was first called Bala and afterwards Salaisa and in Isaias 'heifer of three years' (Isaiah 15:5) because a third earthquake

margin (St. Albans, before Dec. 1214) 'Acrisia*m*. qu*and*o ho*min*es h*abe*nt oculos ap*er*tos . . .' and in CCCC 29, f. 10r b, Additio (s. xii/xiii) 'Aurisia *est* q*u*i spec*ie*s fantasie. q*uando* qu*is* ho*min*es h*abe*nt ap*er*tos oc*u*los . . . hec *etiam* p*os*t dici aurisia'.

259 This comment is misplaced, pertaining as it does to the story of Loth in Sodom which is written on ff. 31r-32r, and particularly to Gen. 19:11 ('et eos, qui foris erant, percusserunt caecitate. . .'), a verse not represented in the OE version. Was the commentator misled by the contents of the picture on f. 30r, which might be interpreted as some people not seeing "what is in hand"? The picture shows Abraham entertaining the three angel guests, while, in the words of Dodwell and Clemoes, *Illustrated Hexateuch*, 24, "presumably Sarah is in the tent on the right doubting and laughing (Gen. 18:9–10)."

260 *Sylwan* consternantem *P*] conternantem *Cl S W T*[p.c.]; the manuscripts are divided between these two readings from Isaiah 15:5: the former ("stampeded heifer") is Old Latin and gives the better sense; the latter is the Vulgate reading, doubtless a reflexive emendation. See no. 125.

swallowed it after the overthrow of the . . . other four cities. . . . Therefore, as long as Loth was in them, the Lord spared him. . . . Jerome says that Loth, fearing that the earthquake was usual, going out, remained in the mountain. . . . And it is believed that some such was done, as in the days of Noe.

123a. (gloss, trailing from OE text into right margin at end of second block of OE text) **ségor:** i*d est* parua

F. 32v *Illustration:* One large frame, heaven rains fire on Sodom. **OE** 5 lines above, 2 below = Genesis 19:23–26. No annotations.

F. 33r *Illustrations:* Two frames: upper, left, Loth's wife as pillar of salt, Loth, with daughters in city, look on grievingly; lower, left Loth and daughter approach a hill, right, Loth in a cave with daughters, who speak together. **OE** = Genesis 19:27–32

124. dicitur etiam uallis salinaru*m*. forte sit ibi sal. vel lapides salis ci*r*ca inueniuntur:˙ (HS 1101C/D)[261]

It is called the Valley of Salts, maybe there is salt there or stones of salt are found around there.

125. Segor. q*ue* & bala. & zoara una de q*u*inq*ue* ciuitatib*us* sodomoru*m* ad p*r*eces loth de incendio | reseruata. q*ue* usq*ue*. n*unc* ostendit*ur*. Meminit hui*us* Isaisas [*sic*] in uisione cont*ra* Moab. (Jerome, SLNH 23.919C; Lagarde 149.28)

Segor, which is Bala and Zoara, one of the five cities of the Sodomites saved by the prayers of Loth from the burning, which is shown up to the present day. Isaiah recalls this in his vision against Moab (Isaiah 15:5).

F. 33v *Illustration:* Two frames: upper, large hill with two openings, in larger Loth is given wine by daughters and in smaller he is sleeping with one; the lower picture repeats. **OE** = Genesis 19:33–37

126.[262] dic*it* ier*onymus* filias posse excusari:˙ quia crediderunt genu*s* humanu*m* defecisse. 7 pietas | posteritatis:˙ i*m*pietate*m* i*n*cest*us* excusauit. s*ed* hoc:˙ | patrem non excusat. Set infidelitas ei*us* | causa fuit incestus. de eode*m* strab*us* ait.[263] ‖ loth:˙ inexcusabilis e*st*. p*r*imo:˙ q*u*ia angelo non credidit. se posse salueri[264] in

[261] A note added in *S β γ T* (Sylwan 102/42, note).

[262] Inside lower frame, 4 lines, continuing to 34r top, 3 lines between two lines of OE at top and upper frame; marginal *signes de renvoi* '+hwær /+hær' and in-text continuation marks referring to where the comment continues on f. 34r.

[263] *Sylwan* ut ait strabus] s. a. *Cl S β γ*; 'strabus' expressed 'strab;'.

[264] *sic*, with 'i' imperfectly altered from some other letter, probably 'e'.

segor. dein*de*: | Quia inebriatus est: et fuit peccatum causa peccati: vel dicit*ur* nescisse fuisse filiam: | putans fuisse uxorem suam:- (HS 1102B/A)

Jerome says the daughters could be excused because they believed that humankind had been destroyed and piety towards posterity excused the impiety of incest. . . . But this does not excuse the father but his infidelity was the cause of the incest. Strabus says the same thing: Loth is not excusable, first because he did not believe the angel that he could be saved in Segor; then because he was drunk and that sin was the cause of his sinning. . . . Or it is said that he did not know she was his daughter, thinking she was his wife.

F. 34r *Illustrations:* Two frames: upper divided into two panels with nearly identical pictures, left birth of Moab, right birth of Amon; lower, Abraham left, King Abimelech enthroned in his palace and surrounded by a military court, has Sarra brought before him. **OE** = Genesis 19:38–20:2

127a. Profectu*s* est abraam de conualle ma*m*bre: in t*er*ram australem. p*er*egrinatus est in geraris. inter cades. unde fulxerunt [*recte* flux-] | aque contradictionis. 7 sur; (HS 1102C)

Abra(h)am set out from the Vale of Mambre to the southern land, . . . he wandered in Gerara between Cades, whence flow the waters of contradiction, and Sur [cf. Num. 20:13 and no. 301a].

127b. (gloss in last line of OE) **abimelech** `rex gerare´ (= HS 1102C, cf. Gen. 20:2)

F. 34v *Illustration:* One frame: In a palace God appears to Abimelech, who is sleeping on a bed, an unfinished drawing of a woman beside him. **OE** = Genesis 20:3–15

128. (margin) [O]n þán tíme hí cwæðe | hære hælder bréder | [w]ære fæderes:[265]

At that time they said their elder brothers were fathers.

[265] MS edge is trimmed, the 'O' is gone: but one can read 'hære' 2x, visible in fiber optic light (and easily on the CD-ROM); the passage makes sense following HS if the second 'hære' is emended to 'wære', as here, or alternatively, if "were" is understood "their elder brothers (were) their fathers"; Crawford's reading (no. 25) "ærcfæderes" is without MS warrant. "Sicut enim dicebant cognatos fratres, sic et cognatas sorores; fratrem vero Aram, patrem suum vocavit, quia senior eo fuerat, secundum usum loquendi, quo majores natu, patres vocamus, minores filios . . ." (HS 1102D-1103A) ("So they called male relatives brothers and female relatives sisters; indeed [Abram] called his brother Aram his father because he was elder to him, according to common usage, whereby those born elder we call fathers, those younger we call sons . . .").

F. 35r *Illustrations:* Two frames: upper, left, Abimelech speaks to Abraham, who appears to be hastening to him, Sarra behind with soldiers, on right Abimelech's gifts of livestock to Abraham; lower, left, in house, birth of Isaac, right, Abraham praying, hand of God extended. **OE** = Genesis 20:15–21:7

129.[266] Abraha*m* fuit. c. annor*um* sara. xc § Exinde. p*os*t totide*m* dies: iud*e*i circu*m*cidunt. ARabes u*er*o; p*os*t .xiii. annos. | q*u*ia eo (. .) te*m*pore: Hismael gentis illi*us* au`c´tor circu*m*cisus fuit.(. .) | Et uocauit eum ysaac i*d est* risu*m*. quia risu*m* fecerat. d*omin*us parentib*us*. i*d est* Gaudiu*m* i*n*opinatum. (HS 1103C) **ii.xlvii.** [A.M. 2047]

Abraham was 100 years old and Sara 90 (cf. Gen. 21:5). After that after just so many days [i.e., eight days, Gen. 21:4] the Jews perform circumcision. The Arabs indeed (circumcise) after 13 years, because at that time Ismael, the founder of his people, was circumcised. And he called him Isaac, that is, 'laughter', because the Lord made laughter for (his) parents, that is, unexpected joy. (cf. no. 120)

F. 35v *Illustrations:* Upper, feast on the ablactation of Isaac, who is at Abraham's right hand; lower, left, Ismael and Isaac playing, right, in a building, Sarra remonstrating with Abraham, hand of God extended. **OE** = Genesis 21:8–13

130.[267] Nota*n*du*m* au*tem* 7 ex priorib*us* et ex p*re*se*n*ti loco. q*uo*d ysaac n*on* sit nat*us* ad quercu*m* ma*m*bre. siue in | aulone. ut i*n* hebreo habet*ur* s*ed* i*n* geraris: u*b*i et barsabee oppidu*m* e*st*: usq*ue* hodie q*ue* p*ro*uincia ante | n*on* multu*m* temp*us* ex diuisione p*re*sidiu*m* palestine. salutaris e*st* dicta. hui*us* rei testis *est* script*ura* q*ue* | ait. et habitauit abraha*m* i*n* t*er*ra philistinor*um*:- (Jerome, HQG 23.969B; CCSL 72, 26.5)

It is to be noted from preceding passages (Genesis 20:1) and the present one, that Isaac was not born at the Oak of Mambre or in the vale [of Mambre] as the Hebrew has it, but in Geraris, where the city of Barsabee is located to the present day, which province not long before the division of the garrisons of Palestine was called 'safe'.[268] There is a witness to this in Scripture which says "and Abraham lived in the land of the Philistines" (Gen. 21:34).

F. 36r *Illustrations:* Two frames: upper, Abraham leaving Hagar and Ismael in the wilderness; lower, right, Ismael, "a good way off" from Hagar, who in middle is

---

266 Top of lower frame to bottom of same frame; code reference in margin 'et exinde' is referring the Latin comment below the OE to OE text at line 5 up, **þam eahteðan dæge.**

267 In the margin 'q T', of obscure significance.

268 That is, the provincial name of the southern part of the Holy Land was in Jerome's day "Palaestina Salutaris."

addressed by an angel with scroll, and on left Hagar, holding Ismael, scoops cup of water from the "waterpit." **OE** = Genesis 21:14–20

131.[269] Qui tollens pane*m*. et utre*m* aquae. i*m*posuit scapule agar. et t*r*adidit ei pueru*m*. | et puer deficeret siti;[270]| et sedit p*ro*cul Quantu*m* arcus iacere potest. ne uideret filiu*m* | Morientem.[271] 7 fleuit | (up in right margin) i*d est* fletu*m* mat*r*is pro | puero | 7 implens | utrem (et *cancelled*) abiit.[272] (HS 1105D)

"Who, taking bread and a jar of water, placed (them) on (Hagar's) shoulder and delivered the child to her" (Gen. 21:14) . . . And the boy grew weak from thirst. . . . "And (Hagar) sat as far away as a bow can shoot" lest she see her son dying "and wept" (Gen. 21:16); . . . that is, the weeping of the mother for the boy; . . . and filling the jar, she left.

132.[273] Sur v*b*i inuenit ang*elu*s ancilla*m* sare. agar int*er* cades. & barth. Extend-it*ur* au*tem* desertu*m* svr usq*ue* | ad mare rubru*m*. q*uo*d ad egipti co*n*finia, p*er*uenit: Porro cades solitudo e*st* sup*er* urbe*m* petra*m*. | Sed. & sc*r*iptura desertu*m* cades co*n*tra facie*m* egipti extendi memorat. ad q*uo*d p*r*imu*m* uenere. ‖ hebrei. rubro[274] Mari transuadato. (Jerome, SNLH 23.919C; Lagarde 149.22)

Sur where the angel found Hagar, the slave woman of Sara, between Cades and Barad. The Desert of Sur extends up to the Red Sea which reaches to the borders of Egypt. Further on, the Solitude of Cades is above the city of Petra. But Scripture also notes that the Desert of Cades extends up to the edge of Egypt, where the Hebrews first came after they crossed the Red Sea.

F. 36v *Illustrations:* Upper, right, Ismael with his bow, left, Hagar with a wife for Ismael; lower, Abraham swearing to the enthroned Abimelech and Pichol. **OE** = Genesis 21:20–26

---

[269] A more-or-less continuous passage, begins in top of ledger upper frame, 1 line, moving to lower ledger of same, 1 short line, with codes indicating relevance to OE, lines 3–4 of middle block; upper ledger of lower frame, 2 lines; 2 marginal areas.

[270] *Signes* relate this line to OE: 7 **þ*æt* wæter asceor|tode þe wæs on ða*m* buteruce.**

[271] *Signes* relate this line to OE **þ*æt* héo nolde geséon hu þ*æt* cíld | swúlte.**

[272] Marginal notes are keyed to the OE text as if it were the text preceding in HS: cf. Claudius: **God sylf gehyrde ðæs cildes stemne** / *margin:* 'id est fletum matris pro puero'; HS: "et exaudiuit Deus vocem pueri, id est, fletum matris pro puero"; Claudius: 7 **héo of þa*m* sealde þa*m* cnápan dríncan** / *margin:* '7 implens utrem abiit'; HS: "deditque puero bibere, et implens utrem abiit." Below the upper frame, within line 4 of the OE, at the insert place of the upper marginal note, there is a partially erased entry, beginning 'i⟨d est⟩ a \\\\\\'.

[273] Bottom three lines, continuing to top line of f. 36v.

[274] The first 'r' is insular.

133.[275] **7 hys módor him genam wíf on egypti / lánde** | de qua nati sunt ei filii xii.[276] principes. tribuum suarum. [quorum][277] apell*ati*one: opida pagi | et t*r*ibus celebrant*ibus* [*recte* -tur]. Et moratus e*st* in solitudine pharam. (HS 1104A/1103D)

. . . **and his mother took a wife for him from Egypt,** from whom were born to him twelve sons, princes of their tribes from whose names are celebrated cities, countries, and tribes. \ "And he remained in the wilderness of Pharan." (Gen. 21:21)

134. Et eduxit eos abraha*m* ad puteu*m*. q*ue*[m] ostenderat de*us* agar. que*m* foderat abraha*m*. ante | .agar eiectam. Et serui abimelech abstulerant illum abrahe. Et restituit ei abime/lech puteu*m*. (HS 1104B)

And Abraham led them to the well which God had shown Hagar, which Abraham had dug before casting out Hagar. And the servants of Abimelech took it from Abraham. . . . And Abimelech restored the well to him.

135a.[278] § dasem urbs assirio*rum*. nobilis. q*u*am extruxit assur int*er* niniuen. & chalac (Jerome, SNLH 23.890B; Lagarde 114.14)

Dasem is a noble city of the Assyrians, which Assur built between Ninevah and Chalach.

135b. dris. id e*st* q*u*ercus. | ma*m*bre. iuxta chebron. q*ue* usq*ue* ad etate*m* i*n*fantie mee. & co*n*stantii regis i*mperium* therebint*us* mon|str`ba´*tur* p*er*uet*us* & annos magnitudine indicans: sub q*u*a habitauit abraha*m*. Miro au*tem* cul|tu ab ethinicis [*sic*] habita e*st* & ueluti q*u*onda*m* [*recte* quodam] i*n*signi nomine co*n*secrata: (*ibid.* 114.16)

Dris, that is 'oak', Mambre, next to Hebron, where up to the time of my childhood and the reign of Emperor Constantius a very ancient terebinth was shown, indicating by its great age that Abraham dwelt under it. By the gentiles it was tended with strange worship, and was once consecrated as with a (certain) special name.

F. 37r *Illustrations:* Upper, Abraham making a covenant with Abimelech by giving him sheep and oxen;[279] lower, right, Abimelech and Pichol leaving, Abraham planting a grove. **OE** = Genesis 21:27–34

---

275 Top second and third lines, written as if continuing OE which immediately precedes in line 1.

276 *Sylwan* f. xii] xii f. *Cl Tr*

277 *recte*; what is written is 'q*u*arīr' or '-ū*m*'.

278 This note is written as if continuous with the next ('chalacdris' written as one word). In margin, 'rda', of obscure significance.

279 All the animals appear to have originally been sheep; one has been altered into an "ox" by a later hand.

136a.[280] Messe regio indie in q*u*a habitauer*unt* `filii´ iectan. filii heber. (Jerome, SNLH 23.908B; Lagarde 136.26; also as no. 90, above)

Messe is a region of India in which live the sons of Jectan, the sons of Heber.

136b.[281] Ofir unde sicut i*n* regnor*um* lib*r*is legim*us* | aur*um* afferebat*ur* Salomoni: fuit au*tem* un*us* de posteris heber. nomine ofir. ex cui*us* stirpe uenientes | a fluuio cofene usq*ue* ad regione*m* indie q*ue* uocat*ur* ieria habitasse refert josephus. a q*uo* puto | & regione*m* uocabulu*m* *con*secuta*m*- (Jerome, SNLH 23.915A/B; Lagarde 144.21)

Ofir, whence, as we read in the books of Kings, gold was brought to Solomon. There was a descendant of Heber, by the name of Ofir, of whom those coming from his family, Josephus says, inhabited the region from the river Cofene to the region of India which is called Jeria, from whom I suppose the region takes its name.

136c. Sofera mons orientis in india. iuxta q*u*am habitauer*unt* | filii iectan. filii hebér. q*u*os joseph*us* refert. a cophene flumine & indie regionib*us*, usq*ue* ad id || locor*um* p*e*ruenisse. V*b*i appellat*ur* regio jeria. S*ed* & classis salomonis p*er* t*r*iennu*m* hinc queda*m* co*m*[282]|mertia deportabat:· (Jerome, SNLH 23.919A; Lagarde 149.1)

Sofera, the eastern mountain in India, next to which lived the sons of Jectan, the sons of Heber, whom Josephus mentions as having come from the river Cophene and the regions of India to that place, where it is named the region of Jeria. But also the fleet of Solomon carried from here a certain amount of trade for three years.

137. (f. 37r, above and below top of upper frame) bersabee. i*d est* puteus septem.[283] sabee. *enim* hebraice:· septem sonat. et ibide*m* p*er*cusserunt | ambo fedus; Vnde etiam[284] bersabee dictu*m* putant. i*d est* puteu*m* iuramenti; sabe. *enim* hebraice iuramentu*m* / d*icit*ur. (HS 1104B/C)[285]

---

[280] The next three items represent collated information about the sons of Heber and are run together, from top of f. 37r to bottom (with continuation marks) and continuing on to f. 37v, as if one note.

[281] Top margin, 2 lines, with cross-shaped continuation mark indicating bottom margin, 2 lines.

[282] 'mer' cancelled and written on next line.

[283] *edd.* septimum

[284] *Sylwan* et] etiam *Cl Tr To T* || sabe] *Sylwan and authorities* sabee

[285] The readings "Bersabee / sabee," "Bersabe / sabe" would make more sense, but the HS tradition has "-ee" in all four places, Claudius being isolated on "sabe." Jerome, *Liber de nom. Heb.*, in the Joshua section (PL 23.808), reverses this: "Sabe, septem vel septies." Thanks to Justin Stover for pointing out the anomaly.

Bersabee, that is 'well of seven'. 'Sabee' is 'seven' in Hebrew; and they both made a covenant at that place, whence it is thought to be called also 'Bersabee', that is 'the well of the oath'. For 'sabe' in Hebrew means 'oath'.

F. 37v *Illustration:* One frame, city right (Bersabee), on the left, God with cross-nimbus and scroll tests Abraham. **OE** = Genesis 22:1–13

138a. (top margin, line 2) Sennaar vn*de* fuit amasphal [*recte* amrafel] q*u*i aduersus reges sodomor*um* bell*um* gessit: (Jerome, SNLH 23.918D, Lagarde 148.29)

Sennaar whence was Amrafel, who made war against the kings of the Sodomites.

138b. Sodoma ciuitas impior*um* diuino igne c*on*su*m*pta iuxta mare Mortuu*m*: (Jerome, SNLH 23.919A, Lagarde 148.31)

Sodom, city of the impious people, was consumed by divine fire beside the Dead Sea.

139a. .ysaac. ut dicit iosephus. xx(. .)v e*s*set annor*um*.

139b. Et abram. c 7 xxv.[286]

Isaac according to Josephus was 25 years old [at the time of the sacrifice]. And Abram was 125 years old.

140.[287] **ðær ðær hí to scéoldon to ofsléane | isáác** ˪ .inter bet`h´el. | et hay: (HS 1105A)

141a.[288] § et reuer|ssus e*st* i*n* ber|sabee. | Hvnc an*ni* [*sic, for* "hoc anno"?] e*st* abraha*m* q*uo*d melcha q*uo*que genuisset filios nachor fr*atr*i suo. hus p*r*imogenit*um* et buz fr*atr*em ei*us*. Et ex hui*us* | g`e´nere e*st* balaam ille diuin*us* ut heb*r*ei t*ra*dunt. q*ui* i*n* libro iob d*icitu*r heliu. Et irat*us* heliu filiu*s* b`a´rachel. buzites. de hui*us* | uidilicet buz desce*n*dens. Camuhel `uero pater *est* damasci-´ p*at*rem syror*um* ip*s*a *enim* uocat*ur* aran. q*ue* hic p*ro* syria posita e*st* legit*ur* in ysaia Caseth `iiii.´ | ad q*uo* casdei. i*d est* caldei. et azau. pheldas. q*uoque* et iedlaph. [*sic*] ac bathuhel de q*uo* nata e*st* rebecca. Hus de cui*us* stirpe ‖ iob desce*n*dit. sic*ut* scriptu*m* e*st* i*n* exordio uoluminis ei*us*. Vir erat i*n* t*er*ra hus: n*om*en ei*us* iob: (cf. Jerome, HQG

[286] The script changes between 139a/b, which are on the same line. Cf. HS 1104C; LJ 153/6 has: "Isaac vero, cum quinque et viginti esset annorum, altare constructo interrogabat. . . ."

[287] In margin, keyed to OE by *signe de renvoi*, cf. no. 142.

[288] Four bottom lines but starting in margin 3 lines up, running to top of 38r, *signes de renvoi* '+hwær /+hær' reference this passage to the picture of the sacrifice on f. 38r, *signe* on lower right; on f. 37v '+hwæ' [*sic*] has been erased three lines below the aforementioned '+hwær'.

23.971B, CCSL 72, 27–28 and Ps.-Eucherius [Claudius of Turin], *Comm. in Gen.*, PL 50.974A/B)[289]

"And Abraham returned to Bersabee (in this year), because Melcha had borne sons to Nachor his brother, Hus the first-born and Buz his brother" (Gen. 22:19–21). And the Hebrews teach that of this one is descended Balaam the prophet, who in the book of Job is called Heliu: . . . "And Heliu the son of Brachel the Buzite was angry" (Job 32:2), of whose [root] of course Buz descends. "Camuel, father of the Syrians" (Gen. 22:21), (is indeed the father of Damascus,) that is called Aran, which is put here instead of Syria, [for the name] read in Isaiah (7:1). Caseth is fourth, from whom Casdaim, that is, the Chaldeans; and "Azau, Faldas, Gethlafach, and Batuel, of whom was born Rebecca" (Gen. 22:22–23). Hus, from whose line Job descends, as is written in the Prologue of this book: "There was a man in the land of Hus, his name was Job" (Job 1:1).

F. 38r *Illustration:* One large frame: in zigzag pattern, from bottom, Abraham leads Isaac, on ass, with two servants across to right, up, to left, takes fire and sword, at top right is interrupted in sacrifice by angel emerging from heaven, on upper left is ram. **OE** = Genesis 22:13–18

141b. (f. 38r, top margin, end of first line) IER*onymus* dic*it*. Male ig*itur* q*u*ida*m* estima*nt* | .eu*m* e*ss*e de gen*er*e esav. Siq*ui*de*m* q*uo*d i*n* fine libri ipsi*us* habet*ur*. eo q*uo*d de syro sermone t*ra*nslat*us* est:· & q*uar*t*us* sit ab esau:· / et reliq*u*a q*u*e ibi co*n*tinent*ur* in hebreis uolominib*us* [*sic*] n*on* habent*ur*:·: (Jerome, HQG 23.971B; CCSL 72, 35.5)

Jerome says: It is incorrect therefore for anyone to think that he [Job] was descended from Esau, since in fact what is contained at the end of this book, to wit, that he is fourth from Esau and the rest, that [version] is translated from the Syriac language and that [statement] is not in the Hebrew books.

[289] This medley of quotations from Genesis 22:19–22, as well as the next item, which is written continuously but with an attribution to Jerome, ultimately trace back to Jerome, HQG, but as worked over in subsequent versions. The sentences from Jerome gloss the separated biblical phrases; this material is frequently found in various orders in numerous later commentaries. All the elements of this passage, including 141a,b are found in Ps.-Eucherius [Claudius of Turin], *Commentarii in Genesim*, PL 50.974A/B; cf. P. Bellet, "Claudio de Turin, autor de los comentarios 'in Genesim et Regum' del Pseudo-Euquerio," *Estudios Biblicos* 9 (1950): 209–23, and M.L.W. Laistner, "Early Medieval Commentaries on the OT," *HTR* 46 (1953): 45–46; cf. CPL 498, CPPM IIA 2187; Bellet's conclusions have been criticized and revised by Michael Gorman, "The Commentary on Genesis of Claudius of Turin and Biblical Studies under Louis the Pious," *Speculum* 72 (1997): 279–329.

142. loc*us enim* ille non d[i]stat á monte moria p*er* iter | unius diei. 7 e*st* inter bethel. 7 hay: | In monte[290] d*ominu*s uidebit. Q*ua*si.[291] Sic*ut* respexit | ysáác i*n* monte: sic uideat nos in hac | angustia. die*m* u*er*o lib*er*ationis ysaac di|cunt hebrei p*r*ima*m* die*m* septembris: (HS 1105A / 1105C)

For this place is not far from Mount Moriah by a one-day's journey, \ and is between Bethel and Hai. . . . "In the mountain the Lord will see" (Gen. 22:14) as if, just as Isaac looked at the mountain, so he may see us in this affliction. The Hebrews say that the day of the liberation of Isaac was the first day of September.

F. 38v *Illustrations:* Two frames: upper, Abraham and Isaac, with walking sticks and entourage, returning to Bersaba; lower, in two panels, left, Abraham weighing out payment for Sarra's burial ground to Effron and two Hittites, right, corpse of Sarra held by Abraham and Isaac. **OE** = Genesis 22:19, 23:1–20

143. (top line, interlined as additions to the OE) `Altero die´ **Abraham ða gecyrde sóna to hys cnápu*m*** `et reuerssu*s* e*st* i*n* bersabéé-´ 7 **férde hi*m* ha*m* swa míd heofonlícre / bletsunge:-** (cf. Genesis 22:19)

The next day **Abraham returned at once to his servants** and returned to Bersabee **and went home thus with a heavenly blessing.**

144.[292] Nunciatu*mque* e*st* ei q*uo*d melcha g`e´nuisset fr*atr*i suo nacho*r*[293] viii. filios. p*r*imogenitu*m*: hus. de ei*us* [*edd.* cuius] | stirpe iob descendit. sic*ut* scriptu*m* e*st*. vir erat i*n* t*er*ra hus nomine iob. et buz fr*atr*em ei*us*. Ex cui*us* genere balaham-[294]| qui s*ecundu*m hebreos d*icitu*r in (. . .) iob eliu buzetes. errant er*go* q*u*i dicunt iob de genere esau: q*uo*d de siro sermone | [*down to lower frame, right panel*] translatus sit: et quod ip*s*e quartus ab esau. | de concubina uero roma:[295] suscep*er*at nachor filios | .iiii^or^. thabée. et gaóm. thaas. et maacha-[296]| Redit [*recte* rediit] aute*m* abraham ad conuallem manbre: | et mortua est sara; i*n* ebron.[297] cu*m* es*s*et. c.xxvii. | annor*um* 7 sepulta e*st* i*n* spe|lunca duplici qu*am* emit | habraha*m*. cccc.[298] siclis argenti | ab effron. (HS 1105D, 1106A)

---

290 Stroke erased above 'e'.

291 *Sylwan* quia] quasi *Cl Tr T*

292 Upper frame, 3 lines, continuing, with places marked, to lower frame right, 9 lines. In the lower portion the style of the script varies.

293 *Sylwan* fr. suo n.] f. s. n. *Cl Tr*; *Cl* order 'viii. filios' not attested.

294 *Sylwan* ex cuius nomine et g.] n. et *om. Cl S β γ δ* || *Sylwan* balaam] balaham *Cl Tr*

295 HS: "Quod enim in fine libri ejus est, quod de Syro sermone translatus sit, et quod ipse quartus ab Esau, in Hebræo non habetur."

296 The phrase is a gloss from Genesis; in PL chapter 59 ("De morte Sarae") starts at "Rediit".

297 *Sylwan* in hebron] ebron *α Tr*. This phrase is not in PL; in Sylwan it falls after "et sepulta est."

298 Erasure above 'cccc'.

"And it was announced to him (Abraham) that Melcha had borne eight children to his brother Nachor, Hus being the firstborn" (Gen. 22:20–21), from his (whose) lineage Job is descended, as it is written, "There was a man in the land of Hus by the name of Job" (Job 1:1) "and Buz was his brother" (Gen. 22:21), from whose race Balaam (was descended), who according to the Hebrews is called in Job, "Eliu the Buzite" (Job 32:2). Therefore they err who say that Job was of the race of Esau, . . . because it was translated from the Syriac language, also that he is the fourth from Esau, . . . by his concubine Roma; . . . and Nachor begot four daughters (Tabee and Gaham, Tahas and Maacha = Gen. 22:24). Then Abraham returned to the Vale of Mambre and Sara died (in Hebron) when she was 127 years old and was buried in a double cave which Abraham purchased from Ephron for 400 shekels of silver (Gen. 23:15).

145. Non peccauit ábraham eme*n*do. nec ille | uende*n*do. sic*ut* nec hodie q*u*i emeret ágrum. | ut faceret cimiteriu*m*. n*is*i forte quia ibi sep`u´lti | erant[299] p*ro*thoplasti. Tamen adam. ⁊ éua iam ibidem sepulti sunt- (HS 1106A)

Abraham did not sin in buying nor he [Ephron] in selling, just as neither does one today who should buy a field in order to make a burial ground, unless perhaps because there were buried the first-created people. . . . For Adam and Eve were buried in that very same place.

146a.[300] IeR*onymus* dic*it*. | § Et tulit uir inaurem. aurea*m*. ⁊ armillas∻ didraginum pond*us* e*st*.[301] bace q*uod* i*n* hoc loco p*ro* didragmo | sc*r*ibit*ur* semuntia e*st*. Secel u*ero* q*u*i latino sermone siclus corrupte scribit*ur*, untie pond*us* habet∻ (Jerome, HQG 23.973B; CCSL 72, 36.25)[302]

Jerome says: And the man took a golden earring (and armlets) of two drachmas' weight. 'Bace', which in this place is written for "two drachmas," is half an ounce; actually a 'shekel', which in Latin is corruptly written 'siclus', weighs an ounce.

---

299 *Sylwan* quia s. erant ibi] quia ibi s. erant *Cl T*

300 Bottom margin, 2 lines, beginning up in left margin; miswritten *signe de renvoi* 'phær' has correspondent 'hær' in lower picture on f. 39r. This *signe* seems in the same script/stint that wrote the OE passage in the margin on facing f. 39r (no. 147). These *signes*, however, fail to correspond, since neither the picture of Abraham's servant on f. 39r nor the surrounding note (no. 148) seem to have anything to do with the content of no. 146a. Similarly, at the end of this extract, there is a continuation mark that has its correspondent at the beginning of the directly facing passage no. 148 (from HS) but there is no apparent textual connection.

301 Edd. "eius."

302 At the end of this passage is another *signe de renvoi* apparently referencing the passage on the top of the lower frame of f. 39r, but it would seem to be misplaced, belonging instead to the passage in the upper frame (no. 146b), another extract from HQG.

F. 39r *Illustrations:* Two frames: Upper, on right Abraham sends his senior reeve to find a wife for Isaac among Abraham's kin,[303] left, the reeve swears by placing his hand under the enthroned Abraham's thigh; lower frame, the reeve with "ten camels" sets out to the land of Nachor. **OE** = Genesis 24:1–19

146b. Tradunt heb*r*ei q*uo*d in sa*n*ctificatione ei*us*. hoc e*st* in ci*r*cu*m*cisione iurav*er*it. Nos[304] au*tem* dicim*us* | iurasse eum in semine abrahe. hoc in ch*rist*o: q*u*i ex illo nasciturus. Erat | iuxta eu*angel*istam mat*th*e*u*m loque*ntem* liber generationis ie*su* | ch*rist*i [d*omi*n*i* *cancelled*] fil*i*i d*avid* fil*i*i a*braham*: (Jerome, HQG 23.973B, CCSL 72.1.1, 36.19; cf. HS 1106C)

The Hebrew tradition has it that he swore according to his sanctification, that is, his circumcision; we would say, however, he swore by the seed of Abraham, that is, by Christ, who from that seed was to be born according to the evangelist Matthew, saying (1:1): "The book of the generation of Jesus Christ, son of David, son of Abraham."

147. (left margin, note to main OE text, lower block of text, line 3) **to náchores** ⁊abraha*m*es | breþer

148. Ad qu*a*m ibat. p*er*rexitq*ue* mesopotamia*m* ad charam. urbe*m* nachor. Multo[305] | q*uidem* labore et tempore.[306] quia i*n* hieme in mesopotamia e*st* luti p*ro*funditas. In estate: aque defectio / in saltibus: latrones:- (HS 1106C/D)

To which (the motherland of Abram) he (Abraham's steward) went and proceeded into Mesopotamia to Haran, the city of Nachor, with much labor and time . . . because in the winter in Mesopotamia the mud is deep and in the summer there is a lack of water and there are highwaymen in the passes.

F. 39v *Illustrations:* Two frames: upper, Isaac comes out to greet the returning reeve, on left, Rebecca veils herself; lower, Isaac leads Rebecca into his mother's tent. **OE** = Genesis 24:20, 24:61–67

149. Josephus dicit. batuelem iam defunctu*m* fuisse: ⁊ uirginem in custodia m*a*tris. ⁊ fr*atr*is. e*ss*e: ⁊ de morte p*at*ris | p*r*edixisse puellam: querenti ad puteu*m* cui*us* e*ss*et filia. ⁊ Moyses dicit. Cucurrit puella i*n* domum m*a*tris. | nuncians que audierat Et p*ro*tulit i*n*aures aureas. ⁊ armillas. ⁊ uasa aurea. ⁊ arge*n*tea. ⁊

[303] The reeve's face is deformed and perhaps worked on by a later hand; a similar deformed face, finished later and looking like a cat's, is on f. 66r.

[304] Altered from 'NoN'.

[305] Code to continuing text in bottom margin.

[306] *Sylwan* tempore et labore] l. et t. *Cl β γ*

uestes dans | Rebecca:· ⁊ mat*ri* quoq*ue* ei*us*[307] ⁊ fr*atr*i ei*us* munera:· (HS 1107B/C, *rearranged*)[308]

Josephus says that Bathuel had already died and the virgin was in the care of her mother and brother and (he says) that the girl foretold her father's death to the one asking at the well whose daughter she was. And Moses says, "The girl ran into the house of her mother" (Gen. 24:28) . . . announcing what she had heard, and he (the servant) brought out the gold earrings and bracelets and gold and silver vessels and clothing, giving them to Rebecca, and he also (gave) gifts to her mother and brother (cf. Gen. 24:28–30).[309]

150. (gloss, OE line 2) **to hys hláforde eode isáác** ˋin gerara´ (HS 1107D)

151.[310].ysaac. xl. erat annor*um* | Rebecca descendit de camelo:· ⁊ tollens teristrum uel pallium albu*m* (. . .) op*er*uit se. ⁊ co*n*nposuit. [*sic*][311] Est (.)aut*em* te|ristrum:· gen*us* arabici uestim*e*nti mulierum:· et hic p*r*imo legit*ur* consensus mulieris | req*ui*situs. et exin*de* pro iure habit*um* e*st*:· ut req*ui*ratur et dimiserunt eam:· (HS 1107D/C)

Isaac was 40 years old.[312] "Rebecca . . . got down from the camel" (Gen. 24:64), and taking her 'teristrum' or white veil, covered and arranged herself. A teristrum is a kind of Arabian covering for women. \ And here is first read of the required consent of the woman, and since then it has been fixed in the law that (a woman's consent to marriage) is required; and "they sent her away" (Gen. 24:59).

152. Abraha*m*:· alia*m* duxit uxore*m*:· nomine cethura*m*. Aiunt hebrei cethura*m* nomen[313] app*e*llatiuu*m* quod i*n*terp*re*tatur | copulata*m*. d*icu*nt *enim* hanc fuisse agar:· que de concubina. mortua sara:· t*ra*nsiuit[314] i*n* coniuge*m*. Josep*h*[us] *etiam* dicit | quod antequam misisset p*ro* uxore filii duxerat eam. Et h*ec* genuit ei lib*er*os vi.[315]| Filii t*ame*n cethure:· a nomine libere:· se saracenos dixerunt:·[316] Et sep*ar*auit eos abraha*m* du*m* uiueret | ab ysaac ad plagam orientalem:· (HS 1108A)

"Abraham married another wife, by the name of Cethura" (Gen. 25:1). The Hebrews say that Cethura (is) a nickname that means 'bound'. They also say that,

---

307 *add. Cl α T*

308 Sylwan 114/46–114/47–114/33–114/32–114/52.

309 The OE skips verses 21–60; this note serves to fill in the narrative.

310 Above top frame, continuing into frame, 2 lines, and, with continuation mark, to lower ledger of this frame, 1 line.

311 *Sylwan* operuit et compsit se] operuit se *Cl W*

312 Phrase unsourced.

313 *Sylwan* esse appellatiuum] esse *om. Cl S β Pa*

314 *Sylwan* transiit] transiuit *Cl Tr*

315 A connecting mark to continuation in lower margin.

316 *Sylwan* se d. s.] se s. d. *Cl β γ*

in truth, this was Hagar, who from being a concubine, following the death of Sara, moved into marriage. . . . Josephus indeed says that (Abraham) had married her before he sent for a wife for his son. And she presented him with six sons. . . . The sons of Cethura freely called themselves 'Saracens' from the name. \ And while she lived, Abraham separated them from Isaac to regions towards the east.

F. 40r *Illustrations:* Two frames: upper, corpse of Abraham (label, see no. 154), flanked by Isaac and Ismael and servants with walking sticks and spade; lower, in two panels, left, Ismael with his descendants, right, corpse of Ismael held by two sons (labeled 'obiit Ismael') **OE** = Genesis 25:5–17

153a. anno abrahe. lxx° v⁚ facta est ei re*pro*missio. anno ei*us* lxxxvi°. nat*us* est hismael. anno ei*us* c^{simo}⁚ | nat*us* est ei ysa`a´c.[317] anno ei*us*. c°(.)xxvii. [*recte* c°.xxxvii] mortua est sara⁚ Isaac. xl. erat annor*um* cu*m* duxit rebecca*m* | uxorem. (HS 1108D-1109A)

Abraham was 75 when the promise was given to him; he was 86 when Ismael was born, 100 when Isaac was born to him, 127 [137] when Sara died. Isaac was 40 when he married Rebecca.[318]

153b. sexagenari*us* erat ysaac q*uando* nati sunt ei paruuli. Viuebat *er*go abraam. 7 adhuc .xv. annus [*sic*] | sup*er*uixit. Joseph*us* sic ait. porro po*st* morte*m* abrahe co*n*cepit uxor ysaac. 7 *cetera*⁚ (HS 1110C)

Isaac was 60 when children were born to him. Abraham continued to live and from this point lived on for 15 years. . . . Josephus says further that after the death of Abraham the wife of Isaac conceived, etc.

154. (in upper picture, label) obit abraham. | natione caldeus. (cf. Eusebius / Jerome, *Chron.* PL 27.111)

Abraham, a Chaldean by birth, died.

155. (following on after OE text, and into lower frame, 4 lines) Tradunt illu*m* hebrei dissinteria mortuu*m* fuisse. | coram cun[c]tis fratrib*us*. i*d est* filiis[319] suis adhuc uiue*n*tib*us* obiit. habitauit au*tem* ei*us* posteritas ab euila usq*ue* | sur. Est au*tem*[320] euila⁚ india. ab euila nepote noe⁚ sic dicta. sur au*tem* *est* solitudo i*n*ter

---

[317] Scribe wrote 'ysacc', cancelled first 'c' and wrote 'a' above.

[318] The comment "Isaac was 40 years old" (= Gen. 25:20) occurs on f. 39v, on 40r, upper comment line 2, and in OE main text, top of 40v.

[319] *Sylwan* coram filiis] coram *om. Cl W Pa*; PL has "fratribus," apparently an emendation to the printed text.

[320] *Sylwan* est uero] est autem *Cl β T*

cades ⁊ barad: | extendens desertum usq*ue* ad MaRe Rubru*m* et egipti confinia: (HS 1109C/D)

According to Hebrew tradition he (Ismael) died of dysentery in front of all his brothers, . . . that is, . . . his sons were still living when he died. His descendants lived from Hevila up to Sur. Hevila is India, and it is so called from Hevila, the grandson of Noe, as it is written (cf. 1 Par. 1:9). Sur is the wilderness between Cades and Barad, a desert extending up to the Red Sea and the borders of Egypt.

F. 40v *Illustrations:* Two frames: upper, right, Isaac praying, hand of God extended, left, God, crowned with cross, blessing the praying Rebecca; lower, birth of Esau ("first born," colored red), going into hands of midwife (to left) and Jacob going into hands of midwife to the right, Rebecca, far right, in childbed. **OE** = Genesis 25:20–26. In the margin opposite the lower ledger of the upper frame, **.ii.cviii.** [A.M. 2108]

156. (brown ink, written in irregular lines in left margin) Nachor abrha*m*es. [*sic*] | breþer `wæs´. bathuel|es feader. ⁊ he istr|[ín]de[321] labane. ⁊ rebé|[c]ca. ysaaces wyf. | ⁊ hy istrínde. | ésau. ⁊ iacob`e´. | iacob hæfde laban`e´s | twá dohtra. lía . ⁊ | rachel, ⁊ hyre | twa ðeówene.[322]

Nachor was Abraham's brother, the father of Bathuel, and he begot Laban and Rebecca, Isaac's wife and they begot Esau and Jacob; Jacob had (to wife) Laban's two daughters, Leah and Rachel and their two bondwomen.

157. § q*uo*d de paruulis nequaq*ua*m dictu*m* e*st*. cu*m* Maior sem*per* p*re*fuit minori. | Sed de populis. ydumei.[323] *enim* q*ui* de esau: futuri erant t*ri*butarii dauitd [*sic*]: q*ui* de iacob. Nisi forte intelli|gat*ur* esau seruisse iacob: du*m* p*er*secutus e*st* eum. | ut lima confert ferro. fornax auro. | flagellu*m* grano: (HS 1110C)

Which was in no way meant of the little boys, since the older was always above the younger.[324] But it is said of the peoples. For the Idumites, who sprang from Esau, were to be the future tributaries of David, who is descended from

[321] The edge is trimmed: the second minim of the 'n' and the tail of the accent over the 'i' can still be read. In the next line, presumably, the first 'c' in 'rebe[c]ca' has also been trimmed away.

[322] 'iacob hæfde . . . ðeówene.' seem to be in a different stint. The comment is unsourced but cf. a similar added marginal note in London, BL, Royal 2.C.i (HS, s. xiii, Rochester), f. 15r: 'Isti laban ⁊ bathuel fr*at*res erant rebecce ⁊ filii batuel filii Nachor fra*te*r Abra*ha*m'.

[323] *Sylwan* idumei] ydumei *Cl W Pa*

[324] cf. Genesis 25:23: "Duae gentes [Esau and Jacob] sunt in utero tuo . . . et major serviet minori." The note comments on the immediately preceding OE: **⁊ se mara deorað þám lǽssan.**

Jacob. Unless perhaps it is to be understood that Esau served Jacob, when he persecuted him, as the file serves iron, the furnace gold, the flail grain.

158. (glosses to lower block of OE text), line 4 up: ⁊ **his nama wæs genémned ésau.** \`i*d est* fortis´; reference mark in line 2 up, gloss word in left margin: ⁊ **hyne mán ne*m*de íacob.** \`i*d est*´ / supplantator. (HS 1110C)

F. 41r *Illustration:* One frame, divided into two panels: left, Rebecca favoring Jacob, who is dwelling in his tent (Gen. 25:27); right, Esau depicted (twice) with each of his two wives. **OE** = Genesis 25:27–28, 26:34–35, 27:1–13

159. (as if continuing the OE) **On ðære ylcan stówe þá bútu abulgan isááce ⁊ rebeccan.** Et licet nollet | .ysaac p*ro*uinciales sue misceri cognitioni:· t*ame*n meli*us* silere decreuit:· (HS 1113A)

In that same place they both [the wives of Esau] **angered Isaac and Rebecca** (Genesis 26:35). And although Isaac did not want his neighbors to mingle with his kin, he thought it was better to be silent.

160.[325] ysaac. c. annor*um* erat. Jacob .xl. | ada filia*m* elom[326] ethei. & oolibama filia*m* ane. filii [*recte* filiam] sebeon euei. basemath \`i*d est* melech´ q*uo*q*ue* filia*m* ismael sorore*m* nabaioth:· | pep*er*it au*tem* ada \`esau´ eliphaz. basemath \`i*d est* melech´ gen*uit* rahuel oolibama edidit. ieus. ⁊ ielom. ⁊ c\`h´ore. Erat au*tem* | the*m*na co*n*cubina eliphaz filii esav. soror lothan-[327] q*ue* pep*er*it ei amalech. ⁊ theman. ⁊ cenez. | Isti filii seir horrei habitatores t*er*re. lothan. ⁊ sobal. ⁊ sebeon. ⁊ anan. dyson. ⁊ esebeon.[328] ⁊ dysan. | hi duces horrei filii seir. i*n* t*er*ra edom. Erat au*tem* soror lotha*m* tha*m*na.[329] Isti duces horreor*um* dux lotha*m*. dux sobal. dux sebeon. dux ana. dux dison. dux eser. dux \`sesebeon´ | dysan. Isti duces horreor*um*. q*u*i imp*er*auerunt in terra seir. (first sentence, cf. no. 153a, the rest = Gen. 36:2–5, 12, 20–21, 22, 29)

Isaac was 100 years old, Jacob 40. "[Esau's wives] Ada the daughter of Elon the Hethite and Oolibama the daughter of Ana, the daughter of Sebeon the Hevite and Basemath, that is Malech, the daughter of Ismael, sister of Nabaioth.

---

[325] This note brings up to this place and summarizes ch. 36, the descendants of Esau, which is mostly ignored in the OE translation, as is most of ch. 26, Isaac's covenant with Abimelech.

[326] 'elom' with a hook over the 'o'; in this passage accents, both flagged types, and hairline types, appear over various vowels in seemingly random fashion. They are not reproduced here.

[327] Genesis 36:12 conflated with 36:22.

[328] Genesis 36:21 has "Eser" as son of Seir, but "Esebon" is mentioned as a son of Gad (hence a descendent of Jacob) at Genesis 46:16.

[329] Connecting marks in margins, labeled 'a/b', going from frame down to bottom edge.

Then Ada bore Esau Eliphaz. Basemath" (that is Melech) "conceived Rahuel. Oolibama brought forth Iehus and Ielon and Core. . . . Themna was the concubine of Eliphaz the son of Esau, (sister of Lothan,) who conceived for him Amalech, and Theman . . . and Cenez. . . . They are the sons of Seir the Horrite, the inhabitants of the land, Lothan and Sobal and Sebeon and Ana, Dyson and Esebeon and Disan. These are the leaders of the Horrites, the sons of Seir in the land of Edom. . . . The sister of Lothan was Thamna. . . . These are the leaders of the Horrites, duke Lotham, duke Sobal, duke Sebeon, duke Ana, duke Dison, duke Eser, duke (Sesebeon) Dysan. These are the leaders of the Horrites who ruled in the land of Seir."

F. 41v *Illustrations:* one frame, in frame Isaac sends Esau out to hunt for him, who, to left of frame, is hunting, and to right of Isaac Jacob is being advised by Rebecca. **OE** = Genesis 27:14–29

F. 42r *Illustrations:* one large frame, with scenes within: above left, Jacob brings kids to cook (cooking fire in middle), above right, Rebecca gives Jacob skins to make him "hairy", middle, Isaac, on a bed, feels Jacob, lower left, Isaac embraces and blesses Jacob, with the apparatus for a meal to the right. **OE** = Genesis 27:29–33. No annotations on ff. 41v-42r.

F. 42v *Illustration:* One offset frame: Esau enters into into Isaac's presence and Isaac realizes he has been deceived, Jacob tiptoeing away on right, outside of frame. **OE** = Genesis 27:33–46, 28:1–2

161.[330] Videns au*tem* esav q*uo*d n*on* libenter aspiceret filias chanaan pater suus∻ yuit ad ismaele*m* `patrum [*for* "patruum"] suu*m*∻´ et | duxit uxore*m* absq*ue* his q*ua*s priu*s* habebat∻ melcch filia*m* ismael filii abraha*m*. sorore*m* Naba|ioth∻ (Gen. 28:6, 8–9)

And Esau, seeing that [his father had blessed Jacob . . . knowing also that] his father did not willingly look upon the daughters of Chanaan, he went to Ismael his (uncle) and took to wife, apart from those he already had, Melech the daughter of Ismael, the son of Abraham, the sister of Nabaioth.

162.[331] § Seyr Mons i*n* t*er*ra edom. in q*uo* habitauit esav. in regione gebalene. Q*u*e ex eo q*uo*d pilosu*s* e*ss*et. ‖ et hispitus. Seyr. hoc e*st* pilosi. nom*en* accepit∻ In q*u*ibus locis ante habitauit. coreus. | q*u*em interfecit chodorlaomor. Meminit montis∻ 7 ysaias in uisione ydumee- (SNLH 23.919B; Lagarde 149.10)

Mount Seir is in the land of Edom, in which Esau lived in the region of Gebalene, which gets its name, Seir, 'hairy', from him because he . . . was hairy and

[330] Supplies text not included in OE version.

[331] Bottom line, continuing to top of f. 43r, 2 lines.

bristly. In which places previously lived Chorraeus, whom Chodorlahomor killed. Also Isaiah recalls Mount [Seir] . . . in his vision of Idumea (Isaiah 21:11).

F. 43r *Illustration:* Large frame divided into two registers: above, Rebecca with Jacob, advising him to flee the wrath of Esau;[332] below, Isaac enthroned, with Rebecca beside him, blesses Jacob. **OE** = Genesis 28:10–17

163. (bottom, 1 line) § ysaac. cxl. anno*rum* erat. (jal *erased*) Jacob. lxxx.[333]
Isaac was 140 years, Jacob 80.

F. 43v *Illustration:* Full-page picture of Jacob's vision of the ladder, God with cross-crown at top, two angels "ascending and descending," Jacob asleep on lower right, no OE.

164. Euigila*ns* iacob. ⁊ p*ro*ph[et]auit de lege. ⁊ templo. ⁊ passione chr*ist*i. que in t*er*ra illa futura erant. Terrib[i]lis e*ni*m. lex. | dom*us* d*e*i. templu*m*. passio chr*isti*: ap*er*tio porte celi. (HS 1114D)

Upon waking Jacob . . . also prophesied concerning the law and the temple and the passion of Christ which were to be in that land. Dreadful is the law, the temple is the house of God, the passion of Christ is the opening of the gates of heaven (cf. Gen. 28:1).

F. 44r *Illustrations:* Two frames: upper, Jacob pouring oil on the titlestone of Bethel; lower, Jacob approaching Laban, who tends his flocks beside his well, Rachel on right. **OE** = Genesis 28:18–22, 29:1–11

165. (at top of upper frame) bethel i*d est* domu*m* dei. Vel hostia*m* dei. p*r*iu*s* *enim* a iebuseis qui eam condidera*nt*: luza uocaba|tur[334] i*d est* nux. *u*el amigdalus. Vel forte copia hui*us* generis arborum est ibi: (HS 1115A)

Bethel, that is 'the house of God' or . . . the 'sacrifice of God'. Previously it was called [Jebus] from the Jebusites who founded it, and it was called Luz, . . . that is 'nut' or 'almond', . . . or perhaps a quantity of this kind of tree is there.

166. (gloss in margin) **laban | nachores súnu** — wæs[335] bat|hueles súne (cf. Gen. 28:5)

---

[332] The picture seems unfinished and confused: the figure to the left whom Rebecca is addressing is tentatively colored blue, while the figure on the right is perhaps merely an unfinished doubling of the other figure.

[333] Unsourced; for the calculation see Genesis 25:26.

[334] *Sylwan* iebus a iebuseis] iebus *om. Cl Tr γ δ* ‖ *Sylwan* uocabatur post luza] l. u. *Cl Tr γ*

[335] Crawford reads "þæt" before 'wæs' but it seems to be an insertion mark.

167. (at top of lower frame) Normann*us* dicit. Que cum aduenisset; amouit iacob lapidem ab ore putei. patet q*uia* non / solus iuit iacob. (HS 1115C)

Normannus says, When she had come Jacob moved the stone from the mouth of the well; this shows that Jacob did not go alone.

F. 44v *Illustrations:* Two frames: upper, left, Jacob and Laban embrace, right, at a table in a house, Jacob points to Rachel on the right and Laban points to Lia on the left, a third unidentified female figure; lower: Jacob and Laban discuss Lia and Rachel. **OE** = Genesis 29:13–28

F. 45r *Illustrations:* Three frames: upper, divided into two panels, right, Jacob receives Rachel as his second wife, Lia to right looks on, left, Laban leaves this scene; middle, Lia and Jacob and their sons: Ruben, Simeon, Levi, Juda; lower, Jacob and Bala and their two sons, Dan and Naptalim. **OE** = Genesis 29:28–29, 32–35–30:1–8 (summary). No annotations on ff. 44v-45r.

F. 45v *Illustrations:* Three frames: upper, Jacob and Zelfa (or Lia) and their two sons, Gad and Asher; middle, Jacob and Lia and their children: Isachar, Zabulon, and Dina; lower, Rachel and Jacob and their infant son Joseph. **OE** = Genesis 30:9–24

168. § Jacob genuit. Joseph nonagesimo s*ecun*do etatis sue anno. ysaac. c. 7 lii. anno*rum* erat-[336]

Jacob begot Joseph in his ninety-second year; Isaac was 152 years old.

169. § Jacob po*st* uiginti annos á laban reuertit*ur*. in t*er*ram chanaan.[337]

Jacob after twenty years returned from Laban into the land of Chanaan.

170. Jeronimo teste in suis ep*isto*lis. Centesim*us* | sexagesim*us* ann*us* ysaac:ʼ Jacob u*er*o centesimus ˋc.ˊ In ve*n*ditione au*tem* filii. cviii. anno*rum* fuit.[338]

By testimony according to Jerome in his epistles: Isaac was 160 years, Jacob 100; Jacob was 108 at the time of the selling of his son.

---

336 Unsourced; the calculation is 92 + 60, cf. no. 153a.

337 Exact wording is unsourced; the information is attributed to Josephus (HS 1119A); cf. LJ 163/23 and no. 171.

338 Not to be found in Jerome's letters. The last part reflects HS 1125A and the *Gloss. Ord.* (as in Sylwan ed. 151/3): "Sciendum quod ante mortem Ysaac duodecim annis uenditus est Ioseph, quod sic probatur. Sexagenarius erat Ysaac cum natus est Iacob, et centum octoginta annorum mortuus est. Ergo centum uiginti annorum erat Iacob in morte patris, in uenditione autem filii centum et octo annorum fuit" ("It is to be known that twelve years before the death of Isaac, Joseph was sold. Which is proven thus: Isaac was sixty when Jacob was born and he died at 180. Therefore Jacob was 120 at the time of the death of his father and 108 at the time of the selling of his son"). See also no. 179.

F. 46r *Illustrations:* Two frames: upper, divided into two panels, right, Jacob entreats Laban for permission to return to his native land (Gen. 30:25), left, speaks to Rachel and Lia (Gen. 31:4); lower, Jacob and his family depart (Gen. 31:17). **OE** = Genesis 30:25–26, 43, 31:1–18

171. Q*u*ia natura ouiu*m* mesopotemie et italie eadem e*ss*e t*ra*ditur. ita: ut bis in anno pariant. vn*de* poeta. bis g*ra*uide | fetu pecudes.[339] Quod autem d*icitu*r ut in uirgis concip*er*ent. (. .) dicit. *enim* iosephus Quod om*ne* tempu*s* quo [*recte* quod[340]] fuit cum / laban; xx. anno*rum* fuit. (HS 1118C, 1119A)

Because the nature of sheep in Mesopotamia and Italy is said to be the same, so that they bear young twice in a year, whence the poet: "sheep twice pregnant with offspring." So also it is said that they conceived by the twigs (cf. Gen. 30:37–42); . . . and Josephus says that the entire time he was with Laban was twenty years.

F. 46v *Illustrations:* Two frames, upper, Laban being informed of Jacob's escape; lower, Laban's dream, with two sleeping figures and God's hand above, a tent to signify Laban's expedition to pursue Jacob (Gen. 31:24) **OE** = Genesis 31:19–28

172a.[341] 7 **gemetton | hyne ón galaad.** § Et est ad t*er*gu*m* phenicis. 7 arabie. collib*us* libani. copulat*us* extendit*urque per* desertu*m* | usq*ue* ad eu*m* locu*m* u*bi* t*ra*ns iordanen habitauit q*u*onda*m* Seon rex amorreor*um*. set. 7 ieremias loq*uitur*: Galáád tu | m*ih*i iniciu*m* libani. A q*u*o monte. 7 ciuitas in eo condita sortita e*st*. uocabulu*m*: q*u*am accepit de amorreor*um* | manu galáád fili*us* machir. filii Manasse. (SNLH 23.898C/D; Lagarde 124.24)

And they encountered him at Galaad. And (Galaad) is . . . behind Phoenicia and Arabia, joined by the hills of Libanus and extending through the desert up to the place across the Jordan where Seon, king of the Amorites, once lived. . . . But Jeremiah (22:6) says, "Galaad, you are to me the head of Libanus." From which mountain the city founded upon it also obtained its name . . . which Galaad, son of Machir, son of Manasse, received from the Amorites.

172b. § Gader. Turris u*bi* habitauit iacob ruben pat*r*is sui | uiolauit (..) thoru*m*. 7 absq*ue* g. litt*er*a in hebreo ader sc*r*ibitur; (SNLH 23.898D; Lagarde 124.32)

Gader, the tower where Jacob lived; Ruben violated the bed of his father; and the letter 'g' lacking in Hebrew, it is written 'ader'.

---

339 'bis grauide fetu pecudes' is from Virgil, *Georgics* 2.150, the last word appearing in only a few MSS of HS and not in PL.

340 que *S Pa*

341 Above lower frame, 1 line, keyed to OE text by *signes de renvoi* (+); connecting mark at 'desertu*m*' to continuing comment in lower margin, 3 lines.

F. 47r *Illustration:* One frame: Laban confronts Jacob. **OE** = Genesis 31:28–44, 53, no annotations

F. 47v *Illustration:* Three frames: upper, right, Laban searching Jacob's tent, left, making a covenant with him; middle, two panels, right, Jacob "offering a sacrifice on the mountain," left, feasting with his kinsmen; lower, right, Laban asleep, left, kissing his grandchildren. **OE** = Genesis 31:53–55

173. Josephus dicit. Vel (. .) p*os*t dici q*uo*d bon*us* c*ur*sor sollicit*us* potuit celerit*er* currendo. solo die t*r*ium dierum it*er*. et labore*m* / p*er*fic*er*e et consummare-[342]

Josephus says, And afterward it was to be said that a good, motivated runner is able by running fast to complete and finish in a single day the work and journey of three days.

F. 48r *Illustrations:* Two frames, upper, Joseph travelling with his entourage, meets angels; lower, Joseph's messengers speak to Esau, enthroned. **OE** = Genesis 32:1–9

F. 48v *Illustrations:* One large frame, Jacob dividing his forces and flocks into two. **OE** = Genesis 32:10–20. No annotations on ff. 48rv.

F. 49r Full-page *illustration* in three registers of Jacob sending flocks and herds to placate Esau, no OE. (Traces of writing along trimmed-off bottom edge.)

174. (top, 1 line) Precesserunt *er*go mun*er*a. (. .) ip*s*e adhuc erat in manaym.[343] (HS 1120C/D)

The presents went before (him); he himself . . . still was in Manaim.

---

[342] The comment is unsourced and rather enigmatic; it seems to refer to Gen. 31:22–23, "It was told Laban on the third day that Jacob fled. . . . and he pursued after him seven days and overtook him in the Mount of Galaad." It may be a reflection of HS 1119C (cf. LJ 164/1): "Josephus dicit: Laban post primum diem cognoscens discessum Jacob et filiarum, persecutus est eos, et in colle procul collocatos invenit eos. Potest dici quia si in tertio die cognovit, tunc post primam [*Sylwan* "primum"] diem dicitur cognovisse, quia tunc egressus nuntius, tertia die venit ad eum, ubi filii pascebant greges, qui separati erant a Jacob itinere trium dierum, ut praedictum est" ("Josephus says: Laban, realizing the escape of Jacob and his daughters after the first day, pursued them, and found them far off on a hill. This can be said because if he knew it on the third day, then after the first day he is said to know it, because that is when a messenger went out and came to him on the third day, where his sons pastured sheep, who were separated from Jacob by a three-days' journey, as was foretold").

[343] *Sylwan* manahim *P*, manahym *S γ*, manain *W*

F. 49v *Illustration:* One large frame divided into two registers, continuing the gifts of animals to Esau, upper, a man herding goats (or sheep), lower, a man herding asses. **OE** = Genesis 32:21–28

175. Fanuel loc*us* in q*u*o iacob tota nocte colluctans. isr*ahe*lis uocabulu*m* meruit. iuxta tor|rente*m* iaboc. Fanuel au*tem* inte*rpre*tat*ur.* facies d*e*i ab eo q*uo*d ibi d*eu*m uiderit∵ (SNLH 23.897C; Lagarde 123.5)

Fanuel, next to the brook of Jaboc, the place at which Jacob wrestled all night, and won the name of 'Israel'. 'Fanuel' is interpreted as 'face of God', from the circumstance that . . . he saw God there.

F. 50r *Illustration:* One frame: Jacob wrestles the angel. **OE** = Genesis 32:28–32, 33:1–14

176.[344] Uir uidens d*eu*m. | IS. *enim* uir. el∵[345] nomen dei est Ra u*ero*∵ uidens d*ici*-*tu*r. vel mens uidens d*eum*. | (. .) Q*uod* (.) q*uod* contra d*eu*m stetit inuict*us* fac*tu*m est ei in signu*m* q*uia* inuict*us* staret / contra fr*at*rem. (HS 1121B)

[In Hebrew 'Israel' means] 'a man seeing God': for 'Is' means 'man', 'El' is a name of God, but 'Ra' means 'seeing', or 'the mind seeing God'. \ That he stood unconquered against God became as a sign to him that he would stand unconquered against his brother.

F. 50v *Illustration:* One large frame divided into two registers: upper, Jacob's family divided among Rachel and Lia as Esau (represented on facing page) approaches; lower, Jacob, represented six times, bows to Esau. **OE** = Genesis 33:14–17

177a.[346]§ Abiitq*ue* de soch`o´t∵ i*n* salem urbem. sichimor*um*[347] i*d est* in sichem. Et forte binomia erat. Moyses ea*m* tunc | t*an*tu*m* uocauit salem. i*d est* consu*m*-mata*m* 7 p*er*fectam. quod ibi femur claudicantis iacob sanatum sit. porro | iacob emit iu[x]t*a* oppidu*m* .c. agnis. 7 habitauit ibi∵ ab emor rege sichimor*um* 7 a filiis suis∵ Et | erecto altari∵ inuocauit fortissimum deu*m* isr*ahe*l. (HS 1122A, abbreviated and slightly rearranged)

And he went away from Soccoth to Salem, city of the . . . Sichomites, that is, into Sichem. . . . And perhaps it had two names. . . . Moses at that time called it all 'Salem', that is 'completed' or 'perfected' because there wounded Jacob's thigh

344 The two sentences, above and in the frame and reversing the order of HS, are perhaps intended as two notes.

345 *Sylwan* hel] el *Cl γ*

346 Bottom, lines 4–2 up, referred by *signes de renvoi* (+) to OE text on f. 51r (no. 177b), second line below frame, with repetition in margin there of opening words, and sign 'hær', which does not have a corresponding "hwær" on f. 50v.

347 *Sylwan* abiit] abiitque *Cl β γ* ‖ *Sylwan* scilicet sichimorum] scilicet *om. Cl W γ*

was healed. After that Jacob purchased by the city [part of a field] for 100 lambs from Emor, king of the Sichomites, and from his sons and lived there and having erected an altar called on the most mighty God of Israel.

178.[348] Scene .*id est* tab*er*nacula. loc*us* in q*uo* habitauit ‖ iacob. regress*us* de mesopotamia. q*ui* li`n´gua hebraica appellat*ur* soch[o]t∴ (SNLH 23.919; Lagarde 149.32)

Scena, that is, 'tabernacle', the place in which Jacob lived having left Mesopotamia, which in the Hebrew language is called 'Soccoth'.

F. 51r *Illustration:* One large frame, informally segmented into three registers, upper, Jacob bows for the seventh time, then embraces Esau, who has dismounted, below, in two registers, Esau's forces. **OE** below picture, upper block, 6 lines of original main text; lower block, supplemental twelfth-century English summary, 4 lines at bottom, running to top of f. 51v = Genesis 33:16–17, 35:1, 5–6, added summary covers 33:18–20; 34; 35:8

179. (top margin, lines 2–3) § ysaac .cl ⁊ x. annor*um* erat. Jacob .c. Joseph .viii. Sciendu*m* q*uo*d an*te* morte*m* ysaac. xii annis uendit*us* est | in egipto. Joseph- .xiii. annis. fuit i*n* egipto Ioseph∴ anteq*u*am ingred*ie*t*ur* domu*m* pharaonis.[349]

Isaac was 160 years old, Jacob 100, Joseph eight; it must be kept in mind that twelve years before the death of Isaac Joseph was sold in Egypt. Joseph was in Egypt thirteen years before he went into the house of Pharaoh.

180. (inserted into OE, line 1 below picture) **Esau férde þa tó seir** `uillam *scilicet* quam de no*m*i*n*e (. .) suo sic dixerat.´ ⁊ **iacob com to sochot** (insert = HS 1121D)

Esau went then to Seir (a town which is so called from his name) and Jacob came to Soccoth.

177b. (margin, with *signe de renvoi*, repeating opening words of passage on f. 50v [no. 177a], bottom) abiit de sochot[350]

---

[348] Bottom line, continuing to top of f. 51r.

[349] Unsourced; cf. nos. 170 and 202.

[350] Note the 'de' ligature here, not in same phrase on f. 50v (no. 177a).

181.[351] and cóm to (. . .) salem cester `et forte binomia erat´[352] on sichem. | *þæt* hís in chanaan lánde. `7´ þar[353] wycnigede. 7 bohte lánd. æt emore (. . . . .) sich`e´mes [*correcting* sichimes] fæder. 7 aræde [*recte* arærde] wéofod | on gódes náme. lían docter dína for hút to hisýen þas landes wyfmén. 7 emores súnu [*corrected from* 'suum'] sichem | ræfode hí. 7 slæp mid híre. hím 7 ælle ís mǽginn to muculum hǽrme. swá seo leden bóc sprycð Genesis.[354] ‖ 7 ræðe se þe wyle. hu ornoslice. iacobes súnes dína hǽre suster hút ledde. 7 emor. 7 sichem ís súne. | 7 haere mǽgum. 7 eác aella þa to hám cómen ofslógon. mid swúrdes écge. 7 gecyrdon gesunde to hǽre | getelde. 7 iacob. 7 ís súnunes [*sic*] mid hære wycstówe ywenden to bét`h´el. 7 hérde gódes náme. On þan tíme | forðferde debbora rebecca fostermoder. 7 heo bebyrigde on nyþéwærðe bethel hunder áne áche. / 7 me cwæð þane steðe áche wóp:

And he came to Salem city (*and perhaps it had two names*) in Sichem. That is in Chanaan land and there (he was) dwelling and bought land from Emor, father of Sichem, and raised an altar in God's name. Leah's daughter Dina went out to see the women of the land and Emor's son Sichem raped her and slept with her, to the great harm of him and all his kinsmen, as the Latin book (Genesis) says, and read it who will how deliberately Jacob's sons led out Dina their sister and slew Emor and Sichem his son and their kin and also all those at home by the sword's edge and returned safe to their tent(s) and Jacob and his sons with their property went to Bethel and praised God's name. At that time Deborah, the fostermother of Rebecca, died and they buried her on the near side of Bethel under an oak and the place is called 'oak weeping' (oak of weeping)

F. 51v *Illustrations:* Two frames: upper, God, with cross-nimbus and scroll, blesses Jacob (labeled 'ie*sus*', 'iacob.') and renames him "Israel", tent to right; lower, God (minus scroll) blesses Jacob and his descendants (labeled '.iacob.'), no tent. **OE** = Genesis 35:9–19

182.[355] *v*el dixit | d*ominus* dic*it* surge | asce*n*de[356] in bet/hel | S*ed* priu*s* s*anct*ifica tuos. (HS 1122D)

[351] In bottom margin, 4 lines, and continuing to top of f. 51v, 4 lines in top margin, and a half line into frame. This English note is written as if continuing the main OE text but it is in a much smaller script and brown ink; comprising a summary of the story of the rape of Dina, omitted from the OE main text and is literally translating selected phrases from Genesis 33, 34, 35 (see ch. 3, 209–11 for discussion). This same hand has inserted 'þa' in a blank space in the original OE text, at the beginning of line 4.

[352] See no. 177a.

[353] The "thorn" is crossed, as is often the case in this passage.

[354] 'Genesis' extends into the margin and is probably a gloss.

[355] Upper left margin, very roughly written in, as is the next comment. This pertains to lower OE text on 51r, line 3, **God spræc to iacobe 7 cwæð to hím arís 7 fár to bethel.**

[356] *Sylwan* s. et a.] et *om. Cl W γ*

. . . or the Lord said, arise, go up into Bethel . . . but first sanctify what is yours (i.e, your family and possessions).

183. (inside upper frame, top left) Et Nota q*uo*d hic uid*etu*r quod t*er*ebint*us* et q*uercus* / sint idem[357](HS 1123A)[358]

And note that this shows that 'terebinth' and 'oak' are the same thing.

184. Habebat *enim* ydola q*ue* rachel furata fu*er*at p*at*ri 7 alia q*ue* simon. 7 leuy rapu|erant a sichimitis. a q*uibus* s*an*ctificandi mu*n*dandi era*nt*[359] | q*ue* omnia effodit iacob subt*er* t*er*ebintu*m*: Que e*st* post | urbe*m* sichem. Tradu*nt* q*uida*m q*uo*d ea tulit dauid in | ier*usa*lem: 7 conflauit in m*ateriam* templi q*uo*d facere dis/ posuerat: (HS 1122D–1123A)

He had the idols which Rachel had stolen from her father and others which Simon and Levi had taken from the Sichemites, by whom they were purified (and) cleansed; \ all of which Jacob buried next to the terebinth, which is behind the city of Sichem. Some say that David took them into Jerusalem and combined them with the materials of the temple which he had planned to make.

185.[360] ʃ Egressu*s* in*de*[361] iacob: uenit uerno tempore ad terram que ducit effratam i*d est* bethléém. 7 e*st* anticipatio. (HS 1123A/B) | b*eata* pr*ius* dicta e*st* effrata. ab uxore caleph q*ue* ibi sepulta e*st*. q*ua*m q*u*ida*m* suspicant*ur* filia*m* fuisse ur et | marie sor`or´is moysi: po*st*ea u*ero* p*ost* fama*m*[362] st*e*rilitate*m* *pro* q*u*a elimelec cum [domo[363]] sua adiit moabitas: cum | reddita fuiss*et* ei incredibilis ub*er*tas: dicta est betleem. q*ue* sonat domus panis (HS 1541D/1542A[364]) § Ibiq*ue*[365] cu*m* parturi-

---

[357] *Sylwan* quia hic] quod hic *Cl W To* ‖ *Sylwan* q. et t.] t. et q. *Cl γ* ‖ *Sylwan* sunt] sint *Cl Tr γ δ*

[358] Collating Gen. 35:8 "[Debora nutrix Rebeccae] sepulta est ad radices Bethel subter quercum" with Gen. 35:4 "at ille [deos alienos] infodit ea subter terebinthum, quae est post urbem Sichem." In HS it is a direct comment on "quercus fletus" and by the physical placement of the note next to the last phrase of the English passage, no. 181, it seems also to serve as a direct comment upon it, in analogous fashion.

[359] Text up to this point unsourced.

[360] Lower frame, 1 line above the upper ledger and 13 lines in the frame, in the blank space to the right of the figure of Jacob; this is a combination of several disparate places in HS to make a continuous suite about Bethlehem and Rachel's death. The mark at the beginning resembles more a *nota*-mark than a paragraph.

[361] *Sylwan* autem] inde *Cl W γ δ*

[362] PL "post famosam."

[363] So PL.

[364] From the "Evangelia" section of HS.

[365] An 'a' above 'ibique' in lighter ink is an index marker, referring to 'b' in left margin below frame opposite original OE account of death of Rachel.

ret | Rachel: que ibi sepulta *est*.[366] Cepit p*er*iclitari. | t*ame*n pep*er*it filium. Egrediente au*tem* anima | *pre* dolore p*artus* Moriens uocauit filiu*m* suu*m* | bennon. i*d est* filiu*m* doloris. Pater u*ero* cum | circu*m*cidit eu*m*: uocauit beniamin-[367]| i*d est* dext*re* filiu*m*. sepulta e*st* er*go* Rachel i*n* | uia q*ue* ducit. beth`l´ee*m* / i*d est* betel /[368] (HS 1123B). Moyses dic*it*. du*m* | *er*go rediret de mesopotamia. 7 n*on*du*m* uenisset | ad p*at*rem adhuc uiuente Rachel. (HS 1125B)

"Thence went out . . . Jacob and came in the spring to the land which leads to Effrata" (Gen. 35:16), that is, Bethlehem, and it is a prolepsis. \ Effrata was already called 'blessed' from the wife of Caleb who is buried there, whom some suppose was the daughter of Ur and Mariam the sister of Moses. Later indeed after the barren famine on account of which Elimelech went with his (family) to the Moabites, when incredible prosperity was restored to it (cf. Ruth 1:1–2), it was called Bethlehem, which means 'house of bread'. \ When Rachel gave birth \ who is buried there \ she began to be in danger but she bore a son. "Giving up the ghost for pain" of childbirth and dying "she called her son 'Ben non[i]', that is 'son of pain'. His father," indeed, when he circumcised him, "called (his son) Benjamin" (Gen. 35:18), that is 'son of the right hand'. Therefore, "Rachel was buried on the road which leads to Bethlehem" (Gen. 35:19), (that is, Bethel). Moses says Rachel was still living when (Jacob) returned from Mesopotamia and had not yet come to his father.

186. Et egressu*s* e*st* fixit tab*er*naculu*m* t*ra*ns turri*m* aber `uel ader´ i*d est* turri*m* gregis. hu[n]c locu*m* d*icu*nt | hebrei. ubi po*st* edificatu*m* e*st* te*m*plu*m*. 7 dictu*m* q*uas*i q*u*oda*m* uaticinio: turri*m* gregis i*d est* congregationis fut*ure* | ad te*m*plu*m*. S*ed* (. . .) ier*onymus* dic*it*. locu*m* e*ss*e iuxta bethlee*m*. uibi [*sic*] vel ang*el*oru*m* grex in (.) ortu d*omi*ni cecinit: uel | (. .) iacob g*re*ges suos pauit: nomen in*de* loco relinq*u*ens: (HS 1123B/C)

"And he went out, and pitched the tent across from the tower Aber (or Ader)" (Gen. 35:21), that is "the 'tower of the flock'." The Hebrews so call this place where afterwards the temple was built, and it is called by a certain kind of prophecy, 'tower of the flock', that is the future congregation (flock) at the temple. But Jerome says the place is by Bethlehem, or where the flock of angels sang at the birth of the Lord, or Jacob fed his flock, hence leaving a name for the place.

---

366 Phrase is brought up to *Sylwan* 147/5 from 147/9.

367 *Sylwan* bennoni] bennon *Cl* α *Tr* ‖ *Sylwan* uero] cum *add. Cl W* γ δ ‖ *Sylwan* et uocavit] et *om. Cl W* γ δ ‖ *Sylwan* filium beniamin] filium *om. Cl* β γ

368 'bethleem' written crudely, as if added in another stint; the insertion mark imposes on the word below. The inserted words 'i*d est* betel' are written outside the present text-space and to the right of the figure of Jacob, and there is an insertion mark after 'bethleem'.

187. Rama. loc*us* e*st* iuxta gabáá. xii° miliario distans á | bethleem. 7 ciuitas e*st* iux*ta* monte*m* sylo.[369] (HS 1544B)

Rama, a place next to Gabaa, 12 miles from Bethelehem \ and the city is next to Mount Silo.

F. 52r *Illustrations:* Two frames: upper, corpse of Rachel, borne by Jacob on right, four male figures on left (her sons and Bala's, including Benjamin?); lower, twelve sons of Jacob. OE = Genesis 35:22–29

188. (in upper frame picture space) erexit iacob titulu*m* sup*er* sepulcru*m* racheli∴ xii la|pides p*er*gr*a*ndes i*n* sign*um* filior*um* suor*um* vno miliario a bethlee*m* est∴[370]

"Jacob erected an inscription upon the tomb" of Rachel (Gen. 35:20), twelve very large stones in recognition of her sons; it is one mile from Bethlehem.

189.[371] Qu`o´d t*ame*n non latuit iacob. Venit *er*go ad ysaac p*at*rem suu*m* i*n* ciuitate ebron. 7 mor|tua*m* iam inuenit matre*m*. Nec multu*m* etiam po*st* aduentu*m* ei*us*. | § et iam mortuam in [*sic*] i*n*uenit. matrem- (HS 1123C)

Because however Jacob did not lie hidden, "He came therefore to Isaac his father in the city of Hebron" (Gen. 35:27), and he found his mother was already dead. Not long after his coming[372] / (and now he found his mother was dead).

190.[373] Hec Jer*onymus*- | Eade*m* au*tem* ciuitas d*icitu*r & mambre. ab amico abrahe ita antiq*uitus* appellata⅂ Et pep*er*it ada esau elifaz. Iste e*st* | cui*us* script*ura* i*n* iob uolumine recordat*ur*. Isti filii esau. 7 isti p*r*incipes eor*um* ip*s*e e*st* edom. et hi filii Seyr. Esau. | edom∴ Seyr. vni*us* nomen e*st* hominis. legam*us* dilige*n*ter deut*er*onomiu*m* u*bi* manifestiu*s* sc*ri*bit*ur* q*uo*mo*do* uen*er*int | filii esau. et int*er*fecerint choreos. Ac t*er*ram eor*um* h*er*editate possederi*nt*⅂ Et fuerunt fillii [*sic*] lothan hori.[374] | 7 ommon. 7 soror lothan. themna. Et the*m*na erat[375] co*n*cubina elifaz filii p*r*imogeniti esau; 7 ex ip*s*a nat*us* e*st* ama|lech. Q*u*od au*tem* d*icitu*r tehman. 7 cenez. 7 am`a´lech sciam*us* po*st*eá regionib*us* ydu*m*eor*um* ex his uocabula imposita∴ ‖ Icc*ir*co au*tem* chorreor[um]. recordat*us* e*st*∴ q*u*ia p*r*imogenit*us* filio-

[369] From the "Evangelia" section; last phrase unsourced.

[370] First part = Gen. 35:20 (cf. HS 1123B), the rest unsourced; cf. L. Ginzberg, *Legends of the Jews* (Philadelphia, 1909–1938), 5:319: "Each of Jacob's sons took a stone and put it on the grave and these twelve stones make up Rachel's tomb" (Lekah 35:20).

[371] In lower frame, top 2 lines, plus a line in lower left corner, in smaller script which repeats part of the comment.

[372] HS continues: "completi sunt dies Isaac centum octoginta annorum," etc. (Gen. 35:28).

[373] Bottom margin, six lines, over to top of f. 52v.

[374] PL incorrectly reads "borri."

[375] Written 'erāt'.

ru*m* esav. ex filiabus eoru*m* acce*per*at concubinam:. (Jerome, HQG, 23.992C-993B; CCSL 72, 56.1)

So Jerome: That same city is called also Mambre from the friend of Abram so called from antiquity.⁊ "And Ada gave birth to Eliphaz" (Gen. 36:4) to Esau. He it is . . . whom scripture records in the book of Job. "These are the sons of Esau and these are the princes of them, the same is Edom and these are the sons of Seir" (Gen. 36:19–20). Esau, . . . Edom, . . . Seir is the name of one man. . . . We may read diligently in Deuteronomy (2:24) where it is written more plainly, how the sons of Esau came and killed Chorites and took their land as a heritage.⁊ "And the sons of Lothan were Hori and Heman and the sister of Lothan was Themna. . ." (Gen. 36:22). "And Themna was the concubine of Eliphaz the firstborn son of Esau and from her was born Amalech. . ." (Gen. 36:12). Because it is said "Theman and Cenez and Amalech . . ." (cf. Gen. 36:11) we may know that these names were later given to the regions of the Idumeans. Therefore it is recorded of the Chorites that the firstborn of the sons of Esau had taken a concubine from their daughters.

F. 52v *Illustrations*: Two frames, upper: corpse of Isaac, carried by Joseph and Esau, with descendants of Jacob and Esau looking on; lower, divided into two registers: above, family of Esau with his two wives and his sons, below, Jacob, with Rachel and nine male figures representing his sons. **OE** = Genesis 36:6–8, 37:1

191a. ✓ad hoc singnu*m* [*sic*] +✓[376] Completi sunt dies ysaac. clxxx. annoru*m*. vel se*cun*d*u*m iosephum. clxxxv. et appositus. | est populo suo plenus dierum. hic t*er*minat*ur* p*r*imus liber iosephi- (HS 1123C/D) | cxx. annorum erat iacob in morte patris. (HS 1125A) | ysaac fili*us* abraha*m* in Gerara natus obiit.[377]| et rediit esau ad montana que dimiserat Et dicta est t*er*ra | ab edom: ydumea que p*r*ius dicebatur bosra. (HS 1123D) ydumea e*st* | in t*er*ra damascena nam et esau habitauit damascum. (HS 1124C; Add. 2) Enum*er*ans *enim* moyses .xii. reges terre | illius. a p*r*imo usq*ue* ad ultimu*m* quem uid*ere* potuit: ait. Et regnauit post bale: iobal filius | zare de bosra. ⁊ hunc d*icu*nt q*u*ida*m* fuisse iob: p*r*onepote*m* esau. (HS 1123D)[378]

"The days of Isaac were completed, 180 years," or according to Josephus, 185 "and he was gathered to his people full of days" (Gen. 35:28–29). . . . Here ends

[376] The correspondent to this "sign" is on f. 59r, margin, no. 191d see comment; the passage here is a medley of HS excerpts, mostly about Esau, written in nine lines that begin above the first frame, lodge in that frame and then over, in, and under the lower frame; see discussion, pp. 352–54.

[377] Repeated on f. 59r, no. 191d; cf. no. 130.

[378] *Sylwan* ydumea ab edom] ydumea *om. Cl To* ‖ *Sylwan* bosra dicebatur] d. b. *Cl W γ* ‖ *Sylwan* in damasco] damascum *Cl S β γ δ* ‖ iobab] iobal *Cl S Tr γ δ*

the first book of Josephus. \ Jacob was 120 years old when his father died. \ Isaac the son of Abraham was born in Gerara and died (there). And Esau returned to the mountains which he had left and the land of Idumea is named from Edom: Idumea, which was first called 'Bosra'. \ Idumea is in the Damascus region and Esau lived in Damascus. \ Moses enumerated twelve kings of that land from the first to the last, which he could see; he said "And after Bela Iobal son of Zara of Bosra reigned" (Gen. 36:33). And some say this was Job, great-grandson of Esau.

191b. (bottom margin, line 4 up) Josephus dicit. q*uo*d amalech filius esau nat*u*-*r*alis | de co*n*cubina: habitauit i*n* parte ydumee q*ue* gabolitis.[379] ⁊ dixit ea*m* amalechite*m*. his u*ero* p*reter*missis: transeundu*m* e*st* ad generacione*m* | iacob. (HS 1124B)

Josephus . . . says that Amalech was the natural son of Esau by a concubine, (she) lived in the part of Idumea which (is called) Gabolites . . . and he called her an Amelechite. Passing over these matters we must proceed to the generation of Jacob.

192. Normanus. legit*ur* in genesi. q*uo*d heliphat p*ri*mogenit*us* esau: genuit de `themna´ *con*cubina: amalech. (HS 1161B "Exodus")

Normanus: It is read in Genesis that Eliphaz was the first-born son of Esau; he begot Amalech of (Themna) the concubine.

191c.[380] Tema met*r*opolis idumee unde | eliphat temanites. et suetam unde baldat suites . bosro*m* i*n* finibus idumee [*corr. from* idunee]. ⁊ arabie. libanus diuidit idumea*m* ⁊ feniciam || in radice cuius oriuntur albana ⁊ fafar flue*n*s secus antiochiam: (HS 1124C, Add. 2)[381]

Thema is the chief city of Idumea, whence Eliphas of the Themanites and Suita, whence Baldad of the Suites. Bosra in the region of Idumea and Arabia Libanus divide Idumae and Phoenicia, from whose sources arise the rivers Alban and Pharphar, flowing beside Antioch.

F. 53r *Illustration:* One frame: Joseph, center, in his "coat of many colors," with his eleven brothers (seven on left, gesturing variously, four on right), speaking to Jacob, right, beside him two wives. **OE** = Genesis 37:2–14

379 *Sylwan* gobolites (emend.)] gabolites *Cl S Tr γ*

380 Bottom margin, lower two lines, continuing at top of 53r.

381 *Sylwan* theman] teman *To*, tema *Cl* || *Sylwan* ydumee] idumee *Cl To* || *Sylwan* eliphaz] eliphat *Cl Tr γ* || *Sylwan* themanites] temanites *Cl To* || *Sylwan* baldach] baldath *S To*, baldat *Cl β* || *Sylwan* bosra] bosron *Cl W Pa* || *Sylwan* ydumee] idumeam *Cl S To* || *Sylwan* pheniciam] feniciam *Cl W γ T* || *Sylwan* in cuius radice] r. c. *Cl γ* || *Sylwan* fluentes] fluens *Cl Pa δ*

193a.[382] Sciendu*m* q*uo*d an*te* morte*m* ysaac .xii. annis uenditus e*st* ioseph. (HS 1125A)

It is to be known that 12 years before the death of Isaac Joseph was sold.

194. (right margin, some lines trimmed) § Questio*:* | Increpauit | eu*m* p*ate*r*:* et ait. | Nu*m*q*ui*d ego | 7 m*ate*r tua e[t] | fr*at*res tui. | adorabim[us] | te sup*er* t*er*ra*m*. | Potuit hoc | dicere co*ng*|rue q*uia* m*ate*r. | adhuc ui|uebat. (HS 1125C)

Question: His father rebuked him and said, "Should I and your mother and your brothers worship you upon the earth?" (Genesis 37:10) He was able to say this fittingly because his mother was still living.

195. (bottom margin) § Job qui 7 Jobab cui*us* p*ate*r zara. et Mater bosrad*:* zara au*tem* fili*us* Ragu`e´l. filii esau. filii ysaac .vi^{tus}[383] ab | abraham rex inclitus in terra edom. (Isidore, *De ortu et obitu patrum*, PL 83.1275D)[384]

Job, also known as Jobab, whose father was Zara and mother Bosrad. Zara was son of Raguel, son of Esau, son of Isaac, the sixth from Abraham, a famous king in the land of Edom.

196. Cont*ra* heb*r*ei asserunt eu*m* de Nachor stirpe generatu*m* vt ia[m] | sup*ra* dictu*m* e*st:* (Jerome, HQG 57.14)

But on the other hand the Hebrews say he (Job) was of the race of Nachor, as was said above.

197. § Jer*onymus* dic*it*. Themna concubina elifaz. mat*er* amalech. fuit. de genere choreor*um* q*ui* ante | ydumeos habitauerunt i*n* t*er*ra seyr. (HQ1P 23.1367 A/B)

Jerome says: Themna the concubine of Eliphaz, the mother of Amalech, was of the race of Horrites who lived in the land of Seir before the Idumeans. (cf. Gen. 36:12)

F. 53v *Illustration:* One frame: A man guides Jacob to his brothers in Dotham. **OE** = Genesis 37:14–28

198. § dothaym. v*b*i inuenit ioseph fr*atre*s suos pecora pascentes. q*ui* et usq*ue* hodie i*n* duodecimo a sebaste | miliario*:* cont*ra* aq*ui*lonis plaga*m* ostendit*ur:* (SNLH 23.890C; Lagarde 115.3)

Dothaim, where Joseph found his brothers feeding their flocks, which to the present day is shown about twelve miles to the north of Sebaste.

---

382 Below rubric, above text, 1 line; occurs also on f. 51r, no. 179, and again on f. 59r, no. 193b.

383 PL "quintus."

384 The substance of the comment originates with Jerome, HQG 57.14.

199.[385] Eosdem uocat madianitas: quos et hismaelitas. Madian *enim* de cethtura filius abrahe. 7 hismael de agar. | et filios de diu*er*sis uxorib*us* legitur ab*ra*ham ab inuicem sep*ar*asse. Forte sep*ar*ati p*r*ius. postea redieru[n]t in unum. || et facti sunt unus pop*ul*us utriq*ue* p*at*ris retinentes nomen. Vel uera e*st* hebreo*rum* op*in*io. qui dicunt agar et | cethuram unam fuisse. 7 ita forte nunq*u*am sep[a]rati[386] fuerunt. (HS 1126 A/B)[387]

He called those Madianites, who are also Ismaelites. For Madian was the son of Abraham by Cethura, and Ismael by Hagar. And it is read that Abraham separated from one another the sons by the different wives. Perhaps they were first separated and afterwards they came back together and were made one people retaining the name of both fathers. Or the opinion of the Hebrews is true, who say that Hagar and Cethura were the same woman and therefore perhaps they never were separated.

F. 54r Full-page illustration, arranged into three informal registers, of the treatment of Joseph by his brothers, top middle, they are stripping Joseph, to right and going down the picture space, casting him into a pit, and, lower part, selling him to a band of Ismaelites; no OE.

200. In ven`di´tione aut*em* filii: cviii. annorum fuit. § aceusaueratq*ue* [*recte* acc-] f*rat*res apud p*at*rem c*r*imine pessimo. | vel de odio in ip*su*m. uel de coitu cu*m* brutis. Vel solum ruben p*ro* concubina p*at*ris. (HS 1125B/C)

At the sale of his son he (i.e. Israel) was 108 years old. . . . And he [Joseph] accused his brothers to his father of the worst crime, either of hate towards himself, or of intercourse with animals. But only Ruben [he excepted] for the sake of his father's concubine.[388]

F. 54v *Illustrations:* Two frames: upper, Reuben by the empty pit rends his clothing, looking back at his brothers; lower, in two panels, left, the brothers daubing Joseph's robe in blood, right, showing it to their father Israel. **OE** = Genesis 37:29–35

385 Bottom, 2 lines, continuing on top of f. 54r.

386 Written 'seperati'.

387 *Sylwan* hysmaelitas] hismaelitas *Cl To T* || *Sylwan* cethura] cethtura *Cl*, cetura *To T* || *Sylwan* ysmael] hismael *Cl Tr* || *Sylwan* separasse Abraham ab inuicem] abraham ab i. s. *Cl β γ* || Forte *add. Cl β γ L* || *Sylwan* retinentes utriusque parentis] u. patris r. *Cl β γ*

388 I.e. remembering he had slept with his father's concubine, Ruben had pity on Joseph, cf. Genesis 35:22 and in HS Joseph reciprocates. For "accusaveratque" cf. Genesis 37:2; that Josephus *falsely* accused his brothers of various crimes and faults is well-established in Jewish lore: see L. Ginzberg, *The Legends of the Jews*, trans. H. Szold and P. Radin (Philadelphia, 2003), 1:328.

201.[389] Erat *enim* tunc[390] in inferno q*u*idam loc*us* beatoru*m*. longe semot*us* a locis penalib*us* qui ob q*u*ietem et separa|tionem[391] ab aliis. sinus dicebatur. sicut sinu*m* maris dicim*us* et dictus est[392] sinus abrahe. q*uia* etiam ‖ abraham ibi erat in sustentatione usq*ue* ad mortem chr*ist*i. (HS 1126C)

At that time there was in 'hell' a certain place of the blessed far removed from the place of punishments, which on account of its quiet and separation from others is called a bosom or haven, as we name the inwelling or bay of the sea, and it is called the 'bosom of Abraham' because Abraham was there in a state of waiting up to the death of Christ.

F. 55r *Illustrations:* Three frames: upper, Jacob mourns Joseph, eleven sons with him; middle, two Midianites sell Joseph to Putifar; lower, Juda with his Canaanite wife (on a bed?) and their three sons. **OE** = Genesis 37:36, 38:1–5

202. Joseph .xvi. annor*um* erat. Jacob. c 7 viii- | Ysaac. c.`l´x 7 viii:· In ue*n*ditione joseph:·[393]

Joseph was 16 years, Jacob 108, Isaac 168 at the time of the sale of Joseph.

203. (gloss to OE, line 3 up) **to anu*m* adolamitiscu*m* mén.** `nomine hiran.´ **7 nam | ðær án chananeisc wíf.** (gloss = HS 1127A, Gen. 38:2)

to a certain odolamitish man named Hiras **and took there a certain Chanaanite wife.**

F. 55v *Illustrations:* Two frames: upper, corpse of Her held by his two brothers, Juda consoles Her's wife Thamar; lower, Thamar in house, left, is told that Juda, right, with Hiras, is coming to Thamnas to shear sheep. **OE** = Genesis 38:6–16

204. § Eman. Termin*us* damasci. sic*ut* in ezechiel legit*ur* ad orient*em* u*er*gens á theman & pal|metis:· q*ue* cet*er*ri [*sic*] int*er*pretes ediderunt thamar. (SNLH 23.897, Lagarde 122.19)

Enan, the border of Damascus as is read in Ezechiel (48:1), towards Theman and Palmetis in the east, which other translators give as 'Thamar'.

---

389 Bottom margin, to f. 55r top. This note is to Genesis 37:35, which in the OE (last line of facing f. 54v) is rendered: **íc fáre to mínum súna to helle**, spoken by Israel. On f. 54r, the "pit" which Joseph is cast into is shaped like a typical Anglo-Saxon hellmouth.

390 tunc *add. Cl S Tr γ δ*

391 Written 'separa-'.

392 *Sylwan* etiam] *om. Cl β*

393 Unsourced, but see no. 179.

F. 56r *Illustrations:* Two frames: upper, Juda gives pledges to Thamar and leaves; lower, when the kid to redeem the pledge is sent to Thamar she cannot be found. **OE** = Genesis 38:16–21, no annotations

F. 56v *Illustrations* Two frames: upper, a messenger tells Juda that the harlot cannot be found; lower, Juda, with staff of judgement, condemns Thamar to be burnt. **OE** = Genesis 38:22–26

205. § Thamna vbi oues suas totondit judas. Ostendit*urque* hodie uicu*s* p*er*gr*an*-dis i*n* finib*us* diospo|leos. euntib*us* elia*m* i*n* trib*u* dan. siue jude. (SNLH 23.924B; Lagarde 156.6)

Thamna, where Judah sheared his sheep. And shown today is . . . a very large town in the region of Diospolis to those traveling towards Aelia [Jerusalem], in the tribe of Dan or Judah.

206. § Legim*us* iuxta heb*rai*ca*m* u*e*ritate*m*. (.)ubi iudas m*e*retr*i*|ce*m* putans thamar∴ dona t*r*ansmittit. et sequester mun*e*ru*m* int*e*rrogat u*b*i e*st* cadesa. Hoc e*st* | scortu*m*∴ Cui*us* habit*us* a cet*e*ris feminis i*m*mutat*us* est. In multis q*u*oq*ue* locis hoc idem repp*e*rim*us*∴ (Jerome, Ep. 78 ad Fabiolam ["42 Mansiones"] 22.716)

We read . . . according to the Hebrew truth (Gen. 38:13–26) where Juda, thinking Thamar a prostitute, sends gifts, and the deliverer of the gifts asked, 'where is cadesa,' that is 'the whore', whose clothing is no different from that of other women. In many places we observe this to be the case.

F. 57r *Illustrations:* Two frames: upper, Thamar, led to the flames, sends her pledges back to Juda, seated as judge; lower, Thamar gives birth to twins, Phares and Zara. **OE** = Genesis 38:27–30, 39:1–2

207. Chasbi u*b*i geminos iude filios thamar edidit. Oste*n*dit*ur* au*tem* nunc loc*us* desert*us* iuxta | odolla*m*∴ in finib*us* eleutheropoleos∴ (SNLH 23.889A; Lagarde 112.18)

Chazbi, where Thamar gave birth to twin sons to Juda. The desert place is today shown near Adolla, on the borders of Eleutheropolis.

F. 57v *Illustration:* One frame: on right, Putifer purchases Joseph and, on left, Joseph attends him and his wife. **OE** = Genesis 39:2–16, no annotations

F. 58r *Illustrations:* Two frames: upper, Putifer's wife holds Joseph's garment pointing at him, her attendants look on at left, Joseph walks away on right, hand of God blessing him; lower, Putifer's wife accuses Joseph to her husband and he has Joseph imprisoned. **OE** = Genesis 39:16–23

208a.[394] `joseph´ xiii. annis fuit ios`e´ph in egipto:· antequam ingredietur domum pharaonis.[395]

Joseph was in Egypt for 13 years before he went into the house of Pharaoh.

F. 58v *Illustration:* One frame, Pharaoh enthroned on right consigns his butler and baker to prison, Joseph seen on left, in the prison. **OE** = Genesis 40:1–19

209. (as if contining last line of OE block and continuing for 1 line) Videbam coram me uitem. 7 in ea | tres fundos. occultos[396] occulos. *scilicet* unde funduntur palmites:· (HS 1128D)[397]

"I saw before me a vine and on it three" shoots, [hidden] eyes (i.e. buds), that is to say, whence are produced young shoots (Gen. 40:9) .

210. (bottom margin) Jer*onymus* dic*it* | § Et ecce uitis i*n* co*n*spectu meo. 7 in uite t*r*es fundi. Tres fundi t*r*ia flagella. et t*r*es ramos siue | `tres et*iam* dies.´ p*r*opagines significant. q*ue* ab illis uocant*ur* sariagim. Et uidebar m*ih*i t*r*ia canistra portare. p*ro* t*r*i*bus* canistris. | *con*dritor*um* tres cofinos farine in heb*r*eo habet*ur*:· (HQG 23.997A, CCSL 72, 59.24)

Jerome says: "And behold a vine in my sight and on the vine three shoots" (Gen. 40:9). . . . Three shoots (are) three scourges and three branches or (rather three days) signify shoots . . . what by them (the Hebrews) are called 'sariagim'. "And I seemed to be carrying three baskets. . ." (Gen. 40:16). For three baskets of 'chondritus' is said in the Hebrew "three 'cophinos' of wheat."

F. 59r *Illustrations:* Two frames: upper, Pharaoh and his court, the baker being hanged on the right; lower, Pharaoh dreaming (labeled 'pharao') **OE** = Genesis 40:20–23, 41:1–7

191d. (margin) +✓[398] | § p*ost* unu*m* annu*m* | ysaac in Gera|ris natus obiit

---

[394] Top, 1 line, above which 'joseph' is written in faint brownish ink.

[395] Unsourced; this note occurs again on f. 59r, no. 208b.

[396] 'oc(c)ulos' is correct. The word 'occultos' has not been cancelled, the error arising from "ocłos" resolved incorrectly (the reading "occultos" in *W*).

[397] Vulgate (Gen. 40:10) has "in qua erant tres propagines (**clystru**), crescere paulatim in gemmas" "on which were three branches which by little and little sent out buds"; the comment is misplaced in relation to OE, dovetailed in after the prophecy to the baker (40:18 **windlas**/canistra), rather than the butler.

[398] Substantially this sentence, with a similar *signe*, occurs in no. 191a on f. 52v, where it says that "at this sign" the days of Isaac are finished; the reference to f. 59r suggests that Isaac died after Joseph had been in Egypt one year. This and the other two repeated notes on this page do the arithmetic: 1 year after the death of Isaac + 12 years before = 13 years that Joseph was sold in Egypt before he confronted Pharaoh; see discussion 352–54, below.

After one year Isaac, who was born in Gerara, died (there).

193b.[399] Scienduⁿ q*uo*d an*te* morte*m* ysaac .xii. annis ue*n*dit*us* e*st* Joseph. (HS 1125A)

It is to be known that twelve years before the death of Isaac Joseph was sold.

208b.[400]§ tredecim. annis fuit ioseph[401] | in egipto anteq*ua*m ingre[die]tur | do-mu*m* pharaonis.

Thirteen years was Joseph in Egypt before he entered into the house of Pharaoh.

F. 59v OE = Genesis 41:8–38; no illustrations or annotations.

F. 60r *Illustration:* One frame, divided into two registers, upper half divided into panels: upper left, Joseph (labeled 'josep', insular 's') being "shaved" or tonsured (Gen. 41:14), prison (?) to the left; upper right, Joseph expounds the dream to Pharaoh; lower register, Pharaoh enthroned, Joseph in a chariot being blessed by hand of God, the people bowing down to him. **OE** = Genesis 41:38–43

211. Triginta anno*rum* erat ioseph. q*uando* stetit cora*m* pharaone. Jacob. c.xxii. anno*rum* erat. (HS 1130B = Gen. 41:46)[402]

Joseph "was thirty years old when he stood" before Pharaoh. \ Jacob was 122 years old.

F. 60v *Illustrations:* Two frames: upper, Joseph and his wife Aseneth before Pharaoh; lower, the people cry to Pharaoh for bread. **OE** = Genesis 41:44–56

212. § de joseph et annis uite ei*us*. Joseph dux egipti. p*er* annos octoginta. | aseneth dece*m* 7 octo anno*rum* Magna 7 speciosa. 7 pulchra ualde | sup*er* om*n*es

---

[399] Above bottom frame, this note occurs also on f. 51r (no. 179) and f. 53r (no. 193a).

[400] In bottom frame, 3 short lines, occurring also on f. 58r (no. 208a), some extra scorings within the picture space for this item. The differences in abbreviations and punctuation in the two copies suggest that this note was brought forward from two different exemplars (from a marginal note in the exemplar HS?).

[401] 'xiii.' is written to the right and a little above this word, and appears to function like the many other "marginal" numerals which call attention to numerals in the texts.

[402] This note matches the main OE text on 60v, where, as here, 'xxx' is placed in the outer margin. The second sentence is unsourced but must be an original calculation based on Bede, DTR 43: "Iacob CXXX an. descendit in Aegyptum. . . ." If Joseph was 30 when he stood before Pharaoh and 39 when Jacob came into Egypt (cf. no. 219), then Jacob was about 122 when Joseph left him and 130 when he came in.

ui*r*gines t*erre*. s*ed* erat p*er* omnia similis filiab*us* he|breor*um*. Erat magna ut sara speciosa ut re|b[e]cca formosa ut rachel- (*Liber de Aseneth*)[403]

Concerning Joseph and the years of his life; Joseph was prince of Egypt for eighty years; Aseneth was eighteen years old, great and attractive and very beautiful above all the virgins of the world. . . . but was in all respects like the daughters of the Hebrews; she was as great as Sara, as attractive as Rebecca, and as beautiful as Rachel.

213. (left margin) p*os*t vii. anno*rum* | fames ingens- | .exoritur.[404]
After seven years a great famine arose.

F. 61r–63r OE = Genesis 42–43:24; no annotations

F. 63v *Illustration:* One large frame in two registers: upper, Joseph's ten brothers bow down to him, offering presents, on right in a small room, Joseph seeks a place to weep for Benjamin; below in two panels, the feast, Joseph's brothers on left, Joseph and the Egyptians on right. **OE** = Genesis 43:25–34, 44:1–2

214.[405] ydioma lingue hebree e*st*: ut eb*r*ietate*m* p*ro* satietate ponat sicut ibi. In stillicidiis suis inebriabit*ur* | germina`n´s. haud dubiu*m* q*u*in terra pluuiis irrigata- (HQG 23.999C/1000A, CCSL 72, 62.3)

It is an idiom of the Hebrew language that it says 'drunkenness' for 'sufficiency', as in this place, "and in its trickling, the new shoots will be inebriated" (cf. Ps. 64:11),[406] where there is no doubt that the earth was watered by rain.

215.[407] P*ro* sacculo perone*m* u*e*l follem habet*ur* in hebreo: P*ro* condi i*d est* poculo. q*uo*d etiam in ysaia legit*ur*. Aquila scip|hum. Symmachus fialam t*ra*nstulerunt: (HQG 23.1000A, CCSL 72, 62.8)

For 'sack' in Hebrew is said 'boot' or 'leather bag'. For 'condy', that is 'cup', which is read in Isaiah (ch. 51), Aquila translates 'scyphulus' [a small wine-cup], and Symmachus 'phiala' [a saucer].

F. 64r–65v OE = Genesis 44:3–45:28; no annotations

---

403 P. Batiffol, ed., *Le livre de la prière d'Aseneth*, Studia Patristica 1–2 (Paris, 1889–1890), 2: 89/12–90/1.

404 Unsourced, cf. Gen. 41:54.

405 Below the picture-frame, 2 lines, a *signe de renvoi* '+' refers back to the end of the upper OE text-block, 7 **hí mán oferdrencte**.

406 Vulgate: "Rivos ejus inebria, multiplica genimina ejus; in stillicidiis ejus laetabitur germinans."

407 In bottom margin, 2 lines; *signe de renvoi* :· refers it to end of lower OE text-block.

F. 66r No OE on page, four-register full-page illustration: top, Joseph gives his brothers tunics, Benjamin receiving more, next register, sends ten laden he-asses and as many she-asses to his father, next, wagons, bottom, the brothers report to their father Jacob/Israel (= Gen. 45:22–28).

216. factu*m*q*ue* e*st* ita. deditq*ue* ioseph singulis binas stolas. stola d*icitu*r a telon q*uod* e*st* longu*m* q*uas*i talaris beniamin.[408] (HS 1133A)

And it was so done. Joseph gave each two tunics. A tunic is so called from 'telon' which reaches to the ankles. Benjamin. . . .

F. 66v *Illustrations:* Two frames, upper, Jacob with his family at Beersheba, being blessed by hand of God; lower, Jacob with his family going into Egypt. **OE** = Genesis 46:1–6; no annotations.

F. 67r *Illustration:* One frame: The wagons sent by Pharaoh to carry Jacob into Egypt. **OE** = Genesis 46:8–34

217. § Herou*m* Ciuitas. in egipto. ad q*u*am occurrit joseph patri suo iacob:- Eliopolis. ciuitas solis. | i*n* egipto:· p*ro* q*u*a in hebreo sc*r*iptu*m* e*st*. ON. In q*u*a petefres sac*er*dos fuit. Meminit hui*us* ezechiel. (Jerome, SNLH 23.896B; Lagarde 121.18, 20, two contiguous entries)

Eroum is a city in Egypt to which Joseph hurried to his father Jacob. \ Heliopolis, the city of the sun . . . in Egypt, for which in Hebrew is written 'On'; in it Petefres[409] was priest: Ezekiel . . . makes mention of this city (Ez. 30:17).

F. 67v Full-page picture space in four registers of Joseph going out to meet Jacob; no OE or annotations.

F. 68r *Illustrations:* Two frames: upper, Joseph sets out in a wagon to meet Jacob; lower, Joseph (labeled 'Joseph') presents "five men . . . the last of his brethren" to Pharaoh (labeled 'pharao', insular 'r'). **OE** = Genesis 47:1–6

218. § Jacob s*ecun*do anno famis ingressus e*st* egiptu*m* cu*m* filiis suis. i*n* me*n*se s*ecun*do. uice|sima p*r*ima die menssis. [*sic*] 7 de[s]ce*n*dit in t*err*a*m* iesse*n*:· (cf. Augustine *Quaest. in Hept.* 34.611, CCSL 33, 89.688; Eusebius/Jerome, *Chronica*, PL 27.145).[410]

Jacob in the second year of the famine went into Egypt with his sons, in the second month . . . (on) the twenty-first day of the month, and descended into the land of Gessen (cf. Gen. 41:46).

408 Scribe misdivides sentence, 'beniamin' being part of the next.

409 The father of Aseneth, Joseph's wife.

410 Probably from a margin or an intermediate source.

F. 68v *Illustrations:* Two frames, Joseph presents Jacob to Pharaoh, Jacob leaves on left;[411] Joseph gives his brothers presents. **OE** = Genesis 47:7–17. Along top of upper picture frame, **ii̅.c.xxx.viii.**[412]

219. Et iosep .xxxix. q*uando* uenit ad eum pater. (HS 1125A)
And Joseph . . . was thirty-nine when his father came to him.

220. Viuebat *ergo* ioseph. post aduentu*m* patris in egipto. | annis septuaginta uno.[413]
So Joseph lived for seventy-one years after the arrival of his father in Egypt.

221.[414] (Sylwan 170/35) Dedit *er*go iosep fr*atri*bu*s* suis poss*essio*ne*m*. in optimo solo t*er*re[415](. . .) ramesses. (169/4) q*u*e tunc: iessem.[416] po*st* thebais dicta e*st* aqua thebei. | quoru*m* legioni p*re*fuit (. . . . .)[417] alie su*n*t thebe.[418] vn*de* thebani. (170/36) Josephus | dic*it*. Concessit ei pharao: ut in heliopolitana urbe conu*er*saretn`u´r [*recte* conuersarentur][419] | illic. *enim* pascua pastores ei*us* habuerant. forte ad t*er*ritoriu*m* heliopoleos:[420] spectabat t*er*ra iessem: (HS 1134D/A/D)

"Joseph therefore gave his brothers a possession in the best place in the land of Ramesses" (Gen. 47:11), \ which then was called Gessen and afterwards Thebes from the waters of Thebes of which (the layperson Maurice, *erased*) headed the legion. The other (city of that name) is Thebes (in Greece), whence 'Thebans'. \ Josephus . . . says that Pharaoh granted to him that they could dwell in the city of Heliopolis; he (knowing) his shepherds had kept pastures [was glad

411 The Vulgate of 47:7 is ambiguous as to who blesses whom: "post haec introduxit Ioseph patrem suum ad regem et statuit eum coram eo qui benedicens illi," but 47:10 is not: "et benedicto rege egressus est foras"; the OE gets it wrong: **Þa bletsode he hine . . . 7 se cyning hine bletsode**; in the picture the crowned and enthroned figure blesses his neighbor, uncrowned and enthroned. The crowned figure is white-haired and may be a last-minute correction of a faulty original design based on the OE text.

412 A mistake for **ii̅.cc.xxx.viii**, A.M. 2238.

413 In Gazaeus' commentary to Cassian, *De incar*, PL 50.191 occurs the following: "detrahere oporteat unum et septuaginta annos, quos vixit Joseph post adventum patris sui in Ægyptum," so the wording is from some ancient source as yet unfound.

414 One line over lower frame and three lines within, rearranged, with references to Sylwan's ed.

415 terre *add. Cl β γ δ*

416 *Sylwan* iessen] iessem *Cl L*

417 In erasure, 'laic*us* mauritiu*s*' (VSC); perhaps erased preparatory to a correction to "beatus mauricius" as in edd. The reference is to the "Theban Legion" commanded by St. Maurice.

418 *h* altered from *e*.

419 *Sylwan* conuersaretur] -entur *Cl S β γ δ*

420 *Sylwan* eliopolitana, eliopoleos] heliopolitana *Cl*, heliopoleos *Cl S*

to be separated from the Egyptians][421] . . . Perhaps the land of Gessen faced towards the territory of Heliopolis.

F. 69r *Illustration:* One frame divided into two registers: upper, Joseph giving the Egyptians food, lower, in exchange for their livestock. **OE** = Gen. 47:18–21, 23–26

222. Effraim q*u*ippe. et Manasse. anteq*ua*m iacob i*ntra*ret in egiptu*m*. 7 famis temp*us* ingrueret. nati s*un*t de ascenech. S*ed* et | illud q*uo*d sup*ra* legim*us* filii Manasse quos gen*uit* ei co*n*cubina syra. Machir. et Machir gen*uit* galáád. filii au*tem* effraim. | fr*atr*is manasse. Suthalaa*m*. 7 Tahaa*m* filii au*tem* suthalaa*m* edem. additum e*st*. (HQG 23.1001A/B; CCSL 72, 49–50)

Before Jacob entered Egypt and the great famine arose, Ephraim and Manasse were born of Aseneth. . . . But also that is added which we have already read of the sons[422] of Manasse "who were born from his Syrian concubine, Machir, and Machir begot Galaad; the sons of Ephraim, the brother of Manasses, Suthalaam and Taam, the son of Suthalaam Edem." (cf. 1 Para. 7:14–15)

223.[423] § ferunt hanc syri*m* fuisse filia*m* | filii laban. q*ue* in egyptu*m* famis i*no*pia ad uenunda*n*du*m* á pat*re* ducta. á Manasse q*ui* horreis p*re*erat mis[er]c*or*diter ‖ suscepta: et pat[ri] cibariis datis. ab eode*m* Manasse i*n* coniugium su*m*pta e*st:* pep*er*itq*ue* ei machir patr|em galáád. `In paralypomenon´ § filii machir hufim 7 Sufim. `unum nomen e*st*.´ et soror eor*um* `*recte* eius´ fuit Mahacha [*the first* 'h' *cancelled*] q*ua*m accepit esron. cum | lx$^{ta}$ e*ss*et annor*um* ex qua suscepit secur `*recte* gab´; Nomen au*tem* sec*un*di salphaad- (QH1P 23.1376 C/D)

They claim this Syrian was the daughter of the son of Laban who, led into Egypt to be sold by her father on account of the scarcity caused by famine, was compassionately taken up by Manasses, who was in charge of the granaries, her father having been given a food allowance; by that same Manasses she was taken in marriage; and she bore to him Machir, the father of Galaad. § In Paralipomenon (1 Par. 7:14–15): the sons of Machir were Hufim and Sufim[424] (that is one name) and their sister (correctly, 'his') was Maacha whom Esron married when

---

[421] PL: "illic enim pascua pastores ejus habebant, sciens gratum esse Ægyptiis separari a se pastores. . ." (cf. Gen. 46:34).

[422] Manasses has only one son, Machir, born of the Syrian concubine, but the uncited first part of the same verse (1 Para. 7:14) mentions another son, "Ezriel."

[423] Bottom 2 lines and to top of 69v, 3 irregular lines with interlining. The irregularity of the writing both in lineation and ductus on the verso seems to be due to an attempt to avoid a flaw in the parchment. This passage is a supplement to no. 222, drawn from a different Hieronyman source; cf. no. 271, a more extended extract from this same place.

[424] Vulgate: "Happhim et Saphan."

he was sixty years old with whom he begot Secur (correctly, '[Se]gab') (cf. 1 Par:2.21). . . . "The name of the second Salphaad" (1 Par. 7:15).

F. 69v *Illustrations:* Two frames: upper, Jacob bringing "all the lands of the Egyptians" into the hands of Pharaoh, Egyptians to left (Gen. 47:20); lower, left panel, Manasses and Effraim (?);[425] right panel, Joseph before Jacob.[426] OE = Genesis 47:27–31, 48:1–2

224.[427] l. 7iiii^or^. annis legit*ur* postea uixisse ioseph in egipto.[428]

It is read that Joseph lived afterward in Egypt for fifty-four years.

225.[429] Sicima iuxta grec*am*. 7 latin*am* co*n*suetud`in´e*m* declinata e*st*. Alioq*u*in i*n* ebreo sichem d*icitu*r ut ioh*annes* q*uo*q*ue* eu*an*g*e*lista testat*ur*. | licet uitiose ut sychar leg`a´t*ur* error i*n*oleuit: et *est* nu*n*c neapolis [*corr. from* neopolis] urbs samaritanor*um*. Q*u*ia ig*itur* sychem ling*ua* hebrea | t*r*ansfert*ur* in humeru*m* pluchre [*sic*] allusit ad n*omen* dicens. Et ego dabo t*ib*i hum*e*ru*m* unu*m*. Arcu*m* hic au*tem* et gladiu*m* iusti|cia*m* [*sic, and edd., for* -iae?] uocat. p*er* q*uam* meruit p*er*egrin*us* 7 aduena. int*er*fecto sychem & emor de p*er*iculo lib*erari*: Vel certe sic ‖ § Jer*onymus* dic*it*[430] | intelligendu*m*. dabo t*ib*i sichima*m* q*ua*m emi i*n* fortitudine mea: H*oc* e*st* i*n* pecunia: q*ua*m multo labore | et sudore q*u*esiui Q*u*od (.) au*tem* dicit sup*er* fra*tre*s tuos: ostendit absq*ue* sorte dedisse eam joseph. (HQG 23.1004A/B; CCSL 72.48.22)

'Sicima' is declined according to Greek and Latin common usage. But in Hebrew it is 'Sichem' as the evangelist John testifies (John 4:5) although it is corruptly read as 'Sychar'; error grew and it is now Neapolis the city of the Samaritans. Because 'Sychem' in the Hebrew tongue is translated by 'on the shoulder' he beautifully alluded to the name, saying "And I will give you a shoulder." . . . Here it is also called the bow and sword (of) justice by which the wanderer and stranger deserved to be freed from peril, Sychem and Emor, having been killed (Gen. 34:26). Or certainly as Jerome says it is to be understood as "I give to you Sichim which I bought in my strength"; that is, with money, which with much

[425] Cf. Gen. 48:1, 5, 8–20; Dodwell and Clemoes refer both panels to Joseph and Jacob. See ch. 6, 322, and note 431 below.

[426] The figures in the lower picture seem touched up or finished by a later (12-century?) hand, as are those of the unfinished upper picture on f. 70v.

[427] Above lower picture, 1 line as if continuing OE. In the margin slightly above this place is '.x.7 vii | c.xl vii.' with confusing separation marks: the numerals refer respectively to **on seofentyne géar** (line 2) and **hundteontig wíntra 7 seofon. 7 xl.** (line 3).

[428] Unsourced; it appears to clash with the information in no. 220.

[429] Lower margin, 4 lines, continuing at bottom of f. 70r, 2 lines, with *signes de renvoi* 'hwær/hær' and crosses.

[430] Written above the main block of writing, alongside the *signe de renvoi*.

toil and sweat I sought; that he also says “upon your brothers” shows that Joseph gave it without a casting of lots.[431]

F. 70r OE = Genesis 48:2–22; no illustrations.

226. (gloss, line 37 of OE) **Ic sille þe anne** [*written* **anme**] **dæl** `i*d est* sychem´ **tofóran þinum broþrum** (cf. HS 1136B)

I will give to you a share that is Sichem **before your brothers.**

227. (bottom margin, end of second line) § Sychar ante | neapolim. iuxta agru*m* q*ue*m dedit iacob filio suo josep: i*n* q*u*o d*omi*n*u*s n*oste*r atq*ue* saluator. s*ecun*d*u*m eu*a*ngeliu*m* ioh*ann*is | samaritane mulieri ad puteu*m* loq*ui*t*ur* ubi nunc ecclesia fabricata est: ex lat*er*e mo*n*tis garizi*m*:- (SNLH 23.923B/C; Lagarde 154.31; last phrase from NLA PL92.1040; CCSL121.176.257, s.v. “Sychem”)

Sychar in front of Neapolis, by the field which Jacob gave to his son Joseph; in which our Lord and Savior, according to the Gospel of John (ch. 4), spoke to the Samaritan woman by the well where now a church has been built \ on the slope of Mount Garizim.

F. 70v *Illustrations:* Two frames: upper, left, Joseph with Manasses and Effraim visit Jacob, and right, Jacob blesses Effraim against Joseph’s will; lower, left, Jacob blesses his sons and indicates, right, that he is to be buried with Abraham and Sarra, depicted in their tomb on right. **OE** = Genesis 49:1, 28–32, 50:1–3

228. His temporib*us* Mortuu*s* est fili*us* pharaonis. de uulnere lapidis beniamin. Et doluit filiu*m* suu*m* phá|rao ualde. et ex dolore `in´firmat*us* e*st*. Et mortuu*s* e*st* pharao annor*um* nonaginta nouem. Et reliq*u*it regnu*m* suu*m* | joseph. Et regnauit ioseph annis .xl 7 viii. in egipto. Et po*st* hec dedit diadema filio[432] pharaonis q*ui*

[431] The placement of this note raises complex issues: it refers, first, to Genesis 48:22 in OE at the bottom of f. 70r, “the portion” given to Joseph by his father indicated by the gloss about Sichem added at line 35 (no.226; cf. also no. 227); second, the comment correlates this with the revenge over the Sichemites (Genesis 34); third, Sichem is interpreted “on the shoulder,” which correlates to the illustration on f. 69v, lower left panel, which shows a man touching his left shoulder with his right hand, which the annotator might have (probably correctly) taken as representing Manasses and Ephraim (Dodwell and Clemoes, *Illustrated Hexateuch*, 30: “Joseph is called to Jacob,” but the picture is of two young men), the pictures on f. 69v seeming to have been touched up or finished by a twelfth-century artist (this retoucher has also worked on the picture on f. 128r); fourth, the comment seems to fill in for the missing text signalled by the remark in the main OE text on f. 70v/3–4: **He hím ræde þa. swa hít on þære ledenbéc awriten is rǽde | þær se þé wille.**

[432] ‘suo’, cancelled after ‘filio’.

| erat ad ubera quando mortuu*s* e*st* pharao. Et ioseph nuncupat*us* est pat*er* ei*us* in t*er*ra egipti;- (conclusion of *Livre de Aseneth*, ed. Batiffol, 114–15)

In these times the son of Pharaoh died from the wound of the stone of Benjamin. And Pharaoh grieved over his son very much and became sick from his grief. And Pharaoh died in his ninety-ninth year. And he left his kingdom to Joseph. And Joseph reigned for forty-eight years in Egypt. And after this he gave the crown to the son of Pharaoh who was a suckling when Pharaoh died. And Joseph was proclaimed his father in the land of Egypt.

229. (lower frame, above upper ledger 1 line, and then within, 3 lines) § Normann*us* dicit. / Cura fuit s*anct*is sepeliri in t*er*ra in qua sciebant chr*istu*m (.) resurrectur*um*. ut cu*m* | eo resurgerent·ʼ distat e*ni*m abrahamium á caluaria·ʼ fere. xxx. milib*us*. | ad littera*m*. de diuisione terre et de statu tribuu*m* fut*uro* p*r*oph*et*auit. ap*er*|tissime uero·ʼ de utroq*ue* chr*ist*i aduentu·ʼ (HS 1135B/C, 1136B)

Normannus says: Care was taken to bury the saints in the (very) earth in which they knew Christ was to be resurrected so that they would rise with him. The tomb of Abraham is thirty miles from Calvary. \ According to the letter (Genesis 49) he prophesied about the division of the earth (among the twelve sons), and about the future state of the tribes, as well as perfectly plainly about the two advents of Christ.

F. 71r *Illustrations:* Two frames: upper, weeping for Jacob; below, two informal registers, above, Joseph gets permission from Pharaoh to bury Jacob in Canaan, lower, the cortege bearing Jacob's body leaves Egypt **OE** = Genesis 50:4–9

230. § Joseph u*ero* p*re*cepit medicis ut co*n*dirent eu*m* aromatib*us* 7 *cus*todierunt eu*m* egyptii·ʼ xl. dieb*us*. Hebrei. saruaueru*nt* [*sic*] | igit*ur*. et ip*s*i i`a´cob[i]·ʼ dieb*us* xxx. 7 ita·ʼ sub a*m*bor*um* *cus*todia. t*ran*sierunt dies .lxx. Aiunt .xxx. dieb*us* eos pla*n*gunt. i*d est* spec*i*ales | missas sub nu*mer*o tot dieru*m* p*ro* eis celebrant. Q*ui*da*m* terci*am* die*m* maxime celebrant. p*ro* sp*irit*u. anima. 7 corp*or*e. Alii·ʼ / septima*m*. q*uia* tr*an*seunt `m´ortui. ad septimam q*u*ietis. vel p*ro* septenario anime. 7 corporis. (HS 1140 C/D)

Joseph commanded the physicians "to embalm him with ointments" (Gen. 50:25) and the Egyptians preserved him for forty days. . . . The Hebrews therefore also attended Jacob personally for thirty days and so under the care of both (Egyptians and Hebrews) seventy days passed. . . . They say that they mourn for thirty days, that is, they celebrate special rites for them under the number of that many days. Some observe the third day most solemnly, for the sake of spirit, soul, and body. Others observe the seventh day because the dead cross over to the seventh resting place, or for the sake of the septenary of soul and body.

F. 71v *Illustrations:* Two frames: above, funeral cortege, with wagons, continues; below, two informal registers, above, mourning in a pavilion for Jacob, Canaanites looking on, below, another scene of funeral cortege. **OE** = Genesis 50:10–13

231. Habitatio au*tem* filior*um* isr*ahe*l qua habitau*er*unt i*n* egipto. 7 in t*er*ra chanaan. ip*s*i 7 patres eoru*m*: | anni quadrigenti t*re*ginta. Qua*m* necessario seq*u*`e´nda*m*. et ip*s*a heb*re*ica u*er*ritas [*sic*] ostendit. | Que narrat caath filiu*m* leui que*m* natu*m* e*ss*e. constat i*n* t*er*ra c`h´anaan uixisse annos centu*m* | t*re*ginta tres. et filiu*m* ei*us* amra*m* patre*m* moysi. centu*m* t*ri*ginta septe*m* annoru*m*. (DTR 90.527 C/D)

"The abode of the sons of Israel which they inhabited in Egypt" and in the land of Chanaan, themselves and their fathers, "was 430 years" (cf. Ex. 12:40). Which is necessarily to be followed and the Hebrew truth demonstrates it, narrating that Caath was the son of Levi, who, it is agreed, was born in the land of Chanaan and lived for 133 years and his son Amram, the father of Moses, for 137 years.

232.[433] Sed timentes bella: deuiauerunt ab itinere | retro.[434] ueneruntq*ue* ad aream adad ubi postea populu*s* murmurans contra d*eu*m. diuino igne consumptus est: | Et planxerunt ibi diebus. vii. 7 *cetera*. (HS 1141A)[435]

But fearing war, they turned back from their journey and they came to the territory of Adad where later the people, murmuring against God, were consumed by divine fire. And they mourned there for seven days, etc.

233.[436] § Jacob filius ysaac natus in t*er*ra chanaan. p*ro*phetans de chr*ist*o et uocatione gentium obiit. ‖ in egipto annor*um* centu*m* quadraginta septe*m*. et sepultus est in cariatharbe: | .Joseph quinq*u*aginta sex. annor*um* erat. (cf. Jerome/Rufinus tr. of Eusebius, *Chronica*, PL 27.147–48)

Jacob the son of Isaac, born in the land of Chanaan, prophesying Christ and the calling of the Gentiles, died in Egypt when he was 147 years old and is buried in Cariatharbe. Joseph was fifty-six years old.

F. 72r *Illustrations:* Two frames: upper, burial of Jacob (labeled 'iacob'); lower, two informal registers, Joseph and his brothers return to Egypt, on horseback and wagons. **OE** = Genesis 50:14–20

433 Above and in lower frame, 3 lines; *signes de renvoi* '+' indicate this pertains to OE three lines up from it: 7 **þær mærlice þæt líc be|hwurfon míd miclum wópe.**

434 *Sylwan* a recto itinere] ab itinere recto *Tr y*

435 A few letters and a partial line beneath erased, apparently the same note as is written overleaf on f. 72r (no. 234).

436 Bottom margin, 1 line, appearing to continue to top of f. 72r, 2 lines.

234. (in upper picture space) et tandem redeundes [*sic*] ad uiam *tran*|sito iordane: sepelierunt- | eum in spelu`n´ca duplici: 7 *cetera*. (HS 1141A)

Finally, returning to the journey, the Jordan crossed, "they buried him in a double cave," etc. (Gen. 50:13)

235.[437] **a** § Filie discurrerunt p*er* muru*m* . hic[438] notat. | q*uia* iosep transeunte p*er* egiptu*m*: mulieres ascendebant muros. ut uid*er*ent | **b** ei*us* pulc*r*itudine*m*. Exasp*er*auerunt eu*m*. 7 iurgati sunt. Inuid*erunt*q*ue* illi habentes iacula: hic[439] de f*ratr*ib*us* ei*us*. vel de | **c** uiris egiptiis.[440] qui iaculis inuidie armati su[n]t. contra eum: sedit i*n* forti[441] arc*us* ei*us* i*d est* in d*omi*no. et i*deo*: dissoluta | sunt uincula brachior*um* 7 manuu*m* ei*us*:[442](.) p*er* manu*m*[443] potentis iacob: i*d est* d*eus*[444] q*ui* est potentia iacob: soluit uincula quib*us* | ligauerant eu*m* f*ra*t*re*s. pastor(.) egressus est: lapis isr*ahe*l. q*uia* de eo (.) ieroboam. q*ui* fortiter rexit isr*ahe*l. i*d est* .x. tribus: ‖ vel pastor toti*us* familie p*atr*is in egipto. hebre*us* h*abe*t in*de*[445] pastoru*m* lapide*m* in isr*ahe*l uberu*m* et uulue. ordo | conuersus.[446] *pro* conceptione et nutricacione [*sic*] ponitur. (HS 1139 B/C)

"The daughters run back and forth on the wall" (Gen. 49:22): this is noted because as Joseph crossed through Egypt women went up on the wall in order to observe his beauty. "They irritated him and were quarreling, those having darts envied him" (Gen. 49:23): here it refers to his brothers or of the men of Egypt who were armed with the darts of envy against him. "His bow rested on the strong" (Gen. 49:24), that is, in the Lord and "therefore the bonds of his arms and hands are loosened through the hand of the mighty one of Jacob" (Gen. 49:24), that is, God, who is the power of Jacob, loosens the bonds with which his brothers bound him. . . . "He came out a shepherd, the stone of Israel" (Gen. 49:24) because from him (came) Jeroboam who strongly ruled Israel, that is, the ten tribes, or (because he was) the shepherd of the entire family of the father in Egypt. The Hebrew says "stone of shepherds in Israel" (Gen. 49:24). . . . "Of the breast and the womb" (Gen. 49:25), the order is reversed . . . it stands for conception and nourishing.

---

[437] Lower frame, 2 lines in upper ledger, 1 line in lower ledger, bottom margin 3 lines, continuing top margin of f. 72v, 2 lines; on f. 72r, marks **a**, **b**, **c** are at the beginning of each segment; the verses commented on (Genesis 49:22–24) are not translated in the main OE.

[438] *Sylwan* hoc] hic *Cl β δ*

[439] *Sylwan* hoc] hic *Cl Tr*

[440] *Sylwan* uel de u. e. *add. Cl L*, marg. *Pa*, add et exp. *T*

[441] *Sylwan* fortitudine] forti *Cl β γ δ*

[442] *Sylwan* illius] eius *Cl β*

[443] *Sylwan* manus] manum *Cl α*

[444] *Sylwan* dei] deus *Cl Tr γ δ*

[445] *Sylwan* tamen] inde *Cl γ T*

[446] *Sylwan* quod] *om. Cl W*

F. 72v *Illustrations:* two frames: upper, Jacob's brothers pleading with him for forgiveness. Between the frames the OE text of Exodus begins, line 3. Lower frame, corpse of Joseph, surrounded by his brothers; **OE** = Genesis 50:20–23, Exodus 1:1–7[447]

236. (margin, and then along top ledger of upper frame) Joseph. centum | annor*um* 7 decem. | obiit. i*n* egipto. | Cui*us* ossa *tran*[s]tule|runt filii isr*ahe*l. | in sichem ciuita|te*m* patris sui. | q*ue* e*st* Neopolis urbs samaritanorum: po*st* cui*us* interitu*m* hebrei egiptiis seruierunt annis centu*m* q*u*adragin/ta Quatuor. (Isidore, *De ort. et ob. pat.*, PL 83.134C/D)

Joseph died 110 years old in Egypt, whose bones the sons of Israel carried to Sichem, the city of his father which is the city of Neapolis of the Samaritans. After his death the Hebrews served the Egyptians for 144 years.

237.[448] § Leui c*entum* annor*um*. 7 xxxvii. obiit. i*n* egipto. Chat fili*us* ei*us*. c*entum* xxxiii^{ta}. amram fili*us* ei*us*. c*entum*.7 xxxvii- | § chaat filiu*m* [*recte* filius] leui genuit- | amram quatuor annis post morte*m* ioseph-[449]

Levi died 137 years old in Egypt. Chaat his son was 133 (when he died) and, Amram his son was 137. Chaat the son of Levi begot Amram four years after the death of Joseph.

238. (7 irregular lines in picture space of bottom frame) Aitq*ue* fr*atr*ib*us* suis asportate ossa mea uobis|cu*m* cumq*ue* adiuras(.)et | eos sup*er* hoc: mortuus est. 7 condit*us* aromatib*us*. | Reposit*us* est i*n* loco[450] in egipto. nec motus: | donec egressi (.) sunt filii isr*ahe*l de egipto. | alii fr*atr*es sec*und*um iosephu*m*: quisq*ue* in obitu suo deferebant*ur*. | 7 sepeliebantur in ebron.[451] post t*ra*ns`l´ati sunt in sichem: (HS 1142A)[452]

And he said to his brothers . . . "carry my bones with you" (Gen. 50:24) . . . and having commanded them about this, "he died and was embalmed. He was buried in a place in Egypt" (Gen. 50:25) nor indeed was he moved until the sons of Israel went out of Egypt. The other brothers, according to Josephus, were car-

[447] The OE text of Exodus begins in lower block, line 3 (8 lines of OE = Exodus 1:1–7, last word of Genesis **lande** appears crowded in, as if the starting place for Exodus had already been determined, which begins with no rubric or other indication of a major section division, just a large colored capital: **Ðis sind israhela bearna naman**. Crawford notes some additional lines at this place recorded by Wanley from Otho B. x, but these lines are not translating Genesis; see discussion, 334–35, below.

[448] Bottom ledger of upper frame, down to top of upper frame, 2 lines.

[449] The exact source of the wording not identified; cf. Ex. 6:16–20, DTR 66.46 (CCSL 123B,471), and HS 1096B.

[450] *Sylwan* loco] loculo *S β γ δ*

[451] *Sylwan* Hebron] ebron *Cl S*

[452] HS "Genesis" (and Sylwan's edition) ends here.

ried off after their deaths and buried in Hebron and afterwards (their bones) were translated to Sichem.

239.[453] **a** § Su`r´rexit igit*ur* rex nouus in egipto:· long[o][454] tempore post mortem iosep. ab illo e*ni*m sub quo fuit iosep. q*ui* p*ro*prio no|mine ne*m*phres [*sic, recte* nephres]:· octauus regnauit ammonophis:· sub quo natus est moyses. regno au*tem* t*ra*nslato ad alia*m* domu*m* || **b** Rex ille ignorauit beneficia iosep:· q*ue* contulerit egipto:· 7 odiebat isr*ahe*l. (HS 1141B/C)

"There arose therefore a new king in Egypt" (Ex. 1:8) a long time after the death of Joseph. Ammonophis reigned as the eighth king after the king under whom Joseph served, whose own name (was) Nephres; Moses was born in the reign of Ammonophis. Because the power had been transferred to another dynasty, that king . . . was ignorant of the benefits Joseph had conferred on Egypt and he hated Israel.

F. 73r *Illustrations:* Two frames: upper, the "new king" among his councilors; lower, two panels, left, taskmasters overseeing Hebrew slaves, in "Phiton," and, right, similar scene, representing "Rameses" (no. 241, written in the frames, also serve as picture labels). **OE** = Exodus 1:8–14

240. (top, first line slightly trimmed) § fiunt au*tem* om*ne*s anni q*ui*b*us* hebrei i*n* egipto fuerunt. ducenti. qu*in*decim. q*ui* ab eo conputant t`e´mpore.[455]| (. .) q*uo* iacob cu*m* filiis suis descendit in egiptum:· Amram gen*uit* Moysen. cu*m* esset anno*rum* sexaginta. / ex matre iochabeth.[456]

All the years in which the Hebrews were in Egypt come to 250, as was calculated from the time when Jacob went down into Egypt with his sons. \ Amram begot Moses when he was 60 years old by his mother Jocabeth.

241. (in lower frame) .phiton. 7 ramesses. Erant q*uidem* i*n* finib*us* egipti- (HS 1141D)[457]

Phiton and Ramesses were certainly in the territory of Egypt.

---

[453] Bottom margin, 2 lines, the separated parts marked 'a', 'b', continuing to middle of f. 73r, bottom ledger of upper frame. Apparently the continuing part is placed where it is on f. 73r so as to serve as a title to the picture of the new pharaoh above it.

[454] An obscured letter at the end of this word, probably 'i' imperfectly altered to 'o'.

[455] Written 'tộmp*er*ore'.

[456] Both parts of this item are unsourced and Amram's years do not correspond with other sources (cf. Julianus Hilarianus, *Chronologia*, PL 13.1100D, Hrabanus, *Comm. in Ex.*, PL 108.11D). The last sentence is fainter, washed off, and incomplete and occurs again as no. 243 on f. 73v.

[457] 'phiton', part of the HS comment, is written over in the left panel as if it were the picture label and the rest is written in the "Ramesses" panel.

242. (bottom margin) § Et quadringentos annos in his miseriis expenderunt i*d est* compleuerunt:- (HS 1142B)

And. . . they spent, that is, filled, forty years in these miseries.

F. 73v *Illustrations:* Two frames: upper, the two midwives before Pharaoh; lower, right, midwives rebuked by Pharaoh, on left, Hebrews multiply. **OE** = Exodus 1:15–22

243. § AMRam genuit Moysen: cu*m* esset annor*um* sexaginta. ex matre iochabeth. et po*st*ea uixit annos septu[a]/ginta septe*m*. (cf. no. 240)

Amram begot Moses when he was 60 years old by his mother Jocabeth \ and afterwards he (Amram) lived 77 years.

244.[458] § Hec nomina filiorum leui p*er* cognationes suas. Gerson. & Caat. & merari. filii gerson. lobem. et | semei. Filii . caat. amram. & isuar. et hebron. 7 oziel. Filii merari. mooli. et mousi: Accepit au*tem* | amra*m* uxore*m* iocabed patruele*m* sua*m*. que `pep*er*it´ ei aaron. 7 Moysen. 7 maria*m*. (= Exodus 6:16–20, '7 maria*m*' from LXX, via HS 1149A?)

"These are the names of the sons of Levi by their kindreds: Gerson and Caath, and Merari. . . . The sons of Gerson: Lobni and Demi. . . . The sons of Caath: Amram and Issar, and Hebron, and Oziel. . . . The sons of Merari: Moholi and Musi. . . . And Amram took to wife Jochabed his aunt by the father's side and she bore him Aaron and Moses" and Mariam.

F. 74rv inserted twelfth-century leaf containing Latin annotations from various sources.

Recto:

245a. Excerpts from Ps.-Jerome, *Quaest. in 1 Paral.* (PL 23): Acham fili*us* carmi: in iosue acham i*d est* coluber insidians. in paralipomenon achar. i*d est* t*ur*bator. Clubai | u*e*l chalubi fili*us* esro*m* filii phares. filii iuda: ip*s*e *est* chaleb *ue*l chaleph fili*us* ieffone. Chaleb ip*s*e duxit uxore*m*. | azuba ex q*ua* nat*us* gerioth. Duxit 7 alia*m* uxore*m* no*min*e ephrata. ex q*ua* suscepit hur uiru*m* Marie sororis | Moysi fr*atr*em uri. auu*m* beseleel. Cenezeus. de loco q*u*i uocat*ur* chanaz. In paralipomenon clubai canis | m*eu*s. in iosue 7 eptatico chaleb canis. Esrom 7 ieffone unu*m* e*st*. Cu*m* mortu*us* e*s*set esrom: ing[r]`e´ssus e*st* | chaleb ad effrata. I*c*ci*r*co uocat*ur* chaleb effrata q*u*ia `caleb´ fuit uir effrate. I*c*ci*r*co d*icitu*r esrom. lx^ta^. annos habuisse | q*uan*d*o* accepit filia*m* uxore*m* machir: ut monstret*ur* per annor*um* num*er*um & de egypto istum[459] egres|sum fuisse: & in terram rep*ro*missionis

[458] Bottom margin, style of writing fluctuates; cf. ch. 4, 241.

[459] Altered from 'egipto illum'.

uenisse. Quia a .xx^{ti}. annis & sup*ra* ad prelium[460] de|scribeba*ntur* usq*ue* ad an-nu*m* sexagesimu*m*. Ab anno sexagesimo & leuite minist*ra*re. & pugna|re milites desineb*an*t. Vnde & romani eos em*er*itos uoca*n*t quia `u*el* d.´[461] ia*m* militare desierunt. (1368A/B)

§In paral*ipomenon* ysai fili*us* obed. i*d est* sac*r*ificiu*m* meu*m* `In regu*m* u*er*o gissai[462] i*d est* sac*r*ificiu*m*.´ Fili*us* ysai abinadab. Ran fili*us* aminadab. In parali*pomenon* symma. | in regu*m* samma. Samma ibide*m*. Symmaa exaudibilis. § In paral*ipomenon* abysa`y´ fili*us* saruie. i*d est* pat*er* sac*r*ificii. | in Regu*m* abysai[463] pa*ter* m*eus* sac*r*ificiu*m*. (1368C)

§ Oazar `*ue*l Gazez´ i*d est* tonsor fili*us* haran[464] filii caleph: ip*s*e e*st* nabal carmel*us*. | Effran. `i*d est* ephrat´ q*u*ia de effraim fuit ab ei*us* no*min*e bethleem effrata uocat*ur*. § Jair iudex q*u*i in iudicu*m* sc*r*ibit*ur* | fili*us* segur `*ue*l at´[465] filii esrom(.): i*c*ci*r*co in iudicu*m* galaadites putat*ur*. & esron dux*it* filia*m* machir pat*r*is galaaht. | uxore*m*. Viculos & lx<sup>ta</sup> ciuitate[s] suscepit iahir in hereditate*m*. eo q*uo*d e*ss*et auia ei*us* filia machir filii manasse. | Assu`u´r fili*us* esron: p*a*t*er* thecue. Thecue e*st* ciuitas: de q*u*a su*m*psit ioab mulier*em* sapie*n*tem. Ona*m* fili*us* iarame|el[466] filii esron accepit no*m*e*n* ona*n* filii iuda q*u*i mortu*us* e*st* 7 in eo differ*unt* q*uo*d fili*us* iude in hebreo p*er* Nvn. | fili*us* u*er*o iarameel p*er* mem sc*r*ibit*ur*.[467] (1369A/B)

Filii ezra. iether. & mered. efer & iaalon. Ezra int*er*pretat*ur* au|xiliu*m*. Ip*su*m eni*m* dic*un*t amra*m* patrem Moysi & aaron `Iether int*er*p*retatu*r residuu*m*. Ip*s*e est aaron.´ Mered rebellans: ip*s*e Moyses. Eser i*d est* fict*us*.[468](. .)| Esr*em*[469] puluis: ip*s*e eldat. Iaalon ylex[470] ip*s*e e*st* medat. ide*m* duo s*un*t q*u*i proph*et*aba*n*t. Tradit*ur* eni*m* Moyse*s* | po*st* accepta*m* lege*m* in he(.)remo. patri iniunxisse ut mat*r*em dimitt*er*et. eo q*uo*d ei*us* amita e*ss*et | filia `e*n*im´[471] fuit leui. po*st* cui*us* discidiu*m*[472] duxisse alia*m* uxore*m* amran fert*ur*: ex q*u*a suscepit hos | duos filios eldad & meldad. Quod u*er*o seq*u*it*ur* genuitq*ue* Maria*m* & sa*m*mai[473]& iesba

---

460 PL "præliandum."

461 i.e., 'uel quid'; PL "qui."

462 Cf. Jerome, *Lib. Int. Hebr. Nom.* (CCSL 72, 36.3): "Iessai insulae sacrificium uel incensum."

463 The scribe has skipped from or confused "Abisai, [filius Sarviae, id est, pater sacrificii]" to/with "[Abisa] pater meus, sacrificium."

464 Altered from 'haron'.

465 I.e., "segat," PL "Segab."

466 'e' written above first 'a'; Vulgate "Jerameel."

467 Written above 'uel bun', i.e., "scribuntur."

468 Written 'ficti*us*'. "Esser fictus" Jerome, LHN 5.25.

469 PL "Effer pulvius."

470 PL "Jalon, lex."

471 On the line 'ł', cancelled; PL has "eo quod illius amita esset."

472 "divorce"; PL has "dissidium," "disagreement, separation."

473 'sammabi', 'b' cancelled.

pat*r*em | est(.)amoa:·[474] Sa*m*mahi[475] mosysen [*sic*] intelligi uolu*n*t. q*u*i int*er*p*re*tat*ur* celestis:· iesba aaro*n* qui | i*n*t*er*p*re*t*ur* collaudatio. pat*r*em estramoha.[476] i*d est* ignem[477] mane*n*te[m][478] eo q*uo*d filii aaron[479] i*n* assiduis sac*r*i|ficiis igne uteba*n*t*ur*. Q*uo*d seq*uitu*r uxor ei*us* iudaia[480] `genuit iered. iudea´ ip*s*a e*st* iochabed mat*er* Moysi. No*min*a u*er*o | q*ue* sequ*untu*r. pene o*mn*ia Moysi no*min*a intelligi uol*un*t q*ui*[a] i*deo* `i´ared uocat*ur*. i*d est* descende*n*s q*uo*d de mo*n*te de[s]ce*nde*rit. | Pat*er* gedor. i*d est* sepiu*m*:· eo q*uo*d q*ua*si q*u*eda*m* sepis[481] lege ci*r*cu*m*[*de*]d*er*it pop*ul*um. (1372B/C) Q*uo*d u*er*o seq*uitu*r. hi au*tem* filii bethia[482] filie pha|raonis. q*ua*m accepit mered:· filia*m* pharaonis icci*r*co i*n* hoc loco 7 mat*r*em Moysi uocat 7 i*n*t*er*p*re*t*atur* filia | d*omi*ni. p*ro*pt*er* bona*m* uolu*n*tate*m* q*uam* in nut*r*iendo puero habuerit. 7 a mared i*d est* Moyse accepta d*icitu*r eo q*uo*d | relictis ydolor*um* cultib*us* ad d*e*i cultutu*m* [*sic*] *con*u*er*sa sit. (1372C/D)

§[483] Charmi pat*er* ceila. et estamoha q*u*i fuit de Machati. Ceila n*omen* loci e*st*:· Machati simili*ter*. Simon | pat*er* amnon. 7 rinma fili*us* fuit estamoha. filii jodia. filii asrael. filii aiaileel.[484] filii chamaz:· | filii sela. filii juda. (1372D-73A)

Acham the son of Charmi: in Joshua (7:1) 'Acham', that is 'snake in the grass', in Paralipomenon (1 Para. 2:7) 'Achar', that is 'disturber'. Clubai or Chalubi the son of Esrom, the son of Phares, the son of Juda (cf. 1 Para. 2:3–9); he is the Chaleb or Chaleph son of Ieffone (Num. 13:7).[485] Caleb . . . took to wife Azuba from whom was born Gerioth (1 Para. 2:18). And he took another wife by the name of Ephrata from whom was born Hur the husband of Mariam, the sister of Moses, and the brother of Uri (1 Para. 2:19–20[486]) and the grandfather of Beseleel (Ex. 38:22); [Caleb] the Cenezite from a place called 'Chanaz'.[487] In Paralipomenon Clubai means 'my dog'; in Joshua and the Heptateuch Chaleb is

[474] Altered from '-hamaha', Vulgate "Esthamo," 1 Para. 4:17.

[475] 'h' altered from 'n'.

[476] Altered from 'estramaha'.

[477] Altered from 'igniis'.

[478] 'manentes', with stroke above 's'; PL "manentem."

[479] Altered from 'airon'.

[480] 'aia' cancelled, 'ea' inserted above; PL "indaia." The source is 1 Para. 4:18: "Uxor quoque ejus [Esthamo] Judaia, peperit Jared."

[481] Altered from 'sepe', PL "sepe."

[482] Altered from 'bethie'.

[483] This passage, marked by a conspicuous change of ductus, though continuing from the same source, is exceptionally corrupt and the selection of passages is broken. The margins are also wider by the width of several letters on each side.

[484] Correctly "Jalaheel."

[485] Cf. L. Ginzberg, *Die Haggada bei den Kirchenvatern: Erster Theil, Die Haggada in den pseudo-hieronymianischen "Quaestiones"* (Heidelberg, 1899), 90–92.

[486] In Paralipomenon Uri is the son of Hur.

[487] Joshua 14:6: "Caleb, filius Jephone, Cenezaeus"; cf. 1 Para. 2:23–24.

'dog'. Esrom and Ieffone is one (name).[488] When . . . Esrom died Caleb went into Ephrata (1 Para. 2:24). Caleb is called 'Ephrata' because he was the husband of Ephrata. Therefor it is said that Esrom was sixty years old when he took as wife the daughter of Machir (1 Para. 2:21) as may be shown by the number of years both that this man came out of Egypt and into the promised land, because from the twentieth year and above to the sixtieth is designated for warfare (cf. Num. 1:3; cf. Lev. 27:3). From the sixtieth year Levites ceased ministering and soldiers ceased fighting, for which reason the Romans call them 'emeriti' because they have stopped doing military service.[489]

In Paralipomenon Isai the son of Obed (1 Para. 2:12), that is 'my sacrifice' (in Kings [1 Kings 14:49] Jessui is 'sacrifice'). The son of Isai was Abinadab. (Aminadab the son of Ran.[490]) In Paralipomenon Simmaa (1 Para. 2:13), in Kings Samma (1 Kings 16:9), Samma being the same person;[491] Symma means 'heard clearly'. In Paralipomenon Abysai is the son of Sarvia (1 Para. 2:16), that is 'father of the sacrifice'. In Kings (2 Kings 2:18) Abysai means 'my father, a sacrifice'.

Oazar (or Gazez) that is 'shearer', son of Haran the son of Caleb, he is Nabal the Carmelite (2 Para. 2:46, 1 Kings 25:3). Ephran (that is Ephrat), because he was from Ephraim; Bethlehem was called 'Ephrata' from his name (cf. 1 Para. 4:4, Mich. 5:2). Jair a judge who in Judges is inscribed the son of Segur (or Segat) the son of Esrom.[492] Therefore in Judges (10:3) he is reckoned of the Galaadites (for) Esron married the daughter of Machir the father of Galaad (1 Para. 2:21). Jair received villages and sixty cities as an inheritance (1 Para. 2:23) because his grandmother was the daughter of Machir the son of Manasses (1 Para. 7:14). Ashur the son of Esron, the father of Thecua (1 Para. 2:24). Thecua is a city from which Joab took a wise woman (2 Kings 14:2). Onam son of Jerameel son of Esron (1 Para. 2:25–26); the son of Juda had the name Onan (1 Para. 2:3) who died and the names differ in this regard, that the son of Juda is written with an 'n' and the son of Jerameel with an 'm'.

The sons of Esra, Jether and Mered and Efer and Jaalon (1 Para. 4:17). Esra is interpreted 'help'. They say he was Amram the father of Moses and Aaron. (Jether is interpreted 'remainder', he is Aaron.) Mered (is) 'rebelling', he is Moses. Eser, that is 'false'. Eser (is) 'dust,' he is . . .Eldad; Jaalon (is) 'holm-oak',[493] he is Medad, and they are the two who prophesied (Num. 12:26–27). It is held that Moses, after he received the law in the desert, commanded his father to put away

[488] Cf. 1 Para. 2:18 "Caleb vero, filius Hesron," Num. 34:19, "Caleb, filius Jephone."

[489] Cf. Avenary, *Revue de Qumran* 4 (1963–1964), 3, and Ginzberg, *Die Haggada*, 92.

[490] So 1 Para. 2:10; the text should read "aminadab filius ran."

[491] I.e., the son of Isai.

[492] 1 Para. 2:21–22 "Post haec ingressus est Hesron ad filiam Machir . . . quae peperit ei Segub. Sed et Segub genuit Jair. . . ." Judges 10:3–4 does not mention the forebears of Jair.

[493] So MS 'ylex,' PL 'lex'.

his mother, because she was his (Amram's) paternal aunt (Ex. 6:20); for she was the daughter of Levi; after whose divorce another woman was brought for Amram to marry; from whom were born these two sons, Eldad and Me[l]dad. And it followed that Mariam and Sammai and Jesba the father of Esthamo were born (1 Para. 4:17). Some want Sammai to be understood as Moses, which is interpreted 'heavenly'; Jesba as Aaron, who is interpreted 'great praise'; father of Esthamo, that is 'enduring fire' because the sons of Aaron used fire in continual sacrifice. So it . . . logically follows that his wife Judaia (Judea gave birth to Iered), is (Jochabed) the mother of Moses. Almost all want the names which follow (1 Para. 4:18) to be understood as of Moses, so that Jared is called 'descending', because he descended from the mountain; the father of Gedor, that is 'of hedges', because he surrounded the people with the law like a kind of hedge. Then follows: "these are the sons of Bethia the daughter of Pharaoh, whom Mered married" (1 Para. 4:18). In this place therefore he called the daughter of Pharaoh 'mother of Moses,' also interpreted 'daughter of the Lord' because of the good will she had in the rearing of the boy. And received by Mered, that is, Moses . . . it is said thereafter, that, abandoning the idol-cults, she was converted to the worship of God.

Garmi the father of Ceila and Esthamo who was of Machati (1 Para. 4:19). Ceila is the name of a place. . . . Machati likewise. Simon the father of Amnon and Rinna (1 Para. 4:20), the son was Esthamo, son of Odaia (1 Para. 4:19?), son of Asrael, the son of Jalaleel (1 Para. 4:16), the son of Cenes, the son of Sela, the son of Juda. (1 Para. 4:21)

245b. § Judas. gen*uit*. phares. Q*u*i gen*uit* esrom. Q*u*i. gen*uit*. aram. Q*u*i gen*uit* amina|dab: Q*u*i gen*uit* naason- Q*u*i gen*uit* salmon. Q*u*i. gen*uit* booz. Q*u*i gen*uit* obed: ex RVTH. Q*u*i gen*uit* | ysai:[494] Q*u*i gen*uit* dauid regem- (as Matthew 1:3–5; cf. also Ruth 4:18–22).

Juda who begot Phares who begot Esrom who begot Aram who begot Aminadab who begot Naason who begot Salmon who begot Booz who begot Obed from RUTH, who begot Isai (Jesse) who begot King David.

246. Saba ciuitas regalis ethiopie. q*u*am joseph*us* a ca*m*bise rege Meroen cognominata*m* ex | sororis uocabulo refert. (Jerome, SNLH 23.922C; Lagarde 153.29)

Saba, a royal city of Ethiopia which Josephus records was named by King Cambises of Meroe from the name of his sister.[495]

F. 74v 35 scored lines, part of a 36th written; quadrata = HS Exodus, parts of Ch. 5 and all of Ch. 6.

---

[494] Ruth 4:22 "Obed genuit Isai, Isai genuit David."

[495] This note links up with material overleaf, f. 74v, line 26.

247. (from Ch. 5) Suscepit *er*go a thermuth[496] alendum puerum & ablactatum:· reddidit filie pha|raonis que adoptauit eum in filium. et dictus est mosis. Egyptii eni*m* | mos:· aquam is: saluatum dicunt. Quem dum quadam die thermuth | obtulisset pharaoni ut & ipse eum adoptaret admirans rex pueri uenus|tatem:· coronam forte qua*m* gestabat:· capiti illius imposuit. | Erat aute*m* hamonis imago fabref*acta*.[497] Puer aute*m* coronam p*ro*ie|cit in terram. & fregit. Sacerdos heliopoleos a lat*er*e regis surgens:· | exclamauit. hic est puer que*m* nob*is* d*eus* occidendum monst*ra*uit. ut | de cet*er*o timore careamus. & uoluit irruere in eu*m*. S*ed* auxilio regis | liberat*us* est. & p*er*suasione cuiusda*m* sapientis q*ui* p*er* ignorantia*m* h*oc* e*ss*e | factum a puero asseruit. In cuius rei arg*umentu*m cu*m* prunas allatas puero | obtulisset:· puer eas ori suo apposuit. 7 lingue su*m*mitate*m* igne corrupit. Vn*de* | 7 hebrei eu*m* impeditioris lingue fuisse autumant. Tante u*er*o ut ait iosephus pulcr*i*tu|dinis fuit. ut n*ull*us adeo seuer*us* e*ss*et q*ui* ei*us* asp*ec*tui n*on* h*er*eret. Multiq*ue* du*m* ce[r]nerent eu*m* | p*er* platea*m* ferri:· ocup*ati*ones in q*uibus* studebant deser`e´rent. |

(Ch. 6) [F]actu*m* e*st* cu*m* adult*us* e*ss*et moyses:· ethiopes uastauer*unt* egyptu*m* usq*ue* ad me*m*phim | 7 mare. Q*uo* circa adu*er*si ad diuinationes egypti. respo*n*sum accep*erun*t ut auxili|atore ut*erentur* hebreo. & uix obtinuer*unt* a t*er*muthe:· ut exercitui que*m* parau*er*at moy|sen p*re*ficerent[498] duce*m* pri*us* p*re*stitis sac*ra*mentis ne ei noc*er*ent. Erat aute*m* moyses uir | bellicosus & p*er*itissim*us* q*ui* fluminis it*er* tanq*ua*m longi*us* p*re*termittens:· p*er* terra*m* duxit | ex*er*citu*m* itin*er*e breuiori ut imp*ro*uisos ethiopas [*recte* -es] p*re*ueniret s*ed* p*er* loca plena ser|pentib*us* it*er* faciens tulit in archis papiriis sup*er* plaustran:· ybices. ciconia*s* | *scilicet* egyptias. nat*ura*l*ite*r infestas serpentib*us* q*ue* rostro p*er* posteriora inmisso aluu*m* | p*ur*gant. Castraq*ue* metatur*us*. p*ro*ferebat eas ut serpentes fugare*n*t & deuorare*n*t | & ita tutus p*er* noctes[499] exercit*us* t*ra*nsibat. Tande*m* p*re*uentos ethiopas expugnans:· | inclusit eos fugientes in ciuitate*m* sabba regia*m*. Q*ua*m post ca*m*bises a no*mine* | sororis sue meroe*m* denominauit.[500] Q*ua*m cu*m* q*ui*a i*n*expugnabilis erat diutius | obsedisset:· iniecit oc*u*los suos i*n* eu*m* tharbis filia regis ethiopu*m* 7 ex condicto | t*ra*didit ei ciuitate*m*. si duc*er*et ea*m* uxore*m* & ita f*act*um est. In*de* e*st* q*uo*d maria & aaron iur|gati sunt adu*er*sus moysen p*ro* uxore ei*us* ethiopissa. Dum aute*m* redire uolu|isset. n*on* adq*u*ieuit uxor. P*ro*in*de* tanq*ua*m uir ast*ro*ru*m* p*er*it*us* imagines[501] sculp[s]it i*n* ge*m*mi*s* h*uius* | efficatie:· ut alt*er*a memoria*m*[502] *con*ferret. Cu*mque* parib*us* anulis i*n*seruisse*t* alt*er*um:· *scilicet* obliuio|ni*s* anulu*m* uxori p*re*buit. Alt*eru*m ip*s*e tulit. ut sic*ut* pari amore:· sic parib*us* anulis | insignirent*ur*.

[496] PL "Terimith."

[497] MS 'fabref*act*am', final 'm' cancelled.

[498] PL "paraverant . . . praeficeret."

[499] PL "noctem."

[500] The source of this sentence is copied directly from Jerome as no. 246.

[501] PL "duas imagines."

[502] Omitted are the words "alteram oblivionem."

Cepit *ergo* mulier amoris uiri obliusci. & tande*m* lib*ere* i*n* egiptu*m* rc/gressus est. (HS 1143D-1144D)[503]

(Ch. 5) She [Moses' mother] therefore took over from Thermuth the nursing of the boy and when he was weaned she gave him back to Pharaoh's daughter who adopted him as a son and called him Moses, in Egyptian *mos* meaning 'water' and *is* 'saved'. Thermuth one day brought him before Pharaoh in order that he might adopt him; the king, admiring the boy's beauty, placed the crown which he happened . . . to be wearing on his head. The image of Ammon . . . was worked into it. But the boy threw it on the ground and broke it. A priest . . . of Heliopolis, beside the king, jumping up exclaimed: "This is the boy whom God has revealed to us to kill, so that we may be without fear from henceforth," and he wanted to rush at him but he was protected with the help of the king and by the persuasion of a certain wise man who claimed that this had been done by the boy out of ignorance. As proof of this, when live coals were brought to the boy, he applied them to his mouth and the tip of his tongue was destroyed by fire. The Hebrews claim this was the source of his speech impediment. Such was his beauty, according to Josephus, that there was nobody so severe as not to be snagged by his looks, and many, when they noticed him walking down the street, dropped whatever they were doing.

(Ch. 6) It happened when Moses was grown up that the Ethiopians devastated Egypt as far as Memphis and the sea. Thereupon, turning to the soothsayers, the Egyptians got the response that they should use the Hebrew as a helper. And with difficulty they got from Termuth that they might set Moses in command of the army he had been raising, he having already sworn the military oath lest they harm him. Moses was a warlike man and very skillful who, avoiding the longer journey down the river, led the army by a shorter route in order to intercept the Ethiopians by surprise. But making the journey through a region full of serpents, in baskets ("arks") of papyrus on carts he carried ibises, that is, Egyptian storks, which are naturally aggressive against snakes, and which, thrusting with their beak in their behind, purge their bowels. And when the camp was about to be laid out, he [Moses] brought the ibises to the front so that they might drive away the serpents and devour them, and thus the army passed through the nights safely. Finally, falling on the cut-off Ethiopians, he confined them as they fled into the royal capital of Sabba, which was later named Meroe for the sister of Cambyses. When it had been invested for a long time, for it was impregnable, the daughter of Tharbis, king of Ethiopia, cast her eyes on him [Moses] and by agreement delivered up the city to him on the condition that he take her as wife, and it was done. Whence it is that Mariam and Aaron quarreled with Moses on account of his Ethiopian wife. When he wanted to leave, his wife would not ac-

[503] This is verbally similar in places to Hrabanus *Comm. in Ex.*, PL 108.15–16, and both Hrabanus and HS are substantially and verbally dependent on Josephus, LJ 2.224–253, passim, 201–3.

quiesce. Therefore . . . like a man skilled in astrology, he carved (two) images on gemstones with this power such that one would confer memory, [the other forgetfulness]. When he put them on a pair of rings, one, the ring of forgetfulness, he offered to his wife; the other he took himself that they might be distinguished by similar rings as by similar love. Therefore the woman began to forget the love of her husband and he freely returned to Egypt.

F. 75r *Illustrations:* Two frames: upper in two panels, right, birth of Moses, left, Moses' mother puts him in basket, her sister standing "a way off"; lower, left, Pharaoh's daughter watches as her two maids lift out the basket, right, the sister of Moses offers to send for a nurse.[504] **OE** = Exodus 2:1–10

248. Name-glosses: upper block of main OE, line 7 **7 hys swustor** `maria´; lower block, line 1 **pharaones dohtor** `thermuth´; line 6 **ðæs cildes swustor** `maria´

249.[505] Et cu*m* plures egiptie admouissent ei uber[a][506] ad lactandu*m* faciem auertebat. (HS 1143D)

And when many Egyptian women brought their breasts near to nurse him he turned his face away.

250. (lower block, interlined above line 6) **7 clipie þé án ebreisc wíf þæt þis cild fedan mǽge** `forte hubera sue gentis sequet*ur*.´ (HS 1143D)

and call for you a Hebrew nurse so that the child may feed perchance he may follow the breasts of her people.

251. (within lower frame) egiptii. *enim* mos:· aquam. is:· saluatu*m* dicunt. (HS 1144A)[507]

In Egyptian *mos* means 'water', *is* means 'saved'.

F. 75v *Illustrations:* Two frames, upper, Moses slays the Egyptian, his dead body on left; lower, Moses intervening between the two fighting Hebrews. **OE** = Exodus 2:11–15

[504] The small male figure with a walking stick must represent a messenger about to be sent.

[505] In bottom ledger of upper frame, with a *signe de renvoi* (a crude '+') that correlates it with OE text in lower block, lines 5–6 (see no. 250). Nos. 248–250 form a suite centering around this OE sentence, from a single continuous HS passage (HS 1143D: "Et cum . . . sequetur") occurring just before that copied as the long extract no. 247.

[506] The final letter an illegible smudge.

[507] Occurs also in no. 247, f. 74v/2–3.

252. (bottom margin) § Et cibor*um* inopia*m* ut ait iosep*hus*. | ui*r*tute tol*er*antie sup*er*abat: 7 uenit ad ciuitate*m* madiam ci*r*ca mare rubru*m*.[508] sic nominata*m*: a quoda*m* filio | abrahe de cethura. seditq*ue* i`u´xta puteu*m*. Erant au*tem* sacerdoti madiam. i*d est* primati. q*ui* antiq*uitus* sacerdotes dicebant*ur* vii. filie q*ui* dicebat*ur* | raguel. agnominat*us* ietro. cognominat*us* cyneus. 7 c*etera*. (HS 1145A/B)

And, as Josephus says, he overcame his scanty supplies of food with the virtue of patience and came to the city of Madian near the Red Sea, so called from a certain son of Abraham by Cethura, and he sat next to a well. There were seven daughters of a priest of Madian — that is chief, who from ancient times were called priests — (he) who was named Reuel, surnamed Jethro, nicknamed Cyneus, etc.

F. 76r *Illustrations:* two frames, upper, left, Pharaoh is informed of Moses' deed and, left, in a little panel Moses is shown fleeing; lower frame, Moses prevents the shepherds from driving away the seven daughters of Reuel. **OE** = Exodus 2:16–20 (there are no annotations on this page but no. 252 on facing page refers to this text and picture in lower frame)

Ff. 76v–78r OE = Exodus 2:21–25, 3:1–22, 4:1–19; no annotations

F. 78v *Illustrations:* Two frames: upper, in two panels, right Moses (horned) with his wife Sephora requests leave from his father-in-law Jethro to return to Egypt, left, he returns with his wife and son Gefron; lower, Moses and Aaron kiss in the wilderness. **OE** = Exodus 4:19–28

253. § Mora*m* t*ame*n faciendi: 7[509] it*eru*m dixit d*ominu*s. Vade in egiptu*m*. quia | mortui sunt q*ui* querebant anima*m* tuam. pharao. s*cilicet* et complices ei*us*. Vel pl*ur*ale p*ro* sing*u*lari | ponitur. si solus pharao querebat: (HS 1147A)

But he (Moses) made a delay and the Lord said a second time, . . . "Go into Egypt because those who sought your life are dead" (Ex. 4:19), Pharaoh, that is, as well as his accomplices; or the plural is used for the singular if only Pharaoh was seeking (his life).

Ff. 79r–80r OE = Exodus 4:29–31, 5:1–23, 6:1–5; no annotations

F. 80v *Illustration:* One frame, in two panels: right, Hebrew foremen complain to Pharaoh (? the enthroned figure is uncrowned), left, Moses and Aaron (with his rod) meet the foremen, the hand of God extended to Moses. **OE** = Exodus 6:5–30

508 The ductus reduces at this point.

509 MS '7t', 't' cancelled.

254. lower block, line 4, English glosses in brown ink, **7 heo gebær | twegen súna** `7 áne dohter´. **moyses. 7 aaron** `7 María´ **and amram**[510]

Ff. 81rv OE = Exodus 6:30, 7:1–19; no annotations

F. 82r *Illustrations:* Large double frame divided into two registers: upper, Moses and Aaron turning the Nile into blood, lower, the Egyptians digging for water. **OE** = Exodus 7:20–25, 8:1–2

255.[511] forte non i*n* omnib*us* s*ed* i*n* his q*ue* (.) maneba*n*t [*recte* manabant] | de nilo. foderuntq*ue* puteos magi. iamnes.[512] et mambres. et dicunt q*uo*d allata est aqua de t*er*ra gessem. qua*m* no*n* | p*er*cussit d*ominu*s plagis. p*ro*pter filios isr*ahe*l. q*ui* habitabant in ea. ioseph*us* dic*it* q*u*ia hebreis erat fluuius pota/bilis. licet e*ss*et mutatus- | vn*de* pocius [*sic*] uidetur q*uo*d alibi quod in nilo aqua fuerit i*n* egipto. Et hec p*r*ima plaga. qua p*er*cussit d*ominu*s egiptum:' (HS 1149C/D)

Perhaps not in all (waters) but in those which remained (flowed) from the Nile. . . . The magi Iamnes and Mambres (2 Tim. 3:8) . . . dug wells and said that water had been brought from the land of Gessen, which the Lord did not punish with plagues on account of the sons of Israel who lived in it. . . Josephus says that the river was drinkable for the Hebrews, even though it had been changed; . . . whence it can be seen that in Egypt there was water from elsewhere than the Nile. And this was the first plague with which the Lord struck Egypt.

F. 82v *Illustrations:* Two frames: upper, God (hand of God) announcing the plague of frogs to Moses and Aaron; lower, in two panels, left, God (hand of God) commanding Moses and Aaron to bring forth the frogs, right, Pharaoh, with his councilors, entreating them to take the frogs away. **OE** = Exodus 8:2–11

256. § Sunt t*ame*n tria genera ranoru*m*. Vnu*m* fluuiale et uocale. aliud minimu*m*. quod calamitu*m* dicit*ur*. q*uo*d si p*ro*iciatur in | os canis:' ommutescit. Terciu*m*:' magnu*m*. et uen[en]osu*m*. quod rubeta dicitur. et uulgo crassantium.[513] et c*etera*. (HS 1150B)

---

[510] Cf. HS 1148D–1149A "filii Amram de Jocabed, Aaron, Moyses et Maria."

[511] Placed at the end of the upper block of OE (and continuing into the upper frame and along the register line), as if continuing the text of Exodus 7:25, which interprets rather than translates the Vulgate: **ac hí** [the Egyptians] **né mihton seofon dágum** 'drincan' **of ðam wǽtere | siððan god hét þæt wǽter to blode gewúrðan**. The inserted correcting word `drincan´ (brown ink) is eleventh-century.

[512] PL has the incorrect isolated reading "Tannes."

[513] PL "exassantium." "Crassantium" is the word in the MSS (e.g., BL Royal 4.D.vii, Royal 7.F. iii, Add. 22491), somewhat obscure, but apparently it means "fat frog"; see Antoine Thomas, "'Crassantus' ou 'Craxantus': nom du crapaud chez Eucheria et ailleurs," *Bulletin du Cange* 3 (1927): 49–58. In his extensive discussion of "crassantus" in Spanish

There are three kinds of frogs: one lives in rivers and is tuneful, another is the smallest, that is called a piper; if it is thrown into a dog's mouth, it becomes silent. The third is large and poisonous, which is called a 'bramble-toad', and folks call it 'crassantium', etc.

F. 83r *Illustrations:* Two frames: upper, in two panels, Moses and Aaron, right, with hand of God, depart from Pharaoh in left panel; lower, in two panels, left, Moses and Aaron bring forth gnats, hand of God above, right, Pharaoh, with his magicians. **OE** = Exodus 8:12–19

257. Sunt a*utem* [s]cynifes. musce adeo subtiles. ut uisum nisi acute cernentis effugiant. Et corpu*s* | cui insidunt*:*[514] ac*er*bo stimulo terebant. [*recte* terebrant.] dixeruntq*ue* pharaoni digitu*s* dei e*st* hic.[515] i*d est* sp*iritu*s dei. Sic. *enim* p*er* dextera*m* filiu*s:* Sic p*er* digitu*m* / sp*iritu*s [sanctus] solet accipi. Hec t*r*ia signa facta sunt p*er* manu*m* aaron. Que secunt*ur:* | uel a d*omi*no tantum queda*m*. Vel p*er* moysen. (HS 1150C)

'Scinefes', gnats, are so tiny that they escape all but the most acutely discerning sight. And the body which they settle on they bore into with sharp stings. . . . "And they said to Pharaoh, this is the finger of God" (Ex. 8:19), that is, the Spirit . . . of God. As it is common to understand through the "right hand" the Son, so through the "finger" is understood the (Holy) Spirit. . . . These three signs which follow were done by the hand of Aaron, or some through the Lord alone, or through Moses.

F. 83v *Illustrations:* Two frames: upper, God (hand of God) tells Moses and Aaron to threaten Pharaoh with plague of flies; lower, Pharaoh, with councilors (right), tells Moses and Aaron to sacrifice. **OE** = Exodus 8:20–29

258. cynomia. i*d est* musca canina quod in psalmo[516] legitur. (HS 1150D)

'Cynomia' (coenomya), that is, a dog flea which . . . is read in the Psalm(s) (Pss. 77:45, 105:31).[517]

F. 84r *Illustrations:* Two frames: upper, in two panels, right, Moses and Aaron sacrifice to God (hand of God), left, Pharaoh hardens his heart; lower, (hand

---

and French sources, Thomas does not notice this HS occurrence, doubtless because of the error in the PL text.

514 PL "insident."

515 The "finger (hand) of God" fortuitously occurs in the illustrations on ff. 82v, 83rv, 84r.

516 PL "psalmis."

517 Cf. Isidore, *Etymol.*, PL 82.471A.

of) God telling Moses and Aaron to go to Pharaoh (?). **OE** = Exodus 8:30–32, 9:1–6

259.[518] Animalia domi saruata.[519] ūn [*recte* non] u*er*o quinta `a´ peste p*er*empta: post: ad pascua educta: | vii[a520] plaga grandine p*er*ierunt.[521]

Animals kept at home not in fact destroyed by the fifth plague, afterwards led to pasture, perished by hail in the seventh plague.

Ff. 84v–86v OE = Exodus 9:6–10:11; no annotations

F. 87r *Illustrations:* Two frames: upper, Pharaoh's servants argue with him to let Moses and Aaron, who stand to right, go; lower (mostly empty), Moses, with Aaron, stretching out his hand to bring on the plague of locusts. **OE** = Exodus 10:12–15

260. dicitur autem loc`u´sta quasi longa hasta. q*uia* longiora retro h*abe*t crura: 7 c*etera*. (HS 1152C)

It is said that locusts are like long spears because they have longer back legs, etc.[522]

Ff. 87v–88v OE = Exodus 10:16–29, 11:1–10, 12:1–19, no annotations

F. 89r *Illustrations:* Large frame divided into two registers: upper, Moses, with Aaron, stretching out his hands to bring on the darkness; lower, in two panels, left, Moses before Pharaoh, right, Moses and Aaron before Hebrews. **OE** = Exodus 12:21–27

261.[523]§ Mensis iste erit uobis p*r*imus in mensibus anni. Hic est aprilis. i*d est* lunatio aprilis. que in martio | sepe inchoat. Hic d*icitu*r ab hebreis nisan. apud egiptios: parimuthi. apud macedones. xaneticus: 7 *cetera*. / § Egipt*us* que p*rius*

---

518 This comment pertains to Ex. 9:19–25, the OE of which occurs on f. 85r/12–85v/5. The pictures on these pages are unfinished and not easily read; Dodwell and Clemoes relate the upper frame to Ex. 9:23.

519 For "seruata"; this spelling also occurs in no. 230.

520 Written 'v`a´ii'.

521 The exact wording is unsourced. Cf. Ex. 9, HS 1151B, "Et mortua sunt animantia Aegypti, quae scilicet erant in domibus, quia quae in pascuis erant, post grandine perierunt"; Augustine, *Quaest in Hept.*, PL 34.607, followed by HS 1151D, has "Congregata quae habes in agro homines enim et jumenta feris inventa grandine morientur."

522 Cf. Isidore, *Etymol.*, PL 82.471A.

523 This note strictly pertains to Exodus 12:2, on f. 88r, but may be seen as pertaining generally to the Passover instructions, ff. 88v-89r.

mesrain[524] post aeria: | ab egipto rege subm*erso*: egiptus dicta est: (HS 1153C, 1153B)

"This will be to you the first of the months of the year" (Exodus 12:2). This is April, that is, the lunation of April, which often begins in March. This is called by the Hebrews 'Nisan', by the Egyptians 'Parimuth' [Pharmuthi], by the Greeks (Macedonians) 'Xaneticus', etc. \ 'Egypt', which was first (called) 'Mesraim', then 'Aerea', is called 'Egypt' from the king of Egypt who was drowned.

262.[525]§ Patriarche au*tem* duodecim nati in mesopo|tamia. conditi sunt in egipto: et egredien|tes filii isr*ahe*l ex egipto portauerunt ossa eor[um] | secu*m* et posuerunt ea in sichem. ut Jero|nimus refert.[526]

The twelve patriarchs, born in Mesopotamia, were established in Egypt, and the sons of Israel, going out of Egypt, carried their bones with them and buried them in Sichem, as Jerome mentions.

F. 89v *Illustrations:* Two frames: upper, in two panels, Moses telling the congregation of Israel to institute the Passover, right, in gabled panel, blood is smeared on the doorposts (hand of God points left but hovers over both panels); lower, the deaths of the firstborn of Egypt, ten figures in irregularly shaped frames, representing tombs. **OE** = Exodus 12:28–33

263.[527] factu*m* e*st* aut*em* q*uo*d nilus preter solitu*m* adhuc inundabat t*er*ram: in qua sepulcru*m* ioseph erat. Tenebant*ur*[528] | aut*em* (.)ex iuramento asportare ossa ei*us*. Habitatio aut*em* filior*um* isr*ahe*l in egipto: fuit cccc.xxx annor*um*. Sed | nomine egipti: i*n*telligend*us* est omnis i*n*colat*us* eoru*m* q*ui* incepit á p*ro*missione abrahe facta in uia mesopotamie ‖ á qua usq*ue* ad legem data*m* tot anni fluxerunt. Solis e*ni*m .cxl iiii. annis: seruiuit[529] isr*ahe*l in egipto. | post mortem ioseph. Quib*us* expletis: eade*m* die egressa(.)e*st* omnis multituto de t*er*ra egipti. quod etiam mira|biliter á deo f*actu*m est. Vel forte eade*m* die qua exiuit abraha*m* ad p*er*egri-

[524] 'r' written and cancelled after this word.

[525] Twelve supplementary rulings have been added within the frame, the top one all across, the rest to the right side (notes 261 and 262 occupy only 8 of these lines). In no. 262 the underlined letters are written in reddish-brown ink, same script.

[526] A summary passage; not found in Jerome with this wording but cf. Jerome, HQG (23.1004A, CCSL 72, 66.4); also cf. nos. 236, 238.

[527] Bottom margin, continuing (with marks) on to f. 90r, bottom; *signe de renvoi* 'hwær +' at beginning refers to OE, line 15 on f. 90r, 'her +': **Witodlice moyses nám iosepes bán mid him.**

[528] '-ur' written out, partially erased, and resolution mark added.

[529] Ambiguously written, with an otiose abbreviation mark: the word could easily be read 'seru*er*unt'.

nandum. et Nota quod hic dicit*ur* / q[ua][530] die egressi sunt. et infra∶ (HS 1155B, C/D)

And it happened that the Nile inundated the land in excess of the usual mark along where Joseph's tomb was located. They were held by their oath to carry away his bones. . . . "The residence of the sons of Israel in Egypt was 430 years" (Ex. 12:40). But by the word 'Egypt' is to be understood all their habitation which began with the covenant with Abraham made on the way from Mesopotamia from which up to the giving of the law so many years have passed. Israel toiled in Egypt after the death of Joseph for only 144 years. When this period was completed, on the same day the whole multitude left the land of Egypt, which was done miraculously by God. Or perhaps was meant that it was the same day on which Abraham left on his wanderings, and note it is said both here and below on which "day they went out" (cf. Ex. 13:3).

F. 90r *Illustration:* One frame: Pharaoh, on left with his court, through an officer, tells Moses and Aaron, who are turning away, to leave with their people (on right). **OE** = Exodus 12:34–42, 13:19–22, 14:1–4

264. (correcting gloss in OE, line 7) **neah sixhundred** \`þusend´[531]

265. (in-text comment at line 18) **⁊ wícodon æt etham** \`ubi*que* et babilonem post facta*m* dicit. dum cambises egiptum uastaret-´ **on þam ytemestan ende þæs | wéstenes.** (HS 1157A[532])

and they dwelt at Etham (it says where also Babylon was later built, when Cambyses laid Egypt waste) **and at the outermost region of the desert.**

F. 90v *Illustrations:* One large frame in three registers: upper, Hebrews, with woman at head, receive vessels from Egyptians; middle, Hebrews with Moses and Aaron at head follow pillar of cloud; lower, they follow pillar of fire. **OE** = Exodus 14:4–5

266. § Non eduxit eos Moyses p*er* palestina*m* cont*er*minam egipto∶ p*ro*pter antiqua*m* molestiam et odiu*m* pat*r*is[533] ne insurgerent philistei | aduersus (.)eos∶ Set circu*m*duxit eos p*er* desertu*m* quod e*st* iuxta mare rubrum∶ hoc mare∶ in duos

530 MS 'q*uia*'.

531 In margin: '.c̄c̄c̄c̄c̄c̄'; cf. Ex. 13:37.

532 Text of HS (1156D-1157A) goes: "Profectique de Sochot venerunt in Etham. Etham ciuitas erant tunc deserta in capite solitudinis, quae a Josepho Lycus dicitur, ubi et Babylonem postea factam dicit, dum Cambyses Aegyptum vastaret," etc. ("'And proceeding from Sochot they came to Etham in the outermost edge of the desert' (Ex. 13:20), which Josephus called Lycus . . . ." The following Additio says that this is not the famous Babylon of Nabuchodonosor, but another, near Mt. Sinai.

533 PL "patrum."

sinus diuiditur:˙ Qui | ab oriente est:˙ p*er*sicus ap*pe*ll*atu*r. q*uia* p*er*se hora*m* ei*us* inhabitant. Alter:˙ arabicus d*icitu*r. Vbi tu*m* nos dicim*us* rubru*m*:˙ Hebreis | habet. cannosum. q*uia* canne in litore abundant. sane ibi coartati sunt filii isr*ahe*l. ex una p*ar*te:˙ erant montes | asp*er*rimi. et inmeabiles. ex altera:˙ Mare. (HS 1156C/D, 1157B/C)

Moses did not lead them though Palestine adjacent to Egypt because of the ancient trouble and hate of their father(s), lest the Philistines rise up against them. But he led them around through the desert which is beside the Red Sea. . . . \ This sea is divided into two gulfs; one, towards the east, is called the Persian Gulf because the Persians live along its coast; the other is called the Arabian Gulf. What we call the Red Sea, the Hebrews call 'Reed Sea' because reeds abound along its shores. Surely, the sons of Israel were trapped there. On one side were the jagged and impassable mountains, on the other the sea.

F. 91r *Illustration:* One frame: Pharaoh, repenting, tells his army to pursue the Hebrews. **OE** = Exodus 14:5–18

267. § Tulitq*ue* trecentos currus p*ro*prios:˙ | et trecentos ab egiptiis. et i*n*secutus e*st* eos. Eq*u*ites q*uoque* duxit. l. `q*u*inquaginta ´ milia. et ducenta milia peditu*m* armatoru*m* ⁊ c*etera*. (HS 1157C)

And he took 300 of his own chariots and 300 from the Egyptians and he pursued them and he led also 50,000 horsemen and 200,000 infantry, etc.

268. Relinq*u*eruntq*ue* egiptu*m* me*n*se xan`c´tico. (*added above in frame* 'i*n* me[n]se aprili.') luna q*u*intadecima po*st* annos t*r*iginta et quadringintos qua*m* pater | n*os*-t*er* abraham uenisset in chananeam. p*os*t iacob aute*m* aduentu*m* in egiptu*m* anno ducentesimo et q*u*into;[534] / i*d est* .xxx. et cccc- (Josephus, LJ 2.318, p. 212)

They left Egypt in the month of 'Xanticus' (in the month of April) on the fifteenth day of the moon 430 years after our father Abraham came into Chanaan, and 215 years after Jacob came into Egypt. That is 430.

F. 91v *Illustrations:* Two frames: upper, divided into four registers, with protogothic writing entered between each segment, the top three show the chariots (depicted as two-axle oxcarts) of Pharaoh in pursuit, the lower the Egyptian foot army, pursuing; lower frame: Moses parting the sea, east wind blowing from right. **OE** = Exodus 14:21–22

269.[535] a § Huic *e*rgo abraha*m* pater septim*us* erat. Erat eni*m* iste filiu*s* amarami. [*sic*] q*u*i fuit de pat*r*e caath. q*ui* nat*us* e*st* de leui. | leui uero de iacob:˙ q*ui* fuit ex

[534] LJ "quintodecimo."

[535] Written on 10 widely-spaced lines in and along ledgers of top four registers and, exceptionally, through the picture spaces, using the pinholes of the chariot wheel designs

isaac filio abraha*m*: leui gen*uit* caath. q*ui* cu*m* pat*re* suo leui. i*n*gress*us* e*st* egiptum. (Josephus, LJ 2.229, p. 200)

b Caath gen*uit* amra*m* q*ui* aaron. q*ui* eliazar. q*ui* finees. Rurs*us* [*sic*] eliazar cu*m* pat*re* suo ááron egress*us* e*st* de | egipto- (Jerome, Ep. 36, Ad Damasum, PL 22.457)

§ Moyses autem erat q*ui*dem anno octogesimo. frat*er* aute*m* ei*us* ááron maior tribus annis existebat. Tamem [*sic*] alia t*ra*nslatio | habet. Quinta p*ro*genine [*sic*] ascend*er*unt filii isr*ahe*l. Moyses e*nim*. q*ui*ntus fuit á iacob. vel p*er* tribu*m* iude: a phares usq*ue* ad salmon. (HS 1156D)

c § Naason[536] p*r*inceps t*r*ib*us* iude: in deserto desc*r*ibit*ur*. Cui*us* fili*us* salmon in terram rep*ro*missionis intrauit. (Jerome, Ep. 36, PL 22.455)

d Q*ui*nq*ue* fuerunt generationes. hebreus. h*abe*t. v*que*.[537] ascenderunt. filii is*rahe*l. (HS 1156D) Judas *enim* gen*uit* pharas (*written above in picture space, with* signe de renvoi ':/' : Q*ui* cu*m* pat*re* suo Juda. ingressus est egiptu*m*). Q*ui* gen*uit* efron. Q*ui* gen*uit* | aram.

e Q*ui* gen*uit* aminadab. Q*ui* gen*uit* naason. qui cu*m* patre egressus est. de egipto: Naason. (d-e = Matthew 1:3–4)

a. From him father Abraham was seventh. He [Moses] was the the son of Amram, whose father was Caath, who was born of Levi, Levi indeed of Jacob, who was of Isaac, son of Abraham; Levi begot Caath, who with his father Levi went into Egypt.

b. Caath begot Amram, who (begot) Aaron, who (begot) Eliazar, who (begot) Phineas. Afterwards Eliazar with his father Aaron went out of Egypt.

Moses was about eighty years old. His brother Aaron was older by three years. But the other translation has: "The sons of Israel went up in the fifth generation from Jacob" for Moses was the fifth from Jacob, or through the tribe of Juda from Phares up to Salmon.

c. Naason is described as a prince of the tribe of Juda in the desert whose son Salmon entered the promised land.

d. Five were . . . these generations, the Hebrew has "the sons of Israel went up five [generations]". Juda begot Pharas (who with his father Juda entered into Egypt), who begot Ephron, who begot Aram,

e. who begot Aminadab, who begot Naason, who with his father left Egypt: Naason.

---

as guide-lines; comments labeled 'a-e', from a medley of sources, Josephus, HS, Ep. 36 of Jerome "Ad Damasum," PL 22.457 (on the use of the latter in these annotations, see ch. 6, 325, 327), and comments as found in the ninth-century Freculphus Lexoviensis, *Chronicon tomi duo* (PL 106.949).

536 Above this word a *signe de renvoi* + that refers to end of e-passage, 'Naason +'.

537 PL "quinque generationes."

270.[538] § a Flauit uentus. uehemens. 7 uertit aqua*m* i*n* siccum. Et diuisu*m* e*st* mare:· | in xii. diuisiones. ut queq*ue* tribus p*er* turmas suas i*n*cederet. Et aduocans Moyses singulas tribus:· a | b s*ecund*um ordine*m* natiuitatis sue:· hortab*atur* eos: ut ip*sum* p*re*eunte*m* sequerent*ur*. Cu*m*q*ue* timuissent intrare. ruben. | Simeon. 7 leui:· Judas p*rimus* aggressu*s* e*st* iter post eu*m*. Vnde 7 ibi meruit regnum. p*ro*fecti sunt *ergo* p*er* mediu*m* ||[539] maris:· [a] Quod uidendes [*sic*] egiptii. i*n*gressi sunt p*ost* eos. Respexit d*ominu*s sup*er* egiptios p*er* columpnam nubis. 7 ignis. | i*d est* [in]tolerabiles imbres:· et graues tonitrus:· choruscationesq*ue* lampantes:·[540] iniecit sup*er* eos. Natura mari*s* | e*st*:· ut quod perit `in´ eo ad p*ro*ximu*m* litus p*ro*iciat. Cu*m ergo* mane iacerent egiptii mortui in litore. patet:· | b quod idem erat `litus´ ex altera montis p*ar*te:· Et tulit isr*ahe*l arma Mortuorum:· (HS 1157D-1158C)

a. The wind blew violently and turned the water into dry land and the sea was divided into twelve parts so that each tribe advanced in its division. And Moses, calling to each separate tribe b. according to the order of the birth of its (eponymous patriarch), addressed them so that they could follow him going forward. And when Ruben, Simeon, and Levi feared to enter, Judas was first to force the march behind him, whence from that time he deserved the kingship. Therefore they made their way through the midst of the sea, . . . a. so, seeing that, the Egyptians went in after them, . . . the Lord looked upon the Egyptians from the pillar of cloud and fire, that is, he cast (un)bearable rain and and heavy thunderclaps, and shimmering lightning upon them. . . . The nature of the sea is that what perishes in it is thrown up on the nearest shore. When therefore in the morning the Egyptian dead lay on the shore (Ex. 14:30), it shows b. that the same kind of shore lay on the other side of the mass of water. . . . And Israel took the arms of the dead men.

F. 92r *Illustrations:* Two frames: upper, crossing of the Red Sea, walls of water represented on each side, unfinished pillar of fire, flanked by Moses and Aaron, vertically divides the frame; lower, six figures crawl on top of an originally empty frame, now filled with twelfth-century notes.[541] **OE** = Exodus 14:23–31

271. In paralyppomen*on* | § Manasse gen*uit* macyr. patre*m* galaad. ex co*n*cubina syra:· filii Machyr. husim.[542] et sussim. unu*m* nom*en* e*st* `et soror ei*us* Maacha´

[538] Bottom frame, top register, 2 lines labeled 'a', bottom margin 2 lines labeled 'b', continuing to f. 92r top, 3 lines labeled 'a' in outer margin + 1 line labeled 'b', in lower ledger of top frame; the purpose of the letters appear to be continuation marks, since this is a single quotation spread over a large area.

[539] In outer top margin of f. 92r is written 'bc' or 'be' of uncertain signficance. Below this is the connecting 'a'.

[540] PL "lampades."

[541] See the comments of Dodwell and Clemoes, *Illustrated Hexateuch*, 34.

[542] MS 'hussim', first 's' deleted.

| Husim.[543] int*erpre*tat*ur* t`h´alam*us*. sussim unct*us*. Nom*en* au*tem* se*cun*di salphaad. Iccirco iste se*cund*us nominat*ur* q*u*ia hi duo principes | erant in tribu Manasse. Id e*st* husim. 7 susim. q*ui* et salphaad. Soror au*tem* ei*us* regina. i*d est* bedan filii hulam. Ali*us* est | iste bedan. et Ali*us* e*st* bedan i*n* Regu*m*. id e*st* samson. bedan int*erpre*tat*ur* in dan. Ista soror regina e*st* debbora. | uxor barach. q*ui* alio nomine lapidoth uocat*ur*. Suthela fili*us* ephraim. [genuit Ezer] et elaad. q*ui* co*n*gregata mul|titudine de isr*ahe*l ascend*ere* nisi sunt in t*erra*m rep*ro*missionis. et i*n* geth philistinor*um* int*er*fecti sunt:· | fr*at*res u*ero* q*ui* ad co*n*solandu*m* ephrachim [*sic*] uener*unt*:· aut eos dicim*us* q*ui* de pat*ri*archis sup*er*erant. aut cognatione*m* | quam frat*er*no nomine sepe nomina[ui]m*us*:· (Ps-Jerome, QH1P 23.1376C/D-1377A; cf. no. 223)

In Paralipomenon (1 Para. 7:14–21): . . . Manasses begot Machir, father of Galaad, by his Syrian concubine. The sons of Machir, Huphim and Suphim, which is one name (and his sister Maacha). . . . Huphim is interpreted 'bridal chamber', Suphim 'anointment'. The name of the second is Zalphaad . . . and the reason this second is so named is because these were two princes in the tribe of Manasses, that is Huphim and Suphim, who is also . . . Zalphaad. And his sister was "Queen," that is of Bedan the son of Ulam (1 Para. 7:17–18). One is this Bedan and the other Bedan is in Kings, that is, Samson. Bedan is interpreted 'in Dan'. This sister, "Queen," is Debbora, the wife of Barach, who is called by the other name of "Lapidoth." Suthela the son of Ephraim [begot Ezer] and Elaad, and when the multitude of Israel were gathered, they strove to ascend into the land of promise, and were killed in Geth of the Philistines; the brothers who indeed came to the consolation of Ephraim we say either are those who survived out of the patriarchs or relations to whom often we gave the name of "brothers."

272a.[544] § Morat*us* est aute*m* isr*ahe*l iuxta lit*us*. vii. dieb*us* 7 cu*m* tympanis. 7 instrume*n*tis musicis:· singulis dieb*us*[545] | ueniebant ad lit*us* 7 cantabant. d*omi*no canticu*m* moysi:· uiri seorsum. 7 mulieres seorsum:· .a. (HS 1158C)

Israel lingered along the shore . . . for seven days and with timbrels and musical instruments every day they came to the shore and sang the song of Moses to the Lord, the men in their group and the women in their group.

F. 92v *Illustrations:* Two frames: upper, Moses leading the people in dancing and singing; lower, Maria (Miriam) leading the women, playing harps. OE = Exodus 15:1–24. At the top, **.ii̅.cccc.liii.** [A.M. 2453].

---

543 Written, apparently, 'Hufim'; 'regina' written 'regma' in both cases.

544 Bottom margin, 2 lines; index letter 'a' at end of this passage, 'b' and 'c' at beginning of lines of comment on verso.

545 'singulis | dieb*us*' written again and cancelled.

272b. .b. Normann*us* dicit. In cui*us* rei memoria: vii. paschalib*us* diebus: cantando redimus ad fontes:- | .c. et terminatur hic: iosephi liber secundus:- (HS 1158C/D)

b. Normannus says in memory of which event for seven days at Eastertide chanting we go to the fonts; c. and here the second book of Josephus concludes.

F. 93r *Illustrations:* Two frames: upper, fountain of Mara, Moses on left, tree being cast into well on right, people drinking; lower, in three registers, above, people come to Elim, Moses on left blesses them; lower two registers show stylized "seventy palm trees of Elim." **OE** = Exodus 15:24–27

273. (within upper frame) § Ibi etia*m* dedit. eis iudicia. nondu*m* t*ame*n in re: s*ed* datur*um* | se p*ro*misit: si obedire sibi (.) uellent. (HS 1159B)

There also he gave them judgements, but not in regard to substance; rather he promised what he would give if they would obey him.

274. (lower frame, on the two internal ledger lines) Exin*de* uenerunt in desertu*m* syn. q*uo*d est inter elim et sina(..)y. ubi plures fecerunt mansiones. | que in nu*m*-*er*is exponentur- (HS 1159C)

From there they came "into the desert of Sin which is between Elim and Sinai" (Ex. 16:1) where they made many stopping places, which are expounded in Numbers.

F. 93v *Illustrations:* One frame in two registers: above, the people complain of their hunger to Moses, Aaron on left; below, the people catch the "quails" sent by God. **OE** = Exodus 16:1–14

275. (top margin) § tricesimo s*cilicet* ab exitu eoru*m* de egipto: qu`a´ndo- s*cilicet* | s*ecun*d*u*m[546] pasca celebrabant*ur*. defecerunt `eis´ uictualia. que tulerant de egipto. et dixserunt: [*sic*] / .xv. i*d est* quinto decimo die.[547] (HS 1159C)

Thirty (days) . . . that is, from their exodus from Egypt when, to be exact, they were celebrating the second Paschal ceremony; the victuals they brought from Egypt had run out for them and they said ["would we had died in Egypt," etc. (Exodus 16:3)]. \ that is, on the fifteenth day (Exodus 16:1).

546 PL: "ab exitu eorum pasca celebrabatur."

547 The phrase is transposed and positioned below the line so as to function as a direct correcting gloss to the OE, lines 1–2: **Þá ferdon hí ðanon on ðam fiftigoðan dǽge þæs æftran | monðes,** 'on the fiftieth day of the second month' (cf. Ex. 16:1).

276. (gloss, line 2 of OE) **þá ferdon hí ðanon on ðam fiftigoðan dǽgc þæs æftran | monðes** `et .xxx.´[548]

277.[549] **drihten ge|sénde swa micel fugelcyn** / de sinu arabico
The Lord sent so many birds from the Arabian Gulf[550]

278.(lower frame, top ledger) ʃ Est aute*m* auis regia. qua*m* Joseph*us* ortigia*m* uocat. Grecus· ortogometra*m*. nos uulgo curleium dicim*us* | .á currendo· (HS 1159D)

[Coturnix] is a . . . royal bird which Josephus calls 'ortygia', in Greek 'orthogometrus', in the vernacular we call it 'curlew', derived from 'currendo', running.[551]

F. 94r *Illustrations:* One frame in two registers: above, Moses and Aaron instruct the people to gather the manna which people begin to do; below, they continue to gather manna. **OE** = Exodus 16:15–23

279. (in frame, 2 lines) Vnde 7 deinceps· mánna dictum est. q*uod* quida*m* indeclinabile putant· alii in p*r*ima. alii in tercia / declinacione ponu*n*t. sicut 7 pasca. che. uel paschatis· 7 ait. M*oyses*. hic e*st* panis dat*us* uobis a domino. (HS 1160A)

[So henceforth it was called 'manna']. Therefore some think it indeclinable, some others place it in the first declension, others in the third, like 'pascha', 'paschae' or 'paschatis'; and Moses said, "this is the bread given to you by the Lord" (Exodus 16:15).

280. (continuing) Quicquid au*tem* seruatu*r*[552] n*on* sabb*ato*. a uermib*us* immortalibus q*uo*s par|turit auaricia corrumpit*ur*. Manna e*st* chr*istu*s. uel u*er*bu*m* ei*us*. unde | uermes fiunt in nob[i]s. ut dicit. Si non uenissem et locut*us* | eis fuissem. peccatu*m* non haberent·[553]

Whatsoever is not kept for the Sabbath is ruined by undying worms (cf. Ex. 17:24) which greed gives birth to. Manna is Christ or his word, whence worms arise in us, as he says: \ "If I had not come and spoken to them, they would not have had sin" (cf. Ex. 16:23–24)

548 I.e., "and the thirtieth" day from the Exodus, as in the preceding comment, correcting the OE.

549 Line 11 of OE, outer margin, with *signe de renvoi*; gloss began to be written above the line, but was washed off and done in margin.

550 The gloss-phrase is at HS 1159D, "et ascendens coturnix, de sinu Arabico." OE: **edisc** | **henna** (corrected in the margin by L'Isle to 'ersc henna') **ðæt ís on leden cuturnix.**

551 OFr. *courleus*; the OED gives a similar etymology.

552 'seruaba*tur*', 'ba' deleted. The usual Vulgate expression is "sabbata custodire."

553 This follows closely Ps.-Augustine, Serm. Supp. 25, PL 39.1795, rather than the *Glossa ordinaria* note derived from it (PL 113.237A); the last sentence is John 15:22.

F. 94v *Illustrations:* Two frames: above, two elders approach Moses and tell him that people (right) gather twice as much manna; below, Moses on left telling the people not to gather manna on the Sabbath, hand of God above him, on right bowl of manna is set in a tent-like structure, hand of God above. **OE** = Exodus 16:23–35

281a.[554]§ Egressus e*st* aute*m* amalech. ut pugnaret aduersu*s* isr*ahe*l. i*n* raphidi*m*. Strab*us* ait. amalech fuit fili*us* hismaelis. a quo | amelechite. q*ui* 7 hismaelite. ip*s*i sunt saraceni. Hos dici[t] iosephu*s*. pugnantes.[555] i*n*habita*n*tes goboth. 7 petram. et | á ci*r*cumstantib*us* conductos ad bellu*m* contra hebreos∻ Econtra legit*ur* in genesi. q*uo*d helephat p*r*imogenit*us* esau∻ ‖ genuit de concubina∻ `thema soror lotham´ amalech. Idem sup*ra* regu*m*. ubi fili*us* doech idumei nuncians dauid Morte*m* | saul∻ ait. amalechites su*m*. forte∻ duo fuerunt. equiuoce.[556] 7 ex his duo populi∻ (HS 1161B/C)

"Amalech went out to fight against Israel in Raphidim" (Ex. 17:8). Strabus says that Amalech was the son of Ismael, from whom (come) the Amalechites, who are also Ismaelites, the Saracens themselves. These according to Josephus were fighting the inhabitants of Goboth . . . and Petra and by the surrounding peoples were led to war against the Hebrews. But on the other hand it is read in Genesis that Eliphaz, the firstborn of Esau, begot Amelech by the concubine (Thema sister of Lotan) (Gen. 36:12). The same above . . . in Kings, where the son of Doech the Idumean, announcing to David the death of Saul, says, "I am an Amalechite" (2 Kings 1:8). Perhaps the two names merely sounded the same and from these two distinct peoples (arose). (cf. no. 282)

F. 95r *Illustration:* One frame: Moses, left, strikes the rock and the people draw water from it and drink. **OE** = Exodus 17:1–13

281b. (upper ledger of frame) § Oreb pars e*st* montis syna. sic dicta. alia e*st* 7 alibi petra oreb. sic dicta∻ p*ro*pter oreb[557] q*ui* occisus est in ea∻ (HS 1161A)

Horeb, . . . part of Mount Sinai, as it is called; another elsewhere is the Rock of Horeb, as it is called on account of [the king of] Horeb who was killed on it (cf. Judg. 7:25).

[554] Bottom 3 lines, continuing to bottom of f. 95r, 2 lines, with *signe de renvoi* and 'hwær/h`a´er' notation, referring to the OE in the lower text block on f. 95r (Exodus 17:8, 13).

[555] MS 'pungnantes', first 'n' cancelled; PL "pugnaces."

[556] PL "equivoci."

[557] PL "oreb regem."

281c.[558] § Ascenderuntq*ue* cum eo:' aaron. et ur uir (.)[559] marie- | T*amen* s*ecun*d*um* paralippomenon fuit filius caleph et marie.[560] auus beseleel. (HS 1161C)

They went up with him, Aaron and Hur the husband of Mariam. Nevertheless, according to Paralipomenon he was the son of Caleb and Mariam . . . the grandfather of Bezeleel.

282.[561]`Ier*onymus* dic*it*´ Et pep*er*it ada esav elifaz. | Iste e*st* cui*us* script*ur*a in iob uolumine recordat*ur*. Et fuerunt filii lothan. horri. 7 ommon. 7 soror lothan themna. Et | erat the*m*na[562] concubina. elifaz filii p*r*imogeniti esav. et ex ip*s*a nat*us* e*st* amalech. *Qu*od au*tem* d*icitu*r them[n]an.[563] 7 cenez. 7 ame/lech. ‖ scia-m*us*. po*st*ea regionib*us* ydu*m*eor*um* ex his uocabula imposita. (HQG 23.992C-993 B/C; CCSL 72, 56.3)

Jerome says: And Ada bore Eliphaz to Esau (cf. Gen. 36:4, 10). . . . This is he whom Scripture mentions in the book of Job (2:11, etc.). . . . "And the sons of Lotan were Hori and Heman and the sister of Lotan was Themna" (Gen. 36:22) . . . "and Themna was the concubine of Eliphaz the firstborn son of Esau and from her was born Amalech" (Gen. 36:12); . . . further it is said "Themnan and Cenez and Amelech" (1 Para. 1:36). . . . We know that afterwards these names were given to the regions of the Idumaeans.

F. 95v *Illustrations:* Two frames: upper, on left Hur and Aaron hold up Moses' arms (labeled '.Hvr. / .Moyses. \ ááron'), on right, the Hebrews defeat the Amalechites; lower, in two panels, right, Moses writes "this deed" in a book as commanded, left, Moses with elders before an altar. **OE** = Exodus 17:14–16, 18:1–4, 7–8

283.[564] Vn*de* 7 seq*uitur*. Ex efraim deleuit eos i*n* amalech. Id e*st* | iosue existe*ns* de t*r*ibu aph`r´aim. deleuit fortes i*d est* i*n*imicos isr*ahe*l in amalech. sic*ut* legit*ur* i*n* exodo. Fugauitq*ue* iosue amalech | i*n* ore gladii. de t*r*ibu ephraim osee filiu*m* Nun. *Qu*em i*n* co*n*sequentib*us* iosue uocat dice*ns*. Vocauitq*ue* Moyses osee filiu*m* | Nún:' Iósue (CD, 23.1325C/D)

---

558 Above and in lower ledger; a *signe de renvoi* links this excerpt to OE, lower block, line 5, **moyses 7 ááron 7 úr**.

559 'e' erased.

560 'et marie' is incorrect and the phrase is not in PL; the authority is 1 Para. 2:19, "And when Azuba was dead, Caleb took to wife Ephrata, who bore him Hur."

561 Bottom margin, beginning towards end of second line, and continuing on top of f. 95v; this note links physically and in matter with no. 281a, but from a different source.

562 MS 'thēna' with incorrect hairline strokes over the minims of 'n'.

563 MS 'thēman'.

564 Beginning in top margin, middle of first line.

Whence also follows: “Out of Ephraim he[565] destroyed them into Amalec” (Jud. 5:14). That is, Joshua, springing from the tribe of Ephraim, destroyed the strong men, that is, the enemies of Israel in Amalec as is read in . . . Exodus: “Joshua put Amalec to flight . . . with the edge of the sword” (Ex. 17:13). . . . “From the tribe of Ephraim Osee the son of Nun” (Numbers 13:9). Whom . . . in what follows Moses calls ‘Joshua’: And Moses “called Osee the son of Nun ‘Joshua’” (Numbers 13:17).

284.[566] Man*us* Erant eni*m* graues:· p*ro* labore orandi. In huius rei fig`u´ra:· sac*er*dos / manus eleuat i*n* missa. ⁊ etia*m* in figura chr*ist*i orantis i*n* cruce:· (HS 1161D)

“For his hands . . . were heavy” (Ex. 17:12) from the labor of praying. In a figure of this the priest lifts his hands in the mass and also as a type of Christ praying on the cross.

285.[567] **Witodlice íc adylgye amaleches gemynd under heo|fone**. q*uo*d in diebus saul impletum est:· (HS 1161D)

Truly I will destroy the memory of Amalech under heaven which was fulfilled in the days of Saul.

286. (bottom margin) Jer*onymus* dic*it* | Po*st* eu*m* i*d est* po*st* iosue:· Saul existens ex t*r*ibu beniamin. p*re*cipiente d*omi*no:· amalech deleuit:· Q*uo*d in sp*irit*u debora de | saule fut*uru*m p*roph*et*a*uit:· q*uo*d ip*s*e e*s*set deletur*us* amalech. sic i*n* lib*r*o samuhelis habes. S*ed* q*uo*d ait. o amalech. i*n* libro non | legit*ur* s*ed* latin*us* int*er*pres sensus gr*ati*a hoc addidit (CD 23.1325D-1326A)

Jerome says: After him, that is, after Joshua, Saul, coming from the tribe of Benjamin . . . as was commanded by the Lord . . . destroyed Amalec. So that in the spirit . . . Deborah prophesied about what was to come concerning Saul . . . that he would destroy Amalec, as you read in the book of Samuel (1 Sam. 15). But . . . what it says, “O Amelech” (Judg. 5:14), is not read in the (Hebrew) book but the Latin translator has added this for the sake of the meaning.

F. 96r *Illustration:* One frame in two panels: left, Moses kisses his father-in-law Jethro, his wife Seffora, and his sons Eliezar and Gerson, looking on, Moses’ encampment on the right, and in right panel, Aaron and the elders eat bread with Jethro, the hand of God extended. **OE** = Exodus 18:8–25

---

565 The subject in the biblical verse is Barac, but it is applied here to Joshua.

566 Above and on top ledger of upper frame, as if continuing the previous note and in the same script. It is awkwardly written across and around the figure of Moses with outstretched arms.

567 In bottom ledger of upper frame, as a gloss to lines 2–3 of OE, with *signes de renvoi.*

287. Sumpsit ietro hostias: de oblatis á Moyse: 7 commedit- | forte tunc sacrificauit Moyses iuxta mont*em* sicut predixerat d*ominus*: | dicit eni*m* iosep*hus* ietro uenisse circa mont*em* ubi i*n* rubo multas / uiderat Moyses uisiones:- (HS 1162A)

Jethro took victims from the offerings from Moses . . . and ate (cf. Ex. 18:12); by chance then Moses sacrificed next to the mountain just as the Lord had foretold. Josephus also says: Jethro came around the mountain where in a bush Moses had seen many visions.

F. 96v *Illustration:* One frame: Moses, left, chosing leaders for the people.[568] **OE** = Exodus 18:25–27, 19:1–15

288. IN hunc modu*m* eccl*esi*a romana | uocauit pl*ur*imos in p*ar*t*em* sollicitudinis. p*r*imates. arehiepiscopos. [*sic*] ep[i]scopos. archidiacones. arcip*re*sbiteros. 7 | minores sacerdotes. leuiora peccata. 7 queda*m* g*ra*u`i´a sed occulta: iudicant. Grauiora u*er*o ap*er*ta: referunt ad | ep*iscopu*m. Adquieuit. Moyses. nec erubuit uir deo plenus: consiliu*m* gentilis. dimisitq*ue* cognatu*m* suum: (HS 1162D)

In this way the Roman church called many into a share of cares: primates . . . archbishops, bishops, archdeacons, archpriests. And the lesser orders judge the lighter sins and some of the serious but private ones; the more serious . . . and public (sins) they reserve to the bishop. And Moses agreed and he was not ashamed, a man filled by God, to follow the counsel . . . of the gentiles, "and he sent his kinsman away" (Ex. 18:27).

F. 97r *Illustrations:* Two frames: upper, Moses leading the people to their encampment at Sinai, and in upper left quadrant, Moses being called by God on the mountain; lower frame, Moses, descending from the mountain (shown on left), speaks to the elders, who are bowing to him. **OE** = Exodus 19:12–15

289. Moyses au*tem* po*st* tres menses egressionis. uenit ad mont*em* syna. | et po*st*qua*m* ieiunando quadraginta dieb*us* et quadraginta noctibu*s* | accepit leg*em*. construxit tab*er*naculu*m* mensib*us* septem:.[569]

Moses three months after the exodus came to Mount Sinai and afterwards, fasting for forty days and forty nights, he received the law, and he constructed a tabernacle in seven months.

---

[568] The picture is difficult to interpret: probably Moses to left, with arms draped, then a "leader" with (counting heads) 19 followers. The annotator at any rate takes the picture as referring to Ex. 18:21, "And provide out of all the people able men, such as fear God, in whom there is truth, and that hate avarice; and appoint of them rulers of thousands, and of hundreds, and of fifties, and of tens."

[569] Unsourced.

Ff. 97v–99r OE = Exodus 19:16–25, chs. 20–22, 23:1–20; no pictures or annotations

F. 99v *Illustration:* One large half-page unframed picture, its spaces now filled with proto-gothic notes: God (labeled 'd*omin*u*s*'), with cross-nimbus talks to Moses, who descends diagonally to right to address the people. **OE** = Exodus 23:20–32, 24:1–3

290.[570] § area orne. id e*st* ier*usa*lin- (SNLH, PL 23.875C, Lagarde 97.9)
The threshing-floor of Orna, that is, Jerusalem.[571]

291.[572] § Pona*m*q*ue* ter*m*inos tuos. á mari | rubro: ab oriente: usq*ue* ad mare palestinu*m*. q*uo*d tirrenum dicit*ur* 7 e*st* ab occi|dente. 7 á deserto: q*uo*d e*st* post bethleem: q*uo*d `*ue*l que´ incipit post tecuam: usq*ue* / ad fluuium. *scilicet* euphraten. que tota regio q*uan*d*o*q*ue* dicta e*st* / judea:- (HS 1168C)
"And I will place your boundaries from the Red Sea" . . . on the east "up to the Sea of Palestine," which is called the Tyrrhenian, on the west, "and from the desert" which is beyond Bethlehem which begins after Tecua "up to the river," namely the Euphrates, which whole region is sometimes called Judea (Ex. 23:31).

292a.[573]§ Hier*usa*lin metr`o´polis. q*uo*nda*m* toti*us*[574] iudee. q*ue* nunc ab helyo adriano cesare. q*uo*d eam | á tyto destructa*m* latioræ[575] situ restaurauerit: helya cogn[o]minata e*st*. Cui*us* op*er*e | f*act*um e*st*. ut loca s*anc*t*am* [*sic*] i*d est* d*om*inice passionis et resurrectionis. s*ed* et i*n*ventionis s*anc*t*e* crucis. q*uo*nda*m* ext*ra*[576] | urb*em* iacentia n*un*c ei*us*de*m* urb*is* muro (. . .) septe*ntr*ionali ci*r*cumdent*ur*: (NLA, PL 92.1037C/D; CCSL 121.172.142)

---

[570] Centered immediately below OE text.

[571] That is, the spot purchased by David that later became the site of the temple (cf. 1 Para. 21:28). This note governs the notes from various sources that follow concerning various places in the Holy Land (granted to Moses and hence to the church); the textual cue seems to be **Bring þine | frumsceattas to godes húse** (Ex. 23:19) at the bottom of f. 99r.

[572] Five lines of varying length in frame below sky; on line 4, the word 'moyses' that seems to begin the line is a picture label, not part of the note.

[573] Nos. 292a-i, rest of notes on f. 99v, 18 lines, and probably continuing on top of f. 100r, 3 lines, and in upper frame 12 lines: various texts written as a group, headed, 'Jer*onymus* dic*it*', on the boundaries of Israel, with a concentration on Jerusalem. 292a is from Bede, NLA but this work was frequently ascribed to Jerome in manuscripts and printed as such in PL 23.1295–1306 (see Laistner, ed., *NLA*, xxxvii).

[574] Written 'toci'.

[575] There are spellings that give signs of an old exemplar, but here the correct reading is "latiore."

[576] Laistner: "infra."

Jerusalem, once the capital of all Judea, which is now named for Aelian Hadrian Caesar, because, destroyed by Titus, he may have restored it on a larger site. Aelia is the name it is known by, by whose [sc. Hadrian's] building program the holy places, i.e., of the Passion and Resurrection of the Lord, but also of the Invention of the Holy Cross, once outside the city, were now enclosed within the northern walls.

292b. § Sex milib*us* bethlee*m* ab ierosolima in meridiano lat*ere* secedit: (Ps.-Eucherius, *De situ Hierosolimae* 11, CCSL 175, 238.56)

Bethlehem is six miles south of Jerusalem.

292c. § Jordanes [*recte* -is] q*uoque* ab eade*m* celi parte iudee t*erre* p*re*te*n*dit*ur*. iiii^{to}. 7 xx^{mo}. | lapide ab elya separatus. (Ps.-Eucherius, *ibid.* 12, CCSL 175, 239.61)

Jordan also is extended over the same low-lying part of the land of Judea, twenty-four miles distant from Aelia (Jerusalem).

292d. § (. .) ARboch scribit*ur*. cu*m* hebreo lega|tur arbe i*d est* iiii^{or}. eo q*uo*d ibi t*res* pat*r*iarche. abraham. | .ysaac. 7 iacob. sepulti s*int*. 7 adam magnus. | ut in ie*s*u libro scriptu*m* est. distat ad meridiana*m* | plaga*m* ab elya. milib*us* circit*er* .xx^{ti}. ii^{obus}. ubi. 7 querc*us* `*ue*l terebint*us*´[577] abraham- | q*ue* 7 mambre. ubi abraha*m* ang*e*los q*u*onda*m* hos|picio suscep*er*it. H*ec* *er*go p*r*imu*m* arbe. pos*t*ea chebron. ab uno- | filior*um* chaleb. sortita uocabulu*m* e*st*. lege u*er*ba dierum. (Hrabanus, *Comm. in Lib. IV Reg.*, PL 109.75C/D–76A)[578]

[Corruptly in our books] is written 'Arboch' when in the Hebrew is read 'Arbe,' that is, 'four', because three patriarchs, Abraham, Isaac, and Jacob are buried there as well as the great Adam, as is written in the book of Joshua (Jos. 14:15). . . . It is about 22 miles to the south of Aelia (Jerusalem), where (is) also the oak (or terebinth) of Abraham, which is Mambre . . . where Abraham once entertained the angels. \ This was therefore at first Arbe and later happened to be called Hebron from one of the sons of Caleb. Read "Words of the Days" (1 Para. 2:42).

292e. § Jericho u*er*o ab ierosolima in oriente*m* estiuum .xiii.[579] milib*us* excurrit. (Ps.-Eucherius, *De situ Hier.* 12, CCSL 175, 239.60)

Jericho is thirteen [18] miles northeast of Jerusalem.

---

[577] Small *signes de renvoi* on the line and above indicating the insertion.

[578] Hrabanus' combined sources are Ps.-Eucherius [Claudius of Turin (d. ca. 840)], *Comm. in Gen.*, PL 50.949A and Jerome, SNLH, PL 23.862B.

[579] Ed. "decem et octo."

292f. § Mare magnu*m* nusq*u*am uicini*us*: q*u*am iuxta[580] ioppen oppidu*m* possidet. q*uo*d .xl[ta]. ab ea in | occasu*m* estiuu*m* milib*us* abe*st*: A dan usq*ue* barsabee p*ro*te*n*dit*ur*[581] longituto t*er*re isr*ah*el.[582] ab aq*u*ilonali plaga | in meridie*m* p*ro*ducta.[583] (Ps.-Eucherius, *ibid.* 13, 14, CCSL 175, 239.69)

The great sea lies nowhere nearer (to Jerusalem) than adjacent to the city of Joppa which is forty miles northwest of it. The length of the land of Israel (Judah) stretches from Dan to Bersabee, measured from north to south.

292g. (bottom line) Utiq*ue* á dan usq*ue* ad bersabee: q*ue* uix. c[tu*m*].xl[ta].[584] miliu*m* spatio i*n* longu*m* te*n*dit*ur* (. .) (Jerome, Ep. 129, "Ad Dardanum," PL 22.1104; CSEL 56, 169.23)

At any rate from Dan up to Bersabee, which extends scarcely 140 miles in length.

F. 100r *Illustrations:* Two frames: upper, the right half set off in a floral frame in which Moses writes down the commandments (label 'Mons syna'), left, sets up an altar; lower, Moses on left in a panel, sends four young men to get sacrificial animals, their heads showing above a blank square. **OE** = Exodus 24:4–5

292h. § AGGay. q*ue* 7 bethel. p*r*iu*s* luza;[585] ad occide*n*tale*m* plaga*m*. uergebat hehe:[586] n*on* multu*m* ab ea distans. Sita e*st* au*tem* | bethel. euntib*us* elia*m* de neapoli in[587] leua parte[588] uie. xii[mo] circit*er* miliario ab elia. (Jerome, SNLH 23.861B; Lagarde 83.30; cf. no. 332)

Aggai, (which is also Bethel, and before that Luz), was situated toward (Hai) on the west side, not very distant from it. Bethel is sited about twelve miles from Aelia, taking the leftward road to Aelia from Neapolis.

292i. § Joppe usq*ue* ad uiculu*m* | n*ostr*um. bethlee*m* xl[ta]. 7 vi. milia s*un*t. Cui succedit uastissima solitudo: plena ferociu*m* barbarorum: (Jerome, Ep. 129, PL 22.1104)

---

580 Ed. "circa."

581 Ed. "praetenditur."

582 Ed. "iudaeae."

583 The wording and phrase-order is considerably changed from the text given in CCSL.

584 Edd.: "centum sexaginta"; var. "CXL."

585 Taken from Genesis 28:19; the changes made to this sentence from the received text of Jerome (in brackets in the translation) are consistent and motivated to account for biblical rather than geographical information.

586 Edd. "uergit bethelis."

587 Written 'neapolím'.

588 MS 'parate', second 'a' cancelled.

. . . (From) Joppa to our little town of Bethlehem are 46 miles, after which succeeds a vast desert full of cruel barbarians.

293. Et xii titulos p*er* xii trib*us* isr*ahe*l. forsan:· xii altaria quos titulos dicit. Vel potiu*s*[589] unum ex. | xii .lapidib*us* et i*n* si*n*gulis singula nomina filior*um* isr*ahe*l scripsit. quasi titulos tribuum:· 7 c*etera*-[590] | misitq*ue* iuuenes. s*cilicet* nadab 7 abyu q*ue* [*recte* qui] fut*u*ri erant sacerdotes. 7 i`m´molau*erun*t d*omi*no pacifica[s][591] uitulos. xii. (HS 1168D)

"And twelve titles, according to the twelve tribes of Israel" (Ex. 24:4); perhaps he says "twelve titles" to mean twelve altars. Or rather, on each of the twelve stones he also wrote one by one the names of the sons of Israel as though they were the names of tribes,[592] etc., and "sent young men," to wit, Nadab and Abiu who were to be priests "and they sacrificed (twelve) calves as peace offerings to the Lord" (Ex. 24:5).

294a.[593] § Iconiu*m*. ciuitas celeb*er*rima li`c´aonie. Et e*st* alt*er*a i*n* cilicia. (NLA, PL 92.1037D; CCSL 121.172.161)

Iconium, a famous city of Lycaonia, and there is another (of that name) in Cilicia.

294b. § Mons oliueti ad orient*em* ierosolime torrente | cedron. int*er*fluente. u*bi* ultima d*omi*ni uestigia. humo imp*re*ssa hodieq*ue* monstrant*ur*. (NLA, PL 23.1301D-1302A; CCSL 121.173.180)

The Mount of Olives to the east of Jerusalem, watered by the stream of Cedron, where the last traces of the Lord impressed in the soil are shown even today.

294c. § Nazareth uiculus | i*n* galilea iuxta mont*em* thabor. un*de* d*omin*us n*oste*r ie*su*s chr*ist*e nazare|nus e*st* uocat*us*.- (NLA, PL 92.1038D; CCSL 121.174.213)

Nazareth, a small town in Galilee next to Mount Thabor, whence our Lord Jesus Christ is called a 'Nazarene'.

294d. § Gethsemani. loc*us* u*bi* an*te* passione*m* saluator | orauit. est au*tem* ad radices montis oliueti.- (SNLH 23.903B; Lagarde 130.22)

589 Written 'pocius'.

590 PL ". . .titulus tribuum duodecim misitque. . . ."

591 *Cl* and PL read "pacifica."

592 Cf. Ex. 39:14 of the breastpiece of Aaron: "And the twelve stones were engraved with the names of the twelve tribes of Israel, each one with its several name."

593 Another series of geographical notes, 294a-m. Resumes on f. 100r in upper frame, 12 lines, diminishing in length to accommodate the picture; in lower frame, 2 lines above, 4 below, and over to 100v, 3 lines at top, 3 lines at bottom.

Gethsemani, a place where before his Passion the Savior prayed; it is at the foot of the Mount of Olives.

294e. § Golgotha. loc*us* caluarie in q*uo* salv`a´tor | p*ro* salute omniu*m* c`r´ucifix*us* e*st*. et usq*ue* | hodie ostendit*ur* in elia. | ad septent*r*ionale*m* plagam | montis syon.: (SNLH 23.903C; 130.25)

Golgotha, the place of Calvary in which the Savior was crucified for the salvation of all. And to this day it is shown in Aelia to the north side of Mount Zion.

294f. § Anameel.[594] Vrb*is*[595] hierusale*m* | s*icut* in zacharie lib*ro* legit*ur*. (SNLH 23.877A; Lagarde 99.10)

Anameel, a city (tower) of Jerusalem as is read in the Book of Zacharias (Zach. 14:10).

294g. Syna mons i*n* regi`o´ne madian. sup*er* arabia*m* i*n* deserto:˙ q*ui* alio no*mi*n*e* coreph[596] uocat*ur*. Vn*de* d*icitu*r. et fecerunt | uitulu*m* in chorep. cu*m* hoc Moyses in syna f*actu*m sc*r*ipserit. (NLA, PL 92.1040; CCSL 121.176.261)

Sinai, a mountain in the region of Madian above Arabia in the desert, whose other name is Horeb, whence is said, "and they made a calf in Horeb" (Ps. 105:19) when Moses will have written that this was done in Sinai.

294h. § I`a´pthice.[597] i*n* t*r*ibu zabulon. n*un*c usq*ue* ioppe uocat*ur* ascens*us* iaphos. et oppidu*m* sicaminu*m* nomine de cesarea | ptholomaide*m* p*er*gentib*us* sup*er* mare:˙ p*ro*pter monte*m* carmelu*m*. jepha[598] dicit*ur*. (SNLH 23.906A; Lagarde 133.32)

Japh(t)ie in the tribe of Zabulon, up as far as Joppa now is called the slope of Japhos. . . . and the city of the Sichamites by the name of Caesarea Ptolemaides by those going over the sea is called Jeptha on account of Mt. Carmel.

294i. § Sydon urbs fenicis i*n*signis. | olim t*er*minu*s* cananeor*um*. ad aq*ui*lone*m* iuxta libani montis ortu*m* sita:˙ et ipsa artifex uitri- liban*us* Mons | phenicis altissim*us*:˙ (NLA, PL 92.1040; CCSL 121.176.269, combined with Jerome, SNLH 908B; Lagarde 136.22)

Sidon, a notable city of the Phoenicians, was once the border of the Canaanites to the north, sited against the beginning of Mount Libanus, "an artificer of glass" (Pliny, *Hist. Nat.* 5.76) / Libanus is the highest mountain of the Phoenicians.

594 Lagarde: "Ananehel."
595 Ed. "turris."
596 PL "Horeb"; Laistner "Choreb," var. "chorep."
597 PL: "Jasthie"; Lagarde: "Iafthie."
598 Edd. "Epha."

294j.[599] § Tyr*us* metropol*is* fenicis i*n* tribu neptali*m*: xx^mo^ p*ro*pe miliario á cesaria philippi: h*ec* q*uo*nda*m* ‖ insula fuit. p*re* alto mari. dcc^ta^ passib*us* diuisa: s*ed* ab alexandro t*er*ra contine*ns* f*act*a e*st* p*ro*pt*er* expugnatione*m* | multis in breui freto aggerib*us* comportatis. Cuius maxime nobilitas conchilio. vel purpura | constat:-(NLA, 92.1040; CCSL121.177.306)

Tyre is the chief city of the Phoenicians in the tribe of Nephtali, about twenty miles from Caesarea Philippi. It "was once an island, separated from the mainland at high tide by 700 feet"; but by Alexander a siege causeway was made by carrying many blocks of material into the narrow straits; "Its greatest distinction consists in the conchilia ('murex') or purple fish" [that produces a purple dye] (citing Pliny, *Hist. Nat.*, 5:76).

F. 100v *Illustration:* One frame: bloody altar on left, Moses facing to right, reads to people from "book of the Covenant" and asperges them with blood. **OE** = Exodus 24:6–11, 29:9–19

294k.[600] § Acheldemach. ager sanguinis: q*u*i hodie monst*rantur* [*recte* monstratur] in elia ad australe*m* plaga*m* montis syon: (SNLH 23.877B; Lagarde 99.20)

Acheldemach, 'field of blood' which today is shown in Aelia on the south side of Mount Sion.

295.[601] § Ac si diceret. Sic p*er*ibit uita ei*us*. 7 sang*u*is ei*us* fundet*ur* q*u*i | uiolabit fedus. h*oc* i*d est* pactu*m* i*nter* nos[602] et deum: (HS 1169A)

But if it said, so his life shall perish and his blood will be spilled who shall violate this covenant, this is the agreement between us and God.

294l.[603] AGER fullonis. et h*oc* in esaysa [*sic*] sc*r*iptu*m* e*st* (. .) ostendit*ur* au*tem* Nu*nc* usq*ue* loc*us* in suburbanis iheru/salem (SNLH 23.876C; Lagarde 98.26)

'Fuller's field,' and this is written in Isaiah (7:3, 36:2) and is shown . . . to the present day the place in the suburbs of Jerusalem.

---

599 Bottom, f. 100r and over to top of f. 100v.

600 Continuing the third line at the top. A cross at end is a continuation mark referring to the note (no. 294l) at the bottom of the page, 'AGER fullonis'.

601 Placed on the top ledger of the frame, as is usual for HS excerpts; this item is not part of the suite of topographical notes.

602 PL "uos."

603 Bottom margin, continuation marks, crosses, at beginning and end of block of text connect it to no. 294k. Several lines up from here in the left margin: 'de Euuangeliis'; this is a title from SNLH, the A-section on the Gospels.

294m.[604] § AENON. Juxta salim ubi baptizabat ioh*anne*s. sic*ut* i*n* eu*a*ng*e*lio cata iohannen sc*r*iptu*m* e*st* et | ostend*itu*r n*un*c usq*ue* loc*us* in octauo lapide scytopoleos ad meridie*m* iuxta Salim 7 iordanen: (SNLH 23.877C, Lagarde 99.22)

Aenon, next to Salim where John baptized as it is written in the Gospel according to John (3:23) and to the present day the place is shown near the eighth (mile)stone to the south of Scythopolis (Beisan), next to Salim and the Jordan.

F. 101r OE 38 lines = Exodus 29:19–41; no pictures or annotations

F. 101v *Illustration:* One large frame, open at top, God, with cross-nimbus, tiara, and book, seated on a mountain, institutes the Sabbath to Moses and the people. **OE** = Exodus 29:42–46, 31:12–17

296.[605] ʃ Est aute[m] sethun: nomen montis. et regionis. 7 arboris. que similis est albe spine in foliis. et est | leuissimu*m* lignu*m*. 7 inputribile. 7 i*n*cremabile. Oleu*m* quoq*ue*: ad luminaria. aromata: in | unguenta. 7 thimiamata. boni odoris. 7 lapides onichinos. itaq*ue* sardonices. 7 ge*m*mas- | faciant mi*hi* sanctuarium. ut inhabitem in medio eorum: ne sit eis labor recurrere. | ad montem huc.[606] `p*r*op*ter* consilia querenda.´ iuxta similtudine*m* tab*er*naculi. quod oste*n*dam tibi facies illud ita:

§ AR`c´ham de lignis sethim facies. que hebraice d*icitu*r heron.[607] Et nota q*uo*d moyses hoc ordine nar|rat. p*r*imo: de eis q*ue* fuerunt[608] i*n* tab*er*naculo.[609] Se*cun*do de tab*er*naculo: tercio: de at*r*io: Josephus uero: econt*ra*. | Ille se*cun*d*u*m ordine*m* co*m*posicionis: Iste s*ecun*d*u*m ordine*m* collacacioni*s*. longitudo ARche: [h]abebat duos | cubitos. 7 semissem: Altitudo similit*er* cubitu*m* 7 semissem.[610] latitudo: cubitu*m* 7 semissem.[611] 7 intelliget*ur* | cubit*us* human*us*: non geometricus. q*uo*d apparet in al(.)tari lateranensi i*n*fra quod dicit*ur* e*ss*e ARcha. etiam[612]| Josephus cubitu*m* uocat hic: duos palmos. 7 d*icitu*r archa. non habuisse pedes. 7

[604] The final enclosing continuation mark (+) at the end of this item.

[605] In the open-topped frame in two blocks, 11 lines of proto-gothic script written in text-space left free above frame, around God-figure and into frame, with other twelfth-century writing within frame at bottom and over to f. 102r, in top of frame; the excerpts are long selections from the "Exodus" section of HS, chaps. 45, 46. The opening code is more like a "nota" than a paragraph.

[606] PL: "hunc."

[607] So MSS; PL "beron."

[608] PL "fecerunt."

[609] Corrected from 'tabernacula'.

[610] With 'sem' written before this word and cancelled.

[611] This section is garbled, differing from the substance of MSS, PL, and the Vulgate (Ex. 25:10), the last reading: "cujus longitudo habeat duos et semis cubitos; latitudo, cubitum et dimidium; altitudo, cubitum similiter ac semissem."

[612] Written 'eciam'.

deaurata e*st* i*n*tus 7 foris- | auro mundissimo. 7 c*etera*. quib*us* ARcha ferebat*ur* nec unqua*m* extr*a*hebant*ur*. In qua:· postposita[613] e*st* testificatio. i*d est* tab|ule i*n* quib*us* scriptu*m* erat test*amentu*m. T*amen*:· (. .)queq*ue* ibi resposita:· testimonia dici possunt. posita e*st* ibi urna au|rea. plena manna:· i*n* testificatione*m*: q*uo*d panem dedisset eis de celo. tabule:· i*n* testificatione*m*:· q*uo*d legem | naturale*m* sopitam in cordib*us*:· suscitauerat in scripto. Virga aaron:· in test*imoniu*m. q*uo*d omnis potestas | a d*omi*no deo est. .deuteronomius:· in testimoniu*m* pacti. q*uo*d dixerat. Omnia que dixerit nobis d*omi*n*u*s faciemus- || Ob hoc dicta est ARcha testam[en]ti. vel testimonii. 7 ob hoc etiam:· taberna|culum testimonii dictum est. Et ideo etiam quia cause p*ro* foribus ei*us* agebantur. et ibi testes pro| ducebantur:·[614] (HS 1169D-1170C)

(from Ch. 45) It [the ark of the tabernacle] is 'setim', the name of a mountain and region and tree, which in its leaves is similar to the whitethorn; it is the smoothest of wood and resistant to decay and burning; "oil for lighting and aromatic ointment and incense of good odor and onyx stones" (Ex. 25:6–7) as well as sardonyx, and gems; . . . "they shall make me a sanctuary so that I shall dwell in the midst of them" (Ex. 25:8); nor shall it be a hardship for them to come back here to the mountain to seek advice "according to the likeness of the tabernacle which I will show to you, thus you shall do" (Ex. 25:9).

(from Ch. 46) You shall make "an ark of setim wood" (Ex. 25:10), which in Hebrew is called 'heron'. And note that Moses narrates in this exact order: first concerning those things that were in the tabernacle; second, concerning the tabernacle itself; third, concerning the court. But Josephus differs, narrating according to the order of composition, Moses according to the order of position. "The length of the ark makes up two and a half cubits. The height is likewise a cubit and a half. The breadth is a cubit and a half" (Ex. 25:10). And a 'human cubit' is to be understood, not a 'geometrical cubit'. That is evident by the altar in the Lateran, below which is said to be the ark.[615] And this, the human cubit, Josephus calls the cubit of two palms' breadth here. And the ark is said to have no feet and to be be covered with the purest gold inside and out, etc. . . . by which [poles] the ark was carried and they were never pulled out. In the ark was placed afterwards the testification, that is, the tablets upon which was written the testament. For whatever is placed there can be called testimony. A golden urn full of manna was placed there in testimony that he gave them bread from heaven; tablets, in testimony that the natural law that slept in their hearts was awakened by the writing; the rod of Aaron, in testimony that all power is from the Lord God; the second law, Deuteronomy, in testimony of the covenant which said: "everything which God said to us, we will do" (cf. Deut. 6:27). From this it is called the ark of the

613 PL "postea posita."

614 'ducu' written before this word and cancelled. The last clause is unsourced.

615 See Erik Thunø, *Image and Relic: Mediating the Sacred in Early Medieval Rome* (Rome, 2002), 160–71.

testament, or tcstimony. From this moreover it is called the tabernacle of the testimony; and for that reason they pled their cases in front of its doors and there witnesses were brought.

F. 102r *Illustration:* One large frame in two registers: above, Aaron and the people worship the golden calf, below, on left they feast and, right, rise up to play. **OE** = Exodus 31:18, 32:1–6

297. (line 3 in frame) Tabernaculu*m* erat domu*s* deo dic[t]ata. quadrata. ⁊ oblonga. t*r*ibus. c`l´ausa parietibus. | aquilonali. meridiano. occidentali. longitudo erat. xxx. cubitor*um*. latitudo: decem. altitudo. x^{m}. (HS 1173D)

The tabernacle was called the House of God, four-sided and rectangular, enclosed by three walls, on the north, south, and west. Its length was thirty cubits, its breadth ten, its height ten.

Ff. 102v–105r OE = Exodus 32:7–35:3; no annotations

Ff. 105v–110v OE = Leviticus; no annotations

Ff. 111r–116v OE = Numbers 1:1–12:15; no annotations

F. 117r *Illustration:* One frame: Moses (horned) sending out a man from each of the twelve tribes to reconnoiter the land. **OE** = Numbers 13:1–5, 17–21[616]

298. Ninive vrbs assirior*um* q*u*am edificauit assur:- egrediens de t*er*ra sennaar. Est. & alia | usq*ue* hodie ciuitas judeor*um* nomine Niniue in angulo arabie. q*u*am nu*n*c corrupte[617] ni|niuen uocant.- (SNLH 23.912C; Lagarde 141.26)

Ninive, a city of the Assyrians which Assur built, leaving the land of Sennaar. There is at the present day another city of the Jews by the name of Ninive in the corner of Arabia which they now corruptly call Niniven.

299. Reblatha Regio babil`on´ior*um*. siue urbs q*u*am nu*n*c antiochia*m* uocant: (SNLH 23.917C; Lagarde 147.22)

Reblatha, a district of the Babylonians, or the city which they now call Antioch.

Ff. 117v–121r OE = Numbers 13:15–16:49; no annotations

F. 121v *Illustration:* One large frame in two registers: above left, God (hand of God) speaks to Moses in a tabernacle, Aaron standing outside in attitude of

[616] All the annotations to Numbers are from Jerome or Ps-Jerome.

[617] Lagarde “conrupte,” PL “correpte,” an emendation [note d]; see Lagarde’s note.

worship, right, Moses gather rods from each tribe; below left, Moses places a rod in the tabernacle, right, "each man takes his rod." **OE** = Num. 16:50, 17:1–2, 17:5, 17:7–11

300. (f. 121v, bottom margin, lines 3–2 up) § Cades. u*bi* fons iudicii e*st*. Est cades barne in deserto. q*ue* coniungit*ur* ciuitati petre. v*bi* occubu`it´ Maria. & Moy|ses rupe p*er*cussa aq*ua*m scicienti [*sic, recte* sitienti] populo dedit. S*ed* et p*r*incipes amalech. ibi a chodollaomor cesi sunt:· (SNLH 23.885A/B; Lagarde 108.21)

Cades, where the fountain of judgement is. It is . . . Cadesbarne in the desert which is in close proximity with the city of Petra . . . where Mariam lay (in the grave) and Moses having struck water from the rock gave it to the thirsty people (Num. 20:1–13). . . . But also the princes of Amelech were killed there by Chodorlahomor (Gen. 14:7).

F. 122r *Illustrations:* One large frame in two registers: above, God's hand bestows priesthood on Aaron and his son; below, right, burial of Maria (Miriam), left, people upbraid Moses (horned) for lack of water, hand of God above Moses. **OE** = Num. 18:1, 20:1–3, 6–8, 10–11

301a.[618] Uidet*ur* m*ih*i i*n* Maria. mortua. i*n* Moyse. ⁊ aaron legi et sacerdotio iudeor*um*. finis inposit*us*. q*uo*d nec ipsi ‖ ad t*erra*m rep*ro*missionis t*r*anscendere ualeant:· nec c*r*edente*m* pop*ulu*m de solitudine hui*us* mundi educe/re- | Et Nota q*uo*d pos*t* morte*m* p*r*ophetie. & aq*ua*s co*n*tradictionis:· idumeu*m* carneu*m* atq*ue* t*er*renu*m* t*r*ansire n*on* possint:· | set egrediat*ur* edom:· + | + Int*er*pretatio q*uo*q*ue* nominis. morti & offense. & negatio t*r*ansitui co*n*uenit. Ubi eni*m* mandatu*m*:· | ibi peccatu*m*. V*bi* peccatu*m*:· ibi offensa. V*bi* offensa:· ibi Mors. Hec e*st* mansio. de q*ua* (. .) psalmista ait. | Co*m*mouebit d*omin*us desertu*m* cades:· Syn au*tem*. sanc*ta* int*er*p*re*tat*ur* cata antifrasin i*n*telligen*dum*. q*uo*mod*o* parce dicun/tur- ‖ ab eo q*uo*d minime parcant. & bellu*m* q*uo*d neq*ua*q*ua*m bellu*m* sit. & luc*us* q*uo*d minime luceat:· (Jerome, Ep. 78, "Ad Fabiolam," "XXXIII Mansio," PL 22.717/716:· CSEL 55, 76.19)

It seems to me that in the death of Mariam. . . . Moses, and Aaron one is to understand an end being imposed on the Law and on the priesthood of the Jews, because they had the power neither to cross over to the promised land, nor to lead the faithful people from the desert of this world. And note well that after the death of prophecy and 'the waters of contradiction' (Num. 20:13) they were not able to cross over the fleshly and carnal Idumea . . . but went out by Edom. Also by interpretation its name is 'for death and offense' and this is fitting for the denial in regard to the passage (Num. 20:18). Where there is a command, there

---

618 F. 121v, bottom line, continuing with 3 lines to top of f. 122r and, with continuation marks (+), to bottom of f. 122r, 3 lines, and continuing to top of f. 122v. Up in the right margin of f. 122r 'xxxiii' to indicate ch. 33 of the source of no. 301a; cf. no. 307a.

is a sin, where a sin, there is an offense, where an offense, there is death. This is the station of which the Psalmist says, "the Lord shall shake the desert of Cades" (Ps. 28:8). Sin (Num. 33:36) is interpreted 'holy', understood as expressed by its opposite; in the same way 'sparingly' is said because they hardly spare at all; and 'bellum' (war/beautiful) which is in no way pretty, and grove ('lucus') which has least light ('luceat').

302. (f. 122r, in margin, insular *r*, brown ink) María[619]

303. (f. 122r, marginal gloss to OE lines 4–5, with *signe de renvoi*) **ǽfter þisum cómon israhela | bearn to ðam westene sín.** / hec e*st* cades.

304. (f. 122r, in frame) § Thuniel \`*ue*l fanuel´ pat*er* Gedor et ezer. pat*er* osa \`*ue*l usa*m*´: filii fuerant[620] hur. fr*atri*s huri. | filii Marie. Gedor u*ero* 7 osa \`*ue*l usi´ no*mi*na locoru*m* sunt. (QH1P, PL 23. 1371B)

Thuniel (or Fanuel) the father of Gedor and Ezer, father of Osa (or Usam), were the sons of Hur, the brother of Huri, the son of Mariam. Gedor and Osa (or Usi) are the names of places (cf. 1 Para. 4:4, 1 Para. 2:19–20).[621]

F. 122v *Illustrations:* Two frames: upper, left, Moses (horned) smites the rock, right, people drink, a woman gives drink to a man; lower frame in two registers, upper left panel, Moses sends two messengers to king of Edom, right panel, king of Edom refuses Moses' request for passage, lower register, the army of Edom (right) bars the way of Moses and the Hebrews. **OE** = Num. 20:14, 17–18, 20–21

305. (lower ledger of upper frame) § Helath regio p*r*incipiu*m* [*sic, for* "-pum"] edom.[622] & ciuitas esav. i*n* decimo á pet[r]\`a´[623] Miliario. co*ntr*a orientem (SNLH 23.896B; Lagarde 121.16)

---

[619] An indexical word (sc. OE line 5, 7 **ðær sweolt maría áárones | swustor**). Because of ink and script classed as an English word.

[620] Corrected from 'fuerunt'.

[621] See no. 245a. The passage connects Mariam, the sister of Moses, to the tribe of Juda through Hur and Huri, the sons of Phanuel of the tribe of Juda. 'Effrata' (= Bethlehem, birthplace of Christ) is interpreted 'sororis Moysi'; cf. Stephen Langton, *Comm. in Para.*, ed. Saltman, 88: "Isti sunt fil[ii] Ur, scilicet predicti Phuniel et Ezer. Unde Rabanus sic dicit: Phuniel et Ezer fratres [filii] fuerunt Hur. Nota quod Gedor et Osa loca sunt a filiis Hur possessa et ab eis dicta. Effrata. Sororis Moysi." ("These are the sons of Ur, namely the aforementioned, Phuniel and Ezer. And so Hrabanus says: 'Phuniel and Ezer were the brothers [sons] of Hur.' Note that Gedor and Osa are places possessed by the sons of Hur and so-called from them. Effrata, of the sister of Moses.").

[622] Scribe wrote 'dedom' and partially erased first 'd'.

[623] Scribe wrote 'pet' and inserted 'a' above: it is not a proper abbreviation.

Elath is the region of (the rulers of) Edom and the city of Esau, about ten miles from Petra towards the east.

306.[624] § Aaron sacerdos in lege pr*imus*. anno quadragesimo egressionis ex egipto. etatis centesimo. uicesimo | tertio. in Kalendis augusti. (`m*en*se q*u*into. p*r*ima die mensis.´) ut Josephus p*er*hibet in arabia. in monte asin [*recte* sina] `*u*el or´ qui nunc petra. | dicit*ur* oreb obiit. Eleazaro filio in locu*m* ei*us* subrogato:[625]

Aaron the first priest in the law, in the fortieth year after the year of the Exodus from Egypt, being 123 years old, on the kalends of August (in the fifth month, the first day of the month) as Josephus says, died in Arabia, in Mount Sinai (or Hor),[626] which is now Petra, called Oreb, his place being taken by his son Eleazar. (cf. Numbers 33:38–39, 20:28)

F. 123r *Illustrations:* Two frames: upper, death of Aaron; lower, in two registers, upper right panel, Chanaanites successfully oppose the Hebrews, who, left panel, make a vow to the Lord (hand descending from heaven), lower register, on left, the Hebrews fight successfully, and on right, sack the Canaanite city. **OE** = Num. 20:21, 28, 30; 21:1–4

307a. (f. 123r, upper outer margin; title to Mansio XXXIV, the text being cited in no. 307b) aaron[627] |in | extremo t*er*re edom. | .xxxiiii^{ta} - | mansio est- (Jerome, Ep. 78, PL 22.717)

Aaron (died) in the outermost land of Edom, it is the thirty-fourth station.

307b. (beg. bottom of 122v, lines 1–2 up, continuing on f. 123r under the upper block of OE text, 4 lines) Morit*ur* au*tem* eo anno q*uo* nouus po|pulus t*er*ra rep*ro*missionis int*ra*turus erat. in extremis finib*us* idumenor*um*: ‖ Et plangit eu*m* pop*ul*us. xxx^{ta}. | dieb*us*. ááron plangit*ur*. i*esu*s non plangit*ur*. In lege descens*us* ad inferos. in euang*e*lio ad paradisum- | t*r*ansmigratio: (Jerome, Ep. 78, "Ad Fabiolam," "Mansio XXXIV," PL 22.717–18)

In that year, when the renewed people was about to enter the promised land, he (Aaron) died in the outermost region . . . of the Idumeans. . . . And the people mourned him for thirty days; Aaron was mourned, Joshua (Jesus) was not mourned. In the Law there is a descent to hell, in the Gospel a passing over to Paradise (cf. Num. 20:30, 33:37–39)

---

624 Bottom, lines 2–4 up; the inserted words (written up in the picture space) are marked with a *signe de renvoi* in text, but misplaced at 'monte'.

625 Unsourced. Cf. LJ 271.24–272.9.

626 Influenced by Gal. 4:25: "Sina enim mons est in Arabia."

627 'aaron' in extreme upper corner, added in brown ink, written with insular 'r'.

308. § Bervth filior*um* iacim i*n* deserto loc*us* in quo obiit aaron:˙ & ostendit*ur* usq*ue* | hodie. in decimo lapide[628] urbis petre. i*n* montis uertice:˙ (SNLH 23.880B; Lagarde 102.21)

Beroth of the sons of Jacan is a place in the desert in which Aaron died (Deut. 10:6), and it is shown to the present day at the tenth milestone from the city of Petra on the top of the mountain (Mt. Hor). (cf. no. 281c)

309. (bottom margin) Rursu*m*q*ue* in eode*m* loco pugnat[629] ex uoto:˙ uictor uincit*ur*. Victi sup*er*ant appellant*ur*q*ue* nom*en* orma. | id est anathema- Cu*m*q*ue* nos d*e*i auxilio. destitutos hostis i*n*uaserit. duxer`it´q*ue* captiuos non desp*er*em*us* | salute*m* s*ed* it*er*u*m* armem*ur*[630] ad p*re*liu*m*:˙ Pot`e´st fieri ut uincam*us* v*b*i uicti sum*us*:˙[631] et i*n* eode*m* loco triu*m*[p]hem*us*. In q*uo* | fuim*us* ante captiui:˙ (Jerome, Ep. 78, "Ad Fabiolam," "Mansio 34," PL 22.718)

Once again, on the same spot, he fought . . . because of his prayer, the victor was vanquished. The vanquished prevail and are given a name . . . 'Horma', that is 'anathema'.[632] . . . And when the enemy attacks us, defenseless as we are, and leads us captive, with the help of God let us not despair of salvation but let us rearm for battle. It can come about that we conquer where we are conquered and triumph in the very place in which before we were captured.

F. 123v *Illustrations:* Two frames: upper, the weary Hebrews speak against God (hand of God) and Moses to the right; lower, the Hebrews are attacked by fiery serpents, Moses on right turning away, hand of God. **OE** = Numbers 21:4–5; no annotations

F. 124r *Illustrations:* Two frames: upper, Moses, left, sets up the brazen serpent; lower frame, two panels, left, Moses sends messengers to the king of the Amorites, who, right panel, refuses him passage. **OE** = Numbers 21:9–10, 21–23, 25, 32

310. (bottom margin) § Esebon. Ciuitas seon regis amorreor*um*:˙ in t*er*ra galaad. q*ue* cu*m* fuisset ante Moabitaru*m*. ab amorreis | belli iure possessa e*st*. Meminit hui*us* hieremias. & ysaias. q*uoque* in uisione co*ntra* Moab. Porro nunc | uocat*ur* esbus urbs insignis arabie. i*n* montib*us* q*ui* s*un*t ab ierico:˙[633] .xx[ti]. ab iordane Milib*us* distans:˙ | fuit au*tem* i*n* t*r*ibu ruben- (SNLH 23.893B; Lagarde 117.29)

---

[628] 'lapide' repeated and deleted by scribe.

[629] PL "pugnatur."

[630] Written "armem*us*."

[631] PL "fuimus."

[632] Cf. Num. 21:3, the Israelites defeat the Chanaanites at Horma, the place where earlier they had been defeated by the Amalechites (Num. 14:41–45).

[633] MS 'hierico', with 'h' cancelled.

Hesebon, a city of Sehon, king of the Amorites (Num. 21:26), in the land of Galaad (Jos. 12:2), which belonged to the Moabites before that; it was possessed by the Amorites by the law of war. Jeremias (48:2) makes mention of this as well as Isaias (15:4) in the vision against Moab. Moreover now it is called Esbus, an important city of Arabia in the mountains which are away from Jericho, twenty miles distant from the Jordan; it was in the tribe of Ruben (Jos. 12:6).

F. 124v *Illustrations:* One large frame in two registers: above, the Hebrews defeat the Amorites, below, in an architectural frame forming two picture spaces and representing the city of the Amorites, in left space Moses speaks to his men about the king of Basan, and in right, Hebrews go out to do battle. **OE** = Numbers 21:33–35

311a. § Edrai. v*b*i int*er*fect*us* e*st* og rex basan. gigas. & potens. omnis*que* illi*us* ce*sus* ex*er*cit*us*. Nunc au*tem* e*st* | adra i*n*signis arabie. ciuitas. in .xx^{mo}. q*u*arto lapide a bostra[634]:- (SNLH 23.893B; Lagarde 118.3)

Edrai, where Og king of Basan, giant and powerful, was killed and his entire army was destroyed (Num. 21:33–35; cf. Jos. 13:12). It is now Adra, an important city of Arabia about twenty-four miles from Bos(t)ra.

311b.[635] § Misor. Ciuitas. óg. regis basan- | significat au*tem* misor loca plana atq*ue* ca*m*pestra: Selcha ciuitas regis og. in regione basanitide. | Sephama. t*er*min*us* iudee. ad solis ortu*m*. Sadala. t*er*min*us* judee: (Jerome, SNLH 23.909C, 920C; Lagarde 137.32, 150.24)

Misor, a city of Og, king of Basan; 'Misor' signifies a flat and level place. . . . Selcha, a city of King Og in the region of the Basanites (Deut. 3:10). Sephama, the border of Judea to the east. Sadala, a border of Judea.

F. 125r *Illustrations:* Two frames: upper, left, God promises victory to Moses and on right Hebrews destroy Og; lower, two panels, left Moses and Hebrews travel to Moab, right, Balaac takes counsel. **OE** = Numbers 22:1–20; no annotations

F. 125v *Illustration:* One frame in two panels: left, servants of Balaac offer gifts to Balaam, right, Balaam's dream, hand of God descending on him. **OE** = Numbers 22:20–35[636]

312. (bottom margin) § fotura. ciuitas t*r*ans mesopotamia*m*. (.)unde fuit balaam. ariolus: (SNLH 23.897D; Lagarde 123.17)

---

634 MS 'ab ostra'.

635 More information on Og, with two extraneous entries also copied.

636 A Hebrew alphabet has been added at bottom of page. It does not appear to be part of the annotation project.

Fotura, a city beyond Mesopotamia, whence came Balaam the soothsayer.

F. 126r *Illustrations:* Two frames: upper, left, Balaam beats his ass, center, the ass speaks to him, right, he worships an angel; lower in two registers, above, Balaam, with his men, is met by Balaac, below, Balaac, with Balaam, worships at "seven altars." **OE** = Num. 22:35–36, 23:1, 8, 11–13

313a. (inside lower frame, above altars) § Fogor. & bethfogor mons moabitaru*m*. ad que*m* balac | rex. adduxit balaam ariolu*m* i*n* sup*er*cilio libiadis- (SNLH 23. 897D; Lagarde 123.20)

Phogor and Bethphogor, a mountain of the Moabites, to which King Balaac led Balaam the soothsayer on the summit of Mount Libiad (Num. 23:27–28; cf. Jos. 13:20, 22, Deut. 34:6)

313b. fogor[637] ciuitas regni edom (SNLH 23.898.B; Lagarde 124.6)

Phogo(r), a city of the kingdom of Edom.[638]

F. 126v *Illustrations:* Two frames: upper, Balaam and Balaac worship at seven altars on Mount Phasga; lower, Balaac builds seven altars for Balaam on mount Phogor. **OE** = Numbers 23:1, 8, 11–14, 25–28; 24:1–2, 10–11

314a.[639] § debongad [*sic*] Castra filio*rum* isr*ahe*l (SNLH 23.891A; Lagarde 115.13,14)

Dibongab is a fort of the sons of Israel.

314b. dismeboan \`Moab´[640]. Id e*st* ad occide*n*te*m* moab∵ iuxta iordanen∵ | co*n*n-tra [*sic*] hiericu*m*∵ v*b*i balaac rex Moab. & maiores natu madian israhele*m* i*n*sidiis decep*er*|unt. In q*uo* loco & Moyses sc*r*ibit deut*er*onomiu*m*∵ (*ibid.*)

Dismoab. It is to the west of Moab, next to the Jordan opposite Jericho, where Balaac king of Moab and the aristocrats of Madian deceived Israel with plots; in which place also Moses wrote Deuteronomy (cf. Num. 33:5; 36:13).

---

[637] Edd. "Fogo."

[638] The commentator is combining in 313a/b Jerome's entries on Fogo(r) from two places in SNLH: "de Numeris et Deuteronomio" and "De Regnorum libris."

[639] In the lower picture frame. 314a/b are two entries written as one, no punctuation between them; unlike the combination of entries in 313a/b, here the combination seems to be an accidental confusion of two contiguous unrelated entries.

[640] This word inserted above is apparently intended as a correction of '-boan'; varr.: "Dysme Moab," "Dismemoab," "Dismae moab."

315. § dannaba Ciuitas balac filii beor. regis edom. p*ost* q*u*em regnauit jobab:·[641] & e*st* usq*ue* hodie uilla dan|nia in octauo Milario areopoleos. p*er*gentib*us* arnon-en- Et e*st* alt*er*a dannaba sup*er* Monte*m* | phegor:· in vii^mo^. lapide esbus:· (SNLH 23.890C; Lagarde 114.31)

Denaba, a city of Balaac, son of Beor, king of Edom, after whom reigned Jobab; . . . and there is to the present day a village called Dannia eight miles from Areopolis for those going toward Arnon. And there is another Dannaba upon mount Phegor, at the seventh milestone from Esbus.

F. 127r *Illustrations:* Two frames, upper, two panels, the Hebrews enter into the space of the daughters of Moab and "commit fornication" (Num. 25:1–3); lower, the fornicators are slain (Num. 25:7–9) **OE** Numbers 25:1–9 ; no annotations but no. 316 on f. 128r seems to be meant to apply to text/illustrations on f. 127r[642]

F. 127v *Illustration:* One large frame divided into three registers, in upper two of the Hebrews slay the disarmed men of the Midianites and in lower the Midianite women who are not virgins **OE** = Numbers 25:16–17, 31:6–18;[643] no annotations

F. 128r *Illustrations:* One large frame divided into two registers: Moses, in upper center, numbers the Israelites gathered around and below him. **OE** = Numbers 31:18, 26:2, 51–62, 64–65

316. (in lower picture space, with reference to f. 127r?) Moab ab uno filior*um* loth. q*ui* uocabat*ur* moab. urbs arabie. q*ue* nu*n*c areopolis d*icitu*r | sic uocata. e*st*. Appellat*ur*. (. .)au*tem* moab ex nomine urbis & regio:. porro ipsa ciu`i´tas[644] | q*u*asi p*ro*priu*m* uocabulu*m* possidet. rabbat moab:· (. . .) id e*st* grandis moab:· (SNLH 909A; Lagarde 137.5)

Moab (is so called) from one of the sons of Loth who was called (Moab); it is a city of Arabia which now is said to be called Areopolis. . . . He is called Moab from the name of the city and region; on the other hand this city possesses its own name, 'Rabbat Moab', that is 'Great Moab'.

641 Edd. "Job," but "Jobab" is right; cf. Gen. 36:32–33: "Bela filius Beor, nomenque urbis ejus Denaba. Mortuus est autem Bela, et regnavit pro eo Jobab filius Zarae de Bosra."

642 Moab is mentioned at Numbers 25:1 in the Vulgate, but the name is not used in the OE, and at 31:12, a verse not represented in the OE. The fornication with the daughters of Moab is mentioned in no. 322.

643 Crawford, *OE Heptateuch*, 331, notes that the textual order of chaps. 31 and 26 are reversed in both the Cotton and Laud manuscripts.

644 Written beyond frame, in margin.

317. Petra ciuitas arabie in *terra* edom. *que* cognominata *est* iectahel. & ab assir`i´is[645] Rece*m* d*icitu*r. | Rece*m* hec *est* petra. Ciuitas arabie. in q*u*a regnauit raam.[646] que*m* inte*r*fecerunt filii isr*ahe*l. | d*icitu*r au*tem* ipse rex q*u*oq*ue* madian- (SNLH 23.915C, 916B; Lagarde 145.9, 146.1)

Petra is a city of Arabia in the land of Edom, which is also named Jectahel (cf. 4 Kings 14:7) and by the Assyrians is called Recem (cf. Num. 31:8). Recem, this is Petra, a city of Arabia in which reigned Raam, whom the sons of Israel killed. It is said he was king of Madian as well.

Ff. 128v–139r OE = Deuteronomy; no annotations to Deuteronomy, which is on unillustrated full text pages except for f. 136v, 137r, 138v.[647]

F. 139v *Illustration:* Full-page illustration, framed to simulate moulding, in three informal registers formed by the mountain, showing bottom left corner, Moses (hand of God, above him) blessing the Israelites, middle, the grieving people, above, right, accompanied by God as a cross-nimbed beardless youth, Moses gazes out right towards the Promised Land (pictured on facing f. 140r), at top left his corpse (labeled 'Moysis obiit') is attended by God (labeled 'd*omin*us').[648] No OE.

318. (upper right of frame) .ii°. Milia. ccccxc^t´i´*um* annor*um* | Moyses obiit.[649]

In the 2490th year of the world Moses died.

319. (bottom margin) § Gain. [*recte* Gai in] Moab. Q*u*od inte*r*pr*etatur* uallis moab iuxta fogor. v*b*i sepult*us est* Moyses:· (SNLH 23.900A; Lagarde 126.19)

Gai in Moab, which is interpreted 'Vale of Moab' next to Phogor where Moses is buried (cf. Deut. 34:6).

320. § Gader. & hui*us* rege*m* inte*r*fecit | I*ESU*S.[650] Turris ubi habitante iacob ruben pat*r*is sui uiolauit thoru*m*:· & absq*ue* g. litt*er*a in heb*r*eo ader | sc*r*ibitur:· (SNLH 23.900D, 898D; Lagarde 127.20, 124.32)

[645] Edd. read "a syris"; two MSS closely related to Claudius, Cambridge, Trinity Coll. O.4.7 (f. 75r) and B.2.34 (f. 72v) read 'ab assiriis'; see ch. 6, 310.

[646] Edd. "rocam," "roacam."

[647] On f. 130r/v (right margin, partially trimmed) a series of added numerals pertaining to the Ten Commandments in the main text, added in a later hand, not that of the annotations.

[648] See the detailed analyis of the opening ff. 139v-140r in Withers, *Frontiers*, 263–72.

[649] Bede, DTR, the expected source, gives 2493 years; 'Moysis obiit' does double duty as the picture label and the completion of the text of no. 318.

[650] The scribe generally uses the "nomen sacrum" for "Josue" (the name "Joshua" is the same as "Jesus" in the Vulgate); this is a surprising but common practice in twelfth-century Jerome manuscripts.

Gader, and Joshua killed its king (Jos. 12:13). . . . The tower where Jacob lived when Ruben violated the wedding chamber of his father; and Hebrew lacking the letter 'g', it is written 'Ader'. (cf. Gen. 35:21–22 "turrem gregis" and Num. 34:4; see no. 186)

F. 140r *Illustration*: Full-page frame, painted to simulate moulding, a stylized diagram of the promised land in five registers, the upper three mostly unfinished outlines, the uppermost being the roof of a pavilion of some sort, the second blank except for colored chevrons on the sides, the third blank and filled with twelfth-century writing, the fourth with stylized trees,[651] the lower a greenish field representing the sea.[652] No OE.

321. § Moyses cu*m* quadraginta annor*um*. in egipto. Quadraginta. in madian. Quadraginta | minus t*r*iginta diebus in heremo. p*re*esset pop*u*lo. Centesimo uicesimo etatis anno. | in Monte abarim cont*ra* ieric`h´o ad iordane*m* ubi nunc est ciuitas abilal. obiit. | sepult*usque*[653] e*st*. a d*omi*no i*n* ualle Moab que est. i*n* arabia. Et non cognouit homo sepul|chru*m* ei*us* usq*ue* i*n* presente*m* diem. hec Nor[. . . . . .][654].Supputa p*er* singulas etates annor*um* nume|ru*m*. ab adam. usq*ue* ad hoc te*m*pu*s*. fuerunt anni. ii°. Millia. (. . .) (Quadriginta Nonaginta.)[655] triu*m* annor*um* Et genera|tiones .xx^{ti}.vii^{tem}. iuxta hebreos. `i*d est* usq*ue* ad moyses. 7 aaron.´[656]

Moses had led the people for forty years in Egypt, forty in Madian, forty (years) less thirty days in the desert. In the 120th year of his life, in Mount Abarim opposite Jericho towards the Jordan where now the city of Abilal is, he died and was buried by the Lord in the Vale of Moab which is in Arabia. "And no man knows his burial place to the present day" (Deut. 34:6). This Nor(mannus says): Count up through the separate ages, and the number of years from Adam to this day, that is, up to Moses and Aaron, were 2493 years and twenty-seven generations according to the Hebrews.

F. 140v *Illustration:* One frame: Joshua commanding the leaders of the people, the hand of God descending on him. **OE** = Joshua 1:1–18

651 Cf. OE text on f. 139r/18 **7 pa[l]m treowa byrig** (Deut. 34:3).

652 **7 eall ðæt lánd oððа yte|mestan sǽ** (Deut. 34:2)

653 Written 'sepult*us*qe*m*'.

654 'Hec Nor[manus]' is written with a different nib and has been partially erased.

655 Words in round brackets are inserted from below.

656 Exact source unknown, cf. Deut 34: 6, Jerome, Ep. 78, "42 Mansiones," Bede, DTR "2493." Similar types of unsourced notes are nos. 23 and 66.

322. § Sattim u*bi* p*o*p*ulus* pollut*us* e*st*. fornicatione fili`a´r*um*[657] moab. Est au*tem* iuxta monte*m* phogor:· unde et | i*esus* exploratores ad inuestiganda*m* & noscenda*m* misit iericho. (SNLH 23.920B; Lagarde 150.14)

Setim, where the people was polluted by the fornication of the daughters (sons) of Moab (cf. Mich. 6:5). It is next to Mount Phogor, whence also Joshua sent out spies to Jericho for reconnaissance and intelligence (Jos. 2:1).

F. 141r *Illustrations:* Two frames: above, left, Joshua sends out two spies who, right, confer with Rahab in her house; below, the king of Jericho sends two men for information to Rahab (in her house), who deceives them by pointing away in the wrong direction. OE = Joshua 2:1–2, 4–10

323. § Iosue p*er* annos uiginti sex. regit | pop*u*lum Iosepho testante. Nam de | annis ducat*us* i*m*pius [*sic, for* "imprimis"?] | s*anct*a sc*r*iptura tacet:· | vixitq*ue* centu*m* et decem. | annos. (unsourced, cf. no. 359, also Jos. 24:29, LJ 320.20)[658]

Joshua ruled the people for twenty-six years, according to Josephus. For about the years of his generalship Holy Scripture is silent; and he lived 110 years.

F. 141v *Illustration:* One frame: right, Rahab lets Joshua's spies down by a rope while on left, pursuing messengers leave empty-handed. OE = Joshua 2:10–21

324. Qui cu*m* mis[i]ss*et*[659] ad raab ut educeret eos:· ab[s]conderat eos in stipula | lini `7 quis q[u]alus[660] canabi secus muru*m*.´ qua*m* siccabat sup*ra* muru[m]:· mentiens eos egressos du*m* | clauderet*ur* porta. (HS 1261C/D)

Who, when they were sent to Rahab to bring them out, she hid them on a hank of flax (and some basket of hemp beside the wall) which she was drying on the wall, lying that they had gone out while the gate was being closed.

---

[657] Altered from 'filior*um*'; "filiorum/filiarum" is a MS variant (Lagarde); cf. the OE text and illustration, upper part of f. 127r, and 149, above.

[658] "et ille quidem talia praesentibus loquens defunctus est, cum vixisset annis centum et decem. quorum cum Moyse quidem pro doctrina utilium rerum commoratus est quadraginta, dux autem post illius mortem viginti et sex fuit, vir nec sapientia indignus nec eorum quae cogitabat ut multis sapienter ediceret inexpertus, sed ubique summus et ad opera periculaque magnanimus audaxque bella disponere et in pace dexter, et in omni tempore praecipua virtute conveniens." ("And [Joshua] having thus spoken to those present, died, having lived 110 years. For 40 of them he lived with Moses for the sake of useful learning; after Moses' death he was their general for 26 years, a man neither despicable in learning nor inexperienced in conveying what he intended to the masses, but everywhere distinguished and in deeds and in danger magnanimous and brave in conducting war and skillful in peace and at all particular times suited for virtue"); cf. no. 359.

[659] Written 'mis(.)ss;' 's' erased.

[660] The 'ua' imperfectly formed.

F. 142–143r OE = Joshua 2:22–24, 3:1–17, 4:1–14; no annotations

F. 143v OE 28 lines, the bottom third left blank, not prepared for a picture[661] = Joshua 4:18–19, 5:1–4, 8–12

325. § Anno p*r*imo sui ducat*us* Josue decima die p*r*imi me*n*sis patefacto. Jordanis alu`e´o. et ret[r]orsum | conu*er*so. p*opulu*m i*n* t*er*ram rep*ro*missionis induxit. et sup*er* lapides duodecim á singulis ducib*us* | de profundo iordanis adductos pascha i*m*molauerunt. Tunc manna cibus | uidelicet quadraginta annor*um* defecit. (Bede, DTR, CCSL 123B.472; for second half cf. Jos. 4:5, 20, 5:9–11, 12)

In the first year of his leadership, in the tenth day of the first month, Joshua opened the passage of the Jordan that had been turned back completely and led the people into the promised land; \ and upon twelve stones brought each by a leader (of a tribe) from the depths of the Jordan they celebrated the pasch. At that time manna, the food of forty years, ceased.

326. § Bunos. hoc e*st* collis p*re*puciot*um* | locus i*n* galgalis. u*bi* ci*rcum*cidit ie*sus* p`o´p*ulum* isr*ahe*l. in s*ecun*do ab ihericho lapide. | Et ostendunt*ur* usq*ue* hodie saxa. q*ue* de iordane illic t*ra*nslata | script*ura* co*m*memorat. .xv. milib*us* ab ierosolima | excurrit:ʼ (SNLH 23.880B; Lagarde 102.25)[662]

Bunos: this is the 'hill of the foreskins', a place in Galgal where Joshua circumcised the people of Israel at the second (mile)stone from Jericho. And shown to the present day are the rocks carried there from the Jordan which Scripture commemorates, fifteen miles out from Jerusalem.

327.[663] § bethsaide. ciuitas i*n* galilea. andréé et petri. 7 philippi ap*osto*lor*um* p*ro*pe stagnum genesareth. | § bethfage. villula i*n* Monte oliueti. ad quam uenit d*ominus* ie*sus*. § bethania. villa in s*ecun*do ab elia milia|rio. in lat*er*e Montis oliueti:ʼ ubi saluator lazaru*m* suscitauit. § betharaba.[664] Tran[s] iordane*m*:ʼ u*bi* ioh*anne*s in | penitentia[m] baptizabat. vn*de* et hodie usq*ue* plures de f*ratri*bus. h*oc* e*st* de nu*mero* c*re*dentiu*m* ibi renasci cupientes. | uitali g*ur*gite (. .) baptizantur:ʼ ‖

[661] Dodwell and Clemoes suggest that the color wash, which is all that is there, was the beginnings of a picture to include the Jordan river. The annotator avoids the color areas.

[662] Final phrase unsourced.

[663] F. 143v, bottom 5 lines, the block is marked with a note (+) that links this to the "Bethsaida" note on f. 144r and indicating continuation to bottom of f. 144r; these blocks are contiguous entries in SNLH consisting of the whole "B" section of "De euangeliis."

[664] Imperfectly altered from 'betharaha'.

beth`s´aida piscina in ier*usa*lem q*ue* uocat*ur*[665] probati `*ue*l ce. *ue*l probatiKH.´[666] et a nob*is* interp*re*tari potest pecualis. Hec q*uin*q*ue* | q*uo*nda*m* portic*us* habuit:˙ ostendunt*ur*q*ue* gemini lac*us*. quor*um* un*us* hibernis pluuiis adimp`l´eri solet:˙ | Alt*er* miru*m* in mo`du*m*´ rubens q*ua*si cruentis aq*u*is antiq*ui* i*n* se op*er*is signa testat*ur*:˙ Nam hostias in eo lauari á |(á)[667] sacerdotib*us* solitas fer`un´t:˙[668] vnde & nom*en* accep*er*it:˙ (SNLH 23.884C/D-885A; Lagarde 107.30–108.15)

Bethsaide, a city in Galilee of the apostles Andrew, Peter, and Philip, near the Sea of Genesareth.

Bethfage, a village on the Mount of Olives, to which the Lord Jesus came.

Bethania, a village on the second mile from Aelia (Jerusalem) on the side of Mount Olivet, where the Savior raised Lazarus. . . .

Betharaba [mentioned only at Jos. 15:6, 15:61, 18:22], across Jordan, where John baptized into penance, whence up to the present day many of the brothers, that is, out of the number of faithful desiring to be reborn there, are baptized in the water of life.

Bethsaida is a pond in Jerusalem which is called *probatice* (or *probatike)* and by us may be intepreted 'of sheep'. This place once had five doorways and twin pools are shown which the winter rains usually fill; another (pool), astonishingly red as if with bloody waters, displays the traces of the ancient practice, for the sacrificial animals used to be washed there by the priests, whence it got its name.

F. 144r *Illustrations:* Unfinished frame meant to be in two registers, the upper apparently of the circumcision of the Israelites by Joshua, the lower the feast of unleavened bread. **OE** = Joshua 5:13–16, 6:1–4

328. (top) § Gergesa. Regio u*bi* eos q*ui* demonib*us* uexabant*ur*. saluator restituit sanitati. hodieq*ue* sup*er* monte*m* | uiculus demonstrat*ur* iuxta stagnu*m* tyb*er*i`a´dis[669] in quo[670] porci p*re*cipitati sunt:- (SNLH 23.903B; Lagarde 130.18)

Gergesa, a region where the Savior restored to health those possessed by demons; . . . and today upon the mountain a little place is shown next to the Sea of Tiberias into which the swine rushed.

---

[665] Lagarde "uocabatur."

[666] I.e., προβατική. After this, on the line, a mark 'ħII^e' is a miswriting of Greek 'KH', with the superscript 'e' being a Latin interpretation of "eta"; the interlined words must be considered an interpretation or correction of this mark.

[667] 'á' is written at the end of the line and again at the beginning of the next and then slightly smudged out.

[668] Edd.: "ferunt"; the scribe has added an irregular mark as if he intended "feruntur."

[669] The superscript 'a' is to the right of the 'd', with an insertion mark below at the right place.

[670] Edd. "quod".

329.[671] Celas. id *est* uallis Josaphath. inter ier*usal*em. et ‖ Monte*m* oliueti. Lege p*ro*phe*ta*m iohel- (SNLH 288A; Lagarde 111.13)

Celas, that is the Valley of Jehosaphat, between Jerusalem and Mount Olivet. Read the prophet Joel (3:2, 12).

F. 144v *Illustrations:* Two areas for frames that have not been marked out: upper, Joshua worships the angel (Jos. 5:13–16), three figures to left are unidentified; lower, unfinished picture, of Ark of the Covenant? **OE** = Joshua 6:12–14

330a. § Emmaus. de q*uo* loco fuit cleophas. cui*us* lucas eu`a´n|gelista meminit. H*ec* e*st* nunc nicopolis:· insignis ciuitas palestine. § (. .) Ephraim. Iuxta de|seretu*m*:· [*sic*] ad q*ua*m uenit d*ominus* ie*sus* cu*m* discip*u*lis suis:· (SNLH 23.896A; Lagarde 121.6, 9)[672]

Emmaus, from which place was Cleophas whom the evangelist Luke mentions. This is now Nicopolis, a notable city of Palestine.

Ephraim, next to the desert to which came the Lord Jesus with his disciples.

330b. § Galilea. due s*un*t galilee. e q*u*ibus una galilea | gentiu*m* uocat*ur*. uicina finib*us* tyrior*um*. u*b*i & salomon. xx[ti].[673] ciuitates donauit. hyra*m* regi tyri. in | sorte t*r*ibus neptalim:· Alter[a]. galilea d*icitu*r ci*r*ca tyb*er*iade*m* & stagnu*m* genesareth in t*r*ibu zabulon:- (SNLH 23.902C; Lagarde 129.24)

Galilee. There are two Galilees, of which one is called "Galilee of the Gentiles," near the territory of the Tyrians, where also Solomon gave twenty cities to King Hiram of Tyre in the allotment of the tribe of Neptali (3 Kings 9:11); the other called Galilea is around Tiberias and the Sea of Genesareth in the tribe of Zabulon.

330c.[674] § fuit au*tem* chana i*n* t[ri]bu aser. v*b*i d*ominus* n*oste*r. ⁊ saluator aquas u*er*tit i*n* uinu*m*. Unde et nathanael uir[675] | isr*ahe*lita. saluatoris testimonio co*n*p*ro*bat*ur*. Et e*st* hodie oppidu*m* i*n* galilea gentiu*m*:· (SNLH 23.887A; Lagarde 110.4)

. . . Cana was in the Tribe of Asher where our Lord and Savior turned water into wine, whence Nathanael, an Israelite who acknowledged the testimony of the Savior (cf. John 1:47). And at present it is a city of the gentiles in the Galilean region.

---

[671] F. 144r, bottom line, to top of 144v.

[672] These two contiguous comments comprise the entire "E" section of "De Evangeliis."

[673] So also PL; Lagarde "uiginti quinque."

[674] Lines 6–7 of upper block of annotations, followed by a continuation mark (+) indicating the next comment, similarly marked, below the picture frame.

[675] Edd. "uerus."

330d. § Ithura [*recte* Iturea]. & traconitidis[676] regio. Cui*us* tetrarcha fuit philipp*us* sicut in euangeliis legun*tur*: (SNLH 23.906D-907A; Lagarde 135.6)

The region of Iturea and Trachonitis, of which Philip was tetrarch, as is read in the Gospels (Luke 3:1).

330e.[677] § Gadara urbs trans iordane*n* cont*ra* scytopoli*m* & tyberiade*m* ad orien`tal´e plaga*m* sita i*n* Monte. ad cui*us* radices | a q*ue* calide eruperunt. balneis sup*er* `*u*el desupra´ [678] edificatis:. (SNLH 23.903B; Lagarde 130.15)

Gadara is a city across the Jordan opposite Scythopolis and Tiberias situated to the east at the foot of the mountain from which issues hot water, baths being built on (or over) it.

330f.[679] Jordanis. fluui*us* diuidens iudea*m*. arabia*m* & aulone*m*. & us*que* | ad mare mortuu*m* fluens. q*ui* po*st* multos circuit*us* iuxt`a´ ier`i´cho mortuo. admixt*us* mari n*omen* amittit. (SNLH 23.904A/B; Lagarde 131.25)

Jordan, a river dividing Judea, Arabia and Aulonis. . . . and flowing as far as the Dead Sea, which, after many meanderings by Jericho, mixed with the Dead Sea it loses its name.

F. 145r *Illustration:* One frame, unfinished: Israelites before Jericho? A line of annotation has been almost entirely trimmed from the top edge. **OE** = Joshua 6:15–19

330g. Selo `*u*el silo´ In tribu ephraim. in q*uo* loco archa testamenti mansit: & tab*er*naculu*m* d*omi*ni. usq*ue* ad | te*m*pora samuhelis. Est au*tem* i*n* decimo miliario neapoleos. in regione. acrabitena.[680] S*ed* & | iude patriarche filiu*m*. selon appellatum legun*tur*: (SNLH 23.921B/C; Lagarde 152.1)

Selo (or Silo) in the tribe of Ephraim, in which place the ark of the testament remained, and the tabernacle of the Lord, up to the time of Samuel. It is about ten miles from Neapolis in the region of Acrabitena. But it is also read that the son of the patriarch Juda was called Selon ("Sela," 1 Para. 2:2).

---

676 So some mss.; edd. "trachonitis."

677 '§ Gadara u' was begun in bottom area of unmarked frame, was erased and moved down to bottom margin.

678 *Sic*; Lagarde reads "desuper."

679 In the facsimile of Dodwell and Clemoes a few letters on the right edge have been covered by the stub of the inserted leaf f. 147; this area is clear in the CD-ROM facsimile.

680 Corr. from 'acrabictena' with the deleted 'c' connected to 't' by an imperfect ligature.

330h.[681] Sona*m* unde fuit illa mulier suna|mitis. Est au*tem* usq*ue* hodie uic*us* in finib*us* sebaste in reg`io´ne acrabitena uocabulo sanim:· (SNLH 23.922B/C; Lagarde 153.18)

Sonam, whence was that Sunamitish woman (3 Kings 1–2). There is to the present day a village on the border of Sebaste in the region of Acrabitena, by the name of Sanim.

330i.[682] Semeron `dicunt´ au*tem* nu*n*c p*ro* ea sebaste[n] uocari oppidu*m* palestine. v*b*i *sancti* ioh*an*is baptiste reliq*u*ie co*n*dite | *sun*t. legim*us* i*n* regnor*um* libris. q*uo*d amri rex isr*ahe*l emerit monte*m* someron a q*u*oda*m* semera [*recte* semer]. | et edificauerit in u*er*tice ei*us* ciuitate*m*. q*ua*m ex nomine d*omi*ni appellauerit semeron.[683] (SNLH 23.920C; Lagarde 150.28)

Semeron, . . . they say a city of Palestine is now called Sebaste[n] for it, where St. John the Baptist's relics were buried. We read in the Book of Kings that Amri, king of Israel, bought Mt. Someron from a certain Semer and built on its summit a city which he named Semeron from the name of its lord (3 Kings 16:24).

330j. Syon:· mons urbis ier*usa*lem. Samaria ciuitas regalis in isr*ahe*l. q*ue* nu*n*c sebaste d*icitu*r. Sed & | om*n*is regio q*ue* circa ea*m* fuit a ciuitate q*u*onda*m* nom*en* accep*er*at. (SNLH 23.923B; Lagarde 154.18, 19)[684]

Zion, a mountain of the city of Jerusalem.

Samaria, a royal city in Israel which now is called Sebaste. But the whole region around it got its name at one time from that city.

F. 145v *Illustrations:* Two frame areas, not marked out: upper, destruction of the inhabitants of Jericho; lower, Rahab and her kin are saved?[685] **OE** = Joshua 6:21–25, 27

331. Excepta e*st* raab. i*n* p*er*pet*u*o isr*ahe*l. ⁊ data. e*st* ei h*e*reditas. i*n* medio isr*ahe*lis. ⁊ duxit ea*m* salmon p*r*inceps milicie in | t*r*ibu iuda. q*uarum* pat*er* ei*us* naason fu*er*at p*r*inceps i*n* t*r*ibu iuda i*n* deserto. de h*e*c h*abe*m*us* i*n* matheo. Salmo*n* a*utem* genu*it* | booz:· de raab. booz G*enuit* obeth ex ruth. obet g*enuit* iesse. iesse G*enuit* d*aui*d rege*m*:·

Rahab is received in Israel in perpetuity and an inheritance is given to her descendants in the midst of Israel (cf. Jos. 6:25). And Salmon the leader of the army took her to wife in the tribe of Juda of which his father Naason was the prince in the tribe of Juda in the desert, concerning which is said in Matthew:

681 Apparently functioning here as a gloss to the previous note.

682 This passage is also copied on f. 147r, as no. 334e.

683 In the Vulgate the names are, of the man, "Somer" and, of the place, "Samaria."

684 Two contiguous comments.

685 So Dodwell and Clemoes, *Illustrated Hexateuch*, 40.

Salmon begot Boaz from Rahab; Boaz begot Obeth from Ruth; Obeth begot Jesse; Jesse begot King David (cf. Matt. 1:4–6).

F. 146r *Illustrations:* Two unfinished frames, upper probably intended for sin of Achar; lower, probably intended for the spies sent to Hai: **OE** = Joshua 7:1–4

332.[686]§ Agai ad occidentale*m* plag*am* uergit | bethelis. n*on* multu*m* ab ea distans:· Sita e*st* au*tem* bethel euntib*us* helia*m*. `*id est* ierus*a*lem´ de neapoli i*n* leua parte uic. | .xii[mo]. c[i]rciter miliario ab helia. & usq*ue* hodie paruus licet uic*us* ostendit*ur*. Sed & eccl*es*ia edificata est:· | Ibi[687] dormiuit iacob p*er*gens mesopotamia[m]- (SNLH 23.861B; Lagarde 83.30)

Agai is on the western side of Bethel not far distant from it and Bethel is situated towards Aelia (that is, Jerusalem) from Neapolis, twelve miles from Aelia on the left side of the road, and up to the present day a little place is shown, and moreover a church was built. There Jacob slept on his way to Mesopotamia.

F. 146v *Illustration:* One unfinished picture space: probably intended for the defeat of the Israelites by the men of Hai. **OE** = Joshua 7:4, 6–7, 10–15

333. § IERVSalem i*n* q*u*a regnauit adonibezec. & po*st* eu*m* tenuere iebusei. e q*u*ib*us* & sortita e*st* uocabulu*m*. Quos | multo po*st* te*m*pore dauid ext*er*minans:· toti*us* ea*m* iudee p*ro*uincie met*ro*polim fabricat*us* e*st*. eo q*uo*d ibi lo|cum te*m*pli emerit. & inpensas ex[s]truct*ure*.[688] salomoni filio dereliquerit:· (SNLH 23.904C; Lagarde 132.7)

Jerusalem in which Adonibezec reigned and after him the Jebusites held it, and from them it got its name, whom David a long time later exterminated. It was built as the metropolis of the entire province of Judea, because he purchased the place of the temple and left the expenses of construction to his son Solomon.

334a. § Maacha regio regis | gesurim.[689] (SNLH 23.911B; Lagarde 140.19)

Maacha, a territory of the king of Gesur (Deut. 3:14, Jos. 12:5, 13:11, 13).

334b.[690] § Mod`e´im uic*us* iuxta diospolim. unde fuerunt. machabei. quor*um* hodieq*ue* ibide*m* sepulc/ra ‖ monstrant*ur*. Satis itaq*ue* miror q*uo*m*o*do antiochie eor*um* reliq*u*ias ostendant. aut q*u*o hoc certo | autore sit creditu*m*. (SNLH 23.911C; Lagarde 140.20)

---

686 This comment is also copied as no. 292h, probably from a different exemplar.

687 Edd. "ubi."

688 Edd. "structure."

689 The Vulgate form is "Gesuri."

690 Bottom line, continuing to top of f. 147r; this note follows directly on the previous one in Jerome's text.

Modim, a village beside Diospolis[691] where the Maccabees were from, whose tombs are shown up there at the present day (cf. 1 Macc. 9:19, etc.). I wonder a bit how at Antioch they display their relics or by what authority may be believed.

F. 147r Inserted leaf, no OE; the series of notes from Jerome's SNLH continues.

334c. (lines 2–3) § Magedan. ad cui*us* fines Matheus euang*e*lista sc*r*ibit d*omi*n*u*m p*er*uenisse. Sed | & Marchus ei*us*de*m* nominis recordat*ur.* Nunc au*tem* regio d*ici*-*tu*r Magdena circa gerasam: (SNLH 23.912B/C; Lagarde 141.20)

Magedan, to whose territory the Lord came according to the Evangelist Matthew (15:39). But also Mark (8:10) recorded the same name.[692] Nowadays the region around Gerasa is called Magdena.

334d. (lines 3–5) § Naim. Oppi|dulu*m* in q*uo* filiu*m* uidue á Mortuis d*omi*n*us* suscitauit. & usq*ue* hodie in s*ecun*do miliario thabor montis | ostendit*ur:* co*n*tra meridiem iuxta endor: (SNLH 23.914B; Lagarde 143.22)

Naim, a little town in which the Lord raised the widow's son from death (Luke 7:11–13) and up to the present day it is shown at the second milestone from Mt. Thabor on the south side of Endor.

334e. (lines 5–8, the underlined words in brown ink[693]) § Someron. Et hanc[694] cepit | ie*sus* rege illi*us* int*er*fe[c]to. dicunt au*tem* n*unc* p*ro* ea sebaste uocari opidu*m* palestine. v*bi* s*anct*i iohannis. | baptiste reliq*u*ie co*n*dite s*un*t. legim*us* i*n* regno-*rum* libris. q*uo*d amri rex isr*ahe*l. emerit[695] monte*m* somer`o´n á | q*u*oda*m* semera. & edificau*er*it in u*er*tice ei*us* ciutate*m:* q*ua*m ex nomine d*omi*ni appellau*er*it se-meron. (SNLH 23.920C; Lagarde 150.28; for translation see no. 330i)

335a.[696](lines 9–17) MENSVRARVM appellationes q*u*ib*us* utim*ur:* s*un*t xii. digit*us*. uncia. palm*us*. sext*us* [*recte* sextans] pes. cubit*us* | grandus [*recte* gradus]. passus. dece*m*peda. actus. stadiu*m*. Miliariu*m*. Minima pars haru*m* me*n*sura-ru*m* | est digit*us*. Siq*u*id eni*m* infra digitu*m* metiam*ur* partib*us* respondem*us*. ut

[691] Cf. no. 337n.

[692] Old Latin texts have "Magadan" or "Magdala"; the Vulgate has "Dalmanutha."

[693] This passage was already copied on f. 145r, as no. 330i. The copying of this passage seems hesitant or confused; the first three words are cancelled and then repeated; the variant form 'Someron' occurs here, where 'Semeron' occurs on f. 145r; nevertheless, as if the same exemplar is being consulted, the variant forms 'sebaste' (for 'sebasten') and 'semera' (for 'semer') are in both places; perhaps the scribe left off because it was noticed that this note had already been copied but was then filled in later using a different ink; the next note (from an entirely different source) continues for two words in the lighter ink.

[694] These three words are written, cancelled by underdotting, and written again.

[695] 'emerit' is correct; it looks as if scribe wrote, or partially wrote, 'emerit*ur*'.

[696] For a discussion of this note and the next, see ch. 6, 311–16.

dimidia*m* aut tercia*m* | parte*m* digiti.[697] Palm*us* habet digitos. vii. [*recte* iiii] uncias. iii. Sext*us* [*recte* sextans] que eade*m* doran [*recte* dodrans] appellat*ur* ha|bet[698] uncias. ix. digitos. xii.[699] In pede porrecto semipedes .ii. palmi. iiii. uncie. xii. | digiti. xxvii. In pede p*ro*strato[700] semipedes. iiii^{or}. palmi. viii. uncie. xxiiii. digiti. xxxii. | Cubit*us* habet sexq*u*ipedes.[701] Sexta[tes] duas palmas. sex[702] passus. pedes. v. dece*m*peda que & | p*er*tica.[703] Act*us* in longitudine habet pedes. centu*m*.[704] Stadiu*m* habet pedes. dcxxxv. | Passus. cxxv. Miliariu*m* passus. cc. pedes. v.[705] (ed. as from the prefatory epistle of "Balbi ad Celsum: Expositio et ratio omnium formarum," ed. F. Blume et al., *Die Schriften der römischen Feldmesser* [Berlin, 1848], 1:94–95; also as Gerbert Aurillacensis, *De Geometria* 15, PL 139.116B)

The names of the measurements that we use are twelve: digit, inch, palm, sixth, foot, cubit, grade, pace, perch, act, stadium, mile. The smallest of these measures is the digit; if we want to measure less than a digit, we go by parts, as a half or a third. [An inch equals one and a third] digits. A palm is equal to seven [four] digits or three inches. A sixth, which is the same as a dodrans, equals [three palms or] nine inches or twelve digits. [A foot equals three palms or twelve inches or sixteen digits.] In an extended foot are two half-feet, (four palms, twelve inches, twenty-seven digits). In a stretched foot are four half-feet, (eight palms, twenty-four inches, thirty-two digits). [In a squared foot are eight half-feet.] A cubit equals a foot-and-a-half, two sixths, six palms, [eighteen inches. A grade has two-and-a-half feet]. A pace has five feet. A ten-foot, which is [the same as] a perch, [has ten feet]. An act has the length of 100 [120] feet [the breadth of 120 feet]. A stadium has 635 [625] feet or 125 paces. A mile [has] 200 [1000] paces, five [thousand] feet [comprise eight stadia].

335b. (lines 18–24) Ad estimandu*m*[706] cui*us*q*ue* rei altitu`di´ne*m*:· sole lucente q*u*ecunq*ue* res illa fuerit sub diuo posita um|bra*m* emitte [*recte* emittit]. sed non sibi equale*m*.[707] Quap*ro*pt*er* umbre illi*us* quota*m* parte*m* uolueris elige:· | deinde ui*r*ga*m* [*ed.* virgulam] huic pa[r]ti coeq*u*a[l]ata*m* [*ed.* coaequalem] in terra*m* statuas. & umbra*m* exinde cadente*m*. seu p*er* pedes. seu | p*er* palmos. seu p*er* uncias.

---

697 Edd: "Uncia habet digitum unum et tertiam partem digiti."
698 Edd.: "palmos iii," etc.
699 *Omitted*: "Pes habet palmos iii, uncias xii, digitos xvi."
700 Edd.: "constrato."
701 *Omitted*: "In pede quadrato semipedes viii."
702 Edd.: "uncias xviii. gradus habet pedes duo semis."
703 Edd.: "quae eadem pertica appellatur, habet pedes x."
704 Edd.: "longitudinis ped. cxx, latitudinis ped. cxx."
705 Edd.: "miliarium habet passus mille, milia pedum v, stadios viii."
706 This rubric appears as a marginal note in other manuscripts when it appears at all.
707 Corr. from 'equeale*m*'; edd. "coaequalem."

diuidas. Si maior inuenta fucrit:[708] quantu*m* uirga [*ed.* virgula] sup*eratur.* tan|tu*m* a si*n*gulis partib*us* q*u*aru*m* me*n*sura*m* uirga [*ed.* virgula] habet subtrahas. Si au*tem* minor[709] quantu*m* uirga | sup*er*at. tantu*m* dictis [*ed.* praedictis] partib*us* adicias. Q*u*od au*tem* in umbra. u*el* [ex] augm*en*tatione accreuerit. | v*el* ex subtractione remanserit, p*ro* me*n*sura illi*us* rei teneto [*ed.* habeto]: (ed. Nicolaus Bubnov, as "Geometria incerti auctoris" in *Gerberti postea Silvestri II Papae, Opera Mathematica (972–1003)* [Berlin, 1899], 323; also as Gerbert Aurillacensis, *De Geometria* 24, PL 139.121D)

For estimating the height of an object, the sun shining: any object placed under the open sky projects a shadow, but not one [always] equal to itself. Therefore choose whatever segment of this shadow you want. Then set up a measuring rod equal to this part in the ground and then divide the shadow cast from it into feet, quarter-feet, or inches. If [the shadow] is found to be longer [than the rod], by however much the [shadow] surpasses the rod, then subtract (part by part) from the shadow whatever measure the rod has. But if [the shadow] is less, by however much the stick is longer, add the [pre]determined parts. What in the shadow either increases [by] augmentation or remains by subtraction, (keep) as the measure of that object.

336a.[710] (lines 25–26) Itabiriu*m* p*ro* q*u*o aq*u*ila & symmach*us*[711] in osee p*r*oph*et*a t*r*anstuler*unt* (. . .) thabor. Est au*tem* mons | thabor in ca*m*po maximo ad orientale*m* plaga*m* legionis. (SNLH 23.906C; Lagarde 134.26)

Itabirium, for which Aquila and Symmachus in the prophet Osee (5:1) translated 'Thabor'. And it is Mt. Thabor in the Campus Maximus in the eastern area of the Legion.[712]

336b. (line 26[713]) Sor Tir*us.* met*r*opolis phenicis: i*n* t*r*ibu neptali*m.* (SNLH 23.923B; Lagarde 154.22)

Sor, Tyre, the chief city of the Phoenicians in the tribe of Napthali.

---

[708] Edd.: "Si major inventa fuerit umbra, quam virgula quantum umbra virgulam superat . . . ."

[709] Edd.: "est umbra."

[710] From this point to the end of the page, the left margin projects about 3 mm. further to the left. Except for the first three items, what follows is a series of extracts from Bede, *Nomina regionum atque locorum de Actibus*, the series continuing onto and through the verso.

[711] After this word 't*r*anstulit', cancelled.

[712] The point of Jerome's comment is that the Septuagint used the word "Itabyrion," whereas Aquila and Symmachus, in their more literal Greek translations, restored the Hebrew "Thabor." See Frederick Field, ed. *Origenis Hexaplorum quae supersunt* (Oxford, 1875; repr. Hildesheim, 1964), 2:947.

[713] Ductus changes at this point from larger to smaller.

336c. (line 26) ERMON. Mons ermon q*u*em phenices cognominant sanir. iam & sup*ra* posit*us*. (SNLH 23.893C; Lagarde 118.11)

Mount Hermon which the Phoenicians call Sanir; referred to here and above (i.e., at Lagarde 90.19)

336d. (lines 26–27) ENdor. In t*r*ibu manasse. dixim*us* | & sup*ra* de endor. q*ue* e*st* iuxta oppidu*m* naim. i*n* cui*us* pates (*recte* portas) saluator filiu*m* uidue suscitauit. Est au*tem* ci*r*ca scytopoli*m*- (SNLH 23.896C; Lagarde 121.29)

Endor, in the tribe of Manasses. . . . we spoke also above of Endor (cf. no. 334d), which is beside the city of Naim within whose gates the Savior raised the widow's son (Luke 7:11–15). It is near Scythopolis.

337a. (lines 28–30) Ásia. regio q*ue* minor cognominat*ur*. absq*ue* orientali parte. q*ua* ad cappadotia*m* sirya*m*q*ue* p*ro*gredit*ur*. undiq*ue* ci*r*cum|data. e*st* mari. Cui*us* p*r*ouincie s*un*t frigia. pamphilia. cili`ci´a. licaonia. Galacia. & alie multe. S*ed* specialit*er* u*bi* | ephes*us* ciuitas e*st*: asia uocat*ur*. (NLA, PL 92.1035B/C; CCSL 121.167.5)

Asia is a region called 'Minor' which extends from its eastern part up to Cappadocia and Syria, and is surrounded on all sides by the sea. Its provinces are Phrygia, Pamphylia, Cilicia, Lycaonia, Galatia, and many others, but especially where the city of Ephesus is, it is called 'Asia'.

337b. (lines 30–32) § ANtiochia. Ciuitas syrie coeles.[714] i*n* q*ua* barnabas. 7 paul*us*. ap*osto*li s*un*t ordinati. | Est & alia [in] pisi`di´a p*r*ouintia. in q*ua* p*re*dicantes ide*m* iudeis dixer*unt*. vob*is* oportebat p*r*imu*m* loq*ui* uerbu*m* dei. S*ed* q*uonia*m | repulistis illud. & indignos uos indicastis eterne uite. & c*etera*: (NLA, PL 92.1035A; CCSL 121.168.29)

Antioch, a city of Coele-Syria in which the apostles Barnabas and Paul were ordained, and there is another (so-called) in the province of Pisidia. . . . preaching in which they said to the Jews: "To you it behoved us to first preach the word of God. But when you reject it and judge yourselves unworthy of eternal life," etc. (Acts 13:46).

337c. (lines 32–34) § Alexandria. ciuitas egipti; q*ue* q*u*onda*m* [No][715]| dicebat*ur* int*er* egyptu*m*. africa*m* & mare. q*u*asi (. . .)[716] claustru*m* posita: in q*ua* beati

[714] 'coeles', along with other symptoms in the Bede series, suggests that the manuscript being consulted is earlier than the main Jerome exemplar.

[715] There is a space for this word at the end of the line but no sign of an erasure.

[716] 'dni' is underdotted and erased.

eu*a*ngelistę[717] Marci tumul*us* hodieq*ue* | uen*er*at*ur* (NLA, PL 92.1034D-1035A; CCSL 121.168.33)

Alexandria, a city of Egypt, which once was called 'No', was positioned like a barrier between Egypt and Africa and the sea, in which the blessed evangelist Mark's grave today . . . is venerated.

337d. (line 34) Apollonia e*st* ciuitas. & ipsa macedonie [*] Est⸵ & alt*er*a ei*us*de*m* nominis i*n* syria⸵[718] (NLA, PL 92.1035; CCSL 121.168.43)

Apollonia is a city and it is of Macedonia / and there is another by the same name in Syria.

337e. (lines 34–35) ASos ciuitas asie maritima. | eade*m* apollonia dicta⸵ (NLA, PL 92.1035C; CCSL 121.168.51)

Asos is a coastal city of Asia. This is called Apollonia.

337f. (line 35) § Beroe. ciuitas in macedonia. q*ue* u*er*bu*m* domini nobiliter accepit. (NLA PL92.1035D; CCSL121.169.51)

Beroe, a city in Macedonia which nobly received the word of the Lord (cf. Acts 17:10, 13).

337g.[719] § Cyrene. ciuitas in | libia.[720] Cui*us* regio etia*m* pentapolitana uocat*ur.* eo q*uo*d. v. urbib*us* maxime fulgeat. beronice. arsinoe. ptolomaide. ‖ apollonia. ipsaq*ue* cyrene. Creta. insula grece. c. q*uo*nda*m* urbib*us* nobilis⸵ un*de* & ecatontapolis dicta[721] e*st*⸵ § Cipr*us* in|sula i*n* mari pamphilio. xv. q*uo*nda*m* oppidis insignis⸵ fam`o´saq*ue* diuitiis. maxime eris. Ibi e*ni*m p*ri*ma [*recte* primo] hui*us* metalli in|uentio. & utilitas fuit. Cui p*ro*ximu*m* e*st* in finib*us* cilitie [*sic*] p*ro*montoriu*m* & oppidu*m* ueneris⸵ Cilicia. p*ro*uintia asie. q*ua*m | cidn*us* amnis

[717] *e*-caudata, the only one in the Claudius annotations? Another sign that the Bede exemplar is old (*i.e.*, pre-mid-twelfth century). At f. 74r, line 8, 'rep*ro*missionis', the apparent hook on *e* is the *pro* abbreviation.

[718] At [*], after 'macedonie', the text skips up from the entry on 'Apollonia' to the previous one on 'Amphipolis' (the capital 'E' suggests the skip is at 'Est' and not at 'altera'): "Amphipolis: ciutas Macedoniae; est et altera eiusdem nominis in Syria. Apollonia: ciuitas et ipsa Macedoniae, et est altera in prouincia Africa quae dicitur Pentapolis" ("Amphipolis is a city of Macedonia; there is another of the same name in Syria. Apollonia: a city and it is of Macdonia and there is another in a province of Africa which is called Pentapolis.") The *punctus elevatus* after 'Est' may betoken the annotator's awareness that there is something wrong with his exemplar.

[719] Beginning at line 35 and continuing to top of f. 147v; four contiguous entries.

[720] In Dodwell and Clemoes the 'li-' is obscured in the gutter, but clear on the CD-ROM.

[721] Corrected from 'dictis'.

int*er*secat. & monte*m* amaná. cui*us* salomon. á syria coele. separat.[722] (NLA, PL 92.1036D; CCSL 121.169.74–84)

Cyrene, a city in Libya whose area is called 'Pentapolitana' because it is resplendent with five cities: Berenice, Arsinoe, Ptolemais, Apollonia, and Cyrene itself.

Crete, a Greek island, formerly notable for a hundred cities, whence it was called 'Hekatompolis'.

Cyprus is an island in the Pamphylian sea, once notable for having fifteen cities and "famous for its riches, . . . especially bronze; there was the first discovery and working of this metal" (Isidore, *Etym.* 14.6.14); nearest to it within the bounds of Cilicia is the promontory and town of Venus.

Cilicia, a province of Asia which the river Cydnos intersects and Mount Amana, which Solomon mentions (Cant. 4:8), separates it from Coele-Syria.

F. 147v continues

337h. (lines 4–6, two contiguous entries) § C`h´aldeor*um* regio. int*er* babilonia*m* & | arabia*m*. tygri & eufraten:׳ § Chanaan. filius cha*m* obtinuit t*er*ra*m* a sydone usq*ue* ad gazam:׳ q*ua*m deinceps iudei | possederunt:׳ eiectis chananeis:׳ (NLA, PL 92.1036C; CCSL 121.170.88–91)

The region of the Chaldees (is) between Babylonia and Arabia, Tigris and Euphrates.

Chanaan, the son of Cham, got the land from Sydon to Gaza, which later the Jews possessed, having expelled the Chanaanites.

337i. (lines 6–9) § Gaza ciuitas i*n*signis palestine q*ue* apud[723] uet*er*es erat t*er*mi-n*us* chananeor*um* | ad meridie*m* antique gaze locu*m* uix fundam*en*tor*um* uestigio[724] demonstrans. Hec au*tem* q*ue* nu*n*c e*st*:׳[725] i*n* alio loco p*ro* | illa q*ue* corruit edificata e*st*:׳ (NLA, PL 92.1037C; CCSL 121.171.131)

Gaza, a famous city of Palestine which among the ancients was the border of the Chanaanites to the south; . . . showing the location of ancient Gaza by the ruins of its foundations only with difficulty. The city that now exists was built in another location in place of the one which fell into ruins.[726]

[722] Ed.: "mons Amanus cuius meminit Salomon a Syria Coele separat."

[723] Brown ink.

[724] Ed.: "uestigia."

[725] Ed.: "cernitur."

[726] This comment appears to be brought up out of order to clarify the previous note on "Chanaan."

337j. (lines 8–14) § Cesaréé. ciuita`te´s due s*unt* i*n* t*er*ra rep*ro*missionis. Vna cesarea palestine in li`t´o|re maris magni sita q*ue* q*uo*nda*m* turris stratonis dicta *est.*[727] S*ed* ab herode rege iudee nobili*us* & pulchri*us*. | & cont*ra* uim maris multo utili*us* instructa:[728] I*n* honore*m* cesaris cesara cognominata *est*. Cui etia*m* templu*m* | in ea marmore albo construx*it* i*n* qua nepos ei*us* herodes ab angelo p*er*cussus e*st*. (. .) corneli*us* cent*ur*io bap|titat*us*. [*sic*] & agab*us* p*ro*ph*et*a zona pauli ligat*us* *est*: § Alt*er*a u*er*o cesarea[729] phylippi cui*us* eu*an*g*e*lii sc*r*ipt*ur*a meminit | ad radices montis libani. v*bi* iordanis fontes sunt: S*ed* & t*er*cia cesarea capadotie. met*ro*polis e*st*: cui*us* lu|cas ita meminit. P*ro*fect*us* e*st* ab epheso: & de[s]cendens cesarea*m*. ascendit & salutauit ecclesiam- (NLA, PL 92.1036A; CCSL 121.170.92)

Caesarea: there are two cities (of this name) in the promised land. One is Caesarea of Palestine located on the shore of the Great Sea, which was once . . . called the Tower of Strato. But equipped more notably and beautifully, as well as more effectively against the power of the sea, by Herod [the Great, 73–4 B.C.], king of Judea, it was named Caesarea . . . in honor of Caesar [Augustus]. For him a temple of white marble was built in it in which his [Herod the Great's] grandson Herod [Herod Agrippa I, d. A.D. 44] was struck by an angel (Acts 12:23), Cornelius the centurion was baptized (Acts 10:24–48), and the prophet Agabus was bound with the belt of Paul (Acts 21:11).

The other is Caesarea Philippi, which the writings of the Gospels mention (Matt. 16:13), at the foot of Mount Libanus, where the sources of Jordan are. . . . But there is also a third Caesarea, the capital of Cappadocia, which Luke thus mentions, "Having left Ephesus and coming to Caesarea, he [Paul] went up and greeted the church" (Acts 18:21–22).

337k. (lines 15–19) § derben[730] ciuitas licaonie p*ro*uintie.[731] Elamite p*r*incipes p*er*sidis. Ab elam filio sem app*e*llati. § [E]Phfesus [*sic*] ama|zonum op*us*. ciuitas in asia. ibi requiescit beat*us* eu*an*gelista iohannes. § Frigida [*recte* Frygia] p*ro*uintia asie: troadi sup*er*|iecta. septent*r*ionali sua parte galatie cont*er*mina. meridiana licaoniæ.[732] & pisidie migdonieq*ue* ab ori|ente cappadotia*m* atting*it*. Due s*unt* au*tem* frigie: q*uarum* maior. Smyrna*m* habet. minor u*er*o yliu*m*. § Fenitia | p*ro*uintia syrie: cui*us* partes s*unt* samaria. & Galilea: & alie plurime regiones:[733] (NLA, PL 92.1037A/B; CCSL 121.171.119–128)

---

[727] The older "est" sign, '÷', is used three times in this passage, alongside the usual sign, 'ē'.

[728] Ed.: "exstructa."

[729] MS: 'cessarea', first 's' cancelled.

[730] Written in slightly larger letters than usual, at left margin.

[731] Ink is brown from this point for the rest of the page.

[732] The digraph 'æ' is a symptom of an older exemplar.

[733] The annotations omit further items about Galilea. "Gaza" has been displaced up; see item 337i.

Derbe(n) is a city of the province of Lycaonia.

Elamites, the princes of the Persians, are so named from Elam, son of Sem.

Ephesus, the work of the Amazons, a city in Asia, where rests St. John the Evangelist.

Phrygia, a province of Asia thrust up against the Troad. Its northern part is next to Galatia; Lycaonia, Pisidia, and Migdonia are on the south, and Cappadocia borders it on the east. There are two Phrygias of which the greater pertains to Smyrna, the lesser to Ilium.

Phoenicia, a province of Syria, whose parts are Samaria and Galilee and many other regions.

337l. (lines 19–22) § Galatia. p*ro*uintia asie. | á gallis uocabulu*m* t*ra*hens. q*ui* in auxiliu*m* á rege bithinie euocati. regnu*m* cu*m* eo fac*t*a[734] uictoria diuiseru*nt* | Sicq*ue* deinde g*r*ecis admixti. p*r*imo gallog*r*eci∵ p*os*tea galathe s*unt* apellati∵ § Grecia p*ro*uintia q*u*eda*m* achaie. | q*ue* á g*r*ecis sc*r*iptorib*us* he(.)las uocata. e*st*∵ in q*ua* atthenar*um* ciuitas e*st*∵ q*u*onda*m* attica dicta. (NLA, PL 92.1037B/C; CCSL 121.171.135–141)

Galatia, a province of Asia taking its name from the Gauls who, called in to help by the king of Bithynia, upon victory made a division with him of the kingdom and so, having become mingled with the Greeks, they first were called 'Gallo-Greeks' and afterwards 'Galatians'.

Greece, a certain province of Achaia which by Greek authors is called 'Hellas', in which the city of Athens is; it was once called 'Attica'.

337m. (lines 22–26) Italia regio & pat*r*ia roma|nor*um* ab italo[735] rege uocabulu*m* t*ra*hens∵ q*ue* ab africo & a borea mari magno cin`c´ta. reliq*ua* alpiu*m* obicib*us* obstru|itur∵ Libie[736] p*ro*ui[n]cie due s*un*t. Vna libia cirenaica∵ de q*ua* dictu*m* e*st*∵ & partes libie q*ue* e*st* ci*r*ca cirenen. Hec por|ta (. . .) egipti[737] in parte africe p*r*ima e*st*∵ & mari libico cognom*en* dedit. Postq*ua*m libia ethiopu*m* usq*ue* ad me|ridianu*m* p*er*tingens oceanum (NLA, PL 92.1037–38; CCSL 121.172.162, 166)

Italy, the region and country of the Romans taking its name from king Italus, which is encircled by Africa and the northern sea and the rest "blocked up by the obstructions of the Alps" (Orosius, *Hist.* 1.2.61).

Libya has two provinces, one Libya Cyrenaica of which it is said, "And part of Libya which is around Cyrene" (Acts 2:10). This gate of Egypt is in part of

[734] Laistner, "CC pacta," PL "peracta."

[735] The 'i' is badly formed.

[736] The capital 'L' is formed poorly, like an *I* or *J*; compare the proper *L* in 'Lidda' two lines down.

[737] Edd. "post egiptum."

Africa and gives the Libyic sea its familiar name; after that is Libya of Ethiopia that extends to the southern ocean.

337n. (lines 26–27) § Lidda ciuitas palestine in litore maris magni sita: q*ue* nu*n*c diospolis | appellat*ur*. (NLA, PL 92.1038B; CCSL 121.173.171)

Lydda is a city in Palestine sited on the coast of the Great Sea, which is now called Diospolis.

337o. (lines 27–29) Medi á madai filio iaphet apellati s*un*t. Sunt au*tem* int*er* flume*n* indu*m* & flume*n* tygru*m* | regiones iste: a monte caucaso. usq*ue* ad mare rubru*m* p*er*tingens[738] aracusia. parthia. assiria. p*er*sida. | & media. q*u*as scriptura sacra uniu*er*sas sepe medie nomine uocat. (NLA, PL 92.1038C; CCSL 121.173.189)

Medes are named from Madai the son of Japheth. "Now these regions" are between the river Indus and the river Tigris, "extending from Mount Caucasus to the Red Sea: to Aracusia, Parthia, Assyria, Persia, and Media, all of which Sacred Scripture frequently calls by the name 'Media'." (Orosius, *Hist.* 1.2.17, 19)

337p. (lines 29–31) § Miletus ciuitas in asia mariti|ma. x. stadiis ab ost`i´o meandri amnis secreta:[739] Vbi paul*us* ephesioru*m* maiores alloq*uitur*. Est & i*n*sula non | ignobil*is* ei*us*de*m* nominis. i*n* mari egeo. u*e*l licaonio:[740] (NLA, PL 92.1038D; CCSL 121.174.209)

Miletus is a city in Asia Maritima, ten stadii removed from the entrance of the river Meander, where Paul addressed the elders of the Ephesians (Acts 20:7). There is also a not insignificant island of the same name in the Aegean or Lycaonian (Ionian) sea.

337q. (lines 31–32) Samo. insula i*n* mari egeo in q*ua* rep*er*ta p*r*ius fictilia | uasa t*ra*dunt*ur*. Vnde & uasa samia appellata s*unt*: (NLA, PL 92.1039; CCSL 121.177.283)

Samos, an island in the Aegean in which previously discovered ceramic vessels are dealt in, hence they are called 'Samian' ware.

337r. (lines 32–35) Pamphilia. p*ro*uintia asie. Paph*us* Ciuitas maritima. in | cipro insula. uen*er*is q*u*onda*m* sacris carminib*us* & poetaru*m* famosa: q*ue* freq*u*enti t*er*re motu lapsa n*u*nc ruinar*um* t*an*tum uesti|giis. q*u*id oli*m* fu*er*it ostendit[.] Pergen ciuitas pamphilie p*ro*uintie. Pisid`i´a p*ro*uintia asie. Philipp*is* ciuitas in p*r*ima | parte macedonie. (NLA, PL 92.1039; CCSL 121.174.223–175.230)

Pamphylia, a province of Asia.

[738] Ed. "pertingentes."

[739] A redundant 'e'added above 'c'.

[740] Edd. "Ionio," varr. "uebionio," "lionio."

Paphus, a maritime city in the island of Cyprus "once famous for its sacred songs of Venus and its poets, which, destroyed by frequent earthquakes, now displays what it once was only by the traces of its ruins" (Jerome, *Vita Hilarionis*, 42, PL 23.50C).

Perge, a city of the province of Pamphylia.

Pisidia, a province of Asia.

Philippis, a city in "the first part of Macedonia" (Acts 16:12).

337s. (line 35) Macedonia p*ro*uintia g*r*ecor*um* nobilissima una. & ui*r*tutib*us* alexandri magni nobilior f*ac*t*a*: (NLA, PL 92.1038B; CCSL 121.174.205)

Macedonia, a very famous province of the Greeks and by the power of Alexander the Great made still more famous.

337t. (line 36) § Patara ciuitas licie p*ro*uincie in asia: (NLA, PL 92.1039; CCSL 121.175.231)

Patara, a city of the province of Lycia in Asia.

337u. (line 36) § Tharsus. ciuitas met*r*opol*is* cilicie p*ro*uincie. paulo ap*osto*lo gloriosa. (NLA, PL 92.1040; CCSL 121.177.304)

Tarsus, the capital city of the province of Cilicia, made glorious by the Apostle Paul.

337v. (lines 36–37) Salamis | ciuitas in cypro insula. n*un*c const`a´ntia dicta. q*ua*m t*ra*iani p*r*incipis t*em*po*re* iud*e*i o*mn*ib*us* int*er*fectis accolis deleuer*unt*: (NLA, PL 92.1039; CCSL 121.176.276)

Salamis, a city in the island of Cyprus now called Constantia which in the time of Emperor Trajan the Jews destroyed by killing all the inhabitants.

337w. (lines 38–40) Smirna ciuitas licie p*ro*uintie in asia. cui*us* lucas ita mem[in]it. & pælag*us* cilicie. & pamphilie nauigantes[741]| uenim*us* in smirna*m*[742] licie: p*ro* quo aliq*ui* codices h*abe*nt uenim*us* in listram que e*st* cilicie: Porro Ieronim*us* | in lib*ro* hebreor*um* no*min*um smirna*m* [*recte* mirram] ponit: & int*er*p*retatur* amaram: (NLA, PL 92.1040; CCSL 121.177.285)

Smyrna, a city of the province of Lycia in Asia, which Luke mentioned thus: "and navigating the sea between Cilicia and Pamphylia, we came to Smyrna in Lycia" (Acts 27:5); for which other codices have, "we came to Lystra which is Cilicia." Furthermore, Jerome, in his "Book of Hebrew Names," puts 'Myrra' and interprets it as 'bitter'.

---

741 'nauiganteS', a large round *-s*; note *æ*-digraph in 'pælag*us*' four words before this.

742 MS: 'smirrnam', second 'r' cancelled.

337x. (lines 40–41) Parthi. int*er* flume*n* i*n*du*m*. q*uo*d ab[743] oriente | & flume*n* tigrim q*uod* / e*st*[744] ab occasu siti *sunt*. ut supra dictu*m* est (NLA, PL 92.1039; CCSL 121.174.218)

Parthians are situated between the river Indus that is . . . from the east and . . . the river Tigris which is from the west, as was said above.

F. 148r *Illustrations:* Two picture spaces with unmarked frames and unfinished pictures: upper, ?Joshua prostrated before the Ark; lower, ?Joshua investigates sin of Achan **OE** = Joshua 7:16, 20–22, 24, 26

338. (bottom, 3 lines) Emecachor.[745] q*uo*d int*er*p*re*tat*ur.* uallis achor: id e*st* tumulat*us* [*recte* tumultus] atq*ue* tu[r]baru*m*. Est au*tem* loc*us* iuxta iericho. | haud p*ro*cul a galgalis. Male *ergo* q*u*ida*m* putant uall*em* ach`r´o [*sic*] a nomine ei*us* q*ui* lapidat*us* est nuncupata*m*:· | cu*m* ille achan dictus sit. & non achor. uel achar.:· (SNLH 23.893C; Lagarde 118.14)

Emechachor, which is interpreted 'valley of Achor', that is, 'uproar' as well as 'of a crowd'. . . . It is a place near Jericho, not far from Galgal. Those are wrong who think the Valley of Achor by its name means 'he who is stoned' since he was called 'Achan' and not 'Achor' or 'Achar' (Jos. 7:24–25).

F. 148v *Illustration:* One large unfinished picture space: the stoning of Achan **OE** = Joshua 7:26, 28:1–8; no annotations

F. 149r *Illustration:* One large unmarked picture space, with two figures begun in upper left, and with underdrawings visible in UV intended to depict Joshua's campaign against Hai. Figure washes.[746] **OE** = Joshua 8:10-12, 14–16, 18–21, 23

339.[747] Agai u*ero* uix parue ruine re(. .)|sident.[748] & loc*us* tantu*mmodo* monstrat*ur.* Et sciendu*m* q*uo*d in hebreo. g. lit*er*am n*on* habet scilicet hoc | nom*en*.

[743] 'a ab', 'a' cancelled.

[744] Diagonal stroke by the scribe.

[745] Varr. "Emec," "Emechachor." Lagarde begins: "Achor. hebraice dicitur Emechachor, quod interpretatur uallis tumultus siue turbarum. . . ."

[746] Dodwell and Clemoes, *Illustrated Hexateuch*, 40–41, say "Joshua lifts up his spear towards, *centre*, the city of Ai, as a signal for the men in ambush (seen on the left under ultra-violet light . . .) to rise against the city, whose inhabitants (seen on the right under ultra-violet light, . . .) have been drawn away by a simulated flight (Jos. 8.18–19)."

[747] In the OE, line 16, the annotator has written 'be' above **hindon**. Cf. the annotator's use of "beside" several times in the English notes, apparently the earliest recorded occurrences of this word.

[748] Two letters erased at end of line, perhaps 'di'.

S*ed* uocat*ur* ai∴ sc*r*ibit*ur*q*ue* p*er* elementu*m* q*uo*d apud eos d*icitu*r ain∴ (SNLH 23.861B; Lagarde 84.1; cf. no. 332)

Of Agai indeed scarcely a ruin remains and only the site is shown. And it is to be known that in Hebrew the letter 'g' is lacking and specifically as concerns this name. But it is called 'Ai' and is written with the letter which among them is called 'ayin'.[749]

340a. (bottom, 4 lines) Tharsis[750] unde auru*m* salomoni deferebat*ur*. hanc putat Joseph*us* tharsu*m* urbe*m* e*ss*e cilicie. Porro | iuxta ezechiele*m* p*r*oph*et*am cart`a´go sentit*ur*. Siq*u*ide*m* in eo loco ubi *secundum*. lxx. int*erpre*tes legim*us* car|tagine*m* in lib[r]`o´ habet*ur*[751] sc*r*iptu*m*. tharsis. Nonnulli india*m* putauer*un*t. Et de hoc ta*m* in libro | ep*istu*laru*m* q*u*as ad marcellu*m* [*recte* -am] sc*r*ipsim*us*. q*ua*m in libris hebraicaru*m* questionu*m* plenius diximus∴ (SNLH 23.925D-926A, Lagarde 157.27)

Tharsis whence gold was brought to Solomon. Josephus thought Tharsis to be a city of Cilicia. But according to the prophet Ezechiel (38:13) it was supposed to be Carthage, if in fact in the place where according to the Septuagint we read 'Carthage' in the book (i.e. Hebrew version) it has been written 'Tharsis'. Some supposed it to be India. And concerning this we have written more fully both in the book of letters which we addressed to Marcella[752] and in the book of Hebrew Questions.

F. 149v Two nearly blank picture spaces; in the lower a later drypoint of someone sacrificing at an altar. OE = Joshua 8:23, 25, 30, 32, 9:1–7

340b.[753] Tarsa[754] vbi asa rex[755] fuit. Tharsilla. vnde fuit manaen. Vsq*ue* hodie e[st] uiculus samaritanor*um* | in regione batanea. q*ui* stersilla [recte thersila] d*icitu*r.

[749] The place is mentioned at Jos. 15:32, 19:7, and 21:16.

[750] This entry has many miswritings: 'Tharsis': an uncancelled 'a' before 'h'; 'salomoni': the first 'o' imperfectly changed from 'a'; 'cartago': scribe wrote 'cartogo' and inserted 'a' above without cancelling 'o'; 'libro': 'li`o´' with no proper abbreviation mark (received text has "hebraeo" here); 'habet*ur*': the 'a' is 'o' imperfectly altered; 'india*m*': the 'a' is blotted; 'marcellū' for '-ā'; 'questionū' written as if '-ionii'. The last four words are written in a contrasting script. In a more general sense, it is not clear why this note is copied here at all since there is no evident connection to the Vulgate or OE text or to the picture.

[751] Edd.: "in Hebraeo scriptum habet."

[752] Ep. 37, CSEL 54.286ff.

[753] These contiguous extracts follow in Jerome's work immediately after "Tharsis" copied on the preceding page and are done in the larger script, with the ductus gradually diminishing in size as the four lines proceed.

[754] Scribe wrote 'Tarsia' and cancelled the 'i'.

[755] The top of the leaf has been trimmed, and an inserted word is partially visible, with an insertion mark; PL has "rex Israel fuit." From 'Vsq*ue*' the trimming impinges

Thesba. vn*de* ort*us est* helias p*ro*phe*t*a thesbites. Theman. Iuxta | ezechiel ciuitas ydumee. Porro[756] ysaias in uisione ea*m* ponit arabie. Meminit hui*us* & jeremias | Abdias (. . . .) sc[r]`i´bit[757] ciuitate*m* esav. S*ed* & un*us* filior*um* ei*us* theman app`e´llabat*ur* sicut sup*ra* dixim*us*: (SNLH 23.926A; Lagarde 158.3,4,6,7)

Thersa where Asa was king [of Israel] (3 Kings 15:21).

Tharsilla, whence was Manahem (4 Kings 15:14). Up to the present day it is a village of the Samaritans in the region of Batanea which is called Thersila.

Thesba, whence came the prophet Elijah the Thesbite.

Theman, according to Ezechiel[758] a city of Idumea. Moreover in a vision Isaiah (21:31) located it in Arabia. Jeremiah also made mention of it. Abdias . . . wrote (that it was) a city of Esau.[759] But one of his sons was called Theman as we said above (i.e., Lagarde 156.3).

F. 150r One blank picture space; **OE** = Joshua 9:7, 11–16, 18, 27

342a.[760] Gabaon. vn*de* gabaonite supplices[761] uener*un*t ad ie*su*m. erat olim met[r]`o´polis. & regalis. ciuitas | eueor*um* ceciditq*ue* in sorte*m* t*ri*b*us* beniamin. & n*un*c ostendit*ur* uilla eode*m* nomine. in iiii^to^. Miliario | bethelis. cont*ra* occidentale*m* plaga*m*. iuxt*a* rama & re*m*mon. u*b*i salomon hostis immolatis. ‖ diuinu*m* meruit oraculu*m*: (SNLH 23.900B/C; Lagarde 127.1)

Gabaon, whence the Gabaonites came to Joshua as suppliants (Jos. 9:6). It was once a metropolis and the royal city of the Hevites and fell within the allotment of the tribe of Benjamin, and nowadays a village of the same name is shown, four miles from Bethel opposite the west side near Rama and Remmon where Solomon, having burnt the offerings, deserved (to receive) a divine oracle (cf. 3 Kings 3:4–5, etc.).

F. 150v One blank picture space; **OE** = Joshua 10:3–9, 11–14, 16–18

342b. § Gabaa*m*. usq*ue* ad hanc bellatu*m* e*st*. cont*ra* tribu*m* beniamin. sic*ut* in | libro iudicu*m* sc*ri*bit*ur*: (SNLH 23.902A; Lagarde 129.2)

Gabaam, right up to it war was fought against the tribe of Benjamin as is written in the Book of Judges (20:31).

into the top line of text.

756 'ydumee' cancelled after 'Porro'.

757 Irregularly written after an erasure, apparently 'i' above with a long insertion mark.

758 Actually Jer. 49:7.

759 Abdias is a general prophecy against Edom/Esau; the comment may be through Amos 1:12.

760 Bottom, 3 lines, continuing to top of f. 150v.

761 'u' imperfectly altered from 'p'.

342c. § Gelboe. Montes alie`ni´genaru*m*. in. vi^to^. lapide. á scythopoli in q*u*ibus & | uic*us* e*st* g*ra*ndis. q*u*i appellat*ur* gelb*us*: (SNLH 23.902B; Lagarde 129.14)

Gelboe, mountains of foreigners on the sixth milestone from Scythopolis in which is a large town called Gelbus.

F. 151r *Illustration:* One full-page frame, with a partially finished picture in two registers, showing, upper, Joshua blessed by hand of God, above, stopping the sun and moon and, below him, the Hebrews defeating the Amorites; in lower register the Hebrews block the cave the kings are hiding in with stones; no OE[762]

343. (written on ledger line within frame, an incomplete inscription) Hi deo[763]

344. Ayalon. vallis atq*ue* p*re*ruptu*m*. sup*er* q*uo*d orante q*uo*nda*m*. ie*s*u sol[764] stetit. juxta uilla*m* q*ue* usq*ue* nu*n*c agalon | d*icitu*r. cont*ra* oriente*m* bethelis. t*r*ibus ab ea milib*us* distans. Porro hebrei affirmant ayalon. uic*us* e*ss*e. | iuxta nicapolim in s*ecun*do lapide. p*er* [*recte* pre] gentib*us* elyam: haud p*ro*cul a gabaa. & rama saulis[765] / urbib*us*: (SNLH 23.868A; Lagarde 89.25)

Ayalon, a valley and cliff upon which once upon a time when Joshua was praying the sun (moon) stopped, near the village which up to the present day is called Agalon to the east of Bethel, three miles distant from it. Furthermore the Hebrews affirm that Ayalon is a place next to Nicapolis at the second milestone (in front of) the peoples of Aelia (Jerusalem), a short distance from Gabaa and Rama, the cities of Saul.

F. 151v *Illustrations:* Two frames, upper, city of Maceda; lower, the Israelite chiefs set their feet on the necks of the five captured kings, Joshua, right, looking on. **OE** = Joshua 10:21–26

345. (top margin) Astaroth (. . .)[766] carnaim i*n* t*er*ra gigantu*m* i*n* sup*er*cilio sodomor*um* quos interfecit chodorlao|mor: Sunt hodie duo castella in batanea noue*m* int*er* se milib*us* sep*ar*ata. int*er* adara*m*. & | abela*m* ciuitates: (SNLH 23.861C; Lagarde 84.5)

---

762 Central figure labeled 'Iosue' in the usual labeling script; 'sol' and 'luna' are labeled in a script that uses insular *r*; it resembles the script of the English note on f. 19v, '7 lasca þé is sarai. | 7 melcha'.

763 Cannot be identified; the morphemes could be English but the proto-gothic form of the 'H' suggests that it was the false start of some Latin inscription.

764 Edd. "luna," see Joshua 10:12.

765 At end of line a smudged 'r'.

766 'est' erased.

Astaroth, Caranim in the land of giants, . . . on the height of the Sodomites whom Chodorlahomor killed. There are today two forts (by this name) in Batanea, . . . separated by nine miles, between the cities of Adaram and Abilam.

346.[767] Chebron q*ue* q*u*onda*m* uocabat*ur* arbe. licet male in g*r*ecis codicib*us* habeat*ur* arboc:̇ Condita e*st* au*tem* | ante sept*e*m annos q*u*am thannis urbs egipti c*on*deret*ur*:̇ dixim*us* de hac & sup*r*a. Fuit au*tem* met*r*opolis | enachim. q*uo*d gigantes & potentes intelligere debem*us*. (SNLH 23.888C; Lagarde 112.4)

Hebron which was once called 'Arbe', although it is badly transmitted in Greek manuscripts as 'Arboc'. It was founded seven years before Tanis, the city of Egypt. We spoke about this also above. It was the city of the Enachim, whom we must understand as immense and powerful.

F. 153r[768] *Illustrations:* Two frames: upper, the slaughter at Eglon; lower, slaughter at Hebron. **OE** = Joshua 10:36–39

347.[769] Ain in t*r*ibu jude. urbs sacerdotib*us* separata. | est au*tem* & usq*ue* hodie uilla bethennim nomine. in s*ecun*do lapide a terebinto | hoc e*st*[770] tab*er*naculai[771] (. . . . .[772]) abraha*m*:̇ q*u*attuor milib*us* a chebo`r´n [*sic*]- (SNLH 23.870D-871A; Lagarde 92.23)

Ain in the tribe of Juda, a city set apart for priests. To this day there is a village by the name of Bethennim at the second stone by the terebinth, this is (by the) tent of Abraham, four miles from Hebron.

---

[767] Bottom, 3 lines; *signe de renvoi* 'hwær' refers to 'hær' on f. 153r, opposite **hebron** in OE text, line 3 up; below this is a fainter 'hwær'. The *signes* show that in the twelfth century ff. 151v-153r were facing pages and that the displacement of f. 152 after f. 153 is at least that ancient; these leaves were displaced until the ninteenth century but the manuscript has since been rearranged into its correct, original order. See Marsden, ed. *The* OE Hept., xlv and 240-41, below.

[768] The order of the leaves as it appears they had at the time the notes were written is followed here, i.e., f. 153 before f. 152. A sixteenth-century hand has written at top of f. 153r: 'read this leafe after the next'.

[769] Cf. Jos. 21:13–16. It is written above the lower picture frame, as if following on the OE in line 3, though actually not textually connected (OE = Jos. 10:36).

[770] Above 'est' is a mark,,resembling the usual continuation mark, but perhaps a confused reflex of the older insular symbol for "est" ,∸, if so, this would represent a stray, since the copy of SNLH being followed did not normally use this symbol.

[771] Written by the scribe 'āī'; *recte* '-a', edd. "a tabernaculo."

[772] 'jacob', cancelled.

348.[773] § dabir in *tr*ibu iuda. que uocaba*tur* ciu`i´tas litt*er*aru*m*. *pre*occupauit gothoniel fr*ater* caleph- | int*er*fectis in ea enachim. fuit au*tem* & ipsa sac*er*dotib*us* separata: Porro gothoniel[774] q*u*ida*m* | arbit*r*ant*ur*. filiu*m* fr*atr*is caleph. (SNLH 23.891B; Lagarde 115.27)

Dabir in the tribe of Juda which is called the city of letters; . . . Gothoniel (Othoniel), the brother of Caleph, seized it, killing in it the Enachim (Jos. 15:14–17). It too was set apart for priests (Jos. 21:15); thereafter they were judged by (G)othoniel, the son of a brother of Caleph (Jud. 3:9–10).[775]

349. § Filistiim q*u*e nunc d*icitu*r iscalon [*recte* ascalon]. & ci*r*ca ea*m* regio palestine: (SNLH 23.897C; Lagarde 123.3)

Filistia, which is now called Ascalon and around it is the region of Palestine.

350.[776] § Geth. In hac gigantes q*u*i uocabant*ur* enachim. & phylistinor*um* accole[777] *per*ma*n*ser*unt*: ostendi*tur*q*ue* || uic*us*. in .v^{to}. miliario ab eleutheropoli euntibus diospolin: (SNLH 23.900C; Lagarde 127.15)

Geth, in this place were giants who were called Enachim and neighbors of the Philistines continued to stay there (Jos. 11:22); and a village is shown at the fifth milestone from Eleutheropolis going towards Diospolis.

F. 153v *Illustrations:* Two frames: upper, slaughter at Asedoch; lower, slaughter at Chades Barnea. **OE** = Joshua 10:40–43

351. asedoch.[778] alia h*ec* e*st* ciuitas. n*on* q*u*e sup*r*a. licet eode*m* nomine | uocet*ur* q*u*am expugnauit[779] q*u*onda*m* ies*us* rege illius int*er*fecto: (SNLH 23.868B; Lagarde 90.3)

---

773 Bottom, 4–2 up; the faint or partially effaced second 'hwær' in the right margin may be intended to refer up to **dabira** in the OE text, f. 153r, line 3 up, as if reusing the 'hær' immediately above. The *signes* have primary reference to the text at the bottom of f. 151v.

774 'h' altered from 'l'.

775 Although the annotator has selected the wrong city here, "Dabir in the tribe of Juda" (Lagarde 115.27) rather than "Dabira, city in the tribe of Dan whose king Joshua slew"(Lagarde 115.19), the intent is in any case to gloss the OE, line 3 up, **Fram hebron hé gecyrde to dabira ðære byrig.**

776 Bottom line, continuing to top of f. 153v.

777 An apparently accidental *i*-like stroke before this word.

778 "Asedoch" (for "Asedoth") is the form in the OE (line 4), which is retouched.

779 'g' altered from 'n'.

Asedoth, this is a different city, not the one mentioned before, although it is called by the same name, which Joshua once took by storm, having killed its king.[780]

352.[781] § Macedæ[782] In hac co*n*clusit ie*sus* q*u*inq*ue* reges. i*n* spelunca[783] quos interfecit cu*m* rege Maceda. q*ue* fuit | in t*r*ibu iude: Et nunc e*st* in octauo miliario eleutheropoleos. *contra* sol*is* ortu[m]: (SNLH 23.909D; Lagarde 138.8)

Maceda: in this place Joshua imprisoned five kings in a cave whom he killed with the king of Maceda; it was in the tribe of Juda (Jos. 10:16–18). And now it is on the eighth milestone east from Eleutheropolis.

F. 152r *Illustrations:* Two frames: upper in two registers, above, left and right, kings are slain, in lower right, kings are hanged upon boughs, lower left, their burial; lower, slaughter at Maceda. **OE** = Joshua 10:28; no annotations

F. 152v *Illustrations:* Two frames: upper, slaughter at Lebna; below, slaughter at Lachis. **OE** = Joshua 10:29–35

353. § Lebna. i*n* t*r*ibu juda ciuitas sac*er*dototal*is*. [*sic*] `q*u*am tenuit ie*sus* rege interfecto-´ n*u*nc e*st* uilla i*n* regione eleutherópolitana q*ue* appal|lat*ur* [*sic*] jobna [*recte* lobna]: Scribit de hac isayas (SNLH 23.907B; Lagarde 135.26)

Lebna in the tribe of Judah, a priestly city (which Joshua held . . . having killed the king), now is a village in the region of Eleutheropolis which is called Lobna; Isaiah (37:8) writes of this.

354. Lachis in t*r*ibu juda. Sed | ha`n´c cepit ie*sus* rege ei*us*[784] int*er*fecto. Meminit hui*us* isayas. et ier*emi*as. n*unc* e*st* uilla in vii^{timo}. mili|ario. ab eleutheropoli euntib*us* daroma*n*:. (SNLH 23.907B; Lagarde 135.21)

Lachis in the tribe of Juda. But Joshua captured this town, having killed its king. Isaiah (36:2, 37:8) mentions it and Jeremiah (34:7). . . . Now it is a village seven miles from Eleutheropolis in the direction of Daroma.

355. Eglon. q*ue* & odolla*m*. In t*r*ibu iudæ:[785] cui*us* rege*m* nomine dabir. i*n*terfecit ie*sus*. Est au*tem*. nunc | uilla p*er*g*r*andis i*n* duodecimo ab eleutheropoli lapide: *con*tra oriente*m*- (SNLH 23.893D-894A; Lagarde 118.21)

---

780 The main text refers to Ashedoth in Jos. 10:40, in the southern lowlands; the "different" Ashedoth, in the hill country, is mentioned in Jos. 13:20.

781 Bottom, 2 lines; this note refers to OE text on f. 152r, which f. 153v was facing in the twelfth century.

782 Edd. '-a'; the archaic and incorrect digraph is perhaps from the exemplar.

783 'speluncas' with final 's' cancelled.

784 Edd. "ipsius."

785 Note digraph.

Eglon, which is also Odollam, in the tribe of Juda, whose king, named Dabir, Joshua killed. It is now a very large village on the twelfth milestone from Eleutheropolis facing east.

F. 154r[786] *Illustrations:* One frame divided into three registers: above, the Israelites defeat the northern kings; middle, hamstring their horses; lower, burn their chariots. **OE** = Joshua 11:1–2, 4–9

356. Asor. ciuitas regis[787] iabin. q*u*am sola*m* i*n*cendit ie*su*s. q*u*ia met*r*opol*is*(.)[788] erat om*n*iu*m* regnor*um* philistiim:· (SNLH 23.868C; Lagarde 90.6)

Asor, a city of the kings of Jabin which was the only one Joshua burned because it was the chief city of all the Philistine kingdoms.

F. 154v[789] *Illustrations:* One frame in two registers; above, slaughter at Asor; below, pillaging of the city; right, in panel with round arch, Joshua? **OE** = Jos. 11:10–23; no annotations

F. 155r[790] No pictures; **OE** = Jos. 12:1, 9–24, 21:41–43, 14:2, 23:1, 7, 24:16–17, 31, 29; no annotations

F. 155v[791] *Illustrations:* One large frame in three registers: above, land divided by lot; middle, Joshua rules the Israelites; lower, burial of Joshua (label 'Josue obiit') with **ii̅ d xix** [A.M. 2519]. **OE** (seven lines above frame; line 7, only first word part of original text) = Joshua 24:29–30, 32

357. (addition to ending of OE text) ⁊ **hit wæs gebloten to iosepes beárna | lande.** ⁊ for ðam ðe jacob hít salde Josepe ís súne at ís fórsyðe

and it was consecrated as land to Joseph's sons, and because Jacob give it to Joseph his son at his death (cf. Jos. 24:32).

786 Some partially blotted words from the OE main text have been written in the upper outer margin and underdotted in the text, 'hím ymbe' | 'fólcum swá'; the script appears to be late twelfth-century but as it is imitative of the main text, the insular letters *h*, *y*, *f*, *w* are more finely formed than those used elsewhere in the annotations.

787 PL "regni."

788 Final '-e' has been erased; the "point" is the remains of the lower loop of the 'e'.

789 Outer margin, three words blotted in text are noted in outer margin and underdotted in text, 'ðær' | 'manegra' | 'fastenu', the letters *ð*, *r*, *g*, *f*, *s* having imitative insular minuscule forms in the usual style of the English annotations.

790 One word, 'cyning', added in margin, the word blotted and underdotted in OE text, line 3; the word is written in a better style than usual for English annotations.

791 In upper outer margin several words blotted or effaced in main text are rewritten: 'lánde'(underlined in main text) | 'ðǽne' (for **dune**?) | 'brohton' | 'ðǽs lándes'. They are in the same script as no. 358, written immediately below in the margin.

358.[792] (margin) ða he cóm fǽrm | mesopotánia lánde. | ǽn wycnígeðe ón | sałím | *þæt* ís in chanaan lánde

when he (Jacob) came from Mesopotamia land, on a wandering in Salem, that is in Chanaan land (cf. Genesis 33:18).[793]

359. (bottom margin, brown, somewhat faded ink) Post hec mortuus est josue cu*m* e*ss*et. c 7 x anno*rum*. *Quo*nia*m* cepit minist*ra*re moysi. erat. xl.iiii. anno*rum*. | et xl annis fuit in deserto. Viginti vi. annis rexit populu*m* trans jordanem sepelierunt eum | in tanmasara q*ue* sita e*st* in mo*n*te effraim: (HS 1272A)

"After these things Joshua died when he was 110 years old" (Jos. 24:29). When he began to serve Moses he was forty-four years old and was in the desert forty years. For twenty-six years he ruled the people across the Jordan. . . . "They buried him in Thamnathsare which is located in Mt. Ephraim" (Jos. 24:30).

360. (still lighter, reddish ink) Et surrexerunt allii [*sic*] q*ui* n*on* noue*r*unt dominu*m* et t*ra*d|dit [*sic*] eos d*omin*u*s* i*n* manu*m* cusan rasathaim regis mesop`ot´amie. 7 syrie. `seruieruntq*ue* ei viii annis´ est .ii. alia mesopotamia un*de* uenit.

And there arose others who knew not the Lord . . . and the Lord gave them into the hand of Cusan-Rasathaim, king of Mesopotamia and Syria and they served him eight years; it is a second, other Mesopotamia out of which he came.[794] (Judges 2:10, 3:8).

F. 156r (inserted leaf, torn so that text to right is lost; restored text is in italics)[795]

1) [..] regnass⟨it⟩ sup⟨er⟩ syche⟨m⟩ .iii⟨bus⟩ ann⟨is⟩ a[*bimelech expulerunt ab urbe 7*

2) t⟨r⟩ibu Et recedens in⟨de⟩ obsedit [*Abimelech oppidum Thebes.*

3) Cu⟨m⟩q⟨ue⟩ turrim expugnar[*et Abimelech 7 mulier fragmentum mole desuper*

4) iaciens fregit cerebru⟨m⟩ [*eius, ait armigero suo. percute me ne dicar interfectus a*

5) femina. q⟨ui⟩a int⟨er⟩fecit eu⟨m⟩ [. *Post abimelech iudicauit israhel* (HS 1282A/D)

6) Thola anni⟨s⟩ xxiii. ex [*issachar iudicauit israhel in*

7) sanir. montis ephraim [*et mortuus est* (cf. HS 1283A)

8) post tholam. jair gala[*adites de tribu Manasse judicavit israhel*

---

792 An irregular box has been drawn around this item.

793 This verse introduces Jacob's purchase of the field of Emor, the burial place alluded to by the previous note.

794 That is, Syria-Mesopotamia, the Bashan Valley with the Yarmuk River and its tributaries that flow into the Jordan just south of the Sea of Galilee.

795 For this leaf resolutions of abbreviations are indicated within angle brackets; missing text, supplied from PL, is in italics.

9) xxii. ann⟨orum⟩ h⟨abe⟩ns xxx [*filios. Eo tempore theseus rapuit helenam, quam rursus rece-*

10) perut [*sic*, *recte* -unt] castor 7 pollux [*capta matre thesei. eo peregre profecto. Fuit eo tempore*

11) Jepte Galadites. uir for[*tissimus pugnator sed filius meretricis habuit uxorem galaad.* (HS 1283A/B/C)

12) philistini.[796] 7 amanite. [*deprimunt israhel ex quibus ammonite debellantur*

13) ab iepte q⟨u⟩i libr⟨o⟩ iudicu⟨m⟩. [*ab etate moysis usque ad semetipsum ait supputari annos ccc.* (Bede, DTR, PL 90.529B) *Post jepthe iudicauit israhel*

14) Abessan. u`e´l e`s´sebon. bethlee[*mita de juda vii. annis. Post abessan*

15) aylon. gabulonitis[797] ann⟨is⟩ [*x iudicauit israhel. Pro quorum damno*

16) supplendo:᷾ eusebiu⟨s⟩. iosue [*nec non samueli et sauli quorum annos scriptura sacra non dicit plures annos*

17) qua⟨m⟩ i⟨n⟩ iosepho legebat anno[*tauit quatenus ab egressu israhel ex egipto usque ad edificationem templi*

18) cccc.lxxx. anno⟨rum⟩ sum[*mum quam scriptura predicat haberet.*

19)[798] § abdon `⟨ue⟩l ieb´ thecuites de astraim [*recte* ephraim] annis octo [*iudicauit israhel* (HS 1285B)

20) [..] SANSON robust⟨us⟩ de t⟨r⟩ibu dan lib⟨er⟩ator i[*srahel*

21) Hacten⟨us⟩ lib⟨er⟩ judicu⟨m⟩ te⟨m⟩pora sign(. . .)at h[*abens annos cc xc ix et iudices xii praeter sangar et barach* (HS 1289D–1290A)

22) [Ue]teri testam⟨en⟩to. iiii. hominu⟨m⟩ nomi⟨n⟩a. [*per angelum nuntiata fierunt. ismael. isaac. josias. samson.*

23) [In] nouo testam⟨ento⟩ .ii°. Joh⟨anne⟩s. 7 ie⟨su⟩s. Moyses (HS 1286, Add. 2)[799]

24) [P]ost samson⟨em⟩: judicauit isr⟨ahe⟩l. heli sac⟨er⟩dos. [*qui non tantum iudex*

25) s⟨ed⟩ sac⟨er⟩dos. Et translato sac⟨er⟩dotio á filiis elea[*zari hic* i^{mus} *de filiis ithamar accepit sacerdotium.*

26) [I]n dieb⟨us⟩ ei⟨us⟩:᷾ facta e⟨st⟩ fames in t⟨er⟩ra. et surrexit elim[*elech de bethlehem effrateus cum uxore sua noemi*[800]

[796] Scribe wrote 'philistimi' and canceled first minim of 'm'.

[797] MS: 'gabnlonites' [*sic*], 'e' altered to 'i'; *recte* "zabulonites."

[798] From this point the writing is written further to the left by a few millemeters and thus the beginnings of some lines are covered by the binding repair strip.

[799] For 'Moyses' see the note to line 11 of the verso.

[800] The lower edge of the second half of this line is partially visible.

27) [C]u⟨m⟩ duob⟨us⟩ filiis suis. maalon. 7 chelion. 7 i⟨n⟩gressus e⟨st⟩ regione⟨m⟩ moabitidem. ut ibi [*pasceretur*

28) Q⟨u⟩o mortuo:· filii ei⟨us⟩ duxerunt uxores moabitidas. orpham. 7 ruth et manseru[*nt ibi .x. annis*

29) [et] mortui s⟨un⟩t ambo sine lib⟨er⟩is. Noemi u⟨er⟩o uidua:· surrexit ut rediret i⟨n⟩ pat⟨r⟩ia⟨m⟩. Ru[801] Rut[*h uero sequebatur*

30) eam: (HS 1293B) Profecteq⟨ue⟩ s⟨un⟩t simul. 7 uenerunt in bethlee⟨m⟩. q⟨u⟩e p⟨r⟩ius dicebat⟨ur⟩ effrata ab ux[*ore Caleb*

31) Hec fuit maria soror moysi. secundu⟨m⟩ q⟨u⟩osda⟨m⟩ 7 t⟨ran⟩slata e⟨st⟩ de sepulc[ro] heremi:· in bet[*hleem* (cf. 1296A, Add. 3)

32) [p]ostqua⟨m⟩ p⟨er⟩cussa e⟨st⟩ lepra. agnominata e⟨st⟩ effrata. i⟨d est⟩ furore⟨m⟩ uidit. i⟨d est⟩ ira⟨m⟩ d⟨e⟩i exp⟨er⟩imen[*to*

33) [cog]nouit:· uel i⟨n⟩terp⟨re⟩tat⟨ur⟩ speculu⟨m⟩. q⟨u⟩ia plaga ei⟨us⟩ omnib⟨us⟩ posita e⟨st⟩ in exemplu⟨m⟩. s⟨ed⟩ tunc p⟨r⟩imo p⟨ro⟩p⟨ter⟩

34) [in]c[r]`e´dibile⟨m⟩ ub⟨er⟩tate⟨m⟩ sibi reddita⟨m⟩:· cepit uocari bethlee⟨m⟩. q⟨uo⟩d e⟨st⟩ dom⟨us⟩ panis. Jer⟨ony⟩m⟨us⟩ dic⟨it⟩ q[*uod*

35) chaleph suscepit de effratha. vr uiru⟨m⟩ marie. et uri anū [*recte* auu⟨m⟩][802] beseleel:· (Add. 3) Erat au⟨tem⟩ ibi

36) uir (.) potens. 7 opulent⟨us⟩ booz:· ⟨con⟩sanguineus elimelech. (HS 1293D) Accepit itaq⟨ue⟩ booz. Ruth:·

37) [in] uxore⟨m⟩ 7 p⟨ost⟩ annu⟨m⟩ `nat⟨us⟩´ e⟨st⟩ ei filiu⟨s⟩ q⟨u⟩em posuit Noemi in sinu suo. uocauit nomen ei⟨us⟩ obeth.

38) hic e⟨st⟩ pat⟨er⟩ ysai:· patris dauid. (HS 1295A/B) **§iī.d.ccc. lxx.**

39) Samu`h´el. ann⟨um⟩ .xii. ut docet josephus. In scriptura e⟨ni⟩m s⟨an⟩c⟨t⟩a q⟨u⟩amdiu p⟨re⟩fuerit mi-

40) nime patet. Ab hoc (. .) te⟨m⟩p[o]ra (. .) p⟨ro⟩ph⟨et⟩aru⟨m⟩ i⟨n⟩cipiunt:· (DTR, PL 90.530B)

41) Saul p⟨r⟩im⟨us⟩ hebreor⟨um⟩ rex ann⟨os⟩ xx. Et hui⟨us⟩ q⟨u⟩ia i⟨n⟩ canonica:· **§ iīdcccxc.**

42) sc⟨r⟩iptura n⟨on⟩ habet⟨ur⟩ de antiq⟨u⟩itatu[m] iosephi tempus regni notauim⟨us⟩. (DTR, PL 90.388–390)

43) Quarta mundi etas. (cf. DTR, PL 90.393)

1) Abimelech ruled over Sychem for three years; they expelled them (the inhabitants) from the city and

---

801 'Ru' cancelled.

802 PL 'Ur genuit'; cf. Ex. 38:22.

2) tribe. And retiring from there Abimelech laid siege to the city of Thebez.

3) When Abimelech had taken the tower a woman throwing a piece of mill-stone from above

4) broke his skull, and he said to his armor-bearer, slay me lest it be said I was killed by

5) a woman, whereupon he killed him. (cf. Judges 9:22–54) After Abimelech Thola judged

6) Israel, a man of Issachar, for twenty-three years in

7) Sanir of Mount Ephraim, and he died. (cf. Judges 10:1–2)

8) After Thola, Jair of the Galaadites of the tribe of Manasses judged Israel

9) for twenty-two years, having thirty sons (cf. Judges 10:3–4). At that time Theseus ravished Helen, whom

10) Castor and Pollux took back, the mother of Theseus having been captured, he (Theseus) being indeed most angry. There was at that time

11) Jeptha of the Galaadites, a very strong warrior but the son of a prostitute, Galaad had a wife. (cf. Judges 11:1)

12) The Philistines and Ammonites oppressed Israel, some of whom were conquered

13) by Jephta who in the book of Judges from the time of Moses to his own was to be reckoned 300 years. After Jephta judged Israel,

14) Abessan or Esebon the Bethlemite of Juda (judged) seven years. (cf. Judges 12:8) After Abessan

15) Ahialon of the [Z]abulonites judged Israel for ten years. (cf. Judges 12:11) To make up a lack

16) of years, Eusebius notes for Joshua (and of Samuel and Saul neither of whose years Scripture speaks), more years

17) than one reads in Josephus, for the sake of the 480 years total

18) from the the exodus of Israel from Egypt up to the building of the temple which Scripture has declared.

19) Abdon (or Ieb) the Thecuite of Ephraim judged Israel for eight years (cf. Judges 12:12–14).

20) Samson the powerful, of the tribe of Dan, the liberator of Israel.

21) Up to this point the Book of Judges shows the times having 299 years and twelve judges besides Sangar and Barach.

22) In the Old Testament the names of four men were announced by angels: Ismael, Isaac, Josia, and Samson.

23) In the New Testament, two, John and Jesus. [Moses]

24) After Samson, the priest Heli judged Israel, who was not so much a judge
25) as a priest . . . and the priesthood having been transferred from the sons of Eleazar, this one [Heli] was the first of the sons of Ithamar to receive the priesthood.[803]
26) In his days there was a famine in the land and Elimelech rose up from Bethlehem Effrata with his wife Noemi,
27) with his two sons, Maalon and Chelion, and went into the region of the Moabites in order to pasture (there),
28) who having died, his sons took there Moabite wives, Orpah and Ruth, and lived there for ten years,
29) and both died without sons. But Noemi, being now a widow, rose up and returned to her own country. But Ruth followed
30) her. They set out together and came to Bethlehem which had earlier been called Effrata from the wife of Caleb.
31) This [Effrata] was Mariam the sister of Moses according to certain people and she had been moved from a tomb in the desert to Bethlehem
32) after she had been struck with leprosy. It is named 'Effrata', that is, 'he sees madness', that is he knows the wrath of God by experience,
33) or it is interpreted 'mirror' because its punishment is placed as an example to all, but then at first because of
34) the incredible fruitfulness given back to it it began to be called 'Bethlehem', that is 'house of bread'. Jerome says that
35) Caleb begot on Effrata Ur the husband of Mariam and Uri grandfather of Beseleel [PL: "Ur begot Beseleel"]. There was moreover there
36) a powerful and rich man, Boaz, the relative of Elimelech. Boaz took Ruth
37) to wife and after a year a son was born to him whom Noemi placed in her bosom. He called him Obeth.
38) He is the father of Jesse, the father of David. A.M. 2870.

---

[803] Explained by Add. 1 (HS 1295B): "Sic certum, quod cum Aaron quatuor habuit filios, duo ex eis in deserto igne perierunt; eorum qui remanserant, major natu fuit Eleazor, cui debebatur sacerdotium, quod duravit usque ad Heli, qui fuit de Ithamar fratre suo." ("So it is indisputable, that when Aaron had four sons, two of them perished by fire in the wilderness; of those who remained, Eleazar was the eldest, who was bound to the priesthood, which lasted until Heli, who was descended from Ithamar his [Eleazar's] brother.")

39) Samuel (ruled) twelve years, as Josephus teaches. In Holy Scripture it is not at all clear how long he ruled.

40) From this time began the age of prophets.

41) Saul, the first king of the Hebrews, (ruled) twenty years. And because this is not mentioned in canonical scripture

42) we have noted the length of his reign from the "Antiquities" of Josephus. A.M. 2890.

43) The fourth age of the world.

F. 156v (inserted leaf, torn so that text to left is lost, restored in italics)[804]

1) . . . . *.ziu*]s apud heb⟨r⟩eo d⟨icitu⟩r apud (nos) mai[*us* . . .[805]

2) *Solomon filius dauid annis xl. qui iv^{to} regni*] sui. anno m⟨en⟩se sec[undo]

3) *templum domino edificare cepit in hierusalem collectis ab egressu israhelis ex egi*]pto annis. cccc.l[xxx ut]

4) *regum quoque liber testimonio est. quod in figuram universi temporis*] q⟨u⟩o in hoc se⟨cu⟩lo chr⟨ist⟩i ed-

5) *ificatur ecclesia que in futuro perficitur. vii annis perfecit & septimo*] octaui anni dedicau[it] (Bede, DTR, PL. 90.531B)

(1–5) . . . . called ['Sivan'] among the Hebrews and by us 'May'. . . .

Solomon son of David (ruled) for forty years, who in the fourth year of his reign, in the second month began to build a temple to the Lord in Jerusalem, 480 years in all from the Exodus of Israel from Egypt as also is the testimony of the Book of Kings (which in a figure of all time over which the Church of Christ is built in the present age which will be perfected in the future) he completed in seven years and dedicated on the seventh (month) of the eighth year.

6) *Mortuus est ergo saul et tres filii eius et armiger illius et uniuersi uiri eius. Viri isti pue*]ri 7 domestici ei⟨us⟩ int[e]ll-

7) *igendi sunt. hi tres filii saul cum eo interfecti sunt. ionathan. abinadab. qui*] & iesui & Melchisua. (Ps-Jerome, QH2R PL 23.1346A) § p⟨ro⟩pt⟨er⟩

[804] The text is clumped into several groups of lines, as indicated here, translations following each clump.

[805] End of line is obscured by paste-over; 'nos' is cancelled. Cf. HS 1354B: "Factum est autem, post quadringentos et octoginta annos egressionis Israel de Aegypto, anno quarto regni Salomonis, mense secundo, qui Zius apud Hebraeos dicitur, apud nos Maius, coepit Salomon aedificare domum Domino. . . ."

8) *iniquitates suas et additur quasi in cumulum peccati sed insuper pithonissam consului*]t. p⟨ro⟩pt⟨er⟩ q⟨uo⟩d occidit eu⟨m⟩ d⟨omi⟩n⟨u⟩s. [hui]us

9) *peccati magnitudinem multi non attendunt. Et regnauit saul ui*]uente Samuele: xviii. a[nn]is

10) *et eo mortuo ii*^{bus} *annis. hos annos sacra tamen scriptura non adno*](t)auit. A samuele p⟨ro⟩prie

11) *incipiunt tempora nominatorum prophetarum sicut a saule tempora*] regum is⟨rahe⟩l: § ysaac. iere. 7 ezec [?].[806] (HS 1323B-1324A)

(6–11) So "Saul died and his three sons and his armorbearer and all his men" (1 Kings 31:6). 'These men' included his slaves and domestic servants. These three sons of Saul were killed with him: Jonathan, Abinadab, who is also (called) Jesui, and Melchisa. § On account of his iniquities also is added, as if the acme of his sins but above them, that he consulted the witch, on account of which the Lord killed him. Many do not pay attention to the magnitude of his sin. And Saul reigned while Samuel was living for eighteen years and for two years after he died. Sacred Scripture does not mention these years. From Samuel properly is begun the time of the named prophets as from Saul begins the time of the kings of Israel. Isaac. jere. *ezec*.

12) *Isboseth autem domi erat qui anno quo saul rex constitutus est natu*]s fuisse d⟨icitu⟩r. q⟨u⟩i etia⟨m⟩ xl$^{\langle ta\rangle}$ annor⟨um⟩ fu[is][-]

13) *se legitur cum regnare cepisset. unde colligitur saul xl annos re*]gnasse: (Ps-Jerome, QH2R, PL 23.1346B)

14) *Quidem tamen dicunt xx annos quibus iudicauit samuel aggregandos*] annis hely magist⟨er⟩ sui. S⟨ed⟩ uer[ius]

15) *anni samuelis cum annis saulis ascribuntur.* (HS 1300D) *Saul enim circiter*] xx annos. regnauit. Isboseth:

16) *uero regnans post patrem iam xl*^{ius} *erat. quod tamen ipsi dete*]rminar[e] conant⟨ur⟩. dice⟨n⟩tes saul c[-]

17) *episse regnare post hely et ponunt in regno saulis an*]nos samuel⟨is⟩. Hebreus sic habet. (HS 1306B) Fi[-]

18) *lius unius anni erat saul cum r*]egnauit. i⟨d est⟩ humilis ta⟨n⟩q⟨ua⟩m paru[u]

19) *lus. ii*^{bus} *autem annis regnauit super israhel. id est iuste rexit populum. In reliquis a*]nnis regni. quasi tyrannus sint (HS 1306A/B)

---

[806] Last three words are unsourced (the last very unclear) but perhaps come from a breviate psalter. Cf. the sample that can be seen in PL 26.1114B: "Abraham, Isaac, et Jacob, Moyses, Jesu Nave, Isaac, Jeremias, Ezechiel, duodecim Prophetae," etc. The isolated word 'Moyses' on the recto, line 23, may have strayed from this group.

(12–19) Isboseth was at home, who it is said was born in the year in which Saul was ordained king, who, it is read of, was fourteen years old when he began to reign, whence it is gathered that Saul reigned for forty years.

Now certain people say that the twenty years Samuel judged are to be added to the years of Hely his teacher. But more truly the years of Samuel are included in the years of Saul. For Saul reigned about twenty years. But Isboseth was reigning after his father about to the fortieth (year), which they try nevertheless to determine themselves saying Saul began to reign after Hely and they place the years of Samuel within Saul's reign. So the Hebrew has it.

Saul was "a son of one year" (1 Kings 13:1) when he reigned, that is, 'humble', much as he was 'a little one' when "he reigned for two years over Israel," that is, he ruled the people justly. For the rest of his reign he was like a tyrant.

20) *Quarta a david usque ad transmigrationem babilonis*] (an)n(o)s iuxta heb⟨ra⟩ica⟨m⟩ ueritate⟨m⟩ cc cc lxx[iii]

21) *iuxta lxx translationem xii amplius. generationes iuxta utrosque codices xvii. Quas ta*]men euangelista matheu⟨s⟩ certi misterii gr⟨ati⟩a. xiiii. ponit:· a[807]

22) *qua uelut iuvenili e*]tate i⟨n⟩ populo d⟨e⟩i regu⟨m⟩ te⟨m⟩pora coep⟨er⟩unt. Hec na⟨m⟩q⟨ue⟩ i⟨n⟩ hominib⟨us⟩ etas apta

23) *gubernando sol*]et existere regno:· **iii.dcccc.l.ii**[808]

24) *Quinta quasi se*]nilis etas. a transmig⟨ra⟩tione babilonis. usq⟨ue⟩ in aduentu⟨m⟩ d⟨omi⟩ni saluatoris in

25) *carnem.*] Generationib⟨u⟩s 7 ipsa. xiiii. porro annis .d.lxxx ix^ne, extenta. In qua

26) *ut graui*] senectute fessa. malis crebriorib⟨us⟩ plebs hebrea q⟨ua⟩ssat⟨ur⟩:·

27) *Sexta*] q⟨u⟩e n⟨un⟩c agit⟨ur⟩ etas. nulla generationu⟨m⟩ ⟨ue⟩l te⟨m⟩poru⟨m⟩ serie certa. s⟨ed⟩ ut etas decrep[ita]

28) ipsa totiu⟨s⟩ s⟨e⟩c⟨u⟩li morte co⟨n⟩sum⟨ma⟩da. [*sic*] Has eru⟨m⟩nosas plenasq⟨ue⟩ laborib⟨us⟩ mundi

29) mundi[809] etates q⟨u⟩iq⟨ue⟩ felici morte uicer⟨un⟩t. Septima ia⟨m⟩ sabbati p⟨er⟩ennis etate suscepti:·

30) octaua⟨m⟩ beate resurrectionis etate⟨m⟩ in qua se⟨m⟩p⟨er⟩ cu⟨m⟩ deo regnent expectant:·- (Bede, DTR, PL 90.521B/C)

---

807 Spaced over to the left of line 21, this is the first word of the next sentence.

808 This date, A.M. 3952, is given by Bede as the date of the Nativity, hence obviously out of place.

809 'mundi' repeated on lines 28–29.

(20–30) The fourth (age) from David to the Babylonian exile, the number of years according to the Hebrew truth being 473, (and) according to the Septuagint twelve more, seventeen generations according to both books. But for the sake of a certain mystery the Evangelist Matthew gives fourteen (generations). From this age, as it were youth, the reign of kings among the people of God began, because this age in men is customarily apt for governing a kingdom. A.M. 3952.

The fifth (age), old age, as it were, is from the Babylonian exile up to the advent of the Savior incarnate, and this has fourteen generations and is then 589 years long, in which age as if exhausted by heavy senility the Hebrew people were weakened by frequent evils.

The sixth (age), which is now in progress, not fixed by a certain number of generations or periods, but like the decrepitude of age it will be consummated by the death of the whole world. These troublous ages of the world, full of torments, some have overcome by a happy death. Having been taken up into the seventh age of perennial sabbath, they look forward to the eighth age of blessed resurrection in which they shall reign forever with God.

31) In has su⟨m⟩ma recidit similit⟨er⟩ de supra posita su⟨m⟩ma eos annos octouiani [*sic*]

32) august[i]. qui s⟨un⟩t post chr⟨istu⟩m natu⟨m⟩. p⟨er⟩tinentes ad sextam aetatem:·[810]

(31–32) Omitted in this summary from the summary above are those years of Octavianus Augustus which fall after the birth of Christ and thus belong to the sixth age.

[810] 31–32 unsourced.

III. English in the Annotations

Doubtless most striking and interesting to Anglo-Saxonists about the Claudius annotations is the fact, noticed independently by each of the present authors, that the majority of the English annotations are translations of excerpts from the *Historia Scholastica*. The discovery of this surprisingly late source and its implications for the original composition of (Old) English towards the end of the twelfth century were the chief factors in the inception of this study. There are thirty-nine of these late twelfth-century English annotations inserted into Claudius B. iv.[1] Most are somewhat discursive, a few relatively long, most rather short, a couple being glosses of only a word or two, with a total yield of only about 900 words and about 220 lexical items plus names. All but a couple have an identifiable and direct Latin source. In almost every case that direct Latin source is the *Historia Scholastica* of Peter Comestor. The original version of this work was composed no earlier than 1169, but it will be shown that the version used by the annotator was the revision issued by the Comestor's pupils about 1180.[2]

The purpose of this chapter is threefold: first, to demonstrate that the direct source is the *Historia Scholastica* itself and not the earlier sources of that work (such as Josephus or Jerome); two, to show that the language of the English notes is in its general lexis, orthography, morphology, and syntax determined by the standards of late West-Saxon, adhering with varying success to eleventh-century canons and not showing predominantly the characteristics of emerging Middle

---

[1] The English notes are printed in the "evidence" (ch. 2) in the positions they occupy in the overall program of predominately Latin notes, their numbers flagged by boldface type. The English notes are: nos. 6a, 7, 10, 14, 15, 16, 18, 25a, 25b, 26, 29a, 34, 36a, 36b, 38, 41, 42b, 42c, 44, 45, 46, 47–48, 50, 51a, 52, 61, 62, 67, 77, 128, 147, 156, 166, 181, 254, 302, 357, 358. An *index verborum* to the English annotations is Appendix 2, 371–80.

Crawford's edition of the notes (1922/23), appearing in *The Old English Version of the Heptateuch* and in "The Late OE Notes of MS (British Museum) Cotton Claudius B. iv," has 29 items, but he overlooks one item (no. 18) as well as several glosses and counts as one an item that on grounds of source is here presented as three (nos. 46–48). The clause added to the end of the main text on f. 155v is not edited among the notes in his appendix, but Crawford includes it in the text and notes as one of the late additions (*OE Hept.*, 400).

[2] For the details regarding the text of the *Historia Scholastica*, see ch. 5, 260–68.

English; and, three, given the combination of the first two conclusions, to demonstrate in detail the compositional strategies and linguistic competencies exhibited by the composer of these extremely late original translations. The linguistic evidence shows that the composer was a speaker of a south-eastern dialect who was attempting to suppress, not entirely successfully, the "natural" elements of his contemporary native tongue in favor of an archaic but respected grapholect. The written performance also seems to indicate that the composer was not very practiced or confident in the writing of English. The larger literary questions of why the annotations were made and how the English notes fit into the overall program of Latin notes in Claudius B. iv will make up the substance of the subsequent chapters.

At the outset, we must continue to stress the well-known fact—still a fact despite the recent upsurge of interest in twelfth-century English[3]—that traditions of writing in English became increasingly tenuous from the turn of the twelfth until well into the thirteenth century, whether the language be called "Old" or "Middle" English. In this study the terms "Old" and "Middle" are avoided as anachronisms. "English" was a well-distinguished register of language separate from "Latin" and "French" and had different uses and social/cultural significations. However infrequently it might have been written, English of the eleventh century and later was obviously a legible language to otherwise literate native speakers of English throughout the twelfth century.[4]

Among the 412 manuscripts and fragments he lists containing Anglo-Saxon, N. R. Ker identifies twenty-eight as being produced after 1100;[5] of these, fifteen are primarily productions of the mid- or later twelfth century or the early thirteenth. All reproduce texts from earlier periods. Clearly, even allowing for

---

[3] A renewed interest signified by the articles in *Rewriting Old English in the Twelfth Century*, ed. Mary Swan and Elaine M. Treharne, CSASE 30 (Cambridge, 2000). See the review of materials and research to date in the introduction to the present book and, in the Swan/Treharne volume, Susan Irvine's article, "The Compilation and Use of Manuscripts Containing Old English in the Twelfth Century" (41–61), which, excellent as it is, gives a somewhat over-optimistic account of the role of English and writing in English during this period. For a more measured brief summary of the situation, see Elaine M. Treharne, "The Dates and Origins of Three Twelfth-Century Old English Manuscripts," *Anglo-Saxon Manuscripts and their Heritage*, ed. Phillip Pulsiano and Treharne (Aldershot, in, 1998), 227–53.

[4] The whole topic is clarified considerably by Elaine M. Treharne, "Reading from the Margins: The Uses of Old English Homiletic Manuscripts in the Post-Conquest Period," in *Beatus Vir: Studies in Early English and Old Norse Manuscripts in Memory of Phillip Pulsiano*, ed. A. N. Doane and Kirsten Wolf, MRTS 319 (Tempe, 2006), 329–58.

[5] N. R. Ker, *Catalogue*, xviii-xix. Ker adds to this (xix) the accidentally omitted B.L. Cotton Claudius D. iii, ff. 55–140, a bilingual "Regula S. Benedicti", written for a female house, perhaps at Winchester; he rather arbitrarily excludes B.L. Harley 6258B (s. xiii^1, provenance unknown), composed of medical treatises in OE: see below, n. 32.

massive destruction of manuscripts, late reproduction of Old English texts represented only a minuscule proportion of writing in England during the period. Judging from the very few manuscripts that can be placed, it would seem that active interest in Old English texts continued only at a few establishments, always monastic, maybe Ely,[6] famously Peterborough,[7] certainly Worcester,[8] but chiefly in the south-east,[9] especially at Rochester and Christ Church, Canterbury.[10]

---

[6] Cambridge, University Library Ii.1.33 (Ker 18), s. xii², mixed homilies and saints' lives, placed at Ely by William Schipper, "A Composite Old English Homiliary from Ely: Cambr. Univ. MS Ii.1.33," *Transactions of the Cambridge Bibliographical Society* 8 (1983): 285–98. Treharne ("Dates and Origins," 239–43) recently challenged this, seeing it as a Rochester or Christ Church product, perhaps carried later to Ely.

[7] Bodleian, Laud Misc. 636 (Ker 346), the "Peterborough Chronicle," written to 1121 by one hand, brought up to 1131 by another, with a third adding 1132–1154; for a recent report on this manuscript see Katherine O'Brien O'Keeffe, *Anglo-Saxon Manuscripts in Microfiche Facsimile* 10, MRTS 253 (Tempe, 2003), 41–44.

[8] Bodleian, Hatton 115, ff. 148–155, s. xii med., prognostications, has glosses by the Worcester "tremulous hand," but Treharne ("Dates and Origins") has recently on paleographical and linguistic grounds placed its origin in the south-east. Bodley 343, mixed homilies, s. xii², which Ker (*Catalogue*, no. 310 [375]) places in the West-Midlands and Irvine ("Compilation and Use," 42) in "the Worcester region"; Worcester Cathedral F. 174 (Ker 398), s. xiii¹, "Ælfric's Grammar and Glossary," extracted from bindings, was written on irregularly-sized and -shaped sheets by the Worcester "tremulous hand" (see Christine Franzen, *The Tremulous Hand of Worcester: A Study of Old English in the Thirteenth Century* [Oxford, 1991], 70–71).

[9] B.L. Cotton Vitellius A. xv, ff. 4–93, s. xii med., the "Southwick Codex," containing the only copy of Alfred's "Soliloquies." It belonged to Southwick Priory in Hampsire in the late thirteenth century; insofar as the basic West-Saxon language is breaking down, the linguistic forms are south-eastern, "predominantly Kentish" (cf. Thomas A. Carnicelli, ed., *King Alfred's Version of St. Augustine's Soliloquies* [Cambridge, MA, 1969], 3–4, 19–21).

[10] Besides C.U.L. Ii.1.33, already mentioned, B.L. Cotton Vespasian D. xiv, ff. 4–169, s. xii med., mixed homilies (Rochester or Christ Church). This contains on ff. 151v-157v what is commonly thought of as the latest Old English, or even the earliest Middle English, a translation of a sermon by Ralph d'Escures (bishop of Rochester 1108–1114, archb. of Canterbury 1114–1122); see Thomas Hahn, "Early Middle English," in *The Cambridge History of Medieval English Literature*, ed. David Wallace (Cambridge, 1999), 82–83. Christ Church manuscripts include the anomalous tri-lingual "Eadwine Psalter," Cambridge, Trinity College R.17.1 (s. xii med.), and two copies of the West Saxon Gospels, B.L. Royal 1 A.xiv, s. xii² bearing the Christ Church pressmark and, copied directly from it, Bodleian, Hatton 38, s. xii/xiii; these manuscripts are referred to more extensively in the analysis of language in appendix 1, below. Elaine Treharne ("Reading from the Margins") gives a slightly longer list, but still quite scanty, all things considered.

The impression of the meagerness of English in this period remains even when one brings into consideration legal and other documents using English. According to David Pelteret,[11] 148 documents with some English exist from after the Conquest; the vast bulk are before 1110 and are boundary formulae and witness-lists. In the reign of the Conqueror (to 1087) the use of official English remains vibrant, with thirty-seven or -eight in his reign, more than any other except Edward the Confessor's, one or two during the reign of William Rufus, seven for Henry I, one for Stephen (to 1154), and only five during the thirty-four-year reign of Henry II (1155–1189), and of these, three are mainly in Latin with an English rights clause. The two remaining are relevant to our concerns: Pelteret 51, an English writ of Henry II (1155 × 1161) "to his bishops, earls, sheriffs, and thegns, French and English, in the shires where Theobald [archb. of Canterbury] and Christ Church have land"; no. 54 (1154 × 1161/1172 × 1189), concerning the same and confirming the previous charter. Most of the royal documents have been preserved in multiple copies so there is not much likelihood that many such documents containing English have disappeared entirely. What remains, in other words, are not chance survivals, but linguistically unusual documents. Like the famous English letters of Henry III of 1258, they are isolated products indicating some special circumstances. Tim Machan has recently argued convincingly that in their use of English the letters of Henry III were a specially "actuated" product of the conflict between the king and his barons, a symbolic harnessing of English to anti-foreigner sentiments to gain a temporary political advantage, not, as is usually explained, to advance a linguistic or national agenda.[12] Similarly, the two above-mentioned charters of Henry II are privileges of Christ Church that duplicate a series of privileges written in English going back to Cnut and renewed by all subsequent kings: it is doubtless the monks themselves who were instrumental in seeing that this ancient lineage of rights was maintained in their original "authentic" form. So we would probably do well to see the few instances of English in the late twelfth century as special instances of the use of English rather than as indicators of a wider realm of English usage of which these are chance survivals.

In any case, it remains that the Claudius notes are unique as belated *original* compositions. All the other extant late twelfth century documents repeat the formulas of earlier grants and deeds in a line going well back into the eleventh century.[13] All the "literary" manuscripts are recopyings of works written

[11] David A. E. Pelteret, *Catalogue of English Post-Conquest Vernacular Documents* (Woodbridge, 1990).

[12] See Tim Machan, *English in the Middle Ages* (Oxford, 2003), 21–69, esp. 62–66.

[13] See Joseph Hall, *Selections from Early Middle English, 1130–1250* (Oxford, 1920), 2:264–65.

in earlier times, showing various minor degrees of linguistic updating.[14] So the English annotations of Claudius B. iv are a crucial component of the scarce evidence for a belated *use* of English writing towards the end of the century, as well as what might be the unique belated example of extended *composition* of English to a West-Saxon standard more than sixty years after the time when someone, most likely a monk of Christ Church, composed an Old English translation of a work by his contemporary, Archbishop Ralph d'Escures (d. 1122).[15] Their nature as English, their possible contextual uses, and what might have actuated their composition in the first place (especially in the face of the overwhelming Latinity of the overall project) are the questions which motivated this book. Answers appealing to their linguistic utility alone will not be convincing. But we must first deal with the question of their source and hence date, then their language, since whatever their nature and purpose, they remain the product of a historically situated linguistic act.

Source: Comestor, "Josephus," and "Methodius"

The date of original composition, within the last two decades of the twelfth century, is guaranteed by their main source. That the English notes are in most cases directly drawn from the *Historia Scholastica* can be seen at a glance by comparing them to their sources as presented in the evidence given in Chapter 2. Wanley and those who followed him accepted at face value the attributions "Josephus" and "Methodius."[16] Only two instances need be put forward here to prove the falseness of these attributions as the direct sources. The first is intended to show that the cited source—"Josephus"—is not the direct source:

> 7. (f. 4v) Joseph*us* cw̄æð. þ*æt* wǽs in syrie on áne felde abute damasco. of rædra yrþe. þ*æt* is mæden yrðe. þ*æt* is uniwemð yrþe. lánd huniréped- þat is cláne land[17]

---

[14] For an argument that some of these manuscripts are new compilations of older material and thus represent original literary activity in English, see Irvine, "Compilation and Use," 41–61.

[15] It occurs in London, British Library, Cotton Vespasian D. xiv, ff. 151v-158r. Less often mentioned and perhaps more significant for issues of the late dating of Old English composition, there are in this same manuscript of the second quarter of the eleventh century two OE versions of extracts from the *Elucidarium* of Honorius of Autun (died ca. 1151), ff. 159r-165r. See Ker, *Catalogue*, no. 209, items 43, 45–46, and Jonathan Wilcox, *Anglo-Saxon Manuscripts in Microfiche Facsimile* 8, MRTS 219 (Tempe, 2000), 61, no. 245, items 45, 47–48.

[16] On the identity and nature of these sources as known in the twelfth century, see ch. 1.

[17] Only "flagged" accents, not hairline strokes, are noted in this discussion.

> Josephus said, that was in Syria in a field near Damascus, of red earth, that is virgin earth, that is uncorrupted earth, land untouched, that is pure land.

At first sight, this indeed closely resembles the Latin Josephus: "Hic autem homo Adam vocatus est, quod nomen Hebraica lingua significat rubeus, quoniam consparsa rubea terra factus est. Talis est enim virgo tellus et vera."[18] But it much more closely resembles Josephus' comment as represented by Peter Comestor, which follows the wording of Josephus closely:

> Similiter sicut hoc nomen Adam fuit proprium illi homini, nunc vero est commune, et Adam sonat rubreus, vel rubra terra, quia, secundum Josephum, de rubea terra conspersa factus est. Talis est enim virgo tellus, et vera, vel rubea . . . (Additio 1. Terra proprie adhuc virgo erat, quia nondum corrupta hominum opere, nec sanguine infecta.)[19]

Though somewhat freely composed, the English is based on the elements presented by the *Historia* rather than by Josephus, as is certain because it uses the Additio[20] which has material not in Josephus. The English takes its attribution from the *Historia* ("secundum Josephum") and is, like the *Historia*, a farrago of definitions, not the smoothly discursive narrative of Josephus: 'of rædra yrþe', "de rubea terra"; 'þæt is mæden yrðe', "talis est enim virgo tellus"; 'uniwemð yrþe' (uncorrupted earth), "nec sanguine infecta"; 'land hunireped' (untouched land), "(terra). . .nondum corrupta hominum opere"; 'þat is clane land', "terra. . .virgo."[21] The English phrases of the first half motivelessly follow the grammar of the

---

[18] "But this man was called 'Adam', because in the Hebrew language the name means 'red', since he was made of compounded red dust. For such is virgin and true earth": F. Blatt, ed., *The Latin Josephus* (Aarhus, 1958), 1.34, p. 128.

[19] "In like manner as this name 'Adam' was proper to that man, now it is indeed common (to all men) and Adam means 'red', or 'red earth', because, according to Josephus, he was made of compounded red dust. Of the same kind is also the 'virgin earth' and genuine, or red. . . . (Add 1: Properly the earth was still virgin, because it had not yet been corrupted by the labor of man, nor polluted by blood.)": HS, PL 198.1071A/B.

[20] The "additiones" consist of material that in most manuscripts of the *Historia Scholastica* is appended as planned "sidebars" to the text, usually in the main hand of the manuscript and in the same script. Not all the manuscripts contain all the "additiones," or the same ones, as they are an accretion of increasingly canonical marginal notations; there seem to be fewer in earlier manuscripts; see ch. 5, 268–69.

[21] Another passage which cites Josephus and follows the words of the Latin Josephus exactly is no. 26; but it is taking it all from the *Historia* (PL 198.1078B), which is citing and attributing Josephus exactly.

Latin, shifting from dative to nominative: 'of rædra yrþe', "de rubea terra"; 'þæt is mæden yrðe', "virgo tellus."[22]

The second example is a "Methodius" note that both shows the misleading nature of the attributions and starkly demonstrates the literalism of the English translations:

> **6a.** (f. 4r) Methodi*us* cw̄æð. adam wǽs gescéopa mán on wlíte óf ðritig wíntra. ⁊ naþeles. on áne dǽge. ⁊ géara ⁊ æfter ðam `án ⁊´ twa wíntra. ⁊ þri wintra. ⁊ alla ða oðron.
>
> Methodius said Adam was created a man in appearance of thirty years and yet in one day and a year and after that (one and) two years and three years and all the others.

The English in itself is rather mysterious and the interlinear insertion 'an ⁊' does not increase intelligibility or confidence. When the source in the *Historia* is collated, though, we see that the English reproduces the Latin word-by-word so closely that a separate translation is not required:

> Et si enim factus est Adam quasi in ætate triginta annorum, tamen fuit unius diei, et anni; et post, duorum annorum, et trium, et sic de cæteris.[23]

That is, though appearing at his creation to be a man of thirty, Adam was actually one, and a year later two, and so on. The final phrase, '⁊ alla ða oðron' obviously represents "et sic de cæteris" and, following the Latin, is probably intended as a dative phrase, but it is unidiomatic and senseless apart from its source and hard to parse due to the decay and ambiguity of the inflexions. Indeed, the English flashes into sense only once the Latin source is compared.

This having been said, "Methodius" is not in fact heading this comment in the *Historia*, which appears within a congeries of comments drawn from the opening of the Pseudo-Methodius: "Sed Methodius martyr oravit . . .".[24] The

---

[22] The "field of Damascus" in which Adam was created is from a later section of the *Historia* (see no. 15, which shares a number of phrases) relating to the death of Abel and burial of Adam and Eve.

[23] HS, PL 198.1076B.

[24] This is the source of (Latin) note no. 3. The point is clearer when the contexts of both sources are compared:

Historia

Sed Methodius martyr oravit, dum esset in carcere, et revelatum est ei a Spiritu de principio, et fine mundi: quod et oravit, et scriptum, licet simpliciter, reliquit, dicens quod virgines egressi sunt de paradiso. § Et anno creationis vitae Adam decimo quinto natus est ei Cain, et soror ejus Chalmana. § *Et si enim factus est Adam quasi in aetate triginta annorum, tamen fuit unius diei, et anni; et post, duorum annorum, et trium, et sic de caeteris.* § Et potuit ante Cain multos genuisse, qui tacentur hic. Post alios quindecim annos natus

English annotator assumes, wrongly, that the whole chapter, generally, depends on Methodius but he does not know, or he does not notice, that the particular sentence he chooses, concerning the apparent age of Adam at his creation,[25] is *not* from Methodius, whereas in no. 25a, taken from this same nexus, the comment is attributed correctly to Methodius, as cited by the Comestor.

The annotator picks and chooses from his *Historia* source freely and recombines various sentences and ideas. Here is another note falsely attributed to "Methodius":

> **16.** (f. 7v) Methodi*us* cw̄æð. adam slép be ís wífe. ⁊ hi gestrínde sunes. ⁊ dohtra.
>
> Methodius said that Adam slept with his wife and begot sons and daughters.

There is nothing to this effect in Pseudo-Methodius—in fact, quite to the contrary: Pseudo-Methodius stresses their virginity—but his opening words might have suggested such a summarizing comment:

> In anno autem xxx^mo^ expulsionis eorum de paradiso genuerunt Cain primogenitum et sororem eius Calmanan et post xxx^mo^ alium annum pepererunt Abel cum sororem eius Debboran.[26]

While the English might merely represent a truism derived directly from Genesis and given a "learned" (mis)attribution, it is more likely a conflation of several passages in the *Historia*, the writer mistakenly thinking that a Methodius comment about the virginity of Adam and Eve properly went with the following comment about the birth of Cain and Chalmana, even though the result directly contradicts the gist of the intervening Methodius comment; the underlined passages could then have produced the English of note 16:

---

est ei Abel, et soror ejus Delbora. § Anno vitae Adam centesimo tricesimo Cain occidit Abel, et luxerunt eum Adam et Eva centum annis. (PL 198.1076B/C)

Pseudo-Methodius

Sciendum namque est, quomodo exeuntes Adam quidem et Eva de paradiso virgines fuisse. In anno autem xxx^mo^ expulsionis eorum de paradiso genuerunt Cain primogenitum et sororem eius Calmanan et post xxx^mo^ alium annum pepererunt Abel cum sororem eius Debboran. Anno autem triginsimo et centisimo vitae Adae occidit Cain fratrem suum Abel et fecerunt planctum super eum Adam quoque et Eva annis c. (ed. Sackur, *Sibyllinische Texte und Forschungen*, 60–61).

[25] In Jewish legend Adam was created like a man of twenty years (see Ginzberg, *The Legends of the Jews*, trans. Szold and Radin [Philadelphia, 2003], 1.58, 60); among other sources, Ginzberg cites Jerome but it is not to be found in Jerome as cited.

[26] Ed. Sackur, 60: "In the thirtieth year after their expulsion from Paradise, they begot Cain the firstborn and his sister Calmana and after another thirty years they gave birth to Abel with his sister Debbora."

> "Adam cognovit uxorem suam sed non in paradiso . . . . Sed Methodius martyr oravit, dum esset in carcere, et revelatum est ei a Spiritu de principio, et fine mundi: quod et oravit, et scriptum, licet simpliciter, reliquit, dicens quod virgines egressi sunt de paradiso. Et anno creationis vitae Adam decimo quinto natus est ei Cain, et soror ejus Chalmana.[27]

The underlined material is in fact the substance of the next OE comment, on the facing leaf (along the bottom left of the picture panel):

> **18.** (f. 8r) Eftter [*sic*] fyftene wíntra. ⁊ is súster chalmana.
>
> After fifteen years also his sister Chalmana.[28]

These incomplete phrases read like part of a gloss.[29]

In one case, the recognition of the correct source has allowed the confident reconstruction of the English text. On f. 34v the trimming of the margin has cut off the first letters of each of the three short lines. Crawford[30] transcribed it "On þan time hi cwæðe wære hælder breder ærcfæderes," probably optimistically aiming at the sense "patriarchs." However, comparison with the corresponding place in the *Historia* suggests the correct restoration:

> **128** [O]n þán tíme hí cwæðe | hære hælder bréder | [w]ǽre fæderes⁖
>
> At that time they said their elder brothers were fathers.

---

[27] HS 1076 A/B; "Adam knew his wife but not in Paradise. . . . But Methodius the martyr prayed when he was in prison and the beginning and ending of the world was revealed to him by the Spirit, and he left a writing, although in a simple style, saying that they (sc. Adam and Eve) went from Paradise as virgins. And in the fifteenth year of the creation of Adam Cain and his sister Chalmana were born to him." The Latin Methodius comment, without the highlighted material before and after, has been copied on f. 3v, bottom (no. 3).

[28] *Historia*, PL 198.1076B: "Et anno creationis vitæ Adam decimo quinto natus est ei Cain, et soror ejus Chalmana. . . . Post alios quindecim annos natus est ei Abel, et soror ejus Delbora." ("And in the fifteenth year of creation of the life of Adam Cain was born to him and his sister Chalmana. . . . After another fifteen years Abel was born to him and his sister Delbora.")

[29] And perhaps for this reason this note is not printed by Crawford. It is written in a picture panel and not correlated to the main text as are the related in-text glosses to the main text on the same page: **Eft** (gl.: ofer oðra xv.) **he ge|strynde abel** (gl: ⁊ suester delbora); the Latin *Historia* source of both no. 21 and of these glosses is copied on the same page, in the right picture panel.

[30] *OE Hept.*, 421; "Old English Notes," 128.

This corresponds exactly to the gist of the *Historia*:[31]

> Sicut enim dicebant cognatos fratres, sic et cognatas sorores; fratrem vero Aram, patrem suum vocavit, quia senior eo fuerat, secundum usum loquendi, quo majores natu, patres vocamus, minores filios. . . .
>
> So as they called male relatives brothers, they called female relatives sisters; indeed [Abram] called his brother Aram his father because he was elder to him, according to common usage, whereby those born elder we call fathers, those younger we call sons.

The Language of the Annotations

Old English manuscripts continued to be copied in certain monasteries throughout the twelfth century. The more than two dozen manuscripts dating from after ca. 1100 which contain substantial amounts of Old English represent copies of works that had been composed in the Anglo-Saxon or immediate post-Conquest period.[32] In general, late scribes attempted to copy earlier Anglo-Saxon exemplars faithfully and the level of correspondence to earlier linguistic standards is high. There was a minimum of transcription into contemporary speech sounds and patterns. Nevertheless certain characteristic minor deviations tended to creep in, involving perhaps unconscious phonological and inflectional changes: certainly such deviations cannot be seen as systematic enough to constitute deliberate linguistic updating. The comparison of a few sentences drawn from an early and a late copy of an Ælfric homily (VIII Kalendas iulii Nativitas Sancti

[31] PL 198.1102D–1103A.

[32] The corpus must be extended to include the translations of Ralph D'Escures and Honorius of Autun, the OE versions of which are usually dated in the first decade of the twelfth century. Another candidate for twelfth-century composition is *Peri didaxeon*, a selection and translation of materia medica from the *Practica* of Petrocellus (ca. 1035), occurring in the late manuscript, London, British Library Harley 6258B, ff. 51v-66v. Ker dates this manuscript as s. xiii[1] and arbitrarily excludes it from the ranks of Anglo-Saxon manuscripts as an early Middle English compilation; but good grounds have been advanced for seeing the translation as earlier (see Linda E. Voigts, "Anglo-Saxon Plant Remedies and the Anglo-Saxons," *Isis* 70 [979]: 250, also A. N. Doane, *Anglo-Saxon Manuscripts in Microfiche Facsimile* 1 [Binghamton: 1994], 44–48, and now Danielle Maion, "The Fortune of the so-called *Practica Petrocelli Salernitani*," in *Form and Content of Instruction in Anglo-Saxon England in the Light of Contemporary Manuscript Evidence*, ed. P. Lendinara et al. [Turnhout, 2007], 494–512, at 500–4).

Iohannis Baptistae, CH.I.25) will illustrate the situation; the differences are bolded in the later text:[33]

A Se Godspellere. lucas awrat on cristes béc. be acennednysse iohannes
G Se Godspellere lucas awrat on cristes be**ch** **beo** ac**æ**nnednysse **j**ohannes

þæs fulluhteres:· þus cweþende; Sum eawfæst godes þegen. wæs gehaten
þæs ful**h**teres þus**s** cweðende. Sum **æ**wfæst godes þ**eig**n wæs gehaten

zacharias. his gebedda wæs geciged elisabeð; . . ..
zacharias. His gebe**d**e wæs gece**gd** Elisabeth. . . . .

A Zacharias him andwyrde; Hu mæig ic þinum wordum gelyfan:· for þan ðe wyt sind
G Zacharias him andwyrde. H**wu** mæig ic þin**e** word**en** gel**e**f**en**? For þan þe wyt synd**en**

forwerede to bearnes gestreone; Se engel cwæð:· ic eom godes heahengel.
forwerede to bearnes gestreone. Se **æ**ngel **cw**⟨**eð**⟩. Ic **ea**m godes he**h** **æ**ngel.

7 dæighwonlice ic stande ætforan his gesihðe:· 7 he me sende to þe þis to cyþene:·
7 dæighw**am**lice ic stande ætfor**e**n his gesihðe. 7 he me s**æ**nde to þe. þis**s** to cy**ð**ene.

nu for þinre geleafleaste. beo þu dumb oð ðæt min bodung gefylled sy;
Nu for þinre **ungeleaffullnysse** beo þu dumb:· o**ðð**et min bodung gefyll**o**d sy.

He þa adumbode 7 swa unsprecende ham gewende;
He þa adumbode. 7 swa un**spechind**e ham gewende.

Altogether, the deviations are not many. We see certain incidental non-linguistic changes in the later text, such as the later type of spelling of 'johannes' and a simplified system of punctuation, as well as the distinctly late abbreviation 'cw̄' for *cweð* or *cwæð*. Sounds that have fallen together are confused in spelling: *be/beo*, *eaw-/æw-*, traditional spelling of digraphs is not always observed: *eom/eam*, spelling is leveled in stressed syllables: *acenned-/acænned-*, *geciged/gecegd*, *sende/sænde*, new pronunciations are spelt: *hu/hwu*, vocalized *ġ* is spelled out: *þegen/þeign* (though this spelling occurs earlier, even in A in this passage), simplification of

[33] A = BL, Royal 7 C. xii (written 990, Cerne Abbas), f. 122rv; G = BL, Cotton Vespasian D. xiv (s. xii med., Canterbury or Rochester), ff. 23v-24r. The former is edited by Peter Clemoes, *Ælfric's Catholic Homilies, The First Series: Text*, EETS s.s. 17 (Oxford, 1997), 379; the latter is edited by Rubie D.-N. Warner, *Early English Homilies from the Twelfth Century MS. Vesp. D. XIV*, EETS o.s. 152 (London, 1917), 19.

consonant clusters is common: *gebedda/gebede*, syllables are syncopated: *geciged/gecgd*, *fulluht-/fulht-*, inflections are simplified or leveled: *gebede/gebedda, wordum/worden*, *gelyfan/gelefen*. The G scribe's south-eastern dialect is probably reflected in *gelefen* for *gelyfan*, *bech* probably reflects Norman orthography, and two vocabulary updatings are evident: *geleafleaste/ungeleaffullnysse* and *unsprecende/unspechinde*. Most of these changes except the last were probably practically unconscious to the scribe and most reflected pronunciation changes. Nevertheless it is obvious that it is the scribe's intention to copy "exactly": in actual fact, he must have copied even more faithfully than the above comparison implies, as intermediate copies probably gradually introduced some of these changes.

Likewise, the composer of the notes in Claudius B. iv probably intended to imitate or achieve a standard of "Old English" approaching that of G. He appears to have been an English speaker of Kentish dialect, one who had a passive familiarity with English as available in written documents that reflected a West-Saxon standard, whether from documents that actually dated from the eleventh century or from later more-or-less accurate copies. Such documents as the annotator could see in the "style" of late West-Saxon provided a standard or touchstone which he appears to aspire to as the correct conventional way of writing English. At the same time, however, the actual execution of the original English notes is very muddled because of two factors: absence of an English exemplar as an exact model and control (as in the case of G), combined with obvious lack of practice and training in the writing of English.[34] Thus the kinds of orthographical irregularities, phonetic confusions, simplifications of inflections, and syntactical innovations which can regularly be observed in twelfth-century copies of Old English exemplars are seen in Claudius in proportionately greater profusion because of the absence of a copy-text and the writer's need to resort to inner linguistic resources rather than learned conventions. The consciousness of a "correct" standard, however, inhibits the annotator from composing strictly in his own language, hence the impression these notes give of being a muddled variety of "Old English" rather than "Middle English."

The linguistic features may be summarized briefly; complete details are laid out in Appendix 1.[35] As is common in twelfth-century copies of Old English, West-Saxon /æ/ is represented by other vowels: at 10.1, *cwað* 50.3, *was* 47.1,

[34] This is true not only linguistically but paleographically as well, as the next chapter will show. This is not to assert that the Claudius annotator was a non-English speaker or entirely unfamiliar with written English as it was passed down from copy to copy, but that he was relatively unpracticed in composing and executing it in writing.

[35] Below, 361–69. An *index verborum*, giving all the forms that occur, is Appendix 2. The citations in the following discussion and in the appendices are to annotation number (as in the edition) and line number (as written in the manuscript). References in this section are to: A. Campbell, *Old English Grammar* (Oxford, 1959); Richard Jordan, *Handbook of Middle English Grammar and Phonology*, trans. and rev.

(h)efter 18.1, 46.1, *her* (*ær*) 62.1, *cweð* 46.3, *feader* 156.3, etc., besides many instances where it remains: *æfter*, *(h)ær*, *cwæþ*, *flæsces*, *wæs*, etc. While the traditional spelling prevails and occurrences of ⟨e⟩ for /æ/ and /æ:/ might represent Kentish unrounding in the scribe's speech (Campbell §288, Jordan §§48(2), 49), the occasional use of *a* for *æ* and reverse spellings (*æn* for *an*, *æc* for *ac*, *lænd*, etc.) suggests a more general transition to Middle English, with ⟨e⟩ for the graph æ representing Latin orthography or Norman influence (cf. Campbell §329(3), Jordan §32). The occasional use of ⟨e⟩ for West Saxon /y/ and /y:/ may be Kentish and a feature of the writer's dialect: *yherden* 44.2 (Kentish, Campbell §200(5), Jordan §40), *-tene* 34.4, *feer* ("fire") 44.5. The unrounding of /y/ to /i/ is generalized in late Old English with a consequent alternation of spellings in ⟨i⟩ or ⟨y⟩ long and short, but here the change is in one direction only: *angynne* 10.1, *belyfen* 50.3, *besyde* 25b.1, *mycele*, *wyfmen*, etc. (no instances of ⟨y⟩ > ⟨i⟩, as if the "y" carries a signification of "Old Englishness" for the writer). There is a general reduction of diphthongs which probably represent phonetic realities in most cases: for /ea/ by breaking > ⟨æ⟩, *ælswa* 50.3, *hærme* 181.4, beside ⟨ea⟩ by palatalization, *gear* (3x), *wingeard* 67.1; we see also *cester* 181.1, *ornos[t]lice* 181.5, *-yrðe* 7.1, West-Saxon ⟨ēa⟩ is spelled /æ/ or /e/, *anhæfede* 10.1, *ræfode* 181.4, *estnysse* 10.1, beside *eac* 2x; probably Kentish are spellings such as *wypen* 25b.1 (= *wēopen*), *ywilcon* 26.2 (= *gewēolcon*) (cf. Jordan §85(2)), and perhaps the doubtful reading *hisyen* 181.3 (for *gesēon*?), all representing reductions of Kentish īo, West-Saxon ēo. Unstressed vowels in non-inflectional syllables are most often merged into a single sound, usually represented as ⟨e⟩: *broþer*, *docter* ("daughter"), etc., beside *wensæm* 10.2, *heriænde*; class II weak *acorede* beside *acorðe* 34.3,4, *wuneda*, etc., beside *ræfode* 181.4., etc.

In inflections, endings are merged and spelled most often ⟨e⟩: *scette* (for *scytta*) 34.2, *agene* (wk. acc.s.m.) 34.2, *ane* (dat. s. m. at 6a.1, dat. s. f. at 181.8; dative plurals vary but are usually spelt with a back vowel, *tæran* 25b.1, *domon* 44.2, *muculum* 181.4, beside *gearen* 46.1). The inflectional system has decayed but is still recognizable, merging most inflectional spellings with ⟨e⟩ and the loss of final ⟨-n⟩ making the language look more idiosyncratic than it actually is. Still, with few exceptions, the system is not functionally simplified and in almost no instances are the endings merely dropped.

The representation of consonants is generally the same as in standard Old English. No orthographic distinction is made in the representation of palatals and velars k/c and g/ȝ as in many documents of the later twelfth century. Several medial orthographical confusions suggest changing pronunciation, *forwæhshe* 44.4, *ymegg`h´e* (for *gemecge*) 50.3, *wuniaghe* 10.3 beside *wunyunge* 10.2. Middle English—but not Kentish—is the loss of velar g medially, *hidraan* 10.3, probably for /ydrauan/ < OE /gedragan/, also *twean* 44.3. There is a general orthographic

---

Eugene Joseph Crook, Janua Linguarum, Series Practica 218 (The Hague, Paris, 1974).

confusion or exchange of **d** for **ð** and vice-versa, which probably indicates not any phonological values, nor always confusion, but application of a sign of "antiquity" by the scribe.[36] Initial inorganic ⟨**h**⟩ is pervasive and gives the text much of its odd look: *hær* 50.3, *heuele* 50.4, *his* (for *is*) 181.2, *hunder* 181.8, etc. This phenomenon extends to the Old English prefix "ge-" which was pronounced and coming to be written **y/i**, so that we have the hypercorrections *hidraan* 10.3 (= *gedrauan* or *gedragan*), *hifunde* 34.1, *hisyen* (probably for *gesēon*). However, the opposite does not happen except in the pronoun "his," spelt ⟨is⟩ 14x beside his 3x.

The syntax of these sentences is usually simple and predominantly SV(O), with the subject often being understood; phrases are paratactically related, with SV often followed by a series of repetitive prepositional phrases as complements. Often the word order follows the Latin, but changes away from Latin are always to SVO order. A few of the sentences show more complex syntax, e.g., the first, freely composed, sentence of no. 34 (i.e., a sentence that does not follow a particular Latin sentence) which is paratactically constructed but with prepositional phrases, an OV inversion, and a dative of destination: "Lamach and his sons invented many kinds of skills, and he was a good archer and with his shooting he slew Cain and with his bow his own man he slew to his great sorrow." There is one instance of the inflected infinitive to express allowance in an otherwise awkward sentence: *flæsces to notiena* 62.1 (= "esus carnium"), and once a gerundive occurs: *eode . . . heriænde godes name* 61.3. These texts exhibit some of the earliest instances of the use of non-stressed *me* as a passive particle, almost always directly translating a Latin passive (e.g., *me red* = "legitur" 41.1).

The vocabulary is overwhelmingly from that of standard West-Saxon, limited though it is by both the brevity of the texts and the restricted subject matter and vocabulary of the chosen Latin excerpts. Certain words stand out as suggesting particular kinds of sources: poetry (*neorxnawanga* 3x), charters (*anhæfede* 10.1 "the end of a furrow as a boundary-marker"), computus (*træenle* 10.4, i.e. *trendel*, "globum"). A few words must be Old English but seem to be first recorded in these notes: *beside*, prep. 3x (O.E. *be sidan*), *smell* "odor" 10.2, *ywilcon* 26.2 (i.e. *gewealcan*) in the eventually dominant meaning, "walk," translating "peragrans." There are a few, but not many, French symptoms: *acordian*, "to be in agreement" at 34.3,4, from Old French *acorder*, occurring also in the *Peterborough Chronicle*; *marbre* 44.4 ("marble") is Old French, the Old English cognate being *marma*, *marmorstan*; *pilires* 44.3 ("pillars") is Old French, the Latin source at this place having "columnis," a word available in Old English and indeed this text has both *columban* and *pilires* as if one or the other required glossing. Finally, one must

---

[36] This also seems to be the explanation of the "flagged" or "OE" type of accents: they occur spasmodically, over long and short syllables, stressed and unstressed syllables, even over consonants! It as if the scribe knew only that an English text ought to have them—he does not always avoid them on Latin words in mixed OE/Latin passages (cf. e.g. no. **10** cited below).

note the use, but probably not the earliest use, of *of* to represent the genitive, on the pattern of Old French *de* in geographical phrases: *in ðan lande of syria* 44.3, 29a.1 (OE would be **in syria-lande*), and *denæ of tæran* ("vallis lacrymarum").

As language performance these notes are very much of their time. They reflect an effort to confect texts that present new wine in old bottles, the very modern *Historia Scholastica* in the prestigious language of the ancient English past. Elaine Treharne has provocatively characterized the use of "Old English" in the twelfth century: "The fact that late West Saxon was always a formal register of language, one that would not commonly be a reflection of *parole*, serves to reinforce the argument about the copying of texts in the twelfth century: adherence to West Saxon . . . is an attempt, as it always was, to use the most prestigious register of language for the composition of written texts."[37] These notes were probably composed by someone who had some familiarity with the types of books in Old English still to be found in the monastic library, perhaps someone who had even been involved in copying old texts or drafting charters based on older English models, but apparently the differing registers of these texts did not matter in the search for usable vocabulary.

Linguistically, the annotations give the impression of a push towards idealized West-Saxon forms derived from various models and a pull towards contemporary Kentish forms during composition, similar to what we can see in Henry II's charter of 1155 ×1161, written in a royal chancery hand:

> ⁊ ic keþe eow þ*æt* ic hebbe heom geunnon þ*æt* hi beon ælc þære lande wurþa þe hi eafdon en Edwardes kinges deȝe. ⁊ on Willelmes kinges mines furþur ealde fader. ⁊ on Henrices kinges mines ealde fader. ⁊ saca ⁊ Socne. on strande ⁊ on Streame. On wudan ⁊ onfeldan. tolles ⁊ theames. grithbriches. ⁊ hamsocne. ⁊ forstalles. ⁊ i*n*fangenesthiafes. ⁊ fleamene frimtha. ofer heore agene men. . . .[38]

A generation later the grant was rewritten, and, surprisingly, the English is somewhat closer to West-Saxon in its vowels and vocabulary, because the writer,

[37] Treharne, "Reading from the Margins," 338.

[38] Ed. Hall, *Selections from Early M. E.*, 1:12, language notes at 2:264–69. He edits the B.L., Harley Charters 111 B. 49, an original copy sealed at the bottom. This is identified as a royal chancery hand by T. A. M. Bishop, *Scriptores regis: Facsimiles to Identify and Illustrate the Hands of Royal Scribes in Original Charters of Henry I, Stephen, and Henry II* (Oxford, 1961), nos. 387, 406, pl. XXV(b). The royal scribe, used to writing Latin, not English, is somewhat mystified by the insular letter-forms, alternating between *þ* and *th*, taking *þ* for *k* in the first couple of instances, making various compromises between insular and Norman *f*, *s*, *r*, using *g* for velar and *ȝ* for palatal but inconsistently; there is also a general tendency towards simplifying dipththongs. But an attempt is made to distinguish the script visually from that of the Latin version immediately above.

who reverts to a monastic bookhand, has consulted an older exemplar and copied it exactly, including an attempt to duplicate the early twelfth-century script.[39]

Like the charter, as we shall see in the next section, the English notes depend heavily on pre-existent models as the enabling framework, but, unlike the charter, they are much freer in thought and composition. The clearly Kentish elements in the Claudius annotations must be the effect of the scribe's own speech, though it could conceivably be the last traces of a tradition of scribal normalization holding on in some old-fashioned way in Canterbury. That being said, the English is still a very weird sort of late West-Saxon which shows an imperfect knowledge of the conventions of that artificial dialect as well as disorganized interference from speech and writing conventions, English, Latin, and French. The vocabulary is generally what is found in standard late West-Saxon, but includes out-of-the-way words from charters, poetry, etc. At least three French words are found, as well as what is probably the French-influenced use of *of* as a quasi-genitive. The disintegration of inflections has gone very far, but the functional inflectional system is maintained. Finally, the Latin influence must not be ignored: the very choice of vocabulary, limited and pale as it is, reflects the style of the source in "Hieronymian" historical writing that carried over into the Comestor's style; this Latin has also influenced the syntax in several instances.

Translation: Strategies and Competence

The confusions and inconsistences of the language are more than matched by those of the composition of the discourse. One has to keep in mind the loneliness of the task: by all the evidence, whoever was composing these notes in English was doing something highly unusual, hardly with living example. Naturally enough, as has already been indicated in the first section, the main strategy of the translator therefore is a simple word-for-word dependence on the Latin source. This shows a knowledge of some basic set protocol for choosing one English word for a Latin one, that is, there is some tradition pertinent to the process. At the same time, the work shows a dependence on the Latin as a prop for getting on with the translation at all, that is, there is a limited competence in English

[39] Compare Pelteret 54, Henry II 1154 × 1167/1172 ×1189 (BL Stowe Charter 43) to Pelteret 51, which it reaffirms and to Pelteret 48, Henry I 1123, to his bishops, etc. (BL Stowe Charter 44) in the time of Archb. William. Pelteret 54 uses Pelteret 48 as the model not only of the language but of the script, as can be seen by comparing Plates XLV and XLIV in W. B. Sanders, *Facsimiles of Anglo-Saxon Manuscripts* (Southampton, 1884), vol. 3. In the earlier document there is a clearer difference between Latin and OE scripts; in the later both the Latin and the Old English resemble the Latin script of the earlier document and there is not so clear a distinction of styles between them.

written discourse, which in these notes often has a certain *ad hoc*, even desperate air, at the same time as a native knowledge of spoken English must be assumed.

> **41.** (f. 10v) Me reð on bóce. þ*æt* adam hæfede .xxx. súnes ⁊ swa fela dohtra. bútan cayn. ⁊ abel.
>
> Legitur Adam triginta habuisse filios, et totidem filias præter Cain et Abel.[40]

A single translation serves both passages equally well:

> It is read in a book that Adam had thirty sons and as many daughters, not counting Cain and Abel.

This selection from an "additio" literally preserves the passive using the incipient ME formal idiom of *men* in its reduced form in one of its earliest recorded occurrences. That it is part of the annotator's idiom, and that he has reasonable facility with both languages, is shown by its use in the next example representing not a passive, but the general subject "quidam":

> **14.** (f. 7v) Me cwæð. þ*æt* hi wære inne neorxnawange vii. tide.
> It is said (somebody said) that they were in paradise seven hours.
>
> Quidam tradunt eos fuisse in paradiso septem horas.[41]
> Some say that they were in paradise seven hours.

No. 14 also shows that the annotator has a range of registers to draw from, for he uses the traditionally poetic word *neorxnawang* for "paradiso" (he uses *neorxnawang* two other times and keeps the Latin word in nos. 10 and 50). While these passages illustrate that the annotator has the capacity to handle English somewhat independently, his freedom is pretty limited by his competence. This limited competence in written discourse is shown by his need at times to find his English lexis from far-flung registers, by his tendency to lapse into Latin consciously or unconsciously, and by the uncertainty of his grammar, orthography, morphology, and syntax, all well illustrated by the next example, which alternates between freely composed discourse and slavishness:

> **10.** (f. 5v) Me red on bóc. be paradisu*m* in eden þ*æt* is neorxna.wanga. eden þ*æt* is inne estnysse. ⁊ inne blisse. eden is at anhǽfede angynne on hésdele þysre wórlde. se stéde is swyþe on suóte breðe. ⁊ swyðe suóte sḿelle.[42] ⁊

[40] PL 198.1080B (Add. 1).

[41] PL 198.1075D.

[42] *smell* does not occur in OE. The substantive in sense of "odor" occurs in a Lambeth Homily (ca. 1175, OED s.v. *smell* 2).

> wénsæm wúnyunge. 7 láng hidráan an héstdele. anlǽnges ðære sǽ, bútan úre wuniaghe. ut usq*ue*. ad lunarem globum attíngit. þ*æt* ís tó þas mónas træenle hí táeh`e´. 7 ðaer þa wæteræ dilúuii ne ne cóme. ðat is Noes floð.

> It is read in a book about paradise in Eden, that is "neorxnawang." Eden that is in pleasure and in bliss. Eden is at a headland (furrow end), a beginning in the eastern part of this world. The place is very much into sweet breath and very sweet smell and pleasant dwelling and extended far into the eastern part along the sea, outside of our country (dwelling) so that it reaches up to the sphere of the moon, that is, to the moon's orbit it draws and there the waters of the flood do not come. That is Noe's flood.[43]

The English is in places so awkwardly composed that a sensible literal translation is difficult. Though the rendering is free and the order is rearranged, the translator resorts to Latin thrice, and then Englishes, respectively, the phrases and the interpretation of the words. On the other hand, the translator ransacks whatever resources are available for English vocabulary, regardless of its traditional registers. Indeed, the translator seems familiar with several genres of Old English writing, for example, 'paradisum' is the poetic 'neorxnawang' and the simple "locus amœnissimus" is a prompt for a string of homiletic cliches. The uncertainly written phrase 'atan hæfede'[44] is taken here as OE *æt anheafda, "at the headland," at the extreme edge, "a prima orbis parte." It is attested only as a charter word, meaning "the end of a furrow" as a field-boundary marker, but may have had wider connotations and may also show the writer's familiarity with charter language as an *ad hoc* source of vocabulary items;[45] "træenle" (i.e., *trendel*) suggests familiarity with the OE computus. Having to draw on so many texts for

[43] *Historia*, PL 198.1067A/B: . . . vel a principio, id est a prima orbis parte. Unde alia translatio habet, paradisum in Eden ad orientem. . . . Ergo idem est paradisum voluptatis quod paradisum in Eden, id est in deliciis. Sed a principio, idem quod ad orientem. Est autem locus amœnissimus longo terræ, et maris tractu a nostra habitabili zona secretus, adeo elevatus ut usque ad lunarem globum attingat. Unde, et aquæ diluvii illuc non pervenerunt. ("or 'from the beginning,' that is from the first part of the world. Whence another translation has 'paradise in Eden to the east.' Therefore the 'paradise of pleasure' is the same as 'paradise in Eden,' that is, in delights. But 'from the beginning' is the same as 'to the east.' It is a most pleasant place hidden from our habitable zone by the long tract of land and sea, so elevated that it reaches the sphere of the moon. And whence the waters of the flood did not reach it.") The phrase in the English "be paradis*um* in eden" is macaronic, but basically Latin, with usual Latin abbreviation signs in 'paradisū' and 'usq;'.

[44] So MS; Crawford, without suggesting an emendation, reads 'atana ðam'.

[45] *an(d)héafdu*, "headland," is only attested in the sense "ridge of earth at the end of a furrow where the plow is turned" and occuring only in cartularies as a field-boundary term (see Bosworth-Toller, Supp., q.v.); there are thirty occurrences copied from earlier charters in the 12th century and later according to the *Dictionary of Old English* (s.v.); the phrase here is taken as representing "a prima orbis parte."

words of mildly technical import from so many diverse registers suggests not competence but a rather shaky grasp of English vocabulary beyond the most basic, and the need to consult whatever written English resources were available to the writer at the time (which might have been considerable in twelfth-century St. Augustine's). The emendation above the line to 'taeh`e´' (taken as subj. of "tēon") suggests shaky familiarity with written Old English norms, while on the other hand the form of 'hidraan' (*gedrauan* < *gedragan*) shows a form naturally tending to Middle English pronunciation. Another instance of this is in no. 38 (f. 10r), where "Septuaginta" is rendered 'þa hundseofentig wenðeres'. The word *wendere* "translator" is very rare but precise, interestingly showing that our translator understood and made plain what "Septuaginta" meant, even showing knowledge of its legendary origins and not mistaking it for a numeral. It occurs as a gloss in the prose Aldhelm *De laude virginitatis*[46] and may reflect consultation with such a manuscript present at St. Augustine's.

Like this one, many of the notes are a curious combination of the learned, the proficient, and the incompetent. The common denominator seems to be the need to have some direct model to work from—very little is freely composed, even though the annotator is venturing out into unknown territory and undertaking original translation, perhaps an isolated single instance in the past two generations. A couple of short passages, on facing pages, illustrates this well.

> **62.** (f. 16v) Næs nán wúna hér ða flode. flæsches to notiéna. ǽc her fyrst.
>
> There was no custom before the flood to eat flesh, but this time [here] at first.
>
> Esus carnium ante diluvium non erat, sed post statim concessus est.[47]
>
> There was no consumption of flesh before the flood, but afterwards it was immediately allowed.

The note is hard to translate and perhaps it is not finished—though it is certainly intended to represent this Additio of the *Historia* and means, however it might be translated, that now, after the flood, was the first time flesh was lawfully eaten. The phrase 'flæsches to notiena', the inflected infinitive to render the Latin past

[46] Ed. Louis Goossens, *The Old English Glosses of MS. Brussels, Royal Library 1650* (Brussels, 1974), 5139 *wenderum* "translatoribus, interpretes"; also A. Napier, *Old English Glosses, Chiefly Unpublished*, Anecdota Oxoniensia: Mediaeval and Modern Series 11 (Oxford, 1900), no. 13.1, 5259. Still extant are glossed Aldhelm manuscripts of Canterbury provenance CCCC 326 (CC, s. x/xi), Royal 5.E.xi (CC, s. x/xi), Royal 6.A.vi (CC, s. x ex.), Oxford, Trinity Coll. 38 (CC or St. Aug., s. x ex).

[47] *Historia*, PL 198.1086D (Add. 1); the English better reflects the revised version than it does the PL ed. (cf. Sylwan, ed. *Scol. Hist*): ". . . hic post statum est et hic primo concessum."

part. "esus," the correct genitive object, and the traditional word-order suggest that an OE model was at hand: cf. "þa underfongen hi ealle æt him hyra horsa to brucenne & notienne."[48] What is more interesting, however, is how this slender reed becomes the basis for the next note, on the facing page, f. 17r, the upper picture of which shows Noe cultivating vines, the lower Noe and his family working a winepress, the following text written on the press:

67. hær ða flode nás ná wíngeard[49]

Before the flood there was no vineyard.[50]

Though a *Historia* citation may be made, it is not the direct source so much as a kind of cue for the English note at this place; there seems to be no Latin source. This is a fascinating note. It is an attempt at free or original composition without the Latin as a support; and as such, it pieces together in reversed order two phrases from the preceding English note on the facing page,

Næs nan wuna / her ða flode

hær ða flode / nas na wingeard.

Apparently written in the same stint, these two notes together suggest that the composer had no confidence in striking out in English without some sort of immediate linguistic model.[51]

A native command of the language that nevertheless betrays limited resources for its written composition is shown by the next example:

50. f. 12r § æfter adames forðsiðe. seth ytwǽmde his ofspríng. frám caynes ofsprínge. þ*æt* hí ywende to hære ybora lánda. ⁊ seth wúneda on ána munte

[48] Gregory, *Dialogues* (ed. H. Hecht, *Bischof Wærferths von Worcester Übersetzung der Dialoge Gregors des Grossen*, BaP 5 [Leipzig, 1900–1907], 2.15.32). No. 62 pertains to Genesis 9:3–4, which in the OE main text is written overleaf, f. 16r/15.

[49] Crawford incorrectly reads "næs."

[50] Cf. *Historia*, PL 198.1087A: Cœpit Noe exercere terram, et plantavit vineam, labruscas naturales per cultum ad usum vineæ trahens, bibensque vinum, sed ignorans vim ejus, inebriatus est. ("Noe began to work the earth and planted a vineyard, bringing the wild grapevine into service for winemaking through cultivation 'and drinking the wine' but ignorant of its strength 'became drunk'.")

[51] Perhaps he took his cue from *Adrian and Ritheus*, no. 17: "Saga me hwa sette ærest wineardas of þe hwa dranc ærest wi[n]. Ic þe secge, Noe" (ed. James E. Cross and Thomas D. Hill, *The* Prose Solomon and Saturn *and* Adrian and Ritheus [Toronto, 1982], 37), a similar saying in the *Prose Solomon and Saturn*, no. 46, *ibid*, 33. *Adrian and Ritheus* is preserved in a mid-twelfth-century fragment bound into British Library, Cotton Julius A. ii, in a hand that is of the "prickly" Canterbury type.

> beside paradise. Cayn in ðon felde þe he ís broþer ofslóh, ǽlswa adam hít hét hær is forðsyðe. þat hí ne scolde hí ymegg`h´e. Jose[phus] cwað. sethes súnes belyfen góde. to ðan seofende ofspri[n]ge. hác seþe hi gewéndon to mycelon heuele. {Enoch se seofende. `man frám adame.´ Noe se tynde.}
>
> After Adam's death, Seth separated his offspring from Cain's offspring, so that they went to their native land. And Seth dwelt on a mountain beside Paradise, Cain in the field where he slew his brother, just as Adam commanded before his death, so that they should not mix there. Josephus said Seth's sons remained good to the seventh generation, but later they turned to great evil. {Enoch the seventh man from Adam, Noe the tenth.}

The *Historia* has:

> Josephus autem dicit quod usque ad septimam generationem boni permanserunt filii Seth, post ad mala progressi sunt.[52] . . . Mortuo Adam, Seth separavit cognationem suam a cognatione Cain, quæ redierat ad natale solum. Nam et pater vivens prohibuerat ne commiscerentur, et habitavit Seth in quodam monte proximo paradiso. Cain habitavit in campo, ubi fratrem occiderat.[53]
>
> For Josephus says that up to the seventh generation the sons of Seth remained good, but afterwards tended to evil. . . . Adam having died, Seth separated his kin from the kin of Cain, which returned to its native soil. For also his father when living had kept (them) apart lest they mix in marriage, and Seth lived on a certain mountain near Paradise. Cain lived in the field where he had killed his brother.

On the whole, the English writing seems in command here, with its employment of idiomatic constructions, such as as an adverbial phrase for the Latin's ablative absolute, a *that*-clause for a relative clause, the transposition of the Josephus comment to the end of the narrative section for clarity, and some added material. The translation of "progressi sunt" ('gewendon') resourcefully captures both the sense of going and changing for the worse implied in the Latin. On the other hand, the transposition of Adam's commandment of separation is poor, since it seems at first glance that he commanded Cain's crime. But the translator here is muddled by simultaneously keeping the phrase about Cain's dwelling-place with

---

[52] *Latin Josephus* 1.72 (132): et isti quidem septem generationibus permanserunt deum iudicantes esse dominum omnium et ad virtutem semper inspicientes, deinde tempore procedente de paternis sollemnitatibus ad mala progressi sunt. . . . ("and these [the Sethites] persevered for seven generations esteeming God to be the lord of all and always looking to virtue as their guide, while as time went on they tended away from the religious observances of their fathers towards evil").

[53] PL 198.1081B, 1081C/D.

its material and trying to remodel the grammar of the Latin and put it last, perhaps for emphasis ("pater. . .prohibuerat ne commiscerentur"/ 'ælswa adam hit het hær is forðsyð. þar hi ne scolde hi ymegg`h´e'). The phrase 'to hære ybora landa' seems an awkwardly literal shift for "ad natale solum." The bracketed words of the last OE sentence are added, comprising well-known information that is often repeated.[54]

The annotator can make a summary that departs from his source, but only with the greatest caution and with the effect of "closing up" the material rather than fully representing it:

> **34.** f. 9v ('Josephus' in left margin): lamech. ⁊ hís sunes hífúnde fæle `cenne´ cræftæs. eác he wés gód scétte. ⁊ mid his scéte ófsloh caym. ⁊ mid is bóhe is `agene´ mán. ofsloh. hím to mycele sorhe. for þa*m* caynes sénne bið acorede seófonfealð wyte. ís bið acorðe septuagies septies. wyten. þ*æt* byð syxti. ⁊ seofontene. saulen. of lámech; forfe[r]den in diluuio:
>
> Lamech and his sons discovered many kinds of skills; and he was a good archer and with his shooting he slew Cain and (with) his bow slew his own man to his great sorrow. Therefore Cain's sin is reckoned for seven-fold (punishment), his punishment is reckoned for seventy-seven times, that is sixty plus seventeen souls from Lamech perished in the flood.

This is a reduction of the much fuller version in the *Historia*, derived from a well-known Jewish midrash:

> Lamech autem, secundum Josephum, res divinas sapienter sciens . . . Lamech vero vir sagittarius diu vivendo caliginem oculorum incurrit, et habens adolescentem ducem; . . . casu interfecit Cain . . . æstimans feram, quem quia ad indicium juvenis dirigens sagittam, interfecit. Et cum experiretur quod hominem, scilicet Cain, interfecisset, iratus illic cum arcu ad mortem verberavit eum. . . . Et ideo cum peccatum Cain punitum esset septuplum, ut diximus, suum punitum est septuagies septies, id est septuaginta animæ, et septem egressæ de Lamech, in diluvio perierunt.[55]
>
> According to Josephus, Lamech was wisely knowledgeable of divine matters. . . . But Lamech, a bowman, having lived long, developed cataracts of the eyes, and having a young man as a guide, accidentally killed Cain . . . thinking him a wild beast whom he killed because he aimed his arrow at the young man's signal. And when he realized that it was a man he had killed, namely Cain, Lamech, angry, then and there beat him (his servant) to death with the bow. And therefore since Cain's sin has been punished

[54] e.g., Isidore, *De ortu et obitu patrum*, PL 83.131.
[55] PL 198.1079C/D.

> seven times, as we said, his was punished seventy-seven times, that is seventy souls, and seven gone forth from Lamech, perished in the flood.

The annotator follows the Comestor's attribution, although it does not appear in Josephus' *Antiquities.*[56] The translator seems to be expurgating the passage, altering "res divinas" to 'fæle cenne cræftes', removing the religious connotations from the practices of this wicked man and perhaps also rationalizing the transition to archery. As he abbreviates the story, the translator also rationalizes the hard-to-understand elements, Lamech's "anger" becomes "sorrow" and his beating his guide to death with his bow becomes the more transparent but technically not inaccurate expression that he killed him "with his bow," while maintaining the two tellings of the same incident. It is interesting that, as in No. 10 above, the freer approach appears along with several resorts to familiar Latin phraseology. It would seem that the word-for-word approach keeps the translator focused on the task of finding an English equivalent word, whereas when he is thinking of the general matter, he slips into the "more natural" Latin. He also slips into "French," or rather his naturalized early Middle English vocabulary, twice using the verb *acorder*, a word found also in English in the Peterborough Chronicle.[57]

Having observed what is probably the full extent of the annotator's abilities for free composition, we should finally note the longest passage of all of them because it shows an apparent, but illusory, freedom of composition that demonstrates well the limits of the annotator's competence; this is the long added summary of parts of Genesis 33, 34, 35, the story of the rape of Dina, omitted, doubtless on grounds of propriety, from the main Old English translation. It occupies the large blank space in the bottom margin of f. 51r (main text is Gen. 33:17), and is made to appear as if it follows directly and continues the narrative in the main text, though it is misplaced in the order of the text.

> **181.** (ff. 51rv) **iacob ferde ða mid ealre hys híwrædene swa him god wisode:** and cóm to salem cester (gl.: et forte binomia erat) on sichem. *þæt*[58] hís in chanaan lánde. ˋ7ˊ þar wycnigede. 7 bohte lánd. æt emore (. . . . .) sichˋeˊmes fæder. 7 aræ[r]de wéofod on gȯdes náme. lían docter dína for

[56] See instead Ginzberg, *Legends* (1909–1938), 1:111, 113.

[57] The verb "acordan" is from OF *acorder* and occurs in the Peterborough Chronicle in the sense "come to an agreement" (an. 1119) and in the sense "reconcile" (an. 1120) (s.v. "accorden," Kurath, *MED*). The sense here is hard to tease out, but must mean something like "the (degree of) punishment agrees with (the degree) of sin."

[58] In this passage all the "thorns" are crossed; 'god' (2×) has a small "c"-shaped note over the 'o', a symbol which this scribe, apparently, entered over all the occurrences of "god" in the main text.

hút to hisýen[59] þas landes wyfmén. ⁊ emores súnu[60] sichem ræfode hí. ⁊ slæp mid híre. hím ⁊ ælle ís mǽgum to muculum hǽrme. swá seo leden bóc sprycð {Genesis.}[61] ⁊ ræðe se þe wyle. hu ornos[t]lice . iacobes súnes dína hǽre suster hút ledde. ⁊ emor. ⁊ sichem ís súne. ⁊ hære mǽgum. ⁊ eác aella þa to hám cómen ofslógon. mid swúrdes écge. ⁊ gecyrdon gesunde to hǽre getelde. ⁊ iacob. ⁊ ís súnunes [*sic*] mid hære wycstówe ywenden to bét`h´el. ⁊ hérde gódes náme. On þan tíme forðferde debbora rebecca fostermóder. ⁊ heo bebyrigde on nyþéwærde bethel hunder áne áche. \[62] ⁊ me cwæð þane steðe áche wóp;

Jacob went with all his household as God showed him and came to Salem City (gl.: and perhaps it had two names) in Sichem, that is in Chanaanland and dwelling there and bought land from Emor the father of Sichem and raised an altar in God's name. Lia's daughter Dinah went out to see the women of the land and Emor's son Sichem raped her and slept with her, to the great harm of him and all his kinsmen as the Latin book [Genesis] says and read it he who will how deliberately Jacob's sons led out their sister Dinah and slew with the sword's edge Emor and Sichem his son and their kinsmen and also all those (who had) come home and returned safe to their tent(s) and Jacob and his sons with their encampment went to Bethel and praised God's name. At that time Deborah, the fostermother of Rebecca, died and she (was) buried on the downward side of Bethel under an oak and the place is called the 'oak of weeping' ("oak-weeping").

Whereas many of the other notes give the appearance of having been translated directly into the book, this note contains symptoms suggesting it was written

[59] The manuscript form appears to be 'hiswen' or 'hisyen', but two letters are malformed: the third letter seems intermediate between an *r* and *s* with long descender, but it could be a badly formed *w*; the fourth letter seems to be a dotted *y* but it could also be a malformed *w*. Crawford ("Old English Notes," 128; *OE Hept.*, 422) prints *hisýen*, which more or less represents the shape of the letters as written and which might be taken as a form of *geseon*. In his EETS edition (168), he prints "hisywen" without comment, but representing three letters where there are only two. The Vulgate has at this place (Gen. 34:1) "Egressa est autem Dina filia Liæ, *ut videret* mulieres regionis illius." Another OE word that is both close to the deformed word and syntactically fits the meaning is *hawienne* "(for) to see," a late prose form (see S-B § 363, Anm. 3). Cf. *Lives of Sts.*, ed. Assmann, 49: "Þa gewearð on anum dæge, þæt hire fostermodor hi het gan mid oðrum fæmnum on feld, sceap to hawienne, and hi dydon swa spinnende." The word is common in the south-eastern twelfth-century copy of Alfred's *Soliloquies*.

[60] Corrected from 'suum'.

[61] Crawford, *Hept.*, 168, no. 3, says 'Genesis' is "seemingly in a later hand." But this is unlikely; it is probably an indexical word or gloss on 'seo leden boc' since it is extended into the margin.

[62] This line is written below the rest of the comment, with a run-on mark and inside the picture-frame.

separately and then copied into the manuscript. As mentioned, the note is misplaced and was probably intended to dovetail into the sentence ending on line 2, thus: *'**sochot. ðæt ys geteld** and com to salem', etc., which would have accorded smoothly with the transition in the Vulgate at 33:17–34:1: "venit in Socoth . . . id est, tabernacula. Transivitque in Salem." Several words seem badly miswritten, even by the standards of these texts, 'wycnigede' (a form of *wicode*?), 'arædе' (*arærde*), 'hisyen/hiswen' (see n. 59), other miswritten insular letters such as several cases of alternation between 'ae' and 'æ', and confusion of insular and caroline 'g' ('mæginn' f. 51v/2), the outbreak of accents, not to mention the automatic Latin reflex of 'suum' for "sunu." This suggests the copying of a hastily-written draft on the part of the writer not that confident of the insular letter-forms that he may be seeing in wax. Yet the care and learning that has gone into it is shown by a Latin gloss ('et forte binomia erat') that appears independently derived from Jerome's implication[63] that Salem had two names, Sichem and Salem: "Sichem et Salem, quae latine et graece Sicima uocata est, ciuitas Iacob."

However smoothly it may read as a freely composed narrative,[64] the note is cobbled together from selected sentences from Genesis 33–35, using the same technique of selection and close translation as when the source is the *Historia Scholastica*. The total impression is of literal bits strung together paratactically with the mark '⁊',[65] a style far from the supple prose of Ælfric. The sentence on Simeon and Levi is enlivened with formulaic interventions: 'ornos[t]lice' and 'mid swurdes ecge'. A line-by-line analysis reveals the method of composition. The first lines represent parts of Gen. 33:18–20 pretty closely:

> and com to salem cester on sichem
>
> "Transivitque in Salem, urbem Sichimorum, quæ est in terra Chanaan"
>
> `⁊´ þar wycnigede ⁊ bohte land. æt emore sichemes fæder.

[63] *De situ et nominibus locorum Hebraicorum*, ed. Lagarde, 148.20.

[64] Crawford ("Old English Notes," n. 1 and *OE Hept.*, 422, n. 1) says of this item "the general style . . . suggests Ælfric as its author, though it is not found in the *original* text of either the Cotton or Laud manuscript." In his edition (168), Crawford places this passage where it belongs textually, after 33:17; but this misrepresents where and how it actually appears on the page, at the bottom of f. 51r after the OE main text's version of Gen. 35:5–6, appearing to dovetail syntactically into the main text, using '**iacob**' as the subject of the note's 'com'. There is a conspicuous *signe de renvoi* at 33:17, f. 51r, level with line 2 of the main OE text (after annotator's added word 'sochot'), but it refers not to this OE annotation, but to the Latin Jerome comment on the facing page.

[65] The ⁊-notae are sprinkled in liberally, in one place producing the syntactically implausible, '⁊ þar wycnigede. ⁊ bohte land', if this is to be taken as a past participle. But it is probably a miswriting of a form of 'wicode'/'wycede' "dwelt."

". . . et habitavit juxta oppidum. Emitque partem agri . . . a filiis Hemor patris Sichem. . . ."

7 aræ[r]de weofod on godes name[66]

"Et erecto ibi altari, invocavit super illud fortissimum Deum Israel."

The Dinah story is greatly abbreviated from the Vulgate, but following the exact same method of word-for-word translations selected from the text so as to supply an epitome of the narrative, these being the most idiomatic phrases among the Claudius English annotations:

lian docter dina for hut to hisyen þas landes wyfmen (S V O)

"Egressa est autem Dina filia Liæ, ut videret mulieres regionis illius"

7 emores sunu sichem ræfode hi 7 slæp mid hire

". . . Sichem filius Hemor . . . adamavit eam, et rapuit, et dormivit cum illa"

him 7 ælle his mæginn to muculum hærme swa seo leden boc sprycð Genesis[67] 7 ræðe se þe wyle.

. . . hu ornos[t]lice iacobes sunes dina hære suster hut ledde 7 emor 7 sichem is sune 7 haere mægum 7 eac aella þa to ham comen ofslogon mid swurdes ecge 7 gecyrdon gesunde to hære getelde.

"(Simeon et Levi) . . . interfectisque omnibus masculis, Hemor et Schem pariter necaverunt, tollentes Dinam de domo Sichem sororem suam."

The last three lines translate Genesis 35:6–8 pretty exactly: and are the most idiomatically composed phrases among the Claudius notes in English:

---

[66] Cf. similar phrases occurring in main OE text of Genesis (by chapter and verse, ed. Crawford, *OE Hept.*, ad loc.):

8:20	7 he arærde an weofod gode
12:7	þa abram arærde ðær an weofod gode
12:8	7 arærde þær an weofod gode
13:4	he ðæt weofod ær arærde
13:18	7 þær arærde weofod gode
22:9	7 he ðær weofod arærde on ða ealdan wisan
35:1	7 arære weofod on þære stowe

[67] This resembles Ælfric's phraseology in similar formulas, e.g. "swa swa hit segð on leden on þære cyninga bocum," Hom. 23.13 (ed. J.C. Pope, *Homilies of Ælfric, a Supplementary Collection*, EETS o.s. 259, 260 [London, 1967], 2:728 ff.).

> ⁊ iacob ⁊ is sununes mid hære wycstowe ywenden to bethel ⁊ herde godes name. (S V dat V O)
>
> "Venit igitur Jacob Luzam, quæ est in terra Chanaan, cognomento Bethel; ipse et omnis populus cum eo. Ædificavitque ibi altare, et appellavit nomen loci illius. . . ."
>
> On þan time forðferde debbora rebecca fostermoder ⁊ heo bebyrigde on nyþewærde bethel hunder ane ache, ⁊ me cwæð þane steðe ache wop.
>
> "Eodem tempore mortua est Debora nutrix Rebeccæ, et sepulta est ad radices Bethel subter quercum; vocatumque est nomen loci illius, Quercus fletus."

It is interesting that this note self-referentially characterizes reading as a hermeneutic and translational activity: 'swa seo leden boc sprycð'. Appeals to reading occur in other contexts, such as riddles (e.g., Exeter Riddle 59.15) presenting "reading" as an essentially difficult task, that is, figuring out the riddle; similar appeals occur, in other formulas, in Ælfric, but referring to reading in *English*, e.g.: "⁊ ic awende hig on Englisc ⁊ rædon gif ge wyllað eow sylfum to ræde."[68] On the other hand, the Claudius annotator seems to take it for granted that normal or proper reading is in Latin, easier than reading (or writing) in English. One recalls Ælfric's words copied at the beginning of this manuscript (f.1v): 'æfre se ðe awent oððe se ðe tæcð of ledene. on englisc. æfre he sceal gefadian hit swa. ðæt ðæt englisc hæbbe his agene wisan. elles hit bið swyðe gedwolsum to rædenne ðam ðe ðæs ledenes wise ne can.'[69] These were words of advice that the annotator must have known, but didn't have the means to implement fully in writing, however facile he might have been in speaking everyday English.

Conclusion

In the final analysis, the notes suggest a writer who is unpracticed and uncomfortable writing English. The writer needs a Latin model to follow more or less word-for-word in order to support the effort of writing English at all. At one point he can be detected using his own English as a model, with slender effect, and there may be other instances of modelling based on Old English sentences, both from this book and others. The few sentences that do not show a Latin source are ill-formed and difficult to interpret. The impression indeed is of

[68] *On the Old and New Testament*, in Crawford, *OE Hept.*, 51.830.

[69] "Always he who translates or interprets from Latin into English must dispose it so that the English has its own proper discourse; otherwise it is very misleading to read for him who does not know the discourse of Latin."

something quite artificial, as if these sentences are expected to be taken as coevals of the older text to back up some urgent claim that is felt to be true but can't be confirmed by documents already available. As such, the English notes seem to be uneasily and artificially concocted not as an occasion for writing and communicating but as marks that complement in some manner the authority of the Latin notes, which are of course drawn from a much younger, indeed quite recent source. Although some of the last "Old English books" were copied to be read by occupants of the monastery who were least competent in Latin, these notes do not suggest translations for the benefit of learners with scant Latin; rather, the totality of the performance suggests fluency in the reading of Latin and standard Old English, whereas the independent *production* of English is the difficult task. Altogether, it is as if the writer expects the reader to see in the English notes some signification other than what they literally communicate.[70] They appear to link symbolically modern learning to ancient traditions as they subsisted in St. Augustine's at the time of their concoction.

Before we can pursue this line of thought further, though, we will have to sort out the question of the scripts, who was writing them and with what possible intentions in mind, for their complex interrelation holds the key to the interrelation of the Latin and Old English texts.

[70] Tim Machan (p.c.) has suggested that the annotator may be enacting the discursive practice of "glossing": "he knows such manuscripts are supposed to have such glosses, so . . . he's going to put them in, much as later university texts almost instinctively seem to generate commentaries — they're the things that tell readers something about the genre and status of what they're reading."

IV. Scripts and Codicology

We have shown that the received view, that several decades separated the writing of the English notes from the Latin, is incorrect, and that all the annotations are from the last decades of the twelfth century. We came to this conclusion by the fact that most of the English notes and about half the Latin stem from a single later twelfth-century source, the *Historia Scholastica*. This then gives rise to the question, how closely are the English and Latin notes connected? Are they in coherent relation to one another? Are they part of a single scholarly project? Were the English and Latin notes written in Cotton Claudius B. iv at more or less the same time, or in different campaigns? How many individuals contributed to the annotations? To approach answers to these questions we must consider in some detail the nature of the scripts added to the book in the late twelfth century and the physical changes made to the original book at about the same time.

Scripts

N. R. Ker said "the text was annotated, mainly in two hands."[1] By "two hands" he means to distinguish one which used insular forms and wrote the English notes, as well as many Latin ones and several in both languages, from another "later-twelfth-century hand" which wrote the remainder of the Latin notes in typical late twelfth-century "proto-gothic" or "Norman" script.[2] There are more

[1] Ker, *Catalogue of Manuscripts Containing Anglo-Saxon*, 178.

[2] In the following discussion, we use the term "Norman" advisedly, not least because it carries an ideological and cultural charge that is central to this study. "Proto-gothic" is the term used by many English-speaking paleographers for the style of writing prevailing in England throughout the twelfth century, though it is sometimes also called "Norman" or "international" script. Though we perforce must use the term, "proto-gothic" seems to us not so apt since it subordinates the distinct and prevailing style of the twelfth century, associated especially with monastic manuscripts in north-east Francia and England after the Conquest, to the term used for the style of writing that emerged contemporaneously with the explosion of non-monastic manuscripts around the turn of the thirteenth century. Contrastingly, and for want of a better term, we label as "insular" those notes in Claudius employing script showing any letter-forms imitative of those distinctive of the Anglo-Saxon national script (see below, 225–37).

than thirty English notes having various "insular" symptoms (as well as a number of brief gloss-like insertions in the original text) and above a dozen Latin or Latin/English notes written in scripts using one or more insular letter forms. So it is true that two obviously different types of writing can be discerned by their formal characteristics, also true that the "insular" writing is in general written in a lighter, brownish ink, while the Norman Latin entries are in a contrasting black ink which can usually be distinguished at a glance in the flesh and in color photographs.[3] But it is clear that a guiding assumption behind Ker's judgment is not true: the insular type of writing is not of "s. xii med." by any stretch since much of it is translated from a work not available before 1180. The two types of writing must be seen as at least roughly contemporary, so that it is an open point as to whether the Old English was inscribed first.

In fact, the script of the annotations is very puzzling: the style of the "insular" script or, one should say, scripts is unpracticed and insecure in appearance. It is basically "proto-gothic" in form and in that regard can be compared to the several scripts of Bodley 343 (homilies, s. xii^2, West Midlands?), though it cannot be compared in terms of assured style and uniform, pleasing appearance on the page. It is variable in ductus, often hesitant in layout and execution, and many of the letter forms are idiosyncratic or unsteady, yet it goes out of its way to look "insular," even "hyper-insular" (unlike the early thirteenth-century Cotton Vespasian A. xxii, probably written at Rochester, which makes no attempt to look insular at all). Like the late twelfth-century script of the Christ Church manuscript of the West-Saxon Gospels in Royal 1.A.xiv, it is "a rough untidy hand,"[4] varying considerably between and within scripts and retaining insular letter forms in a script that is basically foreign to insular writing.

In a different way the Norman script is puzzling: though typical of professional-grade monastic writing in southern England and northwestern France throughout most of the twelfth century and into the thirteenth, it varies in its execution. To put it broadly, it is executed in two ductus in which the letter forms remain very similar but the appearance differs markedly: a smaller ductus which writes most of the *Historia Scholastica* entries, and a larger, which writes most of the "Jerome" entries. It is not easy to decide whether these variations indicate one, two, or more hands participating in the "Norman" script entries,

---

[3] The ink colors are easily distinguished in the CD-ROM that accompanies Wither's book, *The Illustrated Old English Hexateuch, Cotton Claudius B.iv: The Frontiers of Seeing and Reading in Anglo-Saxon England* (London and Toronto, 2007). But this is not so with the black-and-white facsimile that has long been available, C. R. Dodwell and Peter Clemoes, eds., *The Old English Illustrated Hexateuch: British Museum Cotton Claudius B. IV,* Early English Manuscripts in Facsimile 18 (Copenhagen, 1974); nor in the facsimile from microfilm accompanying A. N. Doane, *Anglo-Saxon Manuscripts in Microfiche Facsimile,* Volume 7: *Anglo-Saxon Bibles and the Book of Cerne*, MRTS 187 (Tempe, 2002).

[4] Ker, *Catalogue*, 316.

or a single scribe deliberately varying his handwriting for display purposes, or a single hand writing in two separate campaigns. Certainly the different possibilities, combined with the complexities offered by the insular script entries, bring to mind a number of different writing scenarios and motivations for the annotation project.

One thing that is absolutely clear, however, is that whatever their purpose, the annotations were programmatic and had something to do with enhancing the preexisting Anglo-Saxon book. The added annotations (with minor and incidental exceptions) respect the meaning, appearance, and layout of the pages as they were found: annotations are written into spaces that harmonize with existing layout, text, and pictures. The most common space used for *Historia Scholastica* extracts (both Latin and Old English) is that afforded by the double borders surrounding most pictures, treated as ledger lines to guide the writing of short inscriptions, or within the picture frames when there is plenty of space. Sometimes the space is used quite artfully, as on f. 16v, where a number of extracts are elegantly situated within Noe's rainbow arc, or quite wittily, in the interplay among added text, preexisting text, and pictures, as in the generations of Seth to Noah (ff. 10v–12r, see the discussion below, ch. 5, 276–89). The English notes are in a humbler grade of writing compared to the main Old English text, and in contrasting colors. The Norman scripts (though variously) are written in a large, bold conspicuous ductus that does not subordinate itself as "gloss" to a "text." The Jerome notes, which occur more frequently as the book proceeds, are typically reserved for top and bottom margins (though, admittedly, in the later parts of the book, the Jerome entries are less careful of appearance). Side margins are mainly reserved for numerical annotations and Anno Mundi dating.[5]

The Norman Scripts

Most of the Latin notes (and this is the vast bulk of the notes) are written in "proto-gothic" or "Norman" book hand; these notes are quite distinct in color (dark brown to black), size, ductus, and general aspect from the "insular" notes, written in lighter brown inks and a generally smaller ductus. The scripts of these notes are nevertheless somewhat problematic because it is not easy to decide whether we have the work of one variable hand or two (or more): the script tends to be rather inconsistent, often even within the same entry; moreover, the scripts generally differ according to the contents of the notes, falling into two broad categories, the *Historia Scholastica* entries and entries mainly from the works of Jerome (and Pseudo-Jerome). The *Historia* notes are confined to "Genesis" and "Exodus" and the "Jerome" notes are less frequent towards the beginning, gradually in-

[5] The general *mise en page* of the annotations can be seen, e.g., in figs. 8 and 9.

crease in number, and are heavily concentrated in the second half of the book. Since in general the *Historia* entries are written in a script and ductus quite distinct from the "Jerome" notes, henceforth these scripts will be designated "H" and "J" respectively.[6] The question of whether there is one hand or two bears on the nature of the project: if there is one hand, it must be inferred that different scripts were consistently employed to distinguish different types of material or to lend some other impression, or that the entries were made in several campaigns at widely separated intervals; if the different scripts actually represent separate hands of individual scribes the project was a coordinated one that took considerable institutional cooperation, planning, and consultation. The problem boils down to this: can we find genuine individual differences within a mass of writing that might bear the marks of a single well-regulated "house style"? The general appearance of two separate scripts is consistent, yet the letter forms are so similar in the "H" and "J" scripts that there is very little to separate them formally; differences of detail within integral excerpts basically written in one script or the other often seem greater than differences between separated entries that fall into the "H" and "J" categories by means of general comparison.

Ker has characterized late twelfth-century "Norman" writing thus:[7]

---

[6] Simply on the basis of the gross appearance of script, "H" and "J" passages may be distinguished.

Passages written in the "H" script, by item number, with non-*Historia* passages italicized:

1, 4, 5, 6b, 8, 9a–f, 12, 13a, 13c, 17, 18–22, *23*, 24, *27*, 29b, 30–32, 40, 42b, 51a, 51d–f, 53, 56, 59, 63, *65*, 68, *69*, 70e–f, 72, 75, 81, 85a–b, *86*, 87, 88, *91a*, 92, 93, *96*, 97a–b, 99, 102a–b, 106, 110, 111a–b, 112, 113, 115, 116, *117*, 119, 122–24, 126, 127a–b, 129, 131, 133, 134, 137, 139a, 142, 144, 148–53, 155, 157, 158a–b, 159, 164, 165, 167, 171, 173, 174, 176, 177a, *179*, 180, 182, 183, 185, 187, *188*, 189b, 191a, 192, 191b–c, *195–97*, 199, 200, 201, 203, *208a*, 209, *212*, *213*, *215*, *222–24*, *228*, 230, 232, *233*, 234, 235, 238, 239, 241, 242, *248*, 249–55, 258, *259*, 260, 261, 263, 267, *269*, 270, 272a–b, 273–75, 276, 277–79, 281a–c, 285, 288, 291, 295–97, 324, *336b–d*, *337a–x*, 393.

Passages written in the "J" script, with *Historia* passages italicized:

35a–b, 39c, 42a, 55b, 57, 58, 60, 70, *64*, 66, 71, 73, 74, 78, 80a–b, 82a–b, 83, 84, 89, 90, 91b, 94, 95, 98, 100, 101, 103–05, 107, 109, 117, 125, 130, 132, 135a–b, 136a–c, 138a–b, 139b, 141a–b, 146a–b, 154, 160–63, 168–79, 172a–b, 175, 178, *184*, *186*, 189a, 190, *193a*, *194*, 198, 202, 204–07, 210, 191d, 208b, *211*, 214, 217, 218, 220, 225, 227, 231, 236, 237, 240, 243, 244, 246, 262, 268, 271, 280, 282, 283, *284*, 286, 289, 290, 292a–i, *293*, 294a–m, 298–301, 303–06, 207a–b, 308–10, 311a–c, 312, 313a–b, 314–23, 325–29, 330a–j, 331–33, 334a–b, 334c–e, 335a–b, 336a, 338, 339, 340a, 341, 342a–b, 344–56.

This leaves out of consideration a few ambiguous instances and writing on f. 74 (an added leaf).

[7] N. R. Ker, *English Manuscripts in the Century after the Norman Conquest* (Oxford, 1960), 38–39.

> 1. Straight lines, angles, and shallow curves take the place of full curves in the letters **a, b, c, d, e, g, m, n, o, t**. The taller the script the more obvious the angularity.
>
> 2. The beginning of the minim-stroke, instead of forming a roughly triangular projection to the left, is carefully made like the top of a lozenge. . . .
>
> 3. The common mark of abbreviation, instead of being wavy or cupped, becomes again a straight stroke, as it had been in eleventh century book-hand and always in current writing. For a time some scribes use both kinds of stroke indifferently, whilst others keep the wavy stroke to denote omission of *m* and use the straight stroke to mark contractions and the omission of *n*. The straight stroke often has hair-line terminals.
>
> 4. The bow of rounded *d* is made to coalesce with the back of *e*. The *de* ligature is perhaps the earliest of the numerous bitings of converging strokes which characterize the formal book-hand throughout the rest of its long existence. The rather different biting of double *p* is found much earlier.
>
> 5. The scribes tend to make more of the features which distinguished the mid-century script from earlier writing, the trailing headed *a*, the downward turn at the end of final *t*, and the horizontal foot of the minim.

A comparison of our writing with these criteria suggests that it is at the cusp of this new late style as characterized by Ker, after 1170 /1180 certainly because of the date of the source, and maybe as late as the turn of the century.[8] The very first entry on f. 1v (no. 1) will illustrate many points about the script associated with the bulk of the *Historia* entries (fig. 1):

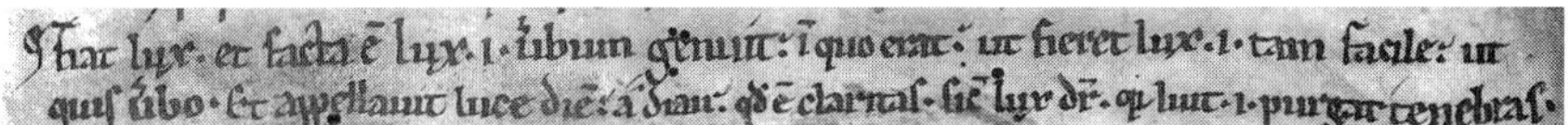

Figure 1: (f. 1v)

[8] The "Norman" scripts of Claudius B. iv can be seen as falling between the dated script of London, British Library, Harley 3038 (1176, St. Mary Bildewas), which still uses the curved abbreviation marks, still has a somewhat rounded openness to the letters, and is using the sideways "z" abbreviation mark, also seen in Claudius (but perhaps from the exemplar), and on the other hand those of the *Historia Scholastica* manuscript British Library Royal 7. E xii (1183, Helenstow nunnery) and the Rochester Catalogue of Books (various hands, f. 2^{A} dated 1202); in the latter two the writing has deteriorated, is uneven within the stint, has introduced predominantly straight abbreviation marks, and is relatively compact in the vertical dimension. The latter has many letter-forms reminiscent of Claudius, especially the repertoire of high s's, the treatment of the feet of minims, the form of the 7-nota. These examples are numbers 86, 87, 88 in S. Harrison Thompson, *Latin Book Hands of the Later Middle Ages, 1100–1500* (Cambridge, 1969).

> § Fiat lux. et facta e*st* lux. i*d est* u*er*bum genuit: i*n* quo erat: ut fieret lux. i*d est* tam facile: ut | quis u*er*bo. Et appellauit luce[m] die*m* á dian: q*uod* e*st* claritas. sic*ut* lux d*icitu*r. q*uia* luit. i*d est* purgat tenebras. (HS 1057B/C)

The ink is dark. The lines of writing are straight, the lower bodies resting on rules. The bodies of the letters are constructed around notional squares but there is still considerable roundness to the curves of **a**, **b**, **e**, **g**, **n**, **p**, **q**; **m** is constructed of minims. There are two varieties of **g**; one, more common, as in 'purgat', has an overall "s" shape with an ovoid upper element, with a looping open lower element finished with a crosshair; the other, as in 'genuit', has an overall "j" shape, the upper loop drawn against the base, the lower element being a plain hook-shape, without the crosshair. The letter-strokes are thick without marked contrast between horizontals and verticals, and the letters are compact, with moderate ascenders and short descenders. But **c** is made with two strokes, the lower a shallow curve, the upper a jabbing thick stroke. **t** has a shallow-curving shaft which at times penetrates the cross-stroke with a spike. **o** tends to be narrow and ovoid, with the upper right side somewhat depressed into the bowl. The only regular pointing is the top of the arm of **r**, the right extension of which bites into the head of following *a*. The **d**, always rounded, varies in form but tends to flick back at the top, though in 'dr̄' it is almost straight. In 'appellauit' *pp* is biting. Minims and the tops of ascenders have either a wedge-shaped projection or a "flag" projecting to the left. There is a "lozenge"-shaped top to the *l* in 'facile' and this is often seen at the tops of ascenders and minims, but not consistently. The bottoms of minims either are finished with a flick to the right or are plain, the longer-drawn descenders tending to turn slightly to the left. There are several varieties of long *s*, either with a horn on the shaft and a thickly-inked top, or unhorned, with a top that is more uniform in thickness with the shaft. The abbreviation mark is the straight stroke, though a wavy upright mark is used in 'u*er*bum'. In other extracts in this script we find the "zigzag" sign for *er*, the "sigma"-shaped nota for *ur*, etc., notae which are standard throughout the century. The "de" ligature occurs frequently on f. 6v, 'de omni', 'de ligno' (no. 12, fig. 2):

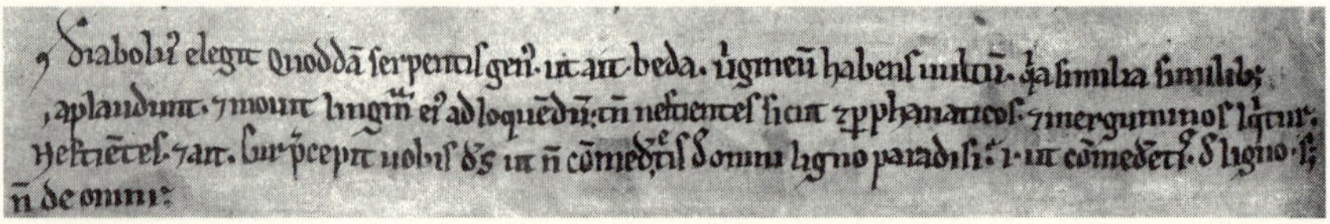

Figure 2: (f. 6v)

As mentioned already, a feature of this script is its variability: in no. 1 (fig. 1), as is often the case (sometimes also at the beginnings of sentences), it begins with a wispy, "sinuous" look and gradually thickens; the ductus varies from medium to small (at 'Et appellauit', etc., a new sentence) and grows larger at the end of the last line, another common characteristic. This single entry thus has three aspects in what must be a single stint. This tendency for thinner, taller strokes to appear at the beginning of sentences is seen in an exaggerated way at the bottom of f. 6v (no. 12, fig. 2), where 'diabolu*s* elegit . . .' and 'Cur p*re*cepit . . .' are of a different character from the rest of the lines, but overall it is not a different script or hand.

Figure 3: (f. 3r)

In the second note (fig. 3), 'Et d*icitu*r sol*:* q*uia* solus lucet.' (HS 1060A), the writing has a more pointed aspect. There is nothing decisively different about the letter-forms from those in fig. 1, but the writing seems more laterally compressed, with a care to make the tops of ascenders more uniform, and to have slightly more exaggerated strokes at the bottoms of *g* and some capitals. An ascender forks ('luna', line 4), but this is extremely rare in Claudius scripts (cf. 'luna' in lines 1 and 2). In 'd*icitu*r' (3x) the abbreviation mark is a flourish shaped a bit like a cursive *n*. There is the same tendency as seen in fig. 1 of the size of the ductus to increase as the writing goes on, but it tends, overall, to be smaller than the writing of normal "H" entries and stands out from it on the page, always making up separate entries.[9] Nevertheless, it is probably a variety of the same script by the same hand, as is seen by a comparison of the writing on f. 66r (no. 216, fig. 4) and f. 1v (no 1, fig. 1). :

Figure 4: (f. 66r)

The "J" script, first seen unambigously at the bottom of f. 14r, makes a striking contrast to the "H" script;[10] there in "H" script is an extract from the *Historia* (HS 1084B) which says Josephus assigns 2656 years between Adam and the ark; immediately following this in very prominent letters with a thicker ductus is a note contradicting this by giving Bede's calculation (fig. 5):

[9] This "pointed" script occurs intermittently, always in *Historia* excerpts; it seems to be the same as "H", with size and height constrained sometimes by the height of the ledgers; clear instances are few in number and clustered: cf. nos. 2, 33, 49, 51b, 118 (larger ductus, marginal note), 120, 216, 219, 221, 229, 256, 257, 265 (interlinear), 266, 287.

[10] A color reproduction of f. 14r is the frontispiece to Dodwell and Clemoes' facsimile.

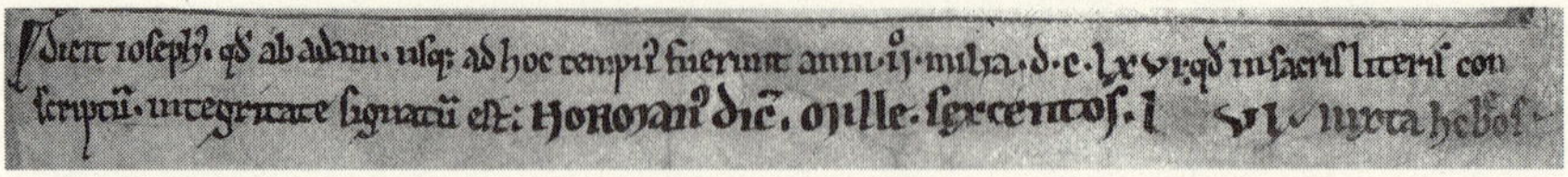

Figure 5: (f. 14r)

NORMAN*US* dic*it*. mille. sexcentos. l vi- iuxta heb*r*`e´os-

The contrast is enhanced because the "H" writing immediately preceding happens to be a bit thinner than usual, and "J" has a "headline" effect because its first word is in capitals; but besides this there is a characteristic employment of a thicker nib and the bodies of letters are about a third larger; yet there seems more to it than this. Turning overleaf, we see a continuation of "J": at the bottom of f. 14v (also from Bede) and on the bottom of f. 15r (fig. 6):

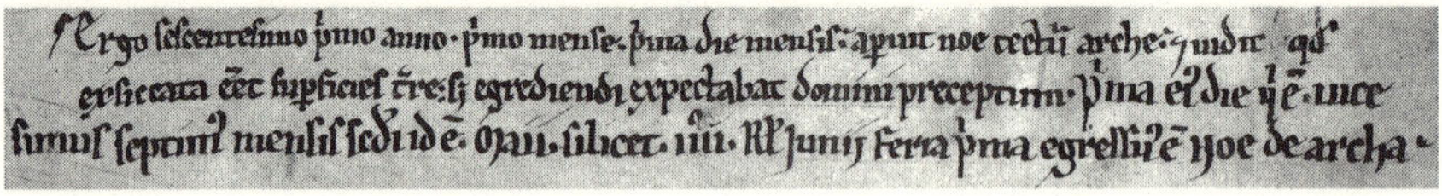

Figure 6: (f. 15r)

where we see "H" and "J", respectively, juxtaposed (no. 59, to 'perceptum', is from the *Historia* [HS 1085C] and no. 60, beg. 'Prima' is unsourced but generally reflects information in Bede's *De temporum ratione*).

As we said, it is very difficult to separate this "J" script from the "H" by formal features, yet it is strikingly different in aspect (see for example the two scripts on f. 21v, fig. 7). In "J" the nib of the pen is consistently broader, there is more verticality, and taller verticals tend to bow a bit to the right; often ascenders in the same word are set akimbo. When there is a line or ledger, the text rides above it a bit and the bowls of *a*'s tend to be raised a bit further still. Minims tend to lean to the right and they are finished at the top with a hairline or lozenge. The bottoms of descenders are left plain, or sometimes trail to a point to the left in a manner not often seen in "H", though they flick to the right frequently as well. The tops of *s* often have a "broken" look. Looking back, we see this larger ductus presented slightly more subtly on the bottom of f. 9v (no. 35a,b, fig. 8), a quotation from Jerome's Epistle 36 to Damasus, while two lines of "H" can be seen above the upper frame and two lines of "pointed" script within the upper frame. The most objective symptoms of difference, such as a more liberal use of capital letters in "J," both before proper nouns and within words (where they virtually never occur in "H"), different systems of abbreviation between "H" and "J," and the use of "&" rather than "7" by "J" are probably because "J" quotations are usually from non-*Historia* sources and

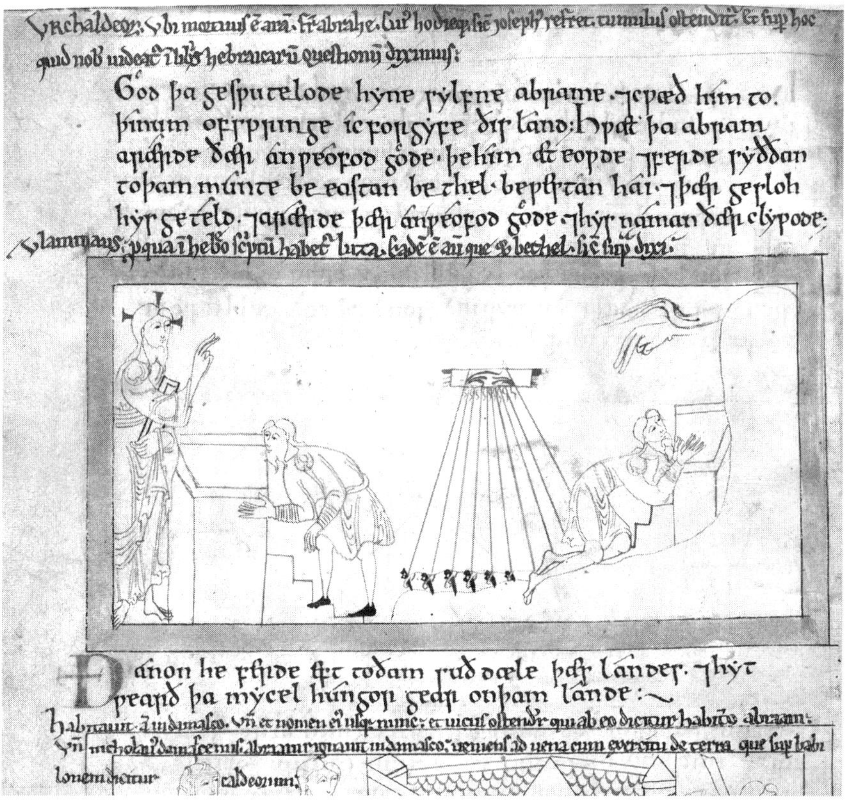

Figure 7: (f. 21v)

hence from different exemplars.[11] The hand or hands writing these scripts must be contemporaneous at any rate, as there are entries showing both scripts, some of "J" which must have been written first and others where "H" is first. The passage at the bottom of f. 14v (fig. 10) is "J", but there are several interventions in the "H" script in brown ink (no. 58, lines 3 and 1 up); added by "H" in brown ink: 'quadraginta octo', 'millia q*u*adrigintes Nonaginta `trium´':

[11] This latter point is well illustrated on f. 16v, where "J" in the rainbow frame (no. 64, lines 5–11) is a long extract from the *Historia* using the 7-nota, while "H", lines 12–13, from Ps.-Bede, uses "&", a sign absent from *Historia*-quotations in any script, except on f. 74v, a special case. The fact that "H" uses straight abbreviation marks and "J" uses both straight and curved is doubtless an effect of the fact that the "H" source(s) were post-1180 while the main "J" source was a Jerome manuscript of mid-century (see below, ch. 6, 309–11). Inconsistencies in "J" entries are presumably the result of the influence of contemporary *usus scribendi*.

Figure 8: (f. 9v)

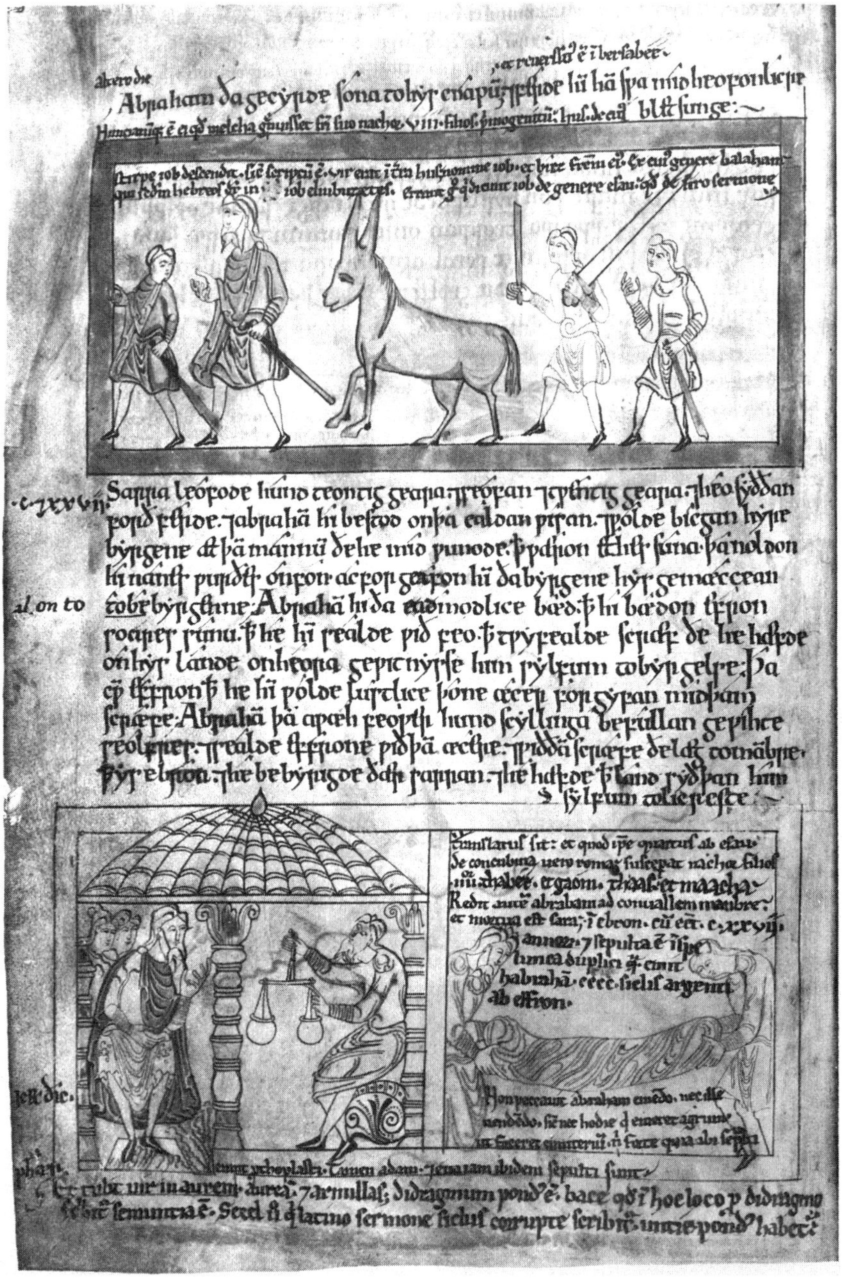

Figure 9: (f. 38v)

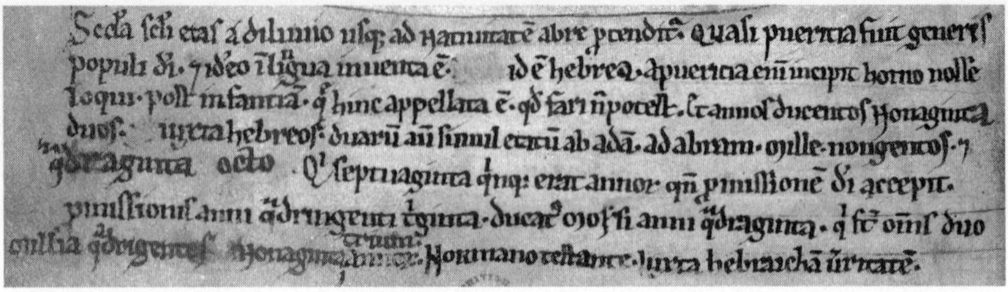

Figure 10: (f. 14v)

On the other hand, on f. 38v (no. 144, fig. 9) the "H" script starts a *Historia* excerpt at the top and carries it continuously down into the right lower picture frame, to '.iiii^{or}'; the next line, also "H", at 'Redit' starts a new *Historia* chapter; between these points in the "J" script is inserted the words 'thabee. et gaom. thaas. et maacha-', a gloss from Genesis 22:24 which is not found in either the printed edition or early manuscripts of the *Historia*.

In fact, many passages seem to be in a mixture of these two scripts. A pastiche of Jerome's Epistle 73 with material from the Gospels and perhaps other sources (no. 66) runs from the bottom of f. 16v to the top of f. 17r (fig. 11).

Figure 11: (f. 17r)

"J" is the main script but additions and corrections are added in the "H" script on f. 16v; the passage in "J" script continues at the top of f. 17r, 'Thare annor*um* septuaginta genuit abram' when suddenly, the text continuing without a break, the script changes to "H": '7 nachor 7 aram' etc. "H" continues to the end of the manuscript line and for another and then the larger "J" script resumes in the margin. The best explanation of the change of ductus in this case is that the writer realized he did not have room to finish the comment neatly in the upper margin and tried to fit it in by reducing size, but when he couldn't fit it all anyhow, gave up and in the margin reverted to the large script appropriate to "Jerome" entries. All these instances could conceivably be the product of two scribes helping, correcting, criticizing, or augmenting each other. But they more strongly suggest that "H" and "J" are not the products of different hands, but variations introduced by the same hand for display purposes, to indicate the different class of sources, or even the same scribe being influenced by or conciously imitating the ductus and script features of his differing exemplars. A single hand seems best to account for the writing on f. 38v (fig. 9), where the "H" script is used for the *Historia* material, the scribe then using his "J" script to indicate an interpolation before returning to the "H" script as he resumed with the next chapter of the *Historia* material—but in the confusion of once making the switch or perhaps because of the length and dispersal of the excerpt, unconsciously reverting to the "J" script as the words of the received *Historia* passage are concluded.

The evidence is often perplexing and ambiguous, and different people might come to different conclusions regarding "one scribe or more." The preponderance seems to be in the direction of a single writer employing different scripts in order to indicate different sources.

The "Insular" Scripts

The term is simply one of convenience, since the script of the English notes is essentially "proto-gothic" and not fundamentally different from that of the "Norman" scripts just discussed.[12] It simply affects the use of certain letter-forms derived from Old English writing, variously, **f**, **g**, **h**, **r**, and **s**, plus the indispensable letters **þ**, **ð**, **wynn**, and **æ**.[13] The first English note (no. 6a), translating the *Historia*, is at the bottom of f. 4r; it demonstrates most of the characteristics of this "insular" script (fig. 12):

Figure 12: (f. 4r)

> .Methodi*us* cwǣð. adam wǽs gescéopa mán on wlíte óf ðritig wíntra. 7 naþeles on áne dǽge. 7 géara[14] | 7 æfter ðam `án 7´ twa wintra. 7 þri wíntra. 7 alla ða oðron.

[12] Insular script in English notes: 6a, 7, 14, 15, 16, 18, 25a, 25b, 26, 29a, 36a, 36b, 38, 41, 44, 45, 46, 47, 48, 50, 51c, 52, 62, 67, 77, 126, 156, 181, 357, 358; Latin/English mixed in insular script: 10, 34, 61; Latin insular script notes: 3, 9c, 11, 13b, 28, 37, 39a, 43, 54, 55a, 70a-f, 72, 79. The annotator has consistently added a 'c'-like mark above the word "God" in the original Old English text, presumably to indicate length, and has done the same in his own script in the four instances of the word (cf. no. 61 on f. 15v, fig. 23).

[13] "All archaizing hands are hybrids," as says M. B. Parkes, "Archaizing Hands in English Manuscripts," in *Books and Collectors 1200–1700: Essays Presented to Andrew Watson*, ed. James P. Carley and Colin G. C. Tite (London, 1997), 101–41, at 101.

[14] At this point there is a mark on the vellum that may be meant as punctuation, but it is not clear.

'Methodius cw̄æð' is in black ink, but the ink has gone brown by 'gescéopa' and tends to get lighter as the pen runs out of ink. The ink occasionally becomes darker even within single letters, e.g., 'óf' is contrastingly dark and in 'dǽge' the lower part of "*a*" and *g* have been retouched with blacker ink, as have the superscript words, which are not from the donor text. The general aspect of the script is that of a small proto-gothic type, showing strong strokes and a jabbing energy, a tendency of the vertical strokes to lean to the right; the pen maintains steady thick/thin contrast between verticals and horizontals; the body of the letters are compact, with short downstrokes; the long line wavers across the page a bit, but is on unruled space. About the letter-forms the following may be noted:

a is a "trailing-headed" caroline/Norman type, varying between an upright *a* with upcurving foot, and a rounder, squatter version, where the head hooks down onto the bowl, which is often somewhat angular;

æ is formed as an *a* with a loop on its back which tends to bite into the following letter so that it is often barely visible;

c is very similar to **e**, two curved limbs with a slight hairline stroke off the top, while

e has a right- and upward curving hairline on its mid-stroke, otherwise similar to *c*;

d and **ð** have the same shape, with a round back whose tip tends to bend back to the right slightly, as in 'adam' (line 1), but is sometimes straight, as in 'ða' (line 2). The stroke on **ð** is an upsloping hairline cutting through the back of the *ð* and finished with a dropping flag; it seems identical in form to the "accents";

f, **h**, **r**, **s**, and **g** are insular in form: **f** is low, its cross-stroke on the writing line and projecting beyond its topstroke, which is pointed and shaped like the top of a caroline *r*, its downstroke flicking to the right; **h** has its feet flicking to the right, a treatment similar to the bottoms of minims: its ascender is topped by a small flag to the left and its right stroke is straight, rather than curving under to the left (as in the "Norman" *h)*; **r** has a downstroke of varying length, but its lower end flicks up sharply to the right; occasionally it has a sloping finial, as in 'æfter' (line 2). **s** is insular in 'scéopa' but with its short downstroke it has the aspect of a caroline **r**, with its right-stroke pointed at the top: a round-topped caroline *s* is used just before, in 'wǽs'; **g** has a flat top, with an *s*-shaped lower member and with a hairstroke finishing it off—it is essentially the "Norman" *g* with a special treatment of the top;

t is two strokes, distinct from **c**, and the upright sometimes protrudes as a spike through the horizontal stroke;

þ is formed like a **p** with an extended upper stroke, the scribe making a long stroke and looping back up to make the bowl (compare *p* in 'scéopa' [line 1] to *þ* in 'þri' [line 2]): the bottom is a flat wedge; *ð* is generally preferred to *þ*;

wynn is distinguished from **p** by having a well formed ovoid loop made as a separate stroke; the bottoms of both flick to the right ('wintra', line 1);

7-note varies, but both strokes are straight, twice with a distinct horn at the end of the upper stroke (line 1).

Abbreviation of letters is by a straight stroke, in this extract used redundantly (as several times elsewhere): 'cw̄æð'.

Minims have a typical proto-gothic "z" form, with a sharp left-stroke at top, curving off at the bottom to the right. Strokes below the line are straight and end either with a sharp rightward flick or plainly. The "accent" is a hairstroke angling up to the right and finished at the top with a dropping flag; accents are applied according to no discernable system. The only punctuation is the point/dot, applied after each natural phrase.[15]

This description of letter forms applies generally to the insular script, but problems arise when detailed comparisons are made to other extracts in English and to the adjacent Latin extracts which would seem to be by the same hand. We see anomalies in the Old English passage representing the *Historia*, on f. 4v (no. 7, fig. 13) overleaf from the one just discussed:

Figure 13: (f. 4v)

> Joseph*us* (..) cw̄æð. *þæt* wǽs in syrie on áne felde abute damasco. of rædra yrþe. *þæt* is mæden yrðe. | *þæt* ís úniwemð yrðe. lánd huniréped, | þat is cláne lanð (cf. HS 1071A/B)[16]

This is written in a uniform light-brown ink. It would seem to be the same script as the passage just discussed, yet it has symptoms which suggest the insecurity of the scribe. The first line is written neatly across the top of the picture, using the frame as a ledger, but the next two lines are juggled inside the picture at a slight angle. Ascenders are taller than in no. 6a (fig. 12), giving the script a more "willowy" or sinuous aspect; they have pointed flags to the left, more pronounced than in no. 6a. Punctuation is phrase-by-phrase, by means of dots, but a "comma" is introduced at the end of the second line. Three abbreviation irregularities occur in no. 7, 'cw̄æð'[17] and the crossed *þ*'s in 'yrþe' and 'þat'. Here occurs the

[15] No. 126, on f. 34v, a marginal comment, is closed with a *punctus elevatus*, as is No. 156 on f. 40v, and the long freely-composed passage no. 181 on f. 51r.

[16] The unflagged hairstroke through the 'd' of 'land' seems accidental (cf. 'cw̄æð' in line 1).

[17] The abbreviation "cw̄" for cwæð/cweð occurs in other late manuscripts, e.g. Cotton Vespasian D. xiv.

insular-appearing dotted y, *v*-shaped with the right-stroke dropping a flag at its top (like an accent stroke) and curving to the left below the line, but the *y*'s in the Norman "H" and "J" entries are also dotted and have a similar form. Insular *s* and *h* are used in the word 'Joseph*us*' along with a Latin abbreviation; insular *r* is maintained throughout, but at 'felde', before the insular *f* in 'of', a caroline *f* is used (a hairstroke to the right off the top) and *s* varies between insular and caroline for the rest. This caroline *s* wobbles between two forms, one with a horn to the left on the straight shaft, and a taller type with a slightly sinuous shaft. Polymorphousness of caroline *s* marks all the scripts of the Claudius annotations. In this extract there seems a slight distinction between *wynn* and *p* ('úniwemð', 'huniréped'), as the bowl of the latter is not touching the shaft at the top. There are two kinds of strokes above letters: hairstrokes (probably added) over *i* and 'abúte' and flagged "accents" over various long and short vowels. In no. 6a (fig. 12) all such strokes are accent-shaped. So, though generally consistent, we see that there is a slight indeterminacy in the way the English script is written from entry to entry.

Such is the predominant aspect of the insular script, subject to all sorts of vagaries, as, for example, on f. 5v (fig. 14): at the bottom, is a long English passage (no. 10), translating the *Historia* (1067A/B), 'Me red on bóc. be paradisu*m*'. This is the same script as in no. 7 (fig. 13), in brown ink, with these observations: *p* in 'paradisū' is distinct from *wynn*, with a hairline stroke closing the top of the angular loop; caroline high *s* is used and among them a form shaped like a tall angular "c", with no horn on the shaft and with an upward curving bottom. In the last phrase, in the word 'is', but nowhere else in the passage, insular *s* is used, with a long, pointed downstroke. Several instances of the 7-note have a pronounced horn at the leftward extension. The *d*'s tend to have straight shafts (fig. 14).

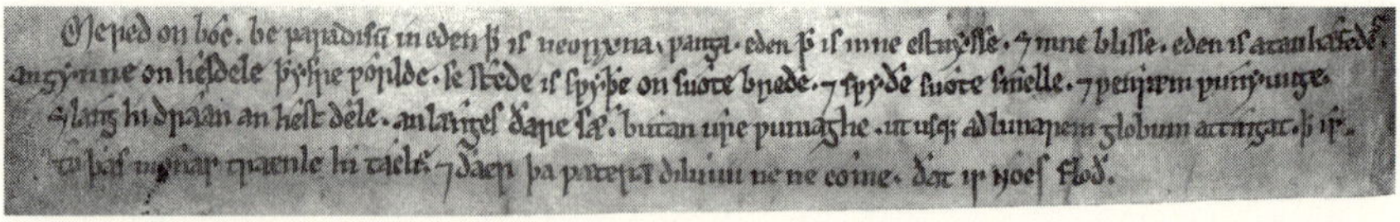

Figure 14: (f. 5v)

The insular script is also used for about a dozen Latin passages. On f. 6v, top (no. 11), the Latin extract is in the same script, in brown ink, with the first *d* having a curved flicked back but the rest straight, and using insular *g* and *r*, as well as standard Latin abbreviation-signs. The Latin marginal note on f. 7r is also in this script, with insular *r*, and it is in the same brownish ink that underlines the apposite main Old English text: **Adam hwær eart ðu.** On f. 3v, in the bottom margin, lines 4–5 up, facing the first Old English extract, is a Latin extract from the *Historia Scholastica* (no. 3) using insular letters (fig. 15):

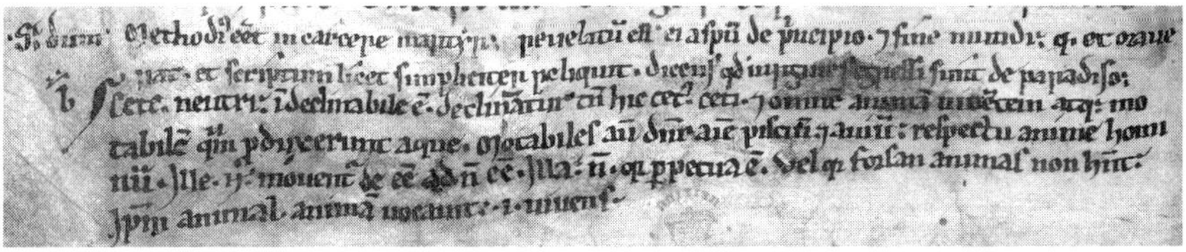

Figure 15: (f. 3v)

> S*ed* dum. Methodi*us* e*ss*et in cárcere martyre:̕ (.) reuelatu*m* est. ei a sp*iritu*m de p*r*incipio. ⁊ fine mundi:̕ q*uod* et oraue|rat. et scriptum licet simpliciter reliquit. dicens q*uo*d uirgines egressi súnt de paradiso:̕

The ink is black, but not as black as the ink of the lines immediately below it (beginning 'Cete. neutri'), written in the "H" script. Its striking peculiarity is the use of insular *r* (after the first caroline *r* in 'carcere'), *g*, and *h*, as well as flagged "accents" over *i* instead of hairline strokes, and an unusual number of other flagged "accents" over the letters. The nib is intermediate between the thickness of the Latin below on f. 3v and the English on the facing page (fig. 12). The letter forms are similar to those described above for passages 6a and 7 (figs. 12 and 13), except that there is, in addition, another form of tall caroline *s*, whose lower part trails off to the left ('dicens') and the ⁊-nota is somewhat curved. Insular *r*, however, is less pointed at the top, and downstrokes are finished sometimes with a deliberate, thickish finial rather than with a flick. Uprights vary between straight, curvy, and leaning to the right, for an incoherent look. It is quite different in aspect from the more delicate and slightly sinuous insular script on f. 4v (fig. 13) but the insular script on f. 4r (fig. 12) strikes a mean between them. The abbreviation marks are a line shaped like a sideways "z" (in 'eēt'), a curved line, and a straight line flicked down at the end for the final "m". The first words of the passage, 'S*ed* dum', are exdented into the margin, suggesting a false start at the beginning of a job, with perhaps some adjusting still to be done; there is also variation between 'ꝗ' and 'qđ' for "quod."[18]

It is not clear why anyone should use insular letters in Latin text at this date. The performance suggests an experimental imitation of vernacular writing that occurs elsewhere.[19] Along the bottom frame of the upper picture on f. 8r (no. 18)

[18] A. Capelli, *Dizionario di abbreviature latine ed italiane*, rev. ed. (Milan, 1990), gives both abbreviations as 12th century, but the second form is usual in the annotations. The PL edition has "oravit" but "orauerat" is found in early manuscripts, e.g. BL Royal 8 C.ix, f. 26r, CCCC 29, f. 5r and Sylwan's 48/7.

[19] This script occurs again on f. 11r (no. 43 and 44, fig. 31), a line of Latin, followed, after an exdent, by a four-line English note, the two taken from separated parts of the *Historia*. They are combined to make a single note about antediluvian writing; the duct and mid-brown ink are identical for both parts (the Latin uses insular *r*), and it is not apparent why one note remains in Latin and the other becomes English, except

is a little note and some glosses,[20] whose Latin source appears lower on the page (no. 21), lower picture, upper right panel (fig. 16):

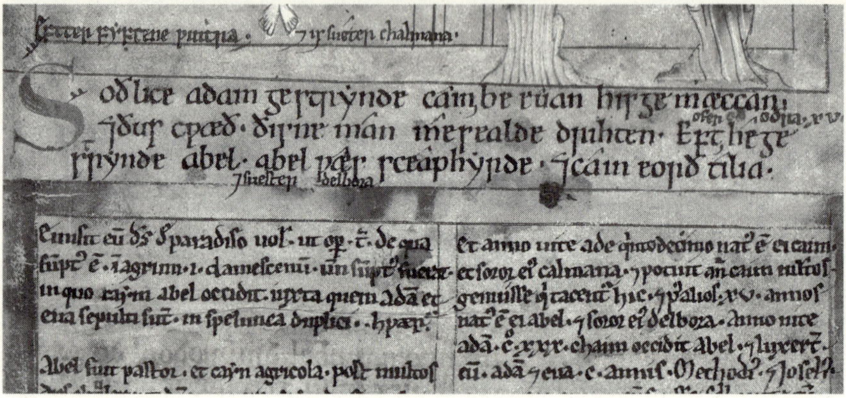

Figure 16: (f. 8r)

> Eftter fyftene wintra. 7 is súeter[21] chalmana (glosses in text: **Eft** gl.: ofer oðra xv. **he ge|strynde abel** gl: 7 suester delbora). (cf. HS 1076B)

It would appear to be in the same insular script, in brown inks (the gloss below being darker), but the first three words are written in a pointed style that gives them a formal appearance, as if a title, and seems further evidence that the scribe was experimenting with various styles of writing. The remaining words are as usual, except that the 7-*nota* and the first (insular) *r* have their downstroke swept conspicuously to the left; the *r*'s are of interest because they vary between round-topped and pointed and may form a missing link between the bulk of the English writing in the "sinuous" script and the Latin on f. 3v (no. 3, fig. 15) which shows this round-topped insular *r*.

Not only the problematic variation of script, but also the convergence of the various scripts, is demonstrated by the first four notes on f. 9r (nos. 26, 27, 28, 29a, fig. 17):

experimentation, unless it is some witty play on the content of the notes. Again, in the middle of f. 14r, in a brown-to-blackish ink, 'dicit Raban⟨us⟩', writing nos. 54, 55a, it uses insular *g* but not insular *r*. It has quite a different aspect from the recurrent "sinuous" script of the English at the top of the page, 'phiarphara' (no. 52). Occasional insular letter-forms occur in picture-labels which seem to be mostly in the "H" script.

[20] Not mentioned by Crawford.

[21] For "suester"; cf. the gloss immediately above the lower frame where the same hand writes 'suester'.

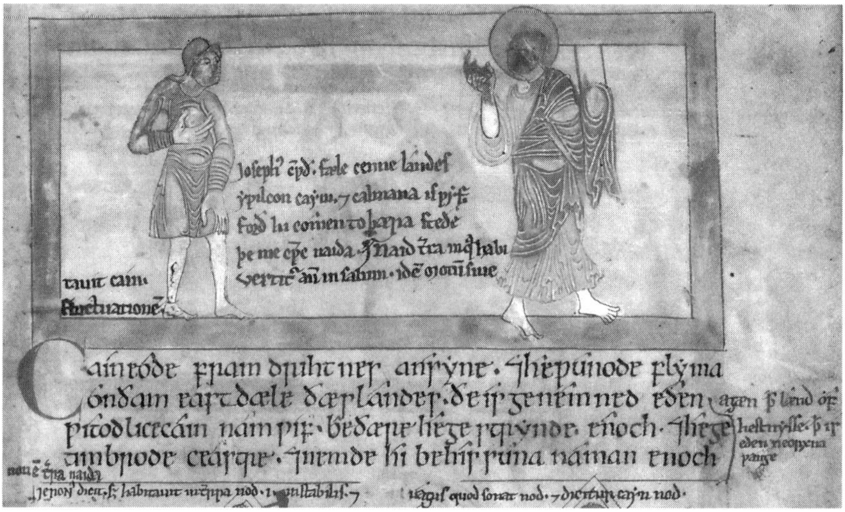

Figure 17: (f. 9r)

On this page Norman and insular scripts seem to exchange roles. At the top, in the upper picture frame, the English comment beginning 'Joseph*us* cwð', representing the *Historia*, is in brown ink, but in a larger and more regular script than usual that seems identical to the "H" script. The different aspect is obvious but the letter forms do not differ formally from previous English passages, except that 'f' and the 'or' ("O2" form) ligature in 'forð' is Norman, giveaways that the hand that wrote this is most comfortable writing Norman/Latin script (the "or" ligature occurs elsewhere in English passages, e.g., no. 34 on f. 9v, 3×). The ductus is not different from the following Latin extract, 'Naid t*er*ra', taken from Jerome, which is, however, in a darker ink. The Latin employs Norman *h* and the *d*'s flick back at the top more, but the letter forms do not otherwise differ. In the English the forms of *æ* are much more distinctly *a* + *e* (spaced apart more than in e.g., no. 6a [fig. 12]) and the *h* of 'hæra' (line 3) is distinctly Norman. Below this block, in the middle picture frame, the Latin comment (no. 28) 'jeron*ymus* dicit' (taken from the *Historia*, along with the attribution) in its aspect is typical of the insular script seen on previous leaves writing English, with its sinuous but disorganized ductus (note incorrect abbreviation and two forms of insular *r* in 'terra'), and insular forms of *g*, straight-backed *d*, etc. But the ink is blackish; is this for display purposes, to indicate the *Historia*, or to harmonize with the better-formed Norman script? The text is erased and faulty, the skipped words 'non e*st* t*er*ra naida', inserted in the same script in brown ink, and in similar brown ink the rather irregularly laid-out English marginal note to the right 'agǽn *þæt* lǽnd' (no. 29a) is in an inconsistent ductus as the script styles exchange roles momentarily.

Scripts that are internally inconsistent appear side by side with scripts that are similar but inconsistent with one another. On f. 10r (fig. 18) are passages in English (nos. 36a, 36b, 38) in contrasting scripts, while 37 and 39a are in Latin but do not clearly separate by style of script from the English:

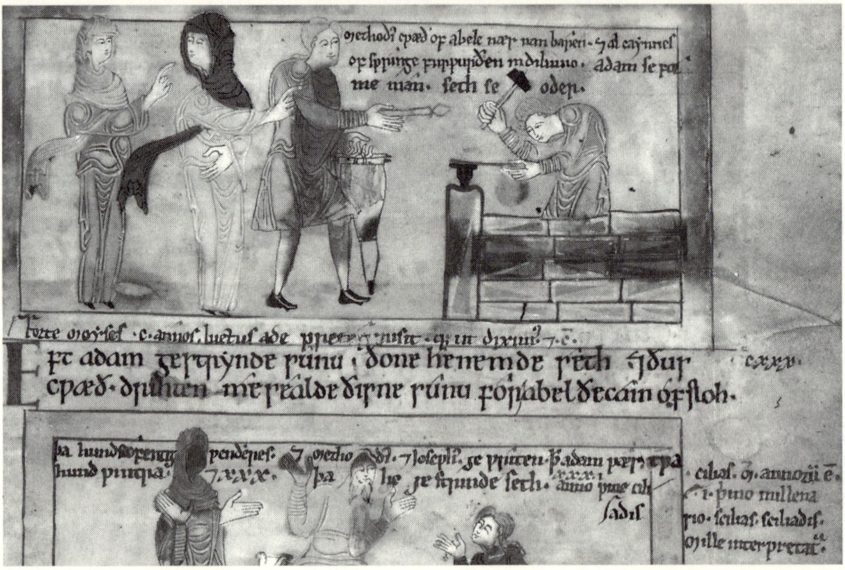

Figure 18: (f. 10r)

> (**36a**) Methodi*us* cwæð of abele næs nan báren. 7 al caynnes | ofsprínge fur-wurðen in diluuio.

> (**36b**) Adam se for|me mán. seth se oder. (cf. HS 1080C)

No. 36a is in the sinuous script, in a dark brown that gets larger and darker as it goes. But 36b, though in a larger and more pointed ductus, is in a lighter ink. Nothing formally distinguishes the scripts, and probably we have here different stints by the same hand, but this second stint looks identical to "H". Below the frame the Latin note, no. 37, 'Forte moyses', is the same script and ink as 36a, with insular *r* but with the curly type of *d* that seems associated with the Latin passages; it includes several random "Old English" accents; "luctus" is mis-written as 'luetus' with the "ct"-ligature nevertheless. No. 38, in English, 'þa hundséofentig wenðeres', is also in brown ink, and is relatively regularly written, though the strokes are thicker than in no. 36a. It seems to be the script of no. 3 (fig. 15) alternating rather violently with "H". The Latin source of this passage is written on f. 8r (no. 22, right lower panel, lines 6–8) and the alternation between scripts may be a result of the scribe flipping back and forth as he translated and copied bits off the page.[22] This certainly seems to be what is happening on the left-hand facing page, f. 7v (fig. 19), where no. 15, 'In syrie. abute damasco' appears disordered as if because the scribe is simultaneously writing and translating from the neatly written Latin source that appears on the right-hand facing leaf (fig. 20, f. 8r, lower frame, left panel, lines 1–4, no. 19, 'Emisit eu*m*').

Figure 19: (f. 7v, no. 15)

Figure 20: (f. 8r, no. 19)

The writing on f. 7v varies in size, and is crowded in with no consideration of appearance or phrasing.[23] The Latin extract has at its end the *signe de renvoi* 'hwær' in the Norman script with Norman *h* and insular *r*, answered by the word 'hær', also with the Norman 'h/r', opposite the English in the outer margin of f. 7v. The 'hwær'/'hær' locations seem to confirm what has already been said, that the Latin

[22] The unsourced Latin comment about *chiliades* in the margin of f. 10r (no. 39a, fig. 18) is in brown ink but is entirely like "H", the *a*'s having a lower head, the *p* a rounder bowl and the long vertical strokes having some "sway" to them. But in the frame, the brief Latin note, '`xxx.´ anno p*r*ime cili|adis' seems to be in the prevailing insular script, though no "insular" letters happen to occur. The last letters, 'adis' have been retraced in black ink and in very black ink is the note in the left bottom of the middle frame (not shown), 'cv. anno*rum*', a fragment from Bede's *De temporum ratione*, in "J" script.

[23] This seems to be the same script as no. 7 (fig. 13), but note the tendency for the tops of ascenders to widen and even fork, different from other examples.

was written first and included an instruction or note to provide a corresponding translation at this place on the facing page.[24]

Conversely, at other places the insular scripts seem to have been written first: for example, on f. 10v (fig. 30, upper right frame, see p. 281) the sinuous insular script in brown ink has two lines, one above the frame and one below, an English comment based on the *Historia* (no. 41), and immediately following it, the first words crowded into the space left after the English, in the larger Norman script and a black ink, is a Latin comment epitomized from Isidore's *De ortu et obitu patrum* (no. 42). Though the English is awkwardly placed, the Norman script tidily accommodates the space available. The same situation obtains, without the layout problem, on f. 9r (fig. 17), where the Latin fits in naturally with the English.

So for all the varieties, there seems to be a single ruling script for the English notes and those Latin notes using insular letters. The only English note that stands apart by script is no. 26 on f. 9r (fig. 17) which seems to be "H" script. But the varieties are such that they seem to reveal not only a single hand behind the English and insular Latin entries, but the same writer who wrote "H". That is, thin nib and brown ink (probably for display purposes), exaggerated ascenders, and otiose accents and abbreviation strokes to achieve an archaic effect do not in the end disguise a single hand trying inconsistently to carry out the difficult task of refashioning an ingrained Norman script into an English one for some temporary purpose.

This is strikingly illustrated in a brief but conspicuous note on f. 5v, no. 9e (fig. 21):

Figure 21: (f. 5v)

§eufrates. 7 tygris. in mare. rubru*m* ferunt*ur*.

This is one of the few direct quotations of Josephus in all of Claudius, that is, Josephus not mediated through the *Historia Scholastica*, and it is stimulated by a remark about the Tigris immediately above, attributed to Josephus but quoted verbatim from the *Historia* (no. 9d). This scholarly supplement to the main source

[24] This may have been among the last of the English passages to have been written, as a kind of afterthought.

is, at a glance, apparently quite different from the insular one written at the bottom of this page (see fig. 14), but the first words are "insular": 'eu*fr*ates. 7 ty*gr*is'. Isolated, these two words have the aspect of the "sinuous" insular script, particularly 'tygris', which leans leftward, but they are also obviously by the same hand of the entire sentence, which is in the "J" script. Could it be that the momentary consultation of an outside source jogged the annotator into using a semi-archaic script?[25]

The key that unlocks seems to be on f. 15. At the bottom of the recto is an *Historia* note in the "H" script (no. 59, fig. 22):

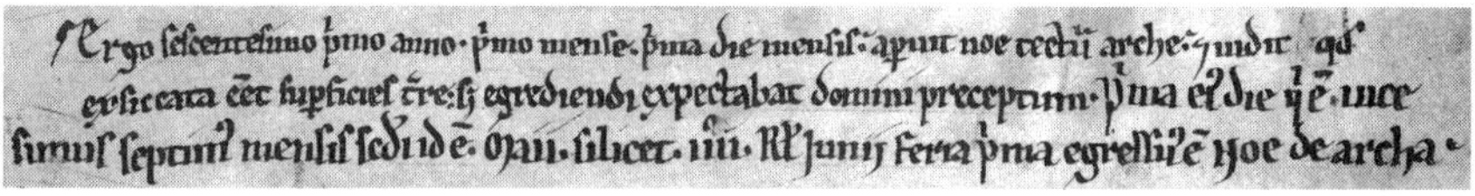

Figure 22: (f. 15r)

> § Ergo sescentesimo p*r*imo anno. p*r*imo mense. p*r*ima die mensis. ap*er*uit noe tectu*m* arche*:* 7 uidit (.) q*uo*d | exsiccata e*ss*et sup*er*ficies t*er*re: s*ed* egrediendi expectabat domini preceptum. (HS 1085C)

This begins in a smaller "pointed" style, as seen in several "H" entries, but the size of the ductus gradually increases and the pointing subsides across the entry until it is written in the full "H" style, the last word, 'preceptum', having a hump of larger letters in its middle, like a well-satisfied python. The next entry is adapted from Bede's *De temporum ratione* and is the normal "J" script in the same black ink (no. 60, fig. 22):

> P*r*ima ei*us* die q*ui* e*st* uice|simus septim*us* mensis s*ecun*di id e*st*. Maii. silicet [*sic*]. iiii$^{o(r)}$. Kł Junii feria p*r*ima egressu*s* e*st* Noe de archa-

The cut of the nib seems to be of the same thickish sort for the letters in both the second line of no. 59 and no. 60. When we go overleaf we see at the bottom a mixed Latin/English extract of the *Historia* (HS 1085b/C, no. 61) written in brown ink and obviously the same script, stint, and ink (cf. the "Norman" *h*'s in 'his hiwscippe', the insular *h* but pointed caroline *r* in 'heriænðe'): yet the scripts on the recto and verso differ widely in aspect (fig. 23):

[25] Perhaps drawn from a manuscript old enough to have been written in insular script?

Figure 23: (f. 15v)

> Manasses damascenus de eisde*m* sic ait. Est sup*er* numada*m* excelsus móns in | armenia: qui baris appellatur. ubi requieuit archa. ⁊ Noe. ⁊ his hiwscippe eode of ðan múnte / heriænðe godes náme.

On the verso the writing is smaller than usual and the nib is more finely cut, but the Latin is the same script as the "H" writing on the recto (no. 59), including the bowed high *s*, the relatively small rightward flicks on the bottom of the minims, the strong rightward curve of the *d*'s, the biting footless *pp* in 'appellatur' with wavering downstrokes (cf. no. 1, fig. 1, 'appellauit'). On the other hand, the English script has a wider-spaced ductus, more conspicuous flicks at the bottom of low strokes (the *pp* in 'hiwscippe' is biting, but the downstrokes are not plain, similarly the foot of the *f* in 'of'). The insular *g* is poorly formed, like a "j". The script is subtly but deliberately modified to distinguish the *Historia* from the "Jerome" and the English from the Latin, but it is all one stint.

The performance of the Claudius scripts is only a more elaborate version of what happens in most late copies made in England of "Cædmon's Hymn" and "Bede's Death Song" and in other late bilingual manuscripts such as Cotton Claudius D. iii (the Winteney "Regula Benedicti"). Often such texts show a contrast between the obsolete English inscriptions and the Latin texts. The Latin is copied in whatever script is normal for the scribe, while the English is most often written in a mannered way that must have been seen as special to the vernacular, as well as perhaps deliberately archaizing. BL Stowe 4 f. 112v (Ker, "s. xii^{2}")[26] shows this well: the scribe highlights the English text by curving many of the lower strokes back to the left, quite unlike his Latin script, but typical of mid-twelfth-century Old English script, besides the very ostentatious and peculiar attempts at insular *g* (mixed with his regular *g*). Much the same can be said of Oxford Bodleian Digby 211, f. 108rb, though not so conspicuously, since the English script, despite formal differences, harmonizes better with the Latin. Durham, Univ. Cosin V, ii. 6, pp. 56–57, also bends the descenders, curves the *s*'s, and gives more openness to the spacing of the letters. This scribe observes the distinction of insular and continental *h*, but does mix insular/caroline *g*'s, *f*'s, etc.; this writing however is "s. xii in.", a time when there was still a lively tradition of

[26] All the examples cited in the next two paragraphs are taken from Fred C. Robinson and E. G. Stanley, eds., *Old English Verse Texts from Many Sources*, Early English Manuscripts in Facsimile 23 (Copenhagen, 1991).

copying Old English. In some copies of "Caedmon's Hymn" and "Bede's Death Song" the same scribe has written the Old English text in an ostentatiously different ductus even though the hand is obviously the same one. This can be seen by comparing the "Caedmon's Hymn" in Oxford, Lincoln College, lat. 31, f. 83r and Oxford, Magdalen College, lat. 105, f. 99r. In Lincoln (which is "s. xii med." according to Ker, note the "hooked" *e*), the hand has written the "Hymn" in the bottom margin in letters perhaps a little narrower than his regular script and has maintained insular forms. But he does not give it a drastically different aspect, though the insular itself gives it a difference. In contrast, the Magdalen scribe, whose hand is a little later than that of Lincoln and rather idiosyncratic in its exuberant flourishes, writes the English in a sidebar surrounded with a decorative frame and exaggerates the heights of ascenders and tops of uncial *d*'s. He actually has not got as good a grip of insular writing as the Lincoln scribe (note caroline *h*, straight and curved *d*'s, continental and insular *g*'s, long and short *r*, long *s* and *f*—an insular *f* in last line—insular and tall *s*). But he has gone out of his way to make it look different and archaic. But the general run of his letters, particularly trailing-headed *a*'s, the angular loop of *g*'s, and treatment of tops of minims and feet show him to be the same scribe, at home with Norman script.

It is in notable contrast that in continental copies of "Bede's Death Song" there is no attempt to distinguish the script or make the text stand out. In English copies where the text is copied as an integral part of the main text, contrast is the rule, suggesting that there was a tradition about how to go about this. So, in Cambridge, St. John's College B. 5, fol. 95r (Dobbie says 14th cent.,[27] but more likely late 13th cent.?), which is the same hand as shown by *a*, *d*, *e*, the script has the same form in both languages, but there is a rounder feel to the English, the main Latin script being more pointed, with longer descenders in caroline *g*, *f*, *s*, while the English retains *wynn* and *þ*, writing 'ær' with an insular *r* and *æ* like an ampersand. However, the scribe does understand that the text has a special status that can be noted by script.[28] Faustina A. v. f. 43r shows that it is not the insular letters *per se* that give the difference of aspect, for although here insular letters are observed very well, the English text does not leap off the page as in some other cases; it is rather the spacing and contrastive treatment of ascenders and descenders that is most important.

[27] Elliott van Kirk Dobbie, *The Manuscripts of Cædmon's Hymn and Bede's Death Song*, Columbia University Studies in English and Comparative Literature 128 (New York, 1937).

[28] On the same opening of Robinson and Stanley, *Old English Verse Texts*, note how in English copies where scripts are not distinguished someone makes a "nota" in the margin beside the English text.

The Inserted Leaves and their Scripts

There are three leaves evidently added in conjunction with the annotation project in order to accommodate extra text. These are folios 74, 147, and 156. The last might be taken as an original leaf but the preponderance of the evidence suggests otherwise.[29]

Cotton Claudius B. iv has an overall page dimension of 325 × 215 mm. It has 20 quires, mostly of eight.[30] Folio 74 is added after the fifth sheet of quire X (a quire of six + f. 74 + f. 76); 69/75, 70/73, and 71/72 are bifolia; the stub of f. 76 projects between ff. 68 and 69 and that of f. 74 between ff. 69 and 70. Folio 147 is added after sheet 5 in quire XIX, an otherwise normal quire of eight, the stub of 147 projecting between ff. 144 and 145. Folio 156 occurs at the end of quire XX (ff. 151–156) and is wrapped around it, traces of f. 156 projecting before and glued to f. 151; probably XX was a quire of 8 with sheets 6–8 cancelled but f. 156 was probably not one of these.

Folio 74 is somewhat smaller in its height than the main pages, being 310 × 212 mm. Folio 147, at 313 × ca. 212 mm., is also not as tall as the book. The inner edge of f. 74 is extended with a strip of parchment serving as the binding tag which projects between ff. 69 and 70. On f. 147 a strip about 13 mm. wide has been glued to the fore-edge and the original membrane is bound into the gutter, which tag, of the same height as the page of f. 147, projects between ff. 144 and 145. On both leaves there are 25 diagonal slash-pricks about 6 mm. apart across the top and bottom. On f. 74 the diagonals run from top left to bottom right, and in the opposite direction on f. 147; in both ranks on both leaves these pricks extend for 158 mm. and are parallel to the writing and perpendicular to the fore-edge. On both ff. 74 and 147 the upper and lower rows of pricks are 298 mm. apart. On f. 74 the pricking nearest to the original inside edge is top 28 mm., bottom 33 mm.; on f. 147 the outermost prick is 33/34 mm. from the edge of the original parchment. It appears that the two leaves were pricked in one operation and then bound into Claudius rotated in relation to each other. It is difficult to see what function these pricks would have served; if they were from a discarded, already partially-prepared leaf that was split and rotated, the pricks should run

[29] Dodwell and Clemoes, *Illustrated Hexateuch*, 15, n. 8, incline to think that f. 156 is a remainder of the original quire, but they allow that it might also have been added in the twelfth century. They report that ff. 154 and 155 "were conjugate."

[30] The collation is **I**^{8} wants 1 (ff. 1–7); **II**^{8} (ff. 8–15); **III**$^{4+1}$ leaf added after 2 (ff. 16–20); **IV-IX**^{8} (ff. 21–68); **X**$^{6+1+1}$ f. 74 12th-century leaf inserted after 5, 1 leaf added after 6 (ff. 69–76); **XI-XIV**^{8} (ff. 77–108); **XV**$^{8+1}$ leaf added after 4 (ff. 108–17); **XVI-XVIII**^{8} (ff. 118–141); **XIX**$^{8+1}$ f. 147 12th-century leaf inserted after 5 (ff. 142–150); ?**XX**$^{8+1}$ sheets 6–8 cancelled, 12-century leaf inserted after 5 (ff. 151–156). Textual rather than physical evidence indicates that another inserted leaf once stood before f. 156; see below, 248, also ch. 6, 333–34.

to at least one of the edges, but they don't.[31] The two leaves are of similar quality: both fairly bright, supple, crisp, and relatively thin, smooth on both sides, making hair/flesh difficult to tell. The two leaves may well have comprised a bifolium at the time of pricking, given the symmetries. On the other hand, if they are excised leaves from quire XX (serving originally as flyleaves), it should be noted that f. 147 resembles in quality f. 152 and f. 74 resembles f. 151. Their smaller dimensions somewhat militates against this possibility. The third inserted leaf (f. 156) is 310 mm. in height, but it appears to have been trimmed at the bottom. It is not pricked at top and bottom as the other late-added leaves were, nor is it likely it was an original flyleaf; it has been wrapped around quire XX. It differs in quality and preparation from the other two inserted leaves and from the Claudius membranes generally.

Folio 74 is separately ruled on recto and verso; lightly on the recto for 39 lines by plummet with double bounding lines on both margins, the writing area being about 270 × 164 mm.; the verso is also plummet ruled, the scoring being somewhat heavier, for 34 lines, with double bounding lines on both margins, the writing area about 270 × 175 mm. There is about 7 mm. between writing rules on the recto, but on the verso the ruling varies, with the top four lines being 7 mm. apart, the rest about 8 mm.

Folio 147 recto and verso are separately ruled by plummet, on the recto for 37 lines, and on the verso for 41. Double bounding lines on the outside edge of the recto and the inside edge of the verso are visible, but trimming, addition of the outer strip to bring the leaf flush with the fore-edge, and close binding make it impossible to detect the opposing bounding lines, if they existed. On the recto, the width from the left edge of the upper block of text to the outer bounding line is 197 mm.; the text area is about 265 mm. high on the recto and about 284 mm. high on the verso. The odd preparation of these leaves may indicate that they consist of prepared charter-materials that have been appropriated for this purpose, for writs and charters were apparently written from rolls of prepared parchment, with the writ (typically wider than long) normally cut off from the roll after it had been filled out.[32] Given their size, match, and

---

[31] Just for comparison, British Library Harley 1524, a St. Augustine's manuscript slightly later than the writing of our annotations, has a page size of 375 × 260 mm. with 62 pricks in the inner and outer margins (outer pricks cut off on many leaves). The rotated leaves of Claudius 74 and 147, if originally from the same sheet, would have been about 434+ × 328 mm. with 60–70 pricks. The information on the St. Augustine's provenance of manuscripts here and on the following pages is taken from N. R. Ker, *Medieval Libraries of Great Britain: A List of Surviving Books*, 2nd ed., Royal Historical Society Guides and Handbooks 3 (London, 1964), 40–47.

[32] See R. C. van Caenegem, *Royal Writs in England from the Conquest to Glanvill*, Selden Society 77 (London, 1959), 109. Writs were economically written, the membrane being no larger than the text absolutely required, the slip usually being about half as wide

preparation, it seems most likely that the person inserting these leaves simply used a couple of already-prepared charter blanks that had been made from a single large membrane.[33]

Folio 156 is a foul half-sheet, with a natural fault sewn up before it was inscribed and probably already slightly irregular on its outside edge before use, as a reconstruction of the text suggests; this leaf is about 10 mm. shorter than the regular leaves; its original width might have been about the same as that of the book, but with an extension wrapped around to the front of the quire and a large diagonal portion subsequently torn off, it is impossible to be sure. The torn-out portion has been supplied to the edges by a later vellum inlay. The leaf is unruled, written on the recto with 43 lines, irregular at the right side, and on the verso there are 32 lines of writing, with several spaces between blocks of text, its left margin appearing irregular as far as it can be seen; this is partly due to irregularity in the membrane which the scribe is avoiding. The beginning of the text on the recto consists of selections from the *Historia Scholastica* so as to make up an epitome of Judges; it begins imperfectly with Abimelech, indicating that the beginning of his story and those of the five judges who preceded him probably occupied an additional added leaf (perhaps a partial leaf) which has become lost. However that may be, this fragile quire, with three cancelled leaves (perhaps excised by the annotator himself), would have been prone to fall apart easily. The original ink foliation and a sixteenth-century notation on f. 153r, 'Read thys leafe after the next', show that in early modern times the positions of ff. 152 and 153 were reversed. That they were already so reversed at the time of the annotations is shown by the fact that on f. 151v a 'hwær/hær' *signe de renvoi* refers a note about 'Chebron' to the Old English text on f. 153r and a note about 'Macedæ' on f. 153v refers (without a *signe de renvoi*) to the Old English text on f. 152r; so it is evident that at the time of the annotations f. 151v faced f. 153r and f. 153v faced 152r; most likely the quire, weakened by the cancellation of its last three leaves, fell apart when it was detached to add f. 156 (and probably another leaf before it) and was incorrectly reassembled *before* the annotator added his contributions.[34] Direct evidence shows that f. 147 was added blank to the book and then filled in.

---

as these pages are tall, typically in the range of 150 to 180 mm. wide; but writ charters were much larger and ordinary writs may have been written, in effect, in a two-column format as regards the width of the roll, the pricking normally trimmed: van Caenegem (Plate IV) shows a writ of Henry I (150 × 375 mm.) in which pricking is visible on the left edge of the face side.

[33] As suggested to Doane by Kathryn Salzer of the University of Tennessee (p.c.). A large Benedictine house at this period would be the bestower of grants as well as the receiver of them.

[34] Ff. 152/153 were rebound in correct order in the nineteenth century. The nineteenth-century pencil foliation has been corrected by another pencil foliation. See Marsden, ed., *The* OE Hept., xlv, for details.

The note on f. 146v 'Mod`e´m uic*us*' begins at the bottom of f. 146v and continues at the top of f. 147r. There is no such direct evidence that f. 74 was added blank. Literary evidence, discussed in a later chapter, suggests it was inserted to anchor the plan of the system of annotations.

At the "doorway" to f. 74, on f. 73v at the bottom, is copied Exodus 6:16–20 (no. 244) written in three lines. This seems to be written in a single stint but is in three distinct styles of script (fig. 24):

Figure 24: (f. 73v)

> a) § Hec nomina filiorum Leui p*er* cognationes suas. Gerson. & Caat. & merari[35]
>
> b) merari. filii gerson. lobem. et | semei. Filii. caat. amram. & isuar. et hebron. 7 oziel.
>
> c) oziel. Filii merari. mooli. et mousi:· Accepit au*tem* | amra*m* uxore*m* iocabed patruele*m* sua*m*. que `pep*er*it´ ei aaron. 7 moysen. 7 maria*m*-

The script changes gradually and subtly, but the last word, 'maria*m*', is totally different in character from 'Hec' at the beginning. Working backwards from the end, the script appears to be "J" type completely, but it morphs more and more to the "H" type as we work back; by the middle of the second line it has changed completely into the "H" type; the first line is mostly in a feathery, thin-lined sort of writing, with an elegant cast, the exact like of which is seen nowhere else in Claudius; there is a definite pointing effect, and the bodies of the letters, rather than forming squares, are slightly rectangular, and the ductus leans slightly left, whereas "H" and "J" tend to lean right. There is an elaborate artificial paragraph of a sort not found elsewhere in the annotations. Yet one cannot point to distinctive, consistent traces of another hand; the bottoms of minims are at first clubbed, but by 'Gerson' they are finished with the usual flick to the right. Puzzling too is the use of '&' in the first half of the quotation and '7' in the second, the form of the ampersand idiosyncratic when in the "H" script. There is no apparent change of ink. The best guess is that the scribe is here experimenting with writing styles, and as this is written immediately before the added leaf f. 74, which shows a variety of styles, it is probably part of that effort.

---

[35] Points where aspect changes within the stint is marked by underlining.

The script of f. 74 presents a crazy appearance. There seem at first glance to be several hands. On the recto (fig. 25), the bottom five lines are clearly "J" script and the next two up "H" tending to "J". The text of lines 1–35 is a collection of extracts from Pseudo-Jerome, *Quaestiones in 1 Paralipomenon* (no. 245a), ending with 'filii juda' (line 5 up). Divisions within the text are acknowledged at 'Acham' (line 1), '§ In para*lipomenon* ysai filiu*s*' (line 11), '§ In para*lipomenon* ab ysa`y'' (line 12), '§ Oazar' (line 13), '§ Jair' (line 14), 'Filii ezra' (line 19), '§ Charmi pa*ter*'' (line 33). 'Filii ezra' is the only of these divisions that represents a substantial skipping of text, and is marked by an extra-large capital rather than by a "paragraph." The script styles do not correspond to these divisions. The upper part of the page, lines 1–20, shows a rather florid script style that is similar to that on f. 73v, line 3 up. Bodies of letters are rectangular, ascenders are forked, and vertical strokes are given jaunty splays and curves; some of the 7-notae have a small bulge or dot on the downstroke that is not quite a cross-stroke (and a mixture of "&" and "7" appear in the passage). The script seems to be trying for elegant flair, so that there is more height and angles to these letters than seen elsewhere, particularly the *a*, which frequently has a short head and triangular bowl;[36] the "Norman" *h* has a "claw" closing it at its bottom. The first line has a "pointed" aspect, with exaggerated ascenders in a "chancery" style and a more elaborate opening initial than found elsewhere in the notes. The ductus varies within lines 1–20 from small to medium. If all the annotations were in this style one would want to date them *after* 1200. Yet telltale signs point to the "H" script: the characteristic "bow" of vertical strokes, the more obvious the longer; the flick to the right to finish minims; the occasional relaxed *d* without such an elaborate curve. And the bottom of the page is executed in blocks of "H/J" script, so the upper writing cannot be later.

In lines 20–21 this script begins to morph into normal "H" script, which continues in lines 22–27 and into 28, when at 'pene o*mn*ia Moysi' it moves back into a variety of the "florid" script. 'Charmi pat*er*' at line 31 is familiar "H" script soon morphing into "J", writing a passage that essentially continues the text from above. The final two lines, clear "J" script, are from Jerome's *De situ et nominibus locorum Hebraicorum* and refer to the content of the passage written on the verso of f. 74 (line 26). This reference to another annotation and the fact that the bottom seven lines are in a wider block than the preceding text suggest that these "H/J" lines were written as an added stint. However, as we shall see, they are part of the same plan. The script styles on the upper portion of f. 74r seem to be an experiment in a certain "elegant" or shall we say "up-to-date" style of writing by the hand that more habitually writes in "H/J" script; this seems reinforced by

[36] This is the form of *a* seen frequently in the Old English notes.

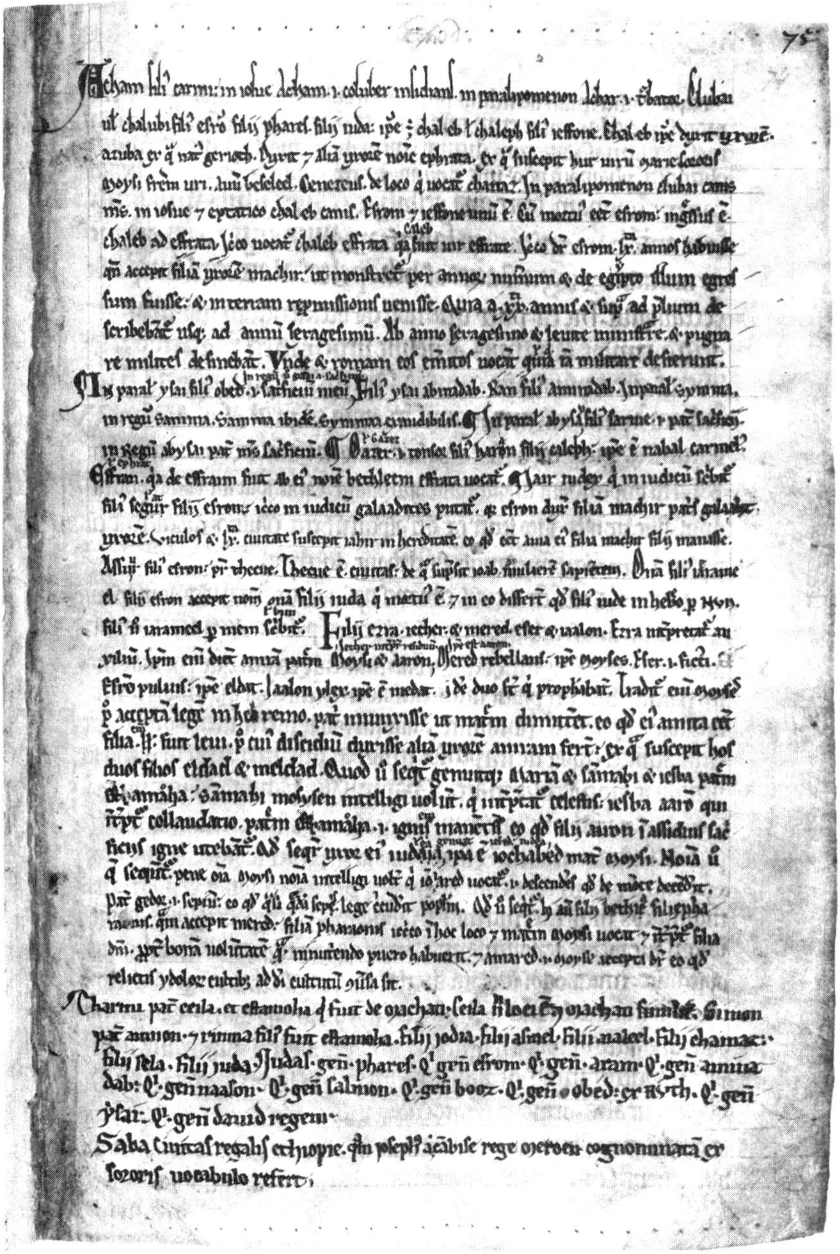

Figure 25: (f. 74r)

the three lines written at the bottom of f. 73v, which show both the florid experiment and the normal script.[37]

The verso of f. 74 (fig. 26) presents a surprising contrast, since it is a version of the large display text often used in deluxe twelfth-century books. The letter forms of this type of script are formally caroline minuscule, but differ from those of the regular Norman scripts not only in size, but in the careful distinction each letter receives, in the large size of the body of the letters in relation to the up- and down-strokes, a general squareness rather than ovoids and minimal curves, carefully-shaped lozenge-tops of minims, greater amount of pointing, thicker verticals leading to greater contrast with horizontals. In its regular use in various manuscripts it is often put in contrast to a medium-size book-hand used for the commentaries and notes written on the same page.[38]

Ker gives two relevant examples from episcopal professions dated 1174 and 1176 which show forms very similar to those on f. 74v.[39] The text on f. 74v is a long continuous extract from Chapters 5 and 6 of the "Exodus" section of the *Historia Scholastica* on the youth of Moses. The script varies in size somewhat, the first four lines being smaller (reflecting the narrower ruling), gradually increases in lines 5–11, and in line 12, after 'obtulisset: puer' settles down into a medium size which has a more current aspect than the previous lines. Lines 5–11 show instances of round *s*, while elsewhere it is always tall. The whole page seems to be all one hand: note particularly the way **t**, formed with two strokes, has a little downward tag at the right of the cross-stroke, and the repertoire of *g*'s, some with an open lower loop with a diagonal cross-hair to the upper loop, others shaped like a figure-eight. An amateurish or experimental air is lent by the variation in the ductus over the page; also notable is the creeping introduction of round-backed *d* as the writing goes on. A date in the late 1170s might be indicated by the alternation of abbreviation strokes between curved and straight varieties. This variation, and the use of "&" whereas in all the other *Historia* extracts the nota is "7," suggest the use of a different exemplar, hence that perhaps this leaf was written earlier as part of some other project and incorporated here.

---

[37] A few letters in the "florid" script may be on f. 151r ('Hi deo'?); or is it the beginning of an English inscription?

[38] This use of large semi-rotunda or -quadrata display script alongside normal minuscule book hand can be seen in the following St. Augustine's books of the late twelfth/early thirteenth centuries in the British Library: Harley 1524 (glossed Pauline epistles), Royal 3.A.i (glossed Numbers), Royal 4. A.ii (glossed Isaiah), Royal 4. A.x (glossed Genesis), Royal 3. A.ii (glossed Leviticus). Though written over a period of years, they appear to have been designed to make up a uniform set for the claustral library. An example of the combination, though the size of the commentary script is smaller than the Canterbury examples, may be seen in Harrison Thompson, *Latin Book Hands*, no. 86, dated 1176, Harley 3038, from St. Mary Bildewas.

[39] *English Manuscripts in the Century after the Norman Conquest*, 37–38, plates 19 b, c.

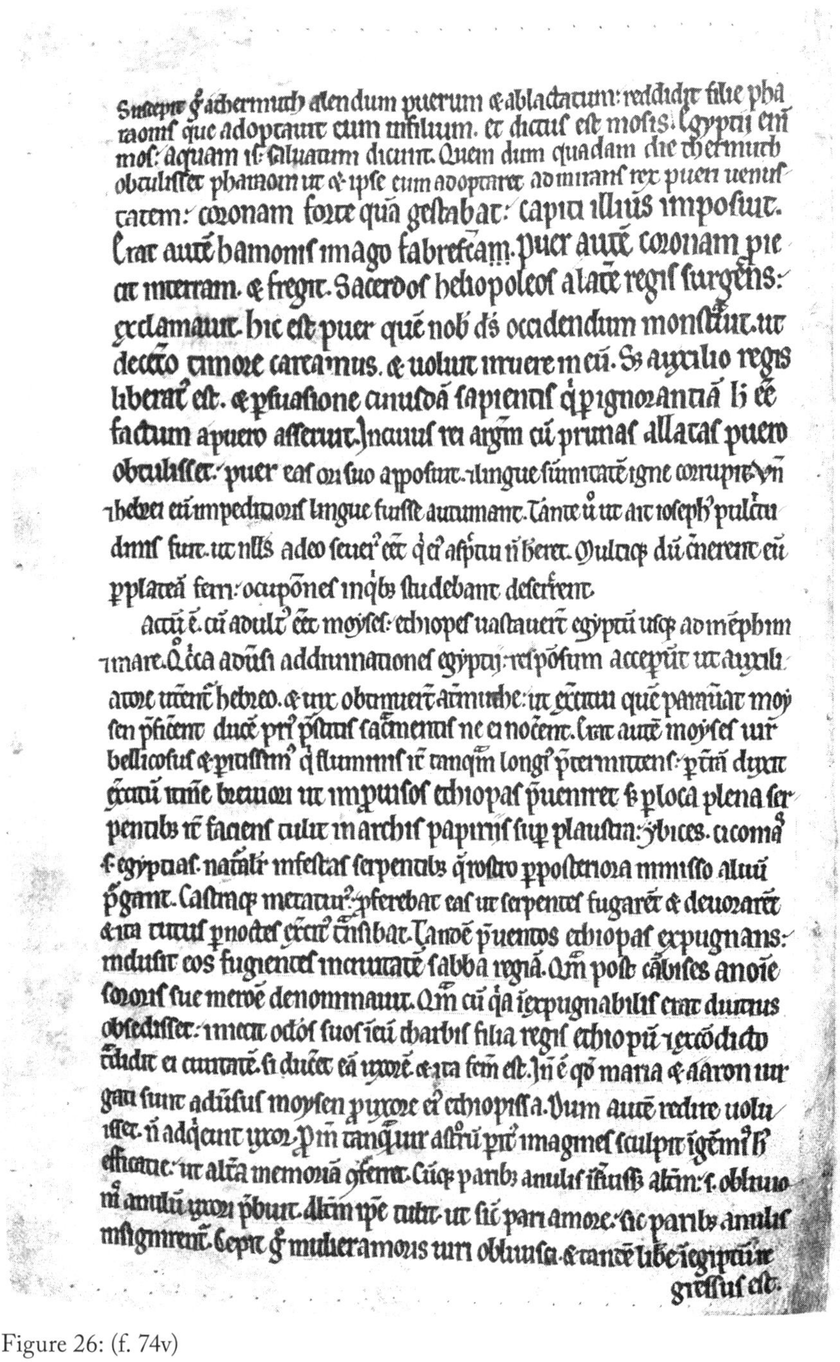

Figure 26: (f. 74v)

Whether the hand is the same as "H/J" is difficult to tell, though the variation or unsteadiness of the ductus, the gradual "cursivization" of the script as it reaches the bottom of the page (note the increasing use of little rightward flicks rather than real finials on downstrokes in line 4 up), the repertoire of tall *s*'s, and the variety of *a* are telltale signs. The ink seems slightly darker on the verso than the recto. Whether the hand of the verso is the same or not, the choice of script suggests a different or unformed purpose, perhaps written before this leaf was fully integrated into the project. Nevertheless, as it is placed, it does seem to be an important part of the overall conception, as will be discussed in Chapter 6.

The scripts of folio 147r (fig. 27) follow the pattern of the annotations as a whole, with a few complications. The excerpt from *De situ et nominibus locorum Hebraicorum* ("Modem", no. 334b) begun on f. 146v continues unbroken in the "J" script to f. 147, which shows that the leaf was added to the book blank and not pre-written. "J" script continues on f. 147r to line 26. The content is surprising, however, lines 9–24 being occupied by apparently unrelated mensural texts (at arrows in fig. 27) of obscure relevance to the prevailing subject-matter (nos. 335a-b, see ch. 6, 311–16 below). The "J" script continues with a couple of Jerome entries and then the "H" script begins in the middle of line 26, perhaps at the fresh Jerome entry 'Sor Tir*us*' (no. 336b), perhaps a little earlier in the line, which is of transitional appearance. Here, if anywhere, someone wishing to posit "H" and "J" as two separate hands could find the best evidence, but the transitional nature of line 26 suggests rather merely a change of pens or a new shift of work. To some extent, the anomalous appearance of the lower part of the recto is merely the effect of wider spacing of the lines of writing. At line 29, 'asia. regio', the program, but not the script, changes, becoming a long series of excerpts from Bede's *Nomina regionum atque locorum de Actibus Apostolorum* going overleaf to the bottom of the verso (nos. 337a–x); though a selection, it represents a good portion of this short work, roughly maintaining the alphabetical arrangement of the original. Perhaps its function is filler, but a case will be made later that it relates to the overall exegetical program of the annotations. On the verso the script is of a mixed character, showing the generally more cursive appearance of "H" but with capital letters in the "J" style. The ink varies on the verso, the sixth line (from 'Gaza'), and all the writing from line 15 on being in brown, with signs of new nibs here and there.

There are indications that the addition of this leaf to the book might have caused some doubt or confusion: the entry on line 5 'Someron' (no. 334e) is begun and its first three words cancelled; and then it is taken up again. Doubtless the hesitation was caused by the realization that this entry had already been written on f. 145r (no. 330i), also in "J" script. On f. 145r the name is 'Semeron', on f.

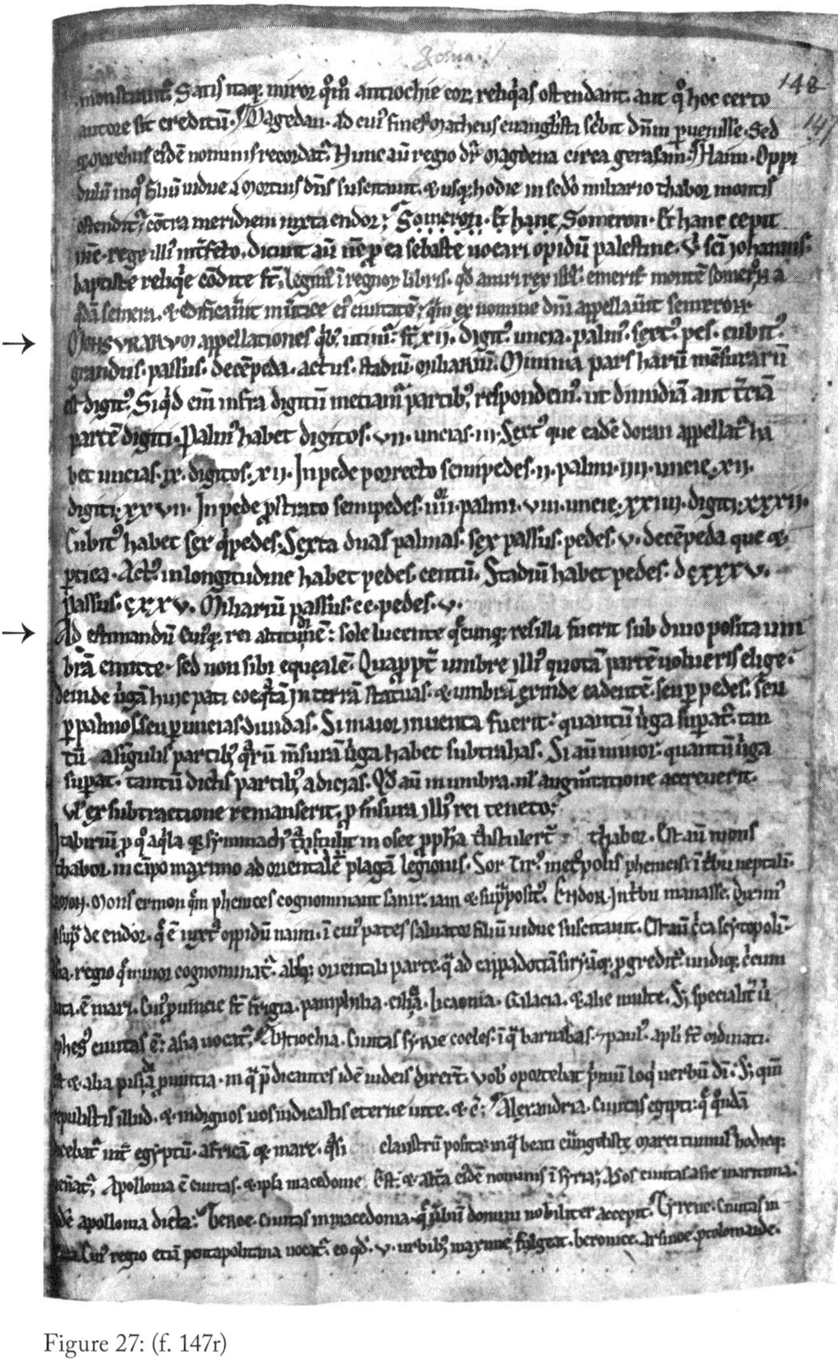

Figure 27: (f. 147r)

147r the attested variant 'Someron'; nevertheless, as if the same exemplar is being consulted, the variant forms 'sebaste' (for "sebasten") and 'semera' (for "semer") occur in both cases, all the points and abbreviations except for 'nunc' also being the same.[40] On f. 147r, the resumption (at the second 'Someron') is in black, but shifts to brown at 'legim*us*',[41] a color which continues for another two and a half lines, into the beginning of the mensural passage (no. 335a).[42]

There is little to be said about the script of f. 156: it is clearly of the "H" type, with the characteristic slight variations that tends to "J" here and there. All the writing is in a dark brown that varies slightly. The text is a medley of sources from the *Historia* and Bede that makes up a kind of "appendix" to the original book, giving a summary of biblical history from Judges to the Incarnation. The textual evidence suggests that there was once another added leaf before f. 156, for the epitome of Judges, via the *Historia Scholastica*, begins at the bottom of f. 155v at Judges 3:8, the beginning of the series of Judges (= approx. HS 198.1273B), and at the top of f. 156r jumps to Judges 9:50, almost exactly the half-way point in the Judges section of the *Historia* (HS 1282D).

The Script and St. Augustine's

One of the few established facts about the external history of Cotton Claudius B. iv is that in the late fifteenth century it was in the possession of the Benedictine house of St. Augustine's, Canterbury. It is clearly identifiable in the St. Augustine's catalogue preserved in Dublin, Trinity College MS 360.[43] Claudius is noted on f. 3, col. 2, no. 34, giving book-description, second folio identification, and press-mark: "Genesis anglic' 2° fo. *and sylðus* d.1.G.1."[44] As was commonly

[40] "Someron"/"Semeron" is an attested variant in the tradition, the other variant words are not (see Lagarde, *Onomastica Sacra*, 150.28). What might have happened is that working on f. 147 the annotator consulted a different exemplar and finding an entry "Someron" thought it was different from "Semeron"; on checking back he saw it was the same except for the headword and cancelled, but then for some reason decided to go ahead with the entry, using the new headword but following what was already written on f. 145r for the rest.

[41] Note the forked ascender of *l*.

[42] The otiose inclusion of this extract on f. 147r is a pretty good indication that the leaf was added to accommodate a previously planned program for which marginal space proved to be insufficient: there are few picture spaces in this part of the manuscript.

[43] Published in James, *Ancient Libraries*, 173–406. James was the first to make this identification (lxxxiv). He dates the fifteenth-century catalogue by internal evidence to 1491 × 1497 (lviii).

[44] James, *Ancient Libraries*, no. 95 (201), and B.C. Barker-Benfield, ed., *St. Augustine's Abbey*, 1:405-06 (no. 95). This manuscript was interlined (between nos. 28 and 29) into the catalogue by a later hand. The significance of this is not clear: was it an oversight,

the practice in monastic libraries, the identity of the volume was guaranteed by copying the first couple of words from the top of the second folio recto into the description: Claudius B. iv has lost its original first folio but the present first folio, originally second, has '7 sylð us' as its first words. It is a reasonable assumption that the manuscript was at St. Augustine's from early times,[45] but there has so far been no evidence to confirm it. The script of the annotations is very distinctive, as must by now be obvious, with its broad, square nib, its high, "bowed" upstrokes and modest downstrokes, its overall "akimbo" or gangly appearance, biting *r*'s, especially before *a*, wide repertoire of *s*'s, right flicking of the bottom of minims, and relative inconsistency within the stint. Hands similar in type to this occur in a number of St. Augustine's books in the British Library datable to the late twelfth century, though none are identical: Cotton Titus A. xxvii, a "Historia Britanniae" with miscellaneous contents, has a number of hands, that on f. 48r similar to ours; Harley 1524, a glossed Pauline Epistles, in display scripts and corresponding book hands shows a number of scribes, some similar to the annotator's; Royal 13.B.viii, Geraldus Cambrensis, has writing in its first half similar in a general way to the Claudius script; in Royal 7.D.ii there is the beginnings of a Latin to Latin/Old English glossary (ff. 18v-19v), with the glosses in a hand of general similarity, though not the same; and Royal 12 B. ix, materia medica, has a general similarity, particularly in the later parts of the book (ff. 116v-117r).

Cotton Nero A. viii, ff. 2–41, contains a chronicle from Christ to 1161 compiled and written in all likelihood at St. Augustine's.[46] At anno 980, f. 30v, it notes 'Hi*c* dedicata e*st* eccl*esi*a beato*rum* ap*osto*lo*rum* petri 7 pauli. 7 rex æthelred in rege*m* *con*secrat*us* e*st*', a reference to the rededication of the abbey by Archbishop Dunstan.[47] An annal for 1081 concerning Archbishop Stigand required more space than the prepared line offered on f. 34r; it has been written by the main scribe of the annals on a supplemental rectangular slip of parchment, 81 × 54 mm., pasted right onto the page by its left edge (fig. 28). The chronicle

---

a late addition, a book not initially considered worth mentioning? Or does its addition to the catalogue show evidence of a very precocious revival of interest in Anglo-Saxon antiquities? This is the only Old English book mentioned in the late catalogue (James, *Ancient Libraries*, lxxxiv), though St. Augustine's may have still held at least one other at this date, e.g., Cotton Tiberius A. vi (an Anglo-Saxon Chronicle); cf. Ker, *Medieval Libraries*, 43; but see his contrary opinion in *Catalogue*, 250. The English annotations themselves imply the presence, or at least availablity, of some other English books at an earlier period.

[45] So Dodwell and Clemoes, *Illustrated Hexateuch*, 16, presume.

[46] Ker, *Medieval Libraries*, 43, places a query beside this item.

[47] *Recte* 978. Susan Kelly, *Charters of St. Augustine's Abbey, Canterbury and Minster-in-Thanet*, Anglo-Saxon Charters 4 (Oxford, 1995), xviii and xiv, n. 9. The event was only vaguely remembered in St. Augustine's tradition: the 14th-century chronicler William Thorne gives 978 in a brief mention (*William Thorne's Chronicle*, ed. Davis, 38).

hand is datable to about 1220.[48] This slip is cut from a membrane containing Ambrose's Letter I.63 to the church of Vercelli, which appears on the dorse (f. 34*v). There were two copies of Ambrose's letters at St. Augustine's according to the late catalogue.[49] The writing appears to be by the same scribe who wrote the Claudius annotations (fig. 29).[50]

One notes pervasive similarities here, particularly with the "J" script, for which a good comparison is Claudius, f. 14v (fig. 8): thick ductus that varies in appearance within the stint (Nero line 5), uneven left justification (Nero lines 3, 5; Claudius lines 1 and 3 up), feet on minims that jerk to the right, short upstrokes have a spur or flag to the left, extra-long understroke of **x**; **b** has a curving horn or flag at the top (Nero '. . .bens' line 3, Claudius 'abram' line 4 up); **st** ligature pinched together (Nero 'iustitie' line 1, Claudius 'testante' line 1 up). High **s** is two-stroke, with two types, one straighter with a more pronounced horn, uncial **d** has a slight flare to the right alternating with a straighter version; the **r** bites into the **a**: Nero 'numeratio*ne*' (3), 'generati. . .' (5); Claudius 'abram', 'q*ua*draginta' (lines 4, 2 up); there is also a tendency for the Nero script to waver between a "strong" and "weak" style (cf. the fifth line) analogous to the alternation between "J" and "H" in Claudius.

If the identity of this hand to that of the Claudius annotations is accepted, this scrap would seem to establish three significant facts: that the writer was a book-scribe and hence the Claudius work probably had some official status for which it was worth taking manpower from other projects; that Claudius B. iv was definitely at St. Augustine's late in the twelfth century; and that the annotation project was carried out there.

---

48 According to Michelle Brown, p.c., 22 February 2002.

49 James, *Ancient Libraries*, 231, no. 381, "Epistolarum Ambrosii liber primus tantum et in eodem libro | Ammonicio Basilii | Tractatus quidam de viciis et virtutibus et | versus Bede de die iudicii cum A / 2o fo. *A dimidia* d.5.G.1"; no. 382, "7 Epistolarum Ambrosii libri ix cum B; 2o fo. *in libro ipsius neque neque* d. 5. G. 1." The fact that no donor is mentioned suggests that these are books from earlier times (cf. James, lxix). A book on Prior Eastry's Christ Church list (ibid., 22, no. 55) contained *inter alia* "Epistola Ambrosii ad U[e]rcellensem Ecclesiam," which corresponds to the address of this letter.

50 The text is from Ambrose, Classis I, Ep. 63 (PL 16.1202B). It appears to be written in two columns, only part of one column remaining, the left edge of the text intact. A transcript of the slip:

1 rex pacis. uerus iustitie rex uenit. Hoc. . . . . .
2 minis i*nter*p*re*tatio. sine pat*re*. sine mat*re*. si[ne]. . . . .
3 sine numeratio*ne*. neq*ue* initiu*m* dieru*m*. nec. . . .
4 bens. Quod et ad filiu*m* dei refert*ur*. Ipse p*r*inci. . . .
5 omniu*m*. Qui matre*m* i*n* illa diuina generat[i]. . . . .
6 pat`r´*em* hoc ui*r*ginis Marie partu ignor[a]. . . . .
7 solo nat*us* ante secula. ex ui*r*gine sola ort[u]. . . . .

added
slip recto →
(f. *34r)

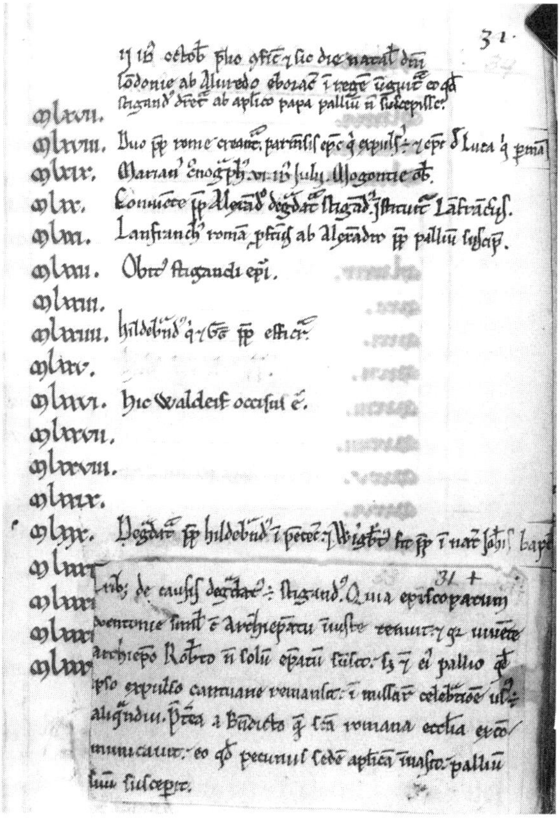

Figure 28: Nero A. viii, f. 34r
By permission of the British Library.

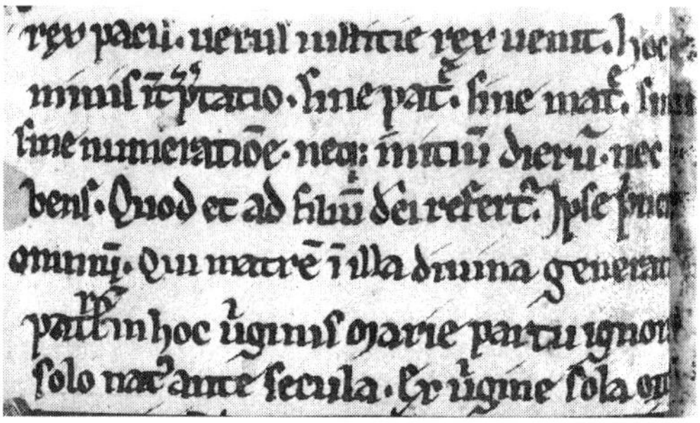

Figure 29: slip verso f. *34v

Conclusion

If it is correct that a single hand, that of a monk of St. Augustine's, has written all of the annotations, one must see the project essentially as the project of a single individual who for some reason has decided to supplement, enhance, interpret, or decorate an old book with the use of more modern books;[51] in the case of the "Jerome" material, the modernity comes from the contemporary compilation of the collection from which the texts have been taken (see below, ch. 6); the *Historia Scholastica* presents a case of a brand-new and hardly digested work being applied to an obsolete text. The variation of handwriting is systematic according to the division of material and therefore must be for purposes of display and/or reference, though there is also the possibility that the writer eccentrically wanted also to give the effect of several hands working on the notes. The only individual name that it is possible to venture is that of "Normannus," presumably a monk of the abbey active in the last quarter of the twelfth century.[52] That he must have been a person of moral or actual authority in the abbey seems a necessary conclusion, since he was able, openly and over some lengthy period of time, to radically modify an impressive book from the previous age and to monopolize for a time several central and up-to-date works necessary for biblical research. That the original book was still valued long after its practical value had abated is suggested by the care and accuracy with which it was annotated in the late twelfth century, as well as by its continued existence in the claustral library three hundred years later.[53]

The added pages testify to the liberties allowed the annotator as well as the elaborateness of the program of notes. Folio 74 suggests work from an early stage of the project, when the scribe may have been experimenting on the recto with different scripts before settling down to those that predominate. The display script on the verso may be somewhat earlier than the other scripts and may have been written before the leaf was added to the book. Indeed, its existence as a loose sheet may have inspired the beginnings of the project. The recto, however, was written after the leaf had been added, as shown by the "experimental"

[51] It is possible to imagine a director controlling a single scribe; or even several "authorities" squabbling over details, a single scribe patiently carrying out orders (perhaps evidenced by the erased "Norman" attributions). But it is more economical to assume that the man who devised the notes also wrote them, given the evidence on the page of improvisation and second thoughts.

[52] On "Normannus" and the Normannus passages, see ch. 7 below.

[53] Is it possible that Cotton Claudius B. iv might owe its existence through the Middle Ages and into the sixteenth century to the interest in the Latin notes rather than the Anglo-Saxon text and pictures? Or perhaps because the presence of the index-like notes made the obsolete text somewhat intelligible?

identity of script on f. 73r and 74r. Folio 147 was certainly added before writing: an excerpt continues from f. 146v onto the added leaf.

In general, the earliest layers would appear to be the *Historia* notes, for they occupy the prime space and on most pages where a guess may be made appear to be written before the "Jerome" notes. The *Historia* annotations cease with "Exodus":[54] was the available copy defective, did the writer lose his extended borrowing privileges, or did ennui set in? The "Jerome" annotations appear to be at first careful supplements to the *Historia* and to the original text; as their frequency gradually increases towards the second half of the book and they eventually take over, they make less careful reference to the original text: was this because of changing purpose, learning, or taste on the part of the annotator, or because of the changing availability of books? Some higher-order thinking was taking place on the page, as is to be gathered from the implied chronological calculation on f. 59r (discussed below, 352-54, fig. 41), constructed out of earlier annotations; this type of activity—and it is not the only instance—suggests that compiler, annotator, and scribe were the same.

The "insular" annotations in English and Latin are concentrated at the beginning of the book, up to f. 18v, except for a few brief incidental notes; the exception is the longish passage on f. 51rv (no. 181) telling the story of Dina, that had been purposely omitted from the Old English original for moral or ideological reasons; so this is a narrative supplement, not an exegetical note, and hence different in kind from the other English notes. After a conspicuous start, the English notes peter out. This configuration suggests that the project began by conceiving of a series of notes in English to "match" the original text. This aspect of the project may have proved too arduous to sustain; certainly most of the notes suggest strain and awkwardness. Perhaps as a result of this the English began almost at once to be supplemented by Latin excerpts written with an affectation of insular features. Some English/Latin insular scripts seem entered in one go (e.g., f. 11r, nos. 43–44, and the entries on the bottoms of f. 15v and 18r). Some of the English entries have errors which show that the scribe was working from notes; others suggest that the scribe was translating on the page from Latin already entered (especially no. 15 on f. 7v, fig. 19). It is evident that at some point in time the entering of Latin *Historia* notes in "H" script overlapped with the English program. But after a little time the English language and the insular script were abandoned, probably as too difficult or recherché to be worth continuing. The Latin program seems extensive, substantially complete. However complete or incomplete, firm or tentative, successful or not, the annotations were conceived as a large-scale, integrated, continuous biblical commentary, founded on the latest up-to-date sources and methods and entered in an ancient book; and it is to the literary aspects of this strange and unique project that we must now turn our attention.

[54] Except that there are two *Historia* notes later in the book, nos. 324 and 392, which might have a source other than the principal manuscript.

V. *Historia Scholastica* and the Annotations

Around the original Old English text in Cotton Claudius B. iv is woven a pattern that shows a thoughtful and learned comprehension and reuse of an ancient and, one would think, totally obsolete book. But for at least one person this was not the case: it was worth a considerable amount of thought and effort to apply to this old book what was at the time very modern learning: contemporary editions of Hieronymian works and copious extracts from a very new, and new type, of biblical commentary, the *Historia Scholastica* of Peter Comestor, chancellor of Paris.

About half the Claudius annotations are exactly-quoted excerpts from the *Historia Scholastica*, as it has long been known, or the *Scolastica Historia* as its recent, and only modern, critical editor entitles it.[1] The original title was perhaps similar to that given in the second-oldest manuscript, Paris, Bibliothèque Nationale lat. 16943 (Corbie, dated ca. 1183), "Hystoria ueteris et noui testamenti." In his prologue, Peter says he composed the book at the request of his *socii*, either those of St. Victor or perhaps the church of Notre Dame. About ten years after the original composition, before 1180, it was revised by his pupils with his approval and received its common title.[2] It was written, most probably, in the late 1160s or early 1170s. The exact date of completion is not known, but the possible range is not great. Peter Comestor was dean of Troyes from at least 1145, the date

[1] Agneta Sylwan, ed., *Petri Comestoris Scolastica Historia: Liber Genesis*, Corpus Christianorum, Continuatio Mediaeualis 191 (Turnhout, 2005) (henceforth Sylwan *Scol. Hist.* or Sylwan ed.). As her title indicates, it comprises only the first section of the complete work, but may stand *pars pro toto*. Its details and conclusions supersede those of the same author's earlier study: "Petrus Comestor, *Historia Scholastica*: une nouvelle édition," *Sacris Erudiri* 39 (2000): 345–82. Although the new edition appeared in March 2005, after the initial version of this chapter had been written, it is the intention of the authors to incorporate her text and textual discoveries into the present chapter and into the apparatus of "Evidence" (ch. 2). We continue to use the traditional uninverted name of the work in this study (often cited as *Historia* or "HS"). For various practical reasons, the text cited throughout this study remains the widely available text of Navarro (1699) reprinted in volume 198, cols. 1054–1644, of the *Patrologia Latina*; important variants taken from Sylwan's edition are noted ad loc. Navarro's text is discussed below, 260.

[2] Sylwan, *Scol. Hist.*, xxxix–xl.

of the earliest extant document in his name.[3] He may have retained this office while studying with Peter Lombard in Paris in the 1160s.[4] He became chancellor of Paris not before 1164 (and hence rector *ex officio* of teaching positions in the cathedral, the nascent University of Paris, for it was the chancellor who had the power of granting or withholding teaching licenses): documents associated with him are dated between 1168 and 1178.[5] It is traditionally held that in 1169 Peter Comestor retired as a canon to the abbey of St. Victor in Paris, based on evidence that he was buried there. He died c. 1178. The *Historia Scholastica* is dedicated to William, archbishop of Sens (1169–1176); Sandra Rae Karp argues that it was written no later than 1169 since the dedication does not mention William's legatine title received in 1169.[6] However this may be, the range can be narrowed downward by the reference in a chronicle entry dated 1173 to the *Historia Scholastica* as already a well-known and widely-diffused text.[7]

The *Historia Scholastica* was composed to meet the growing need for textbooks in the Paris schools[8] and as such was an instant success, becoming by the early thirteenth century one of the three standard university teaching texts, along with Peter Lombard's *Sentences* and the *Decretals* of Gratian; it was glossed

[3] Saralyn R. Daly, "Peter Comestor: Master of Histories," *Speculum* 32 (1957): 62–73, at 65. A more recent summary of the life and works is David Luscombe, "Peter Comestor," in *The Bible in the Medieval World: Essays in Memory of Beryl Smalley*, ed. Katherine Walsh and Diana Wood, Studies in Church History, Subsidia 4 (Oxford, 1985), 109–29. The traditional brief life and works of the Comestor is N. Jung, *Dictionnaire de théologie cathólique* (Paris, 1935), 8:1918–22; a more up-to-date account and bibliography is by Jean Longère in *Dictionnaire de spiritualité ascétique et mystique: doctrine et histoire* (Paris, 1986), 12.2: cols. 1614–26. See also Sylwan, *Scol. Hist.*, x-xiii.

[4] Ignatius Brady, "Peter Manducator and the Oral Teachings of Peter Lombard," *Antonianum* 41 (1966): 454–90, at 483–85; Mark Clark, "Peter Comestor and Peter Lombard: Brothers in Deed," *Traditio* 60 (2008): 85–142; see 120–22 on the reception of the *Historia* in the twelfth and thirteenth centuries.

[5] Brady, "Peter Manducator," 484, who assigns the date of his death as 22 October 1178. Brady's and Daly's accounts of Peter's accession to the chancellorship agree in essentials, but differ on dates by a year or two, cf. Daly, "Peter Comestor," 65.

[6] Sandra Rae Karp, "Peter Comestor's *Historia Scholastica*: A Study in the Development of Literal Scriptural Exegesis" (Ph.D. diss., Tulane University, 1978), 51.

[7] The chronicle of Robert, monk of Auxerre, has only this entry for the year 1173: "Petrus Comestor celebris habetur in Francia, Magistrorum Parisiensium primus, vir facundissimus et in Scripturis divinis excellenter instructus, qui utriusque testamenti historias uno compingens volumine, opus edidit satis utile, satis gratum, ex diversis historiis compilatum" (Léopold Delisle, ed., *Recueil des historiens des Gaules et de la France* [Paris, 1877], 12:298A, cited by Daly, "Peter Comestor," 67).

[8] Alys S. Gregory, "Studies on the Commentaries of Cardinal Stephen Langton," *Archives d'histoire doctrinale et littéraire du moyen age* 5 (1930): 5–151, at 18.

by Stephen Langton about 1193[9] and was repeatedly the subject of *reportationes* (glosses derived from lectures).[10] Its popularity and authority were immense. Although lengthy by modern standards—it occupies nearly 600 columns in the Patrologia Latina—it was designed as a relatively compact and self-contained work dealing with the entire Bible that could fit into one convenient volume. Peter Comestor's original work covers, in order, Genesis, Exodus, Leviticus, Numbers, Deuteronomy, Joshua, Judges, Ruth, 1–4 Kings, Tobias, Ezechiel, Daniel, Judith, Esther, Maccabees, and, as a single section, the Gospels. A few years after the original composition, Peter of Poitiers (d. 1205), successor to Peter Comestor's chair of theology and later also a chancellor of Paris, added a section on Acts (PL 198.1645–1722). In many manuscripts, as virtually a preface to the *Historia*, is included another work of Peter of Poitiers, *Compendium historiae in genealogia Christi*, an abbreviated chronicle with schematic diagrams of the family tree of Christ back to Adam.[11] It draws on the *Historia* and various copies freely interpolate passages from the *Historia*, with which it is so closely associated. The *Historia* was often copied with the *Liber exceptionum* of Richard of St. Victor. In the *Historia* itself coverage is by no means even, the Pentateuch and Gospels receiving the most, and the prophetic books are given short shrift within the sections on Judith, Tobias, and Ezechiel. The reason is that the work is intended as an exposition of the literal level of scripture, as the author makes explicit: "Porro a cosmographia Moysi inchoans, rivulum historicum deduxi, usque ad ascensionem Salvatoris, pelagus mysteriorum peritioribus relinquens" (PL 198.1654).[12]

A word is necessary on what was meant by "literal level." Jerome was the great example of how to do this, and for Jerome and other commentators following his method, including the Victorines Hugh and Andrew who influenced

---

9 Glosses attributed to him in Paris, Bibliothèque Nationale MS. lat. 14417, ff. 125–309: see F. M. Powicke, *Stephen Langton, being the Ford Lectures 1927* (Oxford, 1928; repr. London, 1965), 56.

10 According to Beryl Smalley, *The Study of the Bible in the Middle Ages*, 3rd ed. (Oxford, 1983), 197, n. 4, there is no comprehensive study of the glosses in the manuscripts of the *Historia*.

11 See Philip S. Moore, *The Works of Peter of Poitiers, Master in Theology and Chancellor of Paris (1193–1205)* (Washington, DC, 1936), 97–117. The Latin text is edited from Hamburg, Staats- und Universitätsbibliothek, MS. theol. 2029, ff. 1r-18v, as an appendage to a 15th-century German version in Hans Vollmer, ed., *Deutsche Bibelaufzüge des Mittelalters zum Stammbaum Christi mit ihren lateinischen Vorbildern und Vorlagen*, Bibel und deutsche Kultur . . . I, Der Materialien zur Bibelgeschichte und religiösen Volkskunde des Mittelalters 5 (Potsdam, 1931), 127–88. The text Vollmer used is late and heavily interpolated. As a control, in this study the *Compendium* is cited from British Library Royal 8. C.ix (s. xiii^{in}, Reading Abbey), a large monastic compilation that includes the *Historia* as its second item.

12 "Therefore I traced the historical stream from the cosmographia of Moses to the Ascension of the Savior, leaving the sea of allegory to those who are more expert."

the Comestor so greatly,[13] literalness did not mean a philological/grammatical analysis of the exact meaning of a passage in either Hebrew or Latin, or the full contextual meanings of words and phrases, or an attempt to find the intention of the author, but rather the extra-textual chronology, historical associations and background of what is mentioned in the text, what it is "in reality" beyond the text. This can include explanations of Hebrew words and their Greek and Latin equivalents (as in annotation no. 210) but seldom their connotations and contextual meanings. These commentators in the Christian tradition necessarily saw a split between the literal and allegorical, with the latter always having the greater authority and prestige, and supplying any significant meaning, even though it was not the focus of their exegesis; there was no such divorce in the contemporary Jewish tradition.[14] For the much earlier Jewish author Josephus, the other great influence on literal exegesis in the Middle Ages, this split was not an issue either; he set a different example, to renarrativize the biblical stories completely, supplying the familiar stories with additional events, motivations, themes, subplots, characters that brought them into moral or romantic perspective in a way that accorded with his notions of classical historiography, Jewish tradition, and Hellenistic taste.

In contrast to the *Glossa ordinaria*, which by the preceding generation had stabilized as a standard selection of excerpts from patristic and ecclesiastical authorities to be written as part of a glossed Bible,[15] the *Historia* is a stand-alone work that not merely repeats excerpts from earlier and mostly ancient authorities, but selects its sources critically, often setting them against one another, attempting to integrate "what is known" with the text of the Bible itself so as to create a relatively smooth explanatory meta-narrative of biblical events, things, and persons, a fundamental re-visioning of the usual twelfth-century *glosula* form.[16] It parses various versions of the biblical text and places them in relation to chronological, linguistic, geographic, ethnographic, and social background

[13] This is the main theme of Smalley, *Study of the Bible*, chaps. 3–5.

[14] Herman Hailperin's explanation of the method of Rashi, the famous twelfth-century rabbi of Troyes, is of interest by way of contrast: "As to Rashi's intention . . . what he says, for example, on the first verse of the Book of Lamentations is typical: 'There are many haggadic midrashim, but my purpose is to explain the scriptural passage according to its *peshaṭ*.' It is not easy for one to explain . . . what the word *peshaṭ* suggests as to the meaning of a passage. One might say that it is the sense in which the first author used it—whether his intention was to make the word or words speak concretely, allegorically, parabolically, etc." (*Rashi and the Christian Scholars* [Pittsburgh, 1963], 31–32). Haggadic midrashim explain cruxes by narrative elaboration. This is certainly in the Comestor's repertoire (cf. esp. no. 247).

[15] See the standard account in Smalley, *Study of the Bible*, 56–62.

[16] See Karp, "Peter Comestor's *Historia Scholastica*," 116–17. The *glosula* form was the interspersing of notes right into the text, with marks to indicate separation of main text and gloss. Peter Comestor modified the form by integrating the comments into the

material. Authorities are often named but seldom quoted verbatim; they tend to be paraphrased, combined, and worked into a more-or-less continuous discourse. Most of the sources are traditional within the Church of course, including the familiar literal (and literal parts of) biblical commentaries by Augustine, Ambrose, Bede, and others, with the work of Jerome leading the way; it also leans heavily on the then-popular Latin version of the *Antiquities* of Josephus, who had been adopted in the Middle Ages as an authority with quasi-patristic status.[17] But the sources are also modern, drawing on the recent tradition of literal commentary coming from Victorine scholarship that displayed renewed interest in historical background, the Hebrew text, and Hebrew scholarship. Named by the Comestor are the *Notulae* on the Octateuch (c. 1141) of Hugh of St. Victor; not named but used more intensively is Andrew of St. Victor's commentary on the Heptateuch, probably available from about 1150, drawing on contemporary Jewish research and traditions.[18] Hugh used Hebrew scholarship, but rather defensively, while Andrew tended to use it specifically as Hebrew, without apology. Several scholars have shown how there is a small but significant residue of material in the *Historia* that must be drawn directly by Peter Comestor from living Jewish informants: the Comestor grew up in Troyes, the city of Rashi and in mid-century still the site of a flourishing rabbinical school. The Comestor adopts certain midrashim from Josephus and elsewhere,[19] sympathetically adopts Jewish emphases (for example his favorable view of the Aaronic priesthood), and even adopts methods of exegesis from Jewish informants.[20] What Karp, from whom

---

narrative and by restricting comments to those verses which pertained to the commentator's overall narrative and/or didactic purpose.

[17] Blatt, ed., *The Latin Josephus*, 12–14. On the medieval editions of Josephus, see ch. 1, 7–10.

[18] On Andrew, see Beryl Smalley, "The School of Andrew of St. Victor," *Recherches de théologie ancienne et médiévale* 11 (1939): 145–67, esp. 146–51; Ranier Berndt, *André de Saint-Victor (†1175), exégète et théologien* (Turnhout, 1992), who gives (328–47) a table of passages in the *Historia* directly derived from Andrew's *Expositio super Heptateuchum*.

[19] For example, amidst material drawn directly from Josephus (ed. Blatt, 200–3 [2.230–253]) occurs a midrash explaining Moses' inability to speak well, the episode of the coal of fire on Moses' tongue; this is copied in Claudius on f. 74v, no. 247 (= PL 198.1143D-1144D); another midrash, not garnered from Josephus, occurs in the English note 34 (= HS 1079C/D) on the death of Lamech.

[20] On the possible use of contemporary Jewish informants in the *Historia*, see Hailperin, *Rashi and the Christian Scholars*; Esra Shereshevsky, "Hebrew Traditions in Peter Comestor's *Historia Scholastica*," *Jewish Quarterly Review* 59 (1969): 268–69; S. T. Lachs, "The Source of Hebrew Traditions in the 'Historia Scholastica'," *Harvard Theological Review* 66 (1973): 385–86 (who denies direct contact); the issue is best summed up and analyzed by Karp, "Peter Comestor's *Historia Scholastica*," 197–218. Nevertheless, when all is said, there is a tendency to exaggerate the overall importance of *direct* influence of a living Jewish tradition. The great bulk of Jewish lore is from Josephus or Jerome; modern

these points are drawn, finds most striking and original about the Comestor's approach in the *Historia* is that he does not view Hebrew history and the Old Testament as "shadowy types of truth" essentially cancelled or superseded by the life of Christ and Christian history, but as part of a continuum that runs from the history of the Hebrews into the Evangelical history.[21] In this he is following a strong trend in twelfth-century French biblical scholarship.

From Paris and Troyes, the cities where the Comestor carried out his work, the *Historia* spread rapidly throughout the Norman ambit and beyond; it was one of the most widely popular works of the Middle Ages. How many manuscripts exist is unknown: Stegmüller lists 224;[22] Sylwan says that there are more than eight hundred extant from the twelfth through sixteenth centuries without giving details, but she mentions 180 in France, 77 in Paris, 41 in Munich, 41 in Oxford, 33 in London, 23 in the Vatican, 22 in Cambridge, and 16 in Vienna.[23] Beyond these are dozens of incunables and early prints, from Zainer (Augsburg, 1473) to Navarro (Madrid, 1699).[24] It must be assumed that the *Historia Scholastica* reached great houses in England in the first wave, probably by 1175 at the latest, perhaps initally at St. Albans,[25] but Christ Church and St. Augustine's would certainly have been among them. Several early copies written in England are dateable, the earliest being British Library Royal 7. F. iii, written for the nunnery of Elstow in Bedfordshire, dated 1191/92.[26] British Library, Royal 4. D. vii is a deluxe copy of the *Historia* and Richard of St. Victor's *Liber exceptionum* that was produced at St. Albans at the instigation of Prior Raymond and presented to the abbey by Abbot William (1214–1235); Prior Raymond was deposed in 1215.[27] Another early English copy at Rochester Cathedral, dated around 1190,

---

sources are mostly via Andrew and Richard of St. Victor: see Smalley, *Study of the Bible*, 199, and now Sylwan, *Schol. Hist.*, textual apparatus.

21 Karp, "Peter Comestor's *Historia Scholastica*," 60, 81, 99.

22 F. Stegmüller, *Repertorium Biblicum Medii Aevi* (Madrid, 1954), 4:280–91. This is the tip of the iceberg. For example, Stegmüller lists only four manuscripts in the British Library, but a truer figure is 29 (including fragments) according to the *Index of Manuscripts in the British Library* (Cambridge, 1984–1985), 8:81ff.

23 See the table, *Scol. Hist.*, xxxiii.

24 Ludwig Hain, *Repertorium bibliographicum* (Stuttgart and Paris, 1827), 1b: nos. 5529–40; W. A. Copinger, *Supplement to Hain* (London, 1898–1902), 1: nos. 5530–40, 2: no. 1709, 2b: no. 5532.

25 Sylwan, *Scol. Hist.*, xxxii.

26 Andrew G. Watson, *Catalogue of Dated and Datable Manuscripts, c. 700–1600 in the Department of Manuscripts in the British Library*, 2 vols. (London, 1979), no. 878, 1:152–53, pl. 109. The second quire is gone; it has some but not all additions, written in gloss script in the margins.

27 Rodney M. Thomson, *Manuscripts from St. Albans Abbey, 1066–1235*, 1: Text; 2: Plates (Woodbridge, 1982), no. 28, 1:95–96, plates 240–44. A fifteenth-century table of contents refers the book to donor information in Matthew Paris' *Gesta abbatum monas-*

has recently come to notice.[28] The same St. Augustine's catalogue that mentions Claudius B. iv also lists twenty copies of the *Historia Scholastica*;[29] it is not remarkable that a great house would hold multiple copies of this standard work three hundred years after its composition, but the sheer number of copies suggests the great popularity and indispensability of the work among the monks over the years. Similarly, in the Christ Church catalogue of Prior Eastry (prior 1264–1331), while no copies appear among the claustral books, many personal copies of "Hystorie manducatoris" are listed, the majority shelved beside its companion standard text, Peter Lombard's *Sentences*.[30] One of these still exists, a copy of "s. xii/xiii" Trinity College, Cambridge B.15.5 (342), among "Libri Nigello."[31] Like the Christ Church copies, most of the St. Augustine's copies are listed with their donor's name.[32] Only one St. Augustine's item can be identified with an extant

---

terii Sancti Albani (ed. H. T. Riley, Rolls Series 28.4 [London, 1867], 233–34); Thomson dates the book 'before December 1214'; cf. Watson, *Dated and Datable Manuscripts in the British Museum*, no. 867, 1:150. In both script and decoration it is a full-blown thirteenth-century style deluxe book.

[28] A large-format (330 × 230 mm.) book in double columns, written in proto-gothic script, illuminated and extensively glossed. The source of information, the booksellers "Les Enluminures, Ltd." (Chicago and Paris), indicates that this book has been sold to The Beinecke Library, Yale University (thanks to Sandra Hindman, p.c.).

[29] James, *Ancient Libraries*, 198–200, nos. 45–65, 45 and 46 being a two-volume set "in claustro."

[30] e.g., James, *Ancient Libraries*, nos. 637–38, p. 72, no. 722–23, p. 79, nos. 1047 with 1046, p. 99, no. 1060, p. 100, no. 1181, p. 105, nos. 1171–72, p. 104, nos. 1219–20, p. 107, no. 1340, p. 114, no. 1619 with 1617, p. 134, no. 1651, p. 136 under title "Hystoria scolastica," etc.

[31] James, no. 1084, with the *Sentences*, no. 1085 (p. 101); it is "vellum, 13 3/4 × 10 1/2 inches, ff. 228, double columns of 38 lines, cent. xii/xiii, finely written, from Christ Church." M. R. James, *The Western Manuscripts in the Library of Trinity College, Cambridge: A Descriptive Catalogue*, 4 vols. (Cambridge, 1900–1904), 1:470–71. The "Nigellus" is according to James probably Nigellus Wireker (fl. 1190), perhaps precentor of Christ Church and author of the *Speculum Stultorum*. It was owned at one time by John Parker (red chalk inscription on flyleaf).

[32] At St. Augustine's, by the fifteenth century, the paired shelving of the *Historia* and the *Sentences* had been broken up (books containing the former are nos. 45–65, and the latter nos. 499–542), but some monks from an earlier period (but not earlier than the mid-13th century) can be identified as donors who had owned both, nos. 47/516 (William Bretoun or Britonn, monk, fl. 1287), 49/536.1 (Thomas de Gotele or Gotesle), 50/502 (Henry de Cokeryng, monk, treasurer 1287–1291), 52/513 (Nicholas Maydebroke or de Mekyngbroke), 54/505 (John Pistoris), 55/506 (Nicholas de Bello), 58/518 (cum A), 59/519 (cum B), 60/536.3 (William Byholte, fl. 1297–1320, prior after 1318), 61/501? (Radulph Gatewyk, ordained 1297, monk, infirmarer in 1330; 501 is attributed to "Radulph"). The positive identifications are taken from A. B. Emden, *Donors of Books to S. Augustine's Abbey, Canterbury*, Oxford Bibliographical Society, Occasional

manuscript; unfortunately, it is essentially irrelevant to our purposes since it lacks most of Genesis and Exodus and is of the fifteenth century.[33]

About 179 distinct Latin extracts from the *Historia Scholastica* occur in Claudius.[34] This is in addition to some twenty-four English notes translated directly from it.[35] There are also about nineteen interlinear glosses supplementing the main Old English text that appear to be taken directly from the *Historia*.[36] These are in the "Genesis" and "Exodus" sections[37] and tend to be in clusters on particular pages. About a third of the "Genesis" and rather less of the "Exodus" portions of the *Historia* has been written into Claudius, a rather large amount of text, rivalling the magnitude of the original main Old English text itself.

Until very recently, the textual history of the *Historia Scholastica* was virtually unknown, and the only conveniently available edition was in the Patrologia Latina, volume 198 (ed. J. P. Migne [Paris, 1855]), a reprint of the edition of Emmanuel Navarro (Madrid, 1699). Navarro's edition is uncritical even by the standards of its time, containing no textual apparatus and apparently depending entirely on

Publications 4 (Oxford, 1968), *passim*, who lists other donors of the *Historia* only, John de Barnevile, who donated a number of books of biblical exposition, a senior monk by 1293; Peter De Toynton, prior 1296, Henry Tylmanstone, subprior 1375.

[33] James, no. 65: "Historie scholastice Will. Mongham 2° fo. *cio factum* d.10.G.2": this is now British Library Harley 4132 (s. xv, St. Augustine's *ex libris*; William Mongham, fl. 1452–1469, cf. Emden, *Donors of Books*, 13), as shown by the first words on the second folio, 'cio fcm dogmatizat' etc. The manuscript has a page size of 307 × 200 mm., and a writing area of 212 × 131 mm. in two columns, blind-ruled for 59–61 lines, written in very compact gothic minuscule, with red and blue penwork decoration. It is a working copy which has been very heavily annotated. Unfortunately, half the Genesis and almost all the Exodus section is missing (lacking text corresponding to PL 198.1105D-1194A). James wrongly identifies no. 47 as Harley 4132, which has "2° fo. *est ge creator*."

[34] Nos. 1–5, 8, 9a–c, e–f, 11–12, 13a–c, 17, 19–22, 28, 30–33, 37, 40, 43, 51a–b, e–f, 54, 55a, 56, 59, 61, 63–64, 68, 70a–f, 72, 75–76, 79, 81, 85a, 87–88, 92–93, 97a–b, 99, 102a–b, 106, 108, 110, 112–116, 118–124, 126, 127a–b, 129, 131, 133–134, 137, 140, 142, 144–145, 148–149, 151–153, 155, 157, 158a–b, 159, 165, 167, 171, 174, 176, 177a, 180, 182–187, 189, 191a–c, 192, 193a, 194, 199–201, 203, 209, 193b = 193a, 211, 216, 219, 221, 226, 229, 230, 232, 234–235, 238–239, 241–242, 247, 249–253, 255–258, 260–261, 263, 265–267, 269b–d, 270, 272a–b, 273–275, 278–279, 281a–c, 284–285, 287–288, 291, 293, 295–297, 324, 392.

[35] Nos. 6a, 7, 10, 14, 15, 16, 25a, 25b, 26, 28a, 34, 36a, 36b, 38, 44, 45, 46, 50, 51c, 52, 61, 62, 77, 128.

[36] Nos. 77, 87, 97b, 114, 121, 127b, 140, 150, 158a–b, 180, 181 (repeats 177a), 203, 226?, 248?, 254?, 265, 277, 285. Other 12th-century glosses that do not appear to be from the *Historia* are nos. 29b, 52 (English), 143, 147, 166, 248, 264 (English), 276, 302, 303 (margin).

[37] Except for two isolated occurrences, one on Rahab (no. 324, f. 141v) and one on the death of Joshua on the last regular text page (no. 392, f. 155v).

previous (unidentified) printed editions.[38] It constantly differs in matters great and small from the text as found in Claudius. One's first thought when comparing them is that the Claudius annotator is a careless epitomizer. But in fact the Claudius text of the *Historia* is typical of texts of the late twelfth and early thirteenth centuries current in Norman and English houses, and Navarro's text is particularly bad. There are only a few places where the Claudius text is confused or isolated by a unique reading;[39] it frequently deviates in grammatical connections and the omission of words for brevity's sake from what appears to be the received text of its time and place, but by design, not error. Clearly, the Claudius annotator was faithfully copying from a particular, and fairly good, exemplar.

Agnete Sylwan's recent (2005) critical edition of the Genesis section of the *Historia Scholastica*[40] is the first systematic attempt to write its textual history.[41] Heretofore the classification of manuscripts had never been attempted, and given the tremendous number of manuscripts—more than eight hundred—it probably will remain an impossible task. From the beginning there was contamination by glosses and erroneous *additiones.*[42] Sylwan therefore limited herself to the examination of the "Genesis" portions of twenty-four manuscripts of the twelfth and early thirteenth centuries. She sees two groups, a Champenois and a Parisian. The first consists of fourteen items, nine of which actually orginate in Troyes, Sens, or the rest of the Champagne, the others being from Corbie, Mondsee, France in general, Flanders, and England (Elstow).[43] The second group, of ten items, all originate in Paris, with the exception of Paris, Bibliothèque Nationale 5113, which is Italian. From this list she makes a double exclusion. First, she excludes eight manuscripts which transmit a revision made about 1190 (including Elstow, dated 1191/92), probably at Sens. Five of the eight have Champenois provenance, three were written at Sens. This revision was very influential on the texts used at the university and in the Dutch, French, and German translations, and are thus the basis of the type of texts that mainly circulated throughout the Middle Ages; this version is not important, however, for the establishment of the

---

38 Sylwan characterizes it as a mediocre text, with incorrect rubrics, compared to twelfth-century manuscripts, an abundance of incorrect readings, particularly in the form of glosses and additions, and a long interpolation in the Preface (*Scol. Hist.*, xxxv–xxxvi).

39 Most notably in item 296 (see ch. 2, 139–41).

40 See n. 1 above. The following discussion of the tradition is essentially a summary of Sylwan's observations and conclusions regarding the text of HS as presented in *Scol. Hist.*, xxxvi–lxxxiv.

41 Clark, "Peter Comestor and Peter Lombard," 123–42, in the same year, presented an eclectic edition from five randomly selected early manuscripts of the Prologue and chaps. 1–8 (= PL 198.1054–1063C).

42 For the *additiones* see below, and ch. 3, n. 20.

43 See 260 above and n. 26.

original text, which is her aim. Secondly, she has excluded an incomplete manuscript (Angers, Bibl. mun. 303), and seven turn-of-the century manuscripts exhibiting inauthentic late states of the text.

These exclusions leave eight twelfth-century manuscripts situated at the beginning of the textual tradition and representing two geographical areas; early as they are, their testimony is already characterized by contaminations and errors. The tradition of *Historia Scholastica* "Genesis" is from an archetype ω^1, which is not the original archetype [ω], because all the earliest manuscripts share certain identical errors, Sylwan giving two examples (lxvi):

> Porro cum adoleuissent filii Ysaac, factus est Esau uenator et **Iacob agricola et pastor** in tabernaculis habitabat. (Sylwan ed. 66/1–2, PL 198.1111A)
>
> *recte:* *factus est Esau venator et agricola et Iacob pastor
>
> Et restituit ei Abimelech puteum. Sed in testimonium quod ipse foderat puteum et ablatum [**restituit ei Abimelech**], dedit regi septem agnas. (Sylwan ed. 57/9–12, PL 198.1104B)[44]

The eight early manuscripts chosen by Sylwan fall into two important groups:

> **P** Paris, Bibliothèque nationale, lat. 16943 (Corbie, ca. 1183)
>
> **S** Porto, Biblioteca Publica Municipal, Santa Cruz 42 (Sens or Troyes, s. xii^{ex})
>
> **L** Lyon, Bibliothèque municipale 187 (Paris, s. xii^{ex})
>
> **T** Troyes, Bibliothèque municipale 451 (Paris, s. xii^{ex})

> **Tr** Troyes, Bibliothèque municipale 290 (Troyes, ca. 1185–1200)
>
> **W** Vienna, Österreichische Nationalbibliothek 363 (Mondsee, ca. 1180–1183)
>
> **Pa** Paris, Bibliothèque nationale, lat. 14638 (Paris, St. Victor, s. xii^{ex}/1200)
>
> **To** Tours, Bibliothèque municipale 42 (Paris, s. xii^{ex})

The group **Tr W Pa To** has 129 identical readings (consisting of corrections via the Vulgate, augments, inversions, and other changes), which show that this group was elaborating and correcting the text of **P S L T**, which seems to be the

---

[44] Part of this is no. 134 on f. 36v, but the extract is not copied as far as the otiose repetition.

more original group. **Tr W Pa To** goes back to a common ancestor **Y**, while **P S L T** goes back to an earlier common ancestor **X**. Given that **W** can be dated exactly to 1180–1183, the ancestor **Y** had to be copied before 1180. Sylwan's analysis of these eight manuscripts makes equally clear a regional division, between the Champenois **P S Tr W** (Corbie, Sens/Troyes, Troyes, Mondsee) on the one hand and Paris **Pa To L T** on the other. In three cases **P S Tr W** have readings of the Vulgate, vs. **Pa To L T** which have readings of the pre-Hieronymian Vetus Latina as well as several changes and twenty-one errors in common. On the other hand, **P S Tr W** have six errors in common. There are certain contaminations between the groups which lead Sylwan to the conclusion that the most primitive text is normally transmitted by **P S** with which is often associated **L T** or **Tr W**.

The above data lead Sylwan to the conclusion that the eight manuscripts fall into four pairs: **P S (α)**, **Tr W (β)**, **Pa To (γ)**, **L T (δ)**. But each of these pairs of manuscripts have divergent readings which show that they are not copied from one another. Considered separately, none of these eight manuscripts could be copied directly from any of the others.

The oldest manuscript, **P** Paris, BN Lat. 16943 (Corbie, dated ca. 1183), is distinguished by over four hundred individual readings. Sylwan concludes that this manuscript preserves more purely than any other the Comestor's first version of the work, written before 1170, and that the other lines represent various stages of authorized and unauthorized revision. In **P**, the title, the biblical text, the rubrics, and the chapter divisions are not the same as in other manuscripts and the number of *additiones* is more restrained. In general **P** has an excellent text, often alone giving the right reading against all the other witnesses. Most of its faults are manifestly errors of scribal inattention and the like, rather than transmitted errors (the other witnesses giving the correct readings). In some cases **P** shares errors with the other manuscripts/groups. Other variants are stylistic, readings of **S β γ δ** being introduced to make the style clearer and smoother. The most natural explanation of these is that they are not faults, but deliberate revisions to the rougher style of the original version, made with the author's approval. **P** shows a large number of rare biblical readings which in **S β γ δ** appear revised to accord with Vulgate forms; the **P** readings show the type of readings which the Comestor took from certain glosses and commentaries. The rubrics in **P** tend to be briefer: are they simply abbreviated, or are the rubrics in other manuscripts elaborated? The wording of both series is based on the typical headings in twelfth-century Bibles. **T (δ)** is the only manuscript to preserve a list of chapter headings as well as rubrics in the text. Three of the **T** capitula conform to the rubrics of **P** and not to its own. These **T** capitula probably go back to a more primitive list and conform to the original rubrics that were in **X**, the common ancestor of **P** and **T**. Sylwan concludes that **P** shows the original titles and that the other manuscripts show the titles as they appeared in the revised edition.

From her analysis of these eight manuscripts, Sylwan allows herself the following conclusions: The text which has been transmitted by these witnesses has undergone an evolution which is characterized by retouchings, by a tendency to both abridge and augment the text, by an adaptation of chapter-divisions, by the presence of new or more elaborate rubrics as well as more elaborate *additiones*, and by importing corrections from biblical lemmata and scriptural citations. **P** presents the most primitive text which is identified with the text (**X**) which the Comestor had drafted by about 1170 before he knew it would become an academic book; he had entitled this version "Historia sacre scripture." The other manuscript lines, **Sβγδ**, probably represent what may be called a new edition, a revision of the primitive text, incorporating more accurate Vulgate quotations and smoothed-over grammar, destined to become a teaching text. This revised text (**Y**) was achieved either by the Comestor himself or by others with his approval in the years after 1170. The resulting revision was probably presented to the third Lateran council in 1179. By the year 1180 this edition had been diffused in a great number of manuscripts, supplanting the primitive text which is now preserved only in **P**. Henceforth the title was *Sc(h)olastica Historia*. This (new) edition of the book for use in the schools, prepared in the lifetime of the Comestor, has been preserved in a variety of forms: an integral form, a form contaminated by the primitive text, and a form enriched by later, integral revisions about 1180, after the death of the Comestor, probably in Paris (at St. Victor?). **Tr W** (β) transmits the integral text; **S** presents elements of the revision inserted into the primitive text; **Pa To** (γ) transmits the revised text with the revisions post-1179; **LT** (δ), finally, contains elements of the primitive text, of the text revised before 1179, and of the later revisions. There is, however, a great amount of cross-contamination in every manuscript and no witness is purely of one strain or another. Sylwan in her text attempts to reconstruct **X**, the archetype stemming from the Comestor's original version, most closely represented by **P**.

It needs to be borne in mind that the text of *Historia Scholastica* in Cotton Claudius B. iv must be among the earliest extant and preserves a good portion of the text of "Genesis" (and rather less of "Exodus"). Claudius, as the collation with Sylwan's apparatus in the notes to Chapter 2 indicates, shows the revised integral text **Y** of pre-1179, with many characteristic variants from the γ-strain of the text, stemming from the integral post-1179 revisions; a couple of examples will show this:

No. 4. (Sylwan, ed. 18; PL 198.1061D/1062A)

Sylwan: Cete neutri generis est indeclinabile.
Claudius: Cete. neutri∴ [*om.* S γ] i*n*declinabile e*st*. [↩Pa]

Declinatur: hic cetus, huius ceti. Et omnem animam
declinatur t*ame*n [S β γ δ] hic cet*us*. [*om.* S] ceti. 7 omne*m* anima*m*

uiuentem atque motabilem, quam produxerant aque.
uiue*n*tem atq*ue* motabile*m* qu*a*m p*ro*duxerunt [γ] aque.

Motabiles autem dicuntur anime piscium et auium respectu hominis.
Motabiles au*tem* d*icuntur* a*nim*e pisciu*m*. ⁊ auiu*m*: respectu anime [S β γ δ] hominis.

Ille enim mouentur de esse ad non esse, ista non, quia perpetua est,
Ille. *enim* mouent*ur* de e*ss*e ad n*on* e*ss*e. Illa: [Pa T] n*on* q*uia* p*er*petua e*st*.

uel quia forsan animas non habent,
Vel q*uia* forsan animas non h*abe*nt:

sed ipsum animal uocauerit animam, id est uiuens.
[*om.* S Tr γ δ] Ip*su*m animal anima*m* uocauit. [S Pa γ; ↩ Cl only] i*d est* uiuens-

With the exception of the inversion "animal animam uocauit," all the variants are attested in Sylwan's early exemplars and this is generally the case throughout the Claudius HS-excerpts: that is, the text shows basically the integral revised text as further revised immediately after the Comestor's death. Furthermore, the translations of the English notes are frequently so literal that we can detect the exact textual traditions in the Latin exemplar as indicated in Sylwan's textual notes, converging on the integral revised text but not inconsistent with the features of the Latin extracts:

6a . . . twa wintra. ⁊ þri wíntra [et *add.* S Tr]

10 . . . anlǽnges ðære sǽ . . . [longo maris et terre tractu: Sylwan; PL has "longo terræ et maris tractu," a late δ reading (also S)]

14 [an Additio in S and β γ δ groups]

26 . . . ywilcon caym. ⁊ calmana is wyf [calmana *add.* β]

44 . . . in þan lánde óf syria . . . [*add.* Cl, from *marg.?*; syrica *add.* Tr]

45 . . . swyþe gód enoch . . . [scilicet enoch *add.* Tr]

51c . . . gewemðe hí. wyð cáines dohtra . . . [concupierunt β γ δ; cupierunt Sylwan]

52 [an Additio in β γ δ]

77 (gloss:) þé is sarai [a gloss in S β γ T]

However, the exemplar seems to reflect a yet-later layer of revisions, as shown by No. 122, an *additio* (on "aurisia," a form of blindness), printed in Navarro's edition (PL 198.1100D), but not noticed in Sylwan's apparatus, i.e. it must have been added later: it is not in the dated Elstow manuscript of 1191/92 nor in the late twelfth-century BL Royal 8.C.ix, but it is in the dated St Albans copy of 1214, BL Royal 4. D vii (f. 21r) and in the slightly earlier Cambridge, Corpus Christi College 29 (f. 10r).[45] We must conclude that the exemplar from which Claudius was copied was a "normal" schoolroom copy of *Historia Scholastica*, of the post-1180 revised type, with a few late features that point towards the end of the century.

From the 1180s to the first decade of the thirteenth century the layout and contents of the *Historia Scholastica* were rapidly evolving. Probably from the beginning some copies were laid out in double columns, with clear chapter markings and titles, and with a clear list of capitula. By the 1190s such a layout, together with a markedly square-pointed "gothic" script, was becoming the norm. Some earlier copies, up to the turn of the century, have a more "monastic" layout, written in long lines and in the proto-gothic script prevalent in the twelfth century.[46] Gradually and unevenly, copies were also acquiring the set of more-or-less standard notes that are included in Patrologia Latina as "additiones." Sylwan points out that there is no homogeneity as regards the *additiones* in the various manuscripts, but concludes that twenty-five of the *additiones* were in the original version of the Comestor.[47] Other *additiones* probably stem from the later state of the text or from the definitive revision, and these are marked in Sylwan's notes *more additionis*. In the course of the tradition, *additiones* tended to be touched up or augmented. Early copies sometimes lack these *additiones* altogether, and they differ in text and number from copy to copy. The Claudius annotator certainly used a copy that contained them, or many of them, because he copies a number of them, including several translated into English.[48] The *additiones* most likely evolved out of early indexical and explanatory marginal notes in particular copies; for example, in Royal 8 C. ix, which does not show integral *additiones*, what

[45] Corpus uses the form 'aurisia' like Claudius, against Sylwan's "aorisia" and Navarro's "acrisia"; CCCC 29 has several striking idiosyncratic textual coincidences with Claudius.

[46] Royal 8. C. ix (Reading Abbey, s. xii/xiii) is definitely a monastic copy as shown not only by its *ex libris*, but also by its style of layout, writing, decoration, and contents, which besides the *Historia* includes added extracts from Origen's homilies on Numbers, Jerome's *Adversus Iovinianum*, *Sententie de sancto Augustino*, Walter Map, Odo of Cluny, an abbreviated psalter, and grammatical, herbal, and astronomical notes. The handwriting is very similar in style and date to those of the Claudius annotations. Another remarkable manuscript is British Library Stowe 4, which, though showing abbreviations current at the turn of the century, is written in a deliberately archaizing style, in long lines and a passable "antique" style of anglo-caroline script with no "additiones" and few, probably added, notes. A more modern type of script begins on f. 269r.

[47] Sylwan, ed., lxxvi–vii.

[48] The English are no. 25b = HS 1076D, Add. 1; no. 41 = 1080B, Add. 1; no. 52 = 1084C, Add. 1; no. 62 = 1086D, Add. 1.

is printed in Migne as "Additio 1" to Chapter 33 of "Genesis" is written in the margin of f. 28r against the beginning of Chapter 32 ('Uxor noe puarphuta | Ux`or´ sem; parsia | uxor cha*m*. cetafluia | vxor iaphet; fliua'). In some manuscripts which do have the *additiones*, they remain marginal, often surrounded with boxes or lines, but in later manuscripts they are usually written in sidebars within the text, in the same script and size as the main text and often with elaborate decorative flourishes. Even the mature (1214) and quite elaborate Royal 4 D. vii has *additiones* treated some as marginal glosses and some integrated into text and decoration. In any case, they fairly early became separated from glosses, which continued to accumulate as marginalia, and *additiones* tended to be set apart by borders, or written as "sidebars" as part of the received text. By the end of the twelfth century most complete manuscripts (at least almost all that have survived) have assumed a standard form: medium-format, double-columned, chapters formally laid out and well marked and entitled, stable *additiones*, and, after a short time, an increasingly elaborate, somewhat standardized apparatus of glosses, distinguished by script and layout from *additiones*; these were drawn from the expected ecclesiastical authorities, but also citied more modern sources, as well as "Plato," "Horace," and so on.

The rest of this chapter will be a detailed examination of how the Claudius annotator has utilized this material to deal with one section of the Genesis text: the descendants of Adam. This section is chosen because it shows the most elaborate and intensive interaction of four elements: the original Old English text (*Hept.*), Latin extracts from the *Historia*, English notes based on it, and the picture cycle. We will look both at how this material is treated in the *Historia* and how, faced with the text, the same material is annotated in Claudius, using the *Historia* and other materials. The Claudius annotator seems to be very well acquainted with the nature and contents of the source-text and cites, rearranges, and appropriates it resourcefully and intelligently.

In Claudius, *Historia* extracts are generally placed so that they correlate in topic with what is in the Old English text and/or pictures of the same opening, usually as near to the relevant materials as possible, and often accompanied with a *signe de renvoi*.[49] The relevance of the extract is most often only formal, in the manner of "historical" commentary of the time, as noted already, so that, e.g., the size and distance of sun and moon is noted on the page containing the text of their creation (f. 3r, no. 2) or the grammatical gender of whales is explained near the picture of a large, newly-created fish (f. 3v, no. 4). But this is in harmony with the whole procedure of the *Historia*, which tends to throw miscellaneous material together under topics. When he has larger spaces available, the annotator will

[49] All the citations from the *Historia* which occur in Claudius, both in Latin and English, have been presented in their manuscript order in the "evidence" (Chapter 2) with a minimum of essential comment.

accumulate a number of nominally related extracts, as on f. 16v, where within the rainbow arc are collected from disparate places, not all from the *Historia* either, various comments about Noe's sons. At times the annotator places an extract so that it appears to continue the original Old English discourse (e.g., f. 5v, nos. 9d and 9e). Some serve to fill in narrative gaps in the Old English version, for example, when the Old English skips in the narrative of Rebecca from Genesis 24:30 to 24:61, an extract is chosen that serves to fill in the story (f. 39v, no. 149). There are hardly any places where a moment of thought will not suggest why an extract was chosen and placed as it was, and indeed, that moment of thought may be what the annotator was aiming to provoke.

Here from the *Historia* (in the Patrologia Latina edition) is the entire Chapter 30 of the "Genesis" section ("Epilogum interserit").[50] Passages that have been excerpted for use in Claudius are underlined; biblical quotations are in italics (on the right Claudius folios and note numbers are given; English note numbers are in italics):

Cap. XXX *Epilogum interserit. Hic est liber generationis Adæ* (Gen. V).
Repetit de generatione Adæ, ut integrum ordinem genealogiarum
prosequatur. Unde quidam incipiunt ab Adam primam ætatem; alii a cf. 8r(22),
Seth, quibus assentit Methodius, et ideo hoc dicit, quia de Abel nullus ?10r(*36b*)
natus est, et generatio Cain tota periit in diluvio. *Vixit Adam centum* 10r(*36a*)
triginta annis, et genuit Seth ad imaginem, et similitudinem suam, ipse
ad imaginem Dei, reliqui ad imaginem ejus, Adæ; quod fere idem est.
Vel potius mortalis, mortales. Unde: *Qualis terrenus, tales et terreni* (I
Cor. [X]V). Forte Moyses centum annos luctus Adæ prætermisit, quia 8r(22), bis
ut diximus, Septuaginta et Methodius, et Josephus ducentum triginta 10r(37),
annorum eum fuisse scribunt, cum genuit Seth. Iste genuit Enos, qui 10r(*38*), 8r(22)
Cainam, qui Malaheel, qui Jaret, qui Henoch, qui Mathusalem, qui
Lamech, qui Noe. Sicut ergo in generatione Cain, septimus, scilicet 11v(*45*)
Lamech, fuit pessimus, ita in generatione Seth, septimus, scilicet Henoch, fuit optimus. Et transtulit illum Deus in paradisum voluptatis ad tempus, ut in fine temporum, cum Elia convertat corda patrum in filios (Malach. IV). Judæi tamen causam hujus translationis attribuunt potius septenario, quam sanctitati ejus, quia plures leguntur sanctiores eo, quorum nullus translatus est. In tantum enim aiunt, Deum omnia sub septenario disposuisse, quod etiam dicunt eum septem cœlos creasse, et cuique nomen suum datum, et septem terras, quas David fundamenta montium vocat (Psal. XVII). De annis Mathusalem diversæ sunt opiniones. Secundum computationem LXX, vixit annos quatuordecim post diluvium, sed non legitur fuisse in arca, nec translatus ut
Henoch. Quidam dicunt quod mortuus fuerit ante diluvium sex annis. 11v(*46*)
Hieronymus asserit, quod eodem anno, in quo fuit diluvium, mortuus est, quod etiam diligens computatio annorum ejus, secundum Gen-

[50] This is ch. 31 in Sylwan's edition.

esim, manifestat. Tamen omnes in numero annorum vitæ ejus conveniunt, quia vixit annis nonagentis sexaginta novem. Porro Noe fuit decimus ab Adam, in quo prima ætas terminata est; ita quod et ipse fuerit in ea. Hujus ætatis annos Septuaginta ponunt duo millia ducenta quadraginta quatuor; alii ducenta sexaginta quatuor. Hieronymus 12v(51a) non plene duo millia. Methodius duo millia. Ipse tamen per chiliades sæcula disponit, nec apponit annos si supersint, et ideo nihil certum de numero annorum tradidit.
Additio 1. Henoch quasdam litteras invenit, et quosdam libros scripsit 11r(43) sub quo Adam intelligitur mortuus. (PL 198.1080B-1081A)

"This is the book of the generation of Adam" (Gen. 5:1). It retraces from the generation of Adam so that it may follow the entire sequence of the genealogy in order. Thus some begin the first age from Adam and others from Seth, to which Methodius gives his assent and accordingly says that from Abel nobody was born and the entire lineage of Cain perished in the Flood. "Adam lived 130 years and begot Seth in his image and likeness" (Gen. 5:3), he, Adam, in the image of God and the rest in his, Adam's; which is almost the same. Or rather, from the mortal comes the mortal. For, "What is earthly is also of the earth" (1 Cor. 15:47). Perhaps Moses neglected to mention a period of 100 years of mourning by Adam, because, as we have said, the Septuagint, Methodius, and Josephus write that [Adam] was 230 years old when he begot Seth. Seth begot Enos, who begot Cainan, who begot Malaleel, who begot Jared, who begot Enoch, who begot Mathusala, who begot Lamech, who begot Noe. As therefore in the generation of Cain, the seventh, namely Lamech, was the worst, so in the generation of Seth, the seventh, namely Enoch, was the best. And God translated him into the Paradise of Pleasure for a period of time, so that at the end of time, with Elias he will convert the hearts of the fathers to the sons (Malachai 4:6). The Jews however would rather attribute his translation to his being the seventh, than to his holiness, because one reads of many who are more holy than him, none of whom were translated. And indeed they say that God arranged everything in sevens, so that they even say he created seven heavens and gave each of them its own name, and seven earths, which David called the foundations of the mountains (Ps. 17:8). There are diverse opinions about the years of Mathusala. According to the computation of the Septuagint, he lived for fourteen years beyond the Flood but it is not read that he was in the ark, nor was he translated like Enoch. Some say that he was dead six years before the flood. Jerome asserts that he died in the same year as the Flood, which a careful computing of his years according to Genesis will show. Nevertheless all sources agree on the number of years in his life, that he lived for 969 years. Then Noe was the tenth from Adam in whom the First Age is terminated and so he was within it. Of this Age the Septuagint posits 2244 years; others say 2264, Jerome not quite 2000, Methodius 2000. The latter however arranges the world into 'chiliads,' but does not assign years if they go over the limit (of 1000 years) and therefore he transmitted nothing certain about the number of years carried down by tradition.

Addition 1: Enoch discovered certain letters and wrote certain books, during whose lifetime Adam is understood to have died.

The *Historia* shows a fairly seamless interweaving of sources, story, and comment. In contrast, the Claudius annotator has selected from this material and dispersed it over several pages, freely combining and separating comments, carefully scanning the source text. He is interested in bringing out the chronological material and uses less of the narrative innovations. At any rate, we see the annotator appropriating a particular passage leaving traces of selection, rearrangement, and conflation. When all is done the Claudius annotator has used up all the biblical material of the chapter (considering that some of the material is covered by the main Old English text), excepting the moralizing comment from Paul and the Jewish philosophy about septenaries.

The Comestor's coherence is brought out by considering its building blocks. That the *First age begins with Adam* was a truism since Augustine, with the most popular source of the information being Chapter 66 of Bede's *De temporum ratione.*[51] This is set against the divergent opinion of the frequently cited Methodius, that the *First age begins with Seth* because the original sons of Adam left no lines beyond the Flood.[52] *Adam the image of God, his posterity the image of Adam.* Hrabanus similarly has, "Note how Adam was made to the image and similitude of God, however men were made to the similitude of Adam."[53] Perhaps the Comestor reflects a more elaborate comment such as Bede's, "When, sinning, Adam corrupted this beautiful newness of the divine image in himself, he begot out of himself a corrupt lineage of humankind."[54] But the thrust of Bede's comment is that this corruption gives way to the renewal by the second Adam. The *Historia*'s information seems more specific; *Perkḳî Rabbi Eliezar* 2, which spawned generations of medieval Jewish comment, says "Adam begot [Seth] in his likeness and image, different from Cain, who had not been in his likeness and image. Thus Seth became, in a genuine sense, the father of the human race, especially the father of the pious, while the depraved and godless are descended from

---

[51] Cf. Bede, *The Reckoning of Time*, trans. Faith Wallis (Liverpool, 1999), 356–59.

[52] Methodius says only: "CC^{mo} autem et XXX^{mo} anno primi miliari, quod est primum seculum, natus est Sedh [*sic*] . . . ." (ed. Sackur, 61). Honorius Augustodunensis, *De imagine mundi* (PL 172.165D) says that Cain and his entire lineage perished in the Flood.

[53] "Nota quia Adam ad imaginem et similitudinem Dei factus est, homines autem ad similitudinem Adæ facti sunt" (Hrabanus, *Comm. in Gen.*, PL 107.510A). Sylwan, 57, note, notes the *Glossa Ordinaria*, which has "Ada*m* ad si*mi*litudin*em* dei f*act*us est, alii ad si*mi*litudine*m* adę" (*Biblia Latina cum Glossa Ordinaria*, repr. of Adolph Rusch, Strassburg, 1480/81, ed. K. Froelich and M. T. Gibson [Turnhout, 1992], 33). Methodius has ". . . natus est Sedh vir gigans in similitudinem Adae" (ed. Sackur, 61). This leads him to the bizarre statement that the giants who provoked God were these progeny of the "giant" Seth (62).

[54] "Qui quoniam pulcherrimam hanc nouitatem in se diuinae imaginis peccando corrupit, corruptamque ex se prosapiam generis humani procreavit. . . ." (*In Genesim* 767, CCSL 113A, 26).

Cain."[55] The thrust of the Christian comment, as exemplified by Bede, is continued by the Comestor's citing the key text on this point, 1 Corinthians 15:47, "The first man *was of the earth, earthly*, the second man, from heaven, heavenly," the thematics being further heightened if verse 49 is recalled, as it would be by a monastic reader: "Therefore, as we have borne the image of the earthly, let us bear also the image of the heavenly." The insertion of *one hundred years of mourning by Adam for Abel* before the begetting of Seth not mentioned by Moses (i.e. as the writer of Genesis) is from Methodius,[56] but the more immediate source, as Sylwan suggests, may be the more exactly corresponding words of Fretellus, *Descriptio de locis sanctis*[57] ("Vallis Lacrymarum dicta eo quod centum annis in ea luxit Adam filium suum Abel. In qua et postea monitus ab angelo cognovit Evam uxorem suam, ex qua genuit filium suum Seth. . . .");[58] in any case it is a narrative move with a computational function, to reconcile the LXX's 230 years and the Vulgate's 130 before the begetting of Seth (Gen. 5:3). The Septuagint tradition is specifically invoked by the comment that *Adam* was *230 years old when he begot Seth*, found in Methodius, as cited above, and Josephus: after the death of Abel and flight of Cain "[Adam] had an urgent desire of begetting in his 230th year";[59] "Later to Adam, when he was 230 years old, his son Seth was born. . . ."[60]

The two stories that break the pattern are linked in the comment that *Lamech, the seventh, was worst of the Cainites, Enoch, the seventh, best of the Sethites*; Ginzberg cites *Bereschit Rabbah* (23.2), which sees the culmination of Cainite evil in Lamech, as a killer and bigamist, but Ginzberg also points out that the preponderance of Jewish tradition sees Lamech as a prophet.[61] The source of the remark on Enoch is doubtless also Jewish in origin but survived mainly in the Christian tradition, as in Jude 14, "Now of these Enoch also the seventh from Adam, prophesied. . .," following 1 Enoch (93.3): "I [Enoch] was born the seventh during the first week, during which time judgment and righteousness

[55] Ginzberg, *Legends of the Jews*, trans. Szold (1909–1938), 1:121, 5:149.

[56] "Anno autem triginsimo et centisimo vitae Adae occidit Cain fratrem suum Abel et fecerunt planctum super eum Adam quoque et Eva annis C[a]" (ed. Sackur, 60–61).

[57] Sylwan, *Scol. Hist.*, 58; Rorgo Fretellus of Nazareth, chancellor of Galilee and geographer (d. ca. 1154).

[58] P. C. Boeren, ed., *Rorgo Fretellus de Nazareth et sa description de la terre sainte: Histoire et edition du texte*, Koninklijke nederlandse Akadmie van Wetenschapen, afdeling Letterkunde, nieuwe Reeks 105 (Amsterdam, 1980), 9 (= PL 155.1039B): "The Vale of Tears it is called because in it for a hundred years Adam mourned his son Abel, afterwards in it an angel instructed him to know his wife Eve, from whom his son Seth was born. . . ."

[59] "et vehementer eum generationis amor habebat agentem annos triginta et ducentos. . . ." (LJ ed. Blatt, 132.4).

[60] "Adae siquidem, cum esset triginta et ducentorum annorum, Seth filius natus est. . ." (LJ ed. Blatt, 134.1).

[61] Ginzberg, *Legends of the Jews* (1909–1938), 1:117, 5:145.

continued to endure. After me there shall arise in the second week great and deceitful things. . . ."[62] *Enoch was translated to the Paradise of Pleasure* derives from Malachai.[63] This "translation" of Enoch is a Christian augmentation, while contemporary *Jews attribute Enoch's translation to the septenary*, rather than to his holiness. Ginzberg points out that the legend of the translation of Enoch, while present in intertestamental sources, was favored by Christians, not Jews, and that there is in fact no mention of Enoch in the Tannaim or Talmud.[64] Likewise, *Jews say God arranged everything in sevens, seven heavens, seven earths.* The septenary is an all-pervasive tendency in intertestamental and rabbinic thought; ascent through seven heavens is associated with Enoch in the Slavonic Book of Enoch.[65] *The seven earths are the foundations of the mountains.* "The one earth rises above the other, from the first to the seventh, and over the earth the heavens are vaulted, from the first to the seventh, the last of them attached to the arm of God"[66]— an idea getting support from the traditional Jewish understanding of Psalm 17:8.[67]

Mathusala lived fourteen years beyond the Flood but was not in the ark or translated like Enoch. This point clashes with Jerome, scrutinizing the calculation of the years of Mathusala necessitated by the Septuagint: "When he is said above [in the LXX] to have lived 969 years, there is no question that he lived fourteen

---

62 Ed. James H. Charlesworth, *The Old Testament Pseudepigrapha*, 2 vols. (Garden City, NY, 1983–1985), 1:74.

63 Malachias 4:5–6: "Behold I will send you Elijah the prophet, before the coming of the great and dreadful day of the Lord. And he shall turn the heart of the fathers to the children and the heart of the children to the fathers. . ." The *locus classicus* in medieval tradition is Adso, *De ortu et tempore Antichristi* (ed. Sackur, *Sibyllinische Texte und Forschungen*, 111–12).

64 Ginzberg, *Legends of the Jews* (1909–1938), 5:156–57. For a summary of the Christian tradition, see A. N. Doane, *Genesis A: A New Edition* (Madison, 1978), 255. The Comestor is rather isolated in his statement that Enoch was translated to the Paradise of Pleasure. Most commentators have him translated to heaven, or ambiguously allegorize the event.

65 Ginzberg, *Legends of the Jews* (1909–1938), 1:131–36, 5:158.

66 Midrash ha-Gadol on Genesis 1:16–17, Ginzberg, *Legends* (1909–1938), 1:12. The same note mentions various sources that say the earth rests on pillars, which rest on water, which rests on mountains, which rest on the winds, which rest on storms, which rest on God's arm; the number of pillars varies between seven, twelve, and one; in the Clementine writings, the seven pillars are identified with Adam, Enoch, Noah, Abraham, Isaac, Jacob, and Moses.

67 "Commota est, et contremuit terra; fundamenta montium conturbata sunt." See Mitchell Dahood, *The Anchor Bible: Psalms I, 1–50* (Garden City, NY, 1965), 106. The patristic interpretation (Augustine, Cassiodorus, etc.) of the phrase in Ps. 17:8 is "hope of the proud." There seems to be no connection in Christian tradition with the "seven earths."

years after the Flood, and how could that be true when there are only eight souls saved in the ark?"[68] *Some*, that is Augustine, *say he was dead six years before the Flood*; this is taken directly from Augustine's *Quaestiones in genesim*, tackling the same problem less rigorously than Jerome: "Some fewer, but truer, manuscripts of the Septuagint report that Mathusala died six years before the flood."[69] But, more authoritatively, *Jerome says he died in the same year as the Flood*, his conclusion in the same passage just cited: "And so it was that in the 969th year of his life Mathusala died, at which year the Flood began."[70] The chapter returns to the "First Age" theme with which it began: *Noah was tenth and within the First Age*; a truism that could be gleaned from Augustine, Bede, or anywhere. The numbers assigned to various authorities by the Comestor for the first age are somewhat eccentric, "Septuagint" 2244, "others" 2264,[71] Jerome "not quite 2000." The first number should be "2242," which stems from Eusebius' erroneous calculation, as repeated by Isidore and Bede.[72] The Greek Josephus ("alii"?) gives the correct total for the Septuagint, 2262, while the Latin Josephus gives 2656,[73] obviously a conflation by the translator of the Septuagint number and that of the Hebrew/Vulgate, 1656. The latter is Jerome's number. Methodius placed the Flood at the end of the second millennium.[74] *Methodius arranged the world into "chiliads,"* the Comestor using the terms *chiliad* and *miliarius* interchangeably. The thousand-year period was a popular way of reckoning the ages of the world, but was discouraged by serious chronographers, as the Comestor suggests, because its precision (six ages of a thousand years each) aggravated the problem of millenarianism.[75]

---

68 "Cum autem supra DCCCCLXVIIII annis uixisse sit dictus, nulli dubium est XIIII eum annos uixisse post diluuium, et quo modo uerum est quod octo tantum animae in arca saluae factae sunt?" *Hebr. Quaest. in Gen.* 11.5 (PL 23:947A). Also *Glos. ord.* (ed. Froelich and Gibson, 34–35).

69 "Septuaginta interpretatione Mathusalam in codicibus paucioribus sed ueracioribus sex annos ante diluuium reperitur fuisse defunctus": (PL 34:549).

70 "atque ita fit, ut DCCCCLXIX anno uitae suae Mathusala mortuus sit, eo anno quo coepit esse diluuium": Jerome, *Heb. Quaest in Gen.* (PL 24:947).

71 But this phrase in Navarro/Migne is lacking in Sylwan's text and apparatus and in all the manuscripts seen, as well as Claudius (ed. no. 51a) and is probably a late correction of the preceding erroneous number.

72 Bede, *Reckoning of Time*, trans. Wallis, 358.

73 "duo milia sexcenti quinquaginta sex" (Blatt, ed., 133:22). The Greek Josephus is cited from H. St. J. Thackeray, ed. and trans., *Josephus*, Loeb Classical Library (London and New York, 1930), 4:39, which page has a chart showing the text and the relevant calculations.

74 Ed. Sackur, 63.

75 See Bede, *The Reckoning of Time*, trans. Wallis, 353–61, and Richard Landes, "Lest the Millennium Be Fulfilled: Apocalyptic Expectations and the Pattern of Western Chronography 100–800 CE," in *The Use and Abuse of Eschatology in the Middle Ages*,

And therefore he transmitted nothing certain about the number of years carried down by tradition.

Addition: *Enoch invented letters and wrote certain books. . .* Enoch when translated becomes the scribe of heaven. In Sefer Noah (150–60), Adam had a book of divine secrets which was hidden upon his death and which Enoch found, memorized, and hid again.[76] The conduit for this idea is the near-contemporary Honorius Augustodunensis (d. c. 1151), whose wording the Comestor follows.[77]

This is the Comestor's treatment of the generations from Adam to Seth to Noah. It illustrates his style of commentary, the weaving of many comments into a single discourse forming a pattern analogous to the narrative movement of the biblical text. In Claudius, the openings ff. 10v-11r and 11v-12r contain the original Old English text corresponding to Genesis 5:5–31, the Sethite lineage from Adam to Noe, most of the space being occupied by pictures.[78] On each page, between the picture frames, and sometimes above or below, are written between three and five lines of Old English text corresponding both to the Vulgate of Chapter 5 and to the pictures. For example, on f. 10v there are three picture spaces, on f. 11r and f. 11v two somewhat larger picture spaces, and on f. 12r three, matching in size those on f. 10v. All these spaces are divided vertically into two panels. Alternating with the picture spaces are brief segments of the original Old English text. The pictures follow a formula that is a witty visual riposte to the biblical formula "Vixit autem X *xxx* annis et genuit Y, et genuit filios et filias, et facti sunt omnes dies X *xxx* anni et mortuus est." On the left of each frame is a picture of the enthroned patriarch with his wives to his right and son(s) to his left; on the right of each frame is a scene of his burial. The variants to this pattern reflect the small amount of variation in the text: when the series gets to Enoch, on f. 11v, the right picture is not of his burial (since "ambulauitque cum Deo et non apparuit, qua tulit eum Deus" [Gen. 5:24]) but of his assumption into a blue watery firmament via a ladder, God with cross-nimbus and a book taking him up by the left hand.[79] This picture seems to have the indexical function of orienting

ed. Werner Verbeke et al., Mediaevalia Lovaniensia Series I/Studia XV (Leuven, 1988), 137–209.

[76] Ginzberg, *Legends* (1909–1938), on Enoch the heavenly scribe, 1:129, on Adam's hidden book, 1:156, 5:177. Bede (*De temporum ratione* 66, A.M. 622) says that Enoch wrote certain things of a divine nature, as Jude attests, but also cites with approval Augustine's rejection of the Enoch books.

[77] *De imagine mundi* (PL 172.165C): "Hic [Enoch] litteras reperit et quosdam libros conscripsit. Hujus tempore mortuus est Adam." ("At this time [Enoch] discovered letters and wrote certain books. In his time Adam died."); cf. Sylwan, *Scol. Hist.*, 58.

[78] Recently these genealogical pages have been discussed in detail from a different and complementary angle by Withers in *Frontiers*, 195–221.

[79] The image is, perhaps coincidentally, similar to that of Jacob's ladder on f. 43v; iconographically, there is greater similarity with the ladder that carries angels between Paradise and Heaven in Bodleian MS Junius 11, p. 9.

the user to a place in the text. Facing it is the other variant picture, the middle frame on f. 12r, reflecting a textual variation. Unlike the throne/burial frames this is a single scene, though the patriarch-figure divides the frame vertically. It shows an upright figure in patriarch-guise, doubtless Lamech, sitting between a woman to his right and a young man to his left. They appear to be sitting on a striped sofa, but this is meant to represent a plowed field with its furrows, the middle figure signifying Lamech and the right his son Noe, as the comforter "ab operibus et laboribus manuum nostrarum in terra" (Gen. 5:29).

The twelfth-century annotator thus on these openings found a tidy repeating pattern of corresponding text and pictures. What did he do? For one thing, within the frames each patriarchal corpse has been correctly labeled: (f. 10b) 'adam obiit,' 'seth obiit,' 'enos obiit,' (f. 11r) 'caynan obiit,' 'malaleel obiit,' (f. 11v) 'Jared,' 'Enoch,' (f. 12r) 'mathusalem,' 'ob⟨iit⟩ lamech'.[80] The relevant dates "Anno Mundi" from Bede's Chronicle have been supplied in a large version of the "J" script, so that on ff. 11v-12r we see in the margins the dates from Creation pertaining to Enoch (687), to Mathusala (874), to Lamech (1056).[81] Moreover, these openings have attracted more than the usual share of late notes in English, in the proto-gothic script in its insular guise. The Latin notes on these pages, judging by the way they are fitted into available spaces, appear written after the English annotations have been entered.

The Comestor's treatment of Genesis 5 acknowledges the series of generations but downplays the repetitive patterns and, while formally functioning as commentary on the words of Genesis 5, imposes over it a rich pattern of variation and eventfulness emerging out of a variety of voices that blend into a single discourse and narrative line, even as long-standing ecclesiological "literal" explanations are being set against more novel or "hebraic" sources. On the other hand, the original designers of Claudius, by placement of text and pictures, highlighted the repetitive patterns in Genesis. Faced with materials pulling in such different directions, the annotator disperses the surface of the *Historia*'s text over the receiving pages so as as to disturb, complicate, and enrich both; he does not maintain the interweaving of the *Historia*'s continuous discourse, but by piecemeal selection and rearrangement creates a new patterning out of what must have been perceived as an exploitable series of gloss-worthy moments. Of the two ground-breaking characteristics of the commentary-source, the annotator retains the Comestor's historicism, resisting any monastic top-heavy allegorical

[80] The variant Lamech picture is not labeled; it falls, exceptionally, between two text-segments on f. 12r.

[81] Every A.M. date, Genesis through Joshua, given by Bede (except a couple relating to secular events) has been uniformly entered throughout Claudius, in the appropriate place in the margin. See the detailed discussion of this in the Bede section, ch. 6, 330–33.

"building,"[82] but obliterates the smoothly constructed historical narrative. The annotator brings the obsolete Anglo-Saxon book into the play of contemporary exegetical fashion, but the selective rearrangement of it to illuminate textual details, the display of information in different registers and fields, is backward-looking and effectively refashions the modern text into a resemblance of earlier monastic commentaries, as is shown by a detailed analysis of the annotator's doings on these two openings, ff. 10v–11r, 11v–12r.

Folio 10v has three pictures and the Old English version of Genesis 5:5–11; it has been annotated in two distinct scripts, an insular one with a rather delicate ductus and a thicker and slightly larger Norman one; in the top-right picture panel, showing Adam's death, an English note of two lines is in the insular script, and in darker ink a larger and thicker ductus writes in Latin as if a continuation of the English (nos. 41–42a). The latter script also supplies the picture titles to the burials in the three frames, an intervention in the Old English text, and numerals in the outer margin.[83] The textual intervention is at Genesis 5:6 (line 3 of the Old English), supplying from the Vulgate in a space left blank[84] the age of Seth when he begot Enos, 'hund wintre. 7 v.'[85] The English note, written in the space showing Adam's burial, is an exact translation of Additio 1 of Chapter 29 ("De Seth, et ejus generatione"), and may have been found in his copy as a marginal note towards the end of Chapter 29[86] or between 29 and 30 ("Epilogum interserit," i.e. the generations from Adam to Noe):

> **41.** Me reð on bóce. *þæt* adam hæfede .xxx. súnes 7 swa fela dohtra. bútan cayn. 7 abel.
>
> It is read in a book that Adam had thirty sons and just as many daughters, less Cain and Abel.
>
> Legitur Adam triginta habuisse filios, et totidem filias præter Cain et Abel. (HS 1080B Add. 1)

The translation serves equally well for the English and the Latin. This note shows not merely that the annotator was translating from the *Historia Scholastica* but also that he was using a copy that had the *Additiones* in at least their embryonic, marginal form, that is, a copy that was far enough along in the tradition to have

---

[82] Smalley, *Study of the Bible*, 196.

[83] 'c.v.', 'xc.', refer to the numbers in the text at the corresponding place. '.ccc.xxv.' is the A.M. year of Enos's begetting of Cainan (Bede, *De temporum ratione* 66, A.M. 325).

[84] Not on an erasure according to Crawford, 96.

[85] C.U.L. Ii.1.33 and other manuscripts have "Seth leofode fif 7 hundteontig geara," showing that the annotator did not consult another copy of the Old English text for his wording.

[86] As is the case with Royal 4. D. vii, f. 16a.

acquired that extra feature. The subsequent Latin note in "J" script is fitted exactly into the space after the English note, showing it was written second, as if in a coordinated campaign, or at a later time. It is derived from Isidore, *De ortu et obitum patrum* and is an exact response to the textual and pictorial context:

> 42a. Et sepult*usque est* in cariatharbe. que distat ab ier*usal*em .xxii. milibus ad australe*m* plagam.[87]
>
> And [Adam] was buried in Cariath Arbe, which is twenty-two miles south of Jerusalem.

The same pattern continues on the facing page (f. 11r). The burial scenes and A.M. numbers in the margin, as well as the marginal text numbers, are in the "J" script. In this script, again, are added from the Vulgate the numbers left blank in the Old English version on the fourth original line from the bottom (Gen. 5:18): '**Iared gestrynde enoch ða hé wæs** húnd wíntre. twa and syxtig.'[88] More interestingly, in the insular hand are five lines at the bottom of the page, consisting of two notes, one in English and one in Latin. The first, in Latin and using insular *r*, is the "Additio" to chapter 30 (no. 43):

> 43. Enoch quasdam literas i*n*uenit. quosda*m* lib*r*os sc*r*ipsit. sub q*u*o adam credis mortuus.[89]
>
> Enoch discovered certain letters and wrote certain books. In his time Adam is believed to have died.

This note would have been found on the same or the adjoining page of his *Historia* exemplar as the source of the English note (no. 41) on f. 10v, but in this instance the annotator for some reason did not translate it into English. But in the next line there is an English note (no. 44), in the same script and ink, about Seth's sons from Chapter 28 ("De generationibus Cain"):

> **44.** Sethes súnes yhérden adames wytegunge be twám dómon, ⁊ þa yfu[n]donne creftes ne forwurþon, wríten hí on twám colúmban, þæt bið twéan pilíres,

[87] Isidore: "Sepultus est autem in loco Arbee, qui locus nomen a numero sumpsit, hoc est quatuor [i.e., cariatharbe] nam tres patriarchae ibidem sunt sepulti, et hic quartus Adam. Distat autem locus iste non procul ab Hebron. . . . Est autem civitas sortis Judae in sacerdotibus separata distans ad australem plagam millibus xxii ab Hierusalem" (PL 83.131B).

[88] No. 42c. Crawford does not note this intervention. This verse is worded differently in CUL Ii.1.33: "Iaræd leofode hundteonti geare ⁊ twa ⁊ sixti ⁊ gestrinde Enoh."

[89] PL has "sub quo Adam intelligitur mortuus" ("in his time Adam is believed to have died"); Sylwan and all the seen manuscripts read "creditur"; Claudius is smudged at this place but appears to have 'credis' over an erasure.

Figure 30a: (fol. 10v)

Figure 30b: (fol. 11r)

Figure 31a: (fol. 11v)

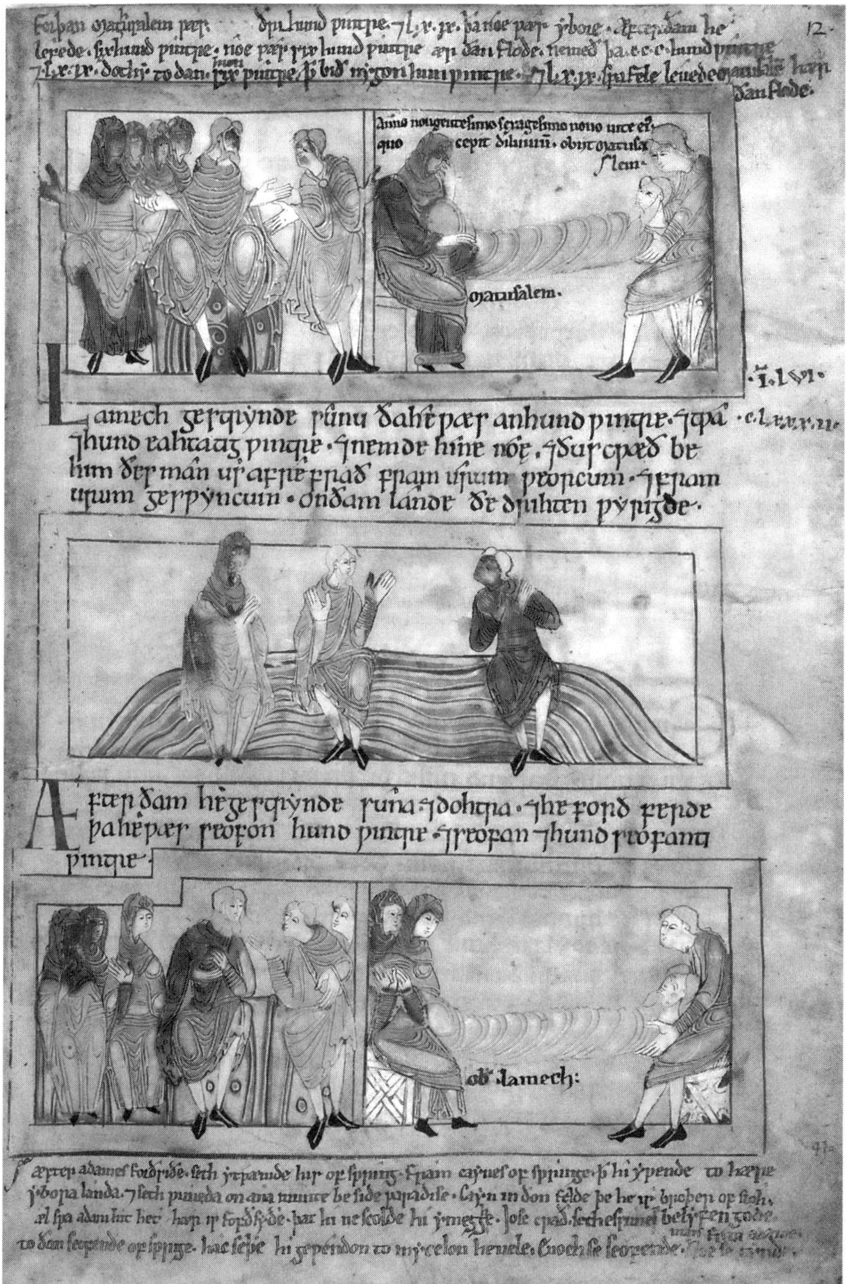

Figure 31b: (fol. 12r)

ín h[w]æder ǽl in þan lánde óf syria. Josephus cw̄æð áne of márbra, oðra of ysódene tíhele. þa áne se flod ne mihte forwæhshe, þa ódra féer ne formélta.

Seth's sons heard Adam's prophecies about two judgments, and lest the invented arts should perish, wrote them on two columns, that is on two pillars, everything on both, in the land of Syria. Josephus said one of them was of marble, the other of fired tile. The one the flood could not dissolve, the other fire could not destroy.

This translation serves for most of the Latin as well:

Et quia audierat Adam prophetasse de duobus judiciis, ne periret ars inventa, scripsit eam in duabus columnis, in qualibet totam, ut dicit Josephus, una marmorea, altera latericia, quarum altera non diluetur diluvio, altera non solveretur incendio. Marmoream dicit Josephus adhuc esset in terra Syriaca. (HS 1079A/B)

The Old English shows an awkward literalness (e.g., "in hwæder æl" = "in qualibet totam") and other features already discussed in chapter 3. But it also shows a keen eye for the odd or fabulous detail in this legend taken by the Comestor from Josephus.[90] And here are combined two pieces of information about antediluvian writing, placing it, as appropriate, amidst the "sons of Seth" even though the *Historia* has disposed it differently. The combination of both languages in the same insular hand seems a deliberate witty play on the subject-matter.

The next opening is in its layout a mirror image of the preceding and continues the genealogical pattern. Again, it is dominated by Old English notes in the insular script. The A.M. and marginal text-numbers, as well as the picture-labels, continue in the Norman script,[91] but on this opening only one short note is in Latin and in the Norman script. The main Old English text presents the genealogy of Adam from Enoch to Noe (Gen. 5:21–31), while the pictures are offset by one, from Jared to Lamech. Into the picture the annotator writes a note in insular script, taken from Chapter 30 ("Epilogum interserit") showing the enthroned Enoch (lower frame, left panel):

45. Eal swa of caymes ofsprínge se seófonde wǽs þúrutlige [lamech[92]] hunwarst. swa wǽs of sethes ofsprínge se seófende þurutlyge swyþe gód enoch.

---

[90] Blatt, ed., 132.

[91] In the lower frame of f. 11v, right panel, the picture is of the Ascension of Enoch, which is in lieu of his death and is duly labeled.

[92] The name 'lamech' written in the margin of v. 11v seems to be in the "insular" script (note the way the second member of the *h* loops up rather than bends in) and pertains to the English note written in the adjoining frame, not to the picture.

Just as from Cain's offspring the seventh, Lamech, was the most thoroughly bad, so of Seth's offspring the seventh was the most thoroughly good Enoch.

Sicut ergo in generatione Cain, septimus, scilicet Lamech, fuit pessimus, ita in generatione Seth, septimus, scilicet Henoch, fuit optimus.[93]

In the spirit of the chapter of the *Historia* from which it is excerpted, the note is placed in Enoch's picture, not Lamech's; the absence of Lamech's name is probably a reflection of the annotator's exemplar ["scilicet lamech" is added in the β, γ, δ groups of manuscripts], rather than an omission; in any case, he required its inclusion and put it in the margin, with a little comma-shaped *signe de renvoi* after 'hunwarst'.

The next annotations are of exceptional interest, for they address Jerome's "famosa quæstio, et disputatione omnium Ecclesiarum ventilata," about when Mathusala died, before or after the Flood; here we see the annotator working out this problem of biblical scholarship in English; he sees that the *Historia Scholastica* is not really satisfactory, for the Comestor leaves it unclear when Methusala died and even appears to entertain the possibility that Methusala lived beyond the Flood. At the bottom of the page and going over to the top of f. 12r is a congeries of notes in the insular script that can be divided into three sections by their sources (nos. 46–48). The first part continues with *Historia*, "Genesis," Chapter 30:

46. fæle cynne wenu[n]ghe me telleð be matusalemes geáren. þa lxx. (*gl:* hundseofentig wríter) cw̄æð þæt he lefede `xiiii. wíntre´ hefter þan flode. hác me ne reð þæt he wéra [*i.e.* wære] in þara árcæ, ne hé ne ferde mid gode swá enóch deða. súme cwæð þæt he forþférde .vi. wíntre hǽr þan flode. Jer*onymus* cw*æð* þán ylcan geáre þe se floð wæs.

Many sorts of opinions are told about the years of Mathusala. The LXX (that is, the seventy writers) said that he lived (fourteen years) after the Flood. But one does not read that he was in the ark or that he went with God as Enoch did. Some said that he died six years before the Flood. Jerome said [he died] the same year that the Flood was.

De annis Mathusalem diversae sunt opiniones. Secundum computationem LXX, vixit annos quatuordecim post diluvium, sed non legitur fuisse in arca, nec translatus ut Henoch. Quidam dicunt quod mortuus fuerit ante diluvium sex annis. Hieronymus asserit, quod eodem anno in quo fuit diluvium mortuus est.[94]

[93] PL 198.1080C/D.

[94] PL 198.1080D-1081A.

The annotator follows the Comestor in writing 'lxx' for the Septuagint and then adds a gloss above the line, 'hundseofentig wríter',[95] and inserts alongside the gloss, above the line, the all-essential words 'xiiii. wintre';[96] these augmentations may be signs of composition or recomposition on the page, an issue which will be taken up in a moment. The next line (last on f. 11v), merely a calculation of the years of Mathusala according to the Vulgate (Gen. 5:25, 28), is unremarkable in itself (the information is in the main Old English version), except that it is attributed to "Norman" in the margin and is a bridge between the *Historia* passage just cited and the next, at the top of f. 12v. This Norman or "Normannus" is a character deserving a discussion of his own (see ch. 7), but for the moment it suffices to say that he was a real person associated with these annotations at St. Augustine's and that the activity here shows that the annotator was unsatisfied with the vague and inconclusive results of the Comestor's note, which leave a possibility that someone besides Noe and his sons survived the Flood. Thus he brings in here *in English* an understanding of Jerome's definitive solution of the problem from the *Hebrew Questions on Genesis*:

> **47–48.** Mathusale*m* gestri[n]de. lamech da he was .c.l.xxx.v.ii. wintre. lamech. nóe þa he wǽs .c.l.xxx.ii wintre || Forþan Mat`h´usalem wæs ðri hund wíntre. 7 l.x.ix. þa nóe wæs ybore. Æfter ðam he léfede. sixhund wintre. nóe wǽs sixhund wíntre ær ðan flode. nemeð þa .c.c.c. hund wíntre 7 .l.x.ix. dot hy to dan six `hun´ wíntre þ*æt* bið nygon hun wintre. 7 l.x.ix. swa fele léuede matusale*m* hær ðan flode.
>
> Mathusala begot Lamech when he was 187 years old. Lamech (begot) Noe when he was 182 years old. Therefore Mathusala was 369 years old when Noe was born. After that he lived 600 years. Noe was 600 years (just) before the flood. Take then 369 years, add it to that 600 years so that it is 969 years, so many (years) Mathusala lived before the flood.

Jerome had written:

> Siquidem et in hebraeis et Samaritanorum libris ita scriptum repperi et uixit Mathusala CLXXXVII annis et genuit Lamech. Et uixit Mathusala, postquam genuit Lamech DCCLXXXII annos. Et genuit filios et filias. Et fuerunt omnes dies Mathusalae anni DCCCCLXVIIII, et mortuus est. Et uixit Lamech CLXXXII annos et genuit Noe. A die ergo natiuitatis Mathusalae usque ad diem natiuitatis Noe sunt anni CCCLXIX: his adde DC annos Noe, quia in sexcentesimo uitae eius anno diluuium factum est: atque

[95] So it is taken to be; the final *r* is like an *n* in that the first stroke has no descender, but the second stroke turns up sharply like an insular *r* rather than an *n*.

[96] Does he write 'wiutre'? If so the words were being copied probably from a draft on wax or one scratched onto the page before being inked.

ita fit, ut DCCCCLXIX anno uitae suae Mathusala mortuus sit, eo anno quo coepit esse diluuium.[97]

Indeed, in the Hebrew and Samaritan books I have found it written "and Mathusala lived 187 years and begot Lamech. And Mathusala lived after he begot Lamech 782 years. And he begot sons and daughters. And all the days of Mathusala were 969 years and he died. And Lamech lived 182 years and begot Noe. Now from the day of the birth of Mathusala to the day of the birth of Noe are 369 years." To these add 600 years of Noe because in the 600th year of his life the flood occurred: and so it was that in the 969th year of his life Mathusala died, in that year in which the flood began.

The point of this question is that when the years given in the Septuagint version are calculated, Mathusala lives fourteen years beyond the flood. The Hebrew and Samaritan versions keep his years within the acceptable range; the calculation is simpler in Norman's version than Jerome's but comes out the same and is certainly based on Jerome's text. The set of notes about Mathusala thus conclude with a final statement that he did not live beyond the Flood. Given that a copy of Jerome's work was at hand for the annotator and was being frequently consulted (see below, ch. 6), Jerome is likely the immediate as well as ultimate source.[98] And indeed, in the proto-gothic script on f. 12r, in the top frame (right) at the burial of Mathusala, is a brief epitome of Jerome's note, perhaps taken from a marginal note in the copy of the *Historia* being consulted:

anno nongentesimo sexagesimo nono uite eius quo cepit diluuium. obiit Mathusalem.

In the 969th year of his life, when the flood began, Mathusala died.

Norman's concern for getting the chronology right according to Jerome, which doubtless reflects a monastic bias in favor of the older text, can be seen also on f. 14r, where the *Historia* note giving from Josephus the A.M. date of Noe's entering the ark as 2656 is immediately "corrected" with the note (no. 57): 'Norman*us*

[97] Jerome, HQG 5.27–28, CCSL 72.8–9 (PL 23.947B/C).

[98] Though one must never rule out that the annotator was taking items from the margin of the *Historia Scholastica* exemplar(s) being consulted. For example, at this place in Royal 4 D. vii occurs a note that, while different in intention (supporting the LXX rather than opposing it), is in the same vein: (f. 16rb) '*Qu*ia cum ccc. clxvii. anno*rum* gen*uit* Lamech 7 Lam*ech*. cu*m* e*s*set. clxxxviii. anno*rum* genuit noe. *Qua*m om*ne*s anni s*un*t. ccc. lv. vsq*ue* ad noe. t*ande*m ad diluuium dc. anni. quib*us* adde .xiiii. 7 h*abe*s annos matussale. dc.ccc. lxix. 7 ita .xiiii. post dilu*uium*' ("because when he [Mathusala] was 167 years old he begot Lamech and Lamech when he was 188 years old begot Noe. In the end all the years are 355 up to Noe, exactly 600 years at the Flood to which add 14 and you have the years of Mathusala, 969 and so 14 after the Flood").

dicit. mille. sexcentos. l (.) vi- iuxta heb*r*eos-' (the A.M. date is also added above this on the same page in probably the same stint).

There is one more English note on this page, at the bottom, under the picture of Lamech, bringing together (and reversing their relative order) two separated passages from Chapter 31 "De causa diluvii" and treating the order of statements rather freely:

> **50.** § æfter adames forðsiðe seth ytwǽmde his ofspríng frám caynes ofsprínge þ*æt* hí ywende to hære ybora lánda. ⁊ seth wúneda on ána munte beside paradise. Cayn in ðon felde þe he ís broþer ofsloh, ǽlswa adam hít hét hær is forðsyðe. þar hí ne scolde hí ymegg`h´e. Jose[phus] cwað sethes súnes belyfen góde to ðan seofende ofspri[n]ge. hác seþe hi gewéndon to mycelon heuele. Enoch se seofende. `man fram adame.´ Noe se tynde.
>
> After Adam's death, Seth separated his offspring from Cain's offspring so they went to their native lands and Seth dwelt on a mountain beside paradise, Cain in the field where he slew his brother. Moreover Adam commanded before his death that they should not mix there. Josephus said Seth's sons remained good to the seventh generation but afterwards they turned to great evil. Enoch was the seventh man from Adam, Noe the tenth.
>
> Mortuo Adam, Seth separavit cognationem suam a cognatione Cain, quæ redierat ad natale solum. Nam et pater vivens prohibuerat ne commiscerentur, et habitavit Seth in quodam monte proximo paradiso. Cain habitavit in campo, ubi fratrem occiderat. / Josephus autem dicit quod usque ad septimam generationem boni permanserunt filii Seth, post ad mala progressi sunt.[99]

The annotator places this quotation on the border between the generation of Seth and the story of the commingling of the two lines. It might have been selected from Chapter 31 because it brings together all the themes—the death of Adam, the line of Seth, the evil and good generations and what is to come—on the next page. The annotator seems to have added the last sentence in his own words, to

[99] PL 198.1081C/D, 1081B. Methodius (ed. Sackur, 61) has, "Et tunc disiuncti sunt ab invicem, hoc est generatio Seth a cognatione Cain, et abstulit Seth suam cognationem sursum in quendam montem, proximos [*sic*] paradiso qui erat." ("And then they were separated from one another, this is the generation of Seth, from the family of Cain, and Seth took his family up to a certain mountain, which was next to Paradise"). Josephus (ed. Blatt, 132) has, "Et isti quidem septem generationibus permanserunt deum iudicantes esse dominum omnium et ad virtutem semper inspicientes, deinde tempore procedente de paternis sollemnitatibus ad mala progressi sunt. . . ."("And these continued for seven generations to keep believing that God was the Lord of all and always considering virtue, until with the passing of time from the religious ceremonies of their fathers they passed on to evil").

emphasize the high points and implicitly, perhaps, nuance the statement attributed to Josephus.

The pages discussed show the annotator's tendency to disperse the information found in the *Historia*. But the work is also constructive and freely recombines materials from the source in order to fashion continuous commentaries that make sense according to different categorizations. We can see this activity well on ff. 7v-8r (fig. 32). The original Old English text of the opening is Genesis 3:19–24, 4:1–2, the Curse, the Expulsion, and the birth of Cain and Abel. The pictures are (f. 7v), upper frame, God confronting Adam, lower frame (left) the Expulsion, (right) Adam with a spade, Eve with what appears to be a pick (or a distaff?); (f. 8r) upper frame (left) cherubim with the flaming sword, (right) two trees, lower frame, (left) a young man (Abel) tending sheep with an older man on the left gesturing with his left hand and with his right holding a spade (Adam); (left) a young man on the right is digging with a spade (Cain), while an older man faces him, holding a pick (Adam). The upper portions of these unusually tall latter panels are thickly filled with Latin notes in the "H" script, taken from different parts of the *Historia*. In the left panel is a note taken from "Genesis" Ch. 24 ("De ejectione eorundem de paradiso, et rhomphæa ignea") concerning "the field, Damascus, whence Adam was taken and where Cain killed Abel and near where Adam and Eve are buried in a double cave" (no. 19); from Ch. 25 ("De generationibus Adæ") how "Abel was a shepherd, Cain a farmer" (= Gen. 4:2, but from HS 1076D) combined with selections from Ch. 26 ("De oblationibus fratrum"), that after many days they offered gifts, Cain of his produce, Abel, *according to Josephus*,[100] of milk and the firstborn of his lambs (HS 1076D), the legend that Adam taught his sons to offer tithes (HS 1077A), the anger of Cain (HS 1077A/B) (no. 20). In the right frame the selection jumps back to Ch. 25, freely selected to make a single coherent comment on the years of Adam when his daughters and sons were born.[101] Then follows from Ch. 30 ("Epilogum interserit") two separated sentences on the age of Adam at the begetting of Seth and the termination of the First Age in Noe. The notes in the frame are concluded by an unsourced calculation on the years from Adam to the birth of Noe. The annotator's rearrangement of the *Historia* extracts has produced a different kind

[100] "nam cum eis placuisset sacrificare deo, Cain quidem de culturae germinationibus obtulerat fructum, Abel autem lac et primogenita gregum. . . ." (Blatt, ed., 130). The italicized phrase is not in Claudius but is in the early manuscripts of the *Historia*.

[101] Compare the different bundling of the information in the *Historia*, ch. 25 (HS 1076B): a) comment on St. Methodius' imprisonment as related to Adam and Eve, b) age of Adam when he begot Cain and his sister Chalmana, c) apparent age of Adam at his creation, d) unmentioned progeny of Adam, e) interval after which he begot Abel and his sister Delbora, f) age of Adam and Eve when Cain killed Abel, g) 100 years' mourning for Abel. Elements b), d), e), f), g) are grouped together on f. 8r. Element a) is on f. 3v (Latin, insular hand, no. 3); element c) is on 4r in Old English (no. 6a).

Figure 32a: (fol. 7v)

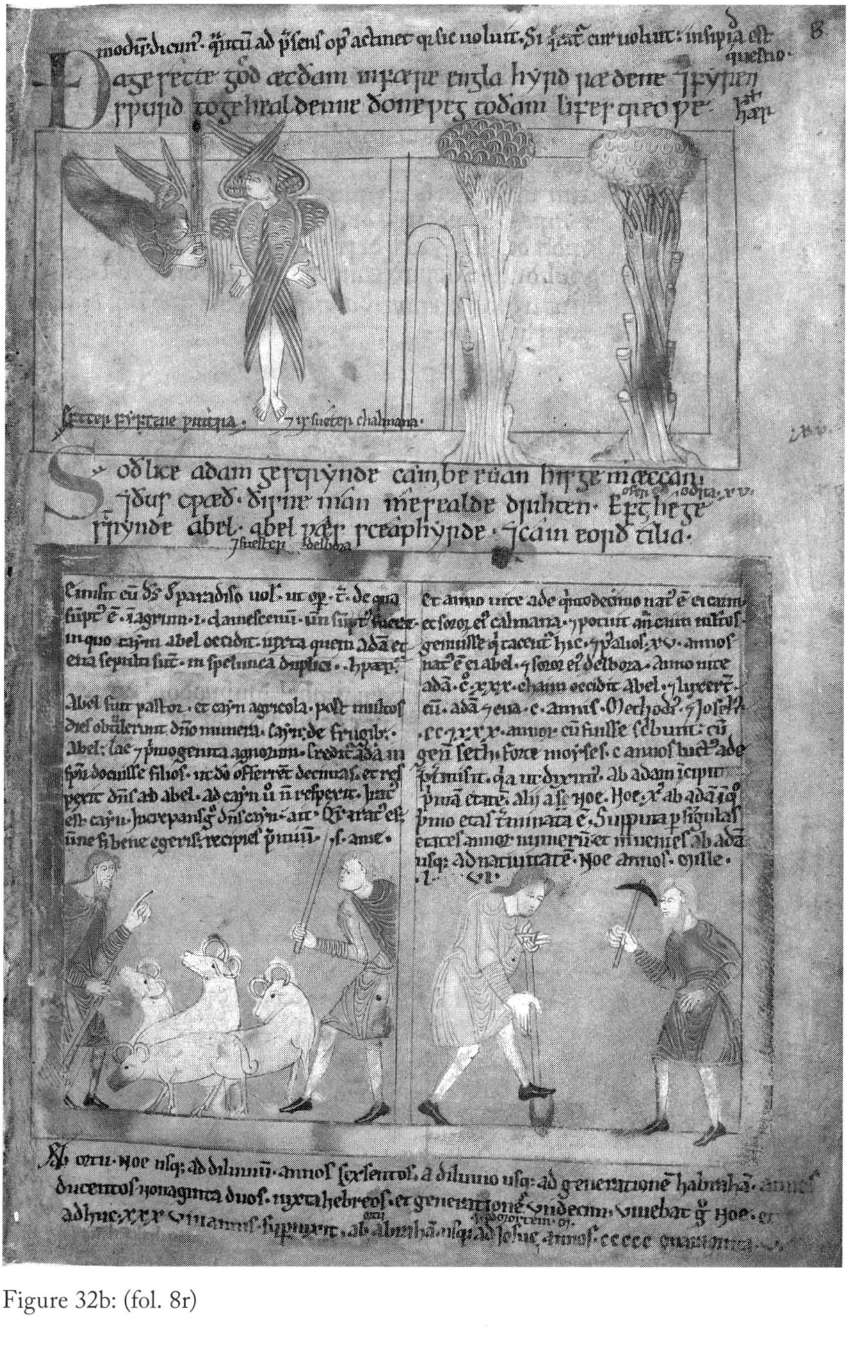

Figure 32b: (fol. 8r)

of coherence, arranged not on narrative logic or the progress of his sources (for example, the Methodius material is grouped together in Ch. 25 at col. 1076A) but a category-logic: In the left panel cullings from the *Historia* present a coherent but not narrative account of the doings of Cain and Abel (nos. 19–20):

Claudius f. 8r left panel

> "And God sent him out from the paradise of pleasure to till the earth from which he was taken" (cf. Gen. 3:23) in the field, that is, of Damascus, whence he was taken in which Cain killed Abel, near which Adam and Eve are buried in a double cave (1075C); "Abel was a shepherd and Cain a farmer; after many days they brought the Lord gifts" (cf. Gen. 4:2, 3), Cain of his produce, Abel [according to Josephus] of milk and the firstlings of his lambs. It is believed that Adam taught his sons by the Spirit that they offer tithes to God (1076D-1077A). "And the Lord had respect to Abel, to Cain truly he had not respect (1077A). And Cain was angry" (cf. Gen. 4:4–5). Speaking loudly, the Lord thus said to Cain: "Why are you angry, if you do well will you not receive?" (cf. Gen. 4:6–7) the reward, namely from me (1077A/B).

In the right panel is information on the generations of Adam, the annotator bringing together similar relevant information from two disjunct chapters:

Claudius f. 8r, right panel

> **A** And in the fifteenth year of Adam's life Cain was born and his sister Chalmana, **B** and before Cain he was able to beget many who are not mentioned here. And after another fifteen years Abel was born and his sister Delbora. In the one hundred and thirtieth year of Adam's life Cain killed Abel and Adam and Eve mourned for a hundred years (1076B). **C** Methodius and Josephus have written that he [Adam] was 230 years old when he begot Seth. **D** Perhaps Moses neglected to mention a period of 100 years of mourning by Adam (1080C). **E** Therefore we say from Adam begins the first age of others up to Noe. **F** Noe is the tenth from Adam, in whom the first age is terminated. (1081A)

Hist. Schol.

from Ch. 25: Sed Methodius martyr oravit, dum esset in carcere, et revelatum est ei a Spiritu de principio, et fine mundi: quod et oravit, et scriptum, licet simpliciter, reliquit, dicens quod virgines egressi sunt de paradiso. **A** Et anno creationis vitæ Adam decimo quinto natus est ei Cain, et soror ejus Chalmana. Et si enim factus est Adam quasi in ætate triginta annorum, tamen fuit unius diei, et anni; et post, duorum annorum, et trium, et sic de cæteris. **B** Et potuit ante Cain multos genuisse, qui tacentur hic. Post alios quindecim annos natus est ei Abel, et soror ejus Delbora. Anno vitæ Adam centesimo tricesimo Cain occidit Abel, et luxerunt eum Adam, et Eva centum annis.

from Ch. 30: Unde quidam **E** incipiunt ab Adam primam ætatem; alii a Seth, quibus assentit Methodius, et ideo hoc dicit, quia de Abel nullus natus est, et generatio Cain tota periit in diluvio. . . . **D** Forte Moyses centum annos luctus Adæ prætermisit, quia ut diximus, Septuaginta et **C** Methodius, et Josephus ducentum triginta annorum eum fuisse scribunt, cum genuit Seth. . . .Tamen omnes in numero annorum vitæ ejus [Mathusala] conveniunt, quia vixit annis nonagentis sexaginta novem. **F** Porro Noe fuit decimus ab Adam, in quo prima ætas terminata est.

All the Historia-text not underlined is used elsewhere by the annotator.[102] In the left panel is collected from diverse places material entirely related to the history of Cain and Abel. In the right, all the material is chronological; the annotator has collocated the "100 years of mourning" from widely separated sections of the *Historia.* The right panel concludes with a sentence not from the *Historia*, "Count up through the individual lifetimes the number of years and you will find from Adam to the birth of Noe is 1056 years." The formula is Hieronymian,[103] though the number is found in Bede's *De temporum ratione*, ch. 66, and is probably a concluding concoction by the annotator himself rather than from a specific source. Section E uses most of the words of the *Historia* but deflects the odd point that it makes ("others [i.e., Ps.-Methodius] say Seth") in favor of the standard view ("first age is from Adam to Noe").

Though these annotations are all in Latin and in the same Norman script, they bear in a special way on the question of the status of the English annotations. The first of them (f. 8r, right panel, top) is:

---

[102] Nos. 3 (f. 3v), 6a (English, f. 4r), 36a (English, f. 10r); The gist of "Tamen omnes . . . sexaginta novem" is represented by the English epitome of Jerome in no. 48 (f. 12r).

[103] Cf. "Supputa per singulas ætates annorum numerum et inuenies ab ortu Sem usque ad generationem Abram trecentos nonaginta annos" (Ep. 73, Ad Euangelum, ed. Hilberg, CSEL 55, 19.10; PL 22.680).

> 19. Emisit eum deus de paradiso uoluptatis. ut operaretur terram de qua sumptus est. in agrum id est damascenum. unde sumptus fuerat. in quo caym abel occidit. iuxta quem adam et eua sepulti sunt. in spelunca duplici.

This (see also detail, fig. 20) agrees exactly with the Old English note on the facing page (no. 15, see also detail, fig. 19), in the right panel of the lower frame, Adam, with spade, and Eve with "pick/distaff," both clothed and being addressed by an angel:

> **15.** In syrie abute damasco. ón áne felde. þanon hé com þær cayn abel ofsloh 7 beside þan wǽs adam. 7 eue. bebyrigde on þan twyfealde scrǽfe.

As can be seen in the reproduction on p. 290, above, this entry is marked in the outer margin of f. 7v with the *signe de renvoi* 'hær' plus a mark consisting of a mid-line horizontal stroke with two dots above answering to the *signe* 'hwær' plus the same mark written immediately after the Latin comment on the facing page. The sequence 'hær/hwær' suggests that the Latin was written first and the English inserted subsequently. Even more interestingly, the Old English is written in a space too narrow and irregular for a good entry and in a most disorganized fashion, suggesting that the writer was *translating as he wrote*, that is, for this note at least, not only does the English writer seem to be taking some sort of cue from the Latin *on the page*, but he translates, at least sometimes, on the fly. But as we saw, on f. 10v, upper frame, right, the Latin is fitted in after the Old English. This comports with the idea already argued at length that the insular and Norman hands were contemporaneous, indeed, one and the same, the annotator appropriating certain spaces, pages, and extracts, as ideas and opportunities offered, leapfrogging himself. The English notes are concentrated in the first part of the book, up to f. 14r, with almost all the notes on ff. 7v-12r being in English. Related to this is the overlap or repetition of part of f. 8r on f. 10r (nos. 37 and 38), a notable and perhaps inadvertent instance of code-switching on f. 10r, when the insular script just below the upper picture begins a passage from the *Historia* 'Forte moyses .c. annos lu[c]tus ade pretermisit quia ut diximus' and continues the same *Historia* passage without a break within the next frame in English: 'þa hundseófentig wenðeres 7 methodius 7 Josephus gewriten þæt adam wæs twa hund wintra. 7 xxx. þa he gestrínde seth'[104] (see fig. 18). This English version more accurately reflects the Comestor's text than when it was written in Latin on f. 8r (as no. 22) and must represent a fresh look at the *Historia* exemplar.

A side-by-side comparison shows the English annotations to be a serious scholarly complement to the *Historia* Latin extracts, involving considerable thought and biblical scholarship. However, the *Historia Scholastica* was a

[104] "The Seventy Writers and Methodius and Josephus wrote that Adam was two hundred and thirty years old when he begot Seth."

brand-new text and as such somewhat on probation to the monastic way of thinking. It appears that by training and tradition the annotator was led to look back to the "real" Jerome as he read Petrus Comestor; certainly it was Jerome (and his various medieval avatars) who provided the annotator with the materials for the rest of the notes, and it is to this material that we now turn.

VI. "Jerome" and the Annotations

About half the notes, and virtually all after Exodus, are drawn from ancient literal commentaries. These are works by or attributed to Jerome, supplemented by a compact collection of Bede's notes on biblical place names and notations according to his Anno Mundi chronology. The annotator assembles these extracts so as to construct in effect a supplement to the *Historia Scholastica* extracts. Though these works greatly predate the annotations, the annotator found and used them in their modern guises, as they came to be edited in the twelfth century; and thus, although by title dozens of works are drawn upon, the annotator probably found nearly all of them in only a couple of books: a one-volume compilation of literal biblical commentaries, some by Jerome, others taken to be by Jerome in the twelfth century; a one-volume compilation of works by Bede on Acts; and a copy of his "Greater Chronicle," forming ch. 66 of *De temporum ratione*—either extracted from the complete work or found in a stand-alone version.[1] Other scattered notes from a variety of sources tend to fall together in stretches sharing the same ductus, abbreviations, and punctuation conventions, suggesting a separate unified source—most likely the margins of one or more copies of the *Historia Scholastica* itself.

"Jerome"

After the *Historia*, the main class of sources, nearly half the annotations in total, are ancient works of geography and chronology, forming a group of works either by Jerome or attributed to him during the Middle Ages. The majority of these texts would have been drawn from a single book available in the St. Augustine's library. Beginning in the late eleventh century and continuing through the twelfth in England and Normandy, most of these works of historical exegesis came to be gathered into single-volume Hieronymian collections that fall into distinct patterns: the "longer" and "shorter" collections.[2] The historical works in

---

[1] See Bede: *The Reckoning of Time*, trans. Wallace, 353–66, esp. 363–64.

[2] The following identification of manuscripts and distribution and identity of contents is culled from the relevant manuscripts and from Richard H. Rouse, Mary A. Rouse, and R. A. B. Mynors, eds., *Registrum Anglie de libris doctorum et auctorum ueterum*

these collections were many of the same ones that the Comestor depended upon heavily; the annotator of Claudius would have been aware of this and would have regarded them as complementary works in the historical register that filled gaps in the *Historia* or which provided him with comments that touched on specific words and passages in the Old English main text.

The "longer collection"[3] contains a mixed anthology of historical/philological and moral pieces that were considered part of the Hieronymian corpus in the Middle Ages; these are all pseudepigraphical, with the exceptions of the *Hebraicae quaestiones in libro Geneseos*, *Liber interpretationis nominum Hebraicorum*, the Epistles to Rusticus and Fabiola (Epp. 125 and 78), and *De situ et nominibus locorum Hebraicorum*, which is a translation by Jerome of a work of Eusebius of Caesarea. In the longer collection the works are arranged, moral works first, historical works second, with the latter arranged more or less in descending order of length. The "shorter" collection, represented by many more manuscripts,[4] is refined down to just the historical and philological works, arranged longer (and genuine) works first, shorter works later. As it happens, we can examine the contents of the "shorter collection" by means of the traces of a St. Augustine's manuscript which was in all probability the very one that the Claudius annotator consulted and used as his exemplar. Though it is now lost, its detailed contents list appears in the same fifteenth-century St. Augustine's catalogue (Trinity College Dublin, MS. 360, f. 14, col. 1) that allows us to identify Cotton Claudius B.iv as a St. Augustine's book:[5]

> Ieronimus de Hebraicis questionibus et in eodem libro | Ieronimus de mansionibus filiorum Isrl | de distanciis locorum | Liber interpretacionum Hebraicorum nominum | Note diuine legi necessarie | De questionibus in lib' Regum | Lib' de questionibus in paralipomenon | de Decem temptacion-

(London,1991), 77–95 and Bernard Lambert, *Bibliotheca Hieronymiana Manuscripta* (Steenbrugge, 1969–1972), vols. 2, 3a, 3b. In the text of this chapter Lambert is cited by volume and item number, in notes and elsewhere by item no. only. Also helpful is R. Sharpe, J. P. Carley, R. M. Thomson, and A. G. Watson, eds., *English Benedictine Libraries: The Shorter Catalogues*, Corpus of British Medieval Library Catalogues 4 (London, 1996).See now B.C. Barker-Benfield, ed., *St. Augustine's Abbey, Canterbury*, 1:505-07.

3 Represented by (A) Alençon Bib. mun. 2 (s. xii, St-Evroult) [plus (S) Madrid, Bibl. nat. 91 (A.101), s. xii, copied directly from A] and (D) Durham Cathedral B.2.11 (s. xi ex, before 1100, Durham).

4 Represented for our period by **(T¹)** Trinity Coll. Camb. B.2.34 (s. xii in., Christ Church), **(T²)** Trinity Coll. Camb. O.4.7 (s.xii in., provenance Rochester, probably written at Christ Church), **(E)** Camb. Emmanuel Coll. 57 (s. xii in.), **(K)** Camb. Univ. Lib. Kk.iv.6 (s. xii), **(Y)** York Minster XVI.i.8 (s. xii, Rievaulx), **(B¹)** Oxford, Bodleian Digby 184 (s.xii), **(B²)** Bodley 808 (s. xii, Exeter), **(M)** Oxford Merton Coll. LI (s. xii).

5 M. R. James, *Ancient Libraries of Canterbury and Dover* (Cambridge, 1903), 220, no. 328, and Barker-Benfield as in n.2.

> ibus | Canticum debbor' | lamentaciones Ieremie prophete | De musicis Instrumentis | de partibus minus notis veteris testamenti | sententie excerpte diuersis opusculis | De mensuris | Ad estimandum cuiusque rei altitudinem | De spera celi | De xij^cim lapidibus | Gesta saluatoris nostri | Conflictus ciuium babilonie et Ierusalem et | de versu *Misericordia et ueritas etc.*

These works can be identified as follows:

1) Jerome, *Hebraicae quaestiones in libro Geneseos* (HQG).[6] This was written between 389 and 391.[7] Concentrating on particular exegetical problems, arranged in the order of the biblical text, each "question" is headed by the relevant extract from Genesis, followed by a brief treatment of literal concerns. These are chiefly linguistic, such as the exact meaning of key Hebrew words, the variants found in the Greek versions (the Septuagint, Symmachus, Aquila, and Theodotion), reconciliation of inconsistencies that have been noticed between statements in a particular Genesis verse and other places in the Bible, and, occasionally, the interpreted meaning of a Hebrew name. It frequently borrows from Josephus' *Antiquities* as well as some contemporary Jewish sources, and avoids allegorical explanations.[8] Twenty extracts from this work occur in Claudius.

2) Jerome, *De XLII mansionibus filiorum Israel in deserto* (Ep. 78, ad Fabiolam).[9] Composed in 400 for a rich Roman widow who met Jerome on pilgrimage to the Holy Land, and more edifying than "scientific," it supplies spiritual interpretations and etymologies of the forty-two "stations" in the order named in Numbers 33 where the Hebrew people stopped during their wandering after the Exodus.[10] Four extracts from this work occur in Claudius.

3) Eusebius of Caesarea, translated by Jerome, *De situ et nominibus locorum hebraicorum* ([SNLH] in the Middle Ages called "De distanciis locorum").[11] Eusebius wrote his treatise ca. 330 and Jerome made the translation about the same time as the *Hebrew Questions*.[12] Though Jerome claims to have revised it, it follows the original closely, with some up-to-date information added. It views the biblical lands from the perspective of the fourth/fifth centuries, when Judaea had

[6] Ed. PL 23.935–1010 and Lagarde, CCSL 72 (1959), 1–56. In the following discussions, the following short references are used: CPL = *Clavis Patrum Latinorum*, ed. Eligius Dekkers (Steenbrugge, 1995); CPPM = *Clavis Patristica Pseudepigraphorum Medii Aevi*, ed. J. Machielsen, 3 vols. (Turnhout, 1990–2003); Lambert = B. Lambert, *Bibliotheca Hieronymiana manuscripta*, 4 vols. ('s-Gravenhage, 1969–1972), cited by volume and item number; see also n. 2.

[7] J. N. D. Kelly, *Jerome: His Life, Writings, and Controversies* (New York, 1975), 153.

[8] See Kelly, *Jerome*, 155–57.

[9] CPL 620, Lambert 1B.78; PL 22.698–724.

[10] See Kelly, *Jerome*, 211–12.

[11] CPL 581, Lambert 2.202; ed. PL 23.859–928, Lagarde, *Onomastica sacra* (1887), 118–90.

[12] Kelly, *Jerome*, 155.

long been a Roman province, rather than from the perspective of biblical times, and one of its chief goals is to correlate contemporary names and places to ancient ones. As an index of place names the main sections are arranged alphabetically, and within each alphabetical section the arrangement is by the order of the books of the Bible, and within these sub-sections the name-entries are roughly alphabetized. There is thus considerable repetition within different sub-headings of names occurring in several biblical books. Entries concentrate on description, topography, and relative location and distance of the place to more prominent places. Claudius draws from this work more extensively than any other except the *Historia*, with more than a hundred extracts.

4) Jerome, *Liber interpretationis nominum Hebraicorum.*[13] Compiled largely from earlier unreliable sources, about the same time as the *Hebrew Questions*, it consists entirely of etymologies, in which Hebrew names are assigned Greek or Latin meanings, in most cases erroneously,[14] and is arranged alphabetically, each letter proceeding through the whole Bible, book by book. It seems not to have been used at all by the Claudius annotator.

5) "Notae diuinae legi necessariae cum suis interpretationibus,"[15] unpublished. After the title, it begins: 'PÞ Hoc in idiomatibus idest proprius locutionibus legis diuinę' and ends 'sed a sole suscipere dicitur quod astro*no*minii diligenter exponunt'. It is a brief treatise on marginal symbols appropriate for marking certain topics or tropes in biblical passages. It is not cited in Claudius.

6a) *Quaestiones Hebraicae in I-III Regum (Malachim)*

6b) *Quaestiones Hebraicae in I-II Paralipomenon (Dabrianim)* (QH1P).[16] This double work is used by Hrabanus Maurus in his commentary on Samuel-Kings, dated 829, and is no earlier than about 800, when a scholiast entered interpretations gathered directly from the Hebrew biblical text into the margins and text of Paris, Bibliothèque nationale lat. 11937 (s. ix in., St. Germain); these were incorporated into 6a (the portion of the Paris manuscript containing the comments on Paralipomenon is lost). Saltman, Martianay, and Berger[17] considered this scholiast, most likely a converted Jew, as the author of both the scholia and the *Quaestiones* on Kings and Paralipomenon. In the ninth and tenth centuries, following the words of Hrabanus, they were attributed to a "Hebreus moderni temporis," or remained anonymous. They acquired their Hieronyman attribution from the eleventh century onwards[18] and are labeled as such in the Hieronyman collections

[13] CPL 58, Lambert 2.201; ed. PL 23. 771–858, Lagarde CCSL 72 (1959), 57–161.

[14] Kelly, *Jerome*, 153–54.

[15] Lambert 3b.404. Copies occur in **T**[1], **T**[2] and **D**.

[16] Lambert 3b.412; CPPM 2349; ed. PL 23.1330–1402.

[17] See Avrom Saltman, ed., *Pseudo-Jerome, Quaestiones on the Book of Samuel*, Studia Post-Biblica 26 (Leiden, 1975), 15–17.

[18] The earliest manuscripts are from Trier (Berkeley, University of California MS UCB 17, formerly Phillips 391, s. xi[2]) and Mainz (formerly Phillips 398, sold 22 May

under discussion, as in Cambridge, Trinity College B.2.34, f. 117r: 'Incipit liber beati Ieronimi presbiteri de questionibus in librum Regum, ~~primum~~.'[19] The commentary on Kings is made up of literal *quaestiones*, midrashim, and etymologies, not unlike Jerome's *Hebrew Questions*, much of it drawn from biblical and rabbinic traditions, sometimes muddled and sometimes fabricated.[20] The commentary on Chronicles, headed in TCC B.2.34 f. 126r 'Incipit liber eiusdem de Questionibus in Paralippomenon', is "to a large extent fragmentary, disjointed, dehydrated, gnomic, and at times completely unintelligible";[21] it is mainly concerned with genealogical matters and for this reason was of interest to the Claudius annotator. Extracts from *Quaestiones Hebraicae in I Paralipomenon* are copied into Claudius at five places, with an extensive series of extracts on the first inserted leaf (f. 74r). A single short entry from *Quaestiones Hebraicae in II Regum* is copied on the final leaf, inserted as f. 156.

7) *De decem temptationibus populi Israel in deserto.*[22] This is a brief treatise appearing in all the eleventh- and twelfth-century Hieronymian collections, a literal midrash on Deuteronomy 1:1–2 concerning the "ten tests" the Lord applied to the Israelites in the desert as extracted from various places in the Pentateuch. Because it utilizes the Hebrew scholia in BN Lat. 11937, Saltman considers it likely that it has the same author as 6a and 6b.[23] The Claudius annotator does not use this text.

8) *Commentarius in canticum Debborae* (CD).[24] This brief commentary on Judges 5:1–24 is in the same *quaestiones* style as 6a; for that reason Ginzberg and Lambert accept it as by the same author, though Saltman is cautious because there are no surviving scholia on Judges.[25] Claudius has two excerpts from this work.

9) *In Lamentationes Hieremiae.*[26] Despite its title, this is a brief allegorical interpretation of the Latin and thence Christian meanings of the letters of the

1913, now untraceable, s. xi/xii); cf. Saltman, ed., *Quaestiones*, 32, 62. The information regarding these manuscripts in Lambert, 3. no. 2, p. 412, is out of date though published later than Saltman. These earliest "Hieronymian" collections are quite different in arrangements and contents from the "longer" and "shorter" collections current in the Norman ambit from the turn of the twelfth century. For a thorough discussion of the later medieval use of the Pseudo-Hieronymian *Quaestiones*, see Saltman, *Quaestiones*, 30–58.

[19] See A. Saltman, "Rabanus Maurus and the Pseudo-Hieronymian *Quaestiones Hebraicae in libros Regum et Paralipomenon*," *Harvard Theological Review* 66 (1973): 43–75, at 44, n. 4 and idem, "Pseudo-Jerome in the Commentary of Andrew of St. Victor on Samuel," *Harvard Theological Review* 67 (1974): 195–253, at 197–98.

[20] Saltman, ed., *Quaestiones*, 17–23.

[21] Saltman, "Rabanus Maurus," 51.

[22] Lambert 3b.409; ed. PL 23.1319–1322.

[23] Saltman, ed., *Quaestiones*, 31.

[24] Lambert 3b.411; ed. PL 23.1322–1328.

[25] Saltman, ed., *Quaestiones*, 31, who cites Ginzberg.

[26] Lambert 3b.460, ed. PL 25.787–792.

Hebrew alphabet. It occurs in all the manuscripts of the "longer" and "shorter" collections but is not used in Claudius.[27]

10) *De diuersis generibus musicorum* ("Ad Dardanum de musicis instrumentis" = Ps.-Jerome, Ep. 23).[28] This is a brief allegorical-Christological interpretation, attributed to Jerome in the medieval tradition,[29] of eight musical instruments named in Daniel and Psalms. The earliest manuscript is Oxford, Bodleian Library, Junius 25 (s. ix, Murbach); the text appears substantially in Hrabanus' *De universo* (PL 111.495–500), dated 849. Opinions have varied as to whether Ep. 23 is Hrabanus' source or confected from his work.[30] But a passage on the organ identical to the text in Ep. 23 has been found in late eighth-century continental Irish manuscripts, suggesting an earlier date for the whole.[31] This is not used in Claudius.

11) "De partibus minus notis Veteris Testamenti (Interpretatio verborum Hebraicorum)."[32] This is a brief unpublished glossary of Hebrew and Greek terms in the Latin Bible beginning "Syntagma, doctrina. Oeconicon, dispensatorem uel secretum," arranged by biblical book. It is not used in Claudius.[33]

12) "Sententie excerpte diuersis opusculis." This is the title given in the St. Augustine's catalogue. Not listed by Lambert, this is an unpublished collection of epitomized extracts mainly from Hieronymian works in the literal vein of interpretation, plus a few other sources. It apparently occurs in only two extant manuscripts, TCC O.4.7, f. 164r-170v, with the same title on its contents list as occurs in the St. Augustine's list and with the incipit: 'Paulus ap*osto*l*us* n*on* ab homini*bus* . . . Ap*osto*l*us* int*er*p*re*tat*ur* missus' and in TCC B.2.34 at f. 173r–179r,

---

[27] A Hebrew alphabet is entered in Claudius at the foot of f. 125v, but it doesn't appear to be connected with the program of annotations.

[28] Lambert 3b.323, CPL 633, CPPM 872; ed. PL 30.213–215.

[29] For example, in TCC B.2.34, f. 268v, it has the title 'Ieronimus ad Dardanum de musicis instrumentis.'

[30] For example, Reinhold Hammerstein, "Instrumenta Hieronymi," *Archiv für Musikwissenschaft* 16 (1959): 117–34, at 117–18, followed by Hermann Josef Frede, *Kirchenschriftsteller: Verzeichnis und Sigel*, Vetus Latina 1/1 (Freiburg, 1981), 372: "wohl aus karolingischer Zeit, vielleicht von Rabanus."

[31] Martin McNamara, *Glossa in Psalmos*, Studi e Testi 310 (Vatican City, 1986), 54–55. Despite its obviously Christian orientation and early medieval style, Hanoch Avenary unconvincingly argues for a direct though lost connection to motifs found in the Dead Sea scrolls ("Pseudo-Jerome Writings and the Qumran Tradition," *Revue de Qumran* 4 [1963–1964]: 3–10).

[32] Lambert 3b.468, CPPM 2506.

[33] It occurs in TCC B.2.34, f. 170r, TCC O.4.7, f. 161r in the manuscripts of the "shorter" collection, as well as in the three manuscripts of the "longer" collection. It also occurs in Rouen, Bibliothèque municipale, A.544 (s. xiii), f. 30r.

with the same incipit;[34] indeed, the texts of the two Trinity manuscripts are virtually identical in contents and order of text, spellings of names, abbreviations, and paragraph marks; the two marginal corrections in the earlier manuscript (B.2.34 at f. 174v/21, 175r/29) appear to have been written by the scribe of O.4.7; in any case the latter has the text right in these places.[35] One interesting passage is the list of aromatics in the same order and most of the wording as that in Haymo of Halberstadt's *Commentarium in Cantica Canticorum* (PL 117.323): 'Ciprus . . . Nardus . . . Crocus . . . Fistula & cinamomu*m* . . . Myrra . . . Aloe . . . Nardus e*st* frutex. . .nardi spicati' (B.2.34, f. 177r/16–177v/1). A copy of Haymo's work is mentioned in the fifteenth-century St. Augustine's list.[36] Given that "Sententie excerpte diuersis opusculis" seems to occur only in the two Trinity (ex-Christ Church) manuscripts and the exemplar of the Claudius annotations, it is not farfetched to suppose it was compiled at either Christ Church or St. Augustine's. In the same spirit as the Claudius annotations, it collects extracts of literal comments on interconnected texts of the Old and New Testaments. However, none of the extracts in this little collection occur in Claudius.

13) "De mensuris."

14) "Ad estimandum cuiusque rei altitudinem." Items 13 and 14 are copied in full in Claudius and are discussed below.[37]

15) "Tractatus de sphaera coeli,"[38] apparently unpublished; incipit: "Adfirmatur coelum rotundum esse iuxta Ecclesiastem," expl. "caritatem consequamur." It is a brief allegorical treatise on the celestial spheres as types of the cross and

[34] Its title in the Eastry catalogue of Christ Church (no. 197) is "Expositio sententiarum ueteris et noui testamenti" (James, *Ancient Libraries*, 39).

[35] The Hieronymian texts drawn on are three of his genuine commentaries on Paul, *Commentaria in Epistolam ad Galatas*, *Commentaria in Epistolam ad Philemonem*, and *Commentaria in Epistolam ad Ephesios*, his *Interpretatio homiliarum Origenis in Cantica Canticorum*, *Commentaria in Esaiam*, *Commentaria in Matthaeum*, his translation of an epistle "Epiphanii ad Johannem," mentioned by title, and Epistle 36, ad Damasum (other extracts from this letter occur in Claudius, but not from this source). Isolated short extracts are from Bede, *De natura rerum* (PL 90.195), Isidore, *Etymologiae* (PL 82.230), Ambrose, *De Spiritu Sancto* (PL 16.723, 751), and Augustine, Epistle 36.4 (PL 33.186) and Sermon 180 (PL 38.973), the last two fathers being mentioned by name, as is Jerome several times. Other extracts can be traced only through what are probably intermediary sources, such as one found in Walafrid Strabo, *Epistola ad Romanos* (PL 114.499), Alcuin, *De diviniis officiis* (PL 101.1271), Rupertus Tuitiensis, *De Trinitate* (PL 167.1312), and Ps.-Bede, *Commentaria in Pentateuch* (PL 91.331–333).

[36] "Quinque libri Salomonis glo. Magistri Hamonis, 2° fo. in textu *et abscondamus*" (no. 135, James, *Ancient Libraries*, 204). Since no donor is mentioned, this may be a manuscript dating to before the mid-thirteenth century.

[37] They are no. 60 in Rouse et al., *Registrum Anglie*, 86.

[38] Lambert 3b.625, Lynn Thorndike and Pearl Kibre, *A Catalogue of Incipits of Mediaeval Scientific Writings in Latin*, rev. and augmented ed. (Cambridge, MA, 1963), no. 30.

occurs in most of the manuscripts of both the shorter and longer collections. It is not used in Claudius.

16) *De xii lapidibus*: Thorndike-Kibre, col. 654,[39] inc. "Iaspis uiridis. super quem fuerit nulla phantasmata timet significat fidem qua et uiridescunt sanctorum animę"; expl. "regia potestate contra omnis incursus constantes." This is a brief summary of the mystical signification of twelve gemstones, which has recently been published. Its editor, Concetta Giliberto, thinks it is an Anglo-Norman epitome of Marbod's popular late eleventh-century poem *Liber lapidum*.[40] It is not used in Claudius.

17) "Gesta saluatoris nostri."

18) "Conflictus ciuium babilonie et Ierusalem."

19) Versus: "Misericordia et veritas."[41]

These final three items were probably added page fillers in blank leaves at the end of the lost St. Augustine's manuscript.

The St. Augustine's manuscript, known only from the late catalogue, is by its contents a typical "shorter collection" of the type found in twelfth-century manuscripts of English and Norman provenance. Table 6.1 synoptically compares its contents to those of Claudius (Cl) and of the extant Hieronymian collections.[42]

---

[39] In TCC B.2.34, ff. 178v-180r, O.4.7, f. 170r-v, also in Durham B.II.11, f. 160v, CUL Kk. iv. 6, f. 21v.

[40] C. Giliberto, "An Unpublished *De Lapidibus* in its Manuscript Tradition, with Particular Regard to the Anglo-Saxon Area," in *Form and Content of Instruction in Anglo-Saxon England*, ed. P. Lendinara et al. (Turnhout, 2007), 249–83, edition at 251–53; the supposed parent text is *Marbodo de Rennes, Liber Lapidum Lapidario*, ed. M. E. Herrera, Auteurs Latins du Moyen Âge 15 (Paris, 2006). Marbod's poem is in the Christ Church inventory of Prior Eastry (prior, 1284–1331), among the claustral books (James, *Ancient Libraries*, 92, no. 955). Herrera dates the poem in the 1090s. As this epitome occurs in the Durham manuscript of "pre-1100" date, it must have been composed, if Giliberto is correct about its source, almost immediately upon the initial dissemination of the poem in England.

[41] Nos. 17-19 are unidentified by us but Barker-Benfield, *St. Augustine's Abbey* 1:507, has recently identified them as texts found together in Edinburgh, National Library of Scotland, Adv. MS 18.5.18 (Rochester, s. xiii in.), no. 17 associated with Evangelia Nicodemi, and 18 and 19 having titles that may be associated with St. Bernard, the short texts "De conflictu duorum regum," beg. "Inter Babylonem et Ierusalem nulla est pax," (PL 183.761C) and Sermo in annuntiatione dominica I on Ps. 84. (PL 183.383A). If copied complete, these texts would have filled one quire of eight.

[42] In Table 6.1 the first column represents the contents as given in the St. Augustine's catalogue; the second column shows the Lambert numbers, the third column notes works represented in the annotations in Cotton Claudius B.iv (Cl). For the other sigla see nn. 3 and 4 above.

Table 6.1

St. Aug. Cat. 328	Lmb	Cl	T^1	T^2	B^1	B^2	M	K	E	Y	A	S	D
1) HQG	200	✓	2r-33v	1–31	1–27	1 --⟩	1–23	1–14	41–65	1 —⟩	1–18	3–20	2–18
2) XII Mansiones	78	✓	33v-47r	31–44	27–38	----	24	14–20	65—⟩	no. 2	----	----	----
3) SNLH	202	✓	47r-77v	45–73	39–65	102–35	68v	32–40	1 —⟩	----	18–35	20–36	19–35
4) LNH	201		79r-114v	74–108	36 --⟩	136	----	21–31	20–40	No. 4	36	37–63	36
5) N.div.leg	404		115r-116v	109									No. 27
6a)QH Reg.	412	✓	117r-37v	112–50	94–129	43–67	34–50	63–82	76–98	No. 5	57–82	64–87	61–71
6b)QHPara.	412	✓	137v-58r	150	129	67	50	82	98	No. 6	82	87	71
7) X Tempt	409		158r-60r	150	129–31	41	90	82–83	98–99	No. 7	82–83	87–88	82
8) Cant Deb	411	✓	160r-64r	152	131–34	91	92	83–84	99–101	No. 9	83–86	88–90	83
9) In.lam. Iere.	460		164r-68v	156	134	96	95	84–86	101	No. 10	86–89	90–93	84
10)Div gen. musc.	323		168v-69v	160		101	99						
11) PM VT	468		170r-72v	161	139						109–10	107	No. 15
12) Ex div. opus			173r-79r	164									
13) De mens		147r	180r	170		✓					✓	✓	✓
14) Rei altitud.		147r	180rv	170							✓	✓	✓
15) De spher. coel.	625		179rv	169	139–47		105		109		96	98	✓
16) XII lapid			179r-80r	178									✓
17) Gesta Salv.													
18) Confl. Jer. & Bab.													
19) Versus													

All the collections have items 1) the *Hebrew Questions*, 3) the *De distanciis locorum*,[43] 4) the *Interpretation of Hebrew Names*,[44] 6a,b) the *Questions on Kings and Paralipomenon*, 7) the *Ten Temptations*, 8) the *Commentary on the Song of Debbora*, 9) *On the Lamentations of Jeremiah*; most have 15) *De sphera coeli*, including all three of the "longer collections." But the "longer collection" lacks 2) the *Twelve Stations* and 10) *De diuersis generibus musicorum*, both also lacking in four of the shorter collections.

Two of the "shorter collections" have identical contents, which are the two already frequently mentioned manuscripts of Trinity College Cambridge, B.2.34 and O.4.7, both probably ultimately from Christ Church, Canterbury.[45] They alone, with the lost St. Augustine's collection, have items 12) *Sententiae excerptae diversis opusculis* and 16) *De xii lapidibus* as well as including the rare item 10) *De diuersis generibus musicorum*, which also occurs in two other "shorter collections" (**B**^{2} and **M**). Item 5) *Notae divinae legi* is found only in the Trinity manuscripts and in the "longer collection" at Durham. Items 13) *De mensuris* and 14) *Ad estimandum* are also found in **B**^{2} of the "shorter collection" and **D** of the longer. When all is said, what stands out is that the St. Augustine's list of contents is identical (except for the final three items, probably added page fillers) with those of the two Trinity manuscripts, one certainly, and probably both, written at Christ Church.[46]

The Trinity manuscripts are closely-related early twelfth-century "shorter" Jerome collections: Trinity College, Cambridge B.2.34 (James 77, siglum **T**^{1}) is a Christ Church Canterbury production, written in the "pointed" or prickly style characteristic of that house, and is doubtless the manuscript listed as item 197 in

---

[43] Except York Minster XVI.i.8.

[44] Except Oxford Merton College LI.

[45] See Richard Gameson, *The Manuscripts of Early Norman England (c. 1066–1130)* (Oxford, 1999): B.2.34 is Gameson's no. 136 ("s. xii^1 Canterbury, Christ Church"); O.4.7 is Gameson no. 167 ("?pre-1124, Rochester").

[46] Though it must be noted that the order of short texts at the end of the collections differs: in **T**^{1} and **T**^{2} the order is 15, 16, 13, 14; in the St. Augustine's item it is 13, 14, 15, 16. The Table of Contents of **T**^{2} is virtually identical in wording to the St. Augustine's list. **T**^{1} has a Table of Contents on f. 1v listing the same works, though the wording is fuller and diverges from the St. Augustine's list and **T**^{2}; The **T**^{1} list includes 'Alphabetu*m* hebreu*m* grecu*m*. cu*m* suis int*er*p*re*tationibus' as on (old) p. 231 (now f. 114v), a short work that might have been left off the St. Augustine's list even if included (as is the case with **T**^{2}, where it is not listed in the contents but appears on ff. 109v–110r, inc. 'Aleph. mille uel doctrina', Lambert 400, CPL 623a, ed. PL 23.1305–1306, also occurring in the "shorter collections" **K**, **B**^{1}, **M** and the "longer" **A**, **S**, **D**); because it lacks a rubric before the text, **T**^{1} does not note item 12, "sententie excerpte diuersis opusculis" though it is present on ff. 173r-179r with the same incipit as in **T**^{2}.

Prior Eastry's catalogue (Christ Church 1284 × 1331);[47] Trinity College, Cambridge O.4.7 (James 1239, siglum T²) is written in round Canterbury-style writing: it was owned by Rochester (ex libris), but may have been written at Christ Church. Both Trinity volumes are plain but nicely produced, medium format, readable volumes suitable for the monastic library.

TCC B.2.34 (T¹) has 181 trimmed leaves, foliated [i] + 180, arranged in 22 quires of 8,[48] leaves 282 × 209 mm. in size. It is written in 29 long lines, in a writing area of 217 × 150 mm.[49] The hand itself is an elegant, consistent early proto-gothic in the "prickly" Christ Church style,[50] using an orangy-brown ink that varies in color. It has decorated initials with fantastic designs in pen and wash with several colors, violet predominating, though these features are neither as fine nor as functional as guides to the reader as those in T². But the capitals are closely related to T² in placement and style, if not in function. The in-text initials and capitals are in reddish-violet ink. The original table of contents is by the main scribe. There are many erasures, and frequent corrections have been added in different contemporary hands, as well as some Greek words in the margins. The binding is early modern (18th century?); there is a mark like '10' painted on the fore-edge.

TCC O.4.7 (T²) has a thirteenth-century Rochester ex libris on f. 1r;[51] but it was probably written at Christ Church Canterbury. The hand is a "mixed hand" of early proto-gothic.[52] James dates this book to about 1120, but perhaps 1130 would be safer. It remains in its original binding, oak boards covered with tawed leather, with the place for a clasp on mid-front-edge and a fastening for a strap on the middle of the back, with four bands in tunnels.[53] The cover is flush with

---

47 Ed. James, *Ancient Libraries*, 38–39: the contents as listed in the catalogue and on the contents list of TCC B.2.34 are identical though their wording is not verbatim.

48 The modern foliation includes the flyleaf and so is one higher than the inked foliation visible on microfilm; the visible foliation is followed in this chapter. The quires are numbered contemporaneously on the last verso of each. Quire X has an additional leaf.

49 Scoring is plummet, 29 lines single bounding scores, outermost vertical extended to top and bottom edges, top three and bottom two horizontals extended to edges.

50 See Ker, *English Manuscripts in the Century After the Norman Conquest*, 25–29.

51 "liber de claustro Roffensi per G. Camerarium" (James).

52 Ker, *English Manuscripts*, 30–33 and plate 10b.

53 Michael Gullick contributed a handwritten note, dated 1 April 1983, which has been put in the Trinity College Library's copy of James's *Catalogue* at O.4.7 ". . .there is nothing remarkable about O.4.7, the Rochester book I saw. And this is so. There is not the slightest doubt that it was bound soon after it was written about 1125 and that it is an exceedingly good example of its type. Some of the details, the shortness of the tabs, the snug fit of the primary bands in the entrance to the tunnels in the board, the weight of the sewing thread, the arrangement of the preliminary gathering of one sheet and the absence of the temporary sewing to be found in other (not all) 12th century bindings, are all valuable" (cited by permission of Mr. Gullick, with thanks).

Tables of contents

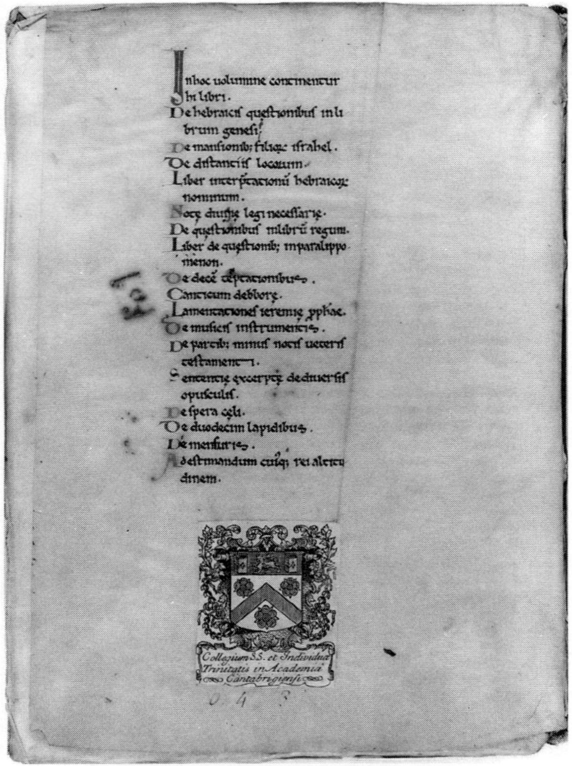

Figure 33: Cambridge, Trinity College B.2.34, f. 1v

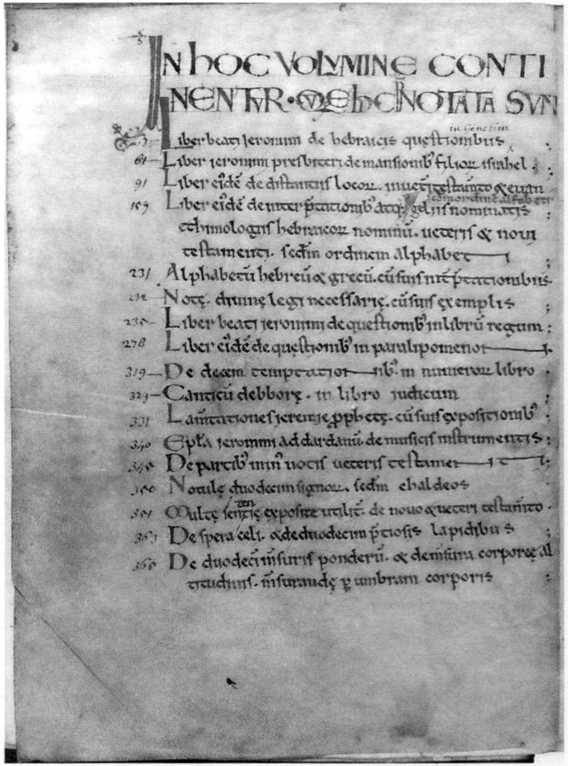

Figure 34: Cambridge, Trinity College O.4.7, flyleaf verso

Used by permission of The Masters and Fellows of Trinity College Cambridge.

the pages, which are 340 × 240 mm. Twenty-one quires of eight are signed on the last verso a-x, ff. 1–168, plus a quire of 4, 3 cancelled, 4 blank (ff. 169–170), plus 2 folios. The book was written by a single skilled scribe in two columns, 32 lines, text area 160 × 240 mm., the column width being about 70mm.[54] There are red rubrics at the beginnings and ends of major texts. Large colored decorated initials at beginnings of texts have fine pale-colored washes and pen work. The fine capitals in red, purple, and green mark text divisions. The script is very black and clear, and the hierarchy of marks and divisions, as well as the columnar structure, is designed for easy consultation. The scribe's own table of contents is on the flyleaf verso.[55] Textually T[2] seems to be a direct copy of T[1], showing at the same time a much improved layout for easier reference compared to the exemplar.[56] The layout of T[1] is more primitive than that of T[2]: it is written in long lines rather than in columns, without a consistent hierarchy of marks and capitals.

The Jerome volume described in the fifteenth-century St. Augustine's catalogue, to judge by its contents, must have been a close relation to the extant Trinity manuscripts from Christ Church, though probably somewhat later in the century, to judge from abbreviations and ligatures as preserved in Claudius (which consistently differ in significant ways from those of the *Historia* extracts), and doubtless had a layout of the more modern type. This lost St. Augustine's Jerome is in all likelihood the immediate source of most of the Hieronymian material copied into the St. Augustine's manuscript, Cotton Claudius B. iv; the Trinity manuscripts give us a pretty exact picture of what the Claudius annotator had in hand as he worked. To explain the texts, pictures, and ongoing biblical texts at hand, Claudius draws from the following "collected" texts that are on the St. Augustine's list: 1) *Hebrew Questions on Genesis*, 2) Epistle 78 *De XLII mansionibus*, 3) *De distanciis locorum* (SNLH), 6a) *The Hebrew Questions on Kings*, 6b) *The Hebrew Questions on Paralipomenon*, 8) *The Canticle of Deborah*, plus the two short mensural texts (13 and 14). These texts have been selected for the evident reason that they are all the texts in the shorter collection that have any bearing on the main texts in Claudius. Two texts not used might at first sight be seen as exceptions to this, 7) *The Ten Temptations in the Desert* and 4) *Interpretation of Hebrew*

---

54 Double vertical bounding scores are on the inner and outer margins of the page, extended to edges; 3 vertical scores in center extended to edges to mark column separation; 3 top and 3 bottom horizontal scores extended to edge.

55 F. 25 is a thirteenth-century replacement of the first leaf of the fourth quire, which shows that books of this type were still in active use beyond the time that the Claudius annotator was working.

56 As Doane found in a practical way while collating texts in T[2] and T[1] over several days. It was much more time-consuming to find particular passages in T[1]. Passages in T[2] are easy to find because of the system of capitalization of place names, hierarchization of letters and entries, consistent paragraphing, darker ink, clearer hand, and double columns.

Names. But 7) primarily concerns Deuteronomy, which is not commented upon at all (that text is without picture space so there is no room for the usual style of annotations in any case); and 4) consists of a plethora of one-word onomastic interpretations that do not match the interests or style of the commentator. So it appears that our annotator has exploited his available Jerome collection fairly systematically.

Textually, these items in Claudius do not conform as closely to those in the Trinity manuscripts as the latter do to each other; presumably the texts of the St. Augustine's volume underwent some revision from lateral sources, particularly as regards punctuation. Because Claudius is freely abbreviating and sometimes epitomizing or making ad hoc connections, disagreements between C on the one hand and T^1 and T^2 on the other do not mean anything. But when C T^1 and T^2 agree against Lagarde's edition (L)[57] it could be significant. Also significant are places where C agrees with L against T^1 and T^2, since this suggests C's text may have been written from a copy corrected from lateral sources. Though T^1 and T^2 regularly differ from C in matters of nominal orthography, punctuation, and abbreviations, they often agree with C in substantive readings against L. The facts, however, including contradictory evidence within single entries, do not support a conclusion that the exemplar of Claudius was textually identical or even particularly close to the texts of T^1 and T^2, though there are many coincidences.[58] In

[57] Lagarde, *Onomastica sacra* (1887). The references are by paragraph and line within paragraph. This edition is reprinted in CCSL 72.

[58] In the following sample of evidence the annotations are listed by their numbers in ch. 2 above. Lagarde's reading is given first, followed after the semi-colon by those of the manuscripts, Claudius (Cl) first, then T^1 followed by T^2. Lagarde's classicising "ae" is changed to "e".

Disagreements of Lagarde against the three manuscripts:

From SNLH: 95: interpretatus; interpretatur 101: probem; probemus 104: uiculus; uicus 132: barad; barth (Cl), barath (T1 T2) 136c: quem; quam 138a: amrafel; amasphal 175: quo Iacob tota; quo tota 294l: autem et nunc; autem nunc 300: ibi occubuit; ubi occubuit 311b: Sadada; Sadala 313b: Fogo; fogor 315: Job; jobab 317: a Syris; ab assiriis / Recem; raam 328: in quod: in quo 330c: cana / uerus; chana / uir 330d: Trachonitis (L T2); traconitidis (Cl T1) 330b: uiginti quinque; xxti. (Cl), uiginti (T1 T2), but in the same extract occurs Galilea (L Cl) Galileę (T1 T2) due sunt (so L Cl, sunt *not in* T1 T2) galilee.

From Ep. 78: 301: possint *et cum multis precibus et conatu uiam non impetrent*, sed (L); italicized words omitted Cl T1 T2.

Contrary evidence, where L Cl agree against T1 and T2:

From SNLH: 162: ex eo; ex ea 172a: Seon rex; rex seon 205: uicus pergrandis; grandis uicus 214: petefres; putrefe (*corr. to* pet- *by* T1) petrefe (T2) 327: mirum; miro 311a: arabie ciuitas; ciuitas arabie, *but in the same extract occurs* a bostra (L T1); ab ostra (Cl) abostra (T2) (note continues).

all likelihood the Claudius exemplar was later than the Trinity copies and under other, lateral, textual influences.

Two small texts, however, are virtually identical in all three manuscripts. The short mensural extracts, 13) "De mensuris" and 14) "Rei altitudinem,"[59] copied in Claudius on the second of the inserted leaves (f. 147r/9–24, nos. 335a and b), are rare and exactly in the form as extracted into the Hieronymian collections; they bear no evident relation to the biblical material but for some reason must have been considered an essential component of the Jerome collection as it was known at Canterbury: in TCC O.4.7 they are written by the main scribe on a final bifolium after the last complete quire, suggesting they were considered an integral and essential part of the ensemble in all three of these sister manuscripts, to be included even at the extra cost of an added sheet. Attributed for a long time to Gerbert of Aurillac, who, became Pope Silvester II (972–1003), they are modified extracts from an older mathematical compilation drawn from "Epaphroditus and Vitruvius"; similar passages occur in a text published by Bubnov under the title *Geometria incerti auctoris.*[60] What is striking is the exact correspondence, in variant wording, omissions, and errors, in multifarious ways that differ from the edited texts, between the two Trinity manuscripts and the lost St. Augustine's as represented by Claudius. Tables 6.2 and 6.3 show these texts, in their Claudius forms, with variants (including capitalization and punctuation) of T^1 and T^2 given beneath, alongside the printed editions (for translations see no. 335 a and b in Chapter 2).[61]

The Claudius scribe sometimes copies the same passage twice; nos. 172b and 320 are apparently taken from different sources, neither of them the same as the Trinity manuscripts:

172b § Gader. Turris ubi habitauit (**T1 T2** habitante) iacob ruben patris sui (sui *om.* **T1 T2**) uiolauit thorum. ⁊ (quę **T1 T2**) absque g. littera in hebreo ader scribitur;

320 Turris ubi habitante iacob ruben patris sui uiolauit thorum; et absque g. littera in hebreo ader scribitur.

[59] The titles in the O.4.7 table of contents are "De mensuris" and "Ad estimandum cuiusque rei altitudinem"; B.2.34 has for the second the title 'De duodecim mensuris ponderum & de mensura corporę altitudinis. mensurandę per umbram corporis'.

[60] Nicolaus Bubnov, ed., *Gerberti postea Silvestri II Papae Opera Mathematica (972–1003)* (Berlin, 1899), 310–65; The extracts correspond to IV.1 and III.9, respectively, the verbal correspondence to IV.1 running only to the word 'miliarium'; the information on measurements was generally known; the wording and order of units resembles that of ch. 3 of the genuine *Geometria* of Gerbert, printed by Bubnov, 57–64. A version of this extract, but with many differences nevertheless, was printed by F. Blume et al., *Feldmesser,* 1:94–95 (see next note).

[61] The first text given is an exact transcription from Claudius. Variations from the edited text are underlined. Places where words in the edited text are missing in Claudius and T^1 and T^2 are marked with three asterisks; variants from T^1 and T^2, including suspensions and punctuation, are given below this passage. Then the edited text is given,

TABLE 6.2

Claudius f. 147r/9–17, no. 335a

No. 13 (f. 147r) MENSVRARVM appellationes q⟨u⟩ib⟨us⟩ utim⟨ur⟩; s⟨unt⟩[a] xii.[b] digit⟨us⟩.[c] uncia. palm⟨us⟩. sext ⟨us⟩[d] pes. cubit⟨us⟩[e] | grandus.[f] passus. dece⟨m⟩-peda. actus. stadiu⟨m⟩. miliariu⟨m⟩. Minima pars haru⟨m⟩ me⟨n⟩suraru⟨m⟩[g] | est digit⟨us⟩. Siq⟨u⟩id[h] eni⟨m⟩ infra digitu⟨m⟩ metiam⟨ur⟩ partib⟨us⟩[i] respondem⟨us⟩. ut dimidia⟨m⟩ aut t⟨er⟩cia⟨m⟩ | *** parte⟨m⟩ digiti. Palm⟨us⟩ habet[j] digitos. vii. uncias. iii. Sext⟨us⟩ que[k] eade⟨m⟩ doran [*sic*] appellat⟨ur⟩ ha|bet[l] *** uncias. ix. digitos. xii. *** In pede porrecto semipedes .ii. palmi. iiii.[m] uncie.[n] xii. | digiti. xxvii. In pede p⟨ro⟩strato semipedes. iiii[or]. palmi. viii. uncie.[o] xxiiii.[p] digiti. xxxii.[q] | Cubit⟨us⟩ habet[r] sexq⟨u⟩iped es.[s] Sexta duas palmas. sex *** passus. *** pedes. v.[t] dece⟨m⟩peda que[u] & | p⟨er⟩tica. *** Act⟨us⟩[v] in longitudine habet[w] pedes. centu⟨m⟩.[x] Stadiu⟨m⟩ habet[y] pedes. dcxxxv. | Passus. cxxv.[z] Miliariu⟨m⟩ *** passus. cc.[aa] *** pedes. v. ***

Variants:

[a]as⟨un⟩t T¹ sunt T² [b]duodeci⟨m⟩ [c]Digit⟨us⟩. T¹ [d]sext⟨us⟩. T¹T² [e]cubit⟨us⟩. T¹T² [f]gradus. T¹T² [g]m⟨en⟩suraru⟨m⟩; T¹T² [h]Siquid T² [i]partib⟨us⟩; T² [j]hab& T² [k]quę T¹T² [l] hab& T² [m]iiii[or] T¹T² [n]uncię T¹T² [o]uncię T¹T² [p]xxiii[or]. T² [q]xxxii[ta] T² [r]hab&. T¹ [s]sesq⟨u⟩ipedes. T² [t]q⟨u⟩inq⟨ue⟩. T² [u]quę T¹, *hook erased?* T² [v]Act⟨us⟩. T¹T² [w]hab& T² [x] c[tu⟨m⟩]. T² [y]hab& [z]c.xxv. T¹ [aa] Miliari⟨um⟩. T²

F. Blume, K. Lachmann, and A. Rudorff, eds.

Mensurarum appellationes quibus utimur sunt duodecim, digitus uncia palmus sextans pes cubitus gradus passus decempeda actus stadium miliarium. minima pars harum mensurarum est digitus: siquid enim infra digitum metiamur, partibus respondemus, ut dimidiam aut tertiam. uncia habet digitum unum et tertiam partem digiti. palmus habet digitos iiii, uncias iii. sextans, que eadem dodrans appellatur, habet palmos iii, uncias viiii, digitos xii. pes habet palmos iii, uncias xii, digitos xvi. in pede porrecto semipedes duo. in pede constrato semipedes iiii. in pede quadrato semipedes viii. cubitus habet sesquipedem, sextantes duas, palmos vi, uncias xviii. gradus habet pedes duo semis. passus habet pedes quinque. decempeda, quae eadem pertica appellatur, habet pedes x. actus habet longitudinis ped. cxx, latitudinis ped . cxx. stadium habet pedes dcxxv, passus cxxv. miliarium habet passus mille, milia pedum v, stadios viii.

TABLE 6.3

Claudius f. 147r/18–24 (no. 335b)

No. 14 Ad estimandu⟨m⟩ cui⟨us⟩q⟨ue⟩ rei altitùdi´ne⟨m⟩; sole lucente q⟨u⟩e cunq⟨ue⟩[a] res illa fuerit sub diuo posita um|bra⟨m⟩ emitte. sed non[b] sibi *** equale⟨m⟩[c]. Quap⟨ro⟩pt⟨er⟩ umbre[d] illi⟨us⟩ quota⟨m⟩ parte⟨m⟩ uolueris elige. | deinde[e] ui⟨r⟩ga⟨m⟩[f] huic pa[r]ti coeq⟨u⟩ata⟨m⟩[g] in terra⟨m⟩[h] statuas. & umbra⟨m⟩[i] exinde cadente⟨m⟩. seu p⟨er⟩ pedes. seu | p⟨er⟩ palmos. seu p⟨er⟩ uncias. diuidas. Si maior inuenta fuerit; *** quantu⟨m⟩ ui⟨r⟩ga[j] sup⟨er⟩at⟨ur⟩[k]. tan|tu⟨m⟩ a si⟨n⟩gulis[l] partib⟨us⟩ q⟨u⟩aru⟨m⟩[m] m⟨en⟩sura⟨m⟩ ui⟨r⟩ga[n] habet[o] subtrahas. Si au⟨tem⟩[p] minor; *** quantu⟨m⟩ ui⟨r⟩ga[q] | sup⟨er⟩at[r]. tantu⟨m⟩ dictis partib⟨us⟩[s] adicias. Q⟨uo⟩d au⟨tem⟩[t] in umbra.[u] u⟨e⟩l *** augm⟨en⟩tatione accreuerit. | v⟨e⟩l ex subtractione remanserit,[v] p⟨ro⟩ m⟨en⟩sura[w] illi⟨us⟩ rei teneto;[x]

Bubnov, ed.

Quaecunque res posita fuerit sub divo, umbram emittit, sed non sibi semper coaequalem. Quapropter umbrae ipsius, quotam partem volueris, eligas. Deinde virgulam coaequalem huic parti in terra statuas et umbram exinde cadentem seu per pedes, seu per palmos, seu per uncias dividas. Si major inventa fuerit umbra, quam virgula, quantum umbra virgulam superat, tantum a singulis, quarum mensuram virgula habet, subtrahas. Si autem minor est umbra, quantum virga superat, tantum praedictis partibus adjicias. Quod autem in umbra vel ex augmentatione accreverit, vel ex subtractione remanserit, pro mensura illius rei habeto.

Variants:

[a]quęcunq⟨ue⟩ T^1T^2 [b]n⟨on⟩ T^2 [c]ęquale⟨m⟩ T^1T^2, Cl *corr. from* equeale⟨m⟩ [d]umbrę T^1T^2 [e]deinde T^1T^2 [f]uirga⟨m⟩ T^1T^2 [g]coęq⟨u⟩ata⟨m⟩ T^1 coęquata⟨m⟩ *with* c *smudged* T^2 [h]terra T^1 t⟨er⟩ra T^2 [i]umbram T^2 [j]uirga T^1T^2 [k]-⟨ur⟩ *stroke is added* T^1, sup⟨er⟩at *(no stroke)* T^2 [l]singulis T^1T^2 [m]quaru⟨m⟩ T^1T^2 [n]uirga T^1T^2 [o]hab& T^2 [p]aut⟨em⟩T^1 aute⟨m⟩ T^2 [q]uirga *written in blacker ink over a large erasure, one letter erased before* u- T^1, á uirga T^2 [r]sup⟨er⟩at *an erasure above* -t T^1, sup⟨er⟩at⟨ur⟩ -⟨ur⟩ *stroke added?* T^2 [s]partibus T^2 [t]aut⟨em⟩ T^1 aute⟨m⟩ T^2 [u]*no point* T^1T^2 [v]remanserit. T^1 remanserit; T^2 [w]mensura T^2 [x]teneto. T^1T^2

Figure 35: Cambridge, Trinity College B.2.34 "Mensurarum" and "Ad estmandum"

Used by permission of The Masters and Fellows of Trinity College Cambridge.

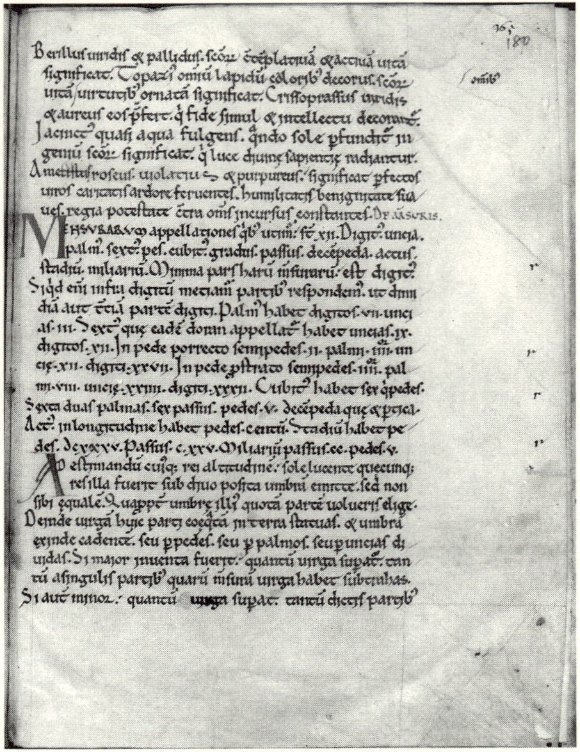

f. 180r

f. 180v

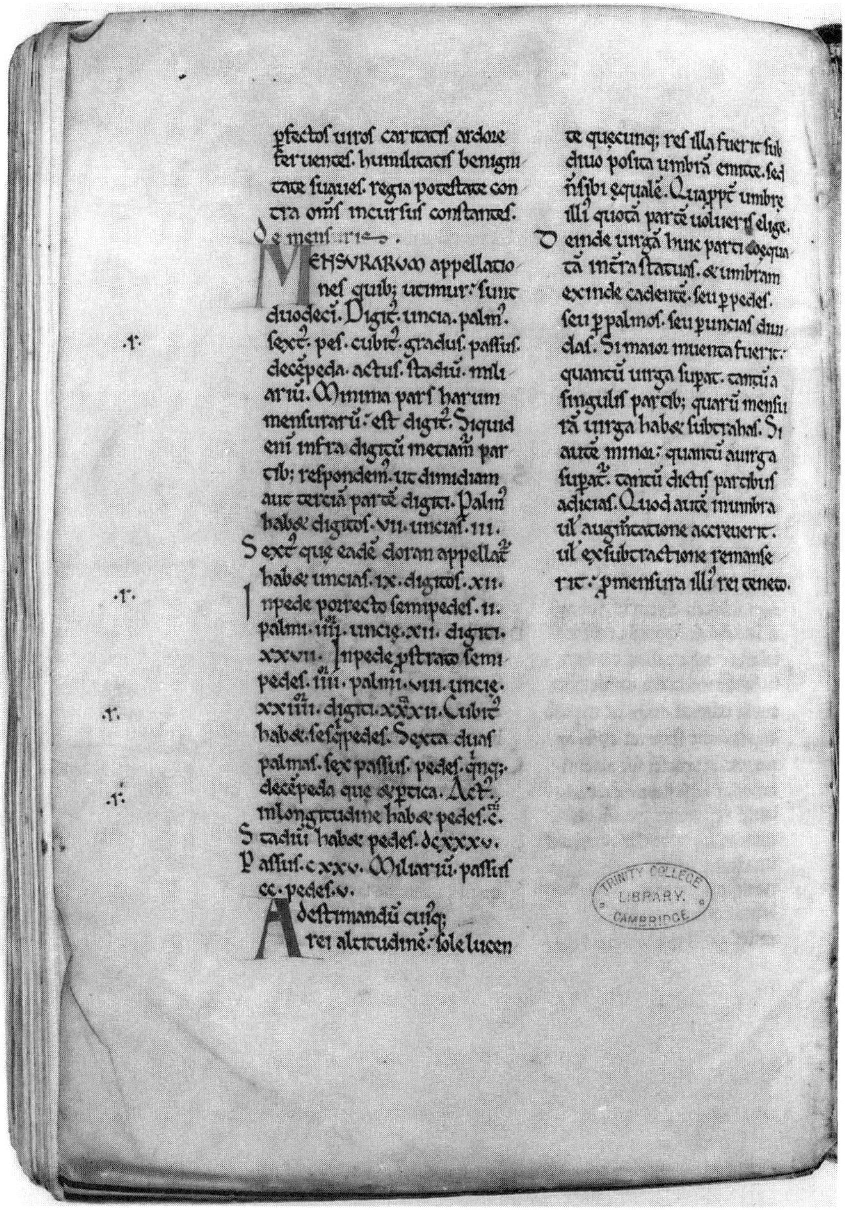

Figure 36: Cambridge, Trinity College O.4.7, f. 170v "Mensurarum" and "Ad estimandum"

As far as these texts go, Claudius, or rather the manuscript Claudius used, could have been a direct copy of T^1 but not of T^2. The erasures in T^1 at the end of the "Ad estimandum" passage (see variants *q* and *r*) bring T^1 into accord with Claudius and seem to link these two manuscripts in some way, perhaps via a corrected intermediary, as does the overwriting of 'uirga' at this same place. The abbreviations and treatment of numbers in T^1 is very close to that of Claudius. T^1 differs more from Claudius than it does from T^2 in matters of pointing and the use of the note 'hab'; obviously all three texts are extremely close to one another against other witnesses as represented by the edition. (See figs. 27 above and 35, 36 below.)

As mentioned, a survey of the sources of the annotations reveals that the Claudius annotator made a systematic use of virtually all the material found in the "shorter collection" that was relevant to the material presented by the Old English main text and the *Historia* extracts that had previously been entered into the book. But whereas the *Historia* annotations cease with Exodus, the Hieronymian notes continue throughout the book. They are not applied in such careful patterns as are most of the *Historia*-derived notes, but are rather linear and connected up largely with place-name cues provided by the main text. Some seem to be added as supplementary to *Historia* notes and may even be calculated in some cases to display the true "originals" of material rewritten by the Comestor. Many of the Hieronymian notes are prefaced by "Jer. dicit." The most striking of these explicit and correct attributions are a couple of the citations of Jerome's *De XLII mansionibus filiorum Israel in deserto* (Ep. 78, ad Fabiolam) which are indicated with almost modern bibliographical accuracy: on ff. 121v-122r a long citation on the death of Maria (Miriam) (no. 301, referring to the Old English text of Numbers 20:1) is accompanied in the upper margin of f. 122r by the mark 'xxxiii', an accurate reference to "Mansio XXXIII," the section of the work from which the citation is taken.[62] Even more explicitly displayed on the next recto is the complete rubric from the same work,[63] added untidily by the same hand in the upper margin: 'aaron in extremo t*err*e edom .xxxiiii^{ta}- mansio e*st*'.[64] Another citation from the same section of this work (no. 309) is at the bottom of f. 123r.The concentration of these three extracts on two adjacent leaves suggests the annotator

words and morphemes missing in Claudius are underlined. The text of no. 13 is from the prefatory epistle of "Balbi ad Celsum," *Balbi ad Celsum Expositio*, ed. F. Blume, et al., *Die Schriften der römischen Feldmesser*, 1: 94–95; the text is also printed in PL 139.121D as Gerbert, *De Geometria*, ch. 24; the text of no. 14 is from Bubnov, *Opera Mathematica*, ed. as "Geometria incerti auctoris," 323; it is also ed. in PL 139.96B-98C. Resolutions of abbreviations are marked with angle brackets.

62 PL 22.716–717, CSEL 55, 76.1.

63 No. 307a/b, referring to Aaron's death, Old English, f. 123r/1–4 = Numbers 20:28–30.

64 PL 22.717, CSEL 55.77.7.

had book in hand at this point, making his own ad hoc connections with the Old English text.[65] The same may be said for the two citations (nos. 283, 286) from the pseudo-Hieronymian *Commentarius in canticum Debborae*, part of the "shorter collection." Both occur on f. 95v and hence are doubtless from a single consult of the exemplar. They are part of an artful ensemble on "Amalech" which brings out the literal, typological, and prophetic valences of Exodus 17:13–14 being rendered by the Old English.

Two Hieronymian comments that appear to be taken directly from his works are of special interest because they involve the English notes and provide comments to the *Historia*, one in Latin, the other translated into English. The first, from *De situ et nominibus locorum hebraicorum*, no. 27, "Naid," pertaining to Genesis 4:16, the exile of Cain, is an addition neatly fitted in (the ductus but not the ink is nearly identical) to an English note (no. 26), itself a translation of the *Historia*, in the upper picture frame on f. 9r (fig. 17): 'Joseph*us* cw*æ*ð. fæle cenne lándes ywilcon caym. ⁊ calmana is wyf. forð hi comen to hæra stede þe me cw*æ*ðe naida';[66] the Latin (no. 27) following has "Naid t*er*ra in q*u*a habitauit cain. Vertit*ur* au*tem* in salum ide*st* motu*m* siue fluctuatione*m*'.[67] The other (no. 48) on f. 12r is the elaboration of the "famosa quaestio" on the age of Mathusala, a note attributed to "Norman," already discussed above (ch. 5, 285–88).

De situ et nominibus locorum hebraicorum (SNLH) is the most frequently used Hieronymian work by far. There are about 110 distinct entries from this work, but closer to 120 when combinations and repeats are taken into account. With few exceptions, these citations are systematically placed either at the top or the bottom of the page, rarely in the picture spaces, which are used, in Genesis and Exodus, for comments drawn from the *Historia*. In Genesis, between f. 9r and f. 70r, there are thirty-six entries from SNLH; in Exodus, between f. 74r and 100v, eleven entries (but only as a medley, see below); in Numbers between ff. 117r and 128r there are fifteen entries; there are no notes to Leviticus at all from any source nor to Deuteronomy, but there are two entries between Deuteronomy and Joshua on f. 139v; in Joshua, between f. 140v and 154r, there are forty-six entries from SNLH. In Genesis and Exodus the main source of notes is the *Historia*, and many of the SNLH annotations can be seen as supplements to the *Historia*. *Historia*-derived notes fail after Exodus and, beginning at f. 117r, in Numbers and Joshua SNLH is the main source of comments.

---

[65] There is an earlier citation from Ep. 78 on f. 56v, referring to Thamar (Old English, line 4 = Genesis 38:24). It has no referencing.

[66] "Josephus says many kinds of land Cain and his wife Calmana passed over; they came forward to their place which is called 'Naid'." This corresponds exactly to HS: "Josephus ait: 'Et multam peragrans terram cum uxore sua Chalmana, collocatus est in loco, qui Nayda nuncupatur in quo ei etiam filii nati sunt'" (PL 198.1078B).

[67] SNLH, PL 23.912D, Lagarde 141.24: "Naid is the land in which Cain lived. Then it was changed into the sea, that is, motion or fluctuation."

The placement of the SNLH notes in the top or bottom margins (only occasionally in the frames) suggests that they constituted a program of their own independent of *Historia* comments; the ductus is generally larger than that of the *Historia* notes, suggesting that the annotator had the Jerome collection in hand and the preset purpose of selecting and placing (mostly) appropriate notes in a pre-determined layout, in a more-or-less single campaign. The *Historia* comments appear to be part of a separate program that was mostly written first but for some reason was not completed. Earlier in Claudius, entries from SNLH frequently seem to be fitted in to conform to already existing entries in English and in Latin from *Historia*: as in the aforementioned no. 27, f. 9r, the extract from SNLH is neatly fitted into the top picture frame after the *Historia*-derived English note; on f. 21v three comments (90, 91a, 91b) are fitted into the ledger-spaces alternating with *Historia* comments. In these earlier parts of the book, as well, the bottom margins have often been appropriated by English and *Historia* notes, as, e.g., f. 25v, where at the bottom the SNLH comment is written in two lines beneath an *Historia* comment so that the rubric 'Jer. dīc' has to be entered up and to the side, next to the *Historia* comment, but in the larger ductus. When the bottom space is clear and there are no competing notes, the SNLH annotations are generally entered boldly across the bottom margins, as for the first time on f. 23r and many times thereafter; if a long entry is begun on the bottom of a verso, it is neatly continued on the bottom margin of the facing recto or, less often, on the top overleaf, a few times on the top of the verso, if begun on a recto. SNLH notes are written more uniformly, both as to ductus and in their consistent placement, than the other Jerome extracts, which sometimes show uncertainty of ductus, or changing ductus, and are more frequently entered so as to accommodate previously written entries.

The Jerome/Eusebius structuring of the notes in SNLH is fairly standard: they are arranged within each letter of the alphabet according to the books of the Bible using the place name as headword; sometimes a place is identified by its location in relation to other places more famous; the place name in Jerome's (Eusebius') time, if different from the biblical name, is often given, and usually some biblical or historical event is associated with it. Typical is the second SNLH entry in Claudius, on f. 20v (no. 84):

> Charan ciuitas mesopotamie t*r*ans edessa*m* que usq*ue* hodie carra d*icitu*r. V*b*i roman*us* cessus [*recte* cesus] e*st* exercit*us*. & crassus dux capt*us*.[68]

In this case its use in Claudius is equally straightforward: it is linked to the occurrence of the name "Charan" in the line of Old English immediately above on

[68] No. 84, PL 23.888B, Lagarde 112.1: "Haran is a city of Mesopotamia beyond Edessa which up to the present day is called Carra, where the Roman army was abandoned [destroyed] and General Crassus captured."

the page (top of f. 20v) **Hi foron oð comon to aran** (= Genesis 11:13, "Haran"). This linking of the note to the text via a headword is in the spirit of Jerome's "literal" style of exposition in SNLH, that is, it is simply an addition of what strikes a modern person as textually extraneous matter.[69] Annotations according to the "headword" principle are sometimes placed correctly despite difficulties the Old English throws up: for example, "Agaylon" (no. 344, Joshua 10:12–13) is placed correctly, at the bottom of f. 151r, even though the Old English copy has corrupted the word to **acheald** (f. 150v/18; Laud MS "achialon"); the annotator is helped by the large picture on f. 151r of Joshua stopping the sun and moon.[70]

Many times the comment is linked to the Old English text via a word within the note, not by the headword itself. For example, 'Ullamaus; p*ro* qua i*n* heb*r*eo scriptu*m* habet*ur* luza. Eade*m* e*st* au*tem* que & bethel'[71] (no. 91b) links to the Old English **bethel** (f. 21v/4) immediately above this comment on the page; the contiguous preceding comment in Jerome's text is entered in the top margin of f. 21v, 'Vr chaldeor*um*' (no. 19a, Lagarde 158.17) which only links as a headword to the same phrase in the Old English text on f. 19v/3, but which has a general contextual relevance where it is entered. Similar is the note at the bottom of f. 24v, 'Damasc*us*. Nobilis urbs fenicis [*sc.* -es] . . .' (no. 101).[72] This links to **fenicen** on the facing f. 25r/4 (Genesis 14:15), and carries with it the rest of Jerome's comment on the "son of Abraham by the slave woman Masec"; by our lights this does not elucidate the passage at hand but it is in the Hieronymian spirit of adding information *literaliter*. It also shows how carefully the annotator is scanning the Old English text, for "Phenicis" does not occur in the Vulgate, only in the Old English version, which must itself have been influenced by Jerome or some work derived from him.[73]

The annotator also adds comments that make up for elisions in the Old English or which are implicit in the text: Genesis 14:18 reads "But Melchisedech the king of Salem, bringing forth bread and wine . . ." whereas the Old English has **Þær com eac melchisedech se mæra godes man se wæs cyning ⁊ godes sacerd.**

[69] Notes with direct headword links to the word in the Old English are nos. 84, 125, 172a, 175, 198, 217, 317, 322, 332, 333, 338, 339, 341, 344, 345, 346, 347, 348, 351, 352, 353, 354, 355, 356.

[70] In this case the picture-elements are labeled by a late twelfth-century hand 'sol', 'luna', 'Iosue' in a style that seems cruder than the generality of the picture-labels; interestingly, the *s*'s have the insular form. The hand seems to be the same that added the English note on f. 19v '7 lasca þé is sarai . ⁊ melcha.'

[71] PL 23.926B, Lagarde 158.17: "Ulammaus for which in Hebrew is written Luz. The same name [Luz] which is also for Bethel. . . ."

[72] PL 23.890B, Lagarde 114.21: "Damascus, the noble city of the Phoenicians."

[73] The most obvious place that the Old English translator might have had resort to is Jerome, HQG (PL 23.960): "Et persecutus est eos usque Dan. Ad Phoenicis oppidum, quod nunc Paneas dicitur." 'fenicen' in the Old English does not derive from an Old Latin reading.

7 **he brohte hlaf. 7 win** (f. 25v/10–11); the geographical omission is made up by three entries from SNLH, f. 25v bottom, 'Sich*em*. 7 sale*m*. . .' (no. 109), f. 26r below the upper picture of Melchisedech, "Salem" (no. 111a)[74] and f. 26r, above lower picture, 'Jebus. ipsa e*st* que et ier*usa*lin', the latter two from sections on Joshua. The relations of these comments are made clear to us by the extract from the *Historia* copied after them on f. 27rv, "And note that whereas Jerusalem was called 'Jebus' up to the time of Melchisedech, by whom it was called 'Salem', after David it was called Jebusalem. But after the 'b' was changed to 'r' it was called 'Jerusalem', as the fortress of Salem. . . ." (no. 112). The annotator was probably motivated to add the Jerome notes as much to illustrate the *Historia* extract as the Old English.

This is one of many indications that the Jerome material was added in a later campaign, after the *Historia* notes had been entered in Claudius. To give one more clear example nearby from many available, on f. 24r/10, between the pictures, the Old English has for Genesis 14 **wið þone dene mambre. þ*æt* ðe ys on ebron. . . .** In a smaller ductus, immediately below on the page, is the *Historia* comment: "Hebron is a city which is named Cariatharbe, that is 'city-four'; for 'arbe' is 'four' and 'cariath' is 'city'. Adam the greatest is buried there, as well as Abraham, Isaac, and Jacob with their wives. . . . Josephus. . . saying that Abram lived by that holm-oak which is called Agygi" (no. 99). Immediately above this, between the ledger line and the bottom of the Old English text is entered in a larger ductus, 'Jer*onymus* dic*it*. ARbe q*ua*tuor. eo q*uod* ibi q*ua*tuor pat*r*iarche sepulti sunt.'[75] Jerome is the source of the comment by the Comestor—the Claudius annotator seems aware of this—and is also appearing to add to the reasons for the city's name, so the extension also serves as gloss on the *Historia* comment.

There are twenty notes taken from Jerome's genuine work, *Hebraicae quaestiones in libro Geneseos* (HQG).[76] All pertain to Genesis except the last (no. 282, f. 95rv), which is to Exodus. Seven are explicitly attributed to Jerome (nos. 80a, 141b, 146a, 190, 210, 225, 282). The comments in this work are entirely literal, but somewhat more expansive and general, and include onomastics, linguistic explanations, resolution of contradictions between biblical passages, and problems of chronological calculation and genealogy. The Claudius annotator is very selective, seldom copying out complete comments, but only pertinent phrases and sentences. For example, no. 100, the "fountain of Cades," Genesis 14:7, is omitted in the Old English and this note fills in the gap, connecting it to the rock that Moses struck water from (Numbers 20:1, 11–13). In several cases extracts

---

[74] This is only the last part of a longer note in SNLH on "Jerusalem" (PL 23.904C, Lagarde 132.6–13).

[75] "Jerome says: 'Arbe' is 'four' because there four patriarchs were buried."

[76] No. 48 is in English; the Latin extracts are nos. 49, 71, 80a, 80b, 96, 100, 117, 130, 141a/b, 146a, 190, 191, 210, 214, 215, 222, 225, 282. No. 141a derives from Jerome through some intermediate source.

from HQG seem to come in clumps, often differ in ductus from the SNLH comments, and were probably written in a distinct but short campaign.

Thus, no. 71 (PL. 951A, Lagarde 11.23): 'He itaq*ue* vii. gentes qu*a*s de japhet. stiripe [*sic*] uenire m`e´moraui. | . ad aquilonis partem habitant';[77] This occurs in the midst of a series of comments drawn from the *Historia* regarding the descendants of the sons of Noe (nos. 70a-f) extending from the bottom of 18r, through 18v and to the bottom of 19r. This group is written in a distinctive small ductus employing the insular form of *g*, and a punctuation mark shaped like a semi-colon. In this script is also the note at the top of 19r (no. 72). The note from Jerome's HQG is squeezed in and the size of the ductus changes from small to large as it goes, probably at 'siblla' [*sic*] but in a different ductus, the familiar "Jerome" one, using the Norman form of *g*. In its original context it is summarizing information, and seems added here to comments already written to perform a similar function, though it does not summarize the actual material that has been entered from the *Historia*.

The HQG comments are often in complex relation with the Old English and the other Latin comments that have been added around it. No. 117 (f. 28r) reads: 'Hic erit rusticus homo manu*s* ei*us* s*up*er om*ne*s. p*ro* Rustico in hebreo sc*r*iptu*m* e*st* faran. q*uo*d in[ter]p*retatu*r onager.'[78] It is the source of the part of the *Historia* gloss written at the bottom,[79] and apparently was chosen by the annotator to serve as an authoritative gloss on it. The Jerome comment is written in a line running along the upper ledger of the lower picture, skipping spaces because the ledger is interrupted by arches. The ductus increases in size as the line advances to the right and then reduces again in size when it returns to the left in the next line, so that it varies in character from both the usual smaller ductus of the *Historia* and the larger of the "Jerome" entries. This folio, 28r, has a cluttered-looking complex of *Historia* comments on Ismael (nos. 115, 116) worked into the margins and ledgers. No. 115 is associated with an erasure and has a *signe de renvoi* linking the "well of Sur" in the comment to **wylsp[r]ing** in line 2; no. 116 is a long comment spread over the page, four lines above the upper picture, one beneath, and two in the bottom margin, with marks indicating that the lowest two lines belong with the word 'prodierant' in the colored arch of the upper picture, and the quotation is continued with signs 'a' and 'b' from above the picture to below it. The HQG extract is fitted into an awkward space still available, seeming to confirm that 1) both the main *Historia* ductus and the "Jerome" ductus are by the same hand; and 2) that the variation of size is a deliberate and systematic matter

[77] "And so these seven peoples, who are remembered as the descendants of Japheth, occupied the regions of the north."

[78] PL 23.963A, Lagarde 23.4: "Here will be the wild man, his hand against all, . . . for 'wild' in Hebrew is written 'faran', which is interpreted 'wild ass'."

[79] 'Hic erit ferus homo; hebreus habet: phara. quod sonat onager. . .' (HS, 198.1097A).

of display to indicate the use of different sources (different books), which here, because of lack of space, cannot be carried out consistently in the Jerome comment.

Nos. 210, 214, and 215 are a cluster of otherwise unusual selections of notes that appear to give an exact gloss to particular Old English words. The effect is spurious of course since the Latin comments are glossing the Vulgate. No. 210, bottom of f. 58v, pertains to the Old English of Genesis 40:10 **þreo clystru** (f. 58v/10) and 40:16 **ðry windlas** (f. 58v/22), Jerome commenting on the Hebrew words for "shoots" and "baskets (of wheat)." No. 214, f. 63v, pertaining to Genesis 43:34, refers from the note below the picture-space to the Old English word just above at line 10, **oferdrencte** with a *signe de renvoi*: '+ ydioma lingue hebree e*st*; ut eb*r*ietate*m* p*ro* satietate ponat sicut ibi'.[80] No. 215, also on f. 63v, to Genesis 44:2, explains that the Hebrew correspondent to "sacculus" may mean "boot" or "leather bag" and provides a *signe de renvoi* before the Latin text and at the end of the Old English line having **sacc** (line 14).

No. 225 shows explicit interest on the part of the annotator in the content of the illustration, a long comment on the place name "Sichem" spreading over the bottom margins of ff. 69v-70r. The Old English text is concerned with Manasses and Ephraim, sons of Jacob, and the only connection seems to be the general one of Sichem's status as a place on the border between the tribes of Manasses and Ephraim. On a textual level, though, the words 'sychem ling*ua* hebrea t*ra*nsfert*ur* in humeru*m*' ("'sychem' is translated from Hebrew as 'shoulder'") link with the lower picture, left panel, on f. 69v, which shows two men (Manasses and Ephraim), the one on the left gesturing and the one on the right emerging from a door (of a town?) and touching his left shoulder with his right hand.[81] The annotator's unusual onomastic interest may have been stimulated by the picture, a picture which appears to have been touched up by a twelfth-century hand.

Although cited in only five places, the pseudonymous *Quaestiones Hebraicae in I Paralipomenon* (QH1P) nevertheless is in some ways the most intriguing of the "Hieronymian" texts used in Claudius because it implies a certain scholarly confidence on the part the annotator, both in respect of the difficulty of the text being used and the special attention given to this somewhat unusual choice of extracts.[82] As mentioned above in the discussion of the texts of the "Shorter Collection," QH1P is elliptical and confusingly organized and deals with the

[80] PL 23.999C, Lagarde 62.3: "It is an idiom of the Hebrew language that it uses 'drunkenness' to mean 'sufficiency'. . . ."

[81] Cf. "Sechem umeri aut labor," Jerome *Liber interpretationis hebraicorum nominum* (Lagarde 10.22); this must be the ultimate source for the gesture in the illustration. Dodwell and Clemoes, p. 30, say this picture shows "Joseph . . . called to Jacob." See the fn. to this item in ch. 2, 102 n. 425.

[82] See above, 93 and Stephen Langton, *Commentary on the Book of Chronicles*, ed. A. Saltman (Ramat-Gan, 1978), 16.

minutiae of Hebrew genealogy and chronology, just the sort of material which seems to have fascinated the annotator. One extract from it on f. 53r probably formed part of a medley on Job's line of descent (no. 197), and as such, it says nothing about the annotator's particular interest. But on f. 69r it was also selected as a gloss (no. 223) expanding on information of Machir son of Manasses from HQG (no. 222), and this entry shows interesting symptoms. It runs from the bottom of f. 69r to the top of the verso. It is clearly part of the same stint that entered the HQG extract; at the '§' the extract from QH1P begins in the same script, carefully written; as it goes overleaf a flaw in the parchment causes space-skipping and irregular lines. There is a belated rubric between the first and second lines 'In paralypomenon', very roughly written, and a couple of interlineations consisting of explicit critical corrections of the exemplar:

r*ecte* ei*us*
et soror eor*um*

r*ecte* gab
ex qua suscepit secur[83]

The disorder of this entry suggests first-draft work and fresh extracting and correcting. Much neater, but showing some of the same symptoms, is no. 271 on f. 92r, that is interlinear interventions and the title 'In paralypomen*on*', in a note which, in part, repeats no. 223, including the same correcting glosses:

unum nomen e*st*. r*ecte* ei*us*
223: filii machir hufim 7 sufim. et soror eor*um* fuit maḥacha q*ua*m accepit esron. cum

´r*ecte* gab`
lx^ta^ e*ss*et annor*um* ex qua suscepit secur; Nomen au*tem* sec*un*di salphaad-[84]

[83] Vulgate "Segub" (1 Para. 2:21–22).

[84] "The sons of Machir were Hufim and Sufim (that is one name) and their sister (correctly 'his') was Maacha whom Esron married when he was sixty years old with whom he begot Secur (correctly '[Se]gab')." This combines the straightforward information of 1 Para. 2:21 with the hopelessly confusing addendum of 1 Para. 7:14–15. The interlineations are taken from the "Glossa ordinaria" or a similar source. The problem that was perceived is that Numbers 26:29 says only "Machir begot Galaad, of whom is the family of the Galaadites," with no mention of other sons and so also Joshua 17:1. Paralipomenon 7:15, after a similar statement, adds "And Machir took wives for his sons Happhim and Saphan." Working about the same time as our annotator, Stephen Langton, *Comm. on Chron.* (ed. Saltman, 103.30–35) settles the crux by taking "Galaad" as a generic name for the single son of Machir, with "Huphin and Suphin" being alternate names.

et soror ei*us* maacha
271: filii machyr. huṣsim. et sussim. unu*m* nom*en* e*st* husim. int*erpre*tat*ur* t`h´alam*us*. sussim unct*us*. Nom*en* au*tem* sec*un*di salphaad.[85]

But no. 271 is a more extensive note on the sons of Manasses and Ephraim (pertaining to 1 Para. 7:14–21) and as such has no bearing on the Old English text at this point, which is the crossing of the Red Sea (Exodus 14:21–31), or any other of the notes in the vicinity, beyond the general connection that this was the moment when the Israelites began their "ascent" to the Promised Land mentioned in the note. Apparently following a different exemplar from no. 223, it seems to reflect the annotator's interest in this particular genealogical node.

No. 304, set in the middle of the picture space on f. 122r, is apparently motivated by its mention of Mariam, sister of Moses, whose death is mentioned at this place in the Old English (line 5, = Numbers 20:1).

Medleys

Some few entries from the works just discussed have no direct connection to the main Old English text, but they generally connect to names or themes in untranslated Vulgate verses, or to matters in the *Historia* or other notes in the vicinity. The annotator doubtless felt it his duty to flesh out gaps and omissions he saw in the Old English, even as already glossed by the *Historia*. A large number of at first puzzling entries occur in series or "medleys" of place names which have typological and/or Gospel resonances and their own logic. By "medley" is meant an ensemble of (usually) short passages from disparate sources showing evidence of having been taken already combined from some source other than the Hieronymian collection. Evidence for these are the extremely miscellaneous and exiguous nature of the selections, abbreviations and notae not commonly used in the ductus being written, Hieronymian passages in the smaller ductus, and arrangement on the page. It is in these medleys of definitely non-*Historia* materials that most of the isolated, seldom quoted sources occur: Hrabanus, Claudius of Turin, Isidore, and, interestingly, Josephus, who is quoted in two instances directly and not via the *Historia*. As source, one obviously thinks of the margins of whatever copy of the *Historia* was available at the time. Despite SNLH having sections on "Exodus," there are relatively few SNLH annotations to Exodus in Claudius, all but one occurring in "medleys."[86]

[85] "The sons of Machir, Huphim and Suphim, which is one name (and his sister Maacha). Huphim is interpreted 'bridal chamber', Suphim 'anointment'. The name of the second is Zalphaad." These interpretations of names do not occur in Jerome's LIHN.

[86] I.e., 290, 292h, 294d-f, h-i, k-l. The only non-medley use of SNLH in Exodus is 246 ("Saba"), a comment on an HS entry.

Ductus and use of the 7-nota, for example, indicate a short medley in the "J" script at the bottom of f. 53r (nos. 195–197), consisting of comments that the annotator found somewhere already combined. No. 196 is from HQG. No. 195 is as Isidore, *De ortu et obitu patrum* (PL 83.1275D). No. 197 is an isolated citation of Jerome's *Quaestiones Hebraicae in I Paralipomenon* (PL 23.1367A/B). The combination refers to the descendants of Esau once again and continues the strain of comments from f. 52r (no. 190) and on the bottom of 52v (nos. 191b, 192, 192c), with supplementary reference to the Old English on f. 52v and, when read together, they make a coherent synthesized comment:

> [195] 'Job qui 7 Jobab cui*us* p*ate*r zara. et mater bosrad; zara au*tem* fili*us* Raguel. filii esau. filii ysaac .vi^tus ab abraham rex inclitus in terra edom. [196] Cont*ra* heb*re*i asserunt eu*m* de Nachor stirpe generatu*m* vt ia*m* sup*ra* dictu*m* e*st*; [197] §Jer*onymus* dic*it*. Themna concubina elifaz. mat*er* amalech. fuit. de genere choreor*um* q*ui* ante ydumeos habitau*er*unt i*n* t*er*ra seyr.'[87]

No. 195 makes Job a descendant of Esau, which Jerome had rejected (cf. no. 141b), and his voice (196) is enlisted here to refute no. 195; no. 197 links the words of Genesis (36:12) to those of Job (2:11). The annotator likely found these three extracts already combined. The ductus is very uneven but apparently of the same stint since the variations occur within the separate segments, not between them; the 7-nota is used in 195 and the "de" ligature in 196, suggesting an exemplar written well into the second half of the twelfth century, that is, in all likelihood, later than the date of the main "Jerome" manuscript he was using, and more like the date of whatever *Historia* manuscript he was following, perhaps in its margin.

A few miscellaneous Jerome quotations which are not from the "shorter collection" occur. On f. 9v, in the large ductus, is a comment (no. 35a) on the seven punishments of Lamech from Jerome's Ep. 36 to Damasus,[88] with the name of the Cainite 'Lamech' conspicuous in the top line of the Old English, but Genesis 4:24, the relevant verse, is not represented in the Old English: 'relege'[89] the comment invites, 'luca*m* euang*e*lista*m*. et i*n*uenies ita esse ut dicim*us*.' And so, taking his own advice, the annotator adds immediately (no. 36b) the words of Luke 3:23, 28 to supply in abbreviated form the "seventy-seven generations"

[87] "Job, also known as Jobab, whose father was Zara and mother Bosrad. Zara was son of Raguel, son of Esau, son of Isaac, the sixth from Abraham, a famous king in the land of Edom. / But on the other hand, the Hebrews say he [Job] was of the race of Nachor, as was said above. / Jerome says: Themna was the concubine of Eliphaz, the mother of Amelech of the race of Horrites who lived in the land of Seir before the Idumeans."

[88] PL 22.455.

[89] Jerome's text has "lege."

from Adam to Christ.[90] Loosely based on Jerome's Ep. 73 and Gospel sources is no. 66 (f. 16v bottom to top of f. 17r), perhaps already found somewhere so composed but written with many interlineations and on the recto with some disorder; it is a long and elaborate comment on the number of years from Sem to Abram. The remaining Hieronymian quotes are from the genuine Ep. 36 (f. 91v, nos. 269 c and d) and the pseudonymous Ep. 129, to Dardanus (f. 99v, no. 292g), but these are both parts of medleys.

This last-mentioned medley on f. 99v is particularly sophisticated and coherent, comprising virtually all the Hieronymian notes to the Exodus section of the manuscript. The Old English text is Exodus 23:20–32, the command to enter and conquer the Promised Land: **nu ic sende minne engel þæt þe // læde in to þære stowe þe ic gegearwode.** Verse 23, which the Old English does not translate, has "And my angel shall go before thee, and shall bring thee in unto the Amorrhite, and the Hethite, and the Pherezite, and the Chanaanite, and the Hevite, and the Jebusite, whom I will destroy." The Jebusite is the inhabitant of Jerusalem, which is conceived in the annotation series as the ultimate goal of this campaign. The annotator, writing in the large "J" script, inserts here a series of citations which both supplies the missing sense and elucidates the ultimate meaning of the passage. Immediately under the block of Old English text, centered and in larger writing, is 'area orne. id*est* ier*usa*lin'. This is a reference from the "De libris regum" section of the letter *A* in SNLH and refers not to 2 Kings 24:16, but through the form of the name in question[91] to 1 Paralipomenon 21:15: the Lord having sent a pestilence upon Jerusalem, "the Lord beheld; and took pity for the greatness of the evil; and said to the angel that destroyed: It is enough. Now stop thy hand. And the angel of the Lord stood by the thrashing floor of Ornan the Jebusite." The "Area Orne" reference thus unites three other passages to 1 Para. 21:15: the angel as it appears on the page in the Old English text (= Exodus 23:20), the angel of Exodus 23:23 that will lead and (by implication) punish the people, and the angel of 2 Kings 24:16, at the moment when Jerusalem is finally acquired for the Chosen People as God relents from the punishment. Following "Area Orne" immediately on the page is an extract from the *Historia* (which was probably written in an earlier campaign) explaining the boundaries of the Promised Land (no. 291), and then nine separate extracts (running to the top of f. 100r) related to Jerusalem and environs (292a-i): Bede's *Nomina regionum atque locorum de Actibus Apostolorum* (292a), Ps.-Eucherius's *De situ Hierosolimae* (292b,c,e,f), Hrabanus's *Commentary on 4 Kings* (292d), Jerome, Ep. 129 ad Dardanum (292g,i), Jerome, SNLH (292h). These extracts are all written in the "J" script as a single unit down through the empty spaces in- and outside the picture spaces on f. 99v and taking up three lines of the top margin

[90] Epistle 36 is cited as nos. 269c/d, but this isolated quote in large "Jerome" script is probably not from a medley or a margin, though neither is it from the "shorter collection."

[91] "Areuna" is the form at 2 Kings 24:16.

of f. 100r; each is introduced with a paragraph mark, and all use the 7-nota. The citation of SNLH is clearly part of this medley and from an exemplar other than the Jerome collection (which uses "&"), while Jerome's Epistle 129 was not part of the Jerome collection and must be from some discrete source, doubtless the medley, which is perhaps from the margins of a copy of the *Historia*. The ductus is smaller here, again suggesting that the variation of ductus between "Jerome" and the *Historia* is a matter of display; that is, while the "Jerome" passages are probably written at a later stage, it would appear that it is the same scribe writing them, and deliberately adopting a style of writing that will distinguish his Jerome contributions in general from his *Historia* quotations.

The use of the larger and smaller ductus to distinguish *Historia* entries from "Jerome" is well illustrated by a medley on f. 91v (no. 269, see fig. 37) which is quite self-consciously done: it consists of excerpts from Josephus, Jerome's Ep. 36 ad Damasum, and comments, doubtless from earlier sources, as found in Freculph of Lisieux's *Chronicon*[92] concerning the genealogy of Moses. These selections are written mostly on the ledgers of the upper picture, giving a rather scattered effect, and are labeled *a* through *e*. In the midst of them, on the fourth line, unlabeled but with a paragraph mark, is a citation of the *Historia*, beginning 'Moyses autem erat q*u*idem anno octogesimo. . .' (HS 1156D) and showing a smaller ductus: presumably it was written first, and the medley was later added around; more of the same section of the *Historia* is written on the eighth line, along the ledger between the wagons and the warriors, 'Quinq*ue* fuerunt generationes. . .', again in the smaller ductus. The 'd' in the margin refers not to this, but to the citation in on the line beginning 'Judas *enim* gen*uit* pharas. . .' showing both the larger ductus and an abbreviation *nota* long out of use. Perhaps the indexical letters were added later, to distinguish *Historia* and non-*Historia* quotations, because the same hand has added before and after the *Historia* notes (a midrash on the crossing of the Red Sea) the symbols 'a' and 'b' in the lower frame, presumably to show that these notes are not part of the genealogical medley above.[93]

Bede

Bede contributes two sources used systematically in Claudius: first, information on places presented in a Hieronymian literal mode drawn from *Nomina regionum atque locorum de Actibus Apostolorum*,[94] and chronological notes drawn from *De*

---

92 PL 106.949. Freculph was a chaplain to Louis the Pious.

93 All of these are presented as one item, no. 269, in ch. 2 above. Other medleys of (mostly) Bedan material are 294 a-j and 337 a-x, the latter occupying much of the inserted leaf f. 147.

94 References are to the edition of Laistner, *Bedae Venerabilis Expositio Actuum Apostolorum et Retractio*, 147–58, repr. in CCSL 121; it is also in PL 92.1033–1040 as the work

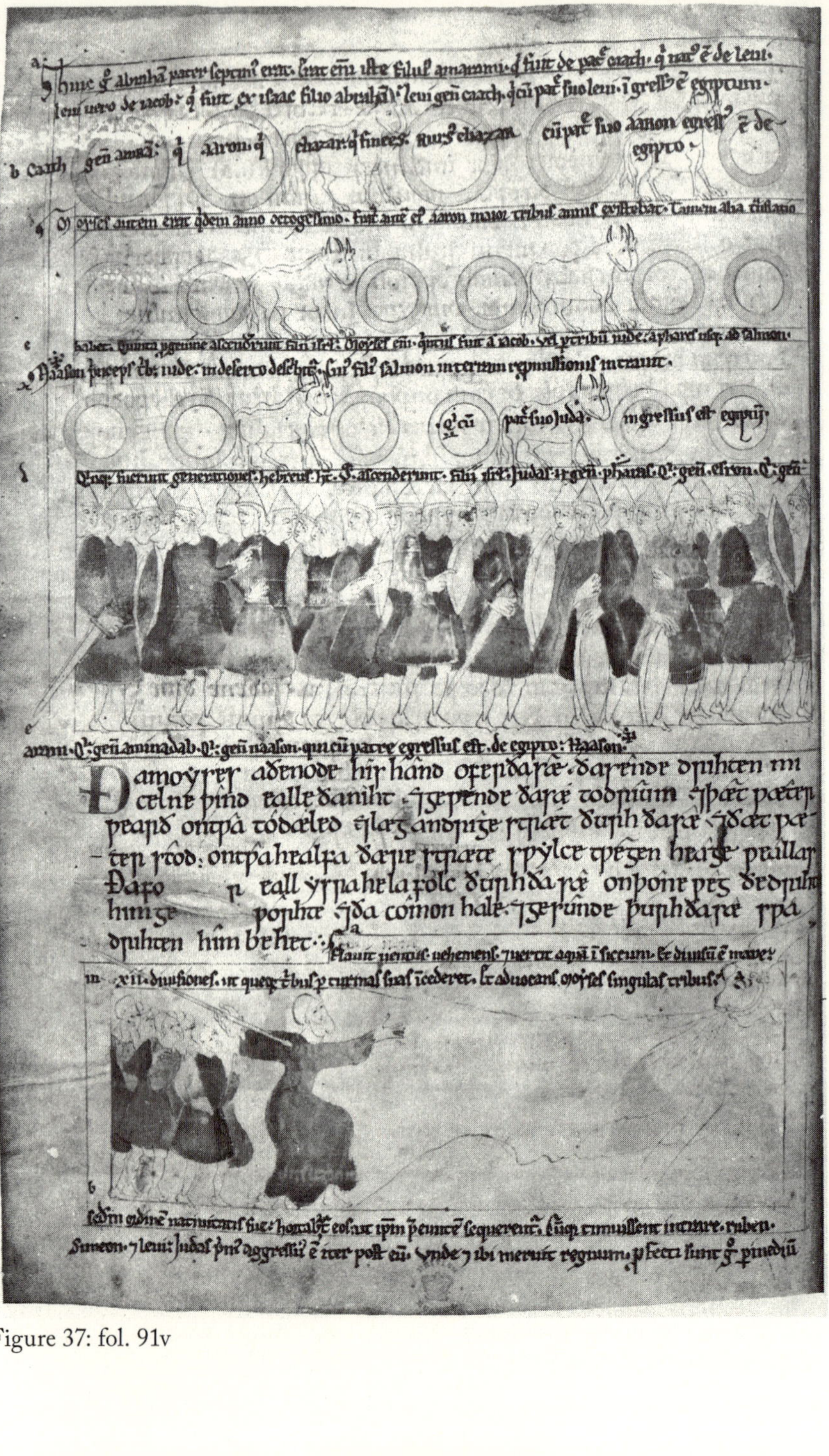

Figure 37: fol. 91v

temporum ratione (DTR), ch. 66, dates "anno mundi" supplied against the events of the Old English text, as well as a sprinkling of comments from that work written throughout the book.[95]

The brief geographical work *Nomina regionum atque locorum de Actibus Apostolorum* (NLA) is a compilation of "Pliny, Jerome, Orosius, Isidore, Adamnan, and [Bede's] own *De locis sanctis*," written for beginning students.[96] It has close textual and codicological links with Bede's *Expositio Actibus Apostolorum* and *Retractio*: Laistner notes that ". . . it is surely significant that in thirteen out of sixteen early MSS . . . the geographical glossary follows immediately after the end of Ex[*positio*], and in eight of these the *explicit* to *Ex* is placed . . . at the conclusion of [NLA]," and he also points out that in the *Retractio* Bede alludes to a geographical remark that is not in the *Expositio* but in NLA.[97] The likely nature of the book consulted by the annotator is shown by the extant manuscript Oxford, Bodleian Library, Bodley 160, of the second half of the twelfth century from the library of Christ Church Canterbury.[98] It contains the Expositio (ff. 1–46r), NLA (ff. 46v-51v), and works of Ivo of Chartres (1050–1115) in a slightly later hand.[99] This typical book of the Christ Church monastic library, with its medium size (273 × 190 mm.), 96 folios, fine, clear script, and careful preparation, with no decoration beyond practical rubrics, gives some idea of how the St.

---

of Bede and in PL 23.1295–1306 among the works of Jerome. It is attributed to Jerome in some manuscripts (Laistner, xxxvii) but the annotator attributes it correctly several times and simply recognized its useful content and "Hieronymian" method and style.

95 In the Claudius edition, items 6b, 39b, 42a (OE), 55b, 57, 58, 231, ?325, as well as several on the final flyleaf. The edition of DTR consulted is that of T. H. Mommsen and C. W. Jones in *Bedae Venerabilis Opera, Pars VI, Opera Didascalica 2*, CCSL 123B (Turnhout, 1972), 461–544.

96 Laistner, *Expositio*, xxxvii.

97 Laistner, *Expositio*, xxxvii.

98 The only possibly related item in the fifteenth-century St. Augustine's catalogue is: "Beda super Actus apostolorum in colleccionibus Wiłłi de Wynchelse cum B": James, *Ancient Libraries*, no. 441. This book, since it is accompanied by the donor's name, must be after the mid-thirteenth century, and was likely a typical collection containing at least the *Expositio* and NLA.

99 Gameson, *Manuscripts of Early Norman England*, no. 643. Though the Ivo of Chartres writing is later, following three blank folios, it is made to harmonize in style and layout with the Bede. The evidence that the manuscript is from Christ Church is the contents list of no. 88 in the Eastry catalogue: "Beda super Actus Apostolorum | *In hoc uol. cont.:* | Descriptio nominum et regionum que continentur in Actibus Apostolorum. | Tractatus Yuonis Carnotensis de ueritate sacramentorum Christi et Ecclesie. | Tractatus eiusdem de Clericatu et eius Officio. | Sermo eiusdem de conuenientia nouorum et ueterum sacramentorum. | Vita beati Iacobi Apostoli" (James, *Ancient Libraries*, 26); not all the works attributed to Ivo can be identified, cf. Ivo Carnotensis, *Sermones*, PL 162.506ff; see the contents list in Gameson (129).

Augustine's book might have looked. Its text differs in many respects from that of Claudius, but might be laterally related to that used by Claudius, as one example will show: Claudius no. 82b (f. 20r) has 'chaldea. uel cedar', the part after the point being a gloss; Bodley 160 (f. 49v/5–8) has 'chadaer' which if not a pure corruption, seems to be a conflation of the original name and gloss.

In Claudius a couple of the extracts are attributed to 'Bede': no. 78 (f. 19v), 82a (f. 20r) at the head of two extracts from NLA; no. 89 (f. 21r) on Damascus is not pertinent to anything in the Old English text except perhaps as an (unmentioned) place Abraham passed by on his wanderings. No. 227 (f. 70r) is an extract from SNLH on "Sychar" (Sichem) with a Bede note added as a gloss on the location of the town. No. 292a (f. 99v, "Jerusalem") heads a medley on towns of the Judean heartland drawn from various sources. Bede extracts (nos. 294a,b,c,g,i,j, f. 100r) comprise most of a medley on places associated with the life of Christ, but other familiar biblical place names are cited. The first ("Iconium") seems out of place. Finally, a large medley (nos. 337a-x) is made entirely of extracts from NLA in alphabetical order, apparently for their own sake, and occupying most of the inserted leaf f. 147. It must be said that the geographical information from NLA is not as well integrated as the Jerome extracts generally are into the overall plan of annotating the main text. On the other hand their presence shows no sign of being insertions or afterthoughts. Most likely they were included to collate the conquests of the Old Testament "Jesus/Joshua" with the places mentioned in the life of the Savior and have a sort of typological function.

Bede's *De temporum ratione* had long been a commonplace text in monastic culture; it exists in hundreds of complete copies, in extracts, in computus, in countless independent epitomes, so that there seems no point in attempting to pinpoint a particular source. Its popularity crested in the Carolingian period, but it continued to be copied in England until the calendar reforms of the sixteenth century.[100] The only section used in Claudius is "The World Chronicle," Chapter 66, which was sometimes omitted from manuscripts of DTR, and sometimes existed in copies as a separate text. The most visually conspicuous Bedan contribution to Claudius is the complete series of "Anno Mundi" numerals added to the margins or in clear picture spaces, appropriately keyed to the text. The particular system used, counting years from the Creation, is not only from Bede but, in the count of years he gives, was devised by Bede.[101] Into the margins the annotator has entered the entire series of A.M. years as given in DTR, Ch. 66, from the

100 See Bede, *The Reckoning of Time*, trans. Wallace, lxxxviii.

101 A.M. reckoning had the ultimate theological purpose of downplaying the effect of "chiliasm," the belief that the world's end would come at the end of six 1000-year periods and hence that it could be predicted. See *Reckoning of Time*, trans. Wallis, 362–63. For the way these numerals appear on the page see the reproductions of ff. 10v-12r in ch. 5 (figs. 30–31).

birth of Seth to the entry into the Promised Land, the only omissions being for A.M. events that have been excluded from the Old English version. The regular method the annotator uses is to write the A.M. number in larger writing and then to draw out into the margin, in smaller writing, the first number that occurs in the DTR entry, but not the rest of the entry it occurs in. This smaller number usually coincides with a number mentioned in the Old English text.[102] Here is the whole series, giving first the A.M. number as in the manuscript, followed by the beginning of Bede's uncopied entry corresponding to the Old English text, with any number in Bede's entry and the OE text drawn out into the margin being italicized:

f. 10r/3 'cxxx.' "Adam annorum *CXXX* genuit Seth. . . ." (DTR 10);

f. 10r/5 '.cc.xxx.v.' "Seth ann. *CV* genuit Enos. . . ." (DTR 11);

f. 10v/7 '.ccc.xxv.' "Enos an. *XC* genuit Cainan. . . ." (DTR 12);

f. 11r/1 '.ccc.xcv' "Cainan an. *LXX* genuit Malalehel. . . ." (DTR 13);

f. 11r/4 '.cccc.lx.' "Malalehel an. *LXV* genuit Iareth. . . ." (DTR 14);

f. 11r/8 '.dc.xxii.' "Iareth an. *CLXII* genuit Enoch. . . ." (DTR 15);

f. 11v/1 'dc.lxxx.vii' "Enoch an. *LXV* genuit Mathusalem. . . ." (DTR 16);

f. 11v/6 '[d]ccc lxx`ii´ii' [trimmed] "Mathusalem an. *CLXXXVII* genuit Lamech. . . ." (DTR 17);

f. 12r/1 'ī.lvi.' (i.e., 1056) "Lamech an. *CLXXXII* genuit Noe. . . ." (DTR 18);

f. 12v (top) 'ī.d.lvi' [this is a mistake for the next item];

f. 14r (lower picture space) 'ī.dc.lvi.' "Noe anno *DC* uenit diluuium mense secundo" (DTR 19);

The items DTR 21–36 correspond to Genesis 11:10–26, which are not in the Old English version in Claudius.[103] The next item (DTR 37) is mistakenly omitted, "M̄DCCCCXLVIII. Thare an. LXX genuit Abraham," the Old English having **Ðare gestrynde abram** (f. 19v/1). The series resumes:

---

[102] There are many other roman numerals drawn out from the Old English text into the margin, unrelated to the DTR numbers; for example, on f. 38v appears 'c. ⁊ xxuii.' referring to the Old English, **hund teontig geara. ⁊ seofan ⁊ twentig geara**; on f. 60r the marginal numeral 'xxx' is drawn out from the Latin comment (no. 211).

[103] These verses are in Cambridge University Library Ii.1.33.

f. 20r (bottom left, in picture space) '.īī.xx.iii' "Tertia mundi aetas a natiuitate coepit Abraham patriarchae. . . ." (DTR 38). This is written directly above a Latin comment (no. 83) on the Third Age;

f. 28r (in upper picture space) 'īī.xxxiiii.' "Abraham an. *LXXXVI* genuit Ismahel. . . ." (DTR 39);

f. 35r (lower picture space) '.īī.xlviii.' "Idem Abraham an. C genuit Isaac. . . ."[104] (DTR 40);

f. 40v/10 '.īī.c.viii.' "Isaac an. *LX* genuit Esau et Iacob. . . ." (DTR 41);

f. 68v/3 'īī.c.xxx.viii.' [*recte* "ĪĪCCXXXVIII"] "Iacob CXXX an. discendit in Aegyptum. . . ."[105] (DTR 43); the 44th and 45th sections of DTR are concerned with secular events;

f. 92v (top) '.īī.cccc.liii.' "Habitatio filiorum Israhel, qua manserunt in Aegypto, fuit CCCCXXX annorum. . .." (DTR 46); this is inserted at the text of Exodus 15:1.

f. 139v 'iiº milia. cccc. xc i`i´ii'; this is written in the picture space showing the death of Moses, with no Old English text on the page. Bede has "ĪĪCCCCXCIII. Moyses annis XL eductum ex Aegypto regit populum Israhel in deserto. . . ." (DTR 47). The eccentric form of the numeral in Claudius suggests a different stint or source; perhaps this number was skipped inadvertently and filled in later.

f. 155v (lower picture space) 'īī d xix.' "Iosue an. XXVI regit populum Israhel" (DTR 48). This is written on the last page of the main Old English text and completes the series.[106] Apart from this series, two further A.M. entries occur, in the notes on the final flyleaf.

Beyond the mere year entries, there are seven extracts from the text of the Chronicle, mostly marking well-chosen liminal moments: no. 6b, noting the First Age from Adam to Noe, no. 231, a genealogical transition from Genesis to Exodus, and no. 325, noting the crossing of the Jordan. No. 39b is a mere sentence fragment. Three notes (55b, 57, and 58) occur on a single leaf, f. 14r, marking the entry into the Ark. Nos. 57 and 58 are both "signed" by "Normannus" (see ch. 7), 57 being just a year note while 58 is a longish compilation of notes on the

---

104 "C" is not drawn out to the margin. **hund wintre** is on line 12.

105 "CXXX" is not drawn into the margin; the Old English has **anhund wintre .7 xxx. wintre.**

106 It is written in a slightly lighter ink next to the picture-label 'Josue obiit', but their position together is apparently coincidental.

Second Age rather pompously annotated 'Normano testante. iuxta hebraicha*m* u*er*itate*m*.'

Planning

Obviously so many entries into so many pages involved a lot of careful planning and research on the part of the annotator. But there also seems to have been a larger, overall plan for the notes, to make them bring out, as the Old English running from Genesis only to Joshua does not, the salvation history implicit in any medieval Christian reading of the Old Testament. This plan is mostly carried out on the inserted leaves. The final flyleaf (f. 156) is covered with an at first sight random collection of disjointed extracts from the *Historia* and DTR. Analyzing this leaf is not made easier by the fact that it has been torn nearly in half so that the upper/outer quadrant is missing; that it has a crude sewing repair in the lower part (which has been avoided by the writing), and that a strip of the inner edge obscured by a binding repair suggests it was a foul sheet in the first place. Nevertheless most of it can be reconstructed with good assurance. The extant part begins imperfectly on the recto with disjointed and slightly epitomized extracts from the *Historia* on the Book of Judges, covering the following "judges"[107]: Abimelech (Jdg. 9, f. 156r/1–5), Thola (Jdg. 10:1–2, f. 156r/6–7), Jair (Jdg. 10:3–5, f. 156r/8), [Castor and Pollux (f. 156r/10)], Jeptha (Jdg. 11–12, f. 156r/11–13), Abesan (Jdg. 12:8–10, f. 156r/14), Ahialon (Jdg. 12:11–12, f. 156r/14), an aside on sources (f. 156r/16–18), Abdon (Jdg. 12:13–15, f. 156r/19), Samson (Jdg. 13–16, f. 156r/20–21), a note on annunciations in the Old Testament (Add. 2, HS 1286D, f. 156r/22–23). This material is extracted (with some breaks and epitomizing) from HS 1282A-1290A and accounts for the second half of the "Judges" section of that work.[108] At line 24 Claudius begins to copy a long continuous passage from the *Historia* on "Ruth" which segues into an epitome that sums up the story (f. 156r/24–38). This is followed by extracts from *DTR*, *Historia*, and other sources with brief notes on Samuel (DTR, f. 156r/39–40), Saul (DTR, f. 156r/41–42), 'Quarta mundi etas' (DTR, f. 156r/43), Solomon (f. DTR, 156v/2–5), Saul's death (HS 1323B-24A), f. 156v/8–11, including a perhaps interpolated note on Saul and Isboseth from the pseudo-Hieronymian QH2R; this is followed by an extract from the beginning of the "Chronicle" section of DTR taking the account quickly through from the Fourth to the Sixth Ages (David to Christ), and the Seventh and Eighth Ages of Sabbath and Resurrection. The plan of this leaf is thus clear: whereas the Old English text ends with the death of Joshua and the translation of Joseph's bones, the annotator supplies a symbolic representation of the rest of the Old Testament history, including a

---

107 See ch. 2, 177–85 for details and exact correlation to the text of the *Historia*.

108 Eleven columns in PL, the wanting first part being ten columns.

relatively detailed sketch of Judges and Kings depending on the *Historia*, up to David and a quick world-chronicle view after that.[109] Folio 156 begins imperfectly, halfway through the judges, and there must at one time have been another inserted leaf covering the first half of Judges. The overall purpose of the final leaf is made explicit by its final entry (f. 156v/31–32): 'In ha[c][110] su*m*ma recidit similit*er* de supra posita su*m*ma eos annos octouiani [*sic*] august[i]. qui s*un*t post chr*istu*m natu*m*. p*er*tinentes ad sextam aetatem;', "Omitted in this summary likewise from the summary above are those years of Octavianus Augustus which fall after the birth of Christ and thus belong to the Sixth Age."[111]

The series of notes on the final leaf show that the annotator has a coherent program and is not just writing in a random selection of items. The annotator is supplementing the original material in the Claudius Hexateuch by quickly advancing the narrative through Judges and the rest of the Old Testament up to the moment of the Incarnation, that is, he completes the material so that the manuscript presents a complete line from Adam to Christ.

From this leaf, we should turn back to the other interventions. The second inserted leaf (f. 147) was inserted blank and continues from the preceding page a series of Jerome notes and then "finishes" the Jerome exemplar by including its final piece, the mensural texts; what was perhaps extra unplanned space was then filled with a long series of excerpts on Bede's book on place names in the Acts of the Apostles, which seemingly serve to function as a typological connection between the locations of the doings of the patriarchs with those of the Apostles, that is, Old and New Testaments are correlated.

The first inserted leaf, f. 74, seems to have a more complex and well-motivated function. One should note, first, that it is set into the book near the beginning of Exodus. In Claudius B. iv, as is well known, the opening of Exodus is flawed.[112]

---

109 On f. 156r, third line up, is written an entry from DTR itself (sec. 76), 'Saul prim*us* hebreor*um* rex ann*i* xx.' with 'ĭĭ d ccc xc' written to the right; on the verso, in the tenth line up, occurs 'ĭĭĭ.dcccc.l.ii'; the text that is written into Claudius is the abbreviated account of the fourth through sixth ages taken from the opening sections of Chapter 66 (DTR 5–8); but the A.M. written there refers to the times of Augustus Caesar: "Anno Caesaris Augusti XLII . . . Iesus Christus filius Dei sextam mundi aetatem suo consecrauit aduentu" (DTR 268); thus the annotator ties up his historical summary with the Incarnation.

110 The manuscript appears to have 'has' but it is not very clear at this place.

111 The passage is unsourced. The spelling of 'aetatem' shows it is taken from an exemplar.

112 Withers, *Frontiers*, 127, presents two possible scenarios to explain this design problem: either the initials marked an illustrated text from which an illustration was omitted deliberately or accidentally at this point, or the initials were being added to an unillustrated text that was being marked up to indicate where illustrations should go. Withers thinks that in either case the problem here is that an intended illustration of the death of Joseph has been accidentally omitted.

Exodus begins on line 13 of f. 72v, two lines below the upper picture space, with an indentation and the large colored capital 'Ð'. Apparently as a result of some confusion, the initial was drawn in at the wrong place by the artist before the text was written, with two lines being left below the frame for a rubric, but when the text of Genesis was being completed it was found it needed to extend into these two lines, plus the indentation space before Exodus (to squeeze in the last word, 'lande'). There is an anomalous large colored capital two lines up from there, in 'Iosep'. In any case, the annotator saw that Exodus needed some sort of opening. One leaf over beyond this is the inserted folio. Its recto contains by far the longest and most perplexing entry of all the notes, a set of extracts from the pseudo-Hieronymian *Quaestiones Hebraicae in I-II Paralipomenon*. The experiments with scripts on this leaf give reason to believe that it was with the set of extracts from this work on the inserted leaf f. 74 that the whole annotating project began. The pre-existing Old English text and pictures run (f. 73v to 75r) from the Egyptian king's injunction to the Hebrew midwives to kill all the male Hebrew children (Exodus 1:15–22) to the birth of Moses (Exodus 2:1–10). The inserted leaf has on the verso two nearly complete chapters from the *Historia* which is a midrash on the early life of Moses; it is written in a large display script of a semi-rotunda type not found elsewhere in Claudius but common enough in St. Augustine's manuscripts (see fig. 26).[113] The writing on both sides of this leaf shows variations that suggest experimentation; the verso has the large display hand, and its text matches the pictures of the birth of Moses on f. 75r, and here it is bound, as facing page. The writing on the recto is mostly a long set of related excerpts from HQ1P written in a ductus that varies considerably over the page, ranging from a smaller florid "chancellery" ductus at the top to the familiar "large" ductus of the Jerome entries in the middle and bottom with several intermediate types. The final entry at the bottom of the recto is "Saba" from SNLH written in the large ductus and relating to material in the Moses story on the overleaf. The obvious changes in ductus do not correspond to changes or breaks in the excerpts but seem to be experiments in writing style by the same hand. At line 33 the excerpt is written with the margin extended to the left; the ductus changes from medium to large within this passage but all parts of it can be matched with various styles in the writing above it on the page (see fig. 25).

The purpose of the manipulation of these extracts, obscure as they are, seems to be to provide a fitting opening for Exodus in the manuscript by joining the genealogy of Moses (he is a Levite) to that of Judah and hence to that of Christ. This is part of the explicit program of twelfth-century historical exegesis, the tracing of the genealogy of Christ from Adam, through the patriarchs, including Moses, whose lineage appears to diverge from that of Christ. The annotator in all probability consulted Peter of Poitiers' *Compendium historiae in genealogia*

---

113 See ch. 4, 244–46, 360n51.

Christi, a brief work that is copied in as a virtual prologue to the *Historia Scholastica* manuscripts from the 1280s onwards. Peter makes the program explicit: "De filiis Jacob numerosa proles descendent; sed de Leui et Juda sufficiat; quia de his descendit christus."[114] Or more compendiously, in his prologue: "seriem sacrorum patrum, a quibus per leviticam et regalem tribum Christus originem habuit."[115] In Claudius the set-up is provided at the bottom of the preceding page, f. 73v, which quotes Exodus 6:20:

> These are the names of the sons of Levi by their kindreds: Gerson and Caath, and Merari. The sons of Gerson: Lobni and Demi. The sons of Caath: Amram and Issar, and Hebron, and Oziel. The sons of Merari: Moholi and Musi. And Amram took to wife Jochabed his aunt by the father's side and she bore him Aaron and Moses and Mariam.[116]

Like the ductus on the following inserted leaf, the ductus varies within the passage, beginning in a rather decorative style and suddenly switching (at 'filii gerson') to the familiar large "J" script (see fig. 24). This fact, plus the function of this quote in setting up what follows, suggests that the leaf had been inserted in Claudius before the recto was written. At any rate, on the recto, the commentary traces the genealogy of the Judaites from Acham son of Charmi (1 Para. 2) to the sons of "Esra" (Hesron, 1 Para. 4:17) a descendant of Judah who is interpreted in 1PHQ as Amran, the father of Moses and Aaron; the text goes on, "Moses, after he received the law in the desert, joined his father as he abandoned his mother, who was Amran's paternal aunt; she was the daughter of Levi." Many of the obscure names in the Judaite line found in the fourth chapter of 1 Paralipomenon are then connected by interpretation to Moses. There follows a note on the daughter of Pharaoh, concluding with an extract that takes the line of ascent back to Judah. The selection of extracts concentrates the commentary on Moses, who in HQ1P is implicitly brought into the lineage of Christ. The Claudius commentator makes the point more explicit by ending this series of extracts with the famous opening of Matthew (1:3–5), which takes the descendants of Judah up to David. This is in the "J" script and may be said, along with the Exodus quote on f. 73v, to frame the extracts from HQ1P.[117] The inserted folio 74 seems to be constructed to provide a "genealogy" of Moses on the recto and a "childhood" of

[114] "From the sons of Jacob will descend numerous progeny; but it is enough to speak of Levi and Juda, because Christ descends from their lines": Peter of Poitiers, *Compendium historiae in genealogia*, ed. Vollmer, 137; Royal 8 C.ix, f. 4v/26a-29a.

[115] ". . . the line of holy fathers, from whom through the levitical and royal tribes Christ had his origin": Vollmer, *Compendium*, 127; Royal 8 C.ix, f. 3r/5–6.

[116] 'et mariam' is an addition taken from the Septuagint or Vetus Latina.

[117] This is not the only time the annotator frames a portion of text with comment: the twins 'farfar fluuius damasci' (f. 21v) and 'abana fluuius damasci' (f. 25v) bracket Genesis 12:7–14:24, the story of Abraham's recognized establishment in the land of Chanaan

Moses full of miracles as a kind of introduction to Exodus, constructed on the analogy to the opening of the Gospel of Matthew, with its genealogy and childhood of Christ. The annotator, in his remodeling of the book at this point, seems to have taken opportunistic advantage of the illustrations, the page falling as it does between the illustrated side f. 73v, with the "two women" (actually representing the Hebrew midwives) echoing the Christian visual theme of the visit of Mary and Elizabeth, and side f. 75r, illustrating the "Nativity" of Moses.

The annotator seems then to have been concerned to almagamate and harmonize, as best he could, all the materials together, original text and pictures, annotations from modern sources, and augmentations of text and structure— to complement a respected old book so that it might be more useful, comprehensive, and modern. It is obvious that an enormous amount of attention, time, and care, as well as intelligence, has gone into the annotation program, with a primary concern being to enhance, not spoil, the overall appearance by the placement and grade of the annotations, which become, as it were, a part of the text itself, rather than a gloss. The old text had certain gaps and lacks. True, it has a formal enough beginning with Ælfric's venerable and learned "Preface" to Genesis which explains the concept of "spiritual understanding" as well as the difficulties and dangers of translation into the vulgar tongue. The added apparatus from the *Historia* and Jerome is almost exclusively, rigorously literal and, while "modern" and illuminating, is probably perceived as perhaps weighing a bit dangerously too much to the "Hebraic" side; hence the other additions, f. 74 which connects Moses to Christ and makes a portal to Exodus with a quasi-Mattheian preface, and f. 147 which connects the place names of IH̄S/Jesu/Joshua in the conquest of Canaan with the place names of IH̄S/Jesus in the familiar locales of the Gospels, and finally f. 156 (along with its lost mate), which knits up all the feast with a resume of the ages from Judges to the Incarnation and beyond, confected from ready-to-hand materials from the *Historia* and Bede.

Overall, then, the annotations show elaborate patterning and planning. We must now turn to such evidence as exists concerning the planner and why such an extensive and laborious plan might have been undertaken to transform this particular ancient book in the first place.

(cf. 4 Kings 5:12). The notes are no. 94 (SNLH 23.898B, Lagarde 124.7) and no. 107 (SNLH 23.876A, Lagarde 97.26).

VII. Normannus at St. Augustine's and those Purloined Letters

All in all, the twelfth-century program of annotations in Claudius B. iv is a very strange production. The book that contains them was in the library of St. Augustine's Abbey, Canterbury, in the late fifteenth century,[1] and we have shown by circumstantial evidence of handwriting and codicology that the book was located there at the time of the writing of the annotations.[2] The English notes are written in an awkward form of English still recognizable as a late example of a grapholectic West-Saxon/Kentish form of English rather than the language of natural contemporary speech. These English notes meticulously translate a "modern" text much later than their ostensible date, dramatized by Ker's dating of them as *mid*-century, somewhat earlier than the composition of the source.[3] They are combined seamlessly in places with direct Latin extracts from the same work to form a running commentary on an illustrated Old English text produced more than a hundred years earlier. And they are combined with extracts from genuinely ancient sources, mostly Jerome, but taken in the main from a single "modern" edition of Jerome's works of historical biblical criticism. There seems to be a programmatic attempt, which is clear only after a close analysis of the contents, to refashion the Old English manuscript originally containing Genesis-Joshua into a simulacrum of a complete "Old Testament" running from Creation to Incarnation. The English notes are written in a deliberately archaizing "insular" script in a different color ink from the other notes; the Latin notes are written in a type of late twelfth-century form of "proto-gothic" script, but the notes drawn from the *Historia Scholastica* are written in a ductus that systematically differs from that of the "Jerome" notes. Moreover, a few of the Latin notes are written using some insular letter-forms. Yet an analysis shows that all the annotations are most likely by a single late twelfth-century hand. Such a strange set of circumstances naturally gives rise to the question: why were these notes added at all? What motivated the performance? It is unlikely that such a systematic, lengthy, elaborate, and learned production was done casually. For answers, we now turn to the

---

1 See ch. 1, 4.

2 See ch. 4, 248–52 (hand), 238–48 (writing onto inserted leaf) and ch. 6, 333–34 (disarranged pages at time of entry of notes).

3 See ch. 1, 6.

mysterious figure of "Normannus" to whom a number of the notes are attributed, although their wording and contents are manifestly from the writings of others.

The name "Normannus" has already been mentioned a number of times in this study, and it has been noticed by a number of scholars dealing with the Old English texts (James, Crawford, Ker, and Dodwell and Clemoes)[4] that some of the notes are attributed to a certain "Norman(nus)." This Normannus is named in ten of the Claudius notes as some sort of authority, in the form "Normannus dicit" or something similar. We need to identify this Normannus more precisely, and we work with the obvious assumption that he was a monk of St. Augustine's instrumental in the annotation project. To look for him at St. Augustine's means looking at the abbey of St. Augustine's itself to see if its history and traditions will reveal clues to the motives behind the annotations. This means taking a moment to review salient features of the abbey's history from its founding to the twelfth century.

There is no modern consecutive history of the abbey, and facts, such as they are, have to be gleaned from a variety of traditional sources. The traditions were self-justifying, forming the authenticating voices of further historical writing. Events as narrated and carried down by oral and written tradition must be seen as colored by particular beliefs, desires, and strategies of writers of later times. The earlier history of St. Augustine's survived mostly by oral tradition, supplemented by a few dozen charters, several spurious. Continuous history is preserved by four later writers: Goscelin of St. Bertin (d. ca. 1095), who came to St. Augustine's late in life and preserved traditions of the eleventh century; Thomas Sprott (later thirteenth century), who compiled a chronicle which remains unpublished and of textually uncertain status; this was substantially followed by the chronicler William Thorne (fl. 1390s) up to 1228; and Thomas Elmham (fl. 1410s) wrote a more critical narrative history up to 806 and then skipped to the time of Abbots Scotland and Wido (1090s), thereafter simply copying documents to 1192.[5] Sprott and Thorne looked back from their thirteenth- and fourteenth-century perches through the highly partisan and protective received traditions of the abbey, but there is no reason to doubt that they were continuing the atmosphere of the late eleventh and twelfth centuries. The keynotes of that atmosphere were pride and anxiety: pride in the antiquity and priority of the house over all others in England, and anxiety that its preeminence, reputation, and privileges were always under threat from the community located a quarter-mile north, Christ Church, under its abbot-archbishop who claimed jurisdiction over St. Augustine's and the home of a more active, distinguished body of monks.

---

[4] See ch. 1, 7, 12.

[5] See Richard Emms, "The Historical Traditions of St. Augustine's Abbey, Canterbury," in *Canterbury and the Norman Conquest: Churches, Saints, and Scholars, 1066–1109*, ed. Richard Eales and Richard Sharpe (London and Rio Grande, 1995), 159–68.

St. Augustine's, officially the Abbey of SS. Peter and Paul, St. Augustine becoming an additional dedicatee about 980, was according to tradition founded by King Æthelbert of Kent for St. Augustine on 9 January 605.[6] It dominated Canterbury for a time, but in 760 lost its chief distinction over the cathedral community, the right of burial of archbishops, and shortly thereafter, with the extinction of the Kentish house, of kings. It was apparently disfavored by the Mercian kings and favored by those of Wessex. It was one, perhaps the only one, of the English monasteries to have enjoyed a continuous independent corporate existence through the ninth and early tenth centuries.[7] It was refounded by Archbishop Dunstan about 980 but for all that did not particularly distinguish itself for learning, personnel, or administration during the Benedictine revival. Although it seems to have weathered various waves of Scandinavian attacks relatively unscathed in the eleventh century, while Christ Church suffered badly, nevertheless Christ Church rose from its ashes and flourished in this period. Christ Church was gradually reformed and monasticized under the archbishops from Dunstan on, themselves monks, and this, combined with the great wealth, prestige, power, and attraction of its being the archiepiscopal seat, meant that it was busier in the world, more intellectually active, and more influential than its more reclusive neighbor. Resentments were inevitable, and from the mid-eleventh century a bitter rivalry arose between St. Augustine's and Christ Church over the antiquity and priority of each, and then, after the Norman Conquest, over privileges and exemptions from the authority of the archbishop. Forged documents and biased in-house historical writing played a good part in Christ Church's battle over the first issue[8] and St. Augustine's over the second.

---

[6] So the chronicle of St. Augustine's of William Thorne, a monk of the abbey (fl. 1375) (*William Thorne's Chronicle of Saint Augustine's Abbey, Canterbury*, trans. A. H. Davis, 8–9). The chronicle is based on an earlier one up to 1228 by the late 13th-century monk Thomas Sprott; the status of the latter work is somewhat mysterious because it remains unpublished, but it is now established that what remains of it is to be found in Cotton Tiberius A. ix and Lambeth Palace MS 419 (Emms, "Historical Traditions," 164). Though later Christ Church tradition tended to claim the priority of its monastic tradition over that of St. Augustine's, Thorne's traditional claim is probably correct: see Nicholas Brooks, *The Early History of the Church of Canterbury: Christ Church from 597 to 1066* (Leicester, 1984), 89–91.

[7] "Indeed, the only important monastery of which we have no information [first half of the 10th century], is St. Augustine's, Canterbury. It is known to have existed as a corporate body at the time, and to have received a gift from Athelstan on the very day of his coronation; how far it was monastic cannot be said, but it would seem that there, and there alone, is it possible that some form of the regular life still persisted. To this positive evidence may be added the absence of any reference to a monk of any existing body as either opposing or assisting the revival" (Dom David Knowles, *The Monastic Order in England*, 2d ed. [Cambridge, 1963], 34–35).

[8] See Brooks, *Early History*, 90, 257–60.

St. Augustine's had its brief triumphs, such as the recovery about 1030 of the relics of St. Mildred and the consequent reconstitution of its lands and convent on Thanet, and the participation of Abbot Wulfric in the papal synod of Rheims (1049) which allegedly resulted in the elevation of the abbot to a rank equal to that of the abbot of Monte Cassino. The next abbot, Æthelsige, was allegedly granted the right to wear the pontifical miter and sandals as a papal sign that St. Augustine's was the premier English monastery, a privilege which however was not exercised for nearly ninety years, until Abbot Roger I assumed them in 1179.[9] Æthelsige was the last Anglo-Saxon abbot, deposed and forced into exile, according to plausible legend because he intrigued against Norman rule, and thus the last to be chosen under the more relaxed jurisdictional rules of the *ancien régime* rather than under the top-down management style of Norman feudalism.[10]

As a result, St. Augustine's had its first Norman abbot imposed rather more quickly than most, about 1070. Scolland or Scotland, previously abbot of Mont St. Michel,[11] governed justly and to the advantage of the house, according even to the highly partisan judgment of William Thorne.[12] Under him the building of the great Norman church began and properties taken after the Conquest were regained. As seen through the eyes of Thorne, Scotland established a pattern that became regular through the rest of the eleventh and the twelfth centuries. A new abbot would be imposed by the king and/or archbishop; the choice would be bitterly resisted by the convent, but eventually accepted; and then, joined by the abbatial candidate, the convent would insist on its ancient privilege of exemption, i.e., that the abbot was to be blessed by the archbishop in the church of St. Augustine's, not the cathedral, and was not to make an oath of obedience to the pontiff. Gradually were added demands for certain advantages in matters of temporal exemptions from taxes and duties. All this the archbishop would refuse and, in high litigious mode, both parties would repair to Rome for papal judgment, the abbot-elect usually in person. Judgment was tilted towards St. Augustine's and away from the archbishop, both because St. Augustine's was assiduous about producing documentation, and because the papal interest was to keep

9 See Kelly, *Charters of St. Augustine's, Canterbury and Minster-in-Thanet*, xxii.

10 According to Thorne's *Chronicle*, trans. Davis, 49–50 he led a popular uprising of the Kentish folk; he was probably conspiring with Archbishop Stigand and other magnates of nationalist sympathies; see Knowles, *Monastic Order*, 103.

11 Emms, "Historical Traditions," 160.

12 Thorne, *Chronicle*, trans. Davis, 50: ". . . [T]he aforesaid king [William] put over the monastery as abbot . . . Scotland, a Norman by nationality, the monks of St. Augustine's putting up with it for the time, though not without bitterness of soul, on account of the tyrannical power of the king, and the weakness of the monastery as was evident on all sides. Scotland, however, is said to have done many great things in his time worthy of praise." Namely, he restored and enlarged the property of the monastery with the king's patronage.

the great abbey an *Eigenkloster* under its direct jurisdiction.[13] By and through this, and also doubtless out of personal interest, the Norman abbots always became good Augustinians in very short order, vociferous in the defense of the abbey's ancient traditions, saints, customs, goods, properties, and privileges against Christ Church, its abbot-archbishop, and, if necessary, the king.

Symbolic of the new order is the story of the translation of the relics of St. Augustine into the just-completed Norman church, as told by Thorne. Upon the death of Scotland, Archbishop Lanfranc intruded an elect, Abbot Wido, in 1091; Wido had been violently resisted by the monks, so violently that a good part of the convent was forcibly dispersed and replaced by Christ Church monks. No St. Augustine's source mentions this.[14] Thorne tries to make it sound as if Wido was St. Augustine's choice, indeed that he had been resisted by Lanfranc, and recounts only that after the saint's body was installed in the church—an ostensible triumph of comity—Abbot Wido came with a few seniors that same night, before the tomb had been completely sealed, and secretly transferred the body, with the head, to an unknown burial place, leaving only a few small bones and a small piece of uncorrupted flesh in the shrine. The body lay hidden for 130 years until it was discovered in the days of Abbot Hugh III (1221) and reinstalled with great honor.[15] The point of this sequence of events seems to be that unlike Wido (who brought honor but not full honor to the saint), Hugh III was freely elected from their own cloister by the St. Augustine's community and was the president of the full restoration of the principal relics as they were known in Thorne's own day.

From the eleventh century, the main defense against intrusions was the abbey's arsenal of documents. Though corporate life was extinguished and the muniments of the house were dispersed at the Dissolution, a fair number of charters pertaining to the abbey itself remain from the Anglo-Saxon period.[16] Most are

---

[13] I.e., "the gradual substitution of the canonical conception of reserved jurisdiction [to the ordinary] for the feudal one of papal *Eigenkirchen*" (Knowles, *Monastic Order*, 584). Knowles shows that the question of monastic privilege and developing canon law to deal with it preoccupied the Roman curia between Gregory VII in 1073 to the death of Alexander III in 1181 (583–91).

[14] It is told in the *Acta Lanfranci*, ed. J. Earle and C. Plummer, *Two of the Saxon Chronicles Parallel*, 2 vols. (Oxford, 1892–1898), 2:290–92; see Emms, "Historical Traditions,"161.

[15] Thorne, *Chronicle*, trans. Davis, 59–60. The reburial in the time of Hugh is told at 189–90.

[16] Kelly, *Charters of St. Augustine's* edits 39 pertaining to St. Augustine's itself and 14 pertaining to its dependent nunnery of Minster-in-Thanet. There may never have been that many more preserved into the Middle Ages. The cartulary PRO E 165/27 of s. xiii & xiv has a list of contents consisting of only 48 pre-Conquest items (see Kelly, *Charters*, li-liv and 189–94). Our discussion of the foundation charters follows Kelly, *Charters*, lxiv-lxv, with other sources of information brought in as indicated.

preserved in copies from the late twelfth century and later, generally gathered in cartularies and copied in chronicles.[17] Many of these are early and unobjectionable. However, the foundational documents are famous forgeries. These consist of three charters of Æthelberht I of Kent dated 605 (Kelly **1–3**) and a privilege of Bishop Augustine (**4**).[18] These are associated with five papal privileges in the names of Boniface IV, Adeodatus, Agatho, and John XII.[19] The only basically genuine item is the Agatho, which asserts papal control over the abbey and has a clause on the free election of the abbot. The purpose of these forgeries was to shore up with written authority the abbey's sincere claims, based, no doubt, on oral tradition, to 1) its seniority as a foundation to Christ Church, and 2) the independence of the abbey from the archbishop. These two claims were at the center of its self-image, pride, and independence of the ordinary's authority.

Forged foundation charter (Kelly) **1** purports to be a grant by Æthelberht, king of Kent, of land east of Canterbury for the foundation of a monastery in honor of St. Peter, "ita dumtaxat ut monasterium ibi construatur, et res quae supra memoraui in potestate abbatis sit, qui ibi fuerit ordinatus" ("so a monastery may be built exactly there, and it is to be forever in the power of the abbot, who is to be ordained there"). The control of the abbey by the abbot and his right to be ordained in it were principal bones of contention from the mid-eleventh century on. The boundaries given coincide with the medieval precincts of St. Augustine's. Diplomatically, it follows a royal charter of the eighth century; its earliest copy is of the fourteenth century, and Kelly thinks it was concocted in the eleventh.[20]

---

[17] The only charters copied about the time of the transactions they record are Kelly **24**, an OE grant of food-rent, about 930, and Kelly **31**, an OE land transaction between Abbot Wulfric (989–1006) and a layman Ealdred, copied into a 6th-century Gospel Book, CCCC 286 (Ker, *Catalogue*, no. 47). One (Kelly **10**) is a ninth-century single-sheet copy of a privilege of 699.

[18] A fifth (Kelly **5**) purports to be a grant of land by King Eadbald to the abbey in 618. Its purpose is to shore up a land claim in the eleventh or twelfth centuries. It is not in purpose or kind associated with Kelly **1–4**.

[19] See Wilhelm Levison, *England and the Continent in the Eighth Century* (Oxford, 1946), 181–82, 187–98. Boniface IV (27 Feb. 611), Birch no. 11, summarized by Thorne, *Chronicle*, trans. Davis, 16; Adeodatus (23 Dec. 673), Birch 31; John XII (22 April 956, the other undated), Birch 915 and 916. All have clauses about the liberties of the abbey that go further than the genuine letter of Agatho (15 May 675), Birch 38: "Igitur postulastis a nobis quatenus vestrum monasterium supranominatum privilegio apostolico decoretur, ut sub jurisdictione sanctae nostrae, cui, Deo auctore deservimus, ecclesiae constitutum, nullius alterius ecclesiae dictioni in posterum submittatur. . . . nullus monachis eisdem praeferatur, nisi quem sibi ex seipsis regulariter praeelegerint patrem. . . ." (Walter de Gray Birch, *Cartularium Saxonicum: A Collection of Charters Relating to Anglo-Saxon History*, 3 vols. [London, 1885–1893], 1:63).

[20] Kelly, *Charters*, 3–9. She thinks it was not copied "in the twelfth and thirteenth centuries because it was felt to have been superseded by **2**" (5). For a fascinating detailed

The next forged charter (Kelly **2**), having the same giver, receiver and date as the preceding, is "a grander version of **1**," which expands the territory granted to the abbey to the east and south and extends the liberty of the abbey to include not just the lands but the monastery itself and everything belonging to it.[21] The anathema invokes the names of SS. Gregory and Augustine themselves. It is a more reckless forgery, drawing on late witness-list formulas and post-Conquest formulas of greeting and "jettisoning the old-fashioned diplomatic of **1**." It was copied many times from the twelfth to the fifteenth centuries and acquired a rubric in the late cartularies showing "that it was being treated as the principal title to the abbey precincts."[22]

The longest of these forged charters (Kelly **3**) is a grant of Æthelberht dated 605 to SS. Peter and Paul of land at "Sturigao alio nomine dictum Cistelet."[23] Though ostensibly only a routine land grant (of parcels long held by the abbey), its purpose, besides shoring up this claim, is to provide the occasion for the fullest and most explicit articulation of the abbey's long-lost right of being the royal burial place ("Ubi etiam mihi et successoribus meis sepulturam prouidi"), as well as the long-contested right of non-interference by any bishop or any king succeeding Æthelberht, of the abbot's perpetual right to rule and to be consecrated within the abbey with the advice of the brethren: "Quod monasterium nullus episcoporum, nullus successorum meorum regum in aliquo ledere aut inquietare presumat, nullam omnino subiectionem in ea sibi usurpare audeat, sed abbas ipse qui ibi fuerit ordinatus intus et foris cum consilio fratrum secundum timorem Dei libere eam regat et ordinet." The witness list is similar in names to **1** and **2** but the form is eleventh-century, there are continental diplomatic elements, and much of the phraseology is from Bede's *Ecclesiastical History*.[24] This document was copied from the twelfth through fifteenth centuries; Kelly thinks it was concocted following a challenge to the other forged charters in 1181.

The fourth document (Kelly **4**), known as the "Bulla Plumbea" because in the Middle Ages it existed as a single sheet with a lead seal, purports to be a charter of privileges granted to the monastery of SS. Peter and Paul directly by Bishop Augustine. It contains the most complete and absolute declaration of the abbey's independence from archiepiscopal and royal control, as Kelly summarizes:

---

discussion of exactly how these documents were confected, see Levison, *England and the Continent*, 174–226.

[21] Edited and discussed, Kelly, *Charters*, 9–13.

[22] Kelly, *Charters*, 11.

[23] Kelly, *Charters*, 13–18. Sturry, to the northeast of Canterbury on the Stour, the name "Sturigao" (i.e. Stour-ge, the latter element like German *Gau*, district) apparently being a genuine ancient form (Kelly, *Charters*, 16, citing Campbell, *Old English Grammar*, 116).

[24] See Kelly, *Charters*, 17, and Levison, *England and the Continent*, 182–83.

> Augustine addresses all future bishops and kings and informs them of the exceptional circumstances of the monastery's foundation before forbidding any interference whatsoever in the monastery itself or the lands and churches dependent on it. . . . The archbishop is to consecrate the abbot (elected by the brethren) in the monastery itself, for the Lord's service rather than his own, and he is to urge him to obey God rather than himself. He is to treat the abbot as a colleague and not as his subordinate. He is not to conduct ordinations or celebrate mass in the abbey church except at the request of the abbot and brethren, and he must not exact any customary dues at all.[25]

This document dates from after the Conquest but before 1120, the approximate date of a copy in BL Cotton Vespasian B. xx (s. xi/xii, a collection of Goscelin's works relating to Canterbury). It was subject to a papal "Inspeximus" in 1178 and passed muster but was seriously challenged in 1181 as being of apparent recent fabrication, because such lead bulls were not used by Cisalpine bishops, and because the writing did not accord with "Roman" style.[26]

More importantly for our purposes, these forgeries extended to their appearance and script as well. While the "originals," such as they were, are lost, they were written in scripts attempting to appear as old as their purported dates. We know this because Thomas Elmham preserves them as actual-size "facsimiles" in his history of St. Augustine's, written probably in his own hand before 1414.[27] He was especially interested in these particular ones because they were the bulwark of the abbey's claims against the archbishop and Christ Church. His facsimiles of Kelly **1** and **2** (see fig. 39), the shorter charters of Æthelberht, are written in a version of "pointed" insular minuscule. Though the ductus resembles his own, the letter forms are mostly carefully shaped to resemble this archaic script. Kelly **4** (fig. 38), the "Bulla Plumbea," is written in a stately uncial that is frequently compared to that of the sixth-century "St. Augustine Gospels" (Cambridge, Corpus Christi College 286),[28] which also may have served as the script-pattern for the original forger. Among Elmham's facsimiles are reproductions of papal documents that can be compared to still-extant papal bulls, and

---

25 Kelly, *Charters*, 21.

26 So Gervase of Canterbury, *Opera Historica*, ed. W. Stubbs, 2 vols., Rolls Series 73 (London, 1879), 1:296, as cited by Levison, *England and the Continent*, 180. Levison (204) shows that the form of the bull could not be before Leo IX (1049–1054), the first pope to use an ordinal number to his name. The seal had on it "Bonifatii papae IIII."

27 See Antonia Gransden, *Historical Writing in England, c. 1307 to the Early Sixteenth Century* (London and Henley, 1982), 345–55, whose discussion of Elmham and his reproduction of the abbey's muniments is generally followed here.

28 For a full description see Mildred Budny, *Insular, Anglo-Saxon, and Early Anglo-Norman Manuscript Art at Corpus Christi College, Cambridge: An Illustrated Catalogue*, 2 vols. (Kalamazoo, 1997), 1:1–50, esp. 6–11; for Elmham's knowledge of this book see 11.

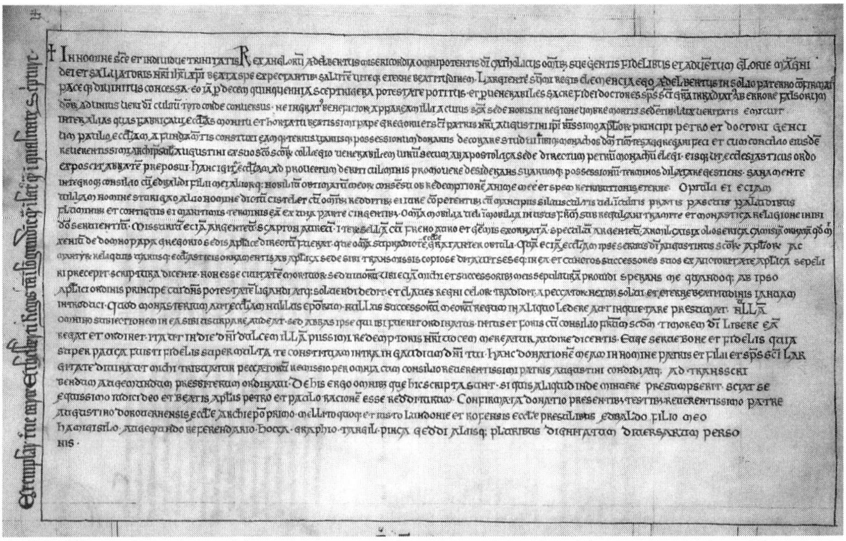

Figure 38: Cambridge, Trinity Hall MS. 1, f. 21v.

Used by permission of The Masters and Fellows of Trinity Hall, Cambridge.

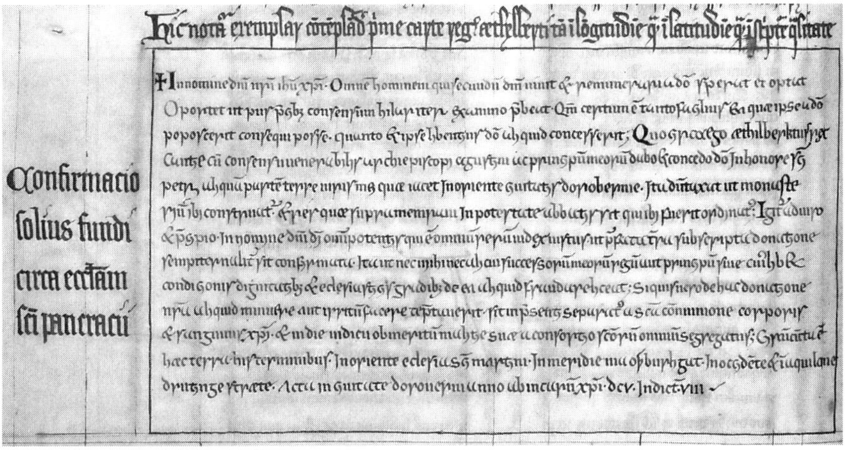

Figure 39: Cambridge, Trinity Hall MS. 1, f. 23r.

Used by permission of The Masters and Fellows of Trinity Hall, Cambridge.

his level of accuracy is high.[29] Elmham's care to reproduce the exact peculiarities of these documents was a reflection of his care for the honor and power of the abbey, which these documents protected by their supposed antiquity, and it was antiquity he wanted to project. We must assume that he accepted their authenticity sincerely. Elmham's activity is remarkable for its quality, but it is not unique; there are traces that the making of facsimiles of older documents took place at various times, for exact copies of lead *bullae* exist in the twelfth-century St. Augustine's cartulary Cotton Vitellius A. ii, ff. 1–19[30] as well as in the "Red Book" of St. Augustine's, Cotton Claudius D. x, ff. 11v, 12r. Most significantly for our purposes, Kelly **3**, the longest of the pseudo-Æthelbertian charters, was, if Kelly is right, forged soon after the year 1181, and is also written in a fine imitation of early uncial.

In that year and since 1176, the abbot was Roger I, a monk of Christ Church. The advent of Roger must have been a relief, following the horrible fifteen-year interregnum of Clarembald, a renegade fugitive monk from Normandy, intruded as abbot by King Henry II. According to Thorne, during Clarembald's time there was extreme factionalism and favoritism, laxity, the improper introduction of boys, and a disastrous piling up of debt and alienation of property, against the explicit rules of the convent.[31] To add to the miseries of this time (1168) there was a disastrous fire which destroyed a good part of the muniments as well as the church.[32] The convent continued to litigate against their unwanted superior and eventually had him deposed by papal intervention. Henry II, offended, took the abbey into his own hands for more than two years, up to the election of Roger. Roger's tenure was long and successful, lasting until 1212, during which time the abbey won papal confirmation of its long-claimed privilege of exemption from the oversight of the archbishop of Canterbury. Though a monk of Christ Church, Roger, like all St. Augustine's abbots-elect, rejected the right of the

---

[29] Michael Hunter, "The Facsimiles in Thomas Elmham's History of St. Augustine's, Canterbury," *The Library*, 5th ser. 28 (1973): 215–20, at 217. Elmham's history, containing the facsimiles, is in Cambridge, Trinity Hall, MS. 1; see M. R. James, *A Descriptive Catalogue of the Manuscripts in Trinity Hall, Cambridge* (Cambridge, 1907), 1–3; see also M. B. Parkes, "Archaizing Hands in English Manuscripts," in *Books and Collectors 1200–1700: Essays Presented to Andrew Watson*, ed. James P. Carley and Colin G. C. Tite (London, 1997), 101–41.

[30] Hunter, "Facsimiles," 218 and pl. VI. Neither in Vitellius A. ii nor in Claudius D. x is an attempt made to reproduce earlier forms of *script* in these charters. The reproductions in figs. 38 and 39 are from digital images kindly suppled by the Librarian of Trinity Hall, Dr. John R. Pollard, facilitated by Dominique Ruhlman, Director of Library Services.

[31] Thorne, *Chronicle*, trans. Davis, ch. 12, 93–100.

[32] Thorne, *Chronicle*, trans. Davis, 94, his exact words being "multe codicelle antique perierunt" (see Emden, *Donors of Books*, 1–2); this could mean only documents were destroyed, but it could have been some part of the library as well.

archbishop to consecrate him in the cathedral or to extract an oath of obedience. "After two journeys to Rome, Roger was eventually blessed by the pope [Alexander III] himself in 1179."[33] Instrumental in his case were the forged charter of Æthelberht, Kelly **1**, and the forged bull **4**. Archbishop Richard rejected their authenticity nevertheless, and the litigation continued until 1183. Gervase of Canterbury thought Roger was trying to escape entirely from the jurisdiction of the ordinary, though Roger was willing to accept "spiritual jurisdiction" over the abbey's priests and clerks (in parishes owned by the abbey).[34] It was in connection with this challenge to the documents, thinks Kelly, that about 1181 the longest of the Æthelberht charters (Kelly **3**) was forged, to make up for the deficiencies of **1** and **4**, criticized in 1179, the first as "erased and overwritten," and the second as looking "too recent."[35] We can see Roger then as presiding over the most elaborate of the famous St. Augustine's forgeries during "the golden age of forgeries." To us, "forgery" denotes a crime: it sometimes did to medieval men and women too, but it often was an act undertaken as a pious duty to accepted traditional truth in the face of documentary inadequacy. As Christopher Brooke puts it,

> Primacy and exemption demanded forgery: in the form in which they were claimed in the eleventh and twelfth centuries they were entirely new ideas, though their protagonists, for the most part, could not realize this. It was incomprehensible to them that earlier generations had not taken greater pains to preserve privileges they must have had. Similarly with land. In England the high watermark of forgery was the period between the new chaos of the Norman Conquest and the establishment of order, or growing legal precision, in the reign of Henry II.[36]

Roger had been elected on St. Dionysius' day, 9 October 1176, William Thorne tells us, the monks of St. Augustine's gathering in chapter to choose this monk of Christ Church. Although this choice was, as usual, imposed by the archbishop, it was an opportune one and represented a powerful moment of renewal; according to St. Augustine's tradition, Roger brought with him as part of the deal "relics of the martyr [St. Thomas à Becket] . . . a great part of the blood which he shed, a certain small portion of head cut away, along with a considerable part of the brain."[37] Such a prestigious beginning could only have highlighted the relief and excitement at finally getting rid of the odious intruder Clarembald. It was a time for new beginnings.

---

[33] Eric John, "The Litigation of an Exempt House: St. Augustine's, Canterbury, 1182–1237," *Bulletin of the John Rylands Library* 39 (1957): 390–415, at 394–95.

[34] John, "Litigation," 395.

[35] Kelly, *Charters*, 18.

[36] Christopher Brooke, "Approaches to Medieval Forgery," in *Medieval Church and Society: Collected Essays* (London, 1971), 100–20, at 114–15.

[37] From Thorne, *Chronicle*, trans. Davis, ch. 13.

In a St. Augustine's manuscript, Gonville and Caius College Library MS. 238, f. 251v (s. xiii), we find a list of the seventy-four monks participating at the election of Roger in 1176. The twenty-fourth listed among them is one named "Normannus."[38] Normannus is a name encountered occasionally in the twelfth century.[39] In a St. Augustine's martyrology, Cotton Vitellius C. xiii, on f. 133r, the obit of "Norman, monk and priest of this place" is recorded at 24 July, in a hand of the turn of the century.[40] Despite a lack of detail concerning the ordinary denizens of St. Augustine's, it is reasonable to suppose that the Normannus at the election, the one mentioned in the obit, and the one whose name appears in the Claudius annotations are all the same person. Normannus occurs twenty-fourth in the election list of seventy-four, suggesting he was a person of some seniority among the brethren.[41] The personnel of St. Augustine's were never that many, varying between about thirty and eighty monks at any one time from the Conquest to the Dissolution, and turnover followed the slow rhythms of lifespans.[42] The years 1176 × 1200 bracket exactly the dates within which we would place the annotations on the internal evidence of source and script. More

---

38 The list is printed by M. R. James, *A Descriptive Catalogue of the Manuscripts in the Library of Gonville and Caius College* (Cambridge, 1907), 1:287. This document is interpreted as the monks at the time of election of Roger I by Emden, *Donors of Books*, 15 and n. 151. First listed is "Willelmus prior," among the last "Rogerus Abbas," seemingly an addition and "very possibly by the same hand [as the rest of the list]" (James).

39 It occurs several times in the Durham "Liber Vitae," Cotton Domitian A. vii, and several times as a surname in the "Black Book of St. Augustine's" (BL Cotton Faustina A. i), a late thirteenth-century cartulary and custumal. The names in question, e.g. Godfrey Norman, Hamo Norman, Robert Norman, Simon Norman, and one person whose christian name is "Norman," occur in the documents of thirteenth-century dates. They are of course all laymen. See G. J. Turner and H. R. Salter, eds., *The Register of St. Augustine's Abbey Canterbury, commonly called The Black Books* 2 vols., British Academy of Records of the Social and Economic History of England and Wales 2–3 (London, 1915, 1924), 2:655.

40 'ix. Kl. Avgs. [24 July] O*bit* Norman*us* | mo*nachus* ⁊ sac*erdos* h*uius* loci.' This entry is in appearance turn of the century and is likely "our" Normannus. On f. 128v, probably entered later, is 'obit Goffridus `Norman´ *frat*er *nost*er,' probably a confraternal layman or *conversus* (see Knowles, *Monastic Order*, 754–55). Abbot Roger's obit is on f. 146v, 'xii. k. noue*m*bris [22 Oct.] Rogerus Abbas Ob. Pie memorie D*omin*us Roger*us* Abb*as* hui*us* loci', showing that the entries continued until at least 1213; however there is no obit for Abbot Alexander (1213–1220) at 4 Oct., which indicates the records ended between 1213 and 1220.

41 It was common practice to arrange lists like this in order of seniority; cf. A. J. Piper, "The Early Lists and Obits of Durham Monks," in *Symeon of Durham: Historian of Durham and the North*, ed. David Rollason (Stamford, 1998), 161–201, at 162.

42 According to J. Cox Russell, "The Clerical Population in Medieval England," *Traditio* 2 (1944): 177–212, at 188, St. Augustine's had 61 monks in 1146, a figure culled from Thorpe's *Chronicle*, trans. Davis, 80, representing a revival from a previous low of

interestingly, it suggests, if it does not require, that Normannus professed during and suffered through much of the long interregnum of Clarembald, a witness to the laxities and depredations, perhaps experienced the fire of 1168, and probably felt, as much as any, an upsurge of morale and energies with the advent of a proper new abbot who brought with him enthusiasm for renewing and extending the prestige and privileges of the house. His contribution to that renewal, we may be permitted to suppose, was his refashioning (whether as designer and writer himself, or as supervisor of another writer) of an ancient English biblical manuscript in a way so as to enhance the prestige and traditions of St. Augustine's.

Here is Normannus' dossier, taken from Claudius B. iv: In English notes derived from the *Historia* and Jerome's *Hebrew Questions* 'Norman' is named on f. 11v (no. 47, these are closely associated with 46 and 48), on the age of Mathusala, and on f. 12v, in a marginal note derived from the *Historia* (no. 51c) as 'N', concerning the pollution of the kin of Seth. Then there are on ff. 14r and 14v (bottom line on each) Latin notes (nos. 57 and 58) derived from Bede's *De temporum ratione*; these have been carefully worked over in two colors of contrasting ink. Though the latter consists entirely of information gleaned from the well-known *De temporum ratione*, it is ostentatiously finished off 'Normanno testante. iuxta hebraicha*m* u*e*ritate*m*', perhaps a phrase picked up from witnessing documents. The name occurs, with all but the initial *N* of the name erased,[43] on f. 20v (no. 86) from Jerome's version of Eusebius' *Chronicle*, all in a larger ductus associated with the Jerome notes. In the smaller "H" ductus are four extracts from the *Historia* in Latin attributed to "Normannus," on f. 44r (lower frame, no. 167), f. 52v (line 2 up, no. 192), f. 70v (above bottom frame, no. 229), and f. 92v (above bottom frame, no. 272b), the last being a liturgical comment. The long entry no. 321 on f. 140r, confected from Deuteronomy 34:6, Jerome's Ep. 73, Ad Fabiolam, and *De temporum ratione*, with perhaps input from Jerome's *De situ et nominibus locorum Hebraicorum*, on the number of years of Moses up to his death, seems to show the original activity of Normannus; 'hec Nor[mannus]' appears in the middle of the entry in what seems a partially erased intervention, though in the same ductus as the passage as a whole.

Of these entries, the most memorable is his research and writing in the English notes nos. 46, 47, and 48 on ff. 11v-12r which compare the Comestor and Jerome on the years of Mathusala, and indeed that whole complex seems to show the selecting and arranging work of Normannus. The name occurs on f. 11v (top) (no. 47), in a note referring back to the preceding English version of the Comestor's inconclusive presentation of the age of Mathusala at the Flood, continuing to the top of f. 12r; this is independent work on Jerome's "famosa quaestio," and it impresses because it involves the scholarly comparison of the *Historia*

30, and in 1423 there were 84. At the Dissolution in 1538 there were 31 monks (Russell, "Clerical Population," 190).

43 The name is clearly visible by video-spectral comparator.

and Jerome's *Hebrew Questions* in order to arrive at an acceptable calculation of the age of Mathusala at the time of the Flood, all written up in English with some facility.[44]

It is pleasant to imagine the hand of Normannus working extensively on f. 12v. On the preceding verso (f. 11v, fig. 31) a very neatly written marginal attribution gives him one of the English comments. Here, though, on f. 12v, the whole page has been worked over carefully. It concerns the sins of the giants (Genesis 5:32–6:10). At the bottom a small script apparently in two stints entered two notes from the *Historia*, one speculating whether the giants were of Noe's time or before and the other on their monstrousness and relation to the Titans (nos. 51e, 51f). The first is keyed by the *signe de renvoi* 'hwǽr'/'hǽr' (Norman *h*, insular *r*) to the original Old English text at line 12 up, ⁊ **hlisfulle weras**; the latter comment is keyed to the Old English original text by the *signe de renvoi* 'ꜳ̆' and inserted at the place where God repents that he created man. But a section of this Latin text is excerpted (see no. 51f) and written up in the margin next to the Old English text it concerns as no. 51d: "[incubi and demons] who are accustomed to take possession of women in rituals." This is very neatly done in a black ink. Above this is a Normannus note in English, in brown ink, also uncommonly neatly done, which is a comment on the gist of the Latin *Historia* note (no. 51b): "In the seven-hundredth year . . . the sons of Seth lusted after the daughters of Cain . . . and the giants were born"; "N[orman]: that is, Seth's sons polluted themselves with the daughters of Cain; from them came the giant men" level to the main Old English text, ⁊ **hi cendon ða synd mihtige fram worulde.**

Normannus seems taken with an interest in chronological questions, as were most literal commentators in the Hieronymian tradition as well as most annotators of twelfth- and early thirteenth-century copies of the *Historia Scholastica*. It is thus tempting to attribute to him the passages in the manuscript involving calculations of years in the lives of the patriarchs, some of these notes being unsourced and unsigned. There is an especially intriguing nexus of comments on f. 59r, three notes in the "J" script (fig. 41), each of which has already appeared earlier in Claudius written in the "H" script:

> 191d (margin) ⋕ |§ p*ost* unu*m* annu*m* | ysaac in Gera|ris natus obiit (unsourced)
>
> 193b (above bottom frame) Sciendu*m* q*uo*d an*te* morte*m*. ysaac. xii. annis ue*n*dit*us* e*st* Joseph. (HS 1125A)
>
> 208b (in bottom frame) § tredecim. annis fuit ioseph | in egipto anteq*ua*m ingre[die]tur | domu*m* pharaonis. (unsourced)

[44] See the detailed discussion, ch. 5, 274–75.

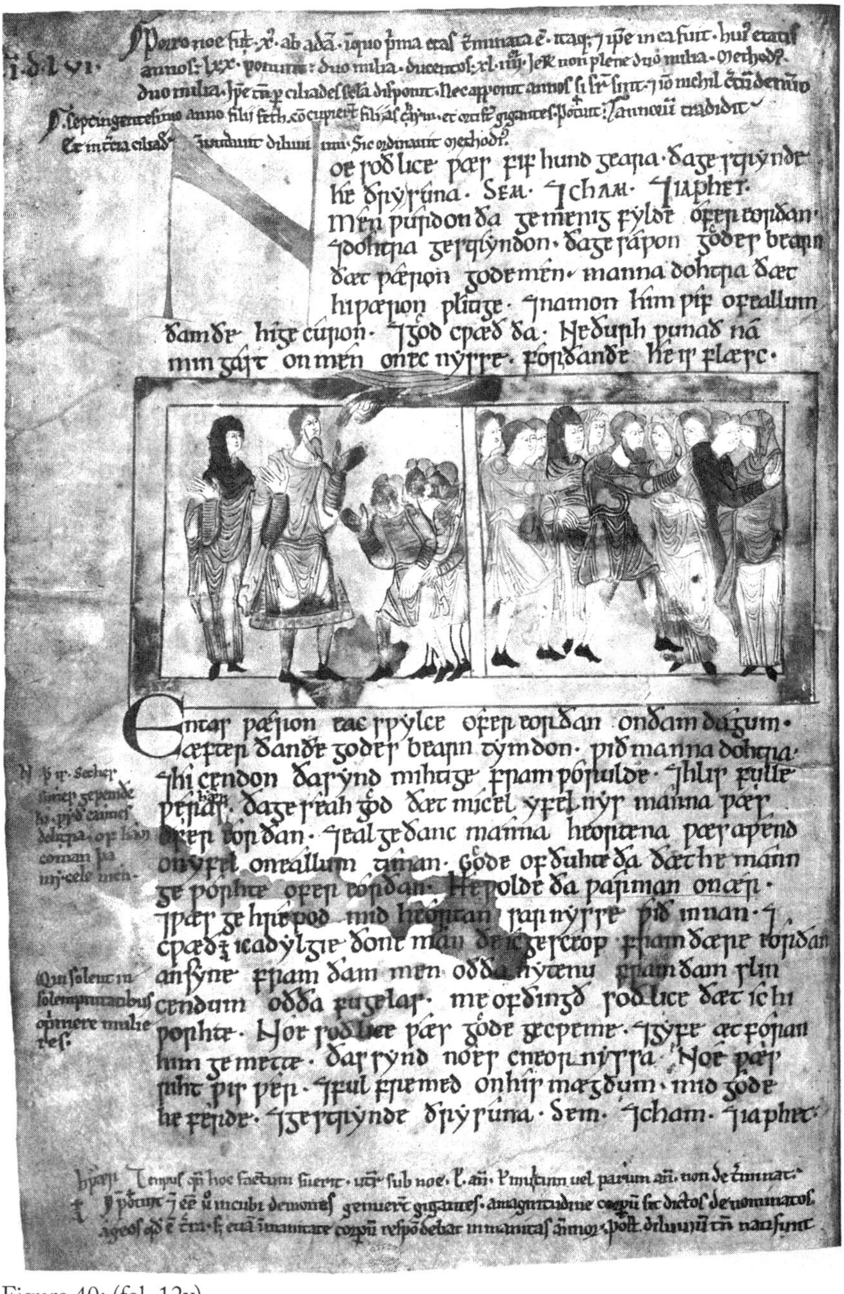

Figure 40: (fol. 12v)

The same text as 191d occurs as 191a on f. 52v in the top picture frame; 193b appears on f. 53r as 193a beneath the rubric at the top; 208b occurs as 208a on f. 58r at the top of the page. In their midst is an attributed Normannus note (f. 52v, line 2 up, no. 192), a Latin *Historia* extract. At the top of this very page, above the picture space showing the burial of Isaac, the "H" script has the note drawing attention to the calculational activity (no. 191a):

✓ ad hoc singnu*m* [*sic*] ✓ ⁜

On f. 59r the "J" script has in the margin given the "signum" plus the repetition of 191a:

⁜ ✓ § post unu*m* annu*m* ysaac in Geraris natus obiit

plus the repeated notes as listed above. The collocations of these three places on f. 59r make up an arithmetical calculation: "Isaac died after Joseph had been in Egypt one year" (191a, 191d), "It is to be known that 12 years before the death of Isaac Joseph was sold" (193b, unsourced, also on f. 53r as no. 193a), "Thirteen years was Joseph in Egypt before he entered the house of Pharaoh" (208b, unsourced, also on f. 58r as no. 208a); in other words the annotator, Normannus?, draws together on f. 59r all the scattered calculations to arrive at the conclusion of 1 + 12 = 13 years that Joseph was in Egypt before he confronted Pharaoh, as if testimony has to be brought forth to bring home the point—it seems like the strategy of a practiced teacher: the reader is encouraged to come to make the calculation for himself by comparing the documents. As the dispersed comments on ff. 52v etc. in the "H" hand stimulate a "Hieronymian" calculation on f. 59r, they call for the "J" script in the latter place, or so at least seems the case.

In the end, it is difficult to say what the attributions mean. Normannus certainly cannot be the author of the vast majority of the Latin comments, which are verbatim extracts from well-known authorities. He might well be the annotator himself. He might have been the local authority selecting particular comments and ordering them to be included. He might be, as we have just suggested, the author of some of the unsourced notes, most of which comprise chronological summaries.[45] He also might be the "author" of the Old English notes, or one of

[45] E.g., nos. 24, 39a, 60, 139 (ref. to Josephus), 153, 163, 168, 169, 170 (falsely attributed to Jerome), 173 (rather enigmatic, falsely attributed to Josephus), 179, 191a (f. 52v) repeated as 191d (f. 59r), 208a (f. 58r) repeated as 208b (f. 59r), 211, 213, 224, 237, 240, 243, 262, 280 (allegorical cast), 289, 318, 331. In addition, the two unsourced notes 230 and 259 appear to be late independent compositions sharing the spelling 'sarvata' for *servata*. But one must allow for some, or many, of the unsourced notes to be derived from the margin of the parent copy of the *Historia Scholastica,*and for the likelihood that for some we simply have not found the source.

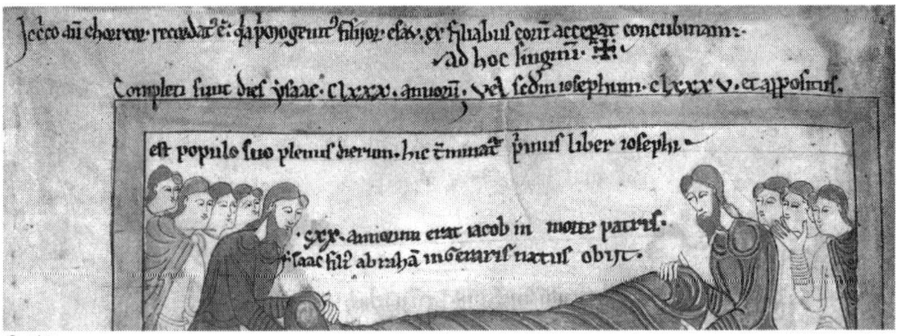

← '*√ad hoc signum* ⁜'

← no. 191a

f. 52v

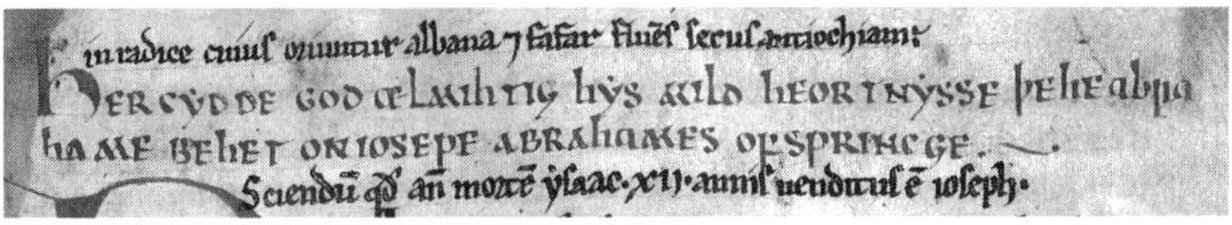

no. 193a

f. 53r

no. 208a

f. 58r

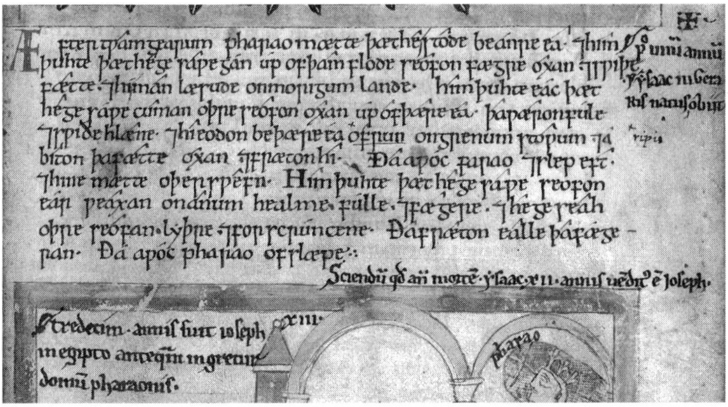

← no. 191d

'⁜ ✓'

← no. 193d

← no. 208b

f. 59r

Figure 41.

them. Alternatively, the "Norman" notes might have been lifted by the annotator from some notebook belonging or ascribed to a person named Normannus. The attributions to Norman[nus] on ff. 11v, 44r, 70v are so positioned in frame or margin that they could be seen as standing outside the text, but they are all still in the same hand and style as the note each is attached to; the rest are integral with the comment, written within the block of text. Why was his name (partially) erased twice? There are otherwise very few erasures or corrections to the annotations. These partially erased attributions (ff. 20v and 140r) might suggest that Normannus's authority was being contested by someone. The latter note is a longish epitome of Jerome's Epistle 73 and *De temporum ratione* in the style of the Mathusala note. Did someone deny his authority or notice that he was not really the author? As a set the Normannus notes have some coherence, for with one exception (the item on f. 44r, no. 167), they show no interest in the biblical narrative or wording, but in extra-textual matters chronological, genealogical, and ecclesiological.

However, when all is said, the congruence of "Normannus," Latin, English translation, diverse scripts, and scholarly criticism of the *Historia* is telling. Though relatively few, the "Normannus" entries involve the annotation-system at every layer as regards language, script-styles, and sources and through the entire book. All this suggests that Normannus was one of the active participants as long as the annotation project lasted. The attributions suggest his importance as a contributor to the project, if not the only one, as compiler and perhaps as the scribe, especially as the paleographical evidence points to all the annotations being in a single hand.

All this may be drawn together to produce a possible scenario for the production of the annotations. Sometime during the reign of Clarembald, when there was in effect no abbot, Normannus must have taken his vows and passed a number of years in the convent during this bitter and tumultuous time. He must have been an assiduous student of the Bible and had probably become familiar with the standard monastic curricula on that subject, but he seems to have been especially interested in the revived literal method associated with the name of Jerome, which suggests he was somewhat *au courant* with the new strands of biblical study taking place among the canons of St. Victor and elsewhere. Perhaps about the time he professed, there was a terrible fire. Bad as it was, it did not destroy the library, for more than fifty manuscripts from before the middle of the twelfth century still exist.[46] However this may have been, there remained among

[46] There are 1837 volumes listed in the late fifteenth-century St. Augustine's list as printed by James (*Ancient Libraries*, 197–406). Of these almost 1300 mention donors' names and these, to go by the identifiable names, are from the thirteenth–fifteenth centuries (Emden, *Donors,* 2). This leaves about 550 unattributed volumes, some of which may have been later cloistral acquisitions; but many, and these the most basic texts of the monastic curriculum, were probably mostly from the twelfth century and earlier. The

the books of the abbey at least one book written in Old English, the great illustrated Hexateuch, Cotton Claudius B.iv.[47] One may suppose that after such a fire the first business must have been surveying the damage and recording the survivors, including a recall of all the books dispersed throughout the monastery. This may have been the occasion when the old Hexateuch written in English came to Normannus's notice. It might also have been the occasion for the acquisition of new books, including the just-published *Historia Scholastica*, which must have begun making its way to England in the decade after the fire. Such a compendious collection of literal comments covering all of Scripture, its unimpeachable sources often evident to a biblical scholar such as Normannus, might have been the inspiration for the annotations. One book that was not lost, apparently, was the abbey's shorter collection of "Jerome" texts, unless it was copied from an older exemplar borrowed for the purpose from Christ Church, Rochester, or some other establishment, of the type we studied in chapter 6. Books in Old English must also have been available to supply the models and vocabulary that are detectable: poetry, computus, charters, homilies. The style of language, that is, rough-and-ready adherence to norms of West-Saxon, we may suppose is a particularly "monastic" sort of English by the mid-twelfth century. The cloistered monks, or at least some of those, and probably those who stuck most faithfully to scriptorium work, must have had little contact with the outside English-speaking world

---

"Jerome" volume that is a centerpiece of this study has no donor listed and was most likely a book of the second quarter of the twelfth century, that is a generation later than the two sister manuscripts in Trinity College, Cambridge (see ch. 6, 306–09). A rough count based on Ker's list shows that of surviving St. Augustine's books, there are 31 from before the eleventh century, 19 from the eleventh, and 12 from s. xi/xii. There are 36 from the twelfth and 12 shown as s. xii/xiii (Ker, *Medieval Libraries of Great Britain*, 40–47)

[47] This is the only book in English listed in the late catalogue. According to Ker, *Catalogue*, xlvi, about 35 extant Anglo-Saxon books appear in Eastry's Christ Church catalogue. Of course there may have been, probably were in Normannus' day, other Anglo-Saxon books at St.Augustine's that did not survive to the time of the late catalogue. But on the face of it, books with Old English were much more prevalent and valued into later times at Christ Church. There seem to be a few books of St. Augustine's that survive with significant amounts of Old English (culled from H. Gneuss, *Handlist of Anglo-Saxon Manuscripts* [Tempe, 2001]): CUL Gg.5.35 (Latin Christian poetry, OE glosses), perhaps CCCC 44, a pontifical (OE added texts), the eighth-ninth century "Corpus Glossary" (CCCC 144) was at St. Augustine's in the thirteenth (ex libris), Durham Cathedral B.III.32 (s. xi^1), a compound manuscript containing Ælfric's "Glossary," with a thirteenth-century table of contents, BL Cotton Cleopatra A. iii (s. x), Latin-OE glossaries, Cotton Domitian A. i (s. x/xi, recipe, booklist), Cotton Otho E. i (s. x/xi, Latin-OE glossary), Cotton Tiberius C. ii (s. ix/x, glossary, scratched glosses in a Bede, "Hist. Eccl."), Cotton Titus A. iv (s. xi^1, bilingual "Reg. Bened."), Cotton Vespasian D. vi (s. x, Latin texts glossed in OE, "Kentish Hymn," etc.), possibly Cotton Caligula A. xv + Egerton 411 (s. xi ex., OE computus, etc.).

of ordinary people. Within the cloister, monks probably spoke mostly Latin or French. Thus "English" meant for them not the natural language that was evolving into Middle English in the abbey's fields and manors, but the ancient language of books, standing ready as models in the cloister library.

The presence in the library of the Anglo-Saxon Old Testament may have struck Normannus as a fitting symbol of the abbey's ancient traditions of learning, and a good vehicle for asserting the abbey's dignities and rights. Refurbishing it would have been an act of piety. Providing it with a literal commentary as a kind of index as well as supplement to the existing translation would have made it more usable. In this vein, leaves were added to provide a proper opening to the story of Moses, advertise the New Testament place-names of the Holy Land, and, on the last leaf, to carry the story to the Incarnation, however sparsely. We may speculate that in order to emphasize the antiquity and prestige of the book, and perhaps to assert a proprietary interest in the kinds of information that had now become available in a compiled and quasi-narrative form in the *Historia*, Normannus's project set out to produce the selected comments from this very new book in the ancient language of English, as a link between the old book, the new learning, and the antiquity of the house owning this artifact. It was a challenge all at once to Jews (to whom the abbey was in ever-increasing debt in Clarembald's and Roger I's time),[48] canons, Paris clerks, and cathedral schools, as well as to Christ Church, with its much more distinguished traditions of writing and learning since the time of Lanfranc. The annotations asserted that this type of information was nothing new to the monks of St. Augustine's, that they had it all along, and they had the English notes to prove how far back and how intimately within their own local traditions deep biblical learning went. Certainly, as we have seen,[49] the selection and arrangement of the extracts "remonasticizes" and denarrativizes the *Historia* being mined as a source of commentary in frames and margins.

Invoking the names of Jerome, Josephus, Hrabanus, et al., all well-established authors of the monastic curriculum, and the conspicuous lack of reference to the "Historiae," or "Magister Petrus," as was all the rage to do among up-to-date clerics, is symptomatic. It looks as if the "modernity" of the source is deliberately being suppressed. The whiff of antiquity the English notes were intended to impart of course technically comprises "forgery," as does the invocation of the name "Normannus" in association with quotations from quite other authorities. All this would be well within the temperament and capabilities of the Augustinian monks. It would also be concocted in a spirit of sincerity: were only the documents there (perhaps consumed by the fire!) the world would know the superior

[48] So Thorne, *Chronicle*, trans. Davis, 110, 136, 182.

[49] See ch. 5, 289–92.

traditions of biblical learning that had been carried on through the centuries at St. Augustine's, the equal of anything going on in present times. The codicology jibes with this, if it is true that the added leaves (ff. 74 and 147) represent materials appropriated from a roll of parchment prepared for the writing of writs and charters;[50] the taste for "authentication" and the materials and skills to carry this out would have been at hand. The obviously deliberate variation of script between "H" and "J" within the Latin notes, the use of "insular script" in both English and Latin, and the use of different-colored ink was well within the range of the textual ethics, paleo-paleographic perceptions, and motor skills of a monk raised in a house that was constantly resuscitating the words and appearance, not to mention existence, of its important documents. Even by the standards of its time, the "forgery" of Old English is rather crudely executed, in retrospect, yet it was done well enough to mislead the greatest English paleographer of the twentieth century, Neil Ker, into dating the English notes a generation too early. The invoking of his own name, sometimes in rather pompous formulations, suggests that Normannus could not resist blowing his own horn, if not his cover, from time to time. He did a good job of confusing the issue, which has lain unnoticed for nine centuries.

The issue of "antiquarianism" that is often raised in connection with late Old English copies does not really begin to encompass the issue, much more profound than *curiositas*, nostalgia, or actual legibility for real audiences. The notes, however useful as information they might be (especially the Latin ones), function as a kind of gigantic certificate of authentication, as on a relic. They are icons of something else besides their linguistic significations: of antiquity, dignity, and learning, authentic and peculiar to the abbey of St. Augustine's. The ancient book guarantees their provenance, and the English of the notes guarantees the antiquity of the learning. However, try as he might, composition of English notes was probably simply too hard for Normannus (or anyone else in the 1180s or '90s) to continue for long, and the impression of antiquity may have been briefly continued with a series of Latin notes written in faux-insular handwriting; eventually that too was abandoned, or perhaps the point had been made. As there was no doubt a practical aspect to the annotations as well, they were extensively continued in normal house script, Normannus's script we may assume, perhaps with a variety of ductus deliberately varied to flag different types of sources, perhaps also to give the impression of the work of several hands, perhaps, more neutrally, the scripts differing primarily because the *Historia* and Jerome notes were done in distinct campaigns of writing.

---

[50] See ch. 4, 239–40.

St. Augustine's was a wealthy house with a well-stocked library, and it never forgot its traditions of quiet, if passive, learning.[51] Its intellectual production lagged behind Christ Church from Lanfranc to Stephen Langton, for it produced no outstanding scholars or writers. As the thirteenth century progressed it fell, along with Benedictinism in general, into mediocrity. But Claudius B. iv lends us a window into the kind of energetic and enthusiastic reception, learning, and compiling that took place there in the person of at least one brother, Normannus, in the last quarter of the twelfth century, whose work, *litterae prolongae apud praesentes*, mingling the far-removed material past with the intellectual present, has subsisted for centuries as "purloined letters," mis-represented, misplaced, and waiting in plain sight to be found.

[51] See Brooks, *Early History*, 266–78, esp. 276, for the valuable comments on the Christ Church library and its pre-scholastic character, with authors and works based in the old monastic curriculum. The same situation would obtain, *mutatis mutandis*, in the St. Augustine's library. In the time of Normannus and into the thirteenth century St. Augustine's was producing a matched Bible set with display quadrata script and bookhand glossing similar to writing in Claudius B. iv (but none of the hands are identical to it): in the British Library is Royal 3. A. i, a glossed one-volume Book of Numbers, apparently written by one scribe, the text in display script, the commentary written in top and side margins and between lines in the same style only smaller; Royal 4. A. ii is a companion to 3.A.i, a glossed Isaiah in the same format and style; Royal 4. A. x is with the previous two, a glossed Genesis, but is of a later date, comments in a small late twelfth/early thirteenth-century hand that is somewhat pointed but still retains features of the mixed style, the text in the older style of round "mixed" hand that relates it to the other two volumes; Royal 3. A. ii is in the same style with the others and apparently part of the same project, a glossed Leviticus. This project must have gone on for fifty years or more.

Appendix I
Analysis of English Language in the Annotations

Orthography/Phonology

Crawford[1] has outlined the orthography as corresponding to phonological values. There is very little to add to his analysis. The data are here set out to underline the contrasts with and deviation from standard late West-Saxon orthography and phonetics. If, in particular instances, deviations are the norm in the notes, that will be stated. The documents that seem to be most relevant comparands are the two late Canterbury manuscripts of the "West-Saxon Gospels," preserved in British Library Royal 1. A. xiv (Canterbury, Christ Church, s. xii) (**R**) and the later copy made from it, Bodleian Library, Hatton 38 (4090) (Canterbury, s. xii/xiii) (**H**). Compared to those documents, the English notes in Claudius B. iv afford only scanty and incomplete data. The analysis of the linguistic forms below follows the format used by Roy Liuzza in his analysis of these two twelfth-century Canterbury copies in his edition of the West-Saxon Gospels.[2]

---

1 "Old English Notes," 124–35.

2 *The Old English Version of the Gospels*, vol. 2, EETS 314 (Oxford, 2000), 175–201. See also his analysis of the texts of these manuscripts in "Scribal Habit: The Evidence of the Old English Gospels," in *Rewriting Old English*, ed. Swan and Treharne, 143–65. Other references in the Appendices are to Joseph Bosworth and T. Northcote Toller, *An Anglo-Saxon Dictionary* (Oxford, 1898) and T. Northcote Toller, *An Anglo-Saxon Dictionary, Supplement* (Oxford, 1921); Campbell, *Old English Grammar*; Richard Jordan, *Handbook of Middle English Grammar and Phonology*, trans. and rev. Eugene Joseph Crook (The Hague, 1974); Bruce Mitchell, *Old English Syntax*, 2 vols. (Oxford, 1985); DOE, Antonette diPaolo Healey et al., *Dictionary of Old English A-F*, CD-ROM version 1.0 (Toronto, 2003). MED, Hans Kurath and Sherman M. Kuhn, eds., *Middle English Dictionary* (Ann Arbor, 1956–2001) and OED, *The Oxford English Dictionary* (Oxford, 1888–1928, rev. ed. 1989).

Vowels and diphthongs of stressed syllables (Liuzza 175–76, §86):

⟨æ⟩ for W-S /æ/: frequently remains, *æfter* (3×) *(h)ær* (2×), *aræ[r]de* 181.2, *cræftæs* 34.1, *cwæþ* 8×, *fæder* (2×), *flæsces* 62.1, *hæfde/hæfede* 156.8/41.1, *mæden-* 7.1, *mægum* ("host") 181.4, *wæs* (13×);

but it alternates with:

⟨a⟩ for /æ/ (a ME symptom): *at* 10.1 357.1, *cwað* 50.3, gsm/n *þas* 10.4/181.3, *was* 47.1 *nas* 67.1

⟨e⟩ for /æ/: *(h)efter* 18.1 46.1, *her* (= *ær*) 62.1, *leden* ("Latin"), 181.4, *cweð* 25a.1 46.3, *creftes* 44.2, *wes* 34.1; probably belonging here is ⟨**ea**⟩ for /æ/: *feader* 156.3 (reverse spelling).

⟨**eo**⟩ for W-S /æ/: *gesceopa* pp 6a.1: this is perhaps an isolated reverse spelling of *gescæpa*, *gescepa* (or a confusion of eo/ea as freq. in **R**, Liuzza §99) or by analogy from the preterit.

Reverse spellings probably are further indications of the ME convergence of /æ/ with /a/:

⟨æ⟩ for W-S /a/: *forwæhshe* 44.4 (cf. Jordan §29.7.2), *æc* (conj.) 62.1 beside *hac* 46.2 50.4.

a+n *anlænges* 10.3, *lænd* 6a.1 beside *land-* 10×, *færm* ("from") 358.1 beside *fram* 50.1 50.4. Those in nasal environments might reflect actual fronting of the vowel, which perhaps takes place in unstressed environments numerous times in **R** and **H** (cf. Liuzza §107, Campbell §379) but only rarely in Claudius (*þane* for *þone* 181.9).

⟨æ⟩ for W-S /a:/: *æn* 358.3; the single example is probably insignificant; in any case, it might stand for *and*. Otherwise W-S ⟨**a:**⟩ remains (but few instances): *an(e)* 6×, *ache* ("oak") 181.8,9, *ham* 181.6, *na(n)* 3×, *napeles* 6a.1; in -**w**- environment, *saulen* 34.5, *-swa* (7); never raised to /**o:**/ (cf. Liuzza, 176–77 §§ 87–88).

⟨a⟩ for W-S /æ:^{1}/ (< WGmc ā): *þar* 181.2, *þara* dsf 10.3 46.2 beside *þær* 3×, *þæra* 26.3; for W-S /æ:^{2}/ (< WGmc ai): *clane* 7.3, *hunwarst* (for *unwǣrst*) 45.2. According to Liuzza the latter is against a purely "Kentish" dialect (Liuzza §89). Also occurs

⟨e⟩ for W-S /æ:^{1}/: *breðe* 10.2, *wera* 46.2 beside *wære* (2×); for W-S /æ:^{2}/ *-dele* 10.2 10.3, *ledde* 181.5, ?*her* 62.1 beside *(h)ær* (5×). Both /æ:^{1}/ and /æ:^{2}/ appear in Kentish as ⟨**e**⟩ (Jordan §§48(2), 49). Evidence of plural prets. of str.

vbs 4 and 5 with ⟨æ⟩ is limited to *cwæðe* 128.1 (in other occurrences vowel is suspended); class 7: *ræðe* (pres. subj.) 181.5.

⟨æ⟩ for W-S /e/: *ycwæþen* pp 25b.1, *fæle* 3×; *træenle* (*trendle*) 10.4 probably belongs here. But ⟨e⟩ for /e/ in *denæ* 25b.1, *ecge* 181.6, *fela/e* 2×, *feld(e)* 3×, *forfe[r]den* 34.5, *forðferde* 46.3, 181.8, *formelta* 44.5, *getelde* 181.7, etc. show that /æ/ and /e/ may be phonemically distinct, though the spelling is often confused. Yet their association may be a Kentish symptom (cf. Campbell §193(d); Liuzza §92).

⟨æ⟩ for W-S /e:/: *slæp* 181.4 beside *slep* 44.1 (cf. Liuzza §93).

⟨æ⟩ for W-S ⟨eo/i⟩ in *hære* ("their") (7×) as the regular form against *hyre* (2×) seems to be a special case of Kentish unrounding, with the spelling stylized to one form (cf. Jordan §70).

⟨a⟩ for W-S /o:/ +r *baren* pp 36a.1 beside *ybore/a* 47.3/50.2; +n *an* 10.3 beside *on* 17×, possibly representing an incipient opening or lengthening (cf. Jordan §35(3)) but more likely an error.

⟨e⟩ for W-S /y/ (< u+i): *cenne* 26.1 34.1, *deða* (= *dyde*) 46.2 *heuele* 50.4, *senne* 34.3, *wensæm* 10.2, *scete, scette* 34.2 beside *cynne* 6a.1. Kentish unrounding (Campbell §288, Jordan §40); similarly, ⟨e⟩ for W-S /y/ (< au+i): *yherden* 44.2 (Kentish, Campbell §200(5), Jordan §40); similarly, when long, *-tene* 34.4 and ⟨ee⟩ for W-S /y:/: *feer* 44.5. The merging of /e/ and /y/ is a feature of the writer's dialect. W-S orthography is preserved in: *bebyrigde* 50.3, *fyrst* 62.1.

Probably related by analogy and perhaps indicating the merging of /e/ with /i/, /y/ (cf. Liuzza §94) is:

⟨e⟩ for W-S /i/: *seþe* 50.4 (but Campbell §217, Kentish *sio-/seoðða(n)*), *lefede* 47.4, *nemeð* (Campbell §216 Kentish *nioman*) 47.4

⟨i⟩ > ⟨y⟩: (Jordan §§ 41, 36) unrounding of /y/ in late OE becomes generalized with spelling alternatives ⟨i/y⟩ (Liuzza §94) but here only in one direction: *angynne* 10.1, *belyfen* 50.3, *besyde* 25b.1, *mycele* (2×), *-nysse* 10.1, 29a.2, *nyþewærde* 181.8, *wyc-* 181.7, *wycnigede* 181.2 358.3 *byð/bið*: for ī: *wycstowe* 181.7, *forðsyðe* 20,3, *wycnigede* 181.2, *wyfmen* 181.3, *wyf* 156.5; OE spelling remains in *blisse* 10.1, *ofspringe* (6×); there seem to be no instances of ⟨y⟩ > ⟨i⟩ or ⟨i:⟩. Here may be mentioned:

⟨u⟩ for ⟨y⟩: *muculum* 181.4 (Jordan §17(1), Liuzza §94).

⟨a⟩ for W-S /ea/: *al* 36a.1 *alla* 6a.2, *salde* 357.1 (Campbell §226, Kt. smoothing); related to this must be:

⟨æ⟩ for W-S /ea/ (by breaking): *ælswa* 50.3, *ælle* 181.4, *hærme* 181.4, *nyþewærde* 181.8 beside **ea** (by palatalization) *gear* 3×, *wingeard* 67.1 which follow W-S orthography (Campbell §260; cf. Liuzza §96 on the general simplification of diphthongs in late 12th-century Canterbury texts).

⟨e⟩ for W-S /ea/: *cester* 181.1, Kentish? (Campbell §187), but cf. Liuzza (§96) who says such spellings may be random, given the variety of representations of front sounds in texts like this.

⟨o⟩ for W-S /eo/: *ornos(t)lice* 181.5; cf. *ornestlyce* in W-S Gospels, which Liuzza (§102) says may be an error, but it probably is a regular reduction, occurring as it does in several texts.

⟨y⟩ for W-S ⟨eo⟩ *(-)yrþe* 7.1 (2×), a Kentish reduction **eo** > **e** > **y**?

⟨æ⟩ / ⟨e⟩ as reductions of W-S /e:a/: *anhæfede* 10.1, *taeh(e)* 10.4, *tæran* 25b.1, *ræfode* 181.4; *hes(t)dele* 10.2 10.3, *estnysse* 10.1, *hesternysse* 29a.2, a general tendency, not Kentish (§§ Jordan 81–82); beside *eac* 2× (Liuzza §98).

⟨y⟩/⟨i⟩ for W-S /e:o/ > Kt. /i:o/: *tynde* (= *tēo[n]ða*) 50.4 *wypen* (= *wēopen*) 25b.1, sim. *bewyppe* 25a.7 (prets. of *(be)wēpan*); *ywilcon* (= *gewēolcon*) 26.2; according to Jordan (§85(2)) in Kentish this represents "a sound approximating /**ie**/ whose two elements originally had equal stress."

⟨ye⟩ for W-S /e:o/ *hisyen* (prob. *gesēon*) 181.3 (MS reading is doubtful) could represent an isolated instance of the Kentish treatment of **ēo** > **īo** > ⟨**ye**⟩ (Jordan §85), if it is not just a freak of spelling.

Vowels of unstressed syllables

Unstressed vowels in non-inflectional syllables appear to have merged into a single sound, variously represented, but most often as ⟨e⟩ whatever the W-S sound/spelling had been: *broþer*, *breþer* (3×), *su(e)ster* (3×), *docter* 181.3, *foster-* 181.8, *wensæm* 10.2, *heriænde* 61.3 *-hæfede* 10.1 (W-S *hēafdu*), class II weak: *acorede* beside *acorðe* (Campbell §389) 34.3,4, *herde* 181.7, *notiena* 62.1, *wuneda* 50.2, beside examples with W-S spelling: *ræfode* 181.4, *ornos[t]lice* 181.5, *wenðeres* 38.1, *tihele* 44.4, *seofon-* 34.3,4; (French) *pilires* 44.3; *muculum* 181.4 vowel harmony? or merely orthographical confusion?; irregular syncope *gewemðe* 51c.2 *uniwemð* 7.2 (e.g. *(un)gewemmed*).

Unstressed vowels in inflectional endings are merged and spelled most often ⟨e⟩:

Subs.: *scette* (= *scytta*) 34.2, *agene* (wk. acc.s.m.) 34.2, *twyfealde* (wk. nt. dat.) 15.10, *ane* (dat.s.m.) 6a.1, *ane* (dat.s.f.) 181.8, dat. *landa* 50.2, *cræftæs* (gen.)

34.1, *denæ* 25b.1, dat. s. *name* 61.3, 181.7, *wæteræ* (nom. pl.) 10.4. Dative plural *gearen* 46.1 but usually back vowel for back vowel: *tæran* 25b.1, *domon* 44.2, *mycelon* 50.4, *muculum* (dat. pl.) 181.4; *cf. mægum* (acc. pl. of *mægen*) 181.5.

Lost final vowel: *cester* (ds) 181.1.

Verbs: inf. *formelta* 44.5, *forwæhshe* 44.4.

pret. 3 s. *deða* (= *dyde*) 46.2 pret. 3 pl. *belyfen* 50.3, *cwæþe* 128.1, *coman* 51c.5 beside pl. *gecyrdon* 181.6, *hifunde* (i.e. *gefundon*) 34.1.

past part. (str.) *ybora* 50.2, *ybore* 47.3 beside *baren* 36a.1, *ysodene* 44.4; (wk.) *hunireped* (= *ungehrepod*) 7.2.

Lost inflection: *cwæð* (pt3p) 46.1,3.

The few compound words show no special reduction of the second element: *mædenyrðe* 7.1 beside *yrþe* 7.1, *neorxnawange* (3×), *twyfealde* 15.10, *seofonfealð* 34.3 *anhæfede* 10.1, *fostermodor* 181.8.

Parasiting: *anhæfede* 10.1, *mycele* 34.3 51c.6 *mycelon* 50.4.

Inflections

The inflectional system of OE has decayed but is still recognizable; with few exceptions, the system is not functionally simplified and in almost no instances are the endings merely dropped (but cf. *uniwemð* 7.2, nom. sing. fem.). Sufficient details are given by Crawford, "Old English Notes," 133–35. The following are to be noted:

str. masc. acc. pl. *mægum*
wk. masc., infl. strong: gen. sing. *monas* ("moons") 10.4
cons. decl. ns *boc*, ds. *boc/boce*;
declension of *sunu*:

nom.	*sunu/e*	*sunes*
gen.		
dat.	*sune*	
acc.	*sune*	*sunes*

ns *breþer*, as *broþer*, np *breðer*; ds *fæder*; ns *docter*, gp *dohtra*, ap *dohtra*; ns *feader*, ds *fæder* 181.2 *fæderes* 128.3.

The few strong adjectives that are used tend to fall together under the ending ⟨e⟩, e.g. dat. masc. sing. *ane* 6a.1, *suote* 10.2; dat. sing. fem. *wensæm* 10.2.

wk. adj. *seo leden boc.*
numeral: *twa* 6a.2 (gen.? masc.) (Kt.? Campbell §683).

Pronouns:

Personal:	*he*	*heo/hi*	*hit*	*hi/hy*
	him	*hire*		*ham*
	hine	*hi*		*hy*
Poss.	*(h)is*	*hyre*		*hære*
Demons.	*se*	*seo/si*	*þæt/ðat*	*þa þa*
	þas			
	ðon/ðan	*ðare/þara*	*þan*	
	ða/ dan	*þæra*		
	ðam			
	þane	*þæt*		*þa*

Infinitives and past parts. of str. verbs end in *-e/-a* (see below).

pret. pl. *cwæð* (2×).

Class III weak, intrusive middle vowel (on analogy of Class II? the eventual ME form) *lefede* 47.4, *hæfede* 41.1 beside *hæfde* 156.8.

Consonants

Representation of palatal consonants is in general as in Old English, e.g.: *cester* 181.1, *ecge* 181.6, *flæsces* 62.1, *geara* 6a.1, *scræfe* 15.10, *scyte*, *scytta* 34.2; there is no distinction of velar / palatal by the variants ⟨k / c⟩, ⟨g / ȝ⟩ as in **H**. The isolated spelling of the velar ⟨ache⟩ ("oak") 181.8,9 is probably Norman influence (Jordan §17.2). Medially there are a couple of orthographical confusions which suggest uncertain or changing pronunciation: *forwæhshe* 44.4, *ymegg` h´e* (i.e., *gemecge*) 50.3 (Norman influence? Jordan §192); nasal environment with loss of /**n**/: *wenughe* (= *wenunge*) 46.1 (Jordan §193), *wycnigede* (from *wician*, but for *wycigede* or *wycigende*?) occurs twice 181.2, 358.3; *wuniaghe* (for *wuniunge*) 10.3 beside *wunyunge* 10.2.

velar **g** lost medially: *hidraan* 10.3 probably representing /ydrauan/ < OE *gedragan* (Jordan §§111.i.a, 186)), a development precocious for Kentish; palatal **g** lost in -**w**- environment: *twean* 44.3.

W-S loss of -**g**- with compensatory lengthening in *mæden-* 7.1 (Campbell §243).

parasiting ⟨-**ig**⟩, as in late OE: *bebyrigde* 15.8, 181.8 (Jordan §190) but text does not show ⟨-**i**⟩ or the early ME vocalizing of palatal /**g**/: *dage* 6a.1; final /-**ig**/ *sixti* 34.4.

⟨**h**⟩ for /**g**/: *sorhe* 34.3, *tihele* 44.4 (Campbell §447).

/**w**/: **s(w)u** for **sweo** *swurdes* 181.6 is late W-S (Campbell §321); later loss of -**w**-: *suster* 18.1 181.5 beside *suester* (Jordan §162(2); cf. Liuzza §117); *saule* 34.5, *swote* 10.2; **hw**-: *hæder* (i.e. *hwæðer*) 44.3 is probably a scribal error.

⟨**u**⟩ for OE ⟨**f**⟩, unvoiced labiodental, is late OE: *heuele* 50.4 *leuede* 47.5 beside *lefede* 46.1 (Campbell §60, perhaps an incipient ME symptom).

loss of /**d**/ in consonant group: *anhæfede* 10.1, *anlænges* 10.3, *træenle* 10.4 (latter occurs in **R**, cf. Liuzza §119).

loss of /**t**/ in consonant group: *hesdele* 10.2, *ornoslice* 181.5.

unvoicing: *dot hy to dan* 47.5.

voicing: frequent spellings such as *cwæðe* for pret. pl. cannot be taken as indicating voicing since the exchange of ⟨**d** / **ð**⟩ is a general orthographical peculiarity of this text and others of the twelfth century (but cf. *forwurþon* 44.4, subj. pret. 3 pl.): ⟨**ð**⟩ for /**d**/ occurs dozens of times probably rather for the sake of the "archaic" appearance of the letter than for any linguistic purpose, e.g.: *hunð* 25a.6, *steðe* 181.3, *floð* 46.3, *ræð(e)* 46.2/181.5, *gewemðe* 51c.2, *deða* (= *dyde*) 46.2, *ycwæðen* pp 25b.1, *forwurþon* 44.2, *acorðe* 34.4 beside *acorede* 34.3, etc.; the inverse is much less frequent: *seofende* 50.4, *tynde* ("10th"), *hæder* (for *hwæðer*) 44.3, *odra* 44.5.

initial unorganic ⟨**h**⟩ is frequent, e.g., *hær* 50.3 67.1 *her* (= *ær*) 62.1, *hac* 50.4, *heuele* 50.4, *his* (for *is)* 181.2, *hut* 181.3, 181.5, *hunder* 181.8, *hefter* 46.1, *hunirepod* 7.2 *hunwarst* 45.2, *hestdele* 10.3, etc.; this affects the prefix *ge*- > *y/i*- > *hi/hy*-: *hidraan* (= *gedragan*) 10.3, *hifunde* 34.1 beside *yfundonne* 44.2 *hisyen* (prob. for *geseōn*) 181.3, beside *gecyrdon* 306, *gesceopa* 6a.1, *ywilcon* (= *gewéolcon*), etc. However, the opposite does not happen except in:

/**h**/ lost regularly in the poss. pron. "his": *is* 14×, beside *his* 3×;

/**h**/ lost in an intervocalic combination: *þurutlige* 45.1,3 (cf. Jordan §196).

⟨**ct**⟩ for /**ht**/: *docter* 181.3 beside *dohtra* 4×.

r metathesis: *færm* (= *fram*) 358.1, *hunwarst* (i.e., *unwrǣst*) 45.2 (Jordan §165).

loss of /**r**/ before dental: *aræde* 181.2 (Jordan §166, rem.).

lack of medial /**n**/: *ahud* (corr. to *ahund*) 25a.2, *yfudonne* 44.2, *ofsprige* 50.4, *gestride* 47.1, *istride* 25a.3, perhaps instances of assimilation (Jordan §173), or as Crawford suggests, scribe's neglect of the abbreviation stroke.

loss of final /**n**/ after unstressed vowel (a ME symptom, cf. Jordan §170): *seþe* (for *siððan*) 50.4, infinitives: *formelta* 44.5, *forwæhshe* 44.4; pp. of str. vbs.: *ybore* 47.3, *ybora* 50.2, *gesceopa* 6a.1; in word w/o sentence stress (Jordan §172): *me* (7×).

/**n**/ infixed in numerals: *seofende* 50.4 (2×), *tynde* 50.4 (WS *seofoðe, teoðe*) (Campbell § 692.7; Kt. *OED* s.v "seventh," "tenth").

intrusion of /**b**/: *columban* (Lat. *columnis*) 44.3 (Campbell § 478).

Syntax and Vocabulary

The word order is predominantly SV(O), the subject often being understood, and where there are several phrases they are paratactic, with SV often followed by a series of repetitive prepositional phrases as complements. In many places the word order is following the Latin but when there is a change from the Latin it is to the SVO order; some longer passages are entirely made of phrases translated with almost no changes of syntax (e.g., no. 50.3). Several selections are relatively freely written, and while restricted mostly to this pattern show more complex syntax, e.g., no. 34; the longest passage, no. 181 (made up entirely of phrases picked here and there from the Latin Bible) has only one sentence which breaks the SV(O) pattern: '. . . hu ornos[t]lice iacobes sunes dina hære suster hut ledde / 7 emor 7 sichem is sune 7 haere mægum 7 eac aella þa to ham comen ofslogon mid swurdes ecge 7 gecyrdon gesunde to hære getelde'.

The early ME use as a passive particle of the word *men* reduced in non-stress position to *me*, almost always directly translating a Latin passive, occurs 7× (10.1, 14.1, 26.4, 41.1, 46.1,2, 181.9): e.g. *me red* = "legitur" (41.1). This form is not recorded in OE before its earliest occurrence in the *Peterborough Chronicle* an. 1137 (cf. MED, s.v. *me*) and begins to appear in mid-century copies of Anglo-Saxon texts.

The inflected infinitive occurs once, to express allowance in a passage that is otherwise awkward: *flæsces to notiena* 62.1 (for "esus carnium"), also perhaps *to hisyen* 181.3. In a freely composed passage the gerundive occurs: *eode . . . heriænde godes name* 61.3.

The dative of destination occurs at 34.3 and 181.4: *7 ælla is mægum to muculum hærme.*

The lexis of these notes is very limited and controlled for the most part by the limited subject and vocabulary of the Latin source(s), a few less-usual words seemingly being lifted from disparate registers: poetry (*neorxnawange* 3×), charters (*anhæfede* 10.1, "the end of a furrow as a boundary-marker"), computus (*træenle* = "globum," 10.4), vernacular homilies (*gewemðe* 51c.2, cf. 7.2, *inne blisse* 10.1). Several phrases are unidiomatic imitations of the Latin and cannot be understood without reference to it: *ælla ða oðron* ("et sic de cæteris") 6a.2, *in hæder æl* ("in qualibet totam") 44.2.

Several words must be OE but seem to receive their first record in these notes:

beside "beside", the earliest recorded use of *be sidan* as a preposition 15.6, 25b.1, 50.2;

smell "odor," 10.2 is not recorded in OE or other Germanic languages, but doubtless represents a word from the earlier language replacing *stenc*. It is recorded about the same time in the Lambeth Homilies in the same phrase as here, "swote smell" (*OED*).

gewealcan = "peragrans" (*ywilcon* 26.2), the eventually dominant meaning of "walk," as used here, is virtually unattested in this sense in OE documents, where it means "to roll."[3]

As is to be expected in a text of this date there are some, but not many, French symptoms:

acordian wk II "be in agreement"? OFr *acorder*. The forms are past participles *(bið) acorede/acorðe* 34.3,4. The exact translation is difficult in context. The word occurs several times in the *Peterborough Chronicle*, at an. 1119, 1120 as a weak II (*MED*, *accorden*), which suggests that it might have been naturalized into OE at a relatively early date. The next two items seem more ad hoc, and occur in the same passage:

marbre 44.4 m/f "marble"; OFr *marbre*, Lat. *marmor*. The OE form of the Latin was *marma*, *marmorstan*.

pilires m. (np) "pillars" 44.3; OFr *pil(i)eres* m. The Latin has "columnis," which is first translated at 44.3 *columban*, a word that occurs several times in OE, and is then glossed, as if necessary to do so, with the French word *pilires*.

of prep. w dat. is used in these notes in literal and transferred senses that occur frequently in OE, "out of a source," "out of a material," "out of a place or direction." But it is also used once in a partitive phrase, 6a.1 *of ðritig wintra*; and thrice it is used in geographical phrases as a substitute for the genitive: 44.3, sim. 29a.1 *in ðan lande of syria* (OE would be **in syria-lande*), 25b.1 *denæ of tæran* ("vallis lacrymarum"). The word-order of the latter may be influenced somewhat by the Latin; the OE would normally be **teara denan* (masc. gen. pl. / fem. acc.). The partitive use may arguably be of frequent occurrence in earlier OE (see Mitchell, *OE Syntax* §1201); whether the "genitive" use is a development of French *de* is a contested point (ibid. §1202–3, which finds no clear instance) but it cannot be dismissed; in any case the instances in our texts are clearly analogous to French usage and late enough that denial of French influence would be difficult.

[3] B-T Supp. gives one gloss instance, "to pass: Gewealcon *emensus*."

Appendix II
Glossarial Index of English

(* *words recorded nowhere else in OE)*

ábútan prep w Lat. ablative "around" abute damasco 7.1 ('in agrum. . .Damascenum') 15.1

ac conj. "but" hac 46.2 50.4, æc 62.1

ác f. "oak (tree)" as ache wop ("oak-weeping," "oak of weeping" 'quercus fletus') 181.9, ds hunder ane ache ('subter quercum') 181.8

ácordian II (OF acorder "reconcile") ?"tally," ?"bring into agreement" pp bið acorede seofonfealð 34.3, pp bið acorðe septuagies septies 34.4 (DOE 2. "to accord, be fitting, be proper" with this passage the only instance [but it occurs in *Peterb. Chron.* an. 1119, 1120])

ác-wóp *see under the separate elements*

æfter prep w dat. "after" 50.1, eftter 18.1, hefter 46.1, æfter þam "after that" 6a.1 47.3, æfter þan 25a.6

ǽn *see* **án** pron *and* **on** prep

ǽr adv "previously," "before" hær 47.5 50.3 her 62.1 [*or for* **her**?]; prep w dat. "before" ær 47.4 hær 46.3 67.1

æt prep w dat. "at" at anhæfede 10.1, at is forsyðe 357.1, "from" bohte land æt Emore ('emitque partem agri a filiis Hemor') 181.2 [*DOE* s.v. æt I.D.6]

ágen adj. "own, proper" asm \`agene´ 34.2

ágén (ongéan) prep w acc. "against, next to" 29a.1

***á-hund** "100" nm ahu\`n´d 25a.2

án pron. "one, a certain one" nsm æn 181.3 dm on ane felde 7.1 15.2, nf ane of marbra ('una marmorea', antecedent is 'columban') 44.3, df hunder ane ache 181.8 af ane ('altera') 44.4; nm a[n] hu\`n´d ? 25a.2 (see **á-hund**)

án num, adj, & subs.: "one" asf ane dohter 254.2, dsm on ane dage 6a.1; adj. "a certain" dsm on ana munte ('in quodam monte') 50.2, dsf ane 181.8; subs? (added, incorrectly, above text) nsm? an 6a.2

an *see* **on**

and conj. spelled out only at 181.1, 42c.1 otherwise always the nota ⁊. Joining words 54x, phrases 15x, joining clauses in paratactic constructions 50x (11x in no. 181); æn 358.3 *for* and?

an-ginn n. "beginning" ds at. . .angynne 10.2

an(d)-héafdu n. (always pl. in documents) "headland," "extreme limit," ("place where the plow is turned," a term to indicate land boundaries in charters) gen at anhæfede angynne ("at the beginning of the boundary" = ?'a primis orbis parte') 10.1

an(d)-langes prep. "along" anlænges ðare sæ ('maris tractu') 10.3

á-rǽran I "raise up" pt3s aræ[r]de 181.2

arc f. "ark" ds in þara arcæ 46.2

be prep w dat. "about, concerning" 10.1 44.2 46.1; "by, beside, with" be is wife 16.1

be-byrgan I "bury" pp wæs bebyrigde ('sepulti sunt') 15.8, sim. ('sepulta est') 181.8

belífan 1 "remain" pt3p belyfen gode ('boni permanserunt') 50.3

beran 4 "bear, give birth" pp nsm baren 36a.1 dsn to ybora landa ('ad natale solum') 50.2, wæs ybore 47.3

***be-síde** (OE be sídan) prep w dat. "beside" beside þan ('juxta quem') 15.6, besyde hebron ('juxta Hebrom') 25b.1, beside paradise ('proximo paradiso') 50.2; cf. the added prefix '**be**hindan' on f. 149r)

be-wópan 7 "beweep," "mourn" pt3p bewyppe ('luxerunt') 25a.7

bliss f-jó "bliss" ds inne blisse ('in deliciis') 10.1

boc f-cons "book" seo leden boc 181.4, ds boc 10.1 boce 41.1

ge-**bora** see **beran**

brǽð m-i "odor" ds on suote breðe 10.2

bróþor m-r "brother" ns breþer 147.2 as broþer ('fratrem') 50.2, np breðer 128.2

bútan prep w acc. "outside of" butan ure wuniaghe ('a nostra habitabili zona') 10.3; "in addition to, besides" butan cayn 7 abel ('præter Cain et Abel') 41.2

bycgan Ii "buy" pt3s bohte 181.2

ceaster f. "city" ds cester 181.1

clǽne adj. "clean, pure" nsn clane 7.3

columne f-an "column, pillar" on twam columban ('in duabus columnis') 44.3

cræft m. "art, invention" ap þa yfu[n]-donne creftes ('ars inventa') 44.2, gs? for pl? fæle `cenne´ cræftæs 34.1

cweðan 5 "say" pt3s cwæð [*usually with a stroke over the 'w' whether the word is abbreviated or not*] 6a.1 7.1 14.1 16.1 44.4 47.1, ('ait') 26.1, ('assentit') 36a.1, ("call") 181.9 cwað 50.3, cweþ 25a.1, ('asserit') 46.3, pt3p cwæðe 128.1 cw⟨æð⟩e 26.4, þa lxx cw⟨æ⟩ð 46.1 sume cwæð ('quidam dicunt') 46.3, pp is ycwæðen 25b.1

cuman 4 "come" pt3s com 15.4 181.1 181.1, pt3p ne ne come ('non pervenerunt') 10.4, pt3p coman ('orti sunt') 51c.5, comen 26.3 181.6

cynn n-ja "kind, type" gp fæle cenne landes 26.1, fæle cynne wenughe 46.1 fæle `cenne´ cræftæs 34.1

cýrran I "turn, return" pt3p gecyrdon 181.6

dæg m. "day" ds on ane dǽge ('unius diei') 6a.1

denu f. "valley" as denæ 25b.1

dohtor f-r "daughter" ns docter 181.3, as dohter 254.2, gp dohtra 41.2, ap dohtra 16.2 51c.4 156.9

dóm m. "judgment" dp domon 44.2

dón anom. "do" pt3s deða 46.2; "add" imp pl dot hy to dan 47.5

dragan 7 "draw along" ppt hidraan (gedragen) 10.3

éac adv. "also" 34.1 181.6

eald adj. "old" comp npm hælder 128.2

eall adj. "all" nsm al caynnes ofspringe 36a.1 dsn ælle is mægum 181.4; subs. npm/n? alla ða oðron ('et sic de cæteris') 6a.2, ælla 181.5, asn in hæder æl ('in qualibet totam') 44.3

eallswá adv. "just as" ælswa ('sicut ergo') 45.1 50.3

éast-dǽl m-i "eastern part" ds on hesdele 10.2 an hestdele 10.3

ecg f-jo "edge (of a weapon)" ds 181.6

eornostlíce adv. "strictly, rigorously, justly" (or, "therefore") ornos[t]lice 181.5

eorðe f-ón "earth" ns yrðe 7.1, 7.2, ds yrþe 7.1

***ést-ness** f. "pleasure" ds Eden. . .inne estnysse ('paradisum voluptati') 10.1 ds hestnysse 29a.2

fæder m-r "father" ns feader 156.3 ds fæder 181.2, np fæderes 128.3

faran 6 "go" pt3s for 181.3

fela n-u (indecl) "many" w 'cynne' + gen. fæle cenne landes 26.1, fæle cynne wenughe ('diversae sunt opiniones') 46.1, fæle `cenne´ cræftæs 34.1, 7 swa fela dohtra ('et totidem filias') 41.2; absol w advbl force swa fele leuede 47.5

feld m. "field" ds felde 7.1 ('in agrum') 15.2 ('in campo') 50.2

féran I "walk" pt3s 46.2

findan 5 "find, discover" pt3p hifunde 34.1 pp apm þa yfu[n]donne cræftes ('ars inventa') 44.2

flǽsc n. "flesh, meat" gs flæsces to notiena ('esus carnium') 62.1

flod m. "flood," the Deluge ns floð 10.4 44.4 46.3, ds (h)ær ðan flode 46.3 47.4 47.5, her ða flode 62.1 67.1; hefter þan flode 46.2

for-feran I "die" pt3p forfe[r]den 34.5 (*see* forð-feran)

forma ord. num., adj. "first" nsm wk forme 36b.1

forð adv "forth" ywilcon . . . forð hi comen 26.3

for-þam conj. "for that reason," "therefore" 34.3, for þan 47.3 for ðam ðe 357.1

forð-feran I "go forth, die" pt3s 46.3, ('mortua est') 181.8

for-meltan 3 "burn up" inf ne formelta ('non solveretur') 44.5

for-síð m. "death" ds 357.1

forð-síð m. "death" ds ('mortuo') 50.1 forðsyðe 50.3

for-þan adv. "therefore" 47.3

for-wascan 6 "wash away, destroy (by water)" inf forwæhshe 44.4

for-weorþan 3 "perish" pt3s furwurðen ('periit') 36a.2; subj pt3p ne forwurþon ('ne periret') 44.2

fóstor-modor f-r "foster-mother" ns fostermodor ('nutrix') 181.8

fram prep w dat. "from" 50.1, 50.4, færm 181.1

fýfýtne num. "fifteen" fyftene 7.1

fýr n-i "fire" ns feer ne (mihte) formelta ('non solveretur incendio') 44.5

fyrst adv. "at first, for the first time" her fyrst 62.1

gán anom "go" pt3p eode 61.2

gear n. "year" ds on ane dage ⁊ geara ('unius diei et anni') 6a.1, geare 46.3; "age, life-span" dp gearen 46.1

ge-sund adj (apm) "safe" or adv "safely" gesunde 181.6

ge-teld n. "tent" getelde ds? or p? 181.7

god m. "God" gs godes 61.3 181.3 181.7, ds gode 46.2

gód adj. "good" nsm 34.2 45.3 npm 50.3

hæder see **hwæðer**

hælder see **eald**

habban III "have" ("have in marriage") pt3s hæfde 156.8, hæfede 41.1

hám m. "home" as to ham comen 181.6

hatan 7 "command" pt3s het 50.3

hé, héo, hit pers pron. "he, she, it" nsm 15.3 34.1 38.2 46.1 46.2 (2x), 46.3 47.1 (2x), 47.3 50.2 156.3 181.1; dsm (ethic) him. . .to hærme 181.4 him to mycele sorhe 34.3 asm hine 25a.7, nsf heo 181.8 hi (sc. Eden) 10.4, dsf hire 181.4, asf hi 181.4, nsn asn hit 50.3 357.1, np(m) hi 50.1 50.3 50.4 128.1 np(m&f) hi 14.2 16.1 26.3 hy 156.6, apm hy 47.5, (reflexive) hi 50.3 51c.3 dp(f) ham 51c.4

hearm m. "harm, injury" ds hærme 181.4

hér adv. "here", "at this time" 62.1? [*or for* **ær**?]

hér *see* **ǽr**

herian II "praise" pt3p herde [*for* herede*?*] 181.7; prp np heriænde 61.3

hidraan 10.3 *see* **dragan**

his, hire, heora poss pron. "he, her, their" (indecl, w following noun) his sunes 34.1 his scete 34.2 his hiwscipe 61.2; is suster 18.1, is wyf 26.2, be is wife 16.1, wyte is ('suum punitum') 34.4, is bohe is `agene´ man 34.3 his ofspring 50.1, is broþer 50.2, is forðsyðe 50.3 is forsyðe 357.1, is mæginn 181.4 is sune 181.5 357.1, is sununes 181.7, hyre twa ðeowene 156.10; hære. . .landa 50.1, [h]ære. . .breder 128.2 hære suster 181.5, hære mægum 181.6, hære getelde 181.6, hære wycstowe 181.7, hæra steðe 26.3

hisyen *see* **séon**

híw-scipe m. "family" ds 61.2

híeran I "hear" pt3p yherden 44.2

hú adv. "how" heading dependent clause w. ind. 181.5

hund n. "hundred" nom. twa hund wintra 38.1 þri hund wintre 47.3, 42b.1, 42c.1 sixhund wintre 47.4 nigon hun wintre 47.5, dat? hunð wintra 25a.6 dm sixhund wintre 47.4 six `hun´ wintre 47.5 ccc hund wintre 47.4

hund-seofontig num. "seventy" (in gloss: hundseofontig writer [= 'LXX', the Septuagint]) 46.1, þa hundseofentig wenðeres ('Septuaginta') 38.1

hunireped *see* **ungehrepod**

hun-warst *see* **un-wǽrst**

hut *see* **út**

hwæðer pron. "each, both" acc. in hæder æl ('in qualibet totam') "everything (written) on each" 44.3

in prep w dat. "in, on" in þan lande 44.3 in þara arcæ 46.2, in ðon felde 50.2, in syrie 7.1 15.1, in chanaan lande ('in terra Chanaan') 181.2 181.5; idiom, w acc. in h[w]æder æl ('in qualibet totam') 44.3, in Eden (= Lat.? 'in Eden') 10.1

inne prep w dat "inside" inne neorxnawange ('in paradiso') 14.2, inne estnysse 10.1, "within" inne blisse 10.1

lǽdan I "lead" pt3p ledde 181.5

land n. "country" gs landes 26.1 181.3, ds 44.2 chanaan lande 181.2 358.5, mesopotamia lande 358.2 landa 50.2, as 181.2, lænd 29a.1; "land," "ground" ns 7.2 7.3

lang adv (for lange?) "for a long time" or adj ("long lasting") lang hidraan 10.3, *see* **hidraan**

lǽden adj. "Latin" seo leden boc 181.4

libban III "live" pt3s lefede ('vixit') 46.1 47.4 leuede 47.5

mǽg m. "kinsman" ap mægum 181.5

mægden-eorðe f-ón "virgin-earth" ns mædenyrðe ('virgo tellus') 7.1

mægen n. "host of picked men" ds mægum 181.4

magan pret-pres (5) "can" subj pt3s ne mihte forwæhshe ('non diluetur') 44.4

man m-cons "man" ns 36b.2 50.4, as 6a.1 34.2, ap 51c.6; ds reduced to passive particle *me*: me red on boc 10.1, me cwæð ('quidam tradunt') 14.1, þe me cwæð ('nuncupatur') 26.4, me reð ('legitur') 41.1, me ne reð ('non legitur') 46.2, me telleð "are told" 46.1, me cwæð ('vocatumque') 181.9

marbre m/f. (OF marbre m.) "marble" ds ane of marbra ('una marmorea') 44.4

me *see* **man**

mecgan I "mix," "commingle (race)" inf ne scolde. . .ymegg`h´e ('ne commiscerentur') 50.3

micel adj "big," "gigantic," "much" dsf to mycele sorhe 34.3, dsn mycelon 50.4 muculum 181.4 npm þa mycele men ('gigantes') 51c.6,

mid prep w dat. "with" mid gode 46.2 mid hire 181.4, mid hære wycstowe 181.7; instr. "by means of" mid his scete 34.2 mid his bohe 34.2 mid swurdes ecge 181.6

móna m. "moon" infl. str. gs monas 10.4

munt m. "mountain" ds munte 50.2 61.2

næs *see* **wesan**

nama m-an "name" ds name 181.3, as heriænde godes name 61.3, sim. 181.7

nán pron. nsm næs nan baren ('nullus natus est') 36a.1 næs nan wuna 62.1 nas na wingeard 67.1

náþélǽs, náþýlǽs adv. "nevertheless" naþeles ('tamen') 6a.1

ne adv. neg part. "not" 46.2 50.3, ne he ne ferde 46.2, with subj. ne forwurþon ('ne periret') 44.2, ne mihte forwæhshe ('non diluetur') 44.4, ne (mihte) formelta ('non solveretur') 44.5; ne ne come 10.4

neorxna-wang m. ds inne neorxna wange ('in paradiso') 14.3, ds? neorxna wange 29a.3, ds? neornxna wanga 10.1

nigon num. "nine" nm nigon hund wintre 47.5

niman 4 "take" imp pl nemeð 47.4

niðeweard adj. "low," "nethermost (side)" on nyþewærde bethel "on the lower side towards bethel" ('ad radices bethel') 181.8

notian II (w gen.) "enjoy, use" inflected inf. flæsces to notiena ('esus carnium') 62.1

of prep w dat. "from" (a material) of rædra yrþe 7.1 of marbra 44.4 of ysodene tihele 44.4, (out of a source) of Abele næs nan baren ('de Abel nullus natus est') 36a.1, of lamech 34.5, of caymes ofspringe 45.1 sim. 45.2, of ham [i.e., him] coman ('orti sunt') 51c.4; "from" (direction away) of ðan munte 61.2; "of" (partitive) of ðritig wintra 6a.1; as substitute for gen. in þan lande of syria 44.3, sim. 29a.1, denæ of tæran ('vallis lacrymarum') 25b.1

ofer prep w acc? "after" ofer oðra xv ('post alios quindecim annos') [*in gloss*] 18.1

of-sléan 6 "kill" pt3s ofsloh ('interfecit') 15.5 34.2 (2x), ('occidit') 25a.2, ('occiderat') 50.2, pt3p ('necaverunt') 181.6

ofspring m. "offspring," "generation" ns ofspringe ('generatio') 36a.2; ds ('in generatione') 45.1 45.2, ('cognatione') 50.1, ofsprige ('ad. . .generationem') 50.4; as ('cognationem') 50.1

on prep w dat. "on," "in" on hesdele ('ad orientem') 10.2, an hestdele 10.3, on suote breðe 10.2, on twam columban 44.3 on. . .munte 50.2; "in" on þan twyfealde scræfe ('in spelunca duplici') 15.9, on ane felde 7.1 ('in agrum') 15.2, on boce 41.1 *beside* on boc 10.1; (locative) on sichem 181.1, on salim 358.3, on nyþewærde bethel 181.8; (temporal) on ane dage 6a.1, on þan time 128.1 181.7; trans. on wlite "in appearance" 6a.1, on godes name 181.3

óðer ord. num., adj. "second" 36b.2; subs. "other" asm? ofer oðra ('post alios') [in gloss] 18.1, nsf ane. . .oðra ('una. . .altera') 44.4, sim. odra 44.5; npn? alla ða oðron ('sic de cæteris') 6a.2

paradis m. "Paradise" (Latin word) with OE inflection dat. beside paradise 50.2; with Latin inflection dat. be paradisum 10.1

pilir m. (OF pil(i)er m.) "pillar" np pilires 44.3

rǽdan 7 "read" pt3s red 10.1, me ne reð ('non legitur') 46.2, sim. 41.1; subj pr3s ræðe 181.5

réafian II "rape" pt3s ræfode ('rapuit') 181.4

sǽ f. ds ðare sæ 10.3

sáwol f. "soul, life, living person" ap saulen 34.5

scræf n-i "grave" ds on þan twyfealde scræfe ('in spelunca duplici') 15.10

scyte m. "shooting" ds scete 34.2

scytta m. "archer" nsm scette ('vir sagittarius') 34.2

sculan pret-pres (6) "must," "ought (to)" subj pt3p ne scolde 50.3

ge-**scyppan** 6 "create" pp wæs gesceopa ('factus est') 6a.1

se, séo, þæt dem. pron. nsm se 10.2 25b.1 36b.1 36b.2 44.4 45.1 45.3 46.3 50.4 (2x) nsf seo 181.4 si denæ 25b.1 nsn 47.5; gsm þas 10.4; gsn þas 181.3; dsm ðon 50.2, ðan 46.1 46.2 46.3 47.4 47.5 50.4 61.2, on þan time 128.1 181.7, ða flode 62.1 67.1, to dan 47.5, dsf ðare 10.3 þara 46.2, dsf/m to þæra steðe ('in loco') 26.3, dsn þan 15.9 44.2, asm þane 181.9 asn 29a.1; npn þa wæteræ 10.4; alla ða oðron 6a.2; treated as npf þa lxx (= LXX, the Septuagint) but followed by singular verb 46.1; subst. dsm þan (sc. felde); 15.7; advbl phr ds æfter ðam "after that" 6a.2 47.3, æfter þan 25a.6; npm 38.1 51c.5 apm þa 44.2 (or conj?) ælla þa 181.6; in place of subject: þæt his in chanaan lande ('quæ est in terra Chanaan') 181.2; expressing a result ðæt byð "that adds up to" 34.4 47.5; nsn at head of defining phrase ("i.e."): þæt is 7.1 7.2 7.3 10.1 10.3 29a.2 51c.1, ðat is 10.4, þæt byð 44.3, þæt wæs 7.1; npm? ða 6a.1; relative se ðe 181.5, þæt is 10.1? 358.5 || þa as nom.s art.? 44.4,5?

sellan Ii "sell" pt3s salde 357.1

seofonfeald adj. nsf seofonfealð 34.3

seofontýne num "seventeen" sixti 7 seofontene 34.4

seofe[n]ðe ord. num. "seventh" nsm seofende 45.1 45.2 50.4; dsm seofende (for wk?) 50.4

séon 5 "see" to hisyen (i.e., geseon) 181.3

séðan 2 "bake" pp dsf ysodene tihele 44.4 (cf. B-T séoþan II (1))

siððа adv. "afterwards" seþe ('post') 50.4

six-hund num. "six" nm 47.4 dm 47.4 47.5

slǽpan 7 "sleep" pt3s slep 16.1, slæp mid hire ('dormivit cum illa') 181.4

***smell** (not recorded in OE) "odor" ds suote smelle 10.2

sorg f. "sorrow" ds sorhe 34.3

sprecan 5 "speak, say" pr3s sprycð 181.4

stede m-i "place" ns se stede ('locus amœnissimus') 10.2, steðe 25b.1 as steðe 181.9, ds taken as fem.? to þæra steðe 26.3

ge-**strýnan** I "beget" (w dat or acc?) pt3s 16.1 gestride lamech 47.1 istr[in]de labane 156.3 þa he gestrinde ('cum genuit') 38.2 istrinde. . .iacob`e´ 156.6

sum indef pron. "someone, a certain one" np sume cwæð ('quidam dicunt') 46.2

sunu m-u "son" ns sunu 181.3 sune 166.2 ds sune 357.1, as sune 181.5, np sunes 34.1 44.2 50.3 51c.2 181.5 sununes 181.6, ap sunes 16.1 41.1

swá adv. "as" 46.2 181.4; "so" swa fela 41.2, sim. 47.5; correlative "thus" ealswa . . . swa 45.2

sweord n. "sword" gs mid swurdes ecge ('gladiis') 181.6

sweostor f-r "sister" ns? suester (*in gloss*) 18.1, ns suster 18.1, as suster 181.5

swíðe adv. "very," "exceedingly" swyð suote smelle 10.2 45.3; adv. or adj.? swyþe on suote breðe 10.2

swót adj. "sweet" dsm on suote breðe . . .suote smelle 10.2

synn f-jó "sin, injury" ns senne 34.3

syxtig num. "sixty" 42c.1 syxti 7 seofontene ("77") 34.4

taehe *see* **téon**

téar m. "tear" dp denæ of tæran 25b.1

tellan Ii "count, consider, think" pr3p me telleð ('are thought') 46.1

téon 2 "pull, lead" subj? pt'3s taeh`e´ (= teah) ('attingat') 10.4

teo[n]ða ord. num. "tenth" nsm tynde 50.4

tíd f. "hour" ap vii tide 14.4

tigel f. "tile, brick" ds oðra of ysodene tihele ('altera latericia') 44.4

tíma m-an "time" ds time 128.1 181.7

tó prep w dat. "to," "towards" to þas monas træenle 10.3, to hæra steðe ('in loco') 26.3, to. . .landa 50.1, to salem ('in Salem') 181.1, to. . .getelde 181.6, to bethel 181.7; "in addition to" dot hy to dan 47.5, transf. to. . .heuele 50.4; "up to" to ðan seofende ofspri[n] ge 50.4; ethic dative to. . .sorhe 34.3, to. . .hærme 181.4; advbl w acc. to ham comen 181.6; w inflected inf to notiena 62.1 to hisyen 181.3

trendel n. "circle, orbit" ds to þas monas træenle ('ad lunarem globum') 10.4

twá num. "two" 42c.1

twǽman I "separate" pt3s ytwæmde ('separavit') 50.1

twégen num. "two" nm twean 44.3 nn twa hund 38.1, g?m twa wintra 6a.2, dm twam 44.2 44.3, af twa dohtra 156.9 twa ðeowene 156.11

twi-feald adj. "two-fold, double" on þan twyfealde scræfe ('in spelunca duplici') 15.10

tynde *see* **teo[n]ða**

þá adv. "then" heading clause 25a.3 358.1; correlative? þa . . . þa 44.4,5 (or arts.?); within clause 47.4 51c.6; conj. "when" 25a.2 38.2, 47.1 47.3, da 47.1

þanon adv. "whence" ('de quo') 15.3

þær adv. "there" ꝥær 181.2 ðaer ('unde. . .illuc') 10.4; conj. "where" 15.5; "lest" ("in that [not]") þar hi ne scolde hi ymegghe ('ne commiscerentur') 50.3

þæt [*written* ꝥ] conj. heading object clause, 41.1, cwæð þæt 14.1 46.1 46.3 50.3; [*written* þæt] 38.1, ræð þæt 46.2; heading consecutive clause, "so that" ('quæ') 50.1, þat 50.3

þe indecl rel part. se ꝥe 181.5, þe ('qui') 77.1, þe. . .wypen ('in quo luxerunt') 25b.1, "(in) which" 46.3 þe se flod wæs ('in quo fuit diluvium') 46.3, in. . .felde þe ('in campo ubi') 50.2; þe me cwæðe ('qui. . .nuncupatur'); 26.4, for ðam ðe "therefore" 357.1

þéowen f-jó "handmaid, female slave" ap ðeowene 156.11

þés, þéos, þis dem. pron. "this" gsf þysre 10.2

þrí num. "three" nm 47.3 gm? þri wintra 6a.2

þrítig num. "thirty" dsm of ðritig wintra 6a.1

***þurh-út-líce** (*sc. OE* þurh-út) adv. "thoroughly" þurutlige 45.1 þurutlyge 45.3

under prep w dat. hunder ane ache 181.8

ungehrepod adj. (*sc.* hrepian II) "untouched" nsf hunireped 7.2

ungewemmed adj. (*sc.* wemman I) "undefiled" nsf uniwemð yrþe ('terra . . . nondum corrupta') 7.2

un-wrǽst adj. "wretched, evil" nsm hunwarst 45.2

úre poss. pron. "our" dat.10.3

út adv "out" for hut ('egressa est') 181.3, hut ledde ('tollentes Dinam de domo') 181.5

wæter n. np wæteræ 10.4

gewealcan 7 "traverse, cross over," = "walk" pt3p ywilcon [gewēolcon] ('peragrans') 26.2

wemman I "defile, corrupt" pt3p gewemðe hi ('concupierunt') 51c.2

wendan I "turn," "go" pt3p hi ywende ('cognation[e] . . .redierat') 50.1, pt3p gewendon to mycelon heuele ('ad mala progressi sunt') 50.4 ywenden 181.7

wendere m. "translator" þa hundseofontig wenðeres ('Septuaginta') 38.1

wénung f. "expectation, (speculative) thought" gp wenughe ('opiniones') 46.1

wéofod mn. "altar" as 181.2

wépan 7 "weep," "lament" pt3p wypen ('luxerunt') 25b.1

wesan anom. "to be" linking pr3s is 10.1 (2x), 10.2 77.1 358.5 his 181.2, in defining phrase, þæt is 7.1 7.2 7.3 10.1 (2x) 10.3 10.4 29a.2 51c.1 þæt byð 44.3; pt3s wæs 7.1 25a.2 25a.3 38.1 45.1 45.2 46.3 47.1 47.3 (2x), 47.4 156.2 166.1, was 47.1, wes 34.1; (as auxil. in pass. constr.) 6a.1 25b.1 pt3p [w]ære 128a.3, wæs (for pl.) 15.7; neg. pt3s næs 36a.1 62.1 nas 67.1; pt3p subj wære ('fuisse') 14.2; pr3s bið acorede 34.3 sim. 34.4, 47.5; subj pt3s wera ('fuisse') 46.2

wician II "to dwell" pt3s *or* pp nms wycnigede [*for* wycigede? *or for* wycigende?] 181.2, sim. 358.3

wíc-stów f. "encampment, (retinue)" mid hære wycstowe ('omnis populus cum eo') 181.7

wíf n. "wife" ns wif ('uxor') 52.1 (3x), wyf 26.2, ds wife 16.1, as rebecca ysaaces wyf 156.5

wífman m-cons "woman" ap wyfmen 181.3

willan anom. v. "to want, wish, desire" subj pr3s wyle 181.5

wín-geard m. "vineyard" ns 67.1

winter m-u "year" gp (partitive) wintra 6a.1, 6a.2 (2x), 18.1 25a.2 25a.5 25a.7 38.2 wintre 46.1 47.1 47.2 47.3 47.4 (2x), 47.5 42b.1 42c.1 acc of time wintre 46.2

wíte n. "punishment" ns wyte 34.4 ap wyten 34.4

witegung f. "prophecy" as wytegunge 44.2

wið prep w acc. "in association with" wyð 51c.3

wlite m-i "appearance" ds 6a.1

wóp m. "weeping" as? ache wop ("oak-weeping") 181.9

woruld f. "world" gs worlde 10.2

wrítan 1 "write" pt3p writen 44.3 gewriten 38.1

wrítere m. np writer [in gloss] 46.1

wuna m-an "custom, usage" ns 62.1

wunian II "dwell" pt3s wuneda ('habitavit') 50.2

wuniaghe for **wuni(n)ge**? *see next word*

*__wuniung__ f. (gerundive of wunian II) "living," "habitation" ns wensæm wunyunge 10.2, ds wuniaghe 10.3

wynsum adj. "pleasant" dsf wensæm 10.2

yfel n. "evil" ds to. . .heuele ('ad mala') 50.4

ylca pron. "(the) same" dsm(wk) þan ylcan geare ('eodem anno') 46.3

ywilcon *see* **wealcan**

Names

Abel nom. 25a.4 dat. 36a.1 acc. 15.5 25a.3 41.2

Abraham gen. abr[a]hames 147.1 156.1

Adam nom. 6a.1 15.7 16.1 25a.2 25a.6 25b.1 36b.1 38.1 41.1 50.3, gen. adames 44.2 50.1, dat. adame 50.4

Bathuel gen. 156.2 166.1

Bethel dat. bet`h´el 181.7, on nyþewærde bethel 181.8

Cain nom. cayn 15.5 25a.2 50.2, caym 26.2, gen. caines 51c.3, caynnes 36a.1 caymes 34.3 50.1 45.1, acc. 41.2 caym 34.2

Chalmana Cain's sister and wife nom. chalmana 18.1, calmana 26.2

Cataphua Cham's wife nom. ('Cathaflua') 52.1

Cham gen. cahmmes 52.1

Chanaan dat. chanaan lande 181.2 358.5

Damascus Lat. abl. abute damasco 7.1 15.1

Debbora nom. 181.8

Delbora Abel's sister nom? (in gloss) 18.1

Dina nom. 181.3, acc. dina 181.5

Eden nom. 10.1 (2×), 29a.3, dat.? 10.1

Emor gen. emores 181.3, dat. emore 181.2, acc. emor 181.5

Enoch nom. 45.3 46.2 50.4

Esau acc.? istrinde esau 7 iacob`e´ 156.7

Eue nom. 15.8 25a.6 25b.1

Fura Japeth's wife nom. ('Fliva') 52.1

Genesis nom. swa seo leden boc sprycð Genesis (probably a marginal gloss) 181.4

Hebron dat. hebron 25b.1

Isaac gen. ysaaces 156.5

Jacob nom. 156.8 181.7 357.1, gen. iacobes 181.5 acc.? istrinde . . . iacob`e´ 156.7

Japeth gen. iaphetþes 52.1

Jeronymus nom. Jer[onymus] 46.3

Jescha *see* **Lasca**

Joseph, son of Jacob dat. 357.1

Josephus (first-century writer) nom. 7.1 26.1 38.1 44.3 Jose[phus] 50.3

Laban acc.? istri[n]de labane 156.4, gen. laban`e´s 156.8

Lamech, descendant of Cain, nom. 34.1 dat. lamech 34.5

Lamech, descendant of Seth, nom. 47.1 acc. 47.1

Lasca, acc. (corruption of 'Jescham' daughter of Nachor) 77.1

Lia gen lian 181.3, acc. lia 156.9

Maria "Miriam" sister of Moses ns (gloss) 302, as 254.2,

Mathusala nom. mathusalem 47.3 47.5 nom./acc.? mathusalem 47.1 gen. mathusalemes 46.1

Melcha (another name of "Lasca") acc. 77.1

Mesopotania dat. mesopotania lande 358.2

Methodius nom. 6a.1 16.1 25a.1 36a.1 38.1

Nachor nom. 156.1

Nayda/Naid land of Nod acc nayda ('Nayda') 26.4

Noe nom. 47.3 47.4 50.4 61.2 gen. noes 10.4 acc. 47.1

Norman nom. 47.1 marginal attribution N[orman]. 51c.1

Paradisum Lat. nom. used for dat. be paradisum 10.1

Parsia Sem's wife ('Pharphia') nom. 52.1

Phiarphara Noe's wife nom. ('Phuaphara') 52.1

Rachel acc. 156.10

Rebecca gen. rebecca 181.8, acc. 156.4

Salem dat. 181.4

Sarai (another name of "Lasca") nom. 77.1

Sem gen. 52.1

Seth nom. 36b.2 50.1 50.2, gen. sethes 44.2 45.2 50.3 51c.1 acc. 38.2

Sichem name of city: dat. cester on sichem ('urbem Sichimorum') 181.1; name of person nom. sichem 181.3, gen. sichemes 181.2, acc. sichem 181.5

Syria dat. in þan lande of Syria ('in terra syriaca') 44.3 in syrie 7.1 ('in agrum scilicet Damascenum') 15.1

List of Works Cited

Primary works cited

Adrian and Ritheus, ed. James E. Cross and Thomas D. Hill, *The* Prose Solomon and Saturn *and* Adrian and Ritheus. Toronto: University of Toronto Press, 1982

Andrew of St. Victor, *Expositio super Heptateuchum*, ed. Charles Lohr and Rainer Berndt. Corpus Christianorum, Series Latina 53.1. Turnhout: Brepols, 1986

Asseneth, ed. Pierre Batiffol, *Le Livre de la Prière d'Aseneth*, 1–115. Studia Patristica 1–2. Paris: E. Leroux, 1889–1890; Marc Philonenko, ed., *Joseph et Aséneth: Introduction, texte critique, traduction, et notes*. Studia Post-Biblica 13. Leiden: Brill, 1968

Augustine, *Quaestiones in Heptateuchum*, PL 34.545

Bede, *Nomina regionum atque locorum de Actibus Apostolorum*, ed. M.L.W. Laistner, *Bedae Venerabilis Expositio Actuum Apostolorum et Retractio*. Cambridge, MA: The Medieval Academy of America, 1939, repr. New York: Kraus, 1970, also ed. Laistner, CCSL 121, also PL 92.1033

———, *De tempore ratione*, ed. T. H. Mommsen and C. W. Jones in *Bedae Venerabilis Opera, Pars VI, Opera Didascalica 2*, Corpus Christianorum, Series Latina 123B. Turnhout: Brepols, 1972; tr. Faith Wallis, *Bede, The Reckoning of Time*. Liverpool: Liverpool University Press, 1999, also PL 90.293

Claudius of Turin, *Commentarii in Genesim*, PL 50.893 [attributed to Eucherius of Lyon]

Fretellus, ed. P. C. Boeren, *Rorgo Fretellus de Nazareth et sa description de la terre sainte: Histoire et edition du texte*. Koninklijke nederlandse Akademie van Wetenschapen, afdeling Letterkunde, nieuwe Reeks, 105. Amsterdam: North Holland, 1980, also PL 155.1037

Gerbert of Aurelliac, ed. Nicolaus Bubnov, *Gerberti postea Silvestri II Papae, Opera Mathematica (972–1003)*. Berlin: R. Friedländer & Sohn, 1899, also as Gerbert Aurillacensis, *De Geometria*, PL 139.91

Glossa Ordinaria: Biblia Latina cum Glossa Ordinaria, repr. of Strassburg: Adolph Rusch, 1480/81, ed. K. Froelich and M. T. Gibson. Turnhout: Brepols, 1992

Heptateuch, ed. S. J. Crawford, *The Old English Version of the Heptateuch, Ælfric's Treatise on the Old and New Testament, and his Preface to Genesis*, EETS, o. s. 160, repr. rev. N. R. Ker. London: Oxford University Press, 1922, rev. ed. 1969; Richard Marsden, ed., *The* Old English Heptateuch *and Ælfric's* Libellus de Veteri Testamento et Novo; *Volume One, Introduction and Text.* EETS 330. Oxford: EETS and Oxford University Press, 2008

Origen, *Hexapla*, ed. Frederick Field, *Origenis Hexaplorum quae supersunt.* Oxford: Clarendon Press 1875, repr. Hildesheim: Olms, 1964

Honorius Augustodunensis, *De imagine mundi*, PL 172.115

Hrabanus, *Commentaria in Exodum,* PL 108.9

———, *De Universo*, PL 111.9

Isidore, *Etymologiarum libri XX.*, in PL 82.73

———, *De ortu et obitu patrum*, PL 83.129

Jerome, *Epistolae,* ed.Isidorus Hilberg, *Epistulae ad Hieronymum.* CSEL 54–56, 59. Vienna: F. Tempsky; Leipzig: G. Freytag, 1910, also PL 22.325

———, *Hebraicae quaestiones in libro Geneseos.* CCSL 72. Turnhout: Brepols, 1958, also PL 23.935

———, *Liber interpretationis Hebraicorum nominum.* CCSL 72. Turnhout: Brepols, 1958, also PL 23.771

——— / Eusebius, *De situ et nominibus locorum Hebraicorum*, ed. P. de Lagarde, *Onomastica sacra*. Göttingen: Horstmann, 1887, also PL 23.859

Ps.-Jerome, *Quaestiones Hebraicae in I-II Paralipomenon*, PL 23.1327

———, *Commentarius in canticum Debborae*, PL 23.1321

Josephus, *Antiquities,* ed. Franz Blatt, *The Latin Josephus, I: Introduction and Text, The Antiquities: Books I-V*, Aarsskrift for Aarhus Universitet 30.1, Humanistisk Serie 44. Copenhagen: Universitetsforlaget I; Aarhus, Munksgaard, 1958

Julianus Hilarianus, *Chronologia*, PL 13.1097

Ps.-Methodius: Ernst Sackur, *Sibyllinische Texte und Forschungen; Pseudo-Methodius, Adso und die Tiburtinische Sibylle.* Halle am S.: Niemeyer, 1898

Marbod of Rennes, *Liber Lapidum. Lapidario*, ed. M. E. Herrera, Auteurs Latins du Moyen Âge 15. Paris: Les belles lettres, 2006

Matthew Paris, *Gesta abbatum monasterii Sancti Albani*, ed. H. T. Riley, Rolls Series 28.4. London: Longmans, 1867

Peter Comestor, *Historia Scholastica,* ed. Agnete Sylwan, *Petri Comestoris Scolastica historia: Liber Genesis.* Corpus Christianorum, Continuatio Mediaevalis 191. Turnhout: Brepols, 2005, also PL 198.1049

Peter of Poitiers, ed. Hans Vollmer, *Deutsche Bibelaufzüge des Mittelalters zum Stammbaum Christi mit ihren lateinischen Vorbildern und Vorlagen*, Bibel und deutsche Kultur...I, Der Materialien zur Bibelgeschichte und religiösen

Volkskunde des Mittelalters 5. Potsdam: Akademische Verlagsgesellschaft Athenaion m.b.H., 1931
Smaragdus, *Collectiones in epistolas et evangelia.* PL 102.15.
Stephen Langton, *Commentary on the book of Chronicles*, ed. A. Saltman. Ramat-Gan: Bar-Ilan University Press, 1978
Thorne, William, *William Thorne's Chronicle of Saint Augustine's Abbey, Canterbury*, trans. A. H. Davis. Oxford: B. Blackwell, 1934

Studies and editions cited

Alexander, Jonathan, *Medieval Illuminators and Their Methods of Work.* New Haven: Yale University Press, 1992
Assmann, Bruno, ed. *Angelsächsische Homilien und Heiligenleben.* Bibliothek der angelsächsichen Prosa 3. Kassel: G.H. Wigand, 1889
Avenary, Hanoch, "Pseudo-Jerome Writings and the Qumran Tradition," *Revue de Qumran* 4 (1963–1964): 3–10
Barker-Benfield, B. C., ed., *St. Augustine's Abbey, Canterbury*, Volume 1, *Introduction, The Catalogue, first part.* Corpus of British Medieval Library Catalogues 13. London: British Library in association with the British Academy, 2008
Barnhouse, Rebecca, and Benjamin C. Withers, eds., *The Old English Hexateuch: Aspects and Approaches.* Kalamazoo: Medieval Institute Publications, 2000
Beckett, Katherine Scarfe, *Anglo-Saxon Perceptions of the Islamic World.* Cambridge Studies in Anglo-Saxon England 33. Cambridge: Cambridge University Press, 2003
Bellet, P., "Claudio de Turin, autor de los comentarios 'in Genesim et Regum' del Pseudo Euquerio," *Estudios Biblicos* 9 (1950): 209–23
Berndt, Rainer, *André de Saint-Victor (†1175), Exégète et théologien.* Bibliotheca Victorina 2. Paris/Turnhout: Brepols, 1991
Birch, Walter de Gray, *Cartularium Saxonicum: A Collection of Charters relating to Anglo-Saxon History*, 3 vols. London: Whiting, 1885–1893
Bishop, T. A. M. *Scriptores regis: Facsimiles to Identify and Illustrate the Hands of Royal Scribes in Original Charters of Henry I, Stephen, and Henry II.* Oxford: Clarendon Press, 1961
Blume, F., K. Lachmann, and A. Rudorff, eds. *Die Schriften der römischen Feldmesser.* 2 vols. Berlin: Georg Reimer, 1848
Bosworth, Joseph, and T. Northcote Toller, *An Anglo-Saxon Dictionary.* Oxford: Oxford University Press, 1898; and T. Northcote Toller, *An Anglo-Saxon Dictionary, Supplement.* Oxford: Oxford University Press, 1921
Brady, Ignatius, "Peter Manducator and the Oral Teachings of Peter Lombard," *Antonianum* 41 (1966): 454–90

Brooke, Christopher, "Approaches to Medieval Forgery," in *Medieval Church and Society: Collected Essays*, 100–20. London: Sidgwick and Jackson, 1971

Brooks, Nicholas, *The Early History of the Church of Canterbury: Christ Church from 597 to 1066*. Leicester: Leicester University Press, 1984

Budny, Mildred, *Insular, Anglo-Saxon, and Early Anglo-Norman Manuscrpt Art at Corpus Christi College, Cambridge: An Illustrated Catalogue*. 2 vols. Kalamazoo: Medieval Institute Publications, 1997

Burchard, Christoph, *Untersuchungen zu Joseph und Aseneth: Überlieferung - Ortsbestimmung*. Wissenschaftliche Untersuchungen zum Neuen Testament 8. Tübingen: J.C.B. Mohr (Paul Siebeck), 1965

Campbell, A., *Old English Grammar*. Oxford: Clarendon Press, 1959

Capelli, Adriano, *Dizionario di abbreviature latine ed italiane*. rev. ed. Milan: U. Hoepli; 1990

Carnicelli, Thomas A., ed. *King Alfred's Version of St. Augustine's* Soliloquies. Cambridge, MA: Harvard University Press, 1969

Cassidy, F. J., and Richard Ringler, eds. *Bright's Old English Grammar and Reader, Third Edition*. New York: Holt, Rinehart, Winston, 1971

Charlesworth, James H., ed. *The Old Testament Pseudepigrapha*. 2 vols. Garden City NY: Doubleday, 1983–1985

Clark, Mark, "Peter Comestor and Peter Lombard: Brothers in Deed," *Traditio* 60 (2005): 85–142

Clemoes, Peter, ed. *Ælfric's Catholic Homilies, The First Series: Text*. EETS s.s. 17. Oxford: Oxford University Press, 1997

Crawford, S. J., "The Old English Notes in B. M. Cotton Claudius B. iv," *Anglia* n.s. 35 (1923): 124–35.

Dahood, Mitchell, ed. *The Anchor Bible: Psalms I, 1–50*. Garden City, NY: Doubleday, 1965

Daly, Saralyn R., "Peter Comestor: Master of Histories," *Speculum* 32 (1957): 62–73

Dekkers, Eligius, ed. *Clavis patrum latinorum*. 3rd ed. Steenbrugis: in Abbatia Sancti Petri, 1995

Doane, A. N., "Anglo-Saxon Bibles and 'The Book of Cerne'," *Anglo-Saxon Manuscripts in Microfiche Facsimile* 7. Tempe, AZ: Arizona Center for Medieval and Renaissance Studies, 2002

———, ["Books, Prayers and Healing"], *Anglo-Saxon Manuscripts in Microfiche Facsimile* 1. Binghamton, NY: MRTS, 1994

———, ed. *Genesis A: A New Edition*. Madison: University of Wisconsin Press, 1978

Dobbie, Elliott van Kirk, ed. *The Manuscripts of Cædmon's Hymn and Bede's Death Song*. Columbia University Studies in English and Comparative Literature 128. New York: Columbia University Press, 1937

Dodwell, C. R., and Peter Clemoes, eds. *The Old English Illustrated Hexateuch: British Museum Cotton Claudius B. iv.* Early English Manuscripts in Facsimile 18. Copenhagen: Rosenkild and Bagger, 1974

Earle, J., and C. Plummer, eds. *Two of the Saxon Chronicles Parallel.* 2 vols. Oxford: Clarendon Press, 1892–1898

Emden, A. B., *Donors of Books to St. Augustine's Canterbury.* Oxford: Oxford Bibliographical Society, 1968

Emms, Richard, "The Historical Traditions of St. Augustine's Abbey, Canterbury," in *Canterbury and the Norman Conquest: Churches, Saints, and Scholars, 1066–1109,* ed. Richard Eales and Richard Sharpe, 159–68. London and Rio Grande: Hambledon Press, 1995

Franzen, Christine, *The Tremulous Hand of Worcester: A Study of Old English in the Thirteenth Century.* Oxford: Clarendon Press, 1991

Frede, Hermann Josef, *Kirchenschriftsteller: Verzeichnis und Sigel.* Vetus Latina 1/1. Freiburg: Herder, 1981

Gameson, Richard, *The Manuscripts of Early Norman England (c. 1066–1130).* Oxford: Oxford University Press, 1999

Giliberto, Concetta, "An Unpublished *De Lapidibus* in its Manuscript Tradition, with Particular Regard to the Anglo-Saxon Area," in *Form and Content of Instruction*, ed. Lendinara et al., 249–83

Ginzberg, Louis, *Die Haggada bei den Kirchenvätern: Erster Theil, Die Haggada in den pseudohieronymianischen Quaestiones.* Inaugural Diss., Heidelberg, 1899

———, *The Legends of the Jews*, tr. Henrietta Szold. 7 vols. Philadelphia: Jewish Publication Society of America, 1909–1938

———, *The Legends of the Jews*, tr. H. Szold and P. Radin. 2 vols. Philadelphia: Jewish Publication Society, 2003

Gneuss, Helmut, *Handlist of Anglo-Saxon Manuscripts: A List of Manuscripts and Manuscript Fragments Written or Owned in England up to 1100.* MRTS 241. Tempe, AZ: Arizona Center for Medieval and Renaissance Studies, 2001

Gorman, Michael, "The Commentary on Genesis of Claudius of Turin and Biblical Studies under Louis the Pious," *Speculum* 72 (1997): 279–329

Goossens, Louis, ed. *The Old English Glosses of MS. Brussels, Royal Library 1650.* Brussels: Palais de Academiën, 1974

Gransden, Antonia, *Historical Writing in England, c. 1307 to the Early Sixteenth Century.* London and Henley: Routledge and Kegan Paul, 1982

Gregory, Alys S., "Studies on the Commentaries of Cardinal Stephen Langton," *Archives d'histoire doctrinale et littéraire du moyen age* 5 (1930): 221–66

Hahn, Thomas, "Early Middle English," in *The Cambridge History of Medieval English Literature*, ed. David Wallace, 61–91. Cambridge: Cambridge University Press, 1999

Hain, Ludwig, *Repertorium bibliographicum.* Stuttgart: J. G. Cottae, 1826–1838; W. A. Copinger, *Supplement to Hain's Repertorium bibliographicum.* London: H. Sotheran, 1895–1902

Hall, Joseph, ed. *Selections from Early Middle English, 1130–1250*. 2 vols. Oxford: Clarendon Press, 1920

Hailperin, Herman, *Rashi and the Christian Scholars*. Pittsburgh: University of Pittsburgh Press, 1963

Hammerstein, Reinhold, "Instrumenta Hieronymi," *Archiv für Musikwissenschaft* 16 (1959): 117–34

Healey, Antonette diPaolo et al., eds. *Dictionary of Old English A-F*, CD-ROM version 1.0. Toronto: Pontifical Institute of Mediaeval Studies, 2003

Hecht, H. *Bischof Wærferths von Worcester Übersetzung der Dialoge Gregors des Grossen*. 2 vols. Bibliothek der angelsächsichen Prosa 5. Leipzig: G. H. Wiegand, 1900–1907

Hunter, Michael, "The Facsimiles in Thomas Elmham's History of St. Augustine's, Canterbury," *The Library*, 5th series 28 (1973): 215–20

Index of Manuscripts in the British Library. Cambridge, England and Teaneck, NJ: Chadwyck-Healey, 1984–1985

Irvine, Susan, "The Compilation and Use of Manuscripts Containing Old English in the Twelfth Century," in *Rewriting Old English*, ed. Swan and Treharne, 41–61

L'Isle, William, ed., *A Saxon Treatise concerning the Old and New Testament*. London: John Haviland for Henry Seile, 1623

James, M. R., "Asenath," in *A Dictionary of the Bible*, ed. J. Hastings. New York: Scribner's, 1898

———, *The Ancient Libraries of Canterbury and Dover*. Cambridge: Cambridge University Press, 1903

———, *A Descriptive Catalogue of the Manuscripts in the Library of Gonville and Caius College*. Cambridge: Cambridge University Press, 1907

———, *A Descriptive Catalogue of the Manuscripts in Trinity Hall, Cambridge*. Cambridge: Cambridge University Press, 1907

———, *The Western Manuscripts in the Library of Trinity College, Cambridge: A Descriptive Catalogue*. 4 vols. Cambridge: Cambridge University Press, 1900–1904

John, Eric, "The Litigation of an Exempt House: St. Augustine's, Canterbury, 1182–1237," *Bulletin of the John Rylands Library* 39 (1957): 390–415

Jordan, Richard, *Handbook of Middle English Grammar and Phonology*, trans. and rev. Eugene Joseph Crook. Janua Linguarum, Series Practica 218. The Hague, Paris: Mouton, 1974

Jung, N. "Petrus Comestor," *Dictionnaire de théologie cathólique*, 8:1918–22. Paris: Librairie Letouzey et Ané, 1935

Karp, Sandra Rae, "Peter Comestor's *Historia Scholastica*: A Study in the Development of Literal Scriptural Exegesis," unpub. Ph.D. diss., Tulane University, 1978

Kelly, J. N. D., *Jerome: His Life, Writings, and Controversies*. New York: Harper and Row, 1975

Kelly, Susan E. ed. *Charters of St. Augustine's, Canterbury and Minster-in-Thanet.* Oxford and New York: Oxford University Press, 1995

Ker, N. R., *A Catalogue of Manuscripts Containing Anglo-Saxon.* Oxford: Clarendon Press, 1957; rev. ed. 1990

———, *English Manuscripts in the Century after the Norman Conquest.* Oxford: Clarendon Press, 1960

———, *Medieval Libraries of Great Britain: A List of Surviving Books.* 2nd ed. London: Offices of the Royal Historical Society, 1964

Knowles, Dom David, *The Monastic Order in England.* 2d ed. Cambridge: Cambridge University Press, 1963

Kurath, Hans, and Sherman M. Kuhn, eds. *Middle English Dictionary.* Ann Arbor: University of Michigan Press, 1956–2001

Lachs, S. T., "The Source of Hebrew Traditions in the 'Historia Scholastica'," *Harvard Theological Review* 66 (1973): 385–86

Laistner, M.L.W., "Early Medieval Commentaries on the Old Testament," *Harvard Theological Review* 46 (1953): 45–46

Lambert, Bernard, *Bibliotheca Hieronymiana Manuscripta.* 4 vols. in 7. Steenbrugge: In abbatia S. Petri, 1969–1972

Landes, Richard, "Lest the Millennium Be Fulfilled: Apocalyptic Expectations and the Pattern of Western Chronography 100–800 CE," in *The Use and Abuse of Eschatology in the Middle Ages*, ed. Werner Verbeke, Caliel Verhelst, and Andries Welkenhuysen, 137–209. Mediaevalia Lovaniensia Series I/ Studia XV. Leuven: Leuven University Press, 1988

Lendinara, Patrizia, Loredana Lazzari, and Maria Amalia D'Aronco, eds. *Form and Content of Instruction in Anglo-Saxon England in the Light of Contemporary Manuscript Evidence.* Fédération Internationale des Instituts d'Études Médiévales, Textes et Etudes du Moyen Âge 39. Turnhout: Brepols, 2007

Levison, Wilhelm, *England and the Continent in the Eighth Century.* Oxford: Clarendon Press, 1946

Liuzza, Roy M., ed. *The Old English Version of the Gospels.* EETS 304, 314. Oxford: Oxford University Press, 1994, 2000

———, "Scribal Habit: The Evidence of the Old English Gospels," in *Rewriting Old English*, ed. Swan and Treharne, 143–65

Longère, Jean, "Petrus Comestor,"in *Dictionnaire de spiritualité ascétique et mystique: doctrine et histoire* 12.2: 1614–26. Paris: Beauchesne, 1986

Luscombe, David, "Peter Comestor," in *The Bible in the Medieval World: Essays in Memory of Beryl Smalley*, ed. Katherine Walsh and Diana Wood, 109–29. Studies in Church History, Subsidia 4. Oxford: Blackwell for the Ecclesiastical History Society, 1985

Machielsen, Iohannes, *Clavis Patristica Pseudepigraphorum Medii Aevii*, ed. idem. 5 vols. Turnhout: Brepols, 1994–2003.

Machan, Tim, *English in the Middle Ages.* Oxford: Oxford University Press, 2003

McNamara, Martin, *Glossa in Psalmos*. Studi e testi 310. Vatican City: Biblioteca Apostolica Vaticana, 1986

Maion, Danielle, "The Fortune of the so-called *Practica Petrocelli Salernitani* in England," in *Form and Content of Instruction* ed. Lendinara et al., 494–512

Marsden, Richard, ed., *The Cambridge Old English Reader.* Cambridge: Cambridge University Press, 2004

———, "Translation by Committee? The 'Anonymous' Text of the Old English Hexateuch," in *The Old English Hexateuch*, ed. Barnhouse and Withers, 41–89

Mitchell, Bruce, *Old English Syntax*. 2 vols. Oxford: Clarendon Press, 1985

Moore, Philip S., ed. *The Works of Peter of Poitiers, Master in Theology and Chancellor of Paris (1193–1205).* Washington DC: The Catholic University of America, 1936

Napier, Arthur, ed. *Old English Glosses, Chiefly Unpublished*. Anecdota Oxoniensia: Mediaeval and Modern Series 11. Oxford: Clarendon Press, 1900

O'Brien O'Keeffe, Katherine, "Manuscripts Containing the Anglo-Saxon Chronicle, Works by Bede, and Other Texts," *Anglo-Saxon Manuscripts in Microfiche Facsimile* 10. Tempe: Arizona Center for Medieval and Renaissance Studies, 2003

Ogle, Marbury B., "Petrus Comestor, Methodius, and the Saracens," *Speculum* 21 (1946): 318–24

Olson, Mary C., *Fair and Varied Forms: Visual Textuality in Medieval Illuminated Manuscripts*. Medieval History and Culture 15. New York and London: Routledge, 2003

The Oxford English Dictionary. Oxford: Clarendon Press, 1888–1928, rev. ed. 1989

Parkes, M. B., "Archaizing Hands in English Manuscripts," in *Books and Collectors 1200–1700: Essays Presented to Andrew Watson*, ed. James P. Carley and Colin G. C. Tite, 101–41. London: The British Library, 1997

Pelteret, David A. E., *Catalogue of English Post-Conquest Vernacular Documents*, Woodbridge: Boydell Press, 1990

Pfaff, Richard William, *Montague Rhodes James*. London: Scolar Press, 1980

Piper, A. J., "The Early Lists and Obits of Durham Monks," in *Symeon of Durham: Historian of Durham and the North*, ed. David Rollason, 161–201 Stamford: Shaun Tyas, 1998

Planta, Joseph, *A Catalogue of the Manuscripts in the Cottonian Library Deposited in the British Museum*. [London]: Hansard, 1802

Pope, J.C., ed., *Homilies of Ælfric, a Supplementary Collection*. EETS o.s. 259, 260. London: Oxford University Press, 1967

Powicke, F. M., *Stephen Langton, being the Ford Lectures 1927.* Oxford: Clarendon Press, 1928; repr. London: Merlin Press, 1965

Robinson, Fred C., and E. G. Stanley, eds., *Old English Verse Texts from Many Sources.* Early English Manuscripts in Facsimile 23. Copenhagen: Rosenkilde and Bagger, 1991

Rouse, Richard H., Mary A. Rouse, and R. A. B. Mynors, eds. *Registrum Anglie de libris doctorum et auctorum ueterum*. London: British Library with the British Academy, 1991

Russell, J. Cox, "The Clerical Population in Medieval England," *Traditio* 2 (1944): 177–212

Saltman, Avrom, "Pseudo-Jerome in the Commentary of Andrew of St. Victor on Samuel," *Harvard Theological Review* 67 (1974): 195–253

———, ed. *Pseudo-Jerome, Quaestiones on the Book of Samuel*, Studia Post-Biblica 26. Leiden: E.J. Brill, 1975

———, "Rabanus Maurus and the Pseudo-Hieronymian *Quaestiones Hebraicae in libros Regum et Paralipomenon*," *Harvard Theological Review* 66 (1973): 43–75

Sanders, W. B., ed. *Facsimiles of Anglo-Saxon Manuscripts*. Southampton: Ordnance Survey, 1884

Schipper, William, "A Composite Old English Homiliary from Ely: Cambr. Univ. MS Ii.1.33," *Transactions of the Cambridge Bibliographical Society* 8 (1983): 285–98

Sharpe, R., J. P. Carley, R. M. Thomson, and A. G. Watson, eds. *English Benedictine Libraries: The Shorter Catalogues*, Corpus of British Medieval Library Catalogues 4. London: The British Library with The British Academy, 1996

Shereshevsky, Esra, "Hebrew Traditions in Peter Comestor's *Historia Scholastica*," *Jewish Quarterly Review* 59 (1969): 268–69

Smalley, Beryl, "The School of Andrew of St. Victor," *Recherches de théologie ancienne et médiévale* 11 (1939): 145–67

———, *The Study of the Bible in the Middle Ages*. 3rd ed. Oxford: Blackwell, 1983

Smith, Thomas, *Catalogue of the Manuscripts in the Cottonian Library, 1696 (Catalogus librorum manuscriptorum bibliothecae Cottonianae)*, ed. C. G. C. Tite. Woodbridge: D. S. Brewer, 1984.

Swan, Mary, and Elaine M. Treharne, eds. *Rewriting Old English in the Twelfth Century*. Cambridge: cambridge University Press, 2000

Stegmüller, Friedrich, *Repertorium biblicum Medii aevi*. Madrid: [n.p.], 1954

Sylwan, Agnete, "Petrus Comestor, *Historia Scholastica*: une nouvelle édition," *Sacris Erudiri* 39 (2000): 345–82.

Thomas, Antoine, "'Crassantus' ou 'Craxantus': nom du crapaud chez Eucheria et ailleurs," *Bulletin du Cange* 3 (1927): 49–58

Thompson, S. Harrison, *Latin Book Hands of the Later Middle Ages, 1100–1500*. Cambridge: Cambridge University Press, 1969

Thomson, Rodney M., ed. *Manuscripts from St. Albans Abbey, 1066–1235*, I: Text; II: Plates. Woodbridge: D. S. Brewer for the University of Tasmania, 1982

Thorndike, Lynn, and Pearl Kibre, *A Catalogue of Incipits of Mediaeval Scientific Writings in Latin*. Revised and augmented ed. Cambridge, MA: Medieval Academy of America, 1963

Thunø, Erik, *Image and Relic: Mediating the Sacred in Early Medieval Rome*, Rome: "L'Erma" di Bretschneider, 2002

Thwaites, Edward, ed. *Heptateuchus, Liber Job, et Euangelium Nicodemi; Anglo-Saxonice. Historiae Judith Fragmentum; Dano-Saxonice*, Oxford: Sheldonian Theatre, 1698

Treharne, Elaine M., "The Dates and Origins of Three Twelfth-Century Old English Manuscripts," in *Anglo-Saxon Manuscripts and their Heritage*, ed. Phillip Pulsiano and eadem, 227–53. Aldershot: Ashgate, 1998

———, "Reading from the Margins: The Uses of Old English Homiletic Manuscripts in the Post-Conquest Period," in *Beatus Vir: Studies in Early English and Old Norse Manuscripts in Memory of Phillip Pulsiano*, ed. A. N. Doane and Kirsten Wolf, 329–58. MRTS 319. Tempe, AZ: Arizona Center for Medieval and Renaissance Studies, 2006

Turner, G. J., and H. R. Salter, eds. *The Register of St. Augustine's Abbey Canterbury, commonly called The Black Book.* 2 vols. British Academy Records of the Social and Economic History of England and Wales 2–3. London: H. Milford for the British Academy, 1915, 1924

Twomey, Michael W., "The *Revelationes* of Pseudo-Methodius and Scriptural Study at Salisbury in the Eleventh Century," in *Source of Wisdom: Old English and Early Medieval Latin Studies in Honour of Thomas D. Hill*, ed. Charles D. Wright, Frederick M. Biggs, and Thomas N. Hall, 370-86. Toronto: University of Toronto Press, 2007

Van Caenegem, R. C., *Royal Writs in England from the Conquest to Glanvill.* Seldon Society 77. London: Quaritch, 1959

Voigts, Linda E., "Anglo-Saxon Plant Remedies and the Anglo-Saxons," *ISIS* 70 (1979): 250–68

Wanley, Humfrey, *Antiquae literaturae septentrionalis liber alter*, in George Hickes, *Linguarum veterum septentrionalium thesaurus*. Oxford: Sheldonian Theatre, 1705.

Warner, Rubie D-N., ed. *Early English Homilies from the Twelfth Century MS. Vesp. D. XIV.* EETS o.s. 152. London: Kegan Paul, Trench, Trübner and Humphrey Milford, 1917

Watson, Andrew G., *Catalogue of Dated and Datable Manuscripts, c. 700–1600 in the Department of Manuscripts in the British Library*. 2 vols. London: The British Library, 1979

Wilcox, Jonathan, "Wulfstan Texts and Other Homiletic Materials," *Anglo-Saxon Manuscripts in Microfiche Facsimile* 8. MRTS 219. Tempe, AZ: Arizona Center for Medieval and Renaissance Studies, 2000

Withers, Benjamin, *The Illustrated Old English Hexateuch, Cotton Claudius B. IV: The Frontiers of Seeing and Reading in Anglo-Saxon England*. London and Toronto: British Library and Toronto University Press, 2007

Wormald, Francis, *English Drawings of the Tenth and Eleventh Centuries*. London: Faber and Faber, 1952

Index

"Ad aestimandum," *see* "Rei altitudinem"
Ælfric:
as a translator of "OE Hexateuch," 1
"Preface to Genesis," 1
Æthelbert, king of Kent, 341
Æthelsige, abbot of St. Augustine's, Canterbury, 342
Alcuin: cited in annotations, 44
Ambrose, St., "Letter to Church of Vercelli" (I.63), 250
Andrew of St. Victor, "Commentary on the Heptateuch," 257–58
"As(s)enath," "History of," 7, 8
extracts from in annotations, 98, 104
Anno Mundi dating, *see* Bede
Annotations in Claudius B. iv:
overall planning of, 333–37
use of *Historia Scholastica* in, 269–95:
use of "Jerome"-texts in, 316–24 *passim*
textual accuracy of, 263
text-type of, 266–68
differences of scripts within Latin, 214–16
"H & J"-scripts, 216–25
English ("insular") scripts, 225–37
insular script in Latin, 228–30
inconsistencies in, 232–34
identity of scripts, 234–36
English language of, 196–200, 361–69
as original compositions, 189–94, 200–11
sources of, 185, 189–94, 293
medleys of texts in, 322, 324–27
Crawford's edition of English notes, 185n1
Greek in, 153
Augustine, St., archbishop of Canterbury, 341
translation of relics of, 343
Augustine, St., bishop of Hippo, *Quaestiones in Heptateuchum*, 99, 120n521, 275
Bede:
anti-millenarianism of, 275
Retractio, 329
Nomina regionum atque locorum de Actibus Apostolorum, 9, 297, 326, 327–30
extracts in annotations from, 47–48, 49, 51, 103, 133, 136–38, 161–68
cited as Jerome, 49
"World Chronicle," 9, 330–33
Anno Mundi dates in, 13, 297, 331–32
cited in *Historia* extract, 21
De temporum ratione, 9, 97n402, 275
extracts in annotations from, 17, 30–39, 105, 152, 177–78, 181, 183–84
see also Pseudo-Bede
Bede's Death Song, 237
Benedictine monasticism: scholarship of, 3, 358–59
Bereschit Rabbah, 273
Berossus, extract from *Historia* attributed to, 51
Brooke, Christopher, 349
Caedmon's Hymn, 236–37
Canterbury, *see* Christ Church *and* St. Augustine's Abbey

Christ Church, Canterbury (monastic cathedral chapter), 3, 341
library of, 360n51
Eastry's library catalogue of, 8n19, 9n23, 261, 303n34, 357n47
hands of, 307
Clarembald, intruded abbot of St. Augustine's, Canterbury, 348
"Clement, Life of," cited in annotations as source, 62
Comestor, Peter, *see* Peter Comestor; *see also Historia Scholastica*
Cotton, Sir Robert, his library, 4
Crawford, S. J., 7
"De Mensuris," 311–16
text in annotations, 158–59
Dunstan, St., archbishop of Canterbury, 249, 341
Elmham, Thomas, 340
facsimiles of documents by, 346–48
Elstow, *see* Manuscripts, London, British Library, Royal 7. F.iii
English in twelfth century:
occurrence of, 188–91
documents, 190, 199
Enoch:
First Book of, 273
Slavonic Book of, 274
Eusebius of Caesarea, 275
Chronica (tr. Rufinus/Jerome), 51, 76, 99, 105
see also Jerome
Flavius Josephus, *see* Josephus
Freculphus Lexoviensis, 123n535, 327
Fretellus, Rorgo, 273
Gazaeus, Alardus, 100n413
Gervase of Canterbury, 346
Giliberto, Concetta, 304
Ginzberg, Louis, 274
Glossa ordinaria, 81n338, 128n553, 258, 272n53, 323n84
Goscelin of St. Bertin, 340
Gratian, *Decretals*, 256
"H"-script," *see* Annotations
Haymo of Halberstadt, *Commentarium in Cantica Canticorum*, 303
Henry II, King, 348
Historia Scholastica, 6, 9
sources of, 259
Jewish influence on, 259–60
establishment of text of (Sylwan), 263–66
typical layout of, 268
additiones, 190n20, 268–69
early diffusion and history of, 256–57, 260–61
copies at Canterbury, 261
method of exegesis, 259–60
treatment of generations of Adam, 270–76
as source of Claudius annotations, 189–94
in combination with Jerome extracts, 316–17
in medleys, 324–27 *passim*
extracts in annotations:
(Latin), 15–141 *passim*, 151, 176–79, 182
(English), 17, 18, 20, 22, 23, 26, 27, 28, 29, 30, 31, 32, 33, 34, 37, 40
Hugh III, abbot of St. Augustine's, 343
Hugh of St. Victor, *Notulae* on the Octateuch, 259
Honorius Augustodunensis, 194n32, 272n52, 276
Hrabanus Maurus, 300, 302, 324
extract in annotations from *Comm. in Lib. IV Reg.*, 134, 326
extract from *Historia* attributed to, 37
Isidore of Seville, 19
extracts in annotations from *De ortu et obitu patrum*;
(Latin), 31n95, 92
(English), 107
see also Pseudo-Isidore
Ivo of Chartres, 329
"J-script," *see* Annotations
James, Montague Rhodes, 7–8
Jerome, St.:
single-volume collection of works of, 9, 297–98
lost copy of at St. Augustine's, 298–304, 309–10

"longer collection," 298, 306
"shorter collection," 298–306
calculation of Methusala's age by, 275, 286–88
cited in *Historia* extracts:
(Latin), 27, 35, 63, 88, 178
(English), 33
cited by Bede in extracts, 167
false attribution of Bede extract to, 49
extracts from *Historia* attributed to, 54, 65
unsourced attribution, 121
false attributions to within a medley, 133n573
extracts in annotations from:
Ep. 36 ("Ad Damasum"), 29, 124, 325, 327
Ep. 73, 41n156
Ep. 78 ("Ad Fabiolam, de XLII mansionibus"), 95, 142, 144, 145, 299, 316
translation of Eusebius' *De situ et nominibus locorum Hebraicorum*, 299–300
method of use in annotations, 317–18
extracts from in annotations, 27, 50, 52, 53, 54, 56, 57, 58 (cited as if Josephus), 64, 68, 69, 70, 79, 82, 84, 85, 92, 94, 95, 99, 103, 113, 135–39, 141, 143, 145–49, 151–61, 168–75
Hebraicae quaestiones in libro Geneseos, 299
methods of use in annotations, 320–22
extracts from in annotations:
(Latin), 34n109, 45, 48, 49, 53, 55, 61, 66, 70, 71, 73, 90, 92, 96, 98, 101–2, 130
(English), 33n108
see also Pseudo-Jerome
Jewish exegesis, 259
Josephus (Latin version of *Antiquitates Iudaicae*), 8–9, 151, 259, 273
literal exegesis of, 258
as (spurious) source of English annotations, 189–90
in annotations:
Historia extracts in annotations attributed to:
(Latin), 19, 25, 40, 74, 91, 117; (English), 18, 27
alluded to in *Historia* extracts, 45, 46, 47, 48, 55, 58, 74–76, 82, 91, 100, 107, 114–15, 118, 127, 128, 129, 130, 132, 140, 177, 179
(English), 32, 34
cited in Jerome extracts, 52, 69, 169
cited as source of a Jerome extract, 58
unsourced citations:
(English), 28n83
(Latin), 70, 83, 123, 144
Greek version compared to Latin, 275
Julius Hilarianus, *Chronologia*, 108n456
Karp, Sandra Rae, 256, 259
Ker, Neil R., 3, 186, 213, 216–18, 244, 359
Laistner, M. L. W., 329
Lambeth Homilies, 369
Lanfranc, archbishop of Canterbury, 343, 358, 360
Langton, *see* Stephen Langton
Latin Josephus, *see* Josephus
L'Isle, William, 4
Liuzza, Roy, 361–69 *passim*
Machan, Tim, 188
Manuscripts:
Alençon, Bibliothèque municipale, 2, 298n3, 305
Berkeley, University Library MS UCB 17 (*olim* Phillips 391), 300n18
Cambridge, Corpus Christi College
MS 29, 62n258, 268
MS 44, 357n47
MS 144, 357n47
MS 286, 344n17, 346
Cambridge, Emmanuel College MS 57, 294n4, 305
Cambridge, Gonville and Caius College Library MS 238, 350

Cambridge, St. John's College B.5, 237
Cambridge, University Library
  Gg.5.35, 357n47
  Ii.1.33, 187n6, 278n85, 279n88, 331n103
  Kk.iv.6, 298, 304n39
Cambridge, Trinity College
  B.2.34, 149n645, 298n4, 300n15, 301–7 *passim*
  B.15.5, 261
  O.4.7, 149n645, 298–309 *passim*
  R.17.1, 187n10
Cambridge, Trinity Hall, MS 1, 346–48
Dublin, Trinity College MS 360, 248, 298–99
Durham, Cathedral Library
  B.II.11, 298n3, 300n15, 304n39, 305, 306
  B.III.32, 357n47
Durham, University Library Cosin V ii.6, 236
Edinburgh, National Library of Scotland, Adv. MS 18.5.18, 304n41
Hamburg, Staats- und Universitätsbibliothek, MS theol. 2029, 257n11
London, British Library
  Add. 22491, 118n513
  Cotton Caligula A.xv + Egerton 411, 357n47
  Cotton Claudius B. iv, *see* Old English Illustrated Hexateuch
  Cotton Claudius D. iii, 188n5, 236
  Cotton Claudius D. x, 348
  Cotton Cleopatra A.iii, 357n47
  Cotton Domitian A.i, 357n47
  Cotton Domitian A. vii, 350n39
  Cotton Faustina A.1, 350n39
  Cotton Faustina A. v, 237
  Cotton Julius A. ii, 204n51
  Cotton Nero A.viii, 249–51
  Cotton Otho B. x, 107n447
  Cotton Otho E.i, 357n47
  Cotton Tiberius A.ix, 341n6
  Cotton Tiberius C.ii, 357n47
  Cotton Titus A. xxvii, 249
  Cotton Titus A.iv, 357n47
  Cotton Vespasian A. xxii, 214
  Cotton Vespasian B. xx, 346
  Cotton Vespasian D.vi, 357n47
  Cotton Vespasian D. xiv, 187n10, 189n15, 195, 227n17
  Cotton Vitellius A. ii, 348
  Cotton Vitellius A. xv ("Southwick Codex"), 187n9
  Cotton Vitellius C.xiii, 350
  Harley 1524, 239n31, 244n38, 249
  Harley 3038, 217n8, 244n38
  Harley 4132, 262n33
  Harley 6258B, 188n5, 194n32
  Harley Charter 111 B.49, 199n38
  Royal 1 A.xiv, 187n10, 214, 361–69 *passim*
  Royal 2.C.i, 77n322
  Royal 3.A.i, 244n38, 360n51
  Royal 3.A.ii, 244n38, 360n51
  Royal 4.A.x, 244n38
  Royal 4.A.xi, 244n38
  Royal 4. D. vii, 62n258, 118n513, 260, 268, 269, 278n86, 287n98
  Royal 7 C.xii, 195
  Royal 7.D.ii, 249
  Royal 7 E.xii, 217n8
  Royal 7. F.iii, 118n513, 260
  Royal 8. C.ix, 259n11, 268
  Royal 12.B.ix, 249
  Royal 13.B.vii, 249
  Stowe MS 4, 236, 268n46
  Stowe Charters 43 & 44, 200n39
London, Lambeth Palace MS 419, 341n6
London, Public Record Office E 165/27, 343n16
Lyon, Bibliothèque municipale 187, 264
Madrid, Biblioteca Nacional, 91 (A.101), 298n3, 305
Oxford, Bodleian Library
  Bodley 160, 329–30
  Bodley 343, 187n8, 214
  Bodley 808, 298n4, 305, 306
  Digby 184, 298n4, 305

Digby 211, 236
Hatton 38, 187n10, 361–69 *passim*
Hatton 115, 187n8
Junius 11, 276n79
Junius 25, 302
Laud Misc. 509, 1n2, 55n221, 319
Laud Misc. 636, 187n7
Oxford, Lincoln College, lat. 31, 237
Oxford, Magdalen College, lat. 105, 237
Oxford, Merton College LI, 298n4, 305, 306
Paris, Bibliothèque nationale de France
lat. 11937, 300–1
lat. 14417, 257n9
lat. 14638, 264
lat. 16943, 255, 264, 265
Phillips 398 (untraceable), 300n18
Porto, Biblioteca Publica Municipal, Santa Cruz 42, 264
Rouen, Bibliothèque municipale A.544, 302n33
Tours, Bibliothèque municipale 42, 264
Troyes, Bibliothèque municipale
MS 290, 264
MS 451, 264
Vienna, Österreichische Nationalbibliothek 363, 264
Worcester, Cathedral Library F. 174, 187n8
York, Minster Library XVI.i.8, 298n4, 305
Manasses Damascenus, extract in annotations (English) from *Historia* attributed to, 39
Marbod of Rennes, *Liber lapidum*, 304
"Methodius" (Pseudo-Methodius *Revelationes*), 9, 272, 273, 276
as (false) source of English annotations, 191–93
extracts in annotations from *Historia* attributed to:
(Latin), 16, 25, 35
(English), 17, 23, 26, 29, 30
cited (Latin), 61
"Midrash ha-Gadol on Genesis," 274n66
Navarro, Emmanuel, editor of *Historia Scholastica* (1699), 255n1, 262–63
Nicholaus Damascenus, cited, 52
Nicholas, Life of, reference erased, 23
Normannus (Norman):
monk of St. Augustine's, 340
present at election of Abbot Roger I, 350
obit, 350
literary activities of, 356–59
as name cited in the OE Hexateuch, 9, 12, 286, 332, 351–58
extracts in annotations attributed to:
(Latin), 38–39, 51, 81, 91, 104, 127, 150
(English), 33–34, 36
Old English Illustrated Hexateuch (BL Cotton Claudius B. iv), 1, 2, 13, 339, 356–57
editing of, 13–15
date of, 6
layout of, 4–5
script of, 2–3, 4
Normannus notes in, 351–52
date of original manuscript, 3
codicological description of, 238
inserted leaves, 238–48, 333–37
cycle of Seth's lineage in, 277–92
see also Annotations
Pelteret, David, 188
Peri didaxeon, 194n32
Perkḳî Rabbi Eliezar, 272–73
Peter Comestor, 6, 255–92 *passim*
corrected by English annotator, 285–87
see also Historia Scholastica
Peter Lombard, 256
Peter of Poitiers, *Compendium historiae in genealogia Christi*, 257, 335–36
Peterborough Chronicle, 207n57, 368–69
Philo Judaeus, cited in annotations, 44
Planta, Joseph, 7
Pseudo-Augustine, 128n553
Pseudo-Bede, extract from *In Pentateuchum Commentarii*, 37
from *Quaestiones super Genesim*, 41

Pseudo-Eucherius, *De situ Hierusolimae*, cited as source, 57, 134, 135
Commentarii in Genesim, 71
Pseudo-Isidore, *Chronica*, 46
Pseudo-Jerome:
Ad Dardanum de musicis instrumentis (Ep. 23), 302
Ep. 129 ("Ad Dardanum"), 135, 326
Commentarius in canticum Debborae, 299
extracts in annotations from, 130, 131
De decem temptationibus populi Israel in deserto, 301
De xii lapidibus, 304
In Lamentationes Hieremiae, 301–02
Notae diuinae legi necessariae cum suis interpretationibus, 300
"De partibus minus notis Veteris Testamenti," 302
Quaestiones Hebraicae in I Paralipomenon, 300–1, 322–24
genealogical import of, 335
extracts in annotations from, 92, 101, 109–13, 125–26, 143
Quaest. Hebr. in libros Regum, 300–1
extracts in annotations from, 181, 182
"Sententie excerpte diuersis opusculis," 302
"Tractatus de sphaera coeli," 303–4
Rabbinical exegesis, 258
Ralph d'Escures, archbishop of Canterbury, 187n10, 189, 194n32
Rashi, 258n14
"Rei altitudinem," 311–16
text of in annotations, 159–60
Richard of St. Victor, *Liber exceptionum*, 260
Roger I, abbot of St. Augustine's, Canterbury, 342, 348
election of, 348–50
St. Augustine's Abbey, Canterbury (St. Peter's and St. Paul's), 3, 12, 340
foundation of, 341
rivalry with Christ Church, 341
resistance to archiepiscopal and royal rule, 342–44
translation of relics of St. Augustine within, 343
documents of, 343–44
forged foundation charters of, 344–48
scripts of, 346–48
library of, 356n46
"Chronicle to 1161" of, 249
catalogue of, *see* Manuscripts, Dublin, Trinity College MS 360
Saltman, Avrom, 300
Scotland, abbot of St. Augustine's, Canterbury, 340, 342
Sefer Noah, 276
Septuagint, 274, 276
cited in annotations:
(Latin), 35, 48, 169
(English), 30, 33
Smith, Thomas, 6–7
Sprott, Thomas, 340
unpublished chronicle of St. Augustine's, Canterbury of, 341n6
Stephen Langton, archbishop of Canterbury, 256–57
Stigand, archbishop of Canterbury, 249, 342n10
Strabus (Strabo), cited, 64, 129
Sylwan, Agneta, editor of *Scolastica Historia* (2005), 255n1, 263–66
Talbot, Robert, 4
Thomas of Elmham, *see* Elmham, Thomas
Thorne, William, 340
Chronicle of St. Augustine's of, 341n6, 342–40 *passim*
Treharne, Elaine, 199
Virgil, *Georgics*, quoted, 82
Wanley, Humfrey, 3, 7, 189
Wido, abbot of St. Augustine's, Canterbury, 340, 343
"West-Saxon Gospels," 361
William, archbishop of Sens, 256
Withers, Benjamin, 2, 3, 12
Wormald, Francis, 3
Wulfric, abbot of St. Augustine's, Canterbury, 342